THE TALKING GREEKS

When considering the question of what makes us human, the ancient Greeks provided numerous suggestions. This book argues that the defining criterion in the Hellenic world, however, was the most obvious one: speech. It explores how it was the capacity for authoritative speech which was held to separate humans from other animals, gods from humans, men from women, Greeks from non-Greeks, citizens from slaves, and the mundane from the heroic. John Heath illustrates how Homer's epics trace the development of immature young men into adults managing speech in entirely human ways and how in Aeschylus' *Oresteia* only human speech can disentangle man, beast, and god. Plato's *Dialogues* are shown to reveal the consequences of Socratically imposed silence. With its examination of the Greek focus on speech, animalization, and status, this book offers new readings of key texts and provides significant insights into the Greek approach to understanding our world.

JOHN HEATH is Professor of Classics at Santa Clara University. He is the author of numerous articles on Latin and Greek literature, myth and culture. His previous publications include *Actaeon, the Unmannerly Intruder* (1992), *Who Killed Homer?* (with Victor Davis Hanson, 1998; revised edition, 2001) and *Bonfire of the Humanities* (with Victor Davis Hanson and Bruce Thornton, 2001).

THE TALKING GREEKS

Speech, Animals, and the Other in Homer,
Aeschylus, and Plato

JOHN HEATH

Santa Clara University

CAMBRIDGE
UNIVERSITY PRESS

CAMBRIDGE UNIVERSITY PRESS
Cambridge, New York, Melbourne, Madrid, Cape Town, Singapore, São Paulo

Cambridge University Press
The Edinburgh Building, Cambridge CB2 2RU, UK

Published in the United States of America by Cambridge University Press, New York

www.cambridge.org
Information on this title: www.cambridge.org/9780521832649

First published 2005

Printed in the United Kingdom at the University Press, Cambridge

A catalogue record for this book is available from the British Library

Library of Congress Cataloguing in Publication data
Heath, John, 1955–
The talking Greeks: speech, animals, and the Other in Homer, Aeschylus, and Plato / John Heath.
p. cm.
Includes bibliographical references (p. 334) and index.
ISBN 0-521-83264-0
1. Greek literature – History and criticism. 2. Speech in literature. 3. Aeschylus – Criticism and
interpretation. 4. Human–animal relationships in literature. 5. Homer – Criticism and
interpretation. 6. Difference (Psychology) in literature. 7. Language and languages in literature.
8. Gods, Greek, in literature. 9. Human beings in literature. 10. Animals in literature.
11. Plato. 1. Title.
PA3015.S74H43 2005
880.9′353 – dc22 2004061594

ISBN-13 978-0-521-83264-9 hardback
ISBN-10 0-521-83264-0 hardback

Contents

Preface and acknowledgments

I wrote most of this book over the past seven summers. Each fall I have returned to classes, where the tolerant smiles and glazed eyes of my freshmen students quickly reminded me that the relevance of the Greeks can easily be lost on the uninitiated – and the scholar. I am fortunate to have spent my academic life teaching bright undergraduates who, with a little coaxing (okay – sometimes with a lot of coaxing), have often joined me in exploring these ancient texts. I thank them.

More pragmatically, I am grateful to two classical journals for permission to publish here revised versions of previously published articles. Part of Chapter 2 appeared as "*Telemachus pepnumenos*: Growing into an epithet," in *Mnemosyne* 54 (2001) 129–57. Chapter 5 is largely based on "Disentangling the beast: Humans and other animals in Aeschylus' *Oresteia*," in *JHS* 119 (1999) 17–47. The editors and anonymous referees involved in these publications were extremely helpful. Santa Clara University generously awarded two of my students summer grants to check references and help create the index. I am much indebted to the University and especially to Tom Garvey and Christine Lechelt.

Several colleagues and friends have offered perceptive insights on individual chapters: Walter Englert, Michelle McKenna, Helen Moritz, William Prior, and Gail Blumberg. Nora Chapman, Mark Edwards, and Victor Hanson read the entire manuscript when it was still a rather unattractive adolescent. Lisa Adams loaned her acumen and acute editorial eye to the penultimate draft. I cannot thank them enough for their many invaluable comments, queries, and suggestions. If this book is still ungainly, it is not their fault. The anonymous readers for the press were open-minded, insightful, and especially helpful in convincing me to eliminate several polemical divagations of which I had grown unhealthily fond. To my editor at Cambridge, Michael Sharp, I feel a particular debt of gratitude for having faith in the intellectual merits of what first crossed his desk as a slightly grumpy analysis of "animals and the Other" in ancient Greece.

Finally, my greatest debt is to Emma, who arrived just when I was starting this book. Her intelligence and optimism are constant sources of inspiration, as well as proof that human nature is not determined entirely by genes. It would also be unforgivable for me not to acknowledge with affection Mel and Andi, whose joyful lives and unhappy fates have served as an impetus for my reflection on the duties we have to all conscious creatures, both articulate and silent.

Introduction

The thesis of this book is embarrassingly unsophisticated: humans speak; other animals don't. This zoological platitude formed the basis – indeed, the motivation – for much of the ancient Greeks' profound and influential exploration of what it means to be human.

It has long been found useful in both literary and anthropological studies to quote out of context Lévi-Strauss' famous observation (he was critiquing totemism) that animals are chosen to convey certain ideas not because they are good to eat, but because they are good to think with.[1] But for the agrarian Greeks, whose hands were dirty from the earth and animals they worked with and struggled against every day, animals were also good to think about. The Greeks were hard-working pragmatists as well as our intellectual and cultural forebears. They were farmers, and their understanding of human nature and animals was shaped by very different "formative" experiences than those of most of us who study them. To take what I hope is an extreme example, my own childhood familiarity with animals in the suburbs of Los Angeles was limited to a series of family basset-hounds (not exactly Laconian hunting dogs), my sister's pet rat, and a blood-sucking half-moon parrot named Socrates, whom my mother, like the Athenian mob 2,400 years before, finally shipped off to Hades with a tainted beverage.

In the United States, where family farmers are no longer "statistically relevant" – where there are more prison inmates than full-time farmers of any kind, and where ranchers are a dying breed[2] – most of us regularly encounter animals only as fuzzy house companions or on our plates. In this, we are very much unlike the ancient Greeks we read and write about. Few of them could afford to feed a mouth that did not help put food

[1] Lévi-Strauss (1969) 162; see Lloyd (1983) 8 n.7.
[2] Hanson (1996) xvi; Schlosser (2001) 8 with 278 n.8, 133–47. It is sobering to remember that not until 1910 did the United States have more industrial laborers than farm workers. A recent survey showed that many of us spend more than 95 percent of our lives indoors; Bekoff (2002) 139.

on the table in return. In a world where food shortage was just one bad harvest away, only the most wealthy could spare the produce to support ornamental creatures. (We will quickly be reminded that the bad boys of archaic literature, Hesiod and Semonides, included most wives under this rubric.) Possession of a "useless" animal was a mark of prestige, a statement of and advertisement for one's status.[3] Alcibiades' large and handsome dog cost seventy minas and served the explicit purpose, according to Plutarch, of drawing attention to his owner's notoriety, especially when Alcibiades whacked off its beautiful tail.[4]

Nor are we much like the Greeks in our diet. The average American eats 197 pounds of meat each year, much of it shrink-wrapped or dispensed in cardboard boxes and buckets.[5] Athens, on the other hand, which may have provided its citizens with twice as much meat as most other cities, probably distributed less than five pounds of beef yearly to individuals in public sacrifices.[6] And the Greeks derived virtually *all* of what they called meat (*krea*) from animals whose throats were slit in religious ritual – cattle, pigs, sheep, and goats. Isocrates at one point (7.29) grumbles that the Athenians create festivals just for the free meat.[7] Nevertheless, the hungry in antiquity

---

[3] See Sallares (1991) 311–13, 383. He observes that the horse in Athens was the prestige animal *par excellence* given its difficult diet, small size, and Attica's lack of good pasture land and unsuitability to cavalry; see Arist. *Pol.* 1289b33–41. Purchasing, maintaining, and equipping a horse were expensive; see Anderson (1961) 136–9; Spence (1993) 183, 272–86, who estimates the cost of a horse alone was equivalent to ten months' wages for a skilled craftsman in classical Athens. The hoplite ethos of archaic and classical Athens was antithetical to horsemanship as well; see Spence (1993) 164–230; Hanson (1995) 114.

[4] *Alc.* 9. "Everyone" in Athens objected to the mutilation. Alcibiades' intention was to give Athenians something notorious to focus on so they would ignore his other faults. Plutarch also observes that Alcibiades sent more horses and chariots to the Olympic Games than any king in Greece; cf. Thuc. 6.16.2.

[5] See Table 1-1 on p. 3 of the U.S.D.A.'s *Agriculture Fact Book 2000*; this includes beef, pork, veal, lamb, chicken, turkey, fish and shellfish.

[6] Jameson (1988a) 105. It is extremely difficult to determine how much meat was eaten at sacrifices – we do not even know if the civic distribution included the wives, children, and dependants of male citizens; see Osborne (1993); Rosivach (1994) esp. 157–8; Garnsey (1999) 100–12. We have no good data on how much meat could have derived from private sacrifices, or how much poultry, fish, ham, or sausage (that is, animal flesh available outside of the sacrificial meal) was eaten; see Isager and Skydsgaard (1992) 94–6. Frost (2001) offers us his own classical Greek recipe for pork sausage. Certainly, old animals frequently became dinner, young males were culled from herds of sheep and goats, and parts of animals inappropriate for sacrifice were preserved in various ways. Thus meat other than that from public rites – estimated by Rosivach (1994) 11–66 to take place 40–5 times each year in fourth-century Athens – was likely to be available in small supplies to some Greeks sporadically during the year, and in famine situations such resources may have been crucial; see Jameson (1983) 9; Gallant (1991) 121–7. The meat from sacrifices was not all eaten on the spot – it would often be sold raw to butcher shops; Jameson (1999) 327–31. Berthiaume (1982) 64–9 argues that there is some evidence for occasional differences between the meat from sacrifices and meat sold in the agora (that is, not all meat came from the altars, although it all seems to have been killed in a religious context).

[7] Jameson (1999) 326.

were willing to eat a wide variety of creatures, and just about every part of a dead animal found its way into the kitchen. The Hippocratic writer of *On Regimen* lists as animals "that are eaten" cattle, goats, pigs, sheep, donkeys, horses, dogs, wild boar, deer, hares, foxes, and hedgehogs.[8] Most Greeks clearly enjoyed animal flesh when they could get their hands on it. Comic drama is awash with animals, references to animal butchering,[9] and drooling couch potatoes who dream of meat-filled utopias. Teleclides in his *Amphictyons* (in Ath. 268b–d), for example, has a character recall the "olden days" when a river of broth (with conduits of sauces), like some modern-day sushi boat, whisked hot slices of meat to lounging diners. But in contrast to the perfunctory fast-food frenzy of today, meat-eating for the Greeks was consistently linked with the social and civic functions of animal sacrifice: vegetarianism and cannibalism were equally freakish perversities that meant the rejection of human community and civilization itself.[10]

Live animals were even more important in the agrarian polis, however, since they were needed for wool, transport, plowing, protection, manure, and edible by-products. Milk and cheese are far more economical for producing calories and protein than animal flesh. There are few less efficient ways of feeding a community than by waiting for animals to turn grain into animal protein – cattle have a feed-protein conversion efficiency of only 6 percent. Greek goats today give six times as many calories in milk as in meat, and nearly three times as much protein. Classical Greeks would

---

[8] Hippoc. *Vict.* 2.46 (6.544–6 L.), cited in Parker (1983) 357, who notes that most of these species are supported by other evidence, although some were eaten only by the poor and in times of food shortage. Porphyry (*Abst.* 1.14) claims that horses, dogs, and asses were not eaten; see Jameson (1988a) 115 n.5 for the ambiguity of the archaeological material. Wilkins (2000a) 17–21 has a rather unappetizing list of the parts of the animal considered edible. An excellent survey of foods eaten in classical Greece can be found in Dalby (1995) 57–92. Fowl were also occasionally sacrificed, and perhaps fish (although most fish seem to have been excluded from regular sacrifice). For the amount of fish likely to have been eaten in classical Greece and its social significance, see Wilkins (1993) and Davidson (1997) 3–35. Fish were a luxury food, oddly enough; see Wilkins (2000a) 293–304. Both mollusk and demersal species of fish have a very low labor input:caloric output ratio; see Gallant (1991) 120–1. On the "absolute coincidence of meat-eating and sacrificial practice," see: Jameson (1988a) 87; Detienne (1989); Durand (1989); but also the cautions of Osborne (1993). The role of animals in sacrifice will be further discussed in Chapter 4. On the heroic diet of Homeric warriors, see Chapter 3.

[9] The dialogue between the Sausage-Seller and the Paphlagonian tanner in Aristophanes' *Knights* (340–497) is especially sharp: McGlew (2002) 98–9 observes that they fight as if "to determine whether the Sausage-Seller can gut the city more completely than the leather maker can tan it."

[10] Holocausts, in which entire animals were sacrificed (and sometimes thrown alive into a fire) to the gods, were rare; Jameson (1988a) 88. Sacrifice and meat-eating were important elements of other ancient Mediterranean cultures in Mesopotamia, Israel, and Egypt. Katz's (1990) comparative analysis of the roles of sacrifice reveals that each culture found quite different meaning in its rituals.

marvel at the golden age world of modern America, where 70 percent of all cereals grown are transformed into burgers, bacon, and chicken nuggets.[11]

The non-human beast in antiquity derived much of its symbolic force from its ubiquitous and very real presence in daily life.[12] Animals were never merely mirrors of ideology but living, breathing, odorous, and unwitting partners in a struggle for survival. These beasts – who often lived right in the house – were a palpable part of the relentless challenge of working with, taming, or being overwhelmed by a difficult environment in an indifferent universe.[13]

We twenty-first-century Westerners, however, often find ourselves so divorced from the natural world that animals have lost much of the evocative power they possessed for the Greeks. Our de-natured, cuddly animals are not so much good to think about or with as good to *sell* with – witness the lucrative industries spawned by Mickey, Garfield, Tony, Simba, Miss Piggy, Willy, Barney, Franklin, and all their furry friends. TV commercials amuse us, and apparently create successful "brand loyalty," with slovenly (but articulate) chickens trying in vain to con their way into the Foster Farms slaughterhouse. We have carefully severed the flesh and blood of nature from the steaks and gravy of culture, thereby attenuating the potency of both. The popularity of zoos (alien to the classical Greeks but which in the United States now draw far more people than professional sporting

[11] Sources for these statistics can be found in Payne (1985) 226, cited in Jameson (1988a) 103; Rifkin (1992) 160–1. Cattle, goats, and sheep do not seem to have been raised solely for meat, but very young animals and those that had already been productive were culled for food; see Burford (1993) 144–59, and especially Rosivach (1994) 79–106. Pigs, raised beyond infancy only for their meat, could thrive on household and garden waste. Hodkinson (1988) 41–7 argues for fairly extensive growing of fodder crops for animals in the classical period, though contra are Skydsgaard (1988) 81 and Isager and Skydsgaard (1992) 103; see Sarpaki (1992) and Garnsey (1992) 151–2 for the importance of legumes in human diet, and Luce (2000) on how vetch came increasingly to be regarded as food for cattle. Even Hodkinson, however, accepts the conclusions of Foxhall and Forbes (1982) 74 that the Greeks got 70–5 percent of their calories from grain alone; cf. Garnsey (1988), whose entire study of famine and food supply in antiquity is based on the availability of grain. Most of the rest of the classical diet derived from milk products, especially cheese from the milk of sheep and goats; Amouretti (2000) provides a recent survey. To judge from bones found in rubbish heaps, the Greeks hunted and consumed wild animals such as deer, boar, bear, partridge, pigeon, and duck. But the labor input:caloric output ratio would have been low; see Gallant (1991) 119–20, and below, Chapter 3, for the ideology of hunting. For animals as traction, see the "Final Discussion" (168–71) in Wells (1992). Sacrificed animals also supplied hides.

[12] This is true for most ancient as well as modern non-industrialized societies; see the articles in Willis (1990).

[13] Even a casual glance at vase-painting and sculpture reveals that the Greeks surrounded themselves with animals in their art as well. And they appreciated a realistically rendered cow as much as anyone: the *Greek Anthology* has more epigrams in praise of Myron's famous bronze heifer (originally standing in the Athenian agora) than of any other work of art; see Klingender (1971) 67.

events[14]) and wildlife documentaries similarly reveals our fascination with an exotic world completely foreign to – and safely locked away from – our quotidian experience.

The usual suspects rounded up in recent classical scholarship are thus not generally the flesh and blood creatures of the farm but those perhaps even more serviceable beasts of the creative imagination used symbolically in Greek literature.[15] With these "constructed" creatures we in classics have grown quite comfortable. The bibliography on the literary use of animals in various classical authors and genres is immense. Merely corralling the scholarship on the creatures in the three authors examined in this study – Homer, Aeschylus, and Plato – has often felt like a Herculean (if not Sisyphean) task. Heroic lions in Homer have been hunted nearly to extinction, ominous serpents de-fanged in the *Libation Bearers*, Plato's horses of the soul broken and saddled. So many eagle-eyed readers have already tracked the animal imagery in Greek literature that one can't help but worry that the once dangerous and magnificent beasts have become a bit familiar, tamed by the frequent scholarly safaris. What can we possibly have left to learn? Can't we just leave the poor critters alone?

Well, no. But in contrast to most previous studies of animals in Greek literature and culture, this book examines neither specific beastly imagery nor the Greek philosophical debates about the nature of non-human animals. In fact, in several chapters animals paradoxically almost disappear entirely. Instead, I pursue the thematic implications of the most obvious and important criterion separating human and non-human animals in Greek thought – the ability to speak. The silence of beasts provided the cultural backdrop against which the Greeks played out their particular visions of what makes a life worth living for humans. This difference between other animals and us was *not* originally thought to be that we possessed rationality, despite what the fourth- and third-century philosophers

---

[14] Arluke and Sanders (1996) 1. They also note that pet owners spend more on animal food than parents spend on baby food each year.

[15] Many books and articles have been written about real animals in specific aspects of Greek life, such as elephants in war (there is an entire website on these creatures alone), hunting, or sacrifice, and about individual species (e.g. dogs, apes, dolphins, horses, snakes, frogs, fish, insects – even polar bears). Some studies borrow modern anthropological approaches (e.g. Csapo's [1993] Geertzian analysis of Greek cockfights). An encyclopedic compilation in German of facts about a wide variety of animals in several ancient cultures is now nearly a hundred years old (Keller (1963), originally published in 1909–13. But as yet there exists no broad analysis of the various roles of animals in the daily life of classical Greece; see Lonsdale (1979) and Bodson (1983) for brief surveys. More recent studies can be found by Martini et al. in: Dinzelbacher (2000) 29–144; cf. Lorenz (2000); Dumont (2001). As de Fontenay's book (1998) reveals, to write a history of animals is to write a history of theology, economics, class, gender, war, and philosophy.

would have us believe. The primacy of reason as a distinguishing criterion derived over time from the far more obvious fact of experience that beasts do not speak. "Dumb" animals do not possess any language. For a human to be made speechless is to become dead, sometimes literally but always culturally – nothing better than a beast. The corpses of Persian dead in Greece, we read in Aeschylus, are mute (*aphôna*), mangled by fish who are poetically and poignantly labeled "the voiceless children" (*anaudôn* . . . *paidôn*) of the sea (*Pers.* 576–80).[16]

Eventually, this lack of speech was connected with irrationality, but that association was a later and secondary philosophical embellishment. If speech is what separates us from the beasts, then the more we master it the more human we become. Equally, the less we are able to articulate our thoughts, the less morally and politically significant we appear. In what becomes a convenient and nearly irreversible cycle, second-class moral and political status can be explained, justified, and maintained by carefully monitoring the opportunity to speak. In ancient Hellas, you are what you can say.[17]

SEPARATING MAN FROM BEAST: GREECE IS THE WORD

Scholars have thoroughly examined the Greek philosophers' endeavors to explain what it is that makes us different from other animals. The Greeks were consumed with this effort, virtually inventing the familiar topos "man alone of the animals is/possesses *x*." Richard Sorabji has documented over three dozen of their answers, including man's unique ability to laugh, distinguish good and bad, know God, do geometry, engage in sex at all seasons (and with other species!), and walk upright, as well as our possession of grammar, shame, and hands.[18] Aristotle alone came up with nearly two dozen different claims for the uniqueness or exceptional character of man.[19] We all are familiar with the answer that many philosophers of the fourth

---

[16] All translations are my own. I have adopted one of the comfortably capricious systems of transliteration of ancient Greek commonly used in classical scholarship.

[17] Speech remains extremely important in modern Greece, where "silence cannot be easily tolerated"; Sifianou (1997) 74–8. After the classical age, language remained a key issue of Hellenic identity. Elites during the Second Sophistic relied on the artificial resuscitation of the language of classical Athens as a source of political authority. Similarly, the lengthy conflict between demotic and *katharevousa* has only recently been sorted out; see Swain (1996) 17–42.

[18] Sorabji (1993) 89–93; see Renehan (1981) 246–52 for the "man alone is . . ." topos. Longo (2000) offers an interesting examination of the emphasis on the uniqueness of the human hand in Greek philosophy.

[19] See Lloyd (1983) 26–35, with his discussion of the contradictory and imprecise nature of many of these claims.

and third centuries settled upon: man possesses the faculty of reason (*logos*) and other animals do not. Humans alone have *logos*, and this assumption in turn shaped the subsequent examination of the various characteristics associated with rationality, such as beliefs, perception, memory, intention, self-consciousness, etc.

Man is a *zôïon logikon*, a rational animal. All other *zôïa* are *alogika*. (Old habits die hard: the modern Greek word for horse is *alogo*.) The philosophical schools did not agree on how reason works, or on its moral consequences, and even Aristotle is inconsistent as to exactly what animals' souls do and do not possess.[20] But as Sorabji demonstrates, Aristotle introduces the "crisis" both for the philosophy of mind and theories of morality by devising a "scientific" structure for denying reason to animals.[21] Plato laid the foundations by narrowing the content of perception and expanding the content of belief. He places tremendous emphasis on *logos*, but he also grants animals a reasoning part of the soul on occasion. Some passages seem to ascribe to non-human animals cognitive and moral capabilities that are human-like. His theory of reincarnation depends upon similar souls within beasts and humans.[22] Moreover, most people in the Platonic view actually lack *logos* in its purest, philosophical sense. *Logos* is required to live the philosophic life, and few of us would qualify. Plato, too, has an incipient scale of being: certain human lives are not merely "like" but actually synonymous with the lives of beasts.[23]

But with Aristotle, the link between *logos* and humans, and the rejection of *logos* from the non-human, becomes explicit. To become fully

[20] Cole (1992) 45–51 shows that there is a tension in Aristotle's ethology: some passages deny, and some grant, intelligence and moral substance to beasts.

[21] Sorabji's (1993) superb book is an exploration of this crisis and its consequences. Earlier important studies of Aristotle on men and animals are Fortenbaugh (1971); (1975) 65–70; Clark (1975) passim; Dierauer (1977) 100–61; Lloyd (1983) 18–57; Preus (1990); see also de Fontenay (1998) 87–101; Lorenz (2000) 220–41. Alcmaeon of Croton (*fl.* early fifth century) was one of the first to differentiate humans from other animals on the basis of our "understanding" (*xuniêsi*) versus their "perception" (*aisthanetai, DK* 24 A5).

[22] See references in Dierauer (1977) 67–97; Renehan (1981) 241; Sorabji (1993) 9–12; Dierauer (1997) 9–10. The best study I have found of Plato's treatment of reason in animals is in an unpublished paper by Cole (1991); see also Preus (1990) 72–4; Pinotti (1994). *Logistikon* in Plato, however, can comprise the whole contents of soul before it enters body. If animals do not have it, then they do not have a soul (cf. *Phdr.* 246b–c; see Rohde [1925] 483 n.40). Later Platonists denied the entrance of the human soul into animals. Proclus, for example, insists that when Plato suggests the soul of Thersites chose the body of an ape (*Resp.* 10.620c) the philosopher means not that the soul entered the body of a beast but took on its character only (*In Platonis Timaeum* 329d); see McDermott (1938) 147 and n.5; Smith (1984). At one point, Plato defines man, etymologically, as the lone creature who looks up at what he has seen and thinks about it (*Cra.* 399c).

[23] Cole (1991); Baldry (1965) 53–5; e.g. *Tim.* 90eff.: if a man fails to make proper use of reason, his soul in its second incarnation will "sink" into that of a woman, bird, four-footed creature, etc.; see also Solmsen (1955) 160–4.

human, we must exercise our capacity for *logos*. It is our definition, our inherent goal, our *telos*. This Aristotelian concept, when linked with Christian metaphysics through various migrations, has been perhaps the single most influential principle in Western religious and ethical thought.

Although this distinction, based upon the possession of reason, has seemed absolutely natural to most Westerners, it is hard to find another culture that has accepted it so completely. As Robert Renehan notes in his study of the Greek anthropocentric view of man, "[t]hat man differs from animals because of his intelligence, so far from being a natural way of looking at things, is an exceptional mode of thought in the history of man."[24] And in fact rationality is *not* the earliest determinant of human uniqueness we find in Greek thought, and it did not go unchallenged, even by Aristotle's successors.

As any first-year student of Greek can testify, *logos* is a tricky word (the LSJ lists over fifty different possible translations). Closely linked to the idea of reason, and more central to the word's basic meaning, is "speech." This noun derives from the same root as the verb *legô*, which means "to gather," "to count," "to recount, tell," and ultimately "to say." The first attested meaning of *logos*, in Homer and Hesiod, has nothing to do with rationality but clearly denotes speech (*Il.* 15.393; *Od.* 1.55–7; Hes. *Op.* 78, 106, 789, *Theog.* 229, 890; cf. *Hymn Hom. Merc* 317–18). When Heraclitus and Parmenides use *logos* not simply as a "verbal utterance" but as something rational – that is, rationality in speech and thought (even outside the human mind and voice) – they set the word on its fateful and well-documented course.[25] It is in this *secondary* development that the word becomes not just the outward form by which inward thought is articulated, but the inward thought itself, the ability to give voice to some reasoned conception (rather than merely to express pleasure and pain, for example). Ultimately, *logos*

[24] Renehan (1981) 239.
[25] See especially Heracl. 1, 2, 50 and Parm. 7. The meaning of *logos* in these passages is disputed, but there is agreement that the word has moved beyond mere articulate language; see Boeder (1959) 82–91; Lincoln (1997), with references to previous scholarship on *logos*. Lincoln shows that *logos* in its early appearances not only refers to speech but in particular to the language of women, as well as the weak, young, and shrewd, that is delightful but also deceptive. The verbal form in Homer more usually means "to gather," but "recount" or "tell" is not uncommon (e.g. *Il.* 13.292; 20.244; *Od.* 3.296; 12.165; 14.197; 23.308); see Janko (1992) ad *Il.* 13.292. The LSJ suggests that the verb first means "say" or "speak" in Hesiod (*Theog.* 27), but the use at *Od.* 203 is very similar; see West (1966) ad *Theog.* 27; Russo (1992) ad *Od.* 19.203. Since I am not interested in the "rational" side of *logos per se* in this study, the long-standing debate over the movement in Greek thought from *muthos* to *logos* is not of immediate concern; see the articles in Buxton (1999) for a recent review of this discussion. Neither do I pursue the philosophical critiques of the inefficacy or limits of *logos*; see Mortley (1986); Roochnik (1990).

comes to mean argument, thought, reason, and dozens of other related ideas.

As we shall see, the most important early Greek vision of the difference between humans and other animals was the most obvious one of all: we talk; they do not.[26] Early Greek has a poetic word, *meropes*, used only as an epithet of humans. It was unclear even to the classical Greeks exactly what the word meant, but later it was thought to derive from two words that signify "dividing the voice," that is, "articulate." Even if this is a false etymology, which it probably is,[27] the invention and promulgation of this derivation itself reveal the natural connection in the Greek mind between speaking and being human.

This link similarly underlies Herodotus' celebrated tale of Pharaoh Psammetichus' test (2.2).[28] Eager to discover which of two nations – Egypt or Phrygia – was the oldest, Psammetichus ordered two newborn children to be raised by a shepherd, who was not to speak a word in their presence. Two years later, both children began to cry out *bekos*, a Phrygian word for bread. The Egyptians immediately conceded that Phrygia was the oldest culture (and, without need of further evidence, claimed second prize). The Pharaonic experiment assumes that philology recapitulates phylogeny. Even without any adult modeling, because the children are human they must eventually speak, and they will utter humanity's primal, "natural" language.

Plato and Aristotle put speech before rationality in important ways, a fact that is often missed or underemphasized. Reasoning for Plato, we should remember, is the silent debate of the soul within itself, and belief is the silent conclusion to a question posed in the inner debate.[29] And although later Platonists such as Plotinus and Proclus would insist on the inexpressibility of the highest truths, and Plato himself emphasized the difficulties of grasping and conveying the highest wisdom, he also demanded that philosophers "give an account" (*logon didonai*) of what they know.[30] Without

---

[26] Good discussions of speech as the defining characteristic of humans in classical thought, with further references, can be found in Dierauer (1977) 32–5; Buxton (1982) 48–62; Thalmann (1984) 78–9; Sorabji (1993) 80–6; Pelliccia (1995) 25–30, 55–79, 103–8. Harrison (1998) argues that the idea that language sets humans apart from animals is less prevalent among the ancient Greeks than in modern times, but even he must admit that there must be a distinction if the analogy of foreign speech with the sounds of birds is to dehumanize the language of barbarians; see below, Chapter 4. Harriott (1982) 13 makes some provocative comments in passing on the significance of animals' inability to speak.

[27] E.g. Hsch.; Schol. on *Il.* 1.250; see Kirk (1985) ad *Il.* 1.250.

[28] See the discussion of Harrison (1998) with references in note 131.

[29] *Tht.* 184d–187b; 189e–190a; *Soph.* 263e; *Phlb.* 38c–e; also Aristotle at *Ath. Pol.* 76b25f.; see Sorabji (1993) 10.

[30] Lloyd (2002) 99.

language, there is no rationality at all. The *logos* denied in adjective *aloga* was originally speech, and only later spread its semantic wings to encompass "irrationality."[31]

Animals obviously do not speak as we do, and this fact was later taken as proof by many philosophers that non-humans had no capacity for language or rational thought. The strength of this link is in fact currently more intensely debated in the scientific literature than ever before, and I will return to it in the Epilogue. Even Aristotle himself, unlike the later Hellenistic philosophers (especially the Stoics), does not provide a sustained discussion of the relation between language and thought. He may have seen language more as a means of developing rationality than as being directly constitutive of it.[32] But in his famous account of the origins of the polis – before his discussion of natural rulers and subjects on the basis of mastery of *logos* (rationality in this case) – he makes clear that no community is possible at all without speech. Humans alone can speak, and speech enables communities to be formed for the pursuit of justice. Language, man's unique endowment, enables him to sort out what is right and wrong:

For nature, as we say, makes nothing in vain, and man is the only animal who possesses speech (*logos*). The *voice* (*phônê*), to be sure, signifies pain and pleasure and therefore is found in other animals [. . .] but *speech* is for expressing the useful and the harmful, and therefore also the just and the unjust. For this is the peculiar characteristic of man in contrast to the other animals, that he alone has perception of good and evil, and just and unjust and the other such qualities, and the participation in these things makes a household and a city-state (polis). (*Politics* 1253a9–19)

Language has its *telos* in pursuing justice, thus making the polis possible. Here, *logos* is speech with an attitude, with an inherent purpose. And the polis, as Aristotle argues here and in his *Ethics*, through its laws and customs habituates humans into the good life. Except as a "creature of a polis" (*politikon zôion*) – and on this almost all Greeks agreed – we cannot be human at all, but must be either a beast or a god.[33]

---

[31] Dierauer (1977) 33; Lorenz (2000) 222.

[32] See: Gill (1991) 174–80; Everson (1994b) 7–8; especially Sorabji (1993) (versus Gill on pages 20–8) for discussion and references; Preus (1990) 85–99 for the Peripatetics. For the Stoics, the connection is secure: the rational animal, the only animal worthy of moral consideration, has linguistic, propositional context to its impressions; see *LS* 53T with 53V, 33A–D; for Stoic language, Long (1971); for rationality, Inwood (1985) 18–41, 66–91. Good on the place of language in the Pyrrhonists is Glidden (1994); Clark (2000) provides an introductory sketch of the significance of animal passions.

[33] For the implications of Aristotle's biological conception of the political animal for human politics, see: Depew (1995); Kullman (1991). Kullman (on pages 99–100) concludes that Aristotle claims that "there are also other animals which are political, but that man is especially political because of his

The success of the polis, the establishment of laws, the rise of justice, the exercise of our humanity – civilization itself – are tied to the use of, and depend upon, speech. We are uniquely cultural beings, and language is both a manifestation and creator of that culture. This connection becomes commonplace in later rhetoric, where command of language makes civilization possible and thus makes Athens, the *locus classicus* of loquacity, superior to other Greek city-states and Greeks superior to other cultures.

For we are in no way superior to other living creatures with respect to the other powers we possess. We are, in fact, inferior to many in swiftness and bodily strength and other faculties. But, since we have developed the ability to persuade each other and to make clear to each other whatever we want, not only have we been set free from living like beasts, but having come together we have founded cities and made laws and invented arts. Nearly everything we have devised the power of speech (*logos*) has helped us accomplish. (Isocrates, *Nicocles* 5–6)

Elsewhere, Isocrates says that Athens uniquely honored speech (*logoi*), since she realized that it is the single endowment that makes us unique among all living creatures. By using this faculty, we have risen above the others (*Paneg.* 48). Athenians are superior to the rest of the world in "those qualities by which the nature of man is superior to the other animals, and the race of the Hellenes to the barbarians, in that you have been better educated than others in wisdom (*phronêsis*) and in speech" (*logoi*; *Antid.* 293–4). Lysias also contrasts the force of "wild beasts" with the duty of men to convince by argument (*logos*; *Fun. Or.* 18–19). Xenophon's Socrates states simply that the power of human expression (*hermêneian)* "makes it possible for us to share all good things with each other by teaching and to take part in them, to lay down laws and administrate the polis" (*Mem.* 4.3.12).[34] Gorgias' *Helen* is the acme of sophistic treatments of the power of *logos*: the word triumphs over action and becomes reality itself.[35]

So it is not surprising that the invention of speech, sometimes combined with the gift of reason, is frequently listed in Greek anthropological accounts as the first human tool that enabled us to climb out of our primeval bestial state. In Euripides' *Suppliants* (201–4), for example, Theseus praises whatever god brought order into our life from disorder and brutishness,

---

speech." Aristotle, as can be seen even from this very brief summary, uses *logos* to mean a wide variety of things; see the convenient surveys in Mortley (1986) 25–30; Roochnik (1990) 23–33. At *Hist. an.* 488a32–b3 Aristotle differentiates animals by the kinds of sounds they make.

[34] Xenophon too (through his character Socrates) is capable of providing numerous "unique" distinctions between man and beast, from voice and hands together to hands and reason together (*Mem.* 1.4.11–14). For Isocrates' "hymn to *logos*," see Poulakos (1997) 9–25.

[35] Segal (1962).

first by instilling reason, then by providing the tongue, the messenger of thoughts (cf. Diod. Sic. 1.2.6; 1.8.3–5). In the famous Ode to Man in Sophocles' *Antigone*, the chorus celebrates that man has taught himself speech and wind-swift thought (354–6). Plato has Protagoras say that man's divine portion was first to be the only creature to worship gods, and second to possess skills such as articulate speech (*Prt.* 322a). Later Hellenistic theories of the origin of language, some no doubt going back to the fifth century, seem frequently to have couched the acquisition of language in the context of the separation of men from other animals.[36] The Romans – and not just the Epicurean Lucretius (5.1028–90) – also paid special attention to language as a civilizing force. Horace says the first creatures who crawled forth on the earth were dumb (*mutum*) beasts, and only with the invention of words and names was progress possible (*Sat.* 1.3.99f.; cf. *Carm.* 1.10.1–14; Cic. *Rep.* 3.2.3; *Carm. epig.* 1528). The rhetorician Quintilian believes that reason (*ratio*) is our greatest gift, but would be useless without speech. In fact, he goes on to state that animals do possess some thought and understanding (*intellectum et cogitationem*), and it is because of their lack of speech that they are called "mute and irrational" (2.16.14–19). Speech makes us human.

Not that all animals are speechless. The Greeks occasionally envisioned a golden age, before the tripartite division of gods, men, and animals became necessary, in which animals could converse with humans. Golden-age visions of the past have always been useful for thinking about the defects of the present and the glories that might yet come to pass. The blissful ages of the past and future, the abode of gods, utopias, Elysian fields, isles of the blessed, distant "barbarian" lands – even dramatic comedy – can all serve the same function of providing a space outside of normal human experience.[37] Animals often play a central role in these imaginary constructions of paradise and the examination of the present.

Sometimes such fantastic places are vegetarian, where even the "wolf also shall dwell with the lamb, and the leopard shall lie down with the kid"

---

[36] There is a great deal of debate about these theories, especially on the later Epicurean ideas versus those of the Stoics (nature versus convention); see Cole (1967) 60–9; also Sikes (1914) 62–5; Dahlmann (1928); De Lacy (1939); Vlastos (1946); Havelock (1957) 79–81; Sacks (1990) 56 and bibliography in Long and Sedley (1990) 488.

[37] For the connections between comedy and various versions of utopia, see Konstan (1995) 15–90; Hubbard (1997); Ruffell (2000). The term 'golden age' itself only shows up in some Latin authors, and gold is not usually associated with it (although Hesiod tells of a golden race); see Baldry (1952). Gatz (1967) lists twenty-three examples. On the difference between social utopias (a goal towards which one may legitimately and hopefully strive) and the golden age, either in the distant past, or far-off (which is a magical, fabulous, fantasy that cannot be a goal or paradigm and was not meant to be), see Finley (1975) 180–1, although this distinction (and others, such as those of Konstan) seems to me to be too severe.

(Isaiah 11.6), although, as Woody Allen adds, the kid won't get much sleep.[38] Meat-eating is usually just one of many elements and practices that are absent from these idyllic locations.[39] Sometimes meat loses its connection with animals altogether. Herodotus (3.18) tells us of a place where meat is thought to grow precooked from earth. This *topos* develops into a comic convention, the perfect parodic extension of the "automatist utopia," in which nature becomes culture. In Pherecrates' *Persians* (130E), we hear of a time when a tree will put forth leaves of roasted kids' guts, and bushes will sprout tender squid and broiled thrushes. Cronus himself, according to Lucian (*Sat.* 7), boasts that there were no slaves in golden days (a common motif), bread already baked and meat already cooked were provided; wine flowed in rivers; milk and honey spurted freely, and (perhaps least likely) all men were good.[40] In some cases, the animals volunteer for suicide missions: Telecleides in his *Amphictyons* (Ath. 268b–c), for example, describes olden days when fish would come to one's house on their own, bake themselves, and serve themselves on tables. Thrushes, already roasted, flew unbidden into waiting mouths. This is guilt-free carnivorism at its best.[41]

Amidst this fantasy, we also occasionally learn that at one time animals could talk. In Plato, for example, the ability of animals to speak long ago would have been beneficial if used – no surprises here – for philosophy. In life under Cronus, we are told, people had leisure and the ability to converse not only with themselves but also with beasts. If we made full use of opportunities with a view to philosophy, talking with animals and one another and learning for the sake of wisdom, then people must have been immeasurably happier than now. But if they ate, drank, and gossiped with each other and animals, merely "telling stories," then the lost opportunity would only have made things worse (*Plt.* 272b–c).[42] Callimachus, adapting an

---

[38] Cf. the Orpheus-like world frequent in Latin (e.g. Verg. *Ecl.* 4.22, 5.60; Sen. *Herc. Oet.* 1060; Claudian *Rapt. Pros.* 2, praef. 25); also Theoc. 24.86f., although this may be interpolated; see Gow (1950) ad loc.; Buchheit (1986).

[39] E.g. snow, clouds, work, disease, slavery, etc.; see Davies (1987a); (1988). Dombrowski (1984a) 19–34 reviews the role of vegetarianism in the golden age.

[40] In *True Story* 1.24 Lucian parodies such stories by describing the unappetizing picture of men on the moon whose noses drip honey and limbs sweat milk. On such "culinary utopias" in Greek comedy, see Fauth (1973); Wilkins (1997).

[41] Sometimes, in an ugly reversal, the natives eat human flesh instead. These cannibalistic associations in the golden age are merely the inverse of the norm – sometimes animals live like humans; at other times humans live like animals. For cannibalism among "primeval man," see Hesiod *Op.* 276–9; Orphic *Fr.* 292K; O'Brien (1985) 274–5; Festugière (1949) 215–20. On this double vision, sometimes even mixed within the same account (as in Theophrastus), see Vidal-Naquet (1986) 286–8.

[42] On Plato's golden age (including the vegetarian world of *Leg.* 782c), see Vidal-Naquet (1986) 285–301; Dillon (1992) 28–30 and 35 n.17 suggests that animal speech was a traditional feature of golden-age theorizing.

Aesopic tale in *Iambus II*, tells how animals once could talk the same way as humans, creatures of "Promethean clay." But a few animals complained about old age and Zeus' rule, whereupon he took away all their voices and added them to mankind. Consequently, humans have become garrulous (*poulumuthoi kai laloi*), and some (especially those not much liked by Callimachus) still speak like beasts. In the preamble to Babrius' Aesopic fables (1–13) we hear of a golden race who lived at a time when the other animals had articulate speech and knew the use of words (*logous*) and held meetings.[43] *The Beasts* by the comic poet Crates included a speaker imagining a return to the "olden days" when there would be no need for slaves – and the fish would jump into the frying pan and tell us when they're done. The chorus of animals, while allowing fish-eating, demanded an otherwise strictly vegetarian diet (14–17E).[44] In Pherecrates' *Miners* (Ath. 268e–269d) we hear of an all-food underworld, where hot slices of sausage lie scattered by the riverbanks, like oysters. Roast thrushes fly around mouths, asking to be swallowed. Here, we find speaking animals combined with the frequent culinary utopias conjured up in Attic comedy. There's nothing funnier than talking meat.[45]

Animals, then, speak in comedy and satire, both on stage and in mock-epics, such as the *Battle of Frogs and Mice*. But they are most famously garrulous in fables, where they converse with gods, humans, inanimate objects, and each other. In our extant examples of the genre, there are more tales involving animals speaking with animals than any other type. Fables are, in the words of one critic, the "true champions of animal eloquence."[46]

The fable has a long Eastern pedigree, the first extant Greek example coming in Hesiod's famous story of the hawk and the nightingale (*Op.* 202–12).[47] Beastly fables – fictional narratives which portray some moral truth by revealing the predictable character traits of humans – take full advantage

---

[43] In a sort of Franciscan natural mysticism, everything was animated by *logos*. Stones spoke, as well as pine needles and the sea; cf. Jubilees 3.27–30 with Osborne (1990) 15–16.

[44] Ceccarelli (2000) 453–5; Ruffell (2000) 481–3. Although, as Wilkins (2000b) 348 points out, there are other indications that *all* meat-eating may be banned.

[45] As Wilkins (1997) 253 notes, "in comedy the food talks back." Animals spoke in the times of Cronus in Cratinus' *Ploutoi* (*Fr.* 363.12–13), at least as read by Ruffell (2000) 476–7.

[46] Dumont (2001) 107. The word "fable" itself derives from a Latin root meaning "to talk." There may have been a tradition in antiquity of dividing fables into two categories, Aesopic (with animals as characters) and Sybaritic (with human beings); Isid. *Etym.* 1.40.2 and Ziolkowski (1993) 18.

[47] See the list in Holzberg (2002) with conclusions on page 19. *Logos, muthos*, and *ainos* were all terms used for fable in classical world; see van Dijk (1997) 124–6; Zafiropoulos (2001) 1–2; Holzberg (2002) 20; also Nagy (1990b) 314–38 and Adrados (1999) 192–200 on the connection of oracles, portents, and similes with fables.

of the most basic vision of animals in antiquity. Their silence forms the essential foundation for these allegorical tales with ethical functions: animals don't talk, so they can be made to say whatever we want in an attempt to understand – as well as critique and influence – our own behavior.[48] In this case, they literally speak and act just like us, abusing language (by lying) to disguise and satisfy their beastly (i.e. human) desires. Interestingly, Aesop was said to have been a Phrygian-born mute and bestial in appearance (he is compared to a frog, monkey, dog, and baboon), a slave who gained speech in a miraculous dream. His inarticulateness, along with his foreign, servile origin and deformed body, makes him the perfect Other to represent the voices of the principal Other.[49] Some scholars have even seen a direct connection between the indirectness of "slave discourse" and the "animal discourse" in the fable – it is the way communication can be made between persons of different status.[50]

Animals talk like us, and act like us, in distant and fictional worlds that help us reflect on ourselves. Their everyday silence makes them extremely useful. And potentially funny, just like the language of all the Others. You can hardly shut up the little critters in the topsy-turvy world of comedy, where slaves, women, and animals rule the roost. Frogs, birds, goats, wasps, storks, ants, bees, as well as sirens, Centaurs, and Amazons are all featured in choruses of Attic comedy. One of Aristophanes' characters remarks that the comic poet Magnes won victories by producing all sorts of voices (*phônas*), apparently both barbaric and bestial, as he plucked, flapped, played the Lydian, buzzed, and dyed himself green to play a frog (*Eq.* 520–4). One of Archippus' comedies – on which Athenaeus wrote a monograph – even presented Athenians with a dancing and singing chorus of fish.[51] As we

---

[48] See especially Zafiropoulos (2001) for the kinds of ethics found in Aesop's fables. As early as Archilochus (*Fr.* 177W) a fox appeals to Zeus for justice, as if the supreme god cares about who is just. Zafiropoulos agrees (28–30) with Nøjgaard's analysis that there are no absolutely consistent "types" of animals in these tales: the lion is not always strong, the wolf crafty, etc. In this way, the animals are like the beasts in Homeric similes; see Duchemin (1960) 397.

[49] See Lissarrague (2000) 136; Holzberg (1996) 633–9, (2002) 76–84, on the *Aesop Romance*, with full references; Zafiropoulos (2001) 10–12. For the similar medieval use of talking animals in fable, see Wackers (1988).

[50] Cole (1991) 48–9; Ziolkowski (1993) 6–10; Rothwell (1995) 233–9; Ford (1999) 38–42; cf. Phaedrus, Book 3, Prologue 33–7. The Greeks did not consider Aesop's tales to be solely children's fare. Socrates, for example, was versifying Aesop as he awaited his death (*Phd.* 60b–61c; cf. Arist. *Rh.* 2.20); see Desclos (1997) for Plato's use of Aesop.

[51] Wilkins (2000b) 347; see the list of animal choruses in Sifakis (1971) 76–7. In comedy, humans can become animals in tolerably humorous ways that may make the transformation less perilous than in other genres; see Silk (2000) 252–5 on Philocleon as "master animal," moving from animal in words to animal in action. But, unlike Silk, I would still suggest that Philocleon's "vitality" and "spontaneity" are meant to be seen as inappropriate in and dangerous to a functioning community.

see so clearly in Aristophanes' *Birds* – a chorus comprised mostly of edible fowl[52] – the beasts can become wonderful tools with which to comment on human politics as well as character, part of the comic exploration of community social, political, and religious codes.

So where does all this lead? It seems that many, but not all, Greeks thought animals lacked reason; none thought they could speak (as least in the same way humans do). Some drew a connection; some challenged it; still others put human thoughts and voices into the usually silent animals in order to pursue their own artistic and political agendas.[53] But the earliest and most central distinction remained the silence of the beasts. As Herodotus asks, "How could a dove utter human speech?" (2.54–7; cf. Diog. Laert. 8.91). When Achilles' horse begins to talk, the carefully differentiated worlds of human and beast are intolerably mixed, and so the Erinyes as guardians of the natural hierarchy put the cosmos back in order by silencing the animal for good.[54]

Greece has been aptly referred to as the "land of *logos*" and Athens as a "city of words" – even "drunk in language" – in recent studies.[55] The ongoing debate about the extent and consequences of literacy in ancient Greece only highlights the significance of the spoken word: all scholars concede that even with the advent of literacy the Athenians remained a remarkably oral society.[56] In no other ancient culture can we find such a premium put on speech, language, and rhetoric, such self-consciousness about the correct means and ethical place of speech in human endeavor. Geoffrey Lloyd concludes his comparison of ancient Chinese and Greek methods of inquiry by pointing out that "the tradition of debate itself stands out as the key institution (of a different kind from those of bureaux

---

[52] Dunbar (1997). Even in this upside-down world of Aristophanes (unlike the vegetarian world of Crates), however, sacrifice of animals will continue both to gods and birds; see Wilkins (2000b) 344–5.

[53] See the Epilogue. The belief that animals can in some sense think turns up already in Presocratics such as Diogenes of Apollonia, Archelaus, Anaxagoras and Empedocles. The first evidence for a systematic discussion of animal intelligence is found in the Peripatetic School, but Plato and Pythagoras (Diels, *Dox. Graec.* 432, 64–5) were said to hold that "the souls of the so-called irrational creatures are rational (*logikai*) but do not actually function rationally because they do not have the power of speech (*to phrastikon*). Thus monkeys and dogs think (*noousi*) but do not speak (*phrazousi*);" Plass (1973).

[54] This passage is examined at the beginning of the next chapter.

[55] Montiglio (2000); Goldhill (1986) Chapter 3, 57–78; O'Regan (1992) 10.

[56] See the recent works, for example, by Gentili (1988) 3–23; Thomas (1989); (1992); Harris (1989); Powell (1991); Steiner (1994), as well as the many responses to the thesis of Havelock (1982) that only with literacy can abstract thought – *logos* – be possible; e.g. Margolis (1983); Adkins (1983); more recently Nails (1995) 139–9; Powell (2002) 21–5; and compare Ornstein's (1997) 34–42 argument that the presentation of phonographic scripts from left to right caused a mental revolution in the left hemisphere of the brain.

or courts) in the situation which most Greek intellectuals operated."[57]
For the Greeks, man *may* be uniquely rational, but ultimately and without
exception he is *homo loquens*, man the talker.[58] Here, then, is a characteristic
of the Hellenic world that is worth exploring in order to understand both
the Greeks and their legacy:

One of the distinguishing features of classical Greek civilization was the value which
it placed upon public argument, debate and disputation. This generalization is truer
of some periods in Greek history than others, and truer of some places than others;
but, by and large, it faithfully reflects a difference between Greece and the other
major cultures of the ancient Near East.[59]

OTHERNESS

The silence of the beasts served as the basis for many of the Greeks'
significant political, social, psychological, and literary self-explorations.
Speech provided the foundations for both rationality and the polis, the
psychological and cultural distinctions of humanity emphasized so frequently by the classical and Hellenistic Greeks. Moreover, as we will see,
the human–speech/animal–silence polarity provided the central framework
for the classical exploration of and justification for the Other that has
been examined so exhaustively over the past three decades. Humans *can*
speak – this was a definition of humanity. So the exercise and control of
speaking became a primary factor in determining both individual and group
status.

There is a difference, of course, between language and speech. One can
know and even master a language and either not be able or choose not to
speak. But, as will become clear in the course of this book, this distinction
is not the important one in the assumptions of the early Greeks concerning

---

[57] Lloyd (2002) 135. This is the more remarkable in that, as Lloyd points out, in most ways the
approaches taken by the two quite different cultures in their pursuit of knowledge actually converge.
His book on the same topic (2002), co-authored with N. Sivin, is entitled *The Way and the Word*, with
each noun standing for the distinctive nature of the Chinese (the *tao*) and Greek (*logos*) principles
of scientific inquiry.

[58] The Romans too remained tied to "the word," as I have tried to show in the case of Ovid's
Metamorphoses; Heath (1992b) 65–87. De Luce (1993) 317 also aptly applies the term *homo loquens*
to the Romans. Some modern and apparently Latinless linguists, trying to capture our exceptional
verbal ability, have labeled our species "homo loquax," which is not quite what they seem to mean;
see Lieberman (1998) and my Epilogue. (This is better than the "homo loquans" referred to by some
anthropologists; see R. Foley [1995] 43.) Goldhill (1986) 75 observes that the spoken word plays an
extended and important role that would be hard to underestimate in fifth-century Athens. On the
therapeutic, almost magical power of "the word" in Greece, see Laín Entralgo (1970).

[59] Buxton (1982) 5; see his discussion on pages 24–7; also Steiner (1967) 36 for other, dissimilar cultures
with metaphysics that "transcend the verbal."

social and political status. What made the crucial difference was control of speech, to use one's language (and this meant Greek) authoritatively and *orally*. [60] Or to *choose* not to use it (a lesson both Odysseus and Telamachus learn well). The key is to be in command of one's speech. Silence means different things at different times and in different situations, different to the Navajo, New Yorker, and Finn. Silence can signal passive powerlessness or the exercise of authority, depending upon the institutional and cultural context.[61] There are different kinds of silence: institutionally determined (e.g. in temples, rituals, taboos), group-determined (e.g. as punishment, in an audience), individually determined (e.g. from deference, anger, contemplation). Moments in religious ceremony among the Greeks were carefully marked by appropriate speech and holy silence. One must know when to speak, shout, pray, and when to hold one's tongue (*euphêmeite*) and not speak the unspeakable (*arrhêta*).[62]

Silence is often associated with passivity and powerlessness, but it also has force if controlled and used in the right settings. Silence can be an active performance, necessarily involving conscious activity. Aeschylus was known for his "silent" characters, who seemed to wait almost endlessly before thundering forth (*Ran*. 911–20). Sophocles, too, was a master of silence. Is there a more powerful control of a scene than Oedipus' extended refusal to respond at all – a "most perfect expression of scorn," as G. B. Shaw referred to such silences – to Polynices' pathetic request for help (*OC* 1254–84)?

The question is not only who can speak, but what can be spoken, how, and in what circumstances. Silence is not merely an acoustic phenomenon, nor is it in total opposition to speech. Communicative silence is deliberately produced or enforced.[63] It is in this light that we will view Spartan "brachylogy" in a later chapter. As Plutarch says, a timely silence can be

---

[60] The Greeks, of course, relied on supplementary forms of communication as well: hand gestures, facial expressions, and body language must all have contributed to creating meaning; see Lateiner (1995); Miller (2000) 188–230; Worman (2002) especially 89–107.

[61] On the different meanings of silence within culture and in different cultures, see especially Jaworski (1993). Kurzon (1998) 5–24 surveys the various connotations of silence in general. For the complexities of power and speech/silence, see the essays in Tannen and Saville-Troike (1985); also Gal (1991); (1995) 170–8; Tannen (1993) 176–8; Watts (1997). Hedrick (2000) esp. 89–170 examines silence and "rehabilitation" in a historiographic context.

[62] The supposed five-year silence of initiates into Pythagoreanism was merely one of the very odd things about this cult; see Casel (1919) 51–5; Mensching (1926); Burkert (1972) 178–9; Montiglio (2000) 9–45. Montiglio (2000) 16–17 shows that *euphêmia* is really speech and silence at the same time, well-omened speech and silencing of ill-omened words that leads to propitious speech.

[63] Walkerdine (1985) 205; Sobkowiak (1997). The inexpressiveness of modern males is apparently notorious, and not just a matter of inarticulateness or an inability to respond to needs of others; see Sattel (1983). On the active nature of silence, see Dauenhauer (1980) 4–6.

better than any speech (*De liberis educ.* 10e; cf. his *Sayings of the Romans*, 207c, which may originate with Simonides, *PMG* 77: "There is a value without risk also in silence"). His entire *De Garrulitate* is a celebration of the power of self-imposed silence. To be talkative – a mere "babbler" – when action is called for, or when silence would better accomplish the task at hand, is equally the sign of brutish behavior: two of the most annoying traits in Theophrastus' *Characters* are "Garrulity" (*adoleschia*) and "Idle Chatter" (*lalia*).[64] But to possess that power of silence, one must be able to determine when and how one speaks. That capacity is exactly what the Other lacks.

I must confess that I was alarmed when I realized that my study of animals was not only leading me *away* from flesh-and-blood creatures, but was also taking me *into* the well-grazed and adjacent fields of structuralism and "alterity." It was certainly never my ambition to add another tome to the tottering stack of investigations of Greek Otherness. I had once even hoped that the appearance of Victor Davis Hanson's examination of Greek agrarianism and farmers, impishly but aptly entitled *The Other Greeks*,[65] would make us think at least twice before proceeding too much farther down that ever-expanding path. So I feel some necessity to justify yet one more exploration of Greek categorical thinking and to situate this book in that oh-so-familiar landscape.

For a while now, it has been commonplace – perhaps it is has become the classical scholar's *modus operandi* (not to mention *vivendi*) – to expose the Greeks' insidious fashion of self-definition through opposition. In 1993, historian Paul Cartledge could publish a book entitled *The Greeks* that was entirely dedicated to illuminating "the ideological habit of polarization that was a hallmark of their mentality and culture."[66] Cartledge's book has seven chapters with the following subtitles: "Us v. Them"; "History

---

[64] See Zeno's snide remarks in Diog. Laert. 7.18; 7.20; 7.23; cf. Pind. *Ol.* 2.86–8, and below in Chapter 6 on the charges against intellectuals such as Socrates that they were "chatterers."

[65] Hanson (1995).

[66] Cartledge (1993a) 12. I choose this particular example because it is the best of its kind, written by one of our most distinguished classical historians. Hellenophobic Otherness studies continue to appear – indeed, Cartledge's book was recently revived (2002) in a new edition. DuBois (2001), for example, manufactures a multicultural Sappho, whose poetry points "toward same-sex love, devotion, memory, toward hybridity, Asian, African, and European beginnings," as the true model of our Hellenic legacy. She opposes her reading of the poet from Lesbos to the well-rehearsed litany of Greek transgressions: "autochthony, a racialized fantasy of purity, a close male citizen body, the subordination of women and slaves, the restriction of women to reproduction and citizen immobility and stability" (72–3); cf. the perplexing self-incriminations of those like Rose (2003) who still wonder if "teaching classics is inherently colonialist," as if Thucydides, Aristophanes, and Euripides did not exist. The sensible comments of Saxonhouse (1996) 72–86 on the thematic function of the Mytilenean debate and the disaster of the Sicilian expedition should be taken as an antidote.

v. Myth"; "Greeks v. Barbarians"; "Men v. Women"; "Citizens v. Aliens"; "Free v. Slave"; and "Gods v. Mortals." The last five chapters lay out the most familiar polarities in current scholarship, but the structure itself invites us into the heart of Otherness studies.

Equally revealing is Cartledge's approach. He acknowledges that his book intentionally focuses on the "pejorative, derogatory, morally loaded" kinds of polarities.[67] The study of Greek culture risks taking on the air of a World Wrestling Federation slug-fest – and with just as much suspense. It can go without saying (but it rarely does) that Western culture's original thug, the Greek male citizen, has been dubbed the brutish winner long before the opponents have entered the ring. What is unfortunate about even such a well-documented, level-headed, and jargon-free study as *The Greeks*, however, is that readers are mistakenly given the impression that this ancient culture was somehow uniquely rotten. It appears that Greece alone – or in a particularly harsh and influential fashion – created and suppressed "marginalized" groups. Even Cartledge, who incorporates only a comparatively modest ideological agenda – he derides classicists who think "we are all ancient Greeks," for example, but also concedes that the Hellenic legacy is one that we must all contend with – feels obligated to conclude with the following paragraph about Greek freedom:

It was, moreover, a freedom that was dearly bought – and this applies in varying degrees to all the hundreds of classical Greek communities, not only to Athens – at the expense of others, the excluded many: free foreigners and women (Greek as well as barbarian), but above all slaves (mainly barbarian but also Greek). Indeed, the exclusion of those various 'out-groups', the collective Other, was arguably the very condition and basic premise of the Classical Greeks' cultural achievements, not least their invention and use of history. If, *pace* Shelley, we are not in fact all Greeks, that may be a just cause of some self-congratulation as well as measured regret.[68]

What is dismissed here, I believe, is the other side, the more exciting and important side, of the Greek examination of the "collective Other." The reason we in California today (to take a wonderfully vulgar example of the West) have two female senators, Hispanic and African-American mayors of many of our major cities, openly gay members of the assembly, nearly unchecked immigration (including an Austrian-born governor), and no ethnic majority at all in a state of over 35 million residents – as well as the international home of technology and "lifestyle innovation" (not usually

---

[67] Cartledge (1993a) 13.
[68] Cartledge (1993a) 182; see Thornton (2000) 7–8 for a brief critique of Cartledge's position.

very pretty) – is because we all *are* Greeks in some crucial fashion. Our vigorous public debate about affirmative action and the rights of illegal aliens and homosexuals rests on the cultural foundations laid out by the Greeks. The discussion of the Other, not merely our discomfort with it, is alive and well thanks to the Greeks: "The keen interest in the other starts with the Greeks. This interest is but another side of the critical examination and interrogation of their own institutions."[69]

This is by no means to deny the dark side of the Greek legacy of exploitation, oppression, and ruthless dynamism. We live daily with the ugly environmental and cultural consequences of our restless search for the faster, cheaper, newer – our Wal-Mart consumerism of the lowest common denominator. We are often rightly disturbed as well by newspaper headlines that highlight how far we still have to go to make our actions meet our social ideals.

But what is most Greek about the Greek attitude towards the Other is *not* the polarities themselves – these existed throughout the ancient Mediterranean, and indeed are still very much visible throughout the world today. The Hebrew Bible repeatedly recites the story of Israelite encounters with the completely unacceptable and ungodly Other (at least as seen by the later writers and compilers) and its necessary rejection. Seth is the Egyptian god of Otherness: foreigners, the barren desert, and chaos were one and the same in Egyptian thought.[70] Persian King Darius did not really entertain the idea of adopting Athenian-style democracy as the result of lively debate within his inner circle. Both he and his son Xerxes wanted little more than to obliterate that annoying Other living at the western edge of their awareness.

What is special about the Greeks is the degree to which they investigated themselves. They took the Other and held it up to constant scrutiny. They sang about it, analyzed it, and even staged it in publicly funded religious festivals. The Greeks had an overwhelming interest in learning more about who they were not, at least in part so they could better understand what made them who they were. In our attempts to understand Greek thought, we should not forget that this process of self-scrutiny created the blueprint for the societal change that has brought about so much amelioration of past injustices. The conversation the Greeks had about themselves helped to produce the *concept* of freedom, as well as the world's most creative and influential examinations of good and evil, an ethical language. If we

---

[69] Castoriadis (1991) 82.
[70] For Egyptian attitudes towards foreigners, see Helck (1964); Vasunia (2001) 8–9 with references.

want to understand the Greeks, our energy may be better spent exploring what is special to them rather than what universal human weaknesses and perversities they exhibit.[71] As Edelstein wrote about Xenophanes, in his age "only a Greek could have discovered and maintained that man is by nature self-reliant and progressive. Outside Greece, the doctrine was unknown, as was the experience in which it was based."[72]

The Greeks oppressed and limited the Other in many, sometimes horrific ways – that too, is part of our heritage. Reality often fell short of the ideal. But that, in the twenty-first century, is no longer news. Exclusionary thinking is *not* what makes the Greeks – or its Western legacy – unique, much less "alien" to us in the modern world; they neither invented nor cornered the market on cultural pathologies. What they did accomplish, at least partly through their tendencies towards polarized thinking, was to discover a way to ask important questions about how life is and ought to be constructed. More on the mark are conclusions such as those of Arlene Saxonhouse, who affirms that the Greeks did not mindlessly adopt static polarities but instead continually questioned "the adequacy of the dichotomies that govern our political lives and ask[ed] whether bifurcations such as those between male and female, young and old, or public and private oversimplify differences and create false and destructive divisions within the city. Or are such boundaries, whether grounded in nature or created by laws, necessary for political and epistemological order?"[73]

The interesting question is therefore *why*? What drove the little men in the rocky Balkan peninsula so long ago to place such emphasis on exploring their identity, especially in such a polarized fashion? What lies behind

---

[71] On freedom, see the convenient survey in Thornton (2000) 162–87; on the good/bad connection with the Other, see Osborne (2000).

[72] Edelstein (1967) 16–17. It will quickly become clear that I side with many recent readers of Greek literature, especially of tragedy, in finding deeply reflective critiques of the very culture that made such art possible. Saïd (1998) 277–84 surveys modern opinions on the relation between tragedy and politics, suggesting that no global interpretative stance adequately accounts for the variety found in the extant tragedies. Gregory (2002) has sympathy for the recent cautions of Griffin (1998, 1999) that the political element of Greek tragedy can be greatly exaggerated, but (quite rightly, I think) concludes that it is justified "to enlist tragic texts as evidence for contemporary attitudes toward questioning authority, whether in the domestic, military, or civic sphere" (quote on page 147); see also Goldhill (2000) 37–41 and Seaford (2000).

[73] Saxonhouse (1992) 2. Her book is an intellectually honest examination of the Greek desire to keep things in neat categories ("pursuit of unity") in face of the threatening chaos of experience ("fear of diversity") – and the subsequent examination of human limitations in attempting to do so. As she shows, we see the Greeks "grappling with the dangers of the extremes on either side" (x). Some of these issues are also examined by Nussbaum (2001). Buxton (1994) 32–4 has a brief and helpful discussion of what he terms Greek tolerance for "self-doubt"; cf. Pelling's conclusion (2000) 188 that we should "notice this readiness of Athenians to be self-critical." These issues will be taken up in detail in later chapters.

their particular dualities? One need not set out to indict these long dead males, nor must one worship all the polarities, ambiguities, and tensions apotheosized by Lévi-Strauss and the Paris structuralists, to appreciate the importance of understanding the meaning of the categories, dualities, and hierarchies in ancient Greek life.[74] The Greeks were consumed with the Sphinx's riddle, the question of what is man and what are and should be the consequences of being human. "I must know my origins (*sperma*), no matter how small!" shouts Oedipus defiantly at those who would stop his search for the truth (*OT* 1076–7).

Jacob Burckhardt noted that the Greek "freedom of mind" produced something remarkable:

Combined with the feeling of community and social cohesion, there was from an early time something higher and more positive – the study and recognition of otherness, the appreciation of what was different, and this was soon extended beyond the limits of the nation itself; it was accepted as mission for humanity.[75]

This heroic quest evoked explorations, as well as justifications and reinforcements, of the differences between men and women, Greeks and non-Greeks, slave and free. And I suggest that underlying this pursuit of self-understanding through juxtaposition is the Greek assumption of the necessity of maintaining a basic but potentially evanescent duality of human and non-human animals.

Greek ideas of humanity, long before philosophers like Aristotle tried to organize them into a coherent system, were based on, and supported and excused by, the human/animal dichotomy. Greek images of the Other, including the divine, were shaped by their understanding that we humans are in most ways, and yet must not act like, animals. This duality permeates Greek thought, a "pronounced dichotomy, whereby man is rigidly

[74] For a concise summary of the Paris School's interest in how culture defines itself in relation to nature, and the use of a grid to integrate and encode gods, humans, animals, and things, see Vidal-Naquet (1986) 1–12; also Dowden (1992) 36–8. Vernant himself sums up the centrality of opposition in this vision of Greek identity: "There is no consciousness of one's own identity without this other who reflects and opposes you by standing up to you. Self and other, identity and alterity go hand in hand and reciprocally constitute each other;" Vernant (1988) ii, translation by Naas (1995) 14; Detienne (1981). Cohen (2000a) 3–13 provides a convenient recent survey of Otherness studies. Seminal for Greek polarized thinking is Lloyd (1966); for the Pythagorean "table of opposites," see Aristotle's *Metaph.* 986a22 and Burkert (1972) 51–2. A good review of the Greek proclivity for ordering human experience by categories can be found in Lloyd (1983) 7–14 and Parker's review (1984) 182–5, which rightly raises a cautionary voice about transposing Mary Douglas' theories to other cultures; cf. Parker (1983) 363–5 and Padel (1992) 138–52. In fairness, Douglas refined her ideas about animal symbolism several times; see e.g. Douglas (1990). Sassi's recent (2001) effort to "reconstruct strategies of exclusion practiced by Greek anthropological discourse" is primarily based upon the Greek practice of pseudo-scientific theories of character.
[75] Burckhardt (1998) 133.

opposed to other animals, [that] has scarcely any rival as a characteristically Greek concept."[76] The human/animal contrast is frequently mentioned in modern scholarship on ancient philosophy, but it has not been of much interest to Otherness scholars focused on the plight of women, slaves, and foreigners. Perhaps this oversight is at least partially because the "oppressed Other" in this case literally has no voice (and no tenured podium from which) to raise an objection.[77]

WHY THE GREEKS?

More than any other ancient culture, the Greeks knew both that we are like the beasts with whom we share space, and in some fundamental way different as well. They did not tend to confuse either the human or divine with animals.[78] As we shall see, when such conflations do occur they signal something dangerous and destructive that threatens to overwhelm us all. The Orphics, Pythagoreans, Cynics – denizens of the Hellenic reject room, with their "confusion" of human, divine, and beast – transgressed the natural order of the Greek world:

When Empedocles [*Fr.* 446] imagines a condition of the organic world where mixed beings exist, he does so in order to contrast our world with the world of accident that preceded it, and thus to throw into relief the normal state of things where human beings are begotten by human beings and animals by animals.[79]

The Egyptians mixed up the human with the beast and the beast with the divine in a fashion that could never be tolerated by the Greeks. Herodotus may exaggerate when he claims that in Egypt animals are without exception held to be sacred, but his account accurately depicts the Greek puzzlement

---

[76] Renehan (1981) 240.

[77] A wonderfully revealing example of the silence of the "animal other" can be found in Lateiner's recent (2003) 429 response to a panel convoked to discuss the "inherent imperialism" in teaching classics. He suggests (wrongly, I think – see below, Chapter 4) that classicists have "largely avoided pressing issues of social justice in ancient politics." Classical monographs, he contends, "can sidestep who was exploited, how roast lamb found its way under Pericles' knife, how cabbage got to Horace's plate, how oysters reached good Trajan's capacious gullet." This well-honed sensitivity to slaves and the subjects of imperialism misses the rather more unfortunate lot of the lamb.

[78] For a recent collection of articles on the "precarious" relationship between men and animals in different cultures, ancient and modern, see Münch and Walz (1998); also Lorenz (2000) for the ancient Mediterranean. A comparison of attitudes towards animals in art and thought in ancient Mediterranean cultures can be found in Klingender (1971) esp. 28–94.

[79] Vidal-Naquet (2001) 133; de Fontenay (1998) 155–6 refers to these sects as "deviations," either too close to the gods or animals. Some Presocratics seem to have entertained the possibility that humans were originally born from different species, although not in a strictly evolutionary sense; for ancient evolutionary theory, starting with Anaximander, see Müller (1980) 41–56; for animals in the Presocratics, see Frenzel (2001).

at an alien culture's attitudes towards both beasts and the divine (2.64–75; cf. Diod. Sic. 1.83; Str. 17.1.38; Plut. *De Is. et Os.* 71).[80] Despite close association with particular animals, the divinities of the Greek pantheon were not theriomorphic (probably ever, but certainly not by the time we run across them). We find no feline Olympians, no ibis-faced heroes, and especially no hawk-headed, sons-of-god *stratêgoi*. Animal worship of virtually every kind is unknown in Greece.[81] Hellenic gods can and do transform themselves into animals: with the protean and concupiscent Zeus around, no maiden in myth would ever be advised to adopt a stray swan or admire a passing bull. But these transformations are manifestations of the gods' power and involvement in the human world, no more surprising than their frequent appearance in the form of particular humans. Even in Homer when a god flits through the air "like a bird," it is usually impossible to tell if this simile refers to a temporary metamorphosis or simply to the speed and ease of flight.[82] The tripartite Hellenic structure of animals–humans–gods – so familiar to those of us in the Western tradition – turns out to be not at all self-evident or universal. Castoriadis concludes his analysis of Greek versions of anthropology with the insight that other cultures reveal no such demand for firm distinctions: "Let us consider, for example, the Jews, the Hindus, the Chinese, or the Indian tribes of America where we observe a 'circulation' among the animal, human, and divine condition – a circulation, not a rupture."[83] The Greeks recognized the possibility of – and so feared – this fluidity. They developed a series of cultural protocols – what eventually became the heart of Western culture – to attempt to limit the overlap and resulting devastation.[84]

In classical Greece, then, there are no sacred cows, hallowed cats, accursed pigs, or mummified baboons.[85] When minor deities like satyrs and Pan

---

[80] Munson (2001) 93–7 makes an elaborate effort to disentangle Herodotus' "fuzzy" and "contradictory" account. Pease's (1955) note on Cicero's (*Nat. D.* 1.43) dismissal of Egyptian theriolatry lists most of the Greek and Roman references to this "*dementia.*"

[81] Burkert (1985) 64–6; he notes that snake worship is a special case (as mentioned below in reference to myths of autochthony); also Lorenz (2000) 206–14. For Dionysus and the river gods, see Forbes Irving (1990) 43–4, and in general his entire discussion 38–50.

[82] For these divine similes/transformations, see Dietrich (1983) 57–8; West (1988) on *Od.* 1.320; Smith (1988) 161–3; Edwards (1991) 29–30 with note 32 for further bibliography.

[83] Castoriadis (2001) 141. Similarly, several of the Celtic gods (e.g. Epona and Cerynnos) took on characteristics of, and were so closely connected to, animals, that they were "something outside the Mediterranean tradition (with the exception of Pan) and must reflect something rather more fundamental in the perception of the position of the animal in relation to the god"; Green (1992) 197.

[84] Hanson and Heath (2001) 28–58.

[85] See Parker (1983) 357–65 for the lack of a category of impure animals or food in Greece. For a thorough history and analysis of food avoidances throughout the world, both ancient and modern,

exhibit animal features, they *behave* like the beasts as well. Hybrid monsters, mostly imports from the East, live on the margins of the Greek world, enemies of civilization to be tamed, exiled, or annihilated. Heracles may have links with the beasts (he dresses like a lion, eats like pig, drinks like a fish, and apparently has a notoriously hairy butt), but these characteristics prepare him all the better for his labors to civilize the world by ridding it of monstrous animals.[86]

The Greeks' acceptance of our inherent links with the animals helps to explain why for the most part they do not seem to have been driven to explain the creation of man in great detail. The compilers of the Hebrew Bible were unable to separate an exploration of humanity from an authorized version of creation (actually two of them), of man fashioned in the image of a god who could not be made into an image. Few Hellenic anthropogonical myths or theories are extant, however, and they do not appear to have been of great collective importance. There was no Greek *Genesis*, although there were full and authoritative accounts of the origins of the gods. Greek creation stories are primarily political, often tales of the autochthonous birth of community founders.[87] And even these tales often emphasized our original links with rather than our separation from other animals. A little known Aesopic tale (240 Perry) informs us that some men behave bestially because they were originally created by Prometheus as animals, but upon Zeus' orders were transformed into humans.[88]

The Greeks were much more interested in exploring the process by which we separated ourselves from the beasts. That is the function of culture; that

see Simoons (1994). Houlihan (1996) 1–10 (with good bibliography) examines the divine bestiary of Egypt; see also Lorenz (2000) 154–71; Teeter (2002). Engels (1999) 23–41 supplies details about sacred cats. On monkeys as recipients of worship in Minoan religion, see Marinatos (1987). We hear of *individual* animals in classical Greece (as opposed to entire species) that are sacred to or strongly associated with a deity in myth or cult (e.g. a deer or bears to Artemis, owls to Athena), and the type of sacrificial animal appropriate for any particular rite was usually carefully regulated. But the Greeks were remarkably free from the animal fetishes and taboos we find in most other contemporary cultures.

[86] For Heracles as beast, culture hero, and god, see Kirk (1974) 206–12; Burkert (1979) 78–98; Padilla (1998) 20–5; Bonnet et al. (1998).

[87] Finkelberg (1998) 105–11 observes that the first fully developed Greek myth of divine creation is not found until Plato's *Timaeus*. In some tales (for example, Cecrops in Athens), founders are part snake as manifestations of their city's claim to the land. Even these city fathers are considered uncanny, however: Cecrops' daughters kill themselves after spying on the serpentine Erichthonius/Erechtheus; see Gantz (1993) 233–8. Blundell (1986) 3–99 provides the most convenient collection and discussion of Greek accounts of the origins of men; see also the classic assemblage of Lovejoy and Boas (1965). For connections between autochthony and politics, see Loraux (2000), and for myths of origins as ethnic boundary makers, J. M. Hall (1997) 51–107. Davies (1987b) astutely links this apparent lack of interest in the creation of mankind to the rarity in Greek sources of the otherwise ubiquitous tales that explain how mankind came to forfeit immortality.

[88] Howe (1999) 235–6.

is why, as Pindar phrased it, *nomos* is king (*Fr.* 146). As recent studies of classical theories of cultural anthropology have demonstrated, there was a wide variety of thought about how we came to be who we are.[89] Often the Greeks envisioned that primitive man lived like beasts and civilization developed slowly from these lowly origins. Other authors argued that there was once a golden age of harmony between animals, men, and gods, from which we have strayed. There were even those who believed that animals lived a life superior to our own, and many authors contrasted our intellectual progress with ethical regress.[90] After all, culture has enabled humans to oppress and kill each other in a systematic fashion rarely found among animals. Still other theories represented some sort of compromise. The philosophical debate concerning the interactions and conflicts of culture and nature (*nomos/phusis*) that heated up in the fifth century is just one of the more familiar manifestations of this Greek fascination with the question of human nature.

In other words, although there was no orthodox theory of cultural anthropology, there was a Hellenic way of thinking about human origins. What is consistent is the insistence that we are like animals, perhaps once virtually animals ourselves, perhaps now closer to them, but in some important way (at least potentially) different. And most Greeks knew that culture, possible only for a "speaking beast," keeps us from devolving, or evolving, into our bestial selves. The trick is to keep the beast at bay long enough to limit the damage we do on this earth. Under the best circumstances, provided only by the bits, spurs, blinkers, bridles, and reins of the polis, we can create meaningful, fully human lives. The Cynics, celebrating the shamelessness of dogs, merely (albeit spectacularly) inverted this Greek effort at separation by appealing to the natural world as a model of behavior. Diogenes is said (Diog. Laert. 6.24) to have frequently observed that in order to live well we require either reason or a halter (*logon ê brochon*). Most Greeks knew we need both.

---

[89] Theories about the beginnings of culture, numerous in later authors, clearly existed in some form in the fifth century; see Blundell (1986) 103–227. O'Brien (1985) argues that the concept of man's "primeval brutishness" cannot be securely dated before the last third of the fifth century. Cole (1967) controversially suggests that Democritus is the central figure who influences later accounts (e.g. those of Diodorus, Vitruvius, Tzetzes, Lucretius, Posidonius); cf. Vlastos (1946). Other scholars have traced these theories back to Xenophanes; see Edelstein (1967); Guthrie (1962) 400–1; (1969) 62–3. Havelock (1957) 106–9 suggests Anaximander and Xenophanes may have already sketched the outline. One of the central texts of contention is Aeschylus *PV* 442–71, 476–506; see Kleingünther (1933) 66–90; Conacher (1977).

[90] For the superiority of animals to men see Lovejoy and Boas (1965) 389–420; Gill (1969); Lilja (1974). Dodds (1973) 1–25 points out that the idea of progress is primarily limited to the fifth century, and that tension between scientific/technological progress and moral regress is common (e.g. in Plato, Poseidonius, Lucretius, and Seneca).

So the more important question for the Greeks became not whence comes man, but whence culture. While it remains true that the "inbuilt pluralism, dialectical agonism, and practical rationality of the polis gave a distinctive twist to the Greek chapter in the history of government,"[91] the more fundamental question is why these cultural protocols were "inbuilt" in the first place.

This fascination with cultural rather than physical anthropology or anthropogony, and the tremendous variety of opinions provided by the Greeks, are unique in the ancient Mediterranean, a central aspect of the "totally exceptional character of the Greeks in relation to all other cultures."[92] For the Babylonians, the boundary separating the animal and human realms was absolute, while among the ancient Israelites there is no evidence of the ideologically charged dialectic between the animal and human worlds that we find among the Greeks.[93] The lack of a certified account of civilization or a divinely sanctioned version of human creation freed the Greeks to ask questions which the advanced civilizations around them could not, both about animals and about themselves. Eric Havelock long ago observed the peculiar luck of the Hellenes: "[H]ad Greek culture, like the Egyptian or Hebrew, been centrally controlled by an organized religion, it is improbable that any notion of man's history would have been allowed to gain currency."[94]

The Greeks had few religious or cultural restraints to prevent them from examining our own animal nature. As I have argued elsewhere, it is in this conception of human nature that we moderns are perhaps most *unlike* the ancient Greeks. We have traded in our bestial natures for angelic souls (or blank slates) that are tainted primarily either by a religious (usually Christian) conception of evil or by nasty societal forces (economic, political, environmental, racial, etc.). In this therapeutic age, we are all victims of something, hoping to reclaim our metaphysical purity through

---

[91] Arnason and Murphy (2001b) 10.

[92] Meier (2001) 56. He finds the origins of the uniqueness among the intelligentsia, whereas I turn to a more basic psychological impulse that might give rise to a culture that could tolerate an intelligentsia.

[93] Katz (1993); Scurlock (2002) examines the role of animals in Mesopotamian religion. Israelite thought is saturated with metaphors taken from herding and agriculture, but they are applied primarily to the relation of the people and their all-encompassing god; see Eilberg-Schwartz (1990) 115–40.

[94] Havelock (1957) 31; see Sourvinou-Inwood's recent (2003) 20–1 discussion of the Greeks' awareness that their own religious understanding was limited and circumscribed. This is not to say that Greek thinkers eliminated the gods or religion from their pursuit of knowledge, of course. But it is going much too far in the other direction to claim, as French (1994) seems to do, that the ventures into natural history by the Presocratics, Aristotle, and Theophrastus are not a scientific advance over what came before and what existed in contemporary cultures around the Mediterranean.

various forms of "chicken soup for the soul."[95] The denial of our own links with the animals – especially cowardly in this neo-Darwinian age – is in part responsible for our overlooking some of the complexities that the Greeks were trying to disentangle.[96] In his examination of classical ideas about human and animal mental capacities and their moral consequences, Sorabji argues that we have in the West until quite recently ignored half of the Greek discussion about our natures – and those of animals. Instead, we have concentrated "on one half, the anti-animal half, of the much more evenly balanced ancient debate."[97] The material fueling this ancient debate was the nearly universal acceptance that we are *all* animals. Given this, then, what makes us – and what *should* make us – different?

OUTLINE OF THE BOOK

The following chapters examine the underlying links between speech (and lack of speech), animals, and human status in representative works of Greek literature.[98] In making a claim that there is a Greek way of viewing the world – particularly when concentrating primarily on Homer and two Athenian authors – I open my argument to the charges of reductionism, essentialism, Athenocentrism, Romanticism, and a whole host of other critical "-isms" that are likely to be hurtful to a sensitive soul. After all, archaic and classical Greece had perhaps as many as 1,500 different city-states, a variety of ethnic enclaves, no idea of nationhood, little consensus in philosophical outlook, a variety of dialects, multifarious constitutions, and 400 years of rapid development between Homer and Plato. Such sweeping claims of "Greekness" threaten to whitewash the delicately nuanced picture of a world "becoming" rather than "coming into" Greece: clearly there is no "single" Greek view of anything.

---

[95] Hanson and Heath (2001) 40–6.
[96] For the moral implications of evolution, see: Rachels (1990); Dennett (1995) 452–521; Pinker (2002).
[97] Sorabji (1993) 1–3.
[98] In some ways, this study can be seen as my attempt to provide a first step towards a supplement of Sorabji's philosophical discussion of the place of animals, in which he suggests that the "story could be still further enriched by attention to non-philosophical texts" (1993) 3. Although I do not ask the same questions as he, and certainly do not approach the literary texts as a philosopher, I think there is much to be learned about these topics by concentrating on the pre-Aristotelian literary tradition. Montiglio's (2000) excellent recent study of the cultural and literary functions of silence in ancient Greece covers some of the same ground as I do, but is not at all concerned with the role animals play in the Hellenic view of speech and humanity. Her examination of language and silence in Greek texts also takes her study quickly through many different texts and genres, whereas I focus in detail on three authors.

In a previous book, I challenged these familiar criticisms of efforts to talk about the Greeks in some comprehensive fashion.[99] Even the crowded freeway of classical scholarship has the need for a variety of on-ramps. Discussing cultural commonalties over time and place does not deny the existence of difference and development as well – the two approaches can be complementary. Jonathan Hall, for example, has recently argued for a far more fluid sense of "Hellenicity" than most scholars have previously found in the evidence. Greek ideas of Greekness, according to Hall's detailed analysis, arose surprisingly slowly. Ideas of ethnic difference, protean in their own right and late in developing, gave way in the fifth century to an Athenocentric scale of cultural difference. Hall is suspicious of studies that evoke a "digital," binary opposition in Greek self-definition, and I think rightly draws our attention to the spectrum of oppositions ("analogic") revealed in our sources.[100]

My own analysis, on the other hand, reveals the links between Greek attempts from Homer to Plato to explore who they are. And rather than focus primarily on what the Greeks say about themselves directly, I also look closely at central literary texts that indirectly reveal the cultural assumptions that support their pursuit of what it means to be human. This examination of the literary "thematization" of these issues – a search for a "poetics of cultural expression" – as well as my interest in continuity of outlook rather than development, will lead me in different directions.[101]

Ultimately, however, each individual attempt to draw broad conclusions about a diverse and complex culture must fall or stand on its own detailed analyses. One way I have tried to support my contention in this book that there is a Greek way of thinking about what it means to be human is to focus very closely on major texts at the beginning, middle, and end of the period. *The Iliad* and *Odyssey* present the first substantial evidence we have for these ideas, and so three chapters are devoted to a close examination of both poems. In claiming that something is Greek, it is crucial to demonstrate that it has been there from the beginning of the evidence and not, say, just in fifth-century Athens. It was the archaic Greeks who first began referring to and thinking of themselves as Greek.[102] I then demonstrate that the same ideas, although dressed in different clothing, appear as central themes

---

[99] Hanson and Heath (2001) 21–8.

[100] Hall (2002); see Buxton's (1982) sensible approach to these parallelisms and analogies frequently found in Greek thought: they are a heuristic device, not a prescription.

[101] And to reach different conclusions on some important points. Hall's thesis, for example, forces him into a titanic effort – one that I think necessarily sinks – to play down the role of language in Greek identity; see Chapter 4.

[102] See the recent summary by Ruprecht (2001) 32–5, but also Hall (2002) passim.

in three plays by the earliest of the three great Athenian playwrights, and also throughout the entire Platonic corpus. Further, I bring in evidence (especially in Chapter 4) found in a wide variety of archaic and classical authors from as many different places (particularly Sparta) and genres as possible to support my argument.

And finally – to be honest – I concede. This is a first attempt to make the case. I hope I have made a good enough argument here about Homer, Aeschylus, Plato, and Athenian culture in general to warrant further detailed exploration of different authors (e.g. Hesiod, Euripides), genres (e.g. the historians and orators) and bodies of evidence (art, for example). Most readers who finish this already long book will be grateful, I think, that I have not attempted the task of closely analyzing every extant Greek text and artifact.

Yet my reading of Greek literary evidence leaves me convinced that one aspect of the Greek world that remained fairly constant over time and place was the centrality of speech in the polis. The editors of a recent collection of papers on "alternatives to Athens," after understandably bemoaning the modern overconcentration on Athens as "extremely unrepresentative of ancient Greek *poleis*," go on to observe that even in non-democratic systems, the assembly still met and the consensual aspect of these communities remained crucial: "Hence persuasion and the cultivation of rhetorical ability were an essential part of political leadership from the time of 'Homeric' society onwards."[103] The Greeks and speech are simply inseparable, and inextricably linked to speech is the Hellenic reflection upon humans and other animals.

Enough of what this book is not. Under scrutiny here are the assumptions about the place of man and animals in the cosmos that inform much of the later, more influential philosophical discussion. First: what did the early Greeks – at least those few whose thoughts we can now read – think made us human? For answers, in Part One I turn to Homer. The opening chapter examines the Homeric poems for that distinguishing characteristic and finds that speech, rather than any mental or psychological ability, is the crucial criterion. If speech is what makes us human, then control of speech becomes an essential determinant of status. Intelligible, cogent, and authoritative speech is the single most consistent criterion in distinguishing between beings of every sort: gods and humans, men and women, Greeks and non-Greeks, the dead and the living. The centrality of authoritative articulation in defining a fully human life was embedded in the Greek mind long before careful philosophical distinctions were made.

The second and third chapters then take up each of the Homeric poems in turn to show how speech is thematically significant to the epics. Control of language demarcates not just the more familiar categories of Other but also distinguishes the young from the mature, the best of the Achaeans from the worst. Telamachus' journey to manhood is traced as a process of developing adult, masculine speech. By the end of the *Odyssey*, he has grown from an ineffectual "child" (*nêpios*) into the deserved bearer of his epithet, *pepnumenos*, "wise" especially with regards to speech. Achilles too must mature, but in a very different fashion, into a "speaker of words" and not merely a doer of deeds. He becomes bestial in every sense of the word, in act and speech, before reemerging in the final book of the *Iliad*. But in brilliant Homeric fashion, the hero's education in the use of language takes him beyond the cultural norms to a manipulation of storytelling for uniquely human instead of primarily competitive purposes. Both epics recount the development of immature young men who cannot control their language effectively into adults who manage their speech in fully human (albeit quite different) ways.

Part One, therefore, attempts to establish that embedded in Greek thought from the very beginning of our evidence is the belief that our power of speech differentiates us – at least potentially – from the rest of the animals, as well as from other humans. Control of language therefore becomes the tool by which we develop and exploit our humanity. Part Two turns to the classical world. A survey of the various categories of Greek Other reveals that what connects them is the loss of their authoritative control of language. The culturally imposed silence associates the Other metaphorically with animals and in turn buttresses and vindicates second-class status. Women, free non-citizens, slaves, barbarians, young and old, and even the gods are all carefully isolated by their association with the silence of animals. Yet in their insistence on free, rational, and open speech as a primary criterion in "creating difference," the Greeks bequeathed to Western civilization the very tool we have used to begin dismantling insti-tutionalized prejudice.

Part Three then examines literature from classical Athens, the home of *logos* and the politicization of polarities. How do the issues raised in our earliest evidence (Part One) and later applied politically and socially (Part Two) play out in classical literature? I examine two representative authors in detail. The first case-study covers the slippery world of Aeschylus' *Oresteia*, where humans and animals are dangerously interwoven in imagery and language itself. Only through the uniquely human application of speech can human, beast, and god be disentangled and the polis invented and maintained, a political space that offers us our best chance of keeping the beast in the halter.

Chapter 6 uses the cultural significance of speech to explore the meaning behind Socrates' fate as depicted in the Platonic dialogues. If to control speech is to exercise one's full humanity, then to be forced into silence is to be reduced in status to some uncomfortable level of the Other. Socrates is portrayed as exaggerating both ends of this dichotomy: to be fully human is not merely to speak, but to converse philosophically. Thus, he is already radically reorienting the significance of speech from its social and political role to a metaphysical tool. But the crisis is more personal: what happens when citizens are driven to silence in the competitive public forum in the land of *logos* by the very process, dialectic, that is supposed to make them more human?

The book concludes with an Epilogue that considers some of the consequences of using animals as the basis for the Other. In some ways, this study is meant to lay the groundwork for further exploration of the history of attitudes towards animals in the West. What are the consequences for animals of this Hellenic definition of humanity and thus of moral worth? As Steve Baker has shown in his study of the "rhetoric of animality," when "animals figure, or can easily be thought of as figuring, in binary oppositions, *they invariably represent that negative in the opposition*."[104] To quiz Lévy-Strauss on what most people take to be the unassailable side of his equation: animals may be good to think with, but are they really all that good to eat? Well, sure they are (as one of my students once replied to this question), "especially with a little barbecue sauce." But this human convenience misses the lion's share of the ethical implications raised by the question. Are animals merely tools for humans to manipulate, not just intellectually but physically (and now even genetically) for our own material comfort? Many Greeks themselves did not think so.

Our Hellenic heritage presents us with two competing values:

1. A traditional view that non-human animals are morally insignificant because of their lack of speech (and therefore reason, which was soon linked to a divine soul);
2. A Western urge to investigate this view rationally, to see if it holds up.

Some of the modern animal-rights movement turns out to be entirely Greek in spirit, hardly "anti-humanistic" as critics mistakenly charge.

---

[104] Baker (1993) 77–119, emphasis in the original; cf. Fudge (2002).

Scientific evidence that derives from Greek ways of thinking, combined with ethical questions that are embedded in our Western blueprint, leads to new knowledge and different answers to old questions: Do no other animals possess language? Can an animal think without speech? Are some other animals rational? Is the rationality of an animal the sole criterion that determines its moral worth? Does mere membership in a rational species suffice to "protect" even those members who are not rational? Professor Sorabji, with no ideological axe to grind, describes the results of his own examination into classical thinking about animals:

I was not at first concerned with any of the moral issues. I was only interested in charting the debate in the philosophy of mind, until I noticed how bad were the arguments designed to show that animals were very different from us. It all sounded rather grand, when Aristotle said that we have reason and they don't. But under pressure, the Stoics retreated to the position that at least they don't have syntax. The moral conclusion was meant to be 'They don't have syntax, so we can eat them.' My embarrassment increased when I noticed that the modern debate, among the followers of Chomsky and critics of the language abilities of chimpanzees, had reached exactly the same point. It has become crucial whether animals have syntax. This, of course, is a question of great scientific interest, but of no moral relevance whatsoever.[105]

As a critic of the hypocritical and West-bashing extremes of Otherness studies, I am aware (and my friends are quick to remind me) of the potential irony in this final effort to link ancient Greek thought with modern morality. Many years ago, my dissertation advisor, a politically active gay man who was to write a well-known book about Greek sexuality, told me that we all end up writing about ourselves. My only thought at the time was that this insight might explain the quality of a lecture I had recently attended on lacunae in Aeschylus. But there is a reason that feminists consider the male–female polarity to be of prime importance in understanding the Greeks, or that Marxists see the free–slave dichotomy as foundational for other relations in antiquity: the fox knows many things, the hedgehog one great one. I find myself daily, at home and at school, listening to the silence of the beasts. I don't know what this means, but it can't be good. A book that was originally intended solely to be a work of literary criticism and not intellectual or social history, much less another exercise in alterity, in the end has metamorphosed into a critical examination of the grand-daddy dichotomy of them all, the *pater familias* of polarity, the Ur-Other. *Hê pronoia d' hê thnêtê kapnos kai phlênaphos*: the gods chuckle at our plans.

---

[105] Sorabji (1993) 2.

One final introductory word. In the following interconnected studies, mostly literary, there is no overt homage paid to any modern theoretical school. There is much in this study that is redolent of structuralism, for example, and my approach often borrows from an impressive body of scholarship. Yet I also think the jargon and extreme formalism found in some structuralist studies are unhelpful, and thus I have abandoned much of what is found in these more subtle applications. No doubt the giants upon whose shoulders I stand will at times grow annoyed by the smell of my socks.

And although much is said here about the links between the ability to speak authoritatively and status, the reader will find no direct references to "discourse analysis" or "speech acts" or "paradigms of power" or "valorization of engendered hierarchies." I have read as much scholarship from as many different perspectives as possible. My debts to this secondary material are many, and are recorded in the notes. My own approach, after a decade of work on the topics in this book, remains comparatively and irredeemably ingenuous. When I suggest that certain kinds of speech lack authority, for example, I mean it in the way that my students, family, and neighbors understand the expression: no one pays much attention to it, is influenced by it, or feels compelled to act upon it. No parent of a teenager will need further explanation. Nor would the Greeks. Certainly, even this mundane definition fits into some theory, but it does not require a label. Every critical stance, in theory, is theoretical. I would hope an innocent reader could make it through the entire book without requiring a manual or, worse yet, a series of mini-lessons on the theoretical underpinnings of my methodology. Learning the rules of these manuals is a career in itself, and a thin one at that, not unlike mastering Esperanto. I have spent most of my effort trying to think about the Greeks, especially Homer, Aeschylus, and Plato, as carefully as possible. I would like to think my priorities have resulted in something worth reading; I am certain that I have could not have spent my time in better company.

PART I

Speech, animals, and human status in Homer

CHAPTER I

Bellowing like a bull: Humans and other animals in Homer

Just before Achilles reenters battle, the angry hero lectures his horses not to leave him dead on the battlefield (*Il.* 19.400f.). This admonition in itself is not so unusual. Hector urges on his steeds with a lengthy petition (*Il.* 8.185–97), and the enterprising Antilochus warns his horses in the middle of a chariot race that they had better run faster if they don't want their throats slit (*Il.* 23.403–16). (Apparently they understand Greek, since "in fear" they immediately pick up the pace.) But in Book 19, as Achilles steps onto his chariot, something quite surprising happens: one of his immortal horses talks back. Not only does the horse converse, but he prophesies the hero's fate in ten perfect hexameters. Nothing in the epic has prepared us for this most famous talking stud in Greek literature.[1] Can animals speak in Homer's epic world?

No, of course not. The poet is at pains to emphasize the singular unnaturalness of the utterance. Achilles is psychologically isolated from the Greek community, denying the validity of gifts, food, burial, and companionship of any kind. His butchery of Trojans over the next three books will reveal him to be part beast, his humanity sacrificed to the passion of revenge. He has dedicated himself to death, both Hector's and thus inevitably his own. Homer brilliantly marks Achilles' separation from all things human by depicting the hero conversing with his steed. As Cedric Whitman observed, "prophecies by horses are calculated to arrest attention."[2] Hera gives the hero's horse the temporary gift of human speech (*audêenta*, 407). The horse does not have the power to speak when or what it chooses – Xanthus is

---

[1] The oddity of Xanthus' prophecy has led some scholars to suggest that Homer has somewhat carelessly adapted an earlier myth, that of Arion, to a new context. Besides the uniqueness of an articulate horse, it has seemed curious to some that Hera grants the ability and the Erinyes terminate it; see Heath (1992a) 397–9 for discussion with bibliography.

[2] Whitman (1958) 271.

no Mr. Ed.[3] The Stoic Chrysippus commented on the replacement of the usual equine sounds (*phônê*) with a human voice (*audê*):

So, too, the poet, when he depicts Achilles conversing with his horses, says that one of the horses spoke, adopting human speech (*anthrôpineî dialektôi*). For he says: "the white-armed goddess Hera made him speak (*audêenta*)" – not because he had no voice before (*aphônon*), or because he did not possess the voice common to horses (*phônên*), but because that is not called *audê*.[4]

The horse, even though immortal, does not have the power to speak. Hera chooses him as momentary instrument of fate. The conversation is an extension of a common function of animals in Greek thought as revealers of the future in the form of prophecies and portents – horses in particular are associated with death and fate.[5] What better way to portray Achilles' detachment from humanity, of his own unacceptable links with the divine and the beast, than to have him conferring with a divine animal right before the crescendo of monstrous violence leading to Hector's death?

Yet even this brief, god-sanctioned violation of the rules of the Homeric world is so serious an offense to universal order that the Erinyes themselves immediately step in to put a halt to the human voice of the animal (19.418). Talking animals are enough of a threat to the ordinances of nature that the cosmic regulators quickly intervene.[6] The gods can bend the rules of nature as known to mortals, perhaps even override fate itself (they threaten to save their favorite warriors from destined destruction, for example). But the poet of the *Iliad* is uncomfortable with the logical and messy consequences of this power, and refuses to let his deities exercise it to any

---

[3] Thus Edwards' (1991) humorous query ad 19.404–17: "One wonders how bards delivered this speech; presumably its solemnity would discourage any equine intonation." Pelliccia (1995) 105–7 convincingly refutes Johnston's claim (1992) that the horses could always speak.

[4] In Galen = *SVF* II.144; trs. Clay (1974) 132; see Labarrière (1984) 39–40 for Aristotle's distinction between *logos* and *phonê*.

[5] See Malten (1914) 179f., 196f.; Rahn (1953) 464f.; Keller (1963) vol. I: 248; Dietrich (1965) 91f.; Richardson (1974) ad 18; Lilja (1974) 72, and Pelliccia (1995) 107–8, with references to other speaking animals in prophecy. This is not the same as a fable; see Van Dijk (1997) 124–6. Edwards (1987) 287–8 is on the mark when he suggests that "probably such warnings occurred in other epics when Achilles or other heroes entered their last battle, and the poet has adapted the scene for the present occasion." I have tried to show elsewhere (1992a) that the horses are part of a series of divine gifts – Chiron's spear, Peleus' armor, Thetis herself – that carry inherent symbolism of mortality and the rift between men and gods. For the connections of Xanthus with previous legends and Homeric themes, see Delebecque (1951) 35. Horses seem to have a special place in the poet's heart – they weep at Patroclus' death, for example (*Il.* 17.426–56); see Nicolay (2001) 54–6.

[6] The bT-scholia on *Il.* 19.404 says the Erinyes appear here in their role of "overseers of things contrary to nature" (*episkopoi gar eisi tôn para phusin*); cf. Heraclitus *Fr.* 94 for the Erinyes as "allies of *Dikê*," who will not allow the sun to overstep its limits. On the role of the Erinyes in epic in general, see Padel (1992) 164–8. All Homeric references are to the *Iliad*, unless otherwise specified.

great degree.[7] So it is with speech. Thus, we are told that the magical golden maids created by Hephaestus are endowed with *noos, phrenes, audê*, and *sthenos* (18.417–20) but they are never shown exercising their human-like organs and characteristics. Instead, they are presented in the epic merely as mechanized crutches. The gold and silver dogs guarding Alcinous' palace (*Od.* 7.91–4), marvelous creations though they may be, are given no mortal characteristics, at least not by Homer, who is careful about such things.[8]

Animals do not speak, an obvious fact of life that holds even in Homer's most exotic locales. Critters bark, bleat, and bellow just like the animals we are all familiar with today. An eagle does converse with Penelope, but only in a prophetic dream with an emphatically human voice (*phônêï . . . broteêï, Od.* 19.545). After killing twenty geese, the eagle flies to the queen and provides an interpretation of his own actions: a bird before, he has returned as her husband to kill the suitors. The combination of prophecy and Penelope's own wishful thinking – some scholars have even suggested she has a certain affection for the fowl[9] – make the eagle's speaking particularly portentous, but there is nothing magical here: it is a fantasy.

Not even in the folk-tale world of Odysseus' distant wandering do we find talking animals. Scylla, with her monstrous heads, can only bark terribly like a newborn puppy (*Od.* 12.85–7). The forbidden meat of Helius' cattle bellows eerily (*memukei*) like live animals (*boôn . . . phônê*, 12.395–6) – this is unpalatable enough. Polyphemus talks to his ram, wishing he had the power of speech (*potiphônêeis*) to tell him where Nobody is hiding (9.456–7), but even this brute does not expect a response.

Animals do not speak in fairyland. If you want to turn men into swine, as Circe teaches us, you can leave their minds (*nous*) unchanged but transform their bodies and voices (*phônên*, 10.239–40). Their minds are useless without

---

[7] Morrison (1997) has suggested that at key junctures there is a hint that "something very different might have happened" than is dictated by fate. But in fact nothing different ever does happen in the action of the epic itself. This is a poetic way of increasing the dramatic tension of a scene while also dealing with a world populated by competing fates and deities. As Jones (1996) 116 concludes, Homer is not a theologian. On the other side of the issue, Pucci (2002) 29–30 suggests that when Zeus contemplates saving Sarpedon (16.433f.) Homer "cunningly" prompts us to think Zeus could save Sarpedon but we know Zeus cannot. But do we? After all, Ganymede, one of the "mortal men," was taken up by the gods to pour wine for Zeus, "so that he could be among the immortals" (20.232–5; and see below for options beyond immediate death available to those in the *Odyssey*).

[8] Despite the ingenuity of the argument by Faraone (1987) 257–80. The dogs are described in divine terms, not human, as "immortal and ageless."

[9] See the arguments against this interpretation in Rozokoki (2001) 2–3. It could be that Penelope has invented the entire dream to explore the character and identity of the stranger she so oddly entrusts with such a personal experience. Lonsdale (1989) 408 notes that the eagle in effect performs the same role as a bird diviner, linking omens, fables, and similes.

speech.[10] This, as we shall soon see, is the same procedure adopted by the gods when they take human shape.

Although the attitudes towards animals expressed by characters may differ in the two epics,[11] there is a consistent portrayal of animals' basic nature: except for their lack of voice, animals in Homer seem to be composed, both physiologically and psychologically (the difference disappears most of the time), very similarly to humans. A close examination of Homeric beasts reveals that the ability to speak separates humans from the rest of the animal world. This criterion of differentiation then provides the foundation for all other categories of human status in the poems.

LANGUAGE AND THE ANIMALS

There is no general word in Homer for animal. *Thêr* and *thêrion*, the closest candidates, refer to wild beasts, and do not include domestic species.[12] In fact, these words (the latter appears only in the *Odyssey*) may not even include birds and fish, or else Laertes would not lament that his son must have perished far from home, devoured by fish, beasts (*thêrsi*), or birds (*Od.* 24.291–2). The strong linguistic demarcation of living beings into gods, humans, and animals so familiar to the classical age is missing one of its key components. No place in Homer can we find that neat tripartite division that becomes a hallmark of later Athenian efforts to differentiate.[13]

[10] This passage is often taken to imply that pigs do *not* usually have *noos* (e.g. Renehan [1981] 254). But what the poet emphasizes is that the men retained that *same noos as before* (*hôs to paros per*). This last expression would be completely unnecessary if animals obviously had no *noos*. The only *noos* available would be men's. In fact, the major point of this transformation seems to be that while they received a pig's body and voice, they did *not* get a pig's mind. Just what that might be like is not of concern to the poet. At 329, Circe tells Odysseus that his *noos* is beyond enchantment, which suggested to some scholiasts that Homer means not that the men's entire *noos* was unchanged, but just the part of the *noos* that likes human beings; see Combellack (1987) 210, 217. Thus, the ancient commentators assumed that both pigs and men had a *noos*; the issue was how much needed to be changed when one becomes a swine; see below for the *noos* of the dog Argus.

[11] Dumont (2001) 73–97 argues that in the *Odyssey* there is room for an affection towards animals that is found only for horses in the more hostile universe of the *Iliad*.

[12] See Körner (1930) 3, and the summary in Dierauer (1977) 7 with n.4; cf. Seiler (1953), esp. 232–3, who sees the contrast between men and animals coming in Greek thought only with Hesiod. The earliest use of *thêr* in the more inclusive sense is found in Archilochus *Fr.* 177W. *Zôion* is first attested in Semonides *Fr.* 13W. Lonsdale (1979) 156 concludes that there is no truly generic word for animals until *to zôion* comes into common use in the fifth century.

[13] E.g. Sophocles' *en thêrsi, en brotoisin, en theois anô* (*Fr.* 941.12; cf. Eur. 346N and the discussion below in Chapter 5 of Aeschylus' Erinyes, whose troubling nature is described as not of gods, men, or beast, *Eum.* 69–70). Hesiod (*Op.* 277) pits fish, beasts (*thêrsi*), and flying birds against humans in terms of their possession of justice (*dikê*). For these animals to eat each other is considered cannibalism by the poet. So although the word *thêr* itself here cannot refer to all animals, there is a dichotomy between human and animal that does not seem to be Laertes' point in the *Odyssey* passage; see Renehan (1981) 254–5; Lau (2000) 8–16.

To understand the place of animals in Homer's world we must look at them case by case – and there are a lot of them, at the last count (by those who count these things) sixty-two identifiable species of animals, all but five restricted to similes.[14]

One of the most notable features of the Homeric epics is the frequent comparison of humans to an impressive menagerie of animals. Clearly, at least on the surface, we have much in common with our furry, scaly, and winged (if less eloquent) fellow creatures. Over half of the similes in the *Iliad* (125/226) have animals as their subject.[15] When we think of these comparisons, we tend to recall most immediately the numerous physical actions and reactions that make the drama, especially on the battlefield, so vivid. Warriors can scarcely move without evoking a zoological double: they stream out like bees, swarm like flies to milk, range like rams, leap like wolves, fight like lions, pursue like hawks, tremble like deer, dart like hawks, screech like vultures, bellow like bulls, flee like locusts before fire, race like a horses, are penned in like lambs or stretched out like worms, and in the *Odyssey* even cling like a bat or have their brains dashed out like puppies.[16] Perhaps we are not surprised that animals possess the same physical properties as humans – such words as *sthenos* (strength), *alkê* (prowess), and *charmês* (joy in battle) are common in the extended similes.[17]

But most significantly, as the reference to the "joy" of animals suggests, Homer was even more interested in the mental and emotional connections between the heroes and their non-human counterparts. References to seats of emotion or psychological or mental states are found in nearly two-thirds of animal similes in the *Iliad*, and in almost two-thirds of these an analogous mental state is mentioned in the surrounding narrative. Homer assumes, then, that animals are motivated by the same emotions and causal thoughts as humans. As a result, they can be credited with such virtues as bravery, industry, and parental devotion.[18] In fact, these similar feelings, motives, and levels of awareness are often the main point of comparison.

---

[14] Lonsdale (1990) 25, with list on pp. 129–31.

[15] Lonsdale (1990) 10. Edwards (1991) 24–41 has an excellent summary of the different forms and functions of Homeric similes and metaphors in general. Minchin (2001a), (2001b, 132–60) expands upon Edwards by using a cognitive perspective to focus on the relationship between imagery and meaning. Metaphors are much less common in the epics; for some examples using animals, see Kokolakis (1981). Stanford (1972) 131 notes that true animal metaphors are limited to only the dog, deer, fly, and lion.

[16] Lee (1964) 65–73 and Scott (1974) 190–205 provide fairly complete lists of animal similes in the epics.

[17] Lonsdale (1990) 133–4; Clarke (1995) 146–8.

[18] Lonsdale (1990) 15, 82; he concludes that there are approximately forty phrases in the animal similes that emphasize the heroic ideal of bravery and its opposite, cowardice; see also Lilja (1974).

There is every reason to believe that Homer found little significant distinction between the mental or emotional lives of human and non-human animals.

Some of Homer's most moving similes involve parental affection and suggest that animals feel and possess consciousness, and do not just behave in the same way as humans. Achilles suffers for others as a mother bird does for her chicks (9.323), and laments the loss of Patroclus like a lion who has lost his cubs (18.318; cf. Odysseus and Telemachus wailing like birds whose young have been taken, *Od.* 16.216; Penelope compared to the grieving nightingale, *Od.* 19.518; and the fear and grief of the negligent doe who abandons her young in the lion's den, *Od.* 4.335 = 17.126). Conversely, Odysseus' men weep upon his return from Circe's cave with a joy similar to that of calves frisking about their returning mothers (*Od.* 10.410; cf. the Trojans' bleating like ewes upon hearing their lambs, 4.433). Warriors defending their positions, or fallen comrades, are frequently compared to similarly defiant animal parents. So Polypoetes and Leonteus defend the Greek wall "like wild boars," rejecting the assault of Asius, who complains to Zeus: these two, he says, are as adamant as wasps or bees that have made their nest (*oikia*) in a path and will not leave their home (*domon*) but stay and defend their young (*teknôn*, 12.167–72). The language makes clear the commonalties, with anthropomorphic terms bringing the insects' actions into the human realm. They have homes, both in the technical and domestic sense, and their offspring are called *tekna*, a standard term for human children as well.[19]

These actions of the non-humans thus are thought to be as complex as those of their human counterparts. The point of the simile is the fierceness of the wasps' defense. Their actions only make sense to the poet if they are instigated by human motives. There is no suggestion here of a hard-wiring of animals' reactions, no effort to distinguish some sort of learned reaction from an instinctual response. Nor do all animals have a single disposition which the poet can simply slap into place as needed,[20] although the frequently timorous behavior of threatened deer, cattle, sheep, small birds, and fish makes an excellent analogy for the feelings of impotence associated with human fear. In similes, as in fables, animals are often chosen for particular "conventional" traits. But even lions – animals usually

[19] Other similes with animals defending their young include 16.259 (wasps), 17.133 (lion), 17.4 (cow), *Od.* 20.13 (dog). Homer uses *tekna* of animal young fairly frequently (e.g. 2.311–15, 11.113, *Od.* 16.216, etc.; cf. the similar double use of *tekos*). For *oikia* of animals, see also 12.221, 16.261 with Fraenkel (1921) 91–4 and Lilja (1974).

[20] *Contra* Lloyd (1966) 184 and Sassi (2001) 38–9.

selected for their courage and fierceness – can be afraid when the occasion calls for it (e.g 17.67; cf. *Od.* 4.792). The "meaning" of individual species not only is linked to the context but also varies depending upon whether they show up in similes, metaphors, formulaic expressions, or the general narrative.[21]

Homeric beasts have wills (e.g. 16.825, 17.112), can yearn (11.161, 24.6), be eager (5.136, 11.239, 13.471), have joy (2.462, 3.23), be proud (6.506–10, 15.263–7) and disappointed (11.555, 17.664). Suggestive too are expressions involving *blemeainôn* ("exulting in," e.g. 12.42, 17.22, 135) and *pepoithôs* ("trusting in," 5.299, 13.471, 17.61, 17.728; *Od.* 6.130) combined with a noun such as *alki* (force) or *sthenei* (strength), which imply a high degree of self-consciousness. The poet assumes that the animals' actions are motivated by the same thoughts and impulses that drive the humans to whom they are compared. The ostensible purpose of animal similes is often not merely to point out how fierce or strong someone is, but to provide insight into the source of that human action. There is no irony intended when a lion or boar is said to possess "manhood" or "manly courage," *agênoriê* (12.46; cf. 12.300, 24.42).[22] The result of this complete overlap in emotional and mental states can be both dramatic and startling. Athena instills the same daring (*tharsos*) into Menelaus that fills a relentless fly that cannot be driven away before it tastes blood (17.569–73). The courage of the fly – perhaps not the first trait one associates with the insect – is the entire point of the simile.

Nevertheless, one need not be a hardcore behaviorist at this point to want further evidence that Homer attributes human faculties to animals to explain similar behavior in his human subjects. We do not always mean exactly what we say, especially when it comes to how we view animals. The rustic chasing a chicken with an axe may very well mumble something to himself like: "So, you think you can get away from me?" or: "You're putting up a brave fight," but that hardly reveals a belief that the fowl has thoughts or feelings that are in any way comparable to those of a human. The implication in the similes is not that humans and the animals are identical in every way. Similes work by bringing disparate objects together that share some particular feature (or features) – the juxtaposition of similarity *and* difference is where meaning is created: in most ways, Menelaus is

---

[21] For an excellent demonstration of this link between the significance of a particular type of animal and the type of literary trope in which it appears, see Faust's (1970) discussion of Homeric dogs.

[22] On the meaning of this word as if it were the intensive *aga-* prefixed to the stem for "man," see Clarke (1995) 152 and n.43, and below in the discussion of non-Greeks.

not a fly. The two domains of a simile cannot overlap entirely.[23] Homer
carefully maintains the basic animal–human distinction on the larger scale,
as can be seen in his avoiding or suppressing tales of metamorphoses.[24]
We will discover that the actual blurring of a hero with his animal analogue
signals a dangerous loss of humanity. But there is another body of evidence
that supports my basic contention that humans in the Homeric world
are remarkably similar to other animals.

Whatever the poet believed was going on when his characters thought
or felt, the same process in the same internal organs is found in all his
living beings. Much has been written about the various "organs" of psychological activity in Homeric man and their connections with speech.
For our purposes here, it will suffice to indicate that despite occasional
assertions in the critical literature to the contrary, Homer was not particularly concerned with separating humans from non-humans in terms of
their biological or metaphysical construction. Although these psychic entities are often distinguished from each other – albeit inconsistently – and
have been identified with various internal organs, they remain remarkably
difficult to pin down, and are probably best considered as metaphorical
terms.[25] For example, *thumos, kardiê, phrenes, noos,* and *psuchê* are all linked
to speech in some way.[26] Moreover, animals possess them all at some point
within the Homeric poems. Deer (*Il.* 4.243–5), wolves (16.156–7), and a
lion (17.109–12) are credited with *phrenes* (cf. *mega phroneonte* of lions and
boars, 11.325, 16.758, 16.824; *oloophrôn* of the same beasts, 15.630, 17.21;
and *kaka phroneôn* of a lion, 10.486, and of wolves and lambs, 22.264).
Beasts frequently have a *thumos* as well, which behaves just like a human
thumos.[27]

[23] Minchin (2001b) 134.   [24] Forbes Irving (1990) 9–12; Vidal-Naquet (2001) 134–5.
[25] Clarke (1999), however, rejects the traditional dualistic interpretation of the body/soul in Homer
and argues that there is a fluid range between both the mental apparatus in the body (physical
organs, such as the lungs, however improperly understood) and the thought and emotions produced
therein. Complete listings and descriptions of these organs can be found in the books and articles by
Sullivan, (especially: 1988; 1989; 1995b; 1995a, 1–122; 1996). Her methodology and conclusions have
been superseded in part by the work on the interchangeability of elements ("semantic degradation")
in certain contexts; see especially Jahn (1987), whose analysis is put to good use in the excellent study
of Pelliccia (1995).
[26] Sullivan (1995b).
[27] Lonsdale (1990) App. B pp. 133–5; Pelliccia (1995) 55–6 and n.89; Clarke (1995) 145–9. See, for
example, *Il.* 11.555, 12.300, 17.664 (lion; cf. *thumoleonta,* 5.639, 7.228), 12.142 (hawk), 12.150 (boar),
13.704 (ox), 16.162 (wolves), 17.22 (boar), 16.468, 17.451 (horse), 17.744 (mule), 17.678 (hare), 22.263
(wolf and sheep), and *Od.* 17.744 (fish). Achilles tells Agamemnon that he has the heart (*kradiê*) of
a deer (1.225). A boar possesses a *kêr* (12.45), and an *êtor* is found in fawns (11.115), wasps (16.264),
and lions (17.111, 20.169); see Cheyns (1985). Stanford (1959) ad *Od.* 1.52 observes that *oloophrôn* in
the *Iliad* is confined to savage animals, but in the *Odyssey* is used to describe gods (e.g. Atlas) and
mortals (e.g. Aietes, Minos).

One often reads that Homeric animals do not have souls like those of humans. Homer does seem reluctant to credit an animal with a *psuchê*.[28] For example, whereas the *psuchê* can fly away from men at death to the underworld (e.g. *Il.* 16.856, 22.362), it is usually the *thumos* that departs from animals to nowhere in particular (e.g. *Od.* 3.455, 11.221). But Homeric expressions for death are varied, and animals share in almost all of them. On one occasion, the *psuchê* does in fact leave the body of an animal, a boar sacrificed by Eumelus: *ton d' elipe psuchê* (*Od.* 14.426). The identical expression is used at *Il.* 5.696 for the fainting of Sarpedon (cf. the same phrase at 16.453 for the hero's imminent death). And the expressions for the loss of *thumos* for both humans and animals at death overlap to such a degree that they are impossible to distinguish. The *thumos* can leave humans in the identical fashion it departs from animals: the phrase used at *Od.* 3.455 of a sacrificed heifer – *lipe d' ostea thumos* – is the same expression used of the death of warriors (*Il.* 12.386, 16.743; *Od.* 12.414; cf. *Il.* 20.406). Anticleia describes the process of human death in this very form (*Od.* 11.221). The phrase applied in *Il.* 23.880 to the death of a dove – *ôkus d' ek meleôn thumos ptato* – is virtually identical to that used earlier of humans (13.671–2, 16.606–7). The *thumos* of a boar is "seized" (12.150) just as a hero is eager to "seize" the *thumos* of an enemy (5.852). In general, the *thumos* of an animal can fly off (*apo d' eptato thumos, Il.* 16.469 of a horse; *Od.* 10.163 of a stag; 19.454 of a boar) in the same way the *psuchê* of a human does (e.g. *Il.* 16.856, 22.362). Anticleia also generalizes that the souls of all humans fly off in similar fashion when they die: *psuchê d' êut' oneiros apoptamenê pepotêtai* (*Od.* 11.222).[29]

Homer does not use these psychological terms with the kind of precision that we moderns would like, and it makes little sense to reject what the text

---

[28] See, for example, the comments of Garland (1981) 49; Rahn (1953) 448f.; Snell (1960) 11–12; Warden (1971) 95–6 n.1. For the soul of animals in Homer in general, see Bremmer (1983) 125–31 and Claus (1981) 62 n.8. West (1961) 134 comments on a likely reference to the soul of a snake in Hes. *Fr.* 96.

[29] In fact, the *thumos* can be thought of as going to the underworld just as the *psuchê* often does (7.330, 16.856, 22.362; *Od.* 10.560, 11.65). Nestor says that if Peleus heard of the Achaeans' cowardice he would pray that his *thumos* "apart from his limbs might enter the house of Hades," *Il.* 7.131. Garland's objection (1981) 49 n.50 that this is part of an unfulfilled statement seems to me beside the point. True, the *thumos* never actually flies off, but Peleus' conditional statement would only have force if the protasis were possible. Kirk (1990) ad loc. calls the use of *thumos* here "casual, not to say careless," but that simply begs the question: would such a statement have seemed absurd to Homer's audience? We have no evidence that it did. Thus, I cannot accept attempts, such as those in Snell (1960) 8–16, to resolve the overlapping qualities of *thumos* and *psuchê* by assuming "contamination" of one passage with another, or postulating different "layers" of tradition. Recent critiques of Snell's theories about Homeric man's fragmentation and lack of self-awareness can be found in: Halliwell (1990b) 37–42; Williams (1993) 21–9 (philosophical); Wirshbo (1993) (philological).

clearly states.[30] Both humans and at least one animal have a *psuchê*, and all species seem to have a *thumos* (as well as every other psychological organ and activity associated with the organs). When alive, then, there is simply no obvious difference between the mental or physical lives of humans and animals. Our examination of similes would lead us to expect this: the entire point of the comparison of actions, emotions, and motivations depends upon a parallel "inner" life of both individuals being compared, the so-called tenor and vehicle.[31] And all living species die in similar fashion. Both the *psuchê* and the *thumos* of animals and humans depart upon death; both can fly away, and both can be imagined leaving the body upon death and moving to the underworld. In fact, Odysseus sees Orion in the underworld driving together the *very same* animals he had killed when alive (*Od.* 11.572–5)!

One possible explanation for the rarity of a reference to a *psuchê* in animals is that the soul in Homer, as Redfield has argued, is the self that exists for others.[32] The *psuchê* appears only upon death, or near death, because humans die not only physically but socially. This is decidedly *not* the case with animals, who are the ultimate representative of nature alone, not culture. When an animal dies, it does not change states, nor does it have a community that needs to deal with such a metamorphosis. It does seem to have a personal connection with a family (e.g. the possession of *oikia, domon, tekna*) that can grieve, but there is no larger community of bees or cattle, for example, that must integrate death and renewal into its concerns. Animals therefore apparently need and have no social selves beyond the family. But this distinction has no metaphysical or moral implications. It seems unlikely, given the fact that an animal can be imagined to have a soul that leaves upon death, that Homer believed this distinction to be a crucial one. Moreover, the poet *needs* animals to die like humans. The plain, unhappy fact of our mortality differentiates us from the gods. Animals are

---

[30] Padel (1992) 12–48, esp. 33–40. Clarke (1999), Chapter 5, seems to me to engage in special pleading in dismissing the obvious import of the poet's description of a *psuchê* leaving a body and going toward the underworld. There is no need to force the epic poet to have a consistency of expression about death that is not there.

[31] For these terms for the objects compared in a simile, see Chapter 5. This is parallel to the uncomfortable situation psychological experimenters find themselves in when defending painful and cruel experiments upon animal subjects. If animals are so different from humans that such treatment is not cruel, then what can the experiments tell us about human experience? And if the lab results are applicable to our lives, then it must be because we have done something that we would never inflict upon ourselves to beings who are like us in relevant ways.

[32] See Redfield (1975) 176–8. Rahn (1967) 98–9 explains the near-absence of an animal's free soul by the indifference to continued existence of animals after death, which really amounts to the same thing. Russo and Simon (1968) emphasize the communal nature of *all* Homeric depictions of the mental life of heroes.

perfect analogues for human warriors in the *Iliad* especially because they die just like we do and react to the threat of destruction with all the same thoughts, fears, desperation, hopes, and courage that so characterize the mortals on the battlefield.

Some critics have thought it significant that animals in Homer do not possess *noos*. But it is not true that animals are consistently devoid of *noos* – at least one animal is described as possessing whatever ability is associated with this "organ" (see below). Moreover, *noos* in the epics never suggests reason as we conceive of it, but rather it refers to recognition, a momentary insight, a realization and instant interpretation. It is not until the sixth and fifth centuries that the word moves towards a meaning of "reason" or "calculation," and even then it must compete with other words of similar meaning.[33] So we must discard the connection between reason and speech that is to become so important in later philosophical thought.

There does appear to be some link between speech and *noos*, just as there is with the other psychological organs. But again, this connection is loose. Odysseus' men, who are turned into swine, retain their *noos* but have the shape and voice (*phônê*) of swine. Achilles' horses are granted a human voice (*audên*) but we hear nothing of *noos*.[34] One famous animal in the *Odyssey*, the long-abandoned dog Argus, is identical to Odysseus' men in having the ability to access *noos* but not a voice:

But then, when he realized [*enoêsen*, that is, possessed a *noos* that enabled him to realize] that Odysseus was near, he wagged his tail and dropped both his ears . . . (*Od.* 17.301–2)

Argus can recognize Odysseus through his disguise – the only time Odysseus is detected without his or Athena's cooperation or without a clue such as a scar.[35] Redfield paradoxically uses this passage as evidence that animals do

---

[33] Fritz (1943) 79–93; Furley (1956) 8; Redfield (1975) 175f. Nagy (1990a) 204–5 defines the verb *noeô* as simultaneously the noticing of signs and the recognition of what they mean. Schmitt (1990) 133, 224 argues that the unity of the person in Homer is formed in the *noos*, the act of perceiving this "Inneren" being called *noein*. Sullivan (1989) suggests the noun has a basic meaning broader than the verb – both of which remain remarkably ill-defined – and notes that (unlike other psychic entities) it has no discernible physical connotation in Homer. Clarke (1999) 119–26, drawing on the extensive study of Jahn (1987) 46–118, concludes that *noos* is different from the other psychological entities because it is not the source or instrument of mental life but the conclusion of the thinking process.

[34] Hephaestus' robots have both (*Il.* 18.419). These robots would provide an interesting case in the modern discussion of artificial intelligence. In what way are they different from humans? Is it their immortality? Cf. Moschus' *Europa* 107–8: Zeus *qua* bull has *noos* like a man but is only lacking human speech (*audê*).

[35] See Goldhill (1988) 17–18, and Russo (1992) ad loc. Since this form of recognition is central to the identification of Odysseus – the recognition of a *sêma* is often a prerequisite for this event, and *noos* is the term for this ability – Homer gives *noos* here to Argus without the intermediate stage of *sêma*;

not possess *noos* or perform the action of *noos* while he also must (rightly) conclude that the dog "in effect performs a human mental act."[36] But the text is clear: Argus here instantaneously recognizes and interprets the "sign" – his master has returned after twenty years. That is just what the verb implies, for humans as well as an animal. The dog reacts like the men transformed into beasts by Circe, who also wag their tails and fawn over Odysseus' men (*Od.* 10. 215–17). This may be as close to the original meaning of *noos* as any response in Homer, if Von Fritz is right when he suggests that the "most primitive function of the *noos* would have been to sense danger and distinguish between friend and enemy," and proposes a possible etymology from the root *snu-* "to sniff."[37]

The inner life of animals is presented almost identically to that of humans in Homer. Non-human animals possess the same psychological and emotional abilities as humans, but are lacking the ability to communicate by voice. This is not to suggest that humans in the epics are thought to be exactly like other animals, just that the poet does not distinguish their psychological constitutions. Homer may take it for granted – as now do even most animals-rights activists – that humans exercise their internal "organs" in a far more complex fashion. But as Pelliccia concludes in his study of these attributes in Homeric animals, they have what we would call intentionality, wills, appetites, and desires.[38] In other words, animals possess most of the elements of consciousness. We are told that Hera gives Achilles' horse the

---

see Nagy (1983) 36–8. De Jong (2001a) ad 17.291–327 observes that in other ways as well the narrator treats Argus almost like a human: he is given a name, an introduction, and a solemn death formula that is used in the *Iliad* of dying warriors.

[36] Redfield (1975) 176–8 n.42; cf. Bremmer (1983) 127. Claus 1981) 62 n.8 suggests that animals' lack of *noos* can be explained as a matter of emphasis. On the Argus episode, see: Rahn (1953) 456–61; Rose (1979); Beck (1991); and especially Goldhill (1988) 9–19, who places the encounter with Argus in a series of scenes of dangerous thresholds watched over by animals.

[37] Von Fritz (1943) 92–3. Frame (1978) makes a lengthy argument attempting to connect *noos* with *neomai*, the mind with the return home, but he must admit (33–5) that even if this etymology is correct, Homer no longer understood the original connection.

[38] Pelliccia (1995) 28. Bonnafé (1984) 95–6 maintains that there is no qualitative difference between men and beasts in Homer, and so a term like anthropomorphism would be anachronistic – animals display a practical intelligence of the same order and the same primary emotions as humans; so also Dumont (2001) 45–6. Griffin (1980) 40 notes that animals are occasionally spoken of in ways that show they are not thought to be entirely different from men; cf. Lilja (1974). Heichelheim and Elliott (1967) 85 emphasize Homer's separation of men from animals, but this is relative to Near-Eastern cultures. Seminal studies of the thematic significance of animals in Homer that I have found particularly helpful are by Rahn (1953) and (1967); Schnapp-Gourbeillon (1981); cf. her brief summary in Bonnefoy (1991) 128–31. Redfield (1975) 131 observes that the gods are conscious creatures but, like animals, are incapable of error, because "no mistake of theirs is irremediable." But some of Homer's similes reveal quite vividly that animal mistakes lead to the destruction of themselves and their entire families. On the dignity with which Homer credits animals in general, see Dietz (2000) 178–85.

power of human speech, but the self-defensiveness, pride, and indisputable logic interwoven through the prophecy seem to derive from the very mind of Xanthus.

There is one irrefutable difference between Homeric animals and humans: animals do not speak. Humans, in fact, can barely keep quiet in the epics: about half of each poem comprises characters' speech.[39] This divergence, although not a moral one, forms the basis for a separation of a variety of groups in the Homeric poems, groups that in the classical period will form the core of the "Other" that has been so thoroughly investigated in scholarship over the past few decades.[40] The use and abuse of language becomes a means of differentiation, usually without the moral implications of later times. Yet, as J.-P. Darmon has observed, the semantic position of animals in the symbolic system of the Greeks remained fairly consistent: much of what is valid for Homer remains valid for the classical period.[41] To understand the use of animals in the Homeric poems is to take a large step towards understanding their application in Greek literature in general.

LANGUAGE AND THE GODS

Perhaps the central reflection in Homeric thought on the nature of our existence here on earth is that in many ways we are really *not* like the very anthropomorphic gods of the poems. Gods live on Olympus, holding "wide heaven" (e.g. *Il.* 20.299; *Od.* 1.67), while men live on the earth (e.g. *Il.* 5.442; *Od.* 6.153) – and are buried in it (e.g. *Il.* 3.243–4, 21.63; *Od.* 11.301). The gods can "do all" (*Od.* 10.305–6; cf. *Il.* 19.90; *Od.* 4.237; 14.445) and "know all" (*Od.* 4.379, 468) – although these powers can be seriously circumscribed on occasion, as the plot demands. The gods live easily, whereas they have woven for humans a wretched life of pain and tragic fallibility (e.g. *Il.* 24.525–6; *Od.* 6.41–6). The Olympians consume nectar and ambrosia, while mortals eat the fruit of the fields (e.g. *Il.* 21.465), especially bread (e.g. *Od.* 8.222, 9.89,

---

[39] 55 percent of the verses in the *Iliad* are embedded in direct speech, 60 percent in the *Odyssey*; see Kelly (1990) 3. Kelly argues from the great disparity in correption found in the speeches and narrative that Greek epic, like that of other Indo-European traditions, derived from proto-epic that was composed entirely of speeches.

[40] For the outlines of how speech defines the Other in Homer, see Bologna (1978) 306–17.

[41] Darmon (1991) 128. See Lloyd (1966), a study of polarities in Greek thought; at page 47 he avers that they appear in Homer in a less developed vision than in the fifth century. Padel (1992) 147–52 rightly notes that before the fourth century the various categories as found in Aristotle are too taxonomic for the fifth century and earlier. But I disagree with her argument that before Plato the animal/demonic non-human is on the outside. She sees tragedy as an exploration of the invasion of the non-human, but I think the Greeks did not in fact differentiate so easily between the metaphors of invasion and release.

191) and cooked meat, and drink wine (e.g. *Od.* 5.196–9). Apparently linked with their divine diet is the *ichor* flowing in the gods' veins, as well as their pleasant immunity to aging.[42] All of these differences are elements of the one insuperable chasm between humans and the gods: the gods do not die, and we do. One of the most common words for gods is a negative formation of our own limitations – *athanatoi*, the "deathless ones," in contrast to us, for whom death is inevitable (*thnêtoi*). The impunity of the fickle immortals offers a foil for the meaningful tragedy of the human condition.[43] But scholars have pointed out one other apparently minor distinction that is worth fleshing out in detail: there are elements of both the intonation and the vocabulary of the gods that are peculiar to the divine.[44] The gods don't talk like we do.

Homeric gods look and sound different from mortals. They are bigger and more beautiful than humans, and so it is only natural that their voices can be louder or more Sirenic. A god's shout sounds as loud as 9,000 or 10,000 men (*Il.* 5.859–61, 14.147–51), sending mortals into panic (e.g. *Il.* 5.862–3, 15.320–1, 18.217f.; *Od.* 24.48–9, 530) or instilling them with strength (e.g. *Il.* 5.92, 11.10–12, 14.151–2). Thus, Hera need not strain when she disguises herself as Stentor, a man whose voice has the power of fifty (*Il.* 5.784–91).[45] The adjective *thespesios*, found in the *Iliad* mainly in the sense of "immensely loud," derives from a meaning of "coming from a god."[46] Artemis is closely associated with loud sounds, earning the description *keladeinê*, "resounding," three times in the *Iliad.*[47] Achilles' divinely aided screams are so overwhelming that they instantly drive twelve of the

---

[42] See *Il.* 5.339–42 with Kirk (1990) ad loc. on the etymological and cultural links between *brotós, brótos, ambroton haima, ambrosiê,* and *ichôr*; also Hainsworth (1988) ad *Od.* 5.93; Janko (1992) ad *Il.* 14.170; Clay (1981–2); and Loraux (1986) 350–4. Excellent on the differences between gods and humans are Griffin (1980) 144–78 and Clay (1983) 133–85; see also Schrade (1952) 144–82. Fraenkel (1975) 54–6 sees in this human/divine contrast the first example in Greek thought of "the mode of polar opposites."

[43] It is significant that the rare suggestion that some mortals may escape death (e.g. Menelaus, *Od.* 4.562–9, and Odysseus, *Od.* 5.135–6.209) is never brought to fruition in the epics; see below.

[44] Clay (1972) and (1974).

[45] For a mortal to have such power is odd by Iliadic standards. It is the kind of detail we might expect from the epic cycle, and the line was omitted in some texts and has been rejected by various critics (see Kirk ad loc.). The reference to Stentor's voice is surely hyperbolic, but it may also be revealing that the ancient readers were not uncomfortable with the amazing, indeed impossible physical feats performed during various heroic *aristeiai*, but recoiled from suggestions of superhuman vocal ability; see McKay (1958) for arguments to retain this line. Griffin (1980) 38–9 discusses the supervoice of Achilles.

[46] So Kaimio (1977) 30–2. In the *Odyssey*, the word retains some of its etymological connections, "beyond human," especially when applied to the dead; see below.

[47] 16.183, 20.70, 21.511 (cf. *Hymn. Hom. Ven.* 18f., 117f.). The word was thought in antiquity to derive from the noise of the chase; see Janko (1992) ad 16.183 and Kennell (1995) 52 for Artemis' association with the competitions in singing hymns (in the form of hunting cries) at Sparta. Due (1965) 2–3,

enemy to their self-destruction (*Il.* 18.228–31). When Iris tells Priam to ransom his son, she speaks softly (*tutthon*) but the king is still gripped with fear (*Il.* 24.169–70). But why exactly does she speak quietly (the expression is unique in Homer)? So that he alone can hear? To try to mitigate the impact of her epiphany? (He later says he saw her as well, 24.223, but he may simply be soothing the fears of a wife worried about his hearing – or his sanity.) Do Priam's limbs grow weak because of the content of the message (not yet delivered), the epiphany, or, as the Greek suggests, the voice itself? Is there something peculiar about the gods' voices besides their volume?[48]

Gods appear to mortals in their full divinity rarely, and only to a few privileged individuals or groups (*Il.* 20.131, 24.462–3; *Od.* 7.201, 16.161). Even then, it is often difficult for us to determine if the god is visible, in disguise, or heard only through the voice. The gods can also appear to chosen individuals within a group, remaining invisible to the rest (e.g. Athena to Achilles, *Il.* 1.198, and to Odysseus, *Od.* 16.159–61). The immortals usually disguise themselves as someone familiar to their visitant, and so they must not only change their appearances to remain unrecognized, but also alter their voices. In the *Iliad*, the formula for this transformation refers to the "body and the tireless voice" (*demas kai ateirea phônên*). When the adjective *ateirês* is applied to the voice, it always refers to a god in the likeness of a man.[49] In the chilling scene when Athena appears to Hector as Deiphobus in front of the walls of Troy, for example, Homer observes that she took the shape and untiring voice of Hector's brother (*Il.* 22.227; cf. 13.45, 17.555). At times, the poet abbreviates the formula by referring solely to the vocal metamorphosis, as when Apollo rouses Aeneas to fight by "likening his voice to Lycaon, the son of Priam" (*Il.* 20.81). Poseidon speaks to Idomeneus by "likening his voice to Thoas, the son of Andraemon" (*Il.* 13.216). The gods in these last two examples must also have changed their shapes if they made a physical appearance as well, but Homer can use the altered voice to stand for the entire transformation.[50]

---

however, thinks it is more likely that it refers to the sounds of wild nature itself. Elsewhere, the adjectival forms of the root modify the west wind (23.208), rivers (18.576, 21.16), and the sea (*Od.* 2.421). The noun and verb signal an inarticulate cry (8.542, 9.547, 18.310, 18.530, 23.869; *Od.*18.402). There is something about Artemis that conjures up loud, natural sounds. See below for the epithet used only of Ares, *briêpuos*, "loud-voiced."

[48] Smith (1988) proposes that the motive for most non-deceptive changes of a god's voice was just this lowering of the divine roar. Bologna (1978) 310 suggests that Iris represents the communication between divine and human, citing Plato's derivation of the name from *eirein* (*Cra.* 408B); cf. Krapp (1964) 137–8 and Richardson (1974) 208–9 for the reactions of onlookers to a divine epiphany.

[49] "Tireless" is the customary translation, but Kaimio (1977) 34 argues that the emphasis should be more on "hard" or "loud" than a temporal connotation of "not wearing out."

[50] The poet can refer merely to change of body as well, as for example at *Il.* 17.323, 21.213; *Od.* 13.288–9.

In the *Odyssey*, we see even more clearly that these references to the gods' speech are not incidental, but rather seem to imply that this completely different kind of intonation is required for a deity to manage a successful masquerade. Five times in the *Odyssey* we find the expression "like Mentor in both shape and voice" to describe Athena's appearance as Mentor (*Mentori eidomenê êmen demas êde kai audên*; *Od.* 2.268, 2.401, 22.206, 24.503, 24.548). As Clay has shown, *audê* in the epic "does not merely denote the vocal production of sounds, but the production of intelligible human speech."[51] There is a separate word, that is, for human utterance, a word applied only to mortal language, never to divine. Only humans and gods modulating their divine voices in human shapes (e.g. Circe and Calypso, each a *deinê theos audêessa*, a "dread goddess of human speech") are associated with this noun or related adjectival form.[52] At *Od.* 6.115f. Odysseus awakens from his waterlogged stupor on the shore of Scheria to the shouts of Nausicaa and her maids. Having just spent seven years with a goddess who used human speech (*audê*), Odysseus is understandably cautious: was it the voice of young women or nymphs that he heard? "Or could it be that I am near people of human speech (*anthrôpôn . . . audêentôn*, 6.125)?" The two words, combined like this nowhere else in Homer, are not tautological. Odysseus hopes at long last to be among humans, not monsters or deities disguised as humans, and the root *audê* is not enough to ensure he has escaped the divine appropriation of human speech. Especially interesting in this context is *Od.* 5.333–5, verses which describe a goddess who saves the shipwrecked hero:

But the daughter of Cadmus, slender-footed Ino, saw him, Leucothea, who formerly was a mortal of human speech, but now in the depths of the open sea has received a share of honor from the gods.

Before, when Ino was human (*brotos*), she used human speech (*audêessa*). But now, as an immortal, she has a new name and apparently a new voice.

---

[51] Clay (1974) 131; see her detailed argument for exceptions that prove the rule; also Baldry (1965) 12 and Hainsworth (1988) ad *Od.* 5.334. Ford (1992) 176–7 amplifies her arguments, looking at other words for sound and voice in Homer. *Phthongos* and *phthongê* are used to mean the distinctive voice of an individual, e.g. of the Sirens, Polyphemus, or even animals (*Od.* 9.167), as well as the voice an individual god assumes (*Il.* 2.791). The voice as mere noise is represented as *phonê* for mortals and animals (e.g. *Od.* 10.239; also of man-made objects, e.g. a trumpet at *Il.* 18.219).

[52] Each of these minor goddesses appears in her true bodily shape, but must still take on a human voice. Loraux (1992) 20 calls the juxtaposition of divine, human voice, and feminine form a "superb oxymoron." See the discussion of Dirlmeier (1967), who believes that the three minor goddesses – Calypso, Circe, and Ino/Leucothea – are so distinct from the Olympians because they represent different layers of the tradition. Nagler (1996) provides evidence that the expression refers primarily to various goddesses of the sea behind whom stands a "shadowy prophetic figure," and so he argues *audeeis* is best understood as "endowed with prophetic speech."

The gods have one voice; humans have another. Gods can imitate mortals, but even mortals with the most "divine" voices – heralds and bards – are limited to *audê*, a merely human voice "like the gods" (*theôi/theois enalinkios audên*; *Il.* 19.250; *Od.* 1.371, 9.4).

Mortals find it extremely difficult to look at any divinity directly, much less see through the gods' disguises. As Odysseus observes, "Who with his eyes could look at a god against his will, whether going here or there?" (*Od.* 10.573–4)[53] Yet the Olympians apparently emanate divinity so strongly that they often find it hard to disguise themselves completely.[54] Just as the gods at times unsuccessfully change their shape, so they occasionally fail to alter their voices sufficiently. When Iris disguises herself as Polites, a son of Priam, to speak to Priam and Hector, she takes on his voice (*phthongên*, 2.791; cf. 13.216). Hector nevertheless recognizes the voice (*theas epos*) as that of the goddess (*Il.* 2.807).[55] On several other occasions, it appears that it is the quality of the voice of Athena that reveals the divine nature of the speaker.[56] Twice, the goddess addresses mortals with no disguise at all, and apparently without appearing visibly, yet they identify her by her voice

---

[53] Cf. *Od.* 17.485–7; *Il.* 5.127–8, 815 for the mist that Athena must remove from Diomedes' eyes for him to distinguish the gods. Ajax the Lesser's boast to the contrary at *Il.* 13.72 is a great bit of characterization, given his post-Iliadic fate; see Janko (1992) ad loc.

[54] Occasionally, they simply seem unable to resist revealing themselves at the last moment. Helen recognizes Aphrodite by her beautiful neck, lovely bosom, and flashing eyes (*Il.* 3.396–7). Rose (1956) 68 suggests that it easier to recognize a deity if the observer comes from a good family, but what hero doesn't? Does Achilles identify Athena by her eyes in the famous scene in Book 1 (*Il.* 1.200)? The brightness often associated with divinity is diminished in the Homeric epic; see Dietrich (1983) 67–8. Poseidon's feet and legs give his divinity away (*Il.* 13.71–2). Homeric Greeks seem to have been more sensitive to the subtleties of the foot than we moderns – Odysseus too is partially recognized by his feet, *Od.* 19.381; see Sowa (1984) 247–9. And though Apollo is transformed into the herald Periphas, Aeneas can tell he is "one of the gods" merely by looking at him face to face (*Il.* 17.334f.). This is an odd passage. Homer tells us that he "knew" Apollo, but Aeneas himself later says only that he recognized "one of the gods"; see Severyns (1966) 101; Dietrich (1983) 66. Is this another example of Homer knowing more about the divine world than the characters (Jörgensen's law)? Athena is especially proud that Odysseus, her protégé in cleverness, did not see through her disguise (*Od.* 13.299f.; cf. Apollo to Achilles, *Il.* 22.9f.). Odysseus protests that the goddess has an unfair advantage in their competition: it is difficult for a mortal to recognize her no matter how clever he is, since she takes on any shape she chooses (*Od.* 13.312–13). Still, he catches on, and by the end of the epic he has little trouble spotting Athena in her Mentor disguise (*Od.* 22.207f.; 24.504; cf. Noemon's comments at *Od.* 4.653–4). Parallels between divine disguises and Odysseus' revelation/recognition are well brought out by Murnaghan (1987) 11–19. For a provocative discussion of the role of epiphanies in Homer that unfortunately gets lost in its own indeterminacy, see Pucci (1987) 110–23; better is his more recent effort (1998) 69–96 to argue that the *Odyssey* "reads" or "rewrites" the "styleme" of the epiphanies in the *Iliad*. An engaging discussion of divine visitation in antiquity and its place in the imagery of the early Christians can be found in Lane Fox (1988) 102–67.

[55] Aristarchus (Arn/A) took this phrase to mean that Hector did not fail to obey (that is, recognize the message), but as Kirk (1985) notes ad loc., the suggestion is that Hector realizes that he is in the presence of the divine.

[56] Clay (1974) 135 and n.26.

(*Il.* 2.182, 10.512; cf. *Od.* 24.535). Hector, too, seems to recognize the voice of Apollo (*Il.* 20.379–80).[57]

These last three instances all use the word *ops* (*opa*) for the voice of the deity, more than half of its occurrences referring to divinities. Although the word itself is "basically a distinctive vocal sound" and is not specifically connected with the gods,[58] it seems to have some links to the divine. The word *euruopa*, a term used twenty-three times to describe Zeus, was interpreted by the Greeks as meaning either "far-seeing" or "far-sounding."[59] It seems to me that Homer is much more interested in the power and quality of the voice of the gods than in their sight, which often fails them. We find no care taken to distinguish divine sight from human sight, whereas Homer knows a specific word for human voice. The poet uses two other words only of the voice of the gods. *Omphê* is the voice used by gods either directly in divine form or in dreams, and *ossa* appears only in connection with Zeus.[60] Zeus, the supreme god who never appears to humans at all, has the supreme voice as well as messengers to deliver his word. Moreover, since the gods seem to have been defined as what humans are not, it makes some sense that humans have one particular word associated with their voice, and that the gods have several less specific terms applied to their speech. It is humans, after all, who are of primary interest to the poet.

Finally, and perhaps most revealingly, the gods not only have their own quality of voice, but some of their own vocabulary as well, and so apparently access to their own language. Four times in the *Iliad* we hear that the gods have a different name for something familiar to mortals (Batieia/Myrine, *Il.* 2.813–14; Aigaion/Briareus, *Il.* 1.403–4; Cymindis/Chalcis, *Il.* 14.291; Scamander/Xanthus, *Il.* 20.74), and twice in the *Odyssey* there are objects which have only divine names (*molu*, 10.305; *Planctae*, 12.61).[61]

---

[57] Cf. 15.246f., where Hector knows one of the gods is in his presence. Achilles seems to recognize Apollo's voice when he addresses the apparently still-disguised god by his correct epithet, *hekaerge* (22.15). At 22.216f., Achilles knows that Athena is addressing him, although it is not clear if the goddess is visible. Odysseus recognizes Athena, although she appears to him in the shape of a woman (*Od.* 20.30–7). Of course, she had descended from heaven and stood over his head as he tried to sleep in the portico of his house, and asked him (still playing the beggar) about his house, wife, and son. Odysseus is no dummy.

[58] Ford (1992) 176; it is used of humans and animals (e.g. *Il.* 3.152, 4.435) as well.

[59] Recent commentators seem to prefer "loud-sounding"; see Kaimio (1977) 70–1; Kirk (1985) ad *Il.* 1.498–9; West (1988) ad *Od.* 2.146; Hoekstra (1989) ad *Od.* 14.235; Montiglio (2000) 72; especially Martin (1989) 51 with n.16; and discussions in Chantraine (1983/4) and Frisk (1960/70). For "wide-gazing," see Clay (1983) 12–13 and Griffin (1980) 179–82 on the "allseeing divinity."

[60] Clay (1974) 135–6; Ford (1992) 175.

[61] For a list of similar distinctions in Greek literature, see West (1966) ad *Theog.* 831. On the origins of these pairs, see: Güntert (1921), esp. 90–115; Heubeck (1949–50); Clay (1972); Kirk (1985) ad 1.403–4. Watkins (1970) attempts to see the language of the gods as a metaphor for "charged" and

Homer, then, draws an important distinction between gods and mortals in their speech: the gods are not merely louder but have a distinctively divine tenor that must be carefully disguised along with their immortal forms. Human speech is distinct enough from the divine to warrant a separate designation. The difference is not merely physiological but cultural as well – the epics reveal remnants of a divine language.

LANGUAGE AND THE DEAD

If humans have a distinct form of speech that in important ways defines their place in the cosmos, what happens when they die? The Homeric picture of the dead is notoriously complex, ambiguous, even contradictory. Nevertheless, the poet is certain (if not perfectly consistent) about one point: the fully dead do not speak like the living. The most common metaphors for dying in Homer involve the loss of sight, as darkness covers the eyes and one "leaves the light of the sun" to "go into the dark."[62] The world of the dead is not primarily dim, however, but unintelligible to the living. Once dead, Homeric souls have no trouble seeing the living or being seen should the opportunity arise, but they do have a great deal of difficulty speaking to them. And the living have just as much trouble hearing the deceased as making physical contact. As Hermes leads the butchered suitors down to the underworld in the last book of the *Odyssey*, these new shades can only squeak like bats (*Od.* 24.5–9). Homer insists that their voices are inarticulate, repeating the verb *trizô* three times in five verses. Only a sharp, high-pitched squeal is emitted.[63] The dead can understand each other, as

"semantically marked" terms. Along similar lines, Suter (1991) 13–25 extends the discussion beyond the mere vocabulary of the gods to all doublets in Homer, and argues that all the "marked" names are associated with the divine. But as Fowler concludes (1988) 98–9, there is no single explanation for all cases of the divine language. The Townleian scholiast on 1.403 notes that such usage lends credibility to the *poet's* access to the divine. Clay's ultimate emphasis on divine knowledge as opposed to speech may go a bit too far (1972). Although humans have no name for *molu* or the *Planktai*, these objects do exist in this world, however difficult they are to access, and may come under human labels in time. There is no strong indication here of a "sphere of knowledge accessible solely to the gods" (131), but rather a much more thorough knowledge of the same world. For an interesting if elaborate attempt to look at the contextual significance of these divine names within the motifs of "polar duality" and "magical help," see van Duzer (New York 1996) 1–47.

[62] On metaphors of light and vision in Hades, the "sightless" place, see: Vermeule (1979) 24–7; Griffin (1980) 90 with n.25; Garland (1981) 46; and most recently Morrison (1999) and Clarke (1999) 241–3. For the etymology of Hades as "invisible" or "sightless," see Ruijgh (1991) 575–6; Beekes (1998); Bremmer (2002) 4. Prier (1989) presents a philosophical interpretation of the significance of sight and appearance in the Homeric world-view. Schofield (1991) 24–5 suggests that Heraclitus' expression "souls sniff in Hades" (*Fr.* 98) is designed to mock Homer's conception of a sightless underworld. But in the Homeric texts, the shades see just fine.

[63] Is the squeaking merely animalistic gibberish, or is it a language of the dead, comprehensible to the deceased, but sounding inhuman to the living? Heubeck's argument (1989) ad *Od.* 11.605, 11.633,

the slain suitors' subsequent conversations with Iliadic heroes reveal, but their words are incomprehensible to the living.

Homer does need the dead to communicate with the living on occasion. The unburied Patroclus uses his voice to remonstrate coherently with Achilles (*Il.* 23.65f.). He has not yet been admitted to the world of the dead, however, and so he can still articulate his complaints – he is recognized by his stature, eyes, and *voice* (*phônê*, 23.65–6). After Achilles agrees to his request for burial (23.95–6), Patroclus' ghost is apparently already more at rest in death, for he quickly flits away from Achilles with an incoherent gibbering (*tetriguia*, 23.100–1) identical to that of the dead suitors. Elpenor, also unburied and seeking final repose, similarly finds no obstacles to conversing with Odysseus (*Od.* 11.60f.). It is significant as well that both dialogues take place beyond the normal realms of human communication, either in a dream (Patroclus) or at the edge of the world (Elpenor). Homer is much more interested in dramatic impact than eschatological consistency. Some ghosts speak when they have to, but the poet is still careful to keep such occurrences beyond the bounds of normal human experience, and limits them to ghosts not yet at rest.[64]

Tiresias' position among the dead is unique. He retains "firm *phrenes*" and has been granted a *noos*. He alone, we are told, has understanding

---

and (1992) 24.5 that the poet is referring to the fluttering of wings rather than the cries of birds is untenable. *Trizô* in the epics always refers to a sharp sound – the backs of Odysseus and Ajax as they wrestle (*Il.* 23.714) or the shrieks (not fluttering) made by eight sparrows *who can't fly* as they are attacked and eaten by a snake (*Il.* 2.314). In post-Homeric Greek the word refers particularly to animal sounds: birds, partridges, locusts, swallows, elephants, mice, as well as the noise from a string, axle wheel, shoe, even the (familiar?) hissing of a person burnt in the fire. "Fluttering" and "whirling" will not suffice. Interestingly, Eustathius (ad *Od.* 24.13f.; cf. ad *Il.* 2.314) says the root is associated with childish weeping (*klauthmurismos*). He thus connects the sounds of the dead with those of children, another group of the Other examined in the next chapter; see Bologna (1978) 312. Sophocles (*Fr.* 879) says that a "swarm" (*smênos*) of the dead comes up "buzzing" (*bombei*); see Cook (1895) for the link between bees and soul. On the inability of the dead to speak properly, see Bremmer (1983) 84–5 and Jahn (1987) 36. Sourvinou-Inwood (1995) 94–106 has made the latest case for taking the *Deuteronekuia* of *Od.* 24.1–204 as post-Homeric, incorporating eschatological ideas (e.g. Hermes as *psuchopompos*, the dead entering Hades before burial) of a later period. Still, the terminology and beliefs about the speech of the dead remain remarkably consistent throughout the epics.

64 True, as Sourvinou-Inwood (1995) 82 n.202 insists, one still needs to explain why the discrepancies would be acceptable to the audience. But it is clear that ideas about death and the dead were extremely varied in early Greece, and there was probably a great diversity of opinion on the matter. Homer's own epics offer various alternatives to the predominant shadowy world of the dead (in addition to the uncomfortable double fate of Heracles at *Od.* 11.601–26; see below): Ganymede (*Il.* 20.231–5), Menelaus (*Od.* 4.561–9; cf. Calypso's offer of immortality to Odysseus, 5.206–10, 23.336), Leucothea (*Od.* 5.333–5), Castor and Polydeuces (*Od.* 11.299–304), and Cleitus (*Od.* 15.250–1) enjoy different fates. Things are even more manifold once one considers other early Greek epics. As Morris (1989) 309–10 concludes, we "do not have to explain every difference between poems as an evolution through time"; see also Bremmer (1994) 101 and Tsagarakis (2000).

(*pepnusthai*) among the dead (*Od.* 10.493–5).[65] He can speak to Odysseus without drinking blood, but he insists on drinking blood anyway. Why? Is Homer uncomfortable with the idea of the ritually interred, even Tiresias, gossiping with the living? Or is it so he can prophesy? The Greek says clearly that he imbibes so that he can "speak the truth" (11.96) – is the emphasis on the verb or the object?[66] Perhaps the dead are not to be trusted (cf. the wonderful debate about the veracity of a dead man in Apuleius' *Metamorphoses* 2.29–30). Anticleia's silence is broken only after she drinks blood – does the blood reinvigorate her body so she can speak, or awaken her mind so she wants to? Or is it so that she, too, will speak the truth, as Tiresias seems to suggest (11.148)?

As is often noted, the dead in Homer are not consistently witless: they must be able to sense and react to rites of blood from which they drink; they are apparently sensitive to the actions of the living; they can be punished by the Erinyes; they have various degrees of power and authority; they fear Odysseus' sword; some even sit in judgment of others.[67] But can the dead speak with the living without the revivifying draught of blood? Tiresias makes what seems to be a universal claim: whoever of the dead drinks the blood will speak, and those who are refused will turn away (147–9). Anticleia is specifically depicted as coming forth to drink before she can speak (11.152–4). Rather than repeating this scene for every subsequent heroine, Homer tells us just once the procedure adopted by his hero to question the women who come flocking to the blood. Odysseus does not allow them all to drink at once, but instead has them drink one at a time as he interrogates them, using his sword to keep them in line (11.228–34).

There is an important lesson here in Homeric composition and poetic art. Homer does not need to remind us each time that blood was imbibed. We have been shown Anticleia's drinking, and have now been plainly told that all the subsequent women drank as well. There is no repetition of

---

[65] The most complete summary of meanings of *phrenes* in Homer is Sullivan (1988) with bibliography; cf. the difficult remarks of Achilles after Patroclus disappears, *Il.* 23.103–4, with Richardson's (1993) note.

[66] That is, is speech here not merely articulation, but power, the ability to "report the verities of the mantic world"? Nagler (1996) 145–8. For the connection between blood and prophecy, and the possibility of the origin of this epic blood-drinking in the practice of oracular consultation of chthonic beings summonable by the offering of blood, see Sourvinou-Inwood (1995) 82–3. Griffith (1997) finds the source of Homer's unusually loquacious dead in influences from Egypt.

[67] For a succinct account of the consciousness of the dead, see Sourvinou-Inwood (1995) 77–94, where she argues there are two concepts at odds in Homeric eschatology: 1) witless shades, which may be an inherited belief from the Mycenaean period; 2) a belief contemporaneous with Homer and his immediate predecessors that the shades are not without some consciousness; see also Tsagarakis (2000) 105–19.

the "drinking" motif, and none is necessary. Anticleia's drinking has thematic significance that is not attached to the other dead. Her shade appears right after that of the unburied Elpenor. This is the first time Odysseus learns of her death, and though he weeps and "grieves deeply," he must demonstrate his characteristic self-control and keep her from the blood until Tiresias appears (11.84–9). Without a sip from the pool, Anticleia apparently does not even recognize Odysseus (11.142–4, 152–4), an additional source of pain to the bereaved son and struggling hero. Once the pathos of this scene is no longer needed, the poet can sustain the dignity of the dead heroines and heroes by limiting the references to the relatively humbling act of imbibing blood with the permission – and at the feet – of Odysseus.[68]

The issues are complex and the picture is often a bit fuzzy, but we can conclude that under normal circumstances the buried dead cannot use articulate speech. They must be reanimated with blood before they can converse with the living. The deceased retain a *psuchê* and *eidôlon*, as Achilles realizes (23.104), but no *audê*, which is never used of the dead (just as it is never used of the undisguised gods). They are only as "witless" as the context requires, but they do not speak with the living without special rites.

In later Greek, and often in Latin, the underworld was known as the "silent regions" and the dead as the "silent ones," or, as the Hesiodic *Scutum* refers to death itself, the place "forgetful of speech" (*lathiphthongoio*, 131). This silence, however, is the absence of articulate speech.[69] To mortal ears, the voices of the dead sound like squeals, a terrifying "screech like birds" (*klangê nekuôn ên oiônôn hôs*, *Od.* 11.605), an awful cry (*thespesiêï iachêi*) which both introduces Odysseus to the dead (11.43) and sends him scurrying away from them in fright (*êchêï thespesiêï*, 11.633). The voices of the dead are linked to the sound of the divine here, at least etymologically, since

---

[68] Sourvinou-Inwood (1995) 81–3 has argued that the dead do not need to drink the blood to speak, at least not in every case. For example, the heroes Odysseus reviews after a brief interlude amidst his Phaeacian audience are not said to have quaffed any blood. But a close examination suggests that it is only in the cases of Achilles and Heracles that Odysseus skips this introduction, and the same selective process as we saw with the heroines is at work here. In addition to specific discussion of the scenes in the eleventh book, Sourvinou-Inwood suggests that epic conventions would require the audience to rely completely upon explicit cues: the audience "would have taken the absence of repetition to entail that the action did not take place." But (as I hope to show in detail elsewhere), the Homeric singer could expect his audience to understand "typical" actions without repeating the introductions explicitly. Johnston (1999) 7–8, in a more recent examination of much of the same material, is apparently unconvinced by Sourvinou-Inwood's argument as well, stating simply that the ghosts are unable to converse in any "meaningful way" until they drink blood.

[69] E.g. Catull. 96.1, 101.4; Tib. 2.6.34; Prop. 2.1.77; cf. *AP* 7.467.8; further references in Bömer (1957) 129–30. On the contrast between the silent and noisy dead, see Stramaglia (1995).

the adjective *thespesios* means "from the divine" (cf. *Il.* 2.599–600 of divine song, and *Od.* 12.158 of the voice of the Sirens).

Finally, it is worth noting the epic use of the word *anaudos*, "speechless." When Odysseus washes ashore, nearly drowned, on Scheria, he is the closest to death that he will come in the epic. His flesh is bloated, and the ocean pours through his mouth and nose. Here, at his physically weakest point in the narrative, Homer describes him as lying on the beach "breathless and speechless" (*apneustos kai anaudos*, 5.456). What better phrase to describe the dead or near-dead in this case, especially given the significance of speech as a defining criterion for the living?[70] Hesiod uses nearly the identical phrase to characterize the gods when they are closest to death. If a "deathless" god violates an oath taken by the river Styx, he lies breathless (*nêutmos*, 795) for an entire year, deprived of nectar and ambrosia (795–7). He remains in a heavy trance, breathless and speechless (*anapneustos kai anaudos*, 797), awaking to an exile of nine years. To be speechless is the equivalent, or at least complement, to being breathless; that is, to be without speech is to be dead, or as close to death as one can come.[71]

The Homeric epics suggest that the distinguishing characteristic of humans is speech – the gods, animals, and even the dead have qualitatively different forms (if any) of articulation that set them apart from living mortals. They can mimic or impersonate human speech for a limited time, but eventually *audê* is relinquished to "those who walk upon the earth" on two feet. It is only natural, then, that a demarcation can be made between humans themselves, based on their speech. We will examine in a later chapter this tendency in classical Athens, where there is often a moral element attached – those who don't speak Greek (e.g. barbarians) or should not speak in public (e.g. women) are somehow less human and thus less worthy of moral or political consideration. But the Homeric texts reveal this

---

[70] His reentry into humanity is specifically marked by the longest act of speech-making in the epics, his recounting of his exploits; see Segal (1994) 19. Boedeker (1984) 67–70 proposes that Odysseus at this point is reduced to "infantile status" – naked, speechless, defenseless, completely exposed to the dangers of nature. His first steps toward recovery are to carry out activities that represent human culture: thinking, constructing, and *talking*.

[71] The one other Homeric use of *anaudos* is also revealing culturally. After Odysseus tricks Circe and subsequently has sex with her, her maids prepare an elaborate meal for him. As it is set before him, he cannot eat, worried as he is about his still-transformed men. Circe rebukes him for his lack of conviviality: "Why do you sit here, Odysseus, like a speechless one (*anaudôi*), eating your heart out and not touching either food or drink?" (*Od.* 10.378). She is offended at his apparent lack of trust and rejection of hospitality (he did sleep with her, after all), so she insults him by comparing him to a person incapable of being part of the community, suggesting that he is as swinish as his silent men (*suôn . . . phônên*, 10.239). But perhaps Odysseus has simply lost his appetite – he is staring at a plate full of meat (372), thinking of his comrades. What, exactly, was on Circe's menu?

underlying assumption about human worth as well, even if not as judg-
mentally as will be found later in Aristotle. Non-Greeks and women are
characterized by their lack of language or, more particularly, their lack
of controlled and authoritative language. Slaves too, by definition, are
deprived of control over most aspects of their lives, and thus Eumaeus
(who knows first-hand) accurately generalizes that Zeus takes away half of
man's worth the day he becomes a slave (*Od.* 7.322–3).

THE LANGUAGE OF NON-GREEKS

Homer's Trojans are remarkably hard to distinguish from the Greeks: they
worship the same gods with the same rites, have similar policy-making
councils, fight with identical tactics, and share equivalent forms of hous-
ing, food, clothing, funerals, and kinship. Even the differences – eastern polygamy, for example – are downplayed.[72] The Trojans do not display the main flaws of barbarian psychology that came to characterize
them in the fifth century: tyranny, immoderate luxuriousness, unrestrained
emotionalism, effeminacy, cruelty, and servility. The main protagonists
in the war, one from Europe and one from Asia, even speak the same
language.[73] This has obvious advantages for the narrative, of course, and

---

[72] Richardson (1993) 16, noting how relatively slight and debatable are the differences between the
warring cultures, lists also the custom of sacrificing horses to rivers (21.130–2) and the dirges of the
Trojans as not typically Greek. For similarities and differences between the Trojans and Greeks, see
Taplin (1992) 110–15, who, however, sees no distinctions in the use of speech and noise (see below) and
especially Hall (1989) 19–55, who demonstrates that many of the pejorative aspects of the "barbarian"
were "invented" after the Persian Wars, and subsequently pushed back on the non-Greeks of the
mythical past. Dowden (1992) 67 seems to suggest that the campaign versus Asia Minor in the *Iliad*
is meant to define Greekness in a positive way and justify encroachment. Sale (1994) argues that
Homer altered the inherited tradition of insolent Trojans ruled by an absolute monarch, in order
to present them as tragic victims of the city's *hamartia*, the corruptibility of the Elders who are the
real rulers of Troy. The Trojans, in this picture, would have a non-Greek form of government and a
different fighting force, made up primarily of amateurs.

[73] This is not true in all of the representations of the Trojans in the post-Persian period, when they
become associated with Asiatics; see especially Soph. *Aj.* 1147, 1262–3; Jüthner (1923) 3; Battegazzore
(1995) 17; Harrison (1998). Watkins (1986) examines the various theories surrounding the language
of the historical Bronze Age Trojans, concluding that it was possibly a Luvian dialect. Homer is often
and rightfully admired these days for his equitable depiction of Greeks and non-Greeks, especially
when the epics are compared to Athenian literature of the post-Persian war era. This was not always
the case in antiquity, however; for the harsh interpretation given to the Trojans and Hector in
particular as arrogant, cruel, cowardly, and foolish in ancient commentaries, see Kakridis (1971) 54–
67 and Richardson (1980). There are still critics who see a negative portrayal of the Trojans as a race
in the *Iliad*, e.g. Pinsent (1984); Hainsworth (1993) ad *Il.* 9.233; Wathelet (1998); see also Rochette
(1997) 40. An earlier argument for Homer's pro-Greek stance in the epic can be found in van der
Valk (1953), supplemented by van der Valk (1985); for bibliography on Homer's "nationalism," see
de Jong (1987b) 12 with n.38. This reading is wrong, I believe – important here is Sale (1989) – as I
hope to demonstrate elsewhere.

remains a dramatic convention to this day when, for example, Nazis are depicted in films as speaking English with German accents.[74] But there *are* differences in language and the ability to control the voice in the epics that suggest speech is an important criterion for differentiation, and the Greeks have better command than non-Greeks. The moral judgment found so often in classical Athenian texts is absent, but the basic pattern is established.[75]

Homer has no generic word for "non-Greek" or "foreigner." Common expressions, such as *allodapoi* and *têledapoi*, refer merely to an origin in a different land and, like all other words used to describe a foreigner or stranger (e.g. *xeinos, allos, allodapos, allotrios phôs*), can be used of strangers either in the opposite camp or on the same side.[76] The word *barbaros* is not found in the epics, but the compound *barbarophônôn*, "of foreign speech," is applied to the Carians (*Il.* 2.867).[77] There is no hint of inferiority here, but once again language forms the distinguishing criterion of Otherness.[78] The few times the poet does choose to speak about foreigners

---

[74] I see that Arnott (1989) 135 has made a similar comparison in describing the coloring of the language in Aeschylus' *Persians*; cited in Harrison (1998) n.45.

[75] This runs against the arguments of: Lévy (1984); Hall (1989) 21–40 with n.64; and Dihle (1994) 1–2, all of whom reject "noise" or "clamor" as a distinguishing criterion between Greeks and Trojans. Thus, I am arguing that Greek self-definition was oppositional before the fifth-century, *pace* J. M. Hall as well (1997) 47–51, and not a construct of the Athenians alone (*pace* Hall [2002] 202–3). What increases is the virility of polarization, not the mechanism. Mackie (1996) provides an extensive genre-based analysis of the differences in the use of language between the Trojans and Greeks. She concludes that the Greeks are more likely to speak publicly in political "blaming," the Trojans are more inclined to less public, more poetic "praising." In her view, the *Iliad* presents an *oikos*-oriented praise culture and an invading, polis-oriented blame culture. I am less concerned about the cultural differences involving subtleties of linguistic self-presentation (and not at all about the literary and generic definitions of these differences) than in the varying abilities to control the use of articulate language in general. Mackie's study thoroughly demonstrates, however, that Homer is both capable of and interested in distinguishing the two cultures through their use of language. For foreign speech in Homer, see Gambarara (1984) 48–52; Werner (1992) 5–7.

[76] Hall (1989) 12–13; Lévy (1991) 67.

[77] There is a water nymph named Abarbareê (*Il.* 6.22), although the word may mean "unmuddy"; see Kirk (1990) ad 6.22. The word *Panellênas* appears at *Il.* 2.530, although its meaning is disputed; Hellenes, in fact, appears only once, in the Catalogue of Ships (2.684); see Lévy (1991) 57–64. Hall (2002) 125–34 argues for the separate and perhaps late development of the meaning of Hellas, Hellenes, and Panhellenes.

[78] See Hall (1989) 9 n.28 for the controversy over the historicity of this passage. On the Carians, see Georges (1994) 14–16, who reasons that the portrait is not completely innocent, since Nastes, one of the Carian leaders, is described as coming to Troy foolishly dressed in gold "like a girl" (2.872); cf. Griffin (1980) 4, the proposition that Nastes serves as a precursor to Paris. The meaning of *barbarophônôn* could be either knowing no Greek or deficient in Greek; see Kirk (1985) ad loc. and Krapp (1964) 107. *Barbaros* itself, as we will see in Chapter 4, will later refer to all non-Greek-speaking people, making the compound redundant; see Strabo's discussion (14.2.27–8) of the meaning of Homer's reference to the Carians. On the Ionian Greeks' ironic role in handing the Athenians the material for emphasizing Asian "difference," see Georges (1994) 60–4, although he underestimates the significance of language in cultural identity (e.g. 130f.).

in general, he consistently focuses our attention on their different language. Four times in the *Odyssey*, non-Greek people are referred to as *allothroous anthrôpous/andras*, "other-speaking humans/men" (*Od.* 1.183, 3.302, 14.43, 15.453). There is no implication of inferiority in these references either, but it is worth noting that the cultural detail chosen to distinguish a people is the way they sound, not where they live or the way they eat, dress, shave, bury their dead, worship, work, marry, or urinate. They are "other-speaking," not "other-living."[79]

A term applied by Ares to the Sintians of Lemnos, *agriophônous*, "of wild speech," is less neutral (*Od.* 8.294). These Sintians were thought to be Thracian or pre-Greek savage tribes on the edge of the Greek world (temporally or spatially; cf. *Il.* 1.594). There is a bit of irony in this description by Ares, himself the most savage and perhaps least favorite of the poet's gods (e.g. *Il.* 5.889–98). Ares is trying to get Aphrodite into bed, and reports that the lame, blue-collar Hephaestus has abandoned his beautiful wife to spend time with the uncivilized folk of Lemnos. Aphrodite deserves better, and here is the swashbuckler Ares himself, eager for the love of "fair-crowned Aphrodite." The epithet "fierce speaking" is meant to sound pejorative, a word that emphasizes the contrast between the misshapen cuckold and the attractive adulterers.[80]

Homer does acknowledge that the Eastern allies of the Trojans speak different languages (*allê d' allôn glôssa poluspereôn anthrôpôn*, *Il.* 2.804; cf. *Od.* 19.175 for different languages on Crete, and *Hymn Hom. Ven.* 162). Perhaps partially as a result of the mixed tongues of the troops, a "din" arose (*orumagdos*, 2.810) with the gathering of the contingents. This Eastern cacophony is a common motif in the epic: the Trojans (and their allies) are noisy, far more likely to create a ruckus than the Achaeans.[81] *Orumagdos*, for example, is a word used to describe the sound of battle (*Il.* 4.449, 8.63, 16.633, 17.424, 17.741) or general noise of men, animals, rivers, stones, etc. Homer frequently convokes the cacophony of war, and the god of war receives the unique epithet (used only twice in Greek, both times of Ares) *briêpuos*, "loud-voiced" (13.521; cf. *Cat.* 10a69). But *orugmados* is most closely associated with the Trojans as they leave for battle or engage in combat (2.810, 8.59, 9.248, 10.539, 17.461). It is never used of the Achaeans alone

---

[79] Rochette (1997) 38 n.9 has a list of Greek compound words with *barbaros* as one element – the other element reveals the area of comparison.

[80] Aphrodite, so often associated with the sweet speech of *Peithô*, may be especially sensitive to language. In her *Homeric Hymn* she explains to Anchises, quite unusually, how she came to be bilingual (113–16).

[81] Benardete (1963) 5–12; so also Colvin (1999) 41–50. For the noises of Greek battle, see Hanson (1989) 152–7.

in the *Iliad*.[82] An excellent example of the contrast is found at *Il.* 8.53f. The Achaeans eat a quick meal and arm themselves for battle. The out-manned Trojans similarly arm, and as they head for the engagement a huge din (*oru-magdos*, 8.59) arises. Is their armor more resonant? Are they shouting? Are we to imagine the polyglottal allies creating an incomprehensible babble? Or is there simply something louder about the Easterners?[83]

This passage can be juxtaposed with two other often-cited passages where Homer contrasts the noisy Trojans with the silent Greeks. At *Il.* 4.422f. the Danaan troops move to battle in such silence (*akên*) that one would think they had no voice (*audên*, 430), silent in fear of their leaders (431). The Greeks speak in established hierarchies, carefully under control – the leaders command; the troops obey. Homer's manipulation of the introductory simile highlights in a paradoxical light the silence of the Greeks.[84] The simile accompanying the Achaeans seems at first to emphasize the sound of the marching army. The Greeks are compared to a series of waves rising up close together on the "resounding" (*poluêchei*) beach, "breaking" on shore with a "great roar" (*megala bremei*), finally "spitting back" the sea foam. The two most recent similes involving the waves of the ocean – both in the second book – explicitly compared the sound of the waves with the shouts of the Greeks at assembly (2.209–10, 394–97; cf. 14.394f., 17.263f.). But Homer misleads us this time. The point of the comparison turns out to be the wavelike *movement* of the troops rather than the sound, the adjectival description of the wave (*epassuteron*, "close together," "in quick succession," 4.423) surprisingly repeated to describe the *visual* impact of the columns of Greeks (*hôs tot' epassuterai*, 427). Homer reverts to the point of his first wave

---

[82] It is used once of Achaeans in the *Odyssey*, where it describes the sound of the Greeks around Achilles' pyre (24.70). It has negative connotations in this epic as well, used only twice elsewhere – of the din of the feasting suitors (1.133) and the ominous sound of wood tossed down by Polyphemus (9.235).

[83] Similarly, when the Trojans attack with the din (*homados*) of the winds mingling with the sea and Zeus' thunder (13.794–9), Nestor deliberates like the *soundless* (*kôphôi*) wave *before* the whirling winds of the storm arrive (14.16–19); see Moulton (1977) 23–4 for this contrasting in simile pairs. *Homados* often refers to the din of war in general (12.471, 16.296, 17.380), but it is especially associated with the Trojans (15.689, 16.295, 7.307; cf. 9.573). At 10.1–16, Agamemnon is distraught at the Trojan fires, music, and "din of men" in contrast to the slumbering Greeks. For the Greeks, a *homados* is closely associated not with war but with the noise of chattering men at an assembly where one is *supposed* to speak (2.96, 19.81). The word is not especially positive: it is used of the mourning for Patroclus (23.234). The verbal form is found only in the *Odyssey*, where it is used five times to describe the suitors' reaction to some startling event (the last occasion being the epiphany of Odysseus and his flying arrows; 1.365, 4.768, 17.360, 18.399, 22.21).

[84] Moulton's analysis (1977) 38–45 of the sequence of similes that includes this passage is excellent. He concludes that the "inconsistencies" of the simile at 4.422f. are the result of a rough attempt to combine two quite different aspects of the narrative situation, sound and movement (44 n.49). I prefer to see it as a deliberate and successful effort on the part of the poet to take advantage of both aspects.

simile in the epic, where the hurried movement of Greeks from assembly to their ships is compared to the swelling of the sea under the winds (2.144–6). We are initially led to believe that the roar of the waves will be like the din of gathering soldiers, and then discover that the motion of the *silent* Greeks is the point.[85] The hush is all the more emphatic – we hear the pounding water and expect to hear the thundering Greeks, but we encounter only ordered silence.

The Trojans, however, cry out like ewes bleating incessantly upon hearing the "voice" (*opa*) of their lambs (4.433–5). Their shout (*alalêtos*) rose through the army, for they did not have one voice or language but mixed tongues summoned from many lands (436–8). The image is not flattering to the Trojans. To be compared to animals – passive, domesticated, female sheep at that – especially in terms of language, would be a direct insult if uttered by anyone but the poet.[86] Whereas the Greeks moved to battle "without pause" (428), the Trojans bleat "without end" (435). The Trojans produce a *throos* and *gêrus*, words for speech that are used only here in the epics. There is something special about the sound of the defenders of Troy. The noun used to describe their tumult, *alalêtos*, is employed carefully by the poet as well. It can be applied to a general noise (*Il.* 14.393), yet it is never used of the Greeks on attack. Twice it is associated with the retreat of the Achaeans (2.149, 18.149), and once with the flight of the Trojans (21.10), but three times it applies to the sound of the Trojans on attack (4.436, 12.138, 16.78). Its only other appearance in Homer is in a description of the shouts of the families of the suitors (*Od.* 24.463). This pattern is repeated throughout the *Iliad*: battle is noisy; Greeks and Trojans alike are clamorous in retreat when loss of discipline is to be expected, but the Trojans on attack are especially obstreperous, vaguely out of control.

The best-known example of this contrast appears at the beginning of Book 3, as Homer sets up the first engagement of warriors for the reader. The Trojans come on with a cry and shout (*klangêï t' enopêï*) like the cry (*klangê*) of cranes when with a cry (*klangêï*) they slaughter the Pygmies.

---

[85] It may also be significant that we do not discover who is being compared to the wave in the simile until immediately after the second appearance of *epassuterai*. Diomedes has just finished speaking, so it seems likely that the simile will describe the Achaeans, but the Greek text does not make this explicit until the wave simile is complete at 427. It is possible that one could have thought the Trojans would be the subject; see Kirk (1985) ad 4.422–8. For varying interpretations of this simile, especially Fraenkel's elaborate series of analogies, see Kaimio (1977) 94–5. On wind and sea similes in general, see Scott (1974) 62–6, and on the sequence of similes in Book 2, Leinieks (1986) 12–15. Hubbard (1981) points out that Homer's tendency to juxtapose similes antithetically, as with sight and sound, may reflect the deep-seated predilection for antithesis in the early Greek mind.

[86] An analysis of Homer's treatment of the troops en masse reveals that the Greeks are more often the aggressive animals; see Hartigan (1973) 230–1.

Apparently, there was a cry much like that of cranes. But the Achaeans come on in silence (*sigêi*), breathing fury, eager to help each other. This last phrase may not mean, as the scholiast interprets, "in the phalanx," but there is certainly a strong contrast implied here, as noted by Kirk (ad loc.; cf. Lucr. 4.116–82), between the disparate noise of the Easterners and the "discipline and resolve" of the Greeks (cf. 2.474, where the Greeks are marshaled as easily as goats). Again, *klangê* is not particularly flattering. The word is used by Homer to refer to sharp sounds – the twang of a bow (*Il.* 1.49), the disordered shouts that must be silenced at a council (*Il.* 2.100), the squeals of pigs (*Od.* 14.412) – but especially the screeching of cranes.[87] The only other occurrences of the word are found in a description of the sound of confusion of the gathering of the Trojans (*Il.* 10.523) and the sound of the dead in the *Odyssey* (11.605), discussed above. The metaphor of the cranes here has a positive, martial side in its association with the attack against the Pygmies, but there is irony here as well. The Greeks are no Pygmies, and their slaughter by the ships will be short-lived. *Klangê* connotes the animal world, which again may have positive associations in terms of strength or courage, but not when it comes to language.[88]

Significantly, *klangê* and other words associated with the sounds of the dead are frequently applied to the Trojans. *Êchê* in the *Iliad* is twice used to describe the sounds of war which arise from both the Greeks and Trojans (13.837, 16.769), but the majority of occurrences refer to the sound of the Trojans (especially of Hector) on the attack (8.159, 12.252, 13.834, 15.590; cf. 15.355). The formula *êchê thespesiê* (of the dead at *Od.* 11.633) is used mostly of the shouts of attackers, and in such cases *always* applies to the Trojans.[89] The Greeks, on the other hand, never raise an *êchê* while on the attack. Similarly the noun *iachê*, outside of the shout of the dead (*Od.* 11.43)[90] is

---

[87] The sound of the Achaeans hastening to battle is also compared to great migrations of cranes and other birds at 2.462–3, but here the reference is not to the shouting but to the sounds of horses and feet and the vast number of troops. For a complex analysis of this passage as a preface to the Paris–Menelaus duel, see Muellner (1990).

[88] The verbal form *klazô* follows a similar pattern. Applied to inanimate objects, such as arrows and the west wind, it also describes the sounds of birds (vultures, eagle, heron) and dogs, as well as the insults of Thersites and the cries of men devoured by Scylla. The only two Greeks to shout (with *klazô*) in attack are Agamemnon and Patroclus, once each – both famously out of control – while the Trojans are five times described as shouting in attack. The verb *klangazô*, Pollux (5.89) tells us, was onomatopoetic for the cry of cranes, and hence was used of the language of the Scythians (Porph. *Abst.* 3.3). Griffin (1980) 4 observes that the Trojans are seen, as soon as they appear in the poem, as "gorgeous, frivolous, noisy; Achaeans, by contrast, are serious and grim." He cites the scholiast ST on 3.2: "Homer characterizes the two armies and does not depart from the representation all through the poem." For the noise of the Trojans, see Kaimio (1977) 22–3.

[89] Kaimio (1977) 30–1.

[90] Some editors find the appearance here objectionable, but see Heubeck (1989) ad loc. The verbal form of the word is used of the combined Greeks on attack twice (4.506, 17.317), however, and is

used to describe the sounds of battle in general (4.456, 14.1), the Greeks (12.144, 15.275, 15.396) and Trojans (16.366, 16.373) in flight, and the Trojans on the attack (15.384, 17.266), but never the Greeks on attack.

Taken by itself, each bit of evidence may be inconclusive.[91] But brought together, they present a consistent picture that cannot be ignored. Homer seems to be careful to distinguish the East from the West on attack, as the Greeks maintain order and discipline. This contrast will later develop into a *topos*, especially after the Persian War, when the noisy and undisciplined East encounters the self-controlled West.[92]

The Trojans are at times noisier than the Greeks, and that seems to be the only significant difference between them. The key is not the sound itself but the appearance of control, both of oneself and of others. Verbal success in the epics, as we shall see in more detail in the next two chapters, comes not merely from the ability to utter a sound (even animals can do that), or even with the possession of articulate language, but only with authoritative speech and one's concomitant power to control one's own speech and silence others. Silent acquiescence signals the acceptance of the authority of another, although, as we will see in the next chapter, the ability to restrain one's own speech is also essential in the *Odyssey*.[93] But in either case, one must first have the opportunity to speak authoritatively, and it is just this ability that is denied to women in the Homeric world.

especially associated with Achilles at his most inhuman; see discussion in Chapter 3. It should be noted that the Greeks are far more likely to shout at assemblies than Trojans, but this is at least in part because the Greeks hold more assemblies than the Trojans.

[91] Examples can be multiplied. An examination of even such a neutral expression as the verb *auô* plus the adverb *makron* shows the same disparities. The phrase is used nineteen times in the *Iliad*, seventeen of these when a hero is either exulting in a victory or rousing his own troops. The Greeks are so described four times (Diomedes, Nestor, Idomeneus, Patroclus). One time, the word describes Agamemnon's attempts to *stop* the Greeks from attacking the Trojans as Hector tries to arrange a truce (3.81). All the other occurrences describe the voices of Trojans, especially of Hector (nine times). The last two appearances are tied closely to Hector's death: he tries to rouse the Trojans as he dons Achilles' armor taken from Patroclus' body (17.183), and he shouts in vain for Deiphobus' (that is, Athena's) help as he faces Achilles.

[92] E.g. Aesch. *Pers.* 399–407; Herodotus. 7.211; cf. Thuc. 4.126.5 for the Illyrians; 1.49.3, 2.89.9 for discipline in general contrasted with clamor; Pi. *Nem.* 3.60; Eur. *Phoen.* 1302–3. For the long-standing tradition of Western military discipline, see Hanson (2001) 279–333. Sale (1994) 83–5 suggests that the noise of the Trojans and their allies derives from their amateur standing: they are not professionals like the Achaeans, but have civilian occupations. Other references to the exceptional noise of Trojans in the *Iliad*: 13.795–801, 15.381–4, 16.364–7, 17.263–6. This Eastern racket should help determine meaning of the debated phrase *abromoi auiachoi* in 13.41. The Trojans, following Hector on attack, like a flame or a tempest blast shout loudly together. Janko (1992) ad loc. rightly sees the reference to noise. Benardete (1963) 8–9, ignoring the evidence of his own article, opts for "silent," as does Hall (1989) 30 and n.89.

[93] Olson (1991–2) 222 n.10; see the next two chapters for more detailed argumentation. As Thalmann (1998a) concludes, slaves (he refers to the *Odyssey*, but his point applies to both epics) are portrayed for their master's sake – everything they do or say serves that purpose.

LANGUAGE AND WOMEN

Penelope's first appearance in the *Odyssey* is evoked by Phemius' sad tale of the Achaeans' *nostoi*. Her objection to the subject of the song is quickly dismissed by Telemachus. Freshly inspired by Athena with "strength and courage," Odysseus' son begins (or continues) his journey to manhood with an abrupt order to his mother:

> Now go to your chamber and attend to your own work, the loom and distaff, and tell your maids to go about their work. But speech will be the care of all men, and especially mine, since the authority in the house is mine. (*Od.* 1.356–9)

Aristarchus athetized these lines, and modern editors (e.g. S. West) are often tempted to follow his lead, primarily on the grounds that Telemachus' statement appears to be untrue: *muthos is* woman's business, as can be seen (it is said) especially in the cases of Helen and Arete. Leaving aside until the next chapter a discussion of the psychological appropriateness of the statement in the context of Telemachus' "maturation," Homer's own characterization of the speech as a *muthon pepnumenon* (361) is noteworthy. These are "wise" words, and at least partially effective ones – Penelope departs in silence, and Athena herself sanctions the event by helping her go to sleep. But what exactly does Telemachus mean by saying that speech is men's concern?

Mortal women can and do speak in the Homeric texts. Even in the male-dominated *Iliad* we hear the words of Briseis, Andromache, Helen, and Hecuba. Of the 677 speeches in that epic, 108 are by women. And by being the object of someone else's speech, they play (like servants and children) a central role even in this martial epic.[94] Odysseus' son, just entering the public world, rudely discharges his mother, but the idea behind his statement is nevertheless valid. Telemachus' point is that women's voices do not carry weight in public matters. Hector can hardly be called a bullying husband, yet his words to Andromache are similarly absolute:

> Now go to your chamber and attend to your own work, the loom and distaff, and tell your maids to go about their work. But war will be the care of all men, and especially mine, of those born in Troy. (*Il.* 6.490–93)

These lines are sometimes said to contrast with those of Telemachus, since the Trojan hero insists not speech but war will be men's affair. But the two

---

[94] De Jong (1987a). Still, as Redfield reminds us (1975) 119–21, women, children, and slaves are all dependent upon men and, along with material possessions, are primarily warriors' property to be fought for.

passages contain virtually the identical sentiment – woman's concern should not be for public matters, and their words carry no public authority.[95] The difference is in the context of the speech and the maturity of the speaker. First, it should be observed that Hector's words are directed not in response to Andromache's speech as a whole, as is sometimes suggested, but more specifically to the final portion of her speech, in which she had offered tactical advice for guarding a weak portion of the walls (6.433–9). These lines were also rejected by Aristarchus, who believed that Hector is replying to Andromache's earlier concerns about the consequences of war.[96] This famous scene can be outlined as follows:

Introduction: Hector smiles at Astyanax as Andromache cries, takes his hand, and speaks (404–6).

1. Worry about Hector's risking death (407–10).
2. Worry about the consequences of Hector's death (410–30), especially the fate of:
   a. Andromache;
   b. Astyanax.
3. Personal Plea: take pity; don't leave; you may die and leave orphan and widow (431–2).
4. Public Plea: tactical advice (wall near fig tree) (433–9).

Hector responds in turn to each point (441) of his wife's concern:

1. He must risk his death, in order to seek glory and avoid shame (441–9).
2. He too worries over the consequences of his death, especially the fate of:
   a. Andromache (450–65);
   b. Astyanax (466–81; this includes the famous helmet scene).
   "Introduction": Andromache smiles and cries; Hector pities her, takes her hand and speaks (482–5).
3. Personal Plea: don't grieve; no man escapes death (486–9).

---

[95] Naerebout (1987) 117.

[96] For his arguments, and reasons for retaining the lines, see Kirk (1990) ad 407–39; also Andersen (1990) 37–9. My argument here provides additional support for their retention. Excellent on this scene is Farron (1979) 22–4. Willcock (1977) 51–2 argues that we can see Andromache inventing a reason for Hector to remain near the walls. Foley (1999) 197 shows how these final lines of Andromache are typologically beyond the traditional lament upon which her scene is built. For a very different analysis of the structure, overly concerned it seems to me with chiasmus and ring-composition but filled with useful insights, see Lohmann (1970) 96–102 and (1988) 34–47. Lohmann's interpretation requires the athetizing of 433–9 in order to maintain his relatively strict schematizing. Such readings will, I think, be supplanted by more subtle analyses based on a different interpretation of the function of ring-composition; see Minchin (1995), (2001b) 181–202, and Nimis (1999). In this case, however, I think ring-composition gives way to one of Hector's other preferred structures for argumentation, the direct rebuttal of points in chronological order. See, for example, Hector's reply (18.284–309) to Polydamas' advice (18.251–83), especially 297–309, with the discussion of Edwards (1991) ad loc.

4. Public Plea: go home and see to women's concerns – war is for men, especially me (490–3).

The pathos of this episode has long earned admiration, and this brief structural analysis can only suggest some of Homer's careful technique. We note in passing the brilliant "interruption" of the Astyanax passage with the helmet scene, the delayed formal introduction to Hector's speech until after this episode (thus making the gestures of affection all the more stirring), the pity which can only be alluded to by the poet because Hector cannot act on his compassion for his wife in the way she so desires by avoiding death in battle. For our purposes in tracing the power of women's speech, we must focus on Hector's last words that address only his wife's logistical concerns. Even the sympathetic Hector rejects outright Andromache's tactical advice. Hector will also foolishly reject Polydamas' similar recommendation, which should carry more authority – perhaps the poet is commenting upon Hector's own prideful inability to listen to good advice from social inferiors.[97] But we are not surprised that women's words have no public authority, no matter how well-intentioned or tactically insightful they may be.

Important and impressive women like Penelope and Andromache are not silenced, but told to use their authority where it is proper – inside the house, commanding the servants, and in Penelope's case, manipulating those importuning her within the house, both the suitors and her husband. Telemachus is trying to put things into their "proper" place at the beginning of the *Odyssey*. The palace of Odysseus has inappropriately become the main sphere of public activity in Ithaca, and Telemachus is responding to Athena's challenge: speech is for men, especially for me, "since the power (*kratos*) in the house is mine." His words are much too sweeping if we take them literally, but he means that the business downstairs is for men. It is not for Penelope to tell the minstrel what song to play – men can make that decision and endure to hear the truth. Of course, some of the wonderful and revealing ironies are that Phemius' song tells of the returns of the Achaeans (the very subject matter of the epic at hand), Telemachus wrongly insists that Odysseus is dead, and Penelope's words do in fact stop the bard. Telemachus is still a novice at speech himself (see Chapter 2). But the point remains that what is meant by speech here is not language itself but speech that becomes action.[98] Recent studies have indicated that while

---

[97] As suggested by an anonymous referee. Kullman (1999) 111 notes that even Hector, who anticipates the archaic polis in its divergent pulls of nobility and community, sides ultimately with the heroic ethos.

[98] See Laird (1999) 1–43, the placement of Telemachus' speech within the broader context of the relationship between speech and power.

there is more room for female and private *muthoi* in the domestic world
of the *Odyssey* than in the *Iliad*, they require the support of physical force,
over which women have little control.[99] What counts is the essential link
between words and their accomplishment, what in the classical age will
become the basis for the ubiquitous dichotomy of word and deed, *logos*
and *ergon*. The frequent taunts between warriors accusing each other of
womanly behavior are aimed at their opponents' lack of action, not speech
(e.g. *Il.* 2.235, 7.96, 236, 8.163, 11.389, 20.252). These insults often combine
various groups of the Other. Children, for example, are found in the same
taunt as women (e.g. *Il.* 7.235, 11.389, 16.7–11). Menelaus brings out the
basic connection of the Other with animals when he refers to the Trojans
as *kakai kunes*, evil bitches (13.623).

Women can even be accused in the Homeric world of talking too much.
In the battle of beggars, Irus accuses Odysseus of talking glibly, "like an old
kitchen woman" (*Od.* 18.26–7). In fact, women's primary activity at feasts
is to make conversation: no Homeric woman (goddesses excepted) is ever
shown eating or drinking in the company of men.[100] The issue is one of
control and influence, and the speech of women does not command that
authority.[101] We can test this theory by examining the presentation of the
two women cited by Stephanie West as examples of powerful females in
speech, Helen and Arete in the *Odyssey*.

Helen's tale is couched in a battle of words.[102] While Menelaus is debat-
ing how best to get Telemachus to reveal his identity (for he seems to know,
4.118–19), Helen bursts into the room and immediately grills her husband

99 Clark (2001); Chaston (2002) 3–9. At a crucial moment, Telemachus will tell Penelope that the bow
     is the concern of men, thus getting her out of the room and preparing the way for the men's work
     of battle (*Od.* 21.350–3). More will be said in the next two chapters about the analysis by Martin
     (1989) of *muthos* as an "authoritative speech act"; Gumpert (2001) 32 errs in assuming for Homer
     that *muthos* implies fiction versus the *logos* of truth.
100 Van Wees (1995) 160; evidence for women's roles at Greek meals is culled by Burton (1998), pages
     144–6 for discussion of the Homeric world.
101 See Barck (1976) 60–2. Farron (1979) 15 shows how Homer "impresses on his audience their
     [women's] desperate helplessness and utter inability to determine the course of events, including
     their own lives" even though the poet does not share the prejudices of his characters and so makes
     them tragic in their ineffectualness. Kakridis (1971) 68–75 argues that women's main function in
     the epic is to try to dissuade men from doing their duty, and thus to form obstacles for men to
     overcome and to create agonizing conflicts in their souls. Blundell (1995) 50, however, reminds us
     that women can also incite their men to fight (e.g. 3.432–6, 9.590–4).
102 Although Austin (1975) 187 sees the Helen/Menelaus exchange as a sincere effort to "caress each
     other's sensibilities" (cf. Murnaghan [1987] 161–2 and n.23), most recent commentators have noted
     the subtle conflict. Good summaries can be found in Goldhill (1988) 19–24 and Olson (1989).
     Worman (2001) 30–6 (also, with some differences, [2002] 56–65) attempts to salvage Helen's
     "mimicry" but misses Menelaus' tone and fails to take account of his not-so-subtle reference to
     Deiphobus.

on each detail (137), announcing that this must be Telemachus. Such impatience to speak is not a virtue, as we shall see later in the case of Achilles.[103] After Pisistratus and Menelaus exchange greetings, the king announces that it is time for food – conversation (*muthoi*, 214) with Telemachus can wait until morning. Helen, however, has other ideas (219). She pours her Egyptian drug in the wine, and tells the men to rejoice in words (*muthois*, 239). She proceeds to give the famous exculpatory account of her meeting with Odysseus in Troy. Helen tells this tale, seemingly about Odysseus' heroics, to her husband and their guests, but her real point is a defense of her own nature and actions in the Trojan War (she uses first-person singular verbs ten times, and first-person adjectives/pronouns eight times). This is her public attempt at rehabilitation, not merely in front of her husband but before the sons of other Achaean heroes. Menelaus is quick to rewrite her effort, however, by providing an unflattering account of her attempted deception of the warriors inside the horse by calling upon them in imitation of their wives' voices (*phônên*, 279). Although it is again ostensibly about Odysseus, the king addresses his entire tale to his wife – she is his audience (five second-person verbs, four second-person pro-nouns/adjectives).[104]

Often overlooked is that both of their stories center on control of speech. Helen claims that she recognized Odysseus but kept her oath not to reveal him to the Trojans. Menelaus' tale, on the other hand, suggests that Helen does not know when to shut up, and it is Menelaus himself, along with Odysseus, who knows when to keep silent.[105] One might even conclude that Helen's use of language at Troy came dangerously close to creating lethal action. Helen's talking had nearly destroyed the Greeks – she had appropriated the male role (ironically, however, through the imitation of other female voices) – and it was only Odysseus' heroic effort to keep the Greeks quiet that saved them. Odysseus, in the end, won the battle of

---

[103] Pedrick (1988) argues persuasively that the entire scene is set up to emphasize Helen's intrusion, since her entrance comes earlier than expected in the normal "type-scene" sequence of women greeting their guests. Similarly, Reece (1993) 80–3 points out that, as with Odysseus' presence at the palace in Scheria, the *anagnorisis* is delayed – the feast is not *immediately* followed by an inquiry into the stranger's identity. Helen simply blurts out the name, and then we must wait for Telemachus' own words some time later.

[104] On the rarity of second-person narration, see de Jong (2001a) ad 4.234–89. Dupont-Roc and Le Bouluec (1976) 32–5 lay out the parallels and inversions between the two narratives. Bergren (1981) 210 thinks that the drug enables Menelaus to tell a painful tale he would otherwise be unable to recall. But the whole passage reads like a duel even before Helen administers the drug. Better is Anderson (1958) 3–5, who speaks of the "smoldering emotions" of the two that need little aid to be brought to the surface.

[105] See Schmiel (1972) 468–9.

speech. Should Helen apply this lesson to herself now? Hadn't Menelaus suggested just minutes ago that this too was *not* the time for talk? Hadn't Helen demonstrated her characteristic impetuosity by breaking into the conversation? Does the cuckolded and frequently trumped husband secretly harbor the desire to clamp his strong hands firmly on the mouth of his garrulous wife, just as Odysseus had nearly throttled Anticlus to keep him quiet? We might recall the words of Menelaus' brother to the greeting of his wife Clytemnestra – Helen's sister – after ten years: your words, like my absence, have been over-extended (Aesch. *Ag.* 915–16).

Perhaps there is no coincidence that the episode silences Helen for another eleven books. And when she does speak again, once more she does so in the context of a battle for control with her husband. As the youths depart from Sparta, an eagle flies by hauling a large white goose. Pisistratus asks Menelaus if this is an omen for them or him. As the cautious king ponders how to answer (15.169–70), Helen once more dramatically jumps in ahead of him (*hupophthamenê*, 171; the verb is used only twice elsewhere in Homer, and never of speech) and supplies an accurate prophecy.

Telemachus has already learned much on his voyage. Raised by females, he must have had his eyes opened during his visit with Nestor. His first wordly encounter presents him with a male so prolix that his wife (3.451–2; 479–80) cannot get a single word in edgewise (but then, who could?). Telemachus then witnesses the ugly little domestic tug-of-war in Sparta. His harsh words to his mother about speech being men's prerogative are reinforced by both positive and negative models at Pylos and Sparta. And so he acknowledges Helen's interpretation in an exaggerated fashion that can only suggest he does not believe it, and then ignores it for the rest of the epic.[106] (Again, since Helen's words are true, perhaps the poet is acknowledging that heroes ignore the words of women at their own cost.) Similarly, one visit with Nestor is enough to teach Telemachus the dangers of too much speech and not enough action, and so he skips out (*Od.* 15.199–201). Bold and confident, Helen can be imagined waging an incessant war with Menelaus for control. But the words of even this most impressive of Homeric women carry no authority by themselves.

The lack of women's verbal authority can be seen even more clearly in the notorious case of Arete, queen of the Phaeacians. Nausicaa advises

---

[106] Ahl and Roisman (1996) 41 observe that heroism in this epic, as seen in Helen's failure and Menelaus' momentary success, is partially determined by "one's ability to seize and exploit the narrative initiative." This applies even more directly to Telemachus' "maturation," as we shall see in the next chapter. Olson (1989) notes how the tales prepare the audience for, and also raise conflicting expectations about, Odysseus' return and encounter with Penelope. So also Andersen (1977), who suggests Menelaus' tale is Homer's invention to allude to Penelope's attempt to identify her guest.

Odysseus that the queen's favor is essential for his return (6.310–15), and Athena in disguise repeats that verdict while reciting the queen's résumé: Arete is of noble birth, good mind, honored like a goddess by the citizens, and accepted as an arbitrator of quarrels "even for men" (7.53–77). But the events of the *Odyssey* suggest that her words too lack authority. Even Athena notes that Arete is honored as no other woman among those who run households *under the authority of their husbands* (*hup' andrasin*, 68). She is important, but there is no female utopia, no primeval matriarchy lurking in Alcinous' palace.[107]

Odysseus does throw himself around the knees of Arete and make his pitch to her for a safe return to Ithaca (7.142–52). But the queen is not the one who responds. After a lengthy silence, Echeneus, an elder "well-skilled in speech," is the first to say something, and he addresses Alcinous.[108] Alcinous gives the orders and addresses the assembly, not his wife, just as we would expect. She is the first to ask Odysseus who he is (237–9), but it is Alcinous who continues to question Odysseus, and who gives orders (Arete's commands are limited to her maids, 7.335; 8.433). Again, this is not to deny Arete's commanding presence. Her sound advice to Odysseus to tie up his chest of goods is quickly accepted (8.443–5). But her final scene in the epic reveals the true nature of women's *muthoi*.

Apparently emboldened by Odysseus' catalogue of heroic and infamous women in the underworld, Arete breaks the silence and addresses the gathered Phaeacians (11.336–41). She praises Odysseus, claiming him as her guest (338), and then commands the Phaeacians to be in no haste to send him

---

[107] See: Fenik (1974) 105–30; Besslich (1966) 143–7; and, for a recent survey of scholarly solutions to the "problematic" issue of the disparity between what is said about Arete and what actually occurs, Whittaker (1999) 142–4. Her answer is that Athena's and Nausicaa's description of the queen is meant to warn Odysseus that he has not yet returned to the real world. Louden (1999) 53–4, 119–20 seconds the suggestion by Doherty (1995) that Odysseus designs his tales to ingratiate himself to Arete, adding that he thereby hopes to win over Alcinous so that "he will more easily be able to reach Arete." This is part of an elaborate and provocative argument that Arete/Nausicaa form a parallel with Circe and Penelope in a thrice-repeated narrative structure that shapes the entire epic. As intriguing as this larger thesis is, the fact remains that Arete in the text itself demonstrates virtually none of the authority referred to by Athena, Nausicaa, or the author. Arete simply does not live up to her billing.

[108] Pedrick (1988) 86–7 shows that Arete's silence is related to the fact that the woman is not usually present at the initial reception of a guest. That is, Arete is intentionally out of place in this reception scene. Her primary reason for appearing, then, is to remain in awkward silence. Alcinous controls Arete by preempting some of the woman's traditional roles (e.g. the giving of gifts at 8.388–93) and through verbal manipulation. De Jong (1995) 134–8 analyzes Arete's silence from a narratological perspective, suggesting it is part of an "interruption pattern" that contributes to our ultimate surprise through her "dangerous" question to Odysseus about the origin of his outfit. See also Olson (1991) for the ambiguities and tensions in Arete's position, as reflected in the use of her name. Reece (1993) 114–15 suggests Arete is modeled on Penelope's similar depiction.

away, but to load him with gifts. Echeneus replies once again with telling directness: what this wise queen has said is on the mark, "but the word and deed (*ergon te epos te*) depend upon Alcinous here" (344–6). It is the man's province to make word become action, and that is exactly what happens. Alcinous insists that his wife's word will indeed hold, "as surely as I live and am lord over the Phaeacians" (348–9). He repeats his wife's suggestion, noting that he himself will see to the gifts, and adds one final (and by now familiar) touch: "But his conveyance will be the care of all men, and especially mine, since the authority in the land is mine" (352–3). He does not tell his wife to go upstairs and supervise her maids – clearly Arete is too important to be so easily dismissed – but he does reassert his own primacy in public matters in the same fashion as Telemachus and Hector.[109] And Odysseus is sensitive enough to note this claim and so addresses his answer to the king, not Arete. In fact, the queen will not speak again in the epic, although Odysseus will have the presence of mind to bid her a formal farewell (13.59–62). Perhaps even here, the status-minded Odysseus reminds the queen of her place, as his last words to her are to enjoy – in her *oikos* – her children, people, and Alcinous the king.

Telemachus' rebuke of his mother turns out to be a brash expression of the cultural norm. In a world where even Hera and Athena can be silenced (if only temporarily) by the wave of the *paterfamilias*, Calypso's legitimate complaint goes unheard, and the clever Circe is outmaneuvered, we should not expect mortal women's voices to command authority. Arete and Helen are impressive and influential women at their respective courts, but their voices require male support to become deed. Penelope, like Helen, is resourceful in act and word – a true match for her clever husband as her "test" of the marriage bed reveals – but even here her authority is limited to the internal world of the *oikos*.[110] As Helene Foley concludes in her

---

[109] *Pace* Wyatt (1989) 238, who remarks that Alcinous adds this phrase "unnecessarily." Martin (1993) 236–7 argues that the phrase "X will be a care to me: I have the power" is always ironic and undercut; so also Thalmann (1998b) 218. I think rather that it is always the sign of emotionally driven overstatement, ironic but nonetheless true. The bow is ultimately the way of differentiating the men, however clever or lucky Penelope was in choosing this means of determining her next husband. Similarly, war really *is* the concern of men, and especially of Hector (*Il.* 6.492–3), even if his statement of that fact, given his fate, is pitiable. We know he will die, but that does not change the truth of his statement. Whose concern is it? Nagler (1993) 249–52 notes that all four appearances of the phrase move from the subordination of women by men to the assertive speaker's command over competitors. Control of *muthos* is control of culture, which Nagler sees (using glasses a bit too modern, I think) as a rejection of peace.

[110] For a survey of recent scholarship on Penelope, and a strong argument for Penelope's "success" (i.e. her *aretê* in terms of beauty, deeds, and reputation), see Helleman (1995). Wickert-Micknat

study of Penelope, "Penelope wins *kleos* as wife, as a person powerless to act except in relation to another, not as a powerful warrior-leader defending his reputation." Women, like animals, have the psychological composition to act virtuously, but they possess no complete *kleos* or authority without husbands.[111] It should come as no surprise, then, that the only characters in the *Odyssey* whose customary winged words may be clipped (*apteros*) turn out to be women.[112]

The lack of language, the defining characteristic of animals in the Homeric epics, is thus redefined as an absence of authoritative speech in those who lack power. Women are born with this cultural deficiency, although some manage to work around it slightly. Men too are born deficient, but they have the chance to outgrow their weakness. In some ways, this acquisition of *muthoi* is the definition of manhood, and thus of the heroic life in general. If to die is to lose the power of speech, then the corollaries might be that to grow up is to gain it, and to live fully is to exercise it. Nowhere are these associations more clear than in the heroic ethos, where to be successful is to be a doer of deeds and speaker of words. But what exactly does

(1982) summarizes the facts that can be gathered about the lives of Homeric women. On women and power, a much-discussed topic in current scholarly discussions, see Easterling (1991). Doherty (1995) 127 sees in Penelope a reaffirmation of gender hierarchy, though Felson-Rubin (1994) 19f. argues for Penelope's creation of plots within the private sphere. Caught in between is Katz (1991). In an effort to give Penelope a form of authority with words she simply does not have, Marquardt (1993) has argued that Penelope's deeds included the writing of messages to the suitors! As Thalmann (1998b) 232 concludes, "Penelope ultimately has little autonomy or power, although she may seem to have some in the immediate situation." He sees this as one of a number of instances in the text where alternative possibilities of social interaction are raised, only to be rejected and the poet's "ideology" reconfirmed; see also Sealey (1990) 147.

[111] H. P. Foley (1995) 108.

[112] For a possible alternate meaning of this phrase, see the next chapter. Eurycleia is an interesting case. We would naturally expect the words of servants to carry little authority. But Olson has pointed out (1991–2) 221 that even though the suggestions of servants are often so reasonable that the master eventually does what the servant advises, it "is all the more striking, therefore, that independent suggestions by servants in the *Odyssey* are routinely rejected immediately when they are made and the servant ordered to do only what he or she has been told." Servants' words cannot carry independent authority, as that would make them equal to their masters. It is heroic men who make words into deeds. Homer may in fact be challenging this very equation, especially in the *Odyssey*, where the moral heroes are mostly servants. And as we have seen several times already, women's advice similarly is often ignored to the hero's cost. This is a debated issue; see Thalmann (1998b) passim. It is no wonder that the proud Eurycleia takes exception to Odysseus' physical restraint of her voice – she is perfectly capable of controlling herself (19.492f.). Her subsequent desire to turn state's evidence on the handmaids may warn us, however, that she is a bit too garrulous (cf. Irus' reference to the kitchen maid) for Odysseus to trust. He does eventually take her up on her offer, even though he dismisses it here. On Telemachus' relationship with Eurycleia and how her "diminishing authority is an essential and necessary condition of his coming of age," see Karydas (1998), esp. 15–16. For Eurycleia's "masculine" perspective (in contrast with Eurynome's disastrous counsel to Penelope), see Pedrick (1994).

it mean to be a speaker of words, and how is this use of language tied into the major themes of the *Iliad* and *Odyssey*? It is to those questions we turn in the next two chapters. We will then be in a position to compare the evidence from Homer – our primary source for early Greek attitudes about status, speech, animals, and human nature – with the views found in the fifth-century "enlightenment" of classical Athens.

CHAPTER 2

Controlling language: Telemachus learns to speak

Polyphemus the Cyclops is the ultimate Other, and as such over the past forty years has been as thoroughly probed as his eye.[1] Although there may still be some critical debate about the origins and significance of the various contradictory aspects of the world the one-eyed giants inhabit, there is general agreement that the episode is one of a series in which Odysseus encounters the super- and sub-human, the non-Greek. The pseudo-pastoralist Cyclopes are the epitome of the uncivilized.[2] They are ignorant of ships and harbors, agriculture, hunting, cooking meat, cities, gift-exchange, laws, assemblies, government, blood sacrifice, and hospitality. Their woolly land, a *potential* golden-age paradise, is characterized by force, hubris, impiety, and cannibalism. Nature overwhelms culture, and Odysseus' triumph is in some way a victory of the civilized over the savage, the Greek over the barbarian, the human over the bestial.

In what has been labeled the most "Odyssean" of all his adventures, the hero displays his cunning intelligence (*mêtis*) in both verbal and non-verbal tricks to overcome his savage tormentor.[3] Intelligence triumphs – or at least mostly triumphs – over force, and self-restraint masters – or for the most part masters – impulse. But more specifically, Odysseus emerges as a "master of language."[4] Odysseus uses his human command of speech to overcome the brutality of the culture-deprived monster. Polyphemus tries to outwit Odysseus in each of their three conversations, and in the first two the Cyclops mistakenly believes he has succeeded. The episode can be read as an examination of the place of language in acting human. The

---

[1] I have gleaned much about this episode from the following studies: Page (1955) 1–20; Podlecki (1961); Brown (1966); Kirk (1970) 162–71; Schein (1970); Glenn (1971) and (1978); Clay (1983) 112–25; Austin (1983), who points out how much of the land of the Cyclopes is defined by negatives; Mondi (1983); Vidal-Naquet (1986) 21–2; O'Sullivan (1990); Reece (1993) 125–42; Segal (1994) 30–3, 202–15; recently and thoroughly, Cook (1995) 93–110.

[2] On the ideological "construction" of the shepherd as the opposite of an agrarian, civilized life, see Shaw (1982–3). The Cyclopes, however, apparently grow grapes and make wine; see below.

[3] Clay (1983) 112.   [4] Cook (1995) 94–6.

key moment is of course the punning use of the name "Nobody" (*outis/mê tis*) which, through a neat trick in Greek, makes *mêtis* ("intelligence") itself the victor. Odysseus prevails through the careful manipulation of language and silence, and nearly destroys himself when he momentarily loses that control. To be fully and successfully human is to manage one's most human characteristic: language.

It is the Cyclops' "deep voice" (*phthongon . . . barun*, 9.257), as well as the monster himself, that first terrifies the Greeks trapped inside the cave. After an initial exchange that reveals just how much trouble Odysseus has stumbled into, Polyphemus asks where the Greek ship has been moored (279–80). Odysseus realizes that he is being tested (*peirazôn*) and is not fooled, answering with crafty words (281–2). This idea of "testing" or "making trial of" someone plays a central role in the return of Odysseus. The root is used many times throughout the epic in the context of identity and discovery.[5] The *Odyssey* can be read as a series of tests passed or failed by its major characters. Telemachus, as we will see, must learn to use language in an adult fashion, moving to adulthood and full humanity from an adolescence "untested in wise words" (3.23). In all these trials, we hear of only two failures: the suitors cannot string the bow, and Polyphemus fails to trick Odysseus. The wily Ithacan sees right through Polyphemus' ploy and tells him the first of several important lies. As a hero in the folktales upon which this entire episode is based, Odysseus is unique in lying to protect his men, and Polyphemus is "uncommonly crafty" to inquire.[6] Homer has drawn attention to this confrontation as a battle of wits, a struggle over who can control language, not merely barbaric brawn versus Greek brains.

The second conversation revolves around Odysseus' famous *outis* trick (355–70). Polyphemus promises a guest-gift in return for some more wine and the name of the stranger. Odysseus gives him the wine and says his name is Nobody, to which the Cyclops replies that he will eat Nobody last as his gift. He naturally believes he has outfoxed the little Greek. Here, the connection with speech, wits, and wine is important. The drunkenness of the giant in the folk-tale is rare.[7] Why is it introduced here? The previous

---

[5] The root is thematically significant especially in the "test" of the bow (21.113, 124, 135, 149, 159, 180, 184, 268, 282, 394, 410), Penelope's testing of Odysseus (19.215, 23.114, 181), and the cautious hero's inquiry into the nature and attitude of native inhabitants (6.126, 9.174 = the Cyclopes), serving men (16.305) and farmers (16.313, 319) on Ithaca, Eumaeus (14.459, 15.304), Penelope (13.336), and Laertes (24.216, 221, 238).

[6] Glenn (1971) 158–9.

[7] Glenn (1971) 161–2, although, as Burgess (2001) 106–8 observes, there are prototypes in which the drunkenness of the giant is stressed.

nights, Polyphemus had fallen asleep without any alcohol. True, we are impressed by Odysseus' cleverness,[8] and one might add that the use of a gift won for respecting a suppliant (196–200) is the perfect tool with which to punish this dean of inhospitality. But wine, as acculturated nature – that is, nature tamed and improved for man's use – is also the correct weapon with which to destroy this beast who does not recognize the differences between culture and nature.[9] Drunkenness is uncommon in the Homeric epics, limited to Polyphemus, Elpenor, and the suitors.[10] One of the brilliantly ironic moments in the *Odyssey* is when the intoxicated leader of the suitors lectures the disguised Odysseus on the dangers of wine (*Od.* 21.293–304). Antinous warns the beggar that wine deluded the Centaur Eurytion and started the battle of the Lapiths and Centaurs. Later in Greek history, this episode came to represent the Greeks against barbarians, but even here in Homer we can sense the similarities between the bestial Cyclops and the half-animal Centaurs.[11] The suitors, Centaurs, and Cyclopes are particularly susceptible to wine, their veneer of civilization so thin that they quickly and easily violate the basic decencies of humanity, especially as represented by the feast. Wine for them represents nature unleashed, barbarity now savaging culture. Bound closely to this psychological vulnerability is their inability to interpret and their slackness with language. The suitors do not recognize Odysseus or understand his words, and they misinterpret or ignore warnings. Polyphemus likewise is linguistically handicapped.

And not just Polyphemus. One of the surprising and often overlooked elements of the story is the response of the rest of the Cyclopes to their

---

[8] Schein (1970) 79–80. Page (1955) considers it to be merely "humorous."

[9] Austin (1983) 21; Cook (1995) 96 with references. *Pace* Shaw (1982–3) 23, who insists that there is no evidence that any of the Cyclopes drank wine, even though it is explicitly referred to at 9.110–11. At 357–9 Polyphemus knows all about the drink, observing that his land produces rich clusters of grapes and conceding that this particular vintage is pure ambrosia and nectar. How else would he know how good it is if he had nothing with which to compare it?

[10] Davies (1997) 101 notes that at *Od.* 3.135–40 Nestor says the Greeks were drunk after the sack of Troy, the only depiction of inebriated Achaean warriors in the epics, and associated with the doomed efforts to return home. But see also *Od.* 9.43–6, where Odysseus' men (great fools!) refuse to obey his orders to flee the land of the Cicones, preferring to lounge on the beach, barbecuing cattle and drinking large amounts of wine. The morality of this tale is not lost even on my sun-loving students (nor is it entirely absorbed by them). Athenaeus (2.38e) quotes Alcaeus and Euripides on how men become beasts under the influence of wine.

[11] Kirk (1970) 152–62. Polyphemus' solo drinking may also be a sign of his lack of civilization, as he inverts the socially integrative function of alcohol in what becomes a "stereotype of otherness"; see Murray (1991) 84. His swallowing the wine unmixed with water is also the mark of a barbarian; see Herodotus 6.84.3 on the Scythians. Centaurs are an interesting mix, since they have human faces and can speak. Perhaps this makes them even more dangerous. Deianira, in Sophocles' *Women of Trachis*, refers to Nessus five times as a "beast" (55, 568–9, 662, 680, 707), but still follows his advice and ends up destroying both Heracles and herself.

wounded friend. When he says that "Nobody is killing me by guile or by force," they are completely fooled and unwittingly make the very cause of Polyphemus' pain – Odysseus' intelligence (*mêtis*) – the subject of their sentence (*mê tis se biazetai*, 410). These round-eyed giants are not the sharpest ogres in the Mediterranean. It is as if Odysseus has given two "linguistically challenged" individuals just enough words to miscommunicate hysterically. The land of the Cyclopes is *not* the land of *logos*.

When viewed in this light, Polyphemus' quaint monologue with his ram becomes thematically significant. Though a few of the folk-tale versions depict the monster addressing his animals, only in Homer does he request that the animal communicate. As the burdened beast struggles last to get out of the cave, the Cyclops wonders why and speaks aloud. Misunderstanding once again, he myopically assumes the animal is grieving for his master's eye. He wishes that the ram could "be of the same mind" (*homophroneois*) and that he had the power of speech (*potiphônêeis te genoio*) to reveal the whereabouts of Nobody (456–7). To our modern, overwhelmingly urban mentality, such a touch may make the Cyclops suddenly more appealing, somehow more human.[12] How cute – he talks to critters! But to the Greeks, and especially in this context, such a wish reveals a grotesque blurring of distinctions between the human and the bestial. This is a pastoral fantasy alien to the georgic mentality of the early Greeks. We do not share *homophrosunê* with animals.[13] The verb Polyphemus uses is found at only one other place in the epic, in the description of the ideal union of a husband and wife wished for Nausicaa by Odysseus (6.183, and by implication found between Odysseus and Penelope). And, as we have seen, the fundamental difference in the Homeric world between humans and animals is their inability to speak. Polyphemus' wish shows once again that he does not recognize the differences between animals and humans, something his ingestion of Odysseus' men has indicated less tastefully but no more significantly.

Homer emphasizes the difference between Polyphemus' animality and Odysseus' humanity in the manner in which the hero escapes. We should not forget that Polyphemus is speaking to the animal that is carrying his

---

[12] E.g. Newton (1983) 138: ". . . but we also feel pity for the Cyclops. Already abandoned by his neighbors, Polyphemus now loses the only living creature to which he feels an attachment." Cf. Clay (1983) 120: "Cyclops, ironically, reveals himself more humane when conversing with his animal than in human society." She cites Eustathius 1639.17, who quotes in this context the proverb of "like to like." This is exactly right – beast to beast; see Dumont (2001) 91.

[13] Segal (1994) 213–24. Four dogs possess *homophrosunê* at *Hymn Hom. Merc.* 194–5; Bolmarcich (2001) also shows that *homophrosunê* is almost exclusively used to delineate a relationship between male comrades.

enemy to safety. Here again, the Cyclops terribly misconstrues the situation. In the traditional folk-tale, the hero usually escapes by crawling out on all fours covered with a sheepskin.[14] He flays the animal and dons the freshly skinned coat, as in Menelaus' acrid disguise among Proteus' seals. But Homer is careful to insure that Odysseus does not take on the symbolic role of four-footed animal. Nor is he to kill an animal without some larger connection to humanity. The ram to which he clings will be sacrificed to Zeus in an (unsuccessful) effort to re-establish the correct relationship with the gods.[15]

Odysseus and his men manage to escape in silence. Humans not only have language but control of it. Odysseus, however, has hidden his identity for too long. In the heroic world, full humanity and heroic singularity can only come from fame, the spread of one's name. Thus, the offer of Calypso ("The Concealer") of immortality on a deserted island is the equivalent of Achilles' abandoned option of a long and inglorious life. But the heroic world has changed since the fall of Troy, vanished in many ways (it lives on primarily in the underworld, frozen in the past lives of dead heroes). Odysseus still has much to learn in his return home. When he shouts out in an effort to regain the heroic identity deprived him by the brutality of Polyphemus and his own necessary disguise as a Nobody, we learn that such efforts can no longer be tolerated in a post-Iliad world. Polyphemus nearly destroys the ship. Silence once again saves the crew, but Odysseus still ignores the evidence – and the whispered pleas of his comrades – and trumpets his name to his victim.

Polyphemus has been tricked by language, and now reveals that he has also misinterpreted the oracle that foretold his downfall. He had expected to be overcome by someone big and strong, by force, not by some little nobody. This is not so much *moral* obtuseness[16] as an inability to speak or listen with necessary skill. Both Polyphemus and Odysseus have misused language and misunderstood the situation, and the last laugh is now on the Ithacan. Polyphemus is able to exercise one aspect of language that is the most

---

[14] Glenn (1971) 167–9; see also Burgess (2001) 106–8.

[15] Some scholars have argued that Odysseus is punished for his own violation of the guest–host relationship, or for various hubristic actions and/or boasts; see: Brown (1966); Friedrich (1987), and especially (1991) for a review of the arguments, with Reece (1993) 142–3; for the counterarguments, see Brown (1996).

[16] Segal (1994) 210–11. He astutely notes (30–3, 202–15), however, that Odysseus' audience, the Phaeacians, as so often in the epic, form the antitheses to the Cyclopes, representing language to excess; see his discussion on pages 12–64 on the Phaeacians in general. For the Phaeacian–Cyclops antithesis as an opposition designed to address issues of overseas exploration and settlement, see Dougherty (2001) 122–42, although I am unconvinced that Odysseus' return home should be read as a "colonial foundation."

elementary, magical, even uncivilized, and most readily available: a curse. Here, language functions at its most basic level – to know and manipulate words, to name, is to control. Odysseus ironically places one tiny bit of real language into the hands of the outwitted brute, and Polyphemus knows how to use it.

This battle of control over language shapes the story of virtually every major character in the Homeric epics. The veteran Odysseus has something to learn as he makes his way back to his wife, son, father, and kingdom. As he reenters the realities of Ithaca, he must shed his associations with both the bestial and the hyper-civilized. A less familiar but even clearer case-study in mastery of language can be found in the marvelous depiction of Telemachus' development throughout the course of the *Odyssey*. A young man struggling to mature, Telemachus grows up before our eyes during the tale of his father's return. In the Homeric world, such maturation means not just becoming a doer of deeds but the controller of speech. Animals play a much less significant role in marking Telemachus' development than for Odysseus, but his journey is more sharply inscribed by his vacillating control of speech. For the moment, then, we will leave Homeric animals in their languageless lairs and focus on the definition of heroic speaking. By mastering the characteristic that most distinguishes humanity from the beast, the hero's son finally fills his father's shoes and becomes fully human.

SPEAKING AND DOING IN HOMER

There are two activities of particular importance to the Homeric hero, two arenas in which superiority can be most clearly established. The often-quoted lines of Phoenix to Achilles set out the challenge directly: "It was to you that the old horseman Peleus sent me on the day when he sent you to Agamemnon, from Phthia, a mere child (*nêpios*), not knowing anything as yet of evil war, neither of gatherings wherein men wax preeminent. For this cause he sent me to instruct you in all these things, to be both a speaker of words and a doer of deeds" (9.438–43; cf. Odysseus' remarks to the fleeing Greeks at 2.200–2). Only two words in Homer are modified by the epithet *kudianeira*, "bringing honor to men," battle (*machê*, eight times) and speech/assembly (*agorê*, once).[17] There is little doubt about what it

---

[17] Thalmann (1984) 180; see especially *Il.* 1.490–1 and 9.374 for Achilles' rejection of heroism by refusing both; cf. Lowenstam (1993) 132–47. Interestingly, *kudianeira* is one of the few purely positive words used to describe war, uttered almost exclusively by characters and only once in simple narrator text; see de Jong (1987b) 222, 224. One need not accept Nagy's insistence on the primacy of a fluid poetic tradition over all else to glean important insights on this dichotomy throughout his early work (1979);

means to be a doer of deeds – to fight successfully in the typical hand-to-hand combat on the plains of Troy. "Always to be the best and superior to others" is the simple, if ultimately impossible goal (6.208, 11.784) in this agonistic society – to risk one's life in battle, be victorious, and gain fame.[18] Nestor, on the other hand, long past his fighting years, is said to "be the best" of everyone in counsel (11.627). What, exactly, makes a "speaker of words"?

The most complete study of this verbal competition is that of Richard Martin, who sees the distinction between *muthos* and *epos* as a central theme of the *Iliad*. *Muthos* implies authority and power, a "speech act" performed at length and usually in public. An *epos* is a mere utterance, usually short, that accompanies a physical act and focuses on the message rather than performance. *Muthoi*, authoritative speech acts, come in three types, all agonistic: commands, boast-and-insult contests, and recitation of remembered events. These contests are marked by their length. According to Martin, performance time (the number of lines allotted to a given speech) is the single most important narrative "sign" in Homer's system for marking the status of a hero or god. Thus, Nestor's and Phoenix's lengthy speeches by definition mark them as authoritative speakers, as do the total 960 verses of Achilles' speech (almost twice as much as either Hector's or Agamemnon's). Speaking to "win out" is the goal of every Iliadic performer. Achilles does this by expanding his speech, just as the author of the poem does. To speak of oneself also lends authority, so Nestor's and Phoenix's autobiographical narratives are inherently effective (although not as close to Homer's own technique as that of Achilles). The main objective is to impose one's verbal presence on the audience.[19]

There is much here of great value for understanding the dynamics of heroic speaking in the epic. I think Martin's insights can be tied more directly into Achilles' "journey" than Martin himself attempts. For I believe that Martin's analysis misses the criticism of this system that is embedded in Achilles' final exchange with Priam. Homer subtly undercuts this heroic self-absorption, this endless expansion for the sake of increasing one's own

---

see also Schofield (1986) and Naas (1995) 47–52. Benardete (1963) suggests that deeds are done by men (*andres*) and words spoken by humans (*anthrôpoi*), but the distinction is not consistent – the real issue is effective speech versus ineffective speech. Van Wees (1992) 95–7, however, downplays this competition for status through eloquence and intelligence.

18 Renehan (1987).

19 Martin (1989); see also Lincoln (1997) 353–62, who concentrates on the *muthos/logos* distinction rather than *muthos/epos* but comes to similar conclusions about the association of *muthos* with power in Homer and Hesiod. Foley (1991) 154–6 observes that *epos* can have power, but must be modified to take on any authority (e.g. by *pukinon*).

status. Achilles learns, unlike anyone else in the text, to employ his verbal skills not to augment his own authority but for personal reasons that derive from his tragic insight. This similarity of *thematic* purpose shared by Achilles and the poet is more significant than the expansion of speech itself as the sign of the hero.[20] In the next chapter, we will see that mere length of speech does not in fact make one a successful speaker at all, if we define success as turning one's words into action. Achilles' speech, as complex as it is, is remarkably unsuccessful. But first we must look more carefully at how one becomes a traditional speaker of words in this heroic world.

In some ways, the references to success in both speaking and fighting become formulaic in the description of the military leaders. Nestor, for example, tells Agamemnon and Achilles that they surpass all the Greeks in *both* counsel (*boulê*) *and* fighting (*Il.* 1.258). While Achilles is unquestionably the finest fighter at Troy, neither man could lay claim to being the best at counsel (indeed, Achilles at least will later concede that others are better speakers, e.g. 18.106). Both, however, have tremendous authority in the assembly. Nestor is also buttering them up, trying to get them to listen to *him* – this is the present challenge for the "best of speakers."[21] Thus, he immediately adds that he himself fought when men were much better than any man now alive (present company included, no doubt!), and they took his advice. The implication is clearly that he is still superior at counsel, at least. Helenus similarly refers to Aeneas and Hector as "the best in every endeavor in fighting and counsel" (6.77–9; cf. Thoas, 15.281–4), although both make disastrous decisions in the war, and Aeneas is certainly not the best fighter. Hector is more honest when he tells Ajax that a god has given the Greek stature, strength, and wisdom, and then quickly adds that Ajax is preeminent with the spear – no suggestion here of superior wisdom or speech (cf. 15.641–3).

[20] I am concerned here with the significance of articulation itself and not directly with the recent interest in the characters as poets, that is, creators of stories who model Homeric tale-telling techniques, of which Martin (1989) is the most thorough. For this aspect of speech in Homer, see the various works of Nagy, especially (1979); Thalmann (1984) 173–82; Murnaghan (1987) 149–75; Ford (1992) 172–97; Pratt (1993) 63–94; Segal (1994) 113–63; the sensible summary of *kleos* by Olson (1995) 1–23; and (with caution) the abstract theoretical discussion in the first chapters of Rabel (1997). Krapp (1964) offers a useful collection of passages, if not much analysis, of references to speech in connection with themes of the epic. Some of the issues raised in these studies will surface in the next chapter in consideration of Achilles' storytelling, in particular to counter Mackie's suggestion (1997) 92 that Achilles' attitude towards narrative is "less advanced" than that of the Odyssean storyteller because he does not transfer his own experience into a tale that gives pleasure or delight. Redfield (1975) 218–23 notes that it is a peculiarity of epic that heroes can "share the perspective of poet and audience and look down upon themselves."

[21] Taplin (1990) 64 notes that we cannot take Nestor as the last word.

Homer and his characters in fact frequently observe that the gods do not grace any individual with every skill: no character in the *Iliad* is allowed to be superior in both public speech and action.[22] In the *Odyssey*, Odysseus is believed to be the best speaker and counselor of the Greeks, a title that he shares occasionally with Nestor (cf. *Od.* 11.512). Athena says as much: he is the best of all men in counsel and speech (13.297–8; cf. 13.332, and Odysseus' self-description at 14.490–1).[23] When Antenor in the *Iliad* compares Odysseus with Menelaus, he concludes that his "words are like snowflakes on a winter's day, and no mortal could vie with him" (*Il.* 3.222–3). Odysseus comes closest to fulfilling the heroic objective of being superior in both word and deed, but only in the post-Iliadic world (*Od.* 2.270–2, 4.328–31, 16.242, 22.226–32). In the *Iliad*, Odysseus himself reminds Achilles that the leader of the Myrmidons is much the best in war, but in counsel "I am best, for I am elder and know more" (*Il.* 19.216–19). Still, Nestor is routinely referred to as the foremost speaker (e.g. 2.370, 11.627), a man who should no longer fight at all.

Why can't a hero be the best at both? Such an individual would probably have so much authority in Homer's world that it would create an untenable political situation. But the poet deals with this issue in a realistic fashion. First, there is the simple fact of life that different individuals possess different skills. Polydamas observes that god has given Hector superiority in the works of war and now he wishes to be better than others at counsel, but he can't do everything. God gives skill at war to one, to another dance, lyre, song, and into another Zeus puts a good mind from which many men get profits and which saves many (13.726–34). Homer agrees with Polydamas' assessment, informing us that although Hector and Polydamas were born on the same night, one far excels in words, and the other with a sword (18.251–2; see the similar words of Odysseus to Euryalus, *Od.* 8.167f.; cf. *Il.* 3.65–6, 23.669–71). Nevertheless, Hector's bullying wins the day over Polydamas' prudent advice. Although Homer often seems to equate good advice with excellence in words, the audience may be "fools" (*nêpioi*) and fail to be persuaded, and thus follow inferior counsel.

But the most frequently implied reason that a great warrior is not a great speaker is that good speaking and advice-giving come with age.[24]

---

[22] Solmsen (1954).

[23] Eurycleia says the beggar is like Odysseus in shape, voice, and feet (19.380–1). Dale (1982) argues that the *epêtês* Athena uses to describe Odysseus at 13.332–4 is connected with *epos* and means preeminence in *muthoi*, just as *anchinoos* in the same passage refers to preeminence in *boulê*.

[24] Especially good on the links between age and speaking is Dickson (1995); Falkner (1995) 14–22; cf. Eustathius 407.15–16: "the young are not ready of speech"; see also Falkner (1989) esp. 26–30.

Youth is associated with a certain ineffectuality of speech – skills need to be learned and, especially, experience needs to be gained. It is a compliment to Menelaus, then, when Antenor notes that he is fluent, brief but clear, not long-winded but to the point "even though he was younger [than Odysseus]" (3.213–15). That is, although not in the same league with Odysseus, he spoke well for one his age.

At the other end of the life span, the elderly have lost their powers at fighting and must make their contributions through sage advice. Nestor frequently begins his speeches by contrasting his former vigor with his present weakness.[25] Words spoken in the present must be backed up by deeds of the past in order to have authority. Nestor's rambling accounts of his youthful battles make his words credible, a connection he makes explicit more than once. Of the eight paradigmatic exhortations in the *Iliad*, four are from the mouth of Nestor and *all* of these refer to his previous exploits (1.254, 7.124, 11.656, 23.626). At 4.310–25, for example, the poet concludes that Nestor gives advice from his knowledge of battles in the past. Agamemnon wishes that the evil old age that now presses down upon the king of Pylos would oppress other soldiers, and that Nestor had their youth. Nestor agrees, wishing he had his former strength, "but in no way do the gods grant to men all things at one time." The young men will wield spears, and he will urge them on with verbal counsel, for such is the office of elders. In general, then, Homer introduces what will become the typical pessimistic view of old age in Greece.[26]

The elders of Troy sit at the Scaean gates, the "wise" (*pepnumenô* as two are labeled, 3.148) leaders who "in old age had ceased from battle, but were excellent speakers, like cicadas who settle on a tree in the woods and lift their delicate voices" (3.150–2). Kirk (ad loc.) suggests that there may be a bit of "affectionate irony" here as well, a reference to the ceaselessness of the old men's talk. This loquacity is one of the primary characteristics of Nestor as well, and it is possible that he is introduced with a similarly gentle irony: "Nestor stood up among them, the sweet speaker, the clear-voiced speaker of Pylos, from whose tongue flowed speech sweeter than honey" (*Il.* 1.248–9). The repetitious description captures the graceful loquacity of the old Pylian

---

De Jong (2001a) ad 2.324 notes that youth is regularly associated with recklessness and impetuosity (Telemachus, Pisistratus, and Nausicaa are exceptions), and reminds us that the youth of the suitors is repeatedly stressed; see also Belmont (1967). On the political ramifications of youth, still of interest is Jeanmaire (1975) Chapter 1, especially 19–20. Casevitz (1998) argues that the Trojans are depicted as old, with the young killed and/or separated from their elders. The union of old and young makes the Greeks eventually victorious.

[25] Pedrick (1983) 58; Alden (2000) 74–111.   [26] See Byl (1976) and below, Chapter 4.

with perfection.[27] Once a great warrior, he has followed the *cursus honorum* of a long-lived Homeric hero, now aiming for the preeminence in speech that is the prerogative (*geras*) of the elderly (4.318–25; cf. 7.157; 11.668f.). He is now considered to be the best counselor among the Greeks (2.370; 11.627; cf. 7.324–5 = 9.93–4). It is no surprise, then, that Nestor most often and most clearly articulates the superiority of seniors in the assembly: "Obey me; you are both younger than I" (*Il.* 1.259). He praises Diomedes' speech in the assembly and announces that the young warrior is best in battle and counsel . . . among those his own age. Diomedes speaks wisely (*pepnumena*) for a youth, but Nestor is older and will set everything out (*Il.* 9.53–61; cf. 2.555). Even the "ageless" gods acknowledge the significance of relative age, as Poseidon tells the younger Apollo that he is elder and knows more (calling the archer god *nêputi*', "foolish," as well; *Il.* 21.439–41; cf. 13.355, for Zeus's being born first and knowing more than Poseidon). It is in this context that Iris reminds Poseidon that the Erinyes "always attend the elder" (*Il.* 15.204).[28]

A dying hero, having been deprived of Nestor's opportunity to age gracefully, descends rapidly in his final breaths through the expected diminution of the two powers. First, with the lethal wound comes the expected loss of the power to act. The word *oligodraneôn*, often translated as "feeble" but etymologically meaning able "to do little," is used only three times in the Homeric poems, each time in this context. The final speeches of both the fading Patroclus and Hector are introduced by it (16.843, 22.337), as are the words of Hector after his foreshadowing faint (15.246). Having lost the ability to be a doer of deeds, the mortally wounded hero retains only the other half of his heroic definition, the power to speak. The three greatest heroes to die in the *Iliad*, Sarpedon, Patroclus, and Hector, also all share

---

[27] Cf. 4.293; see Kirk (1985) ad loc. and Dickson (1995) 101f. for other possible reasons for the long introduction. Richardson (1990) 38–9 suggests that the lengthy introduction gives the stamp of approval by the narrator on the worth of Nestor's ensuing speech, thereby making the subsequent rejection of it all the more poignant. *Agorêtês* is associated with age: it is used twice of Nestor, once of the elderly Trojans on the wall, and once by Nestor of "old man Peleus" (7.126). The other three references (to Telemachus, Thersites, and Achilles/Agamemnon) appear to be sarcastic. For a positive assessment of Nestor's prolixity and loquacity in general, see Martin (1989) 101f. *Ligus* is a key component of Homer's "sonorous" heroes (replaced in classical oratory with *lampra*, "luminous"); see Montiglio (2000) 144–8.

[28] For the claim that the older necessarily know more, cf. 3.205, 9.161,19.219; cf. Echeneus among the Phaeacians, *Od.* 7.155f., 11.342f. Of course, the claim to be older, with its implication of being necessarily wiser, can be an empty boast. Agamemnon tacks on to his long list of recompense to Achilles the condition that the younger warrior submit to him, since Agamemnon is "more kingly and older," 9.160–1. Thus I disagree with Hainsworth that the emphasis in the Greek expression in verse 161 is not on age but ancestry. Odysseus, truly the better speaker, wisely leaves out this line.

one similar formulaic line upon their expiration (it is used nowhere else in the epics): "And as he spoke (*eiponta*) death's end covered him" (16.502, 16.855, 22.361). The last element of their humanity, of their very existence, to disappear, is speech. This connection between death and speech makes for great drama as well, of course, for the heroes' final words are full of tragic significance. But only the greatest warriors, those whose mortality becomes thematically meaningful before Achilles' great awakening in Book 24, are shown losing both aspects of their claim to living a significant life.

Those who are least heroic, on the other hand, are frequently characterized as ineffectual speakers – glib, perhaps, but with no authority. Pathetic Dolon uniquely stammers (*bambainôn*; see Hainsworth [1993] ad 10.375); the hated Ares is accused of whining (5.889); children babble (e.g. 5.408), and the bombastic beggar Irus moans with a verb (*mêkaomai*) and in a formula (*kad d' epes' en koniêïs makôn, Od.* 18.98) that are otherwise limited to animals.[29] Most famously, the deformed and despised Thersites is beaten into silence (cf. Homer's description of the tipsy Elpenor as gifted with neither strength nor brains, *Od.* 10.552–3). Thersites' case is revealing. The episode is set up as a battle for authoritative speech between Odysseus and the misshapen Thersites (2.211f.). The issue is not so much the nature of what is said but who can impose his will upon the army. The words and phrases Homer uses to describe Thersites' verbal nature characterize him as a man as well, matching his physical deformities. But Thersites' speech, albeit abusive, is reasonably well-organized, brief, and echoes many of Achilles' seemingly valid complaints about Agamemnon; and his main argument for going home has been favorably anticipated by the troops' attempted mass exodus.[30] Still, Odysseus characterizes his misshapen adversary as loud, senseless, verbose, abusive, competitive, and taunting. The troops agree, delighted that this "word-flinging humiliator" (*lôbêtêra epesbolon*) will no longer quarrel with shameful words. The soldiers see this as a crowning achievement on Odysseus' résumé: he has proven himself a leader in speech and action before (*boulas . . . polemon*, 273), but this deed, the silencing of Thersites, is the best (275). Why? Because, as Martin puts it, Thersites "does not have the heroic martial performance record needed to back up his words."[31] Can this limping man of the people really lay claim to having captured cities and given booty to Agamemnon, to be one whose captive brings ransom to the king (2.226–33)?

Silence in the *Iliad*, then, is usually a sign of youth, inexperience, lack of authority, and death. Although attentive listening to a leader is commendable in a council or assembly, sitting in silence is only for the anonymous multitude who are not expected to speak. In this competitive world, the "charisma of Homeric speakers can indeed be assessed by their ability to impose silence upon others without ever suffering this humiliation themselves."[32]

In the *Odyssey*, on the other hand, the power of speech is equally balanced by the power of silence. Withholding language intentionally – and it is essential that one have a choice – is just as likely to lead to success as the correct manipulation of language. Not only self-restraint, but as I. J. F. de Jong has shown, "unspoken thought" is a central factor in the epic, lying "between words and deeds."[33] I would tweak her argument slightly by suggesting that these hidden thoughts are still means to deeds, just as words and silence are. What is special about the *Odyssey*'s presentation of speech is that it is applied to a particular goal that is inherently worthy, namely the return home of a hero, king, husband, father, and son. The best speech is not merely well-ornamented or lengthy, but it aims at a worthwhile outcome and succeeds. Odysseus is, as we have seen, already well-known for his speaking. His travels will teach him the values of self-control. But Telemachus provides the best window through which to view the place of speech in this post-Iliadic world. He represents the Homeric vision of youth, inexperienced in both word and deed. He must grow up in order to help his father reestablish himself and regain his identity as king, husband, father, and son. Telemachus *learns* to be a speaker of words, to fulfill his epic destiny as a man "wise in speech."

---

[31] Martin (1989) 111. Kouklanakis (1999) 42–5 argues that Thersites violates the norms of "blame expression" (here following Nagy) and agrees that he does not have the record of deeds to back his speech. Thersites' reputation also counts against him: he is a known troublemaker, and his speech is clearly not interpreted by his fellow Greeks as aimed at the common good.

[32] Montiglio (2000) 55, part of an excellent discussion (especially 46–56, 60–8, 77–9). She concludes that a silent response always highlights a state of tension and forced submission; see also her earlier article (1993). Person (1995) examines the formula for a "dispreferred response" that introduces a delay before an account of this silence and then a reply that usually disagrees with what has been said before.

[33] (1994).

NÊPIOS AND PEPNUMENOS

A critical consensus has emerged over the past forty years that through the course of the *Odyssey* Telemachus grows up.[34] Scholars often disagree on just when, in which ways, how successfully, and with what thematic significance this maturation unfolds, but it has become increasingly clear that in a variety of ways Homer has carefully marked for his audience the stages of Telemachus' growth. Deborah Beck has recently demonstrated that Homer even manipulates the introductory verses of the speeches of both Telemachus and Odysseus to parallel the development of the young man into his father's son.[35] She examines the reunion of the two in Book 16 and their subsequent actions, focusing on speech introductions containing the phrase "the mighty strength of Telemachus" (*hierê is Têlemachoio*, used seven times in the epic, six of which are found in Books 16–22), which always shows Telemachus actively engaged in dissembling to the suitors or for their benefit. She concludes that "the language for Telemachus changes in the same way as the character himself does: it recognizes, or at any rate parallels, his reunion with his father and his subsequent increase in maturity."[36]

I want to suggest that Homer uses Telemachus' much more frequent epithet, *pepnumenos* – applied to him forty-six times in the epic – in a similar and even more pervasive fashion to mark points in Telemachus' maturation

---

[34] Two early and representative interpretations of Telemachus' journey are Austin (1960) and Clarke (1967) 30–44; most subsequent scholarship follows more or less in their footsteps, e.g. Jones (1988), who sees Telemachus' journey as a pursuit of his own identity in terms of his father's famous characteristics: endurance, restraint, intelligence, and deception. An important argument, with bibliography, against the apparent development of Telemachus through the first four books of the epic, is chapter 4 in Olson (1995). He steers a middle course, suggesting that Telemachus undergoes no fundamental personal growth since he has in fact already changed sometime shortly before the *Odyssey* begins. Still, he does see a change in Telemachus' actions. By the end of Book 1, Telemachus has moved out "of a passive acceptance of his world and into an active and engaged relationship with it and thus with storytelling (especially 1.358–9). All the same, to speak of him as 'developing' on an internal level over the course of this scene is to mistake Homer's real interests and concerns. In fact, Telemachus is the same from first to last here; what has changed by the end of Book 1 is that he has begun to act on the feelings and desires he has had from the very start, which is to say he is attempting to live out what he takes to be his father's story in his own person. Not until Book 16 does he really escape the impotence and isolation . . ." (78–9). I have no quarrel with this analysis, but find that these *acts* themselves in the opening books represent development. One is measured in the Homeric world by actions, both physical and verbal. Homer is not interested in internal maturation *per se*, but the degree to which Telemachus takes on the words and deeds of his father and becomes the man he is destined to be. And of course, as Race (1993) 80–1 observes, although Telemachus gains confidence and maturity, he never departs from his essential ethos (defined primarily by his scrupulous regard for hospitality); see also Thalmann (1998b) 206–22.

[35] Beck (1998–9).

[36] Beck (1998–9) 135. On the general topic, see Edwards (1970).

that begin long before the reunion of father and son. Most importantly, *pepnumenos*, while difficult to define, is not as "relatively colorless" as Beck suggests, but is in fact the very characteristic that marks Telemachus' successful journey to adulthood. The epithet, that is, belongs to the Telemachus of the tradition, the "final" version of the adult Telemachus who is hinted at with each speech introduction along the way.[37] One way Homer has framed this maturation is by showing us Telemachus' shedding of childhood as embodied in the word *nêpios* (with its various connotations) and his concomitant development into being truly *pepnumenos*. Telemachus becomes an adult at least in part by learning to manage his language in adult – in Odyssean – fashion, becoming skilled at speech and making his words become actions. He, in effect, "earns" his distinctive epithet by the end of the *Odyssey* as his epithet is gradually actualized.[38] To develop into an adult male leader is to become fully human, and this accomplishment is marked by mastering humanity's unique possession of speech.

Before turning to Telemachus' growth from a *nêpios* into a *pepnumenos* speaker, we must look more carefully at what these strangely slippery words mean in Homer's epics. Agamemnon, discussing family matters in the

---

[37] A parallel use of epithets can be found in the speed epithets of Achilles. These keep the swiftfooted Achaean of tradition in the mind of the audience even though his speed will not be an issue until Books 22 and 23, only to be downplayed in Book 24 where Homer moves the hero beyond the norms of his epithet; see Dunkle (1997) and Burgess (1995) for the connection between Achilles' swiftness and his death. In the language of scholarship on oral poetry, particularly as worked out by Foley (1991), (1999) esp. 208–16, this is "traditional referentiality." The uttering of a noun–epithet formula, whether suitable or not in that instance, refers not merely to the character of the particular moment but rather summons the character as found in the tradition. As Foley says, when *podas ôkus Achilleus* appears, his entire mythic presence is immanent (1999) 141. Bakker (1997) 156–83 expands on this interpretation. He argues that instead "of ascribing a property to an absent referent, noun–epithet formulas make this absent referent present, conjuring it, in its most characteristic form, to the there and now of the performance, as an essential part of the universe of discourse shared between the performer and his audience" (161). He refers to such a conjuring as an "epiphany" of the epic figure effected by the performance out of the timeless world of the myth. Though he thereby downplays the significance of an individual appearance of a noun–epithet formula in a given context, as does Foley, I think these insights can be applied to a diachronic study of a poem. That is, an epithetic phrase can both conjure up the inherent meaning (or not) and be intentionally manipulated by the poet in a specific context for specific thematic purposes. Sale (2001) 65–71 notes that the experience of frequent repetition within the poem itself serves the function of creating a traditional figure. The poet can always choose to use an epithet when meter and syntax permit; when he does, it may or may not be relevant. The audience hears the epithet and makes its own inferences. Similarly, in his examination of oral poetics, Edwards (1997) 283 prudently notes that in specific instances of these repetitions it "remains a matter of individual [reader's] choice; which is, of course, just as it should be."

[38] Important comments on Telemachus' "maturation" are made by Martin (1993) 234–6, who, building on his previous work (1989) on the *Iliad* discussed above, ties this development to the term *muthos* as an authoritative speech act. Also excellent on the connections between *nêpios*, speaking, and maturation is Scheid-Tissinier (1993) esp. 1–13.

underworld with Odysseus, assumes that Telemachus, a mere child at Penelope's breast when the war began, a *nêpios*, is now firmly established as one
of the men (*Od.* 11.448–50). This is exactly the transformation Telemachus
is attempting to accomplish during the course of the *Odyssey.* So what,
exactly, does the word imply? *Nêpios* and its compounds can simply denote
the young ("child, infant, offspring" e.g. Astyanax at *Il.* 6.366, 6.400, 6.408,
22.484, 22.502, 24.726; cf. the expression *nêpia tekna* – literally "childish
children," but perhaps "feeble" – used sixteen times in the epics, including
three times of animal young), which must be Agamemnon's primary meaning here. But these words are also often used to characterize an adult acting
in a childish, thoughtless, or improvident fashion – "fool" is the common
translation, although the difference between "foolish" and "childish" can
be difficult to distinguish.

More to the point, the word *nêpios* may refer etymologically to a child's
inability to speak. Richard Janko has renewed the contention that the
word may be the equivalent of the Latin *infans*, "one who cannot speak."[39]
Professor C. Ruijgh has pointed out to me in correspondence that there is
a semantic problem with this etymology, since the basic meaning of *êpuô*
is something like "to call or speak loudly," and even infants are capable
of calling out. Indeed, the verb is used to describe the sound of the wind
(*Il.* 14.399), Polyphemus' cry (*Od.* 9.399), and the ringing of a lyre (*Od.*
17.271). But Prof. Ruijgh also suggests the etymology can be maintained if
the original meaning of *êpuô* was "to speak loudly and clearly like adults
do." Arcadian *apuomai* ("to summon, to prosecute") and the Homeric *êputa
kêrux* (*Il.* 7.384) may imply the idea of formal speech characteristic of adults
(cf. *Od.* 10.83, where herdsmen call and answer each other). Prof. Ruijgh
concludes that if this etymology is correct, *nêpios* should be explained as a
hypocoristically shortened form of *nêputios* < *naputios*.

The most thorough treatment of the Homeric use of *nêpios* is that of
Edmunds, who prefers a derivation from a root meaning "to join" or "connect."[40] Her main argument against linking *nêpios* with speech, besides the
linguistic awkwardness discussed above, is that nothing in the Homeric
poems suggests that the inability to speak is the essential characteristic of

---

[39] (1992) ad *Il.* 13.292–4, 15.362–4; Hesychius glosses *nêputios* with *aphônon.* Janko believes this is
likely if the word derives from *n-* and *apyô* (Homeric *êpuô*); see Hoekstra (1989) ad *Od.* 14.264
citing Heubeck (1970) 70–2; though cf. Hainsworth ad *Il.* 9.491 (citing Chantraine, but Chantraine
[1983/4] is unsure, as is Frisk [1960/70]); for a summary, see Ingalls (1998) 17 n.18. The digamma
on *epos* makes the straightforward etymology from a negation of the root for speaking difficult. The
fact that Greeks could take *nêpios* to mean not speaking, even if perhaps a false etymology, is almost
as significant as the legitimate etymology. For Latin *infans*, see Néraudau (1984) 53–6.
[40] Edmunds (1990).

a person who is *nêpios*. This point is well-taken, but there may have been an original etymological connection between *nêpios* and speech that was not obvious by Homer's time.[41] The English "baby" presents an interesting parallel. Originally a direct imitation of and comment upon an infant's inability to speak articulately (cf. the etymologies of barbarian, prattle, babble), then a general description of a period of age, and finally used of adults who behave in an inappropriate, childish fashion (as well as a frequent hypocorism in popular songs). Most people using the term today either as an insult or an endearment have no idea, I would imagine, of its etymological significance. Early Greek may also have defined the very young as the "not-speaking (as adults do)," just as we saw it defined foreigners as "other speakers."

Not surprisingly, children (*nêpia tekna*) in a heroic world are pitiable, weak, fearful, foolish, ignorant, careless of war, and incapable of distinguishing between words and things. The seven comparisons of warriors to children in Homeric similes all reveal futile, inappropriate, or ineffectual actions.[42] Children clearly have no authority. This impotency is connected not merely to their physical weakness and political subservience, but also closely to their lack of forceful speech and their inability to put words into action. Thus Nestor reprimands the Greeks for speaking in public assembly like foolish children (*nêpiachois*) who do not care for the work of war (*Il.* 2.337–8; cf. Idomeneus' words to Meriones, *Il.* 13.292–4). Menelaus rebukes his squire with "you were not a fool (*nêpios*) before, but now you talk foolishly (*nêpia*) like a child (*pais*)" (4.31–2).

For a warrior to be categorized as *nêpios* is to have his worth challenged, his status as adult male impugned, his decisions criticized. He is usually in a state of tragic ignorance or headed for disaster when Homer calls him this, especially if the character is in the midst of giving or obeying a calamitous speech (e.g. the case of Patroclus at *Il.* 16.35–47; cf. *Od.* 9.44, 442, 22.32, 370). Of the thirty-eight times it applies to an adult in Homer, in twenty-seven cases that person will soon perish.[43] The poet himself uses the word fourteen times to refer to the deluded behavior of his characters, always

---

[41] Cf. the use of *noos* to refer to homecoming discussed by Frame (1978) 33–5. He makes a lengthy argument that *noos* is connected with *neomai*, the mind with the return home, but must concede that Homer no longer understood the original connection.

[42] Scott (1974) 74; see the excellent survey of Ingalls (1998).

[43] Edmunds (1990) 60–97. She concludes that it describes "some kind of failure of mental perception," which Ingalls (1998) 32–4 refines as "those who are unintelligent or unknowing; those who put their trust in the wrong things or are deceived; and finally those who unknowingly take some action which will bring them harm." Vermeule (1979) 113 and 237 n.36 observes that *nêpioi* have limited perception that will bring death, although one does not always remain a *nêpios*.

in the nominative or third person. The word, then, can mark the unusual intrusion of the poet in passing judgment on his actors with emotional coloring.[44] Telemachus, as we will see, must leave behind his status as *nêpios*. He can no longer remain "childish," a young man who has put little thought into his words or actions, whose speech carries little weight and who may easily be doomed. The issue is not one simply of silence versus speech but, as in the case of women in the Homeric world, one of making words become deeds, of not merely substituting language for action.[45]

Pepnumenos is more difficult to pin down. Hainsworth (ad *Od.* 8.388 and *Il.* 9.57–8) suggests that it "denotes one who observes the courtesies of life, especially in speech . . . It is seldom used of the great heroes (cf. 4.190 of Menelaus), but is a regular description of youthful or subordinate characters . . . who know their place." This is a good but slightly misleading definition that can be refined. *Pepnumenos* and the other perfect forms related to it refer to a wisdom that comes through experience and age, and is very closely connected with speech.[46] Characters associated with this word include the Trojan elders, heralds, Diomedes, Meriones, Hermes, Nestor, Menelaus, Odysseus, Tiresias, and Laertes.[47] Though often merely formulaic, as Hainsworth also notes, it is frequently used to describe someone

---

[44] Griffin (1986) 40; cf. de Jong (1987b) 86–7, who reveals the various levels of narrative one must work through to grasp the various connotations of the word; Janko (1992) ad *Il.* 16.46–8.

[45] Older warriors, the repository of wisdom and advice because of their former deeds, are very aware of the dangers of separating the two activities. They must therefore constantly remind their younger compatriots of their previous exploits (e.g. Nestor's many tales; see especially the connection between the battles of his youth and the cogency of his advice at *Il.* 4.310–25). MacCary (1982) 212, putting it slightly differently, observes that "so many insults begin with the epithet *nêpie*, which seems to suggest that . . . the object of derision cannot distinguish between word and deed."

[46] On the doubtful etymology of the word, see Hainsworth (1988) ad *Od.* 8.388. Kirk (1990) on *Il.* 5.697, citing Chantraine, suggests that attempts to disassociate *pepnumenos*, along with *pinutos* and *ampnunthê*, from *pneô* may be misdirected. Such forms as *ampnunthê/empnunthê* (*Il.* 14.436) and *ampnuto/empnuto* (*Il.* 22.475, *Od.* 5.458, 24.349) mean "he recovered his breath, became conscious again." Clarke (1999) 84–5 with n.57 sees a connection between drawing air into the lungs and this key word for "sound reflective thinking." This "thinking as a result of inhaling" derives from his theory that Homer presents breath combining with bodily fluids as a description of deepening thought. As Prof. Ruijgh has suggested to me, the verb has a physical meaning with the mental connotation of consciousness, so a metaphorical use *pepnusthai* in the sense of "having become conscious, being conscious" seems possible. This definition works well with my interpretation, since Telemachus' epithet would represent the final stage of his maturation as a fully conscious and capable adult. On the intimate connection of *pepnumenos* with speech, see Austin (1975) 74–8, who translates "prudent, sensible, intelligent"; Vivante (1982) 108; Dickson (1990) 42; and especially Dale (1982) 208, who concludes that *pepnumenos* manifestly implies proficiency in speech. She observes that of the some eighty occurrences of the word, at least seventy-three are applied to a person speaking, about to speak, or whose abilities as a speaker are being remarked upon, or to the content of the speeches themselves. She also points out that the possible etymology from a root meaning "to investigate" would be especially appropriate for Telemachus.

[47] Beck (1998–9) 125 suggests that the usage of *pepnumenos* in the *Odyssey* is more complex and less clearly generic than it is in the *Iliad*, where it generally does in fact appear "primarily in speech introductions

who has spoken or is about to speak wisely, and sometimes characterizes such a speech itself. There can be no doubt, for example, about the significance of Polydamas *pepnumenos* (*Il.* 18.249). Homer tells us that Polydamas alone looked both back into the past and forward into the future (250). This last expression implies that Hector's coeval has the adult wisdom that only comes with experience. Menelaus, to the approval of both Greeks and Trojans, concludes that "the minds of younger (*hoploterôn*) men are always lightweight, but in whatever an older man takes part he looks both back into the past and forward into the future" (*Il.* 3.108–10).[48] Polydamas is wise beyond his years. Born on the same night as Hector, he is far the best in speech, just as the son of Priam is with the spear. His advice to the Trojans to retreat to the city, although labeled as sound by the poet (18.313), is dismissed angrily by Hector, who mistakenly addresses him as *nêpie* (295) and warns him not to share such advice ever again. The Trojans shout in acclaim for Hector. *Nêpioi*, Homer calls them all, for Athena took away their wits (311). There is, then, a kind of natural antithesis between these two words that surround Telemachus. Under the best circumstances, Homer suggests, Polydamas' superior counsel would have been, in fact should have been, accepted. In this case, the usually *pepnumenos* speaker does not make his words into actions, and disaster ensues.

Pepnumenos is the mark of a man who has reached mature judgment and can speak and act accordingly. Antilochus provides the perfect example of a young man who has only recently been admitted to the ranks of the *pepnumenoi*. Good friends with Menelaus and second only after Patroclus in the heart of Achilles, Nestor's son is the youngest of the main Achaean fighters (*Il.* 15.569) and the first to kill a Trojan (4.457–62). In fact, the three features most commonly associated with Antilochus are his youth (23.306, 587–90, 756, 787–92), his swiftness afoot (15.570, 18.2, 23.756; cf. *Od.* 3.112, 4.202), and his characteristic quality of being *pepnumenos*. Still, his youthfulness can on occasion nearly overwhelm his adult qualities. When he learns of Patroclus' death, his sorrow silences (*amphasiê*) him,

for various peripheral young men." I would argue that the word carries more complexity in the *Odyssey* primarily because it is so intimately connected with Telemachus, and therefore each reference to it can easily resonate with one of the main themes of the epic. And, as I show below, we are in fact already given a preview of its richness in its association with Antimachus in the *Iliad*.

[48] Aristarchus athetized these lines, but see Kirk (1985) ad loc. Similarly, the "old hero" Halitherses "alone looked back into the past and forward into the future" (*Od.* 24.452). Here, he tries to dissuade the Ithacans from attacking Odysseus, supporting the previous argument of Medon who "knows *pepnumena*" (*Od.* 24.442). So *pepnumenos* is closely associated once again with experience, speaking well, and giving good advice. The only other utterance of the expression "past and forward into the future" comes from Achilles, as he presciently observes that Agamemnon does not understand the consequences the hero's withdrawal from battle will have for the Greeks (*Il.* 1.343–4).

and his "rich voice" is checked (17.695–6). Penelope too is struck with
amphasiê as these same two verses are used to describe her reaction to news
of Telemachus' departure (*Od.* 4.704–5). Eurycleia also has her "rich voice"
checked upon her recognition of Odysseus, although she recovers enough
to speak (at which point, Odysseus checks her rich voice by threatening to
throttle her, *Od.* 19.471–81).[49] That is to say, Antilochus comes dangerously
close to reacting like a woman at this point, a comparison that would hardly
place the young man in the ranks of doers of deeds and speakers of words.
Still, unlike Penelope, who collapses into premature mourning, Antilochus
manages to fulfill Menelaus' orders.[50]

Antilochus' actions in Book 23 further reveal his tenuous grasp on the
claim to full manhood. His underhanded maneuvering during the chariot race evokes a cry of betrayal from his friend Menelaus: "Falsely did
we Achaeans say that you were wise" (*pepnusthai*, 23.440). The king of
Sparta directs more formal charges against Antilochus after the race is over,
accusing him of cheating and addressing him as *prosthen pepnumene*, "wise
before" (23.570). Like so much else in Homeric society, being *pepnumenos*
is not an objective reality but something that is earned, granted to a hero
by his peers, and can just as easily be taken away. And it is crucial for
young warriors to earn this approval, which is why Menelaus challenges
Antilochus in this fashion.

This treatment of the adjective reveals that the poet is very much aware
of the association of *pepnumenos* with the son of Nestor. Even if the epithet appears in some places as formulaic filler without great significance,
Homer can manipulate its appearance for thematic purposes.[51] In introducing Antilochus' apology, Homer uses for only one of four times in the *Iliad*

---

[49] The minor character Eumelus, after being thrown from his chariot by Athena during the funeral
games, is the only other character to whom this formula is applied (*Il.* 23.396–7). As Edwards (1991)
notes ad 17.695, one does not expect Eumelus to speak again after this, and he does not.

[50] This last point was suggested by one of the anonymous readers. Antilochus is in many ways a
doublet of Patroclus, who also responds "like a girl" according to Achilles (*Il.* 16.7–11). Both are
killed by Trojan leaders who are then slaughtered by Achilles, and both are buried with Achilles; see
Willcock (1983). Taplin (1992) 255–6 points out that Achilles smiles for the first time in the epic at
Antilochus (23.556–7). Parry (1989) 308 has some brief comments on the epithet and Antilochus. For
Antilochus as the embodiment of *mêtis*, Odysseus' trait of cunning intelligence, see Detienne and
Vernant (1991) 11–26. Minchin (2001b) 58–9 analyzes Antilochus' performance in Book 23 in light
of the "protest-format," one of the "scripts" that Homer's narrative is founded on that are generated
by cognitive structures organizing the storage of memory.

[51] Especially relevant here is the discussion of Martin (1993); see also the work of Lowenstam (1993)
13–57 on Homer's careful sensitivity to epithets. Cosset (1983) and Tsagarakis (1982) 32–46 argue
that even the various "ornamental" adjectives used for Odysseus (e.g. *polumêtis*, *polutlas*) acquire a
specific meaning in certain contexts and are changed to suit the environment; see also Cosset (1985);
cf. de Jong (1987b) 136. Still of value is Whallon (1969) 1–70, who does not believe epithets of major
heroes are relevant to the context very often, but that they are true to some essential feature of the

a formula otherwise closely associated (forty-three times) with Telemachus in the *Odyssey*: *pepnumenos antion êuda*, "wise Antilocus spoke in return" (23.586). And Antilochus does reveal himself to be wise in speech, as he makes a full apology to Menelaus, blaming his youth (587–95) and offering full restitution and punitive damages. Menelaus subsequently affirms Antilochus' reenrollment into the ranks of the worthy adults, as the king of Sparta forgives the son of Nestor since "before this you were neither foolish or thoughtless, but just now your youth overcame your wits" (23.602–4). Antilochus had proven himself to be familiar with adult protocols before – this minor slippage can be forgiven. His reception of a gift from Menelaus reestablishes him as a junior member in the "club" of Achaean leaders.[52] As if to make it official, Antilochus produces one final speech that demonstrates his right to the title *pepnumenos*. When he takes the last prize in the foot race, he observes how the gods have shown honor to the older generation, for it would be hard for anyone to contend with Odysseus – except for Achilles, of course (23.787–92). This cleverly ingratiating speech – he praises his elders while flattering the young Achilles – earns him an extra half-talent of gold from the appreciative master of ceremonies.

The youthful Antilochus, then, walks close to the boundaries of the adult world. At some crucial moment, a young man leaves behind childish activities and inefficacious prattle (*nêpios*) and enters the public world of heroic action linked to authoritative speech (*pepnumenos*). His goal is to remain in that effective world, but foolish decisions and improvident actions can reduce him to a passive state akin to childhood, womanhood, and senescence – the world of the beast. This fluidity is one of the challenges that make the heroic culture so tricky to maneuver in, that make the constant threat to status both inevitable and dangerous. *Pepnumenos* signifies more than "potential" or "promise," more than the characterization of the "yet-too-young and preheroic,"[53] or the word could not be applied to Tiresias, Odysseus, and Menelaus, among many other well-respected adults. It is a goal to be obtained, a status to be recognized by others, and a label to be retained. That is why it is so frequently associated with young men, the members of a heroic society who are most eager for the initial recognition that they are indeed "men."

character. An excellent summary of current scholarly debate on the "meaning" of formulaic epithets is Edwards (1997) 272–7.
[52] Menelaus' gift also protects him from a possible accusation of greed, as an anonymous reader pointed out to me.
[53] So Austin (1975) 77 and Lateiner (1995) 147.

Most representative of this pursuit is Telemachus, who is not ready for the adult world at the beginning of the *Odyssey* but whose speech is nevertheless introduced by the formula *pepnumenos antion êuda* – "wise Telemachus replied in turn" – forty-three times in the epic, beginning with his very first speech (and the epithet is applied to him three other times as well). How is this possible? Is the epithet merely formulaic, with no real connection to the text? If not, then why this seemingly inappropriate label? Does Homer use an epithet all along that is properly only associated with the mature Telemachus? To what end? Recent studies in the use of noun–epithets have focused our attention on such speech introductions, when the character is represented as doing what the poet himself does, utter authoritative speech:

In other words, if an epithet is a miniature-scale myth, a theme summoned to the narrative present of the performance, then, like any myth, it needs a proper (one could say, "ritual") environment for its re-enactment. One such environment, most frequent and best known, is constituted by the introductions of direct speech.[54]

Why, then, is a stumblingly *pepnumenos* Telemachus presented so frequently in the epic? Hanna Roisman has argued that the epithet refers to "straightforwardness" and "sincerity" in speech. In her view, being *pepnumenos* is the opposite of telling lies, and so Telemachus must outgrow his epithet and learn to be *kerdaleos*, a person typified by his father who possesses "resourcefulness exemplified by an immediate response to a situation at hand with one's own interest uppermost in mind."[55] This is an intriguing suggestion: Telemachus does in fact become more Odyssean in his speech over the course of the epic. But the epithet remains his to the very end, even after he becomes thoroughly "resourceful," and it will be argued here that *pepnumenos* is tied not only to the manner of Telemachus' speech but also to its impact – authoritative, effective, adult, both direct and indirect, sincere and deceptive, both spoken and "silent."

TELEMACHUS EARNS HIS EPITHET

Telemachus begins the epic wisely, yet revealingly, by *avoiding* public speech (1.157). In his private conversation with Athena/Mentes, he admits that he is convinced that Odysseus is dead, and he appears to be resentfully resigned to

[54] Bakker (1995) 111.

[55] Roisman (1994) 10. In a somewhat similar vein, Adkins (1960) 37, 61–2 includes *pepnumenos* among the "quiet virtues" that are ultimately unnecessary for a man to be "good" (*agathos*) since it creates too much moderation to be of help in the selfish pursuit of the exercise of virtue (*aretê*). Whallon (1961a) 126–7 analyzes *pepnumenos* in the context of Telemachus' learning to take action and, like Olson, sees no change in the young man until Odysseus shows up.

his present lot. When Athena wonders if he is the son of Odysseus, Homer applies for the first time the familiar formula for his response (*tên d' au Têlemachos pepnumenos antion êuda*), 1.213. Telemachus in his "wisdom" cannot even say for certain that Odysseus is his father – that is only what his mother and others say. It is no coincidence that the first appearance of this epithet appears in a passage that raises the question of the young man's identity. He must come to accept his heritage, emulate his father, protect his household, speak and act as a Homeric male adult – in short, grow into his epithet by becoming a public figure, gaining self-confidence and authority in speaking as well as by supporting his father in his vengeance upon the suitors. Athena prods him on his way. He is to go to ask about his father, to learn of his fate (1.279f.): "There is no need for you to keep on with childish ways (*nêpiaas*), since you are no longer of that age" (296–7). It is in this context that Telemachus' harsh response (*pepnumenos antion êuda*, 345) to his mother must be taken. When he barks that *muthoi* will be the concern of *men* (358–9), he is taking his first rough stab at growing up. This is the easiest place to do it, setting himself above women, especially his mother. It is no surprise, then, as commentators often note (e.g. West ad 1.297), that Penelope is seized with wonder (360). But less often is it observed that Homer's next line confirms and approves Telemachus' fledgling efforts: "For she laid to her heart the wise word (*muthon pepnumenon*) of her son" (361). The young man has just begun to act in accordance with his mature character, at least in speech. He will have to learn to back up these words with the personal experience of action.[56]

The poet immediately marks Telemachus' new efforts by introducing his words to the suitors with a significant alteration of the customary formula. Rather than his familiar "response" (*antion êuda*), Telemachus does not wait to reply to others but instead opens the conversation himself: *pepnumenos êrcheto muthôn* (367). This rare formula[57] introduces a new side of Telemachus, as he calls for a public assembly, the first in twenty years, so he can speak a word to the suitors. The suitors too marvel at his speech, biting their lips. Antinous snidely (and with unwitting irony) refers to him as a "lofty orator" (*hupsagorên*, 385; cf. 2.85, 303, 17.406 with 2.200 and 20.274) seemingly taught by the gods to speak so boldly. And indeed Telemachus already displays the first signs of his father's crafty speech. He cleverly hides

---

[56] Thalmann (1984) 159–60.

[57] It is used only once elsewhere by Homer, when it is applied to Telemachus upon his return to Ithaca, as he creates his first plot to save himself and his guest from the suitors (*Od.* 15.502). A similar expression, *pepnumenos êrch' agoreuein*, introduces the "wise" Polydamas as he begins to speak in the Trojan assembly (*Il.* 18.249).

from the suitors that he was visited by Athena (1.420) and urged by her to become a second Orestes, subtly deflecting Eurymachus' interest in the identity of the stranger.

Although he has begun his journey towards earning his epithet, he has far to go. Telemachus is eager to speak at the assembly (2.36), but it is the herald who knows *pepnumena* (2.38).[58] Heralds, masters of speech, are often associated with this adjective, but the juxtaposition here seems to point to Telemachus' comparative weakness. He is still innocently direct and poignantly ineffectual in his speech as he tries in vain to prove his maturity.[59] He tells Antinous that it was bad enough that in the past when he was still a child (*nêpios*) they wasted his possessions (2.312–13). But now he is grown and has gained knowledge by *listening* to others (2.314). He alludes for our benefit to his conversation with Athena, of course, but his emphasis on listening to the *muthos* of others rather than creating it is significant. He will try to kill the suitors, he also announces, and go to Pylos without their approval. Such directness, although bold, is certainly counter-productive at that moment and carries no weight with the suitors, who continue feasting, scoffing at his attempt to join the world of adult males (2.322–4). Telemachus' travels in Books 3–4 introduce him more directly to the correct models of *pepnumenoi*, in preparation for the appearance of his father.

Athena/Mentor urges Telemachus to go straight to Nestor, for he is especially "wise" (*mala gar pepnumenos esti*, 3.20). But "wise" Telemachus of the next verse (3.21) immediately reveals how far away from deserving that epithet he is: "I am not yet experienced in wise words (*muthoisi . . . pukinoisin*). Moreover, it is embarrassing for a young man to interrogate an elder" (3.23–4). He has not yet learned the delicate negotiation between respect for elders and participation in their world that we saw Antilochus working through in the *Iliad*. In fact, after sadly recalling the death of his son (3.111), Nestor politely – and surprisingly – compares the words of Telemachus to those of Odysseus: "For to be sure your speech is fitting, nor would one say that a younger man could speak so fittingly" (3.124–5).[60] Yet Telemachus has done little to earn this praise. Nestor has just finished

---

[58] Nagler (1974) 100–2 makes the nice observation that Telemachus' position is marked here by his attendance by two dogs rather than aides. Austin (1975) 61 points out that Telemachus is never called simply *pepnumenos* in other characters' speeches, but usually referred to as a *pepnumenon teknon* or similar variants. Telemachus must become in the eyes of the other characters the person Homer has envisioned him being all along.

[59] Scodel (2001) 315 observes, though, that the sheer fact of his speaking in a public assembly changes the whole "game": none of the suitors can now simply marry Penelope and move into Odysseus' house.

[60] On the inappropriateness of these lines, see West (1988) ad 3.120–5.

praising Odysseus since he "far excelled in every trick, your father, if in fact you are his son" (3.121–3). Telemachus' speech, his first in such an environment, is notable for its lack of subtlety, and leaves enough room in Nestor's mind to doubt the truth of his claim to be of Odysseus' blood. Rather, it is Antilochus' brother, Pisistratus, who has joined the ranks of the *pepnumenoi* and can serve as a more direct model than the aged Nestor. This kind of wisdom, as we will see, seems to run in families.

The disguised Athena rejoices in "wise" Pisistratus, who has the sense to respect her seniority in a speech of greeting (3.52). And Menelaus too recognizes the maturity of Pisistratus. The king of Sparta, after Pisistratus mentions the death of Antilochus, praises the wisdom of Telemachus' companion: "My friend, truly you have said everything a *pepnumenos* man could say or do, even one who is your elder. Clearly you are from such a father, that you speak *pepnumena*" (4.204–6). Pisistratus is there to guide Telemachus to becoming like his father as well, a son "wise and valiant with the spear" (211). When Telemachus is too diffident to respond to the king and queen after his recognition (he had only replied to Nestor after Athena put courage in his heart to ask of his father, 3.75–8), it is Pisistratus who steps in (4.156–67). He explains to Menelaus that Telemachus takes it ill to show *epesbolias* (4.159) in the presence of one whose voice they both delight in as in a god's. The noun, a *hapax*, means "uninitiated speech" according to West (ad loc.), although it later can mean virulent abuse. At *Il.* 2.275 *epesbolon* is used to describe Thersites, so the reference here appears to signal the possibility of Telemachus' failure to construct an appropriate and ingratiating speech.[61]

Pisistratus, the son and brother of *pepnumenoi*, has become the model for Telemachus. Perhaps it is no coincidence that when Telemachus does not reply, his new friend usurps not merely his role but his formula. Instead of the expected answering formula for Telemachus – this will not work here because Telemachus does not say anything in response – we find one for Nestor's son (*ton d' au Nestoridês Peisistratos antion êuda*, 4.155). Standing in place of Telemachus is Pisistratus' patronymic, reminding us of his hereditary "wisdom." And replacing Telemachus' epithet is Pisistratus himself (cf. *Od.* 15.48, where Telemachus wakes Pisistratus to try to leave Sparta precipitately).

Telemachus needs further coaching to elicit the kind of authoritative speech his epithet promises but does not yet evoke (*pepnumenos* is applied

---

[61] Speaking well and gracefully (*kata kosmon*) is the key to this side of *aretê*, as Adkins has shown (1972). Telemachus is not up to the challenge at this point.

to him eight times in Books 3–4). Menelaus is also held up as a model for Telemachus. Both Nestor (3.328) and Pisistratus (4.190) in the presence of Telemachus call the king *pepnumenos*. Moreover, we are introduced to Menelaus in the *Odyssey* by his prudent hospitality and forceful rejection of behavior characteristic of a *nêpios*. When his squire Eteoneus asks if he should receive or dismiss the guests, the king responds with anger: "You were not *nêpios* before this, Eteoneus, son of Boethous, but now like a child you speak *nêpia*" (4.31–2).[62] Menelaus' character, as well as the entire episode at Sparta, is designed for Telemachus and the audience, who desire to know more about Odysseus (who waits just off-stage).[63] Telemachus learns much about speaking and doing, as well as about talking and keeping silent, from his squabbling hosts, as we saw in the previous chapter.

It seems that this exposure to *pepnumenoi* – as well as the adventure itself – does have an effect on the young Telemachus.[64] The morning after the tongue-tied son of Odysseus witnesses Menelaus in action, he is ready to make his request. Perhaps with some insight, or at least as encouragement, Menelaus addresses his guest as "the hero (*herôs*) Telemachus," the first character to use this epithet (4.312).[65] *Pepnumenos* Telemachus immediately informs his host that he has come to learn the news of his father. His tactful response to Menelaus' request that he remain at Sparta longer, while still unguileful, also earns praise from his host as the speech of one of good blood (4.611). His responses in Book 15 introduced by his familiar formula reveal a greater concern for his familial possessions (15.86–91) and a degree of optimism that his father may still be alive (15.154–9, 15.179–81; though cf. 15.265–70, which may just be cautious speech to a stranger). He, rather than Pisistratus, receives gifts as he grows out of his role of mere passenger

---

[62] A *nêpios* is unlikely to be able – and perhaps even to be willing to – negotiate the intricacies of the customs of hospitality. It is no surprise that violators of the feast are frequently called *nêpios* for their unseemly acts and inappropriate speech (e.g. the mutinous comrades of Odysseus, 1.8, 9.44, Polyphemus, 9.419, 442, and the suitors, 22.32, 370). Telemachus too must come to accept his role as corrector of the wrongs of the suitors. As a young adult, he can no longer allow his father's (and thus his) household to be abused; to continue to do so would label him a *nêpios*. Penelope still sees him in this light before his return. As she tells the phantom Iphthime, "And now my dear child left in a hollow ship, a mere child (*nêpios*), knowing nothing of the toils of battle or the councils of men" (4.817–18).

[63] Lowenstam (1993) 182–4 suggests that Menelaus is *pepnumenos* here because he, like Odysseus, has suffered and wandered. Thus, Menelaus in some ways foreshadows Odysseus. This is true, insofar as both Odysseus and Menelaus serve as models for Telemachus; see Felson (2002) 149–52 for Menelaus.

[64] Here I disagree with Olson (1995) 85; see also Scott (1917). Schmiel (1972) views the five speeches at Sparta – carefully arranged by the poet in ascending order, from the most gauche to the most clever – as an object lesson for Telemachus.

[65] De Jong (2001a) ad 4.312 suggests that Menelaus' use of the epithet may reveal that the narratees note Telemachus' progress to maturity.

and takes over as commander. This further development is marked by the second of the alterations from his traditional formula of response. After disembarking, Telemachus does not reply to his comrades but once again initiates the conversation (*pepnumenos êrcheto muthôn*, 15.502). This time, however, he does not merely arrange for a public speech as in Book 1. Now, he takes action. He will not sail directly to the city, but plans to visit his lands first. This unusual effort (see Eumaeus' words of surprise, 16.27–9) is another sign of growing maturity: a concern for his possessions, an avoidance of a possible hostile reception, and an opportunity to learn what has happened while he has been away. Though still young, comparatively weak, and intimidated by the suitors (16.68–89), he is ready for the appearance of his father, the final stage in his growth to manhood. And his dealings with Theoclymenus reveal that he can now take responsibility for another.[66]

Book 16 presents Telemachus' transition from fatherless adolescent to son of the hero he has never known. Before the recognition, he remains unsure about his mother's intentions, admitting both to Eumaeus and the stranger that he is still young (*neos*), lacking the strength to defend himself against the many suitors.[67] He demonstrates the caution that he has inherited from both sides of his family by accepting only gradually that his father really has returned, yet within 150 verses he is not only plotting with Odysseus but giving him advice as well (16.311–20). Although *pepnumenos* is used six times in the book, first in his replies to Eumaeus and the "stranger" (16.30, 68, 112, 146) and finally to his father (240, 262), it is the radical alteration to his customary name and epithet that is significant by the end of the book.[68] Telemachus is quickly tied to his father when, after Odysseus warns him to tell no one of his arrival "if you truly are my son of my blood" (16.300–4), Homer introduces Telemachus' reply with a line unique in the Homeric corpus: "Then his illustrious son spoke to him in reply" (16.308). This phrase emphatically marks Telemachus' role as son that is found with increasing regularity through the rest of the epic.

But perhaps even more interesting is the omission of Telemachus' name at this crucial moment. Telemachus' journey to manhood will not – in fact *cannot* – consist simply of a heroic declaration of his arrival, of stepping openly into the mature world to which he has been denied access. Rather,

---

[66] De Jong (2001a) ad 15.222–88. Millar and Carmichael (1954) 61–2 argue that Telemachus reveals himself to be fully *pepnumenos* by the time of his reunion with Odysseus (16.308), but at this point Telemachus still has much to prove.

[67] Minchin (2002) 18–20 points out that Telemachus' awkwardly independent manner of delivering the news to Laertes (16.130f.) of his return to Ithaca also reflects the waywardness of youth.

[68] Convincingly demonstrated by Beck (1998–9) 132–4. De Jong (2001a) 385 notes that more than in any other book of the epic, Odysseus is referred to here as "father" and Telemachus as "son."

as Odysseus himself has learned, hiding the truth of one's identity – and the truth of one's strength and knowledge – has great rewards in the post-Iliadic world. Careful silence, interior conversations, and monologues when no one is present are part of virtuous speech in the *Odyssey*, a kind of speech that Odysseus and his son are innately prepared to exploit.[69] Telemachus is to become a man not by earning his eternal fame – the glorification of his name – in individual combat, as in the ethos of the *Iliad*. Rather, he will fulfill his role by acting in disguise, like his father, masking his intentions, his abilities, his knowledge, his very maturation. His sudden urge to act must now be tempered by obeying his father's explicit instructions to endure Odysseus' humiliations (*Od.* 16.274–7).

This "filling the father's shoes" is the definition of masculine maturation in the Homeric poems – a father prays that his son will be like him, only better. Hector hopes that Astyanax will be preeminent and strong, rule Troy, be successful in battle, and "far exceed his father" (*Il.* 6.476–81; cf. Hector's own pride in fighting for his father, *Il.* 6.446, and Lycaon to Pandarus, 5.197–200). Even the dour Achilles in the underworld rejoices that his son took his place at the forefront of Achaean fighters (*Od.* 11.538–40), just as his own father had enjoined upon him similar success (*Il.* 9.438–43; cf. Hippolochus' famous advice to Glaucus, *Il.* 6.206–10, and Agamemnon's invidious contrasting of Diomedes to his father, *Il.* 4.370–400). A father's greatest hope is that his son will surpass him, even if, as the disguised Athena tells Telemachus, "few sons are like their fathers: more are worse; few are better" (*Od.* 2.276–7).[70]

To be sure, the *Odyssey* can be read as a comment upon that tradition in several ways. Telemachus must learn to be a fighter, but since his father is so much more than that, he too must grow into a much more complex role than that of Neoptolemus. For that matter, the passage with Hector and Astyanax is painfully ironic in itself – Hector wishes for his son just those characteristics that will lead him to his own death, and thus ultimately to Astyanax' brutal murder. His very gentleness with his wife and son seems to ask us to reflect upon the father's prayer. As William Thalmann has recently pointed out, Telemachus' journey is further complicated by the awkwardness that he must learn to assert his own claim to manhood

---

[69] De Jong (1994). She seems to suggest that Odysseus undergoes no development here (cf. [2001a] ad 1.113–18), but she does discuss Telemachus' maturation in terms of his becoming like his father in the control of speech. On Odysseus' silence as a model of behavior for his son, see Montiglio (2000) 257–75.

[70] See Redfield (1975) 111; Felson (2002) 36–7, and the end of the next chapter. Bloodlines seem to be important primarily on the male side, but Penelope's mastery of unspoken words makes it all the more likely that their son will develop in that direction; de Jong (1994) 39–44.

while at the same time cooperating with and being subordinate to his father.[71] But unlike Thalmann, who sees this dilemma as a reflection upon an "irreconcilable ambiguity" in the culture – part of the poet's effort to impose an aristocratic ideology that raises alternatives to the cultural norms only to reject them – I believe the entire construction of Telemachus' journey is a positive revision of the heroic "ideal." Sons do in fact usually grow up in the shadow of a father (or paternal substitute), whether this presence be benign or perverse, omnipresent, remote, or invisible. War deprives fathers of the opportunity to play their "normal" role. Odysseus' absence, Achilles' fate and post-mortem atavism, and Hector's impending death and selective vision all comment upon this disruption. The *Odyssey* presents us with a necessarily syncopated version of how things "should" be. Telemachus' "subordination" is not primarily political but rather a reflection of the usual tension between the needs both to be independent of the father and yet to be like and guided by him. The father–son relationship is central to the definitions of both characters: Odysseus alone of Homeric heroes refers to himself as the father of a son (*Il.* 2.260, 4.354), rather than the son of a father. Despite whatever irregularities or difficulties may be presented by their sharing space and authority, the three generations of males are clearly and happily reunited by the end of the epic.[72]

At the end of Book 16, after father and son have laid out their plans, Eumaeus returns to the hut. Athena has retransformed Odysseus, fearing that the swineherd may recognize him and race off to tell Penelope (16.457–9). In other words, even the goddess realizes the difficulty of maintaining the silence she has requested of Odysseus and Telemachus.[73] Telemachus addresses Eumaeus, his speech introduced again with a line (unique in the poems) that emphasizes his growing confidence in the presence of his father (460). The son speaks first (*proteros*), and wants to learn of the suitors (461–3). He takes charge, discarding his "replying" for the moment, trying to elicit information that will aid the plot while simultaneously directing attention away from the stranger. He had sent the swineherd off solely to

---

[71] Thalmann (1998b) 206–22.

[72] I don't see the "brotherly" nature of the relationship between Telemachus and Odysseus suggested by Murnaghan (2002) 149–52.

[73] Athena has no reason to doubt Eumaeus' loyalty. I think we may also be able to see here the separation of Telemachus from Eumaeus. Eumaeus has clearly functioned as something of a substitute father. This relationship is signaled by the use of the affectionate *atta*, applied five times in the *Odyssey*, always by Telemachus to the swineherd, three times in the first 130 verses of Book 16 (Achilles uses it in his reply to Phoenix at *Il.* 9.607; cf. 17.561 to Athena, disguised as Phoenix). When Telemachus' real father arrives, Eumaeus becomes less essential. He is a loyal slave of noble heritage but not the father Telemachus needs to grow up. Yamagata (1998) provides a quick overview of various father-figures for Telemachus, including Eumaeus (278–9).

inform his mother that he had returned in safety – no mention was made of the suitors (130–4, 147–53). Now he makes no inquiry at all about this task or his mother's condition, but wonders what the news is from the city. Eumaeus seems slightly annoyed at these questions, since his mission had not been to "run about" (*katablôskonta*, its only appearance in Homer) the city asking and inquiring (465–6). Eumaeus may have seen the suitors arrive, but he is not certain. Amazingly, at the announcement of this news – welcome indeed to the eager son and patient father – Telemachus, who so often replies in the epic, does not say a word: "So he [Eumaeus] spoke, and Telemachus in his royal strength smiled as he caught the eyes of his father; but he avoided the swineherd" (476–7). Beck observes that this "unexpected use of answering language emphasizes Telemachus' self-control in keeping silent, an unusual ability that Odysseus also has."[74] Telemachus proves that he is growing worthy of his epithet by acting in a fashion (that is, by *not* answering) that directs the poet to leave it aside. By not replying at all, he is developing into the "wise" speaker he must become to mature fully. The correct action here is not to say anything, to remain silent (as his father is doing now), to protect his father's disguise, hide his own superior knowledge, and share his first conspiratorial moment with his father as they wait to destroy the newly arrived suitors.[75]

There is now something more formidable about Telemachus' speech, and it does not go unnoticed. Penelope breaks into tears and between sobs asks what he has learned about his father. "Wise" Telemachus does not answer her question, but tells her to bathe, dress, return to her upper chamber and vow perfect hecatombs to the gods should Zeus bring about vengeance. Penelope is more than amazed this time, for she is stunned into absolute silence as "her word remained unwinged" (*apteros*, 17.57). Homer signifies the growth in Telemachus' authority through Penelope's responses. When her son first shocked her with his curt dismissal in Book 1, she apparently ignored his commands to "busy herself with the loom and distaff" and instead simply wept for Odysseus and fell asleep (1.360–4). Now she reacts to Telemachus' much more specific orders to bathe, dress, and vow to the gods by doing exactly these things (17.58–60). All four uses of *apteros . . . muthos* involve Telemachus after his return to Ithaca (19.29,

---

[74] (1998–9) 133. She focuses on the new epithet phrase for Telemachus – his "own honorific epithet" – which I do not find as significant as the absence itself of the more usual answering phrase. Indeed, there is no answering phrase at all.

[75] They will communicate through gazes and gestures from now on: 20.385–6, 21.129, 431. On the function of Book 16 as a set-up for Odysseus' ironically "divine" manifestation to the suitors, see Kearns (1982).

21.386, 22.398; cf. his silencing of Eumaeus, 17.393–5). Even the suitors immediately notice a difference (17.61–6). Silencing others and being able to keep silent when necessary, as well as speaking when it is most effective, are essential characteristics shared by the father and his rapidly maturing son.[76] And Telemachus continues to develop his self-restraint. Although tempted to cry out when Antinous nails Odysseus with a footstool, he instead merely shakes his head "in silence" (*akeôn*) and plans "evils" (*Od.* 17.489–91). Soon he will be using language to further his father's goals.

Most significant is the juxtaposition of *nêpios* and *pepnumenos* over the final six books of the epic. Here, Telemachus sheds the remnants of his childhood and becomes an adult member of the community and full male descendent of the house of Laertes. First, he demonstrates his burgeoning confidence by manipulating his own epithet. As Odysseus is about to fight Irus, the disguised hero asks the suitors to swear an oath not to interfere. After they give their word, Telemachus addresses his father, assuring him that the suitors, Antinous and Eurymachus, are both *pepnumenô* (18.65). They are, of course, neither "wise" nor men of prudent speech, and the father and son must have enjoyed the irony.[77] It is worth noting that Odysseus tries at some length to warn the least offensive suitor, Amphinomus, to leave the palace before the imminent arrival of "Odysseus": "Amphinomus, indeed you seem to me to be *pepnumenos*" (18.125–50). But the poet adds that Athena did not allow him to escape his fate, "binding" him to be slaughtered by the "hands and spear of Telemachus" (18.155–7). Telemachus, in effect, will lay proper claim to the epithet that Amphinomus does not earn.

Particularly interesting in this light is the conversation between Penelope and her son after the fight. She chastises Telemachus for allowing such sport, accusing him of acting inappropriately and immaturely: "Telemachus, no longer are your mind and thoughts unimpaired. Even as a child (*pais*) you devised better counsel; but now, when you are grown and have come to the prime of your youth . . . no longer are your mind and thoughts fitting" (18.215–17, 220). She suspects that her son, old enough in years to act like an adult, may still be the boy (*pais . . . nêpios*) he was before he left Ithaca,

---

[76] Some scholars believe that *apteros* is the equivalent of *pteroenta*, "winged," and does not mean "without wings"; for a discussion, see Fraenkel (1950) ad. *Ag.* 276; Russo (1992) ad *Od.* 17.57; R. D. Griffith (1995) 1–5 with bibliography. If this is a correct interpretation of the phrase, then the "winged words" belong to Telemachus, not the women. This reading would be almost as emphatic, since Telemachus' speech earns a unique adjective for its powerful flight. Most commentators take it to mean unexpressed words, following Latacz (1968); see, most recently, Montiglio (2000) 272–3.

[77] Edwards (1966) 165 notes that the epithet is never attributed to any of the suitors – except here – even though many have names metrically similar to that of Telemachus.

skilled in neither adult works nor words (4.817–18). In his mother's eyes, Telemachus' behavior suggests that he has not earned the right to be called *pepnumenos*. "Wise" Telamachus replies: "I don't resent you for being angry. But now I myself am aware and know each of these things, the good and the base. Before this I was still *nêpios*. But I am not able to discern all *pepnumena*, for these men confuse me, sitting on all sides plotting evil, and I have no helpers" (18.227–32). This is a wonderfully mature response. He acknowledges that Penelope is right – the rules of hospitality have been broken. And he wants her to know that now, unlike before, he is very much aware of what is going on. But his abandonment of childhood and engagement with adulthood mean that he can speak to a purpose, and (son of Odysseus that he is) this means that he can lie. True, he cannot think of all wise things, but allowing his father to fight Irus was the wise thing to do as they wait for the opportunity for revenge. And his insistence that there are no helpers for his cause is of course quite untrue – Odysseus is very much present. By denying his epithet, he takes one more step towards earning it. Ironically, his very control of language has brought him closer than ever to the actual maturity he here claims to be lacking.[78]

Telemachus is also speaking ever more forcefully. When the suitors once again hurl a footstool at his father, Telemachus this time thinks not of tears but speaks out. He tells the suitors that they are mad, bloated, and drunk, and then politely asks them to leave (18.406–9). The suitors bite their lips in amazement at his bold speech. But instead of the harsh and sarcastic response that followed the last time Telemachus evoked such lip-biting at the beginning of the epic (1.381–7; 1.381–2 = 18.410–11), one of the suitors now seconds Telemachus' words and suggests that they depart, leaving the stranger in the house. Telemachus' speech is now closer to becoming action.

Books 18 and 19 describe the pivotal points in Telemachus' transformation. In Book 19, at his father's bidding, Telemachus tells Eurycleia to shut the women in their rooms while he puts away Odysseus' tarnishing weapons. "I was still *nêpios*," he explains, but now he cares what happens to his heirlooms (19.19–20). Eurycleia approves of his new concern for the household, and is struck speechless (her word is unwinged) by "wise" Telemachus' response. He is now in control of his speech, using

---

[78] Line 18.229 with *nêpios* was rejected by Aristophanes and Aristarchus. Roisman (1994) sees Telemachus' maturation into a clever speaker occurring later, in Book 20. Similarly, Hoffer (1995) argues that Telemachus competes successfully in Book 21 for the role of master of ceremonies by "pretending" it is obvious that he should be in charge. I am in agreement with these scholars and others who find a different – and successful – Telemachus, although I find a more gradual change; *contra* is Martin (1993), who sees Telemachus as failing to fill his role as *polumêtis* and thus representing the end of the tradition.

language effectively to accomplish what he once thought impossible – taking vengeance upon the suitors under the tutelage of his father. And in case we have forgotten that the son is becoming the father, Homer soon after has Penelope refer to Odysseus, still in disguise, as a *pepnumenos* man, so very wisely does he speak all *pepnumena* (19.350–2). This is an unusual epithet for Odysseus, appearing only once elsewhere at 8.388, when Alcinous says the stranger in front of him seems to be *pepnumenos*. The poet himself never uses it of his major character, and its double application within three lines is striking. Odysseus is a *pepnumenos* man, both here and in general – his words are wise and do result in action (Penelope immediately carries out his suggestion, for example). His major characteristic is found in the famous manner (*polutropos, polumêtis*) by which he accomplishes his goals, however. He and his son accomplish their goals differently, and so do not share the same major epithets. In a delightful reversal, the wife recognizes in her (disguised) husband the distinctive and inchoate qualities of her son.

By now, it has not escaped Penelope that Telemachus is no longer *nêpios* and irresponsible, but has come to the limits of his youth (19.530–2).[79] Telemachus seconds these words when rebuking Ctesippus for flinging an ox hoof at Odysseus: "Therefore let no one behave unseemingly in my house. For now I am aware of and know each of these things, the good and the base. Before this I was still *nêpios*" (20.308–10). These words momentarily silence the suitors. Telemachus is speaking with more authority than ever, proving he is no longer a child, laying claim as it were to his epithet *pepnumenos*, which Homer immediately restores to him as he lies about the fate of his father (20.338f.). A suitor "at last" speaks out, once again surprisingly siding with Telemachus and asking that no more violence be directed against the stranger.

De Jong sees Telemachus' outburst here as the one slip in his acceptance of Odysseus' injunction to endure his plight.[80] True, he does not follow his father's words to the letter, but the son is also trying to establish his own position as an adult by protecting his rights as man of the house. Two competing currents pull on Telemachus as he struggles towards his father. One requires him to grow up to help Odysseus, but the other demands some degree of separate identity from this same parent. Just before this passage, Telemachus assures the beggar, in words directed at the suitors,

---

[79] Murnaghan (1992) 263 concludes that when Penelope announces the contest among the suitors she (wrongly) imagines that the bow will bring her a new husband, allowing her to leave the house so the newly mature Telemachus can take over his rightful place.
[80] (1994) 38–9.

that he will ward off the insolent intruders' insults and blows because it is his father's house – his as a matter of inheritance. He then warns the suitors to stop their insolence (20.262–7). Clearly, this admonition too would be a violation of his father's orders, but we are meant to see Telemachus' growth into his role. Homer marks this moment by having the suitors "bite their lips" for the third and final time in the epic, marveling at his "bold" words (20.268–9 = 1.381–2 = 18.268–9). This time, Antinous himself, the most unrepentant suitor, replies that they should accept his word, "though it is difficult" and embodies a threat. In fact, Antinous fulminates in return, announcing that if Zeus had allowed it (a clear reference to their attempt to waylay the ship of Telemachus), they would have "stopped him before now in the halls, sharp-voiced speaker though he is" (20.271–4). Telemachus can now control his speech, talking when he deems it necessary and keeping silent when it will benefit his father's cause – and his own. When the suitors try to abuse and provoke him by insulting the beggar (20.351–83), he ignores their words completely. Instead, he can watch his father "in silence," constantly waiting for the right moment when he can put his hands on the intruders (20.384–6).

Telemachus continues to demonstrate his growing maturity. To the amazement of all, he sets up the axes properly, although "he had never seen them before" (21.120–3). He then proves to himself – and to his father – that he is worthy of the family name by showing that he is capable of stringing Odysseus' bow (21.128). The four attempts summarize nicely the great effort he has exerted over the past twenty books to reach manhood. But even more significant is his quick adjustment to his father's nod of disapproval. Although he desperately wants to shoot the arrow through the axes (21.126–9), he adopts Odysseus' unstated plan and sets the bow aside without hesitation.[81] To the gathered suitors, before whom he had been so eager to prove himself, he now dissembles beautifully, adopting the pose of his former adolescence:

Oh my, in truth even after this I will be cowardly and feeble, or I am too young (*neôteros*) and do not yet trust my hands to defend me against a man, when someone grows angry first. But come on, you who are superior to me in strength, test out the bow, and let us finish the contest. (21.131–5)

Telemachus can now lie as he needs to, pretending to be the same ineffectual boy we met in Book 1. He can use his youth to his own advantage, leading the suitors to their destruction. How far he has come from his whining in

---

[81] The suggestion by Felson (1999) 97–8 that this episode refers to "traces of an unrealized plot" is not helped by the conjuring of Freudian issues.

the assembly in Book 2 about his genuine powerlessness and inexperience: "For no man is found here, such as Odysseus was, to ward off destruction from the house" (2.58–9). Now there are two men "such as Odysseus was" in the house.[82]

Telemachus has reached a comfortable independence from his mother and a mature understanding with his father. When Penelope in two separate speeches tries to intervene in the stringing of the bow, attempting to arrange for the "stranger" to give it a try (21.312–19, 331–42), "wise" Telemachus will have none of it. He tells her that no man of the Achaeans has a better right than he to give or deny it to whomever he wishes, and none shall stop him. And as for her, she is to go to her familiar room, loom, distaff, and handmaids, for "the bow will be the concern for men, all but especially for me" (21.344–53). And Penelope is once again amazed, laying to heart the *muthon pepnumenon* of her son and doing what she is told.

His maturity is further signaled when he kills the handmaids. Odysseus had ordered them all to be struck down with swords, but Telemachus comes up with a more creative plan, instead hanging them by a ship's cable. Some readers have been appalled at the speech and actions of "mild" Telemachus, seeing in them a sign of his immaturity or cruelty.[83] But Telemachus' motives are perfectly in line with the thoughts of the other characters. He states that the maids deserve no "clean death" because they poured reproaches on him and his mother and they slept with the suitors (22.462–4; cf. the loaded moral vocabulary he uses to describe the suitors to Nestor, 3.205–9). Eurycleia cites the same crimes: the maids did not respect her or Penelope (22.425), and they walked in "shamelessness" (22.424). More importantly, Odysseus gives identical reasons for their punishment: they dishonored him (22.418) and misbehaved sexually (22.444–5). When he had first witnessed the traitorous maids' behavior, he had struggled to restrain

---

[82] Segal (1994) 55–6 sees the bow episode as vindicating Telemachus' right of succession, proving his identity as Odysseus' son. Thalmann (1998b) 206–33, in accordance with his thesis that Telemachus' maturation into his father's son actually reflects the rejection of certain possibilities (e.g. the independence of the son) in the family dynamics in an honor-based society, sees in Telemachus' obedience in not stringing the bow a "relapse" into childishness. His pretence of impotence in fact cloaks a reality. There is nothing in the text, however, to suggest that there is any regression here at all.

[83] E.g. Heubeck (1992) ad 22.462. I can find no hint in the text of a "moment of regression" in Telemachus' journey, or that his "brutal" treatment "cleanses" his image of "mother wife" that suits a "world without women mentality or phase," as is suggested by Felson-Rubin (1994) 72, 86–7. Thalmann (1998b) 72 argues that Telemachus puts women to such a painful death because their sexuality has threatened Odysseus' social prestige: "No wonder Odysseus is outraged." But it is Telemachus who comes up with the means of punishment. As Halverson (1985) 142 observes, the crime of the slaves is disloyalty not just to Odysseus *per se*, but to his entire household. De Jong (2001) ad 22.444–73 charts the similarities and differences between Odysseus' orders and how they are executed.

his impulse to rush out and slaughter them on the spot (20.5–21). There are no signs from Homer that Telemachus' speech is inappropriate.

As for the manner of the maids' deaths, the poet himself treats the maids with particular contempt by comparing them in graphic fashion to animals (22.468–73). The twelve hanging servants are compared to thrushes or doves that fall into a snare as they hurry towards their resting place (*aulin*). Instead, a hateful bed (*koitos*) welcomes them. The word for bed here is used at ten other places in Homer, always of a comfortable place for human sleep, occasionally for sleep itself. This ironic transference of *koitos* to the animal world serves to tighten the analogy between the doves and the women, since the latter have abused their place of sleep, as Telemachus noted just a few lines before (464). Similarly, *aulis* has appropriate meanings in both the human world (a place to set down tents, *Il.* 9.232, its only other appearance in Homer) and the animal kingdom (a place for cows to sleep, *Hymn Hom. Merc.* 71; *Hymn Hom. Ven.* 168). The verb used to describe the maids' final kicks (*êspairon*) applies to the death throes of animals (fish, fawns, lambs, bulls, snakes) more often than to human activity.[84] Whatever we may think of Telemachus' actions, Homer does nothing to make us feel that the maids did not deserve their fate or that he wants us to disapprove of the way they die – or even the much more gruesome dispatching of Melanthius that follows.[85]

Telemachus' innovative slaughter of the maids, and thus his new independence even from his father, is marked by another unique substitution for his familiar introductory formula as he begins to speak about their fate. For

---

[84] See Sideras (1971) 79. De Jong (2001a) ad 22.468–72 links their deaths to the all-pervasive bird imagery that accompanies Odysseus' return and revenge. Fulkerson (2002) 341–3 makes the interesting suggestion that since hanging is the traditional method of female suicide, Telamachus' actions reveal the cultural expectation that the women *should* have hung themselves from shame.

[85] Collins (1998) 114–20 maintains that the death of Melanthius reveals no overt criticism of Telemachus but forces us to question the *alkê* Telemachus has learned in the *Odyssey*, especially since the execution is unlike the death of any warrior in the *Iliad*. But that difference is surely one of the points. Melanthius is not a warrior but a traitorous slave. Odysseus nearly strangles the loyal Eurycleia. Slaves did not have rights, and traitors were not subject to regular forms of punishment; cf. Menelaus' words about Aegisthus at *Od.* 3.258–61, and Segal (1994) 14–15. Davies (1994) 534–6 contends that this is not an execution but a punishment (that may, of course, result in death), and also objects to the "despicable" act. But the real contrast is with Antinous' unfulfilled threat against Irus should the beggar lose his "duel" with the disguised Odysseus (18.79–87). Irus has done nothing to Antinous to deserve such a fate. For a survey of interpretations of this scene, see Newton (1997). He thinks Odysseus must have ordered the deed, and sees the treatment of the goatherd as a sign of Odysseus' growth, with Melanthius representing the hero's earlier foolish and reckless self. Odysseus is also distanced from the deed – we never do really learn who ordered the act – which shows Odysseus' alignment with the theodicy of Zeus. The same could apply to Telemachus. In fact, the act is presented as part of Telemachus' *aristeia*, not Odysseus'. The son has just demonstrated his independence from his father, and the text suggests that Telemachus is the one giving the orders (546–4). He and the two loyal male servants perform the deed.

the first and only time in the epic, Telemachus is described formulaically as beginning what looks like a public speech: "And wise Telemachus began to address (*êrch' agoreuein*) them" (22.461). Heubeck (ad loc.) observes that the line is more appropriate to meetings and assemblies or social gatherings than to the present situation: all seven other appearances of *êrch' agoreuein* introduce speakers amidst a gathering of fellow speakers. Its introduction here, in this slightly awkward setting, marks Telemachus' new public and social role. In effect, Telemachus is granted his own mini-assembly, at which he is sole speaker and authority – he states his decisions and others obey. He has become a prince, but not a king. The very moment he comes to full maturity is also the moment his father regains his position as political leader and senior male in the household. To mark this transition, Homer introduces Telemachus with a very uncharacteristic formula. Telemachus' journey is not towards complete independence, but to his full position within the family and community. He is at last his father's son, loyal but capable of independent decisions, speech, and action in support of Odysseus.

The last three appearances of the traditional formula bring this journey to a close. At 23.123, "wise" Telemachus acknowledges and accepts his place by telling his father that he will follow him anywhere, under any circumstances. Meanwhile, as if to remind us of Telemachus' genetic predisposition to his new-found authority, Penelope's very first words to Odysseus after the test of the marriage bed define him as *pepnumenos*. She asks him not to be angry, since in all other things he has "always been most wise of men (*malista | anthrôpôn pepnuso*, 23.209–10). And it seems to run in the family, for Laertes becomes the only other character in the *Odyssey* to warrant the familiar epithet formula when he responds to Odysseus in the final book: *ton d' au Laertês pepnumenos antion êuda* (24.375).

Finally, the entire male lineage is connected by the epic's last reference to "wise" Telemachus. Odysseus, pleased at Athena/Mentor's presence when the angry families of the suitors approach, tells his son that it is time to bring no disgrace to the house of his fathers (24.506–9). Then Telemachus *pepnumenos* replies that his dear father will not see him bringing any dishonor to the family name (24.510–12). Laertes proudly chimes in: "What a day this is for me, dear gods! I rejoice completely. My son and my son's son are contending with each other for *aretê*" (24.514–15). Laertes, truly of the old school, sees in his son and grandson noble warriors vying to be preeminent. Like Hector and Achilles, he believes the mark of adulthood to be success in battle.

And as if to mark the end of this heroic vision, Athena gives the enfeebled Laertes one last moment of old-fashioned Iliadic glory: he brings down

Eupeithes with one spear-toss from his rejuvenated hand. As his son and grandson – the latter now poignantly labeled merely the "illustrious son" (526) – leap into the fray, however, the world suddenly changes. Athena shouts, telling the enraged Ithacans to cease from "painful war." They do, terrified, and turn back to the city. But Odysseus, Trojan War veteran, is caught up in moment:

Much-enduring, godlike Odysseus shouted terribly, crouched and then swooped down like a high-flying eagle. (24.537–8)

These verses, although reflecting common Homeric imagery, are in fact distinctive and evocative. Odysseus shouts aloud "terribly," a seemingly familiar picture from the *Iliad*, although the phrase is used only twice elsewhere in the Homeric poems (*Il.* 8.92; *Od.* 8.305), and never simply as a war cry without subsequent words. Verse 538, "a powerful one" (Richardson ad *Il.* 24.308–11), brings home the epic connotations of the moment. Eagle similes are not uncommon in the epics, of course, but this is the only one in the *Odyssey* – the other four appear in battle scenes of the *Iliad* (15.690, 17.674, 21.252–3, 22.308).[86] Most significantly, the entire verse appears at only one other spot in the entire Homeric corpus, *Iliad* 22.308, to describe Hector's final lunge at Achilles. These two passages contain the only uses of the expanded adjective *hupsipetêeis* for the more common *hupsipetês*.[87] Odysseus' willful charge into battle against the families of the suitors is potentially linked to Hector's fateful decision to meet his doom head on. The *Odyssey* is no tragedy, however, and war in this poem must give way to peace. As Athena was there to guide Achilles to triumph in battle, so is she here to assure Odysseus' restoration to home and community. Zeus, who began the epic with a discussion of divine justice, finishes it off with a flaming thunderbolt. Athena tells "much-enduring" Odysseus – his distinctive epithet used here for the last of forty-two times in the epics – that

---

[86] Moulton (1977) 135–9 places the simile in the wider context of bird imagery in the epic as related to the hero's homecoming. He observes that this is the only eagle comparison in the *Odyssey*, and suggests that two of the similes in the *Iliad* are not connected with "offensive valor in battle." This is strictly true, but both are in martial contexts. Menelaus' glance is compared to that of an eagle as the warrior urges on his fellow Greeks in mid-battle to fight for the body of Patroclus (17.674). Achilles' leap is compared to the swoop of an eagle as the war-crazed hero races away from the onslaught of the river (21.252–3). Although in retreat, Achilles is in the midst of his most lethal attack in the epic. For birds and bird omens in the *Odyssey*, see: Fitzgerald (1963) 479–83; Podlecki (1967); Anhalt (2001–2). For eagle omens in the *Iliad*, see Bushnell (1982) and Anhalt (1995).

[87] A "high-flying" eagle appears in an omen at *Od.* 20.240–6 (cf. *Il.* 12.200–7, 13.822) and without the adjective at *Od.* 2.146–54, 15.160, 19.536–50 (cf. *Il.* 24.314). Almost equally rare are *oimêsen* (only at *Il.* 22.140, as Achilles rushes upon Hector) and *aleis* (only at *Il.* 16.403 and 21.571, both in battle scenes). The vocabulary and setting of this verse are distinctly Iliadic.

he, too, must leave off war. And he does, joyfully (24.545). The Trojan War is over at last.[88]

Telemachus' maturation, then, can be seen as his acceptance of his heritage, and this development is revealed at least partially through his becoming the *pepnumenos* son of Odysseus that his epithet has promised he would be. He outgrows his childish silence and ineffectual whining and becomes a "wise" speaker who can put his words into action. But this wisdom in speech in the *Odyssey* involves not just knowing when and how to speak, but also when not to. Telemachus cannot reveal the truth of his father's arrival – he must hide it even from his mother, allowing Odysseus to suffer physical and verbal abuse from the hated suitors all the while. This is another of Odysseus' lessons as well – he must set aside some of the heroic presumptions of the *Iliad* and become a master of a more subtle *post-bellum* dynamic. His instinct for heroic self-identification is challenged during his wanderings, especially by Polyphemus. His refusal to leave the cave and later to remain a non-heroic "Nobody" results in the death of six of his crew members, nearly destroys the entire ship, and ultimately is responsible for his extended wanderings. His actions on Ithaca require a different ethos, one for which he is uniquely suited, and that requires patience and cautious speech in the pursuit of long-term results. As Athena tells him: "But have heart, for you must, and tell no one – no man or woman, no one at all – that you have come back from your wandering, but in silence, submitting to the violence of men, endure many griefs" (13.307–10). It is Athena's plan, and he must learn to accept being "unknown to all mortals" (13.397). The world of the *Odyssey* requires successful navigation of both speaking and silence. As the episodes of the Trojan horse and Polyphemus suggest, and most of the last half of the epic reveals, successfully controlling speech often means controlling oneself, one's desires, appetites, as well as speech.[89] Odysseus must learn when to lie and when to tell the truth, a lesson he only fully understands after he tells one final, unnecessary falsehood that nearly breaks his father's heart.[90] In the *Iliad*, however, the goal is more often directly competitive – to silence not just your enemies, but

---

[88] Burnett (1998) 42 suggests that retaliation gives way to a new civic order, much as in the *Oresteia*. For recent readings of Odysseus' negotiation of his heroic/Iliadic nature – which often leads to failure – and his suppression of his heroic identity, see Finkelberg (1995) and Cook (1999).

[89] On Odysseus' self-restraint, especially as connected with diet, see Cook (1995) 56–65; for his control of speech and its significance for other characters, see Montiglio (2000) 256–75.

[90] See Wender (1978) 56–7 on the cruelty of Odysseus, and Rutherford (1986) 161–2 on how the trick backfires, showing Odysseus that there is a time also for openness and trust. He seems to learn at last from his mother's tale of dying from grief for her son; though cf. Falkner (1989) esp. 42–8, and Dimock (1962) 120 on the "fruitfulness" of this pain in establishing Odysseus' identity. For a summary of interpretations of Odysseus' motivation in this awkward scene, see West (1989) 125–27

your allies as well. As in so many other ways, it is the tragic Achilles who is forced to transcend the cultural expectations about the use of language as well. But that is another tale altogether.

and Scodel (1998) esp. 9–16. Scodel argues that Odysseus tests Laertes because he needs his father as an ally and thus is trying to prepare him to fight. But if this is so, he stops at just the wrong moment – Laertes is at his weakest, fainting, groaning, and fouling himself with dust in mourning. I think rather that Odysseus *breaks down* at this point in his fabrication. He stops in mid-lie because he cannot stand to see his father suffer, as Homer's unique phrasing of Odysseus' pain at this moment makes clear (24.318–20). Heubeck (1992) ad 318–19, who defends these lines, aptly draws our attention to the similar verses in Odysseus' meeting with Penelope (19.203–12). But the differences between the two passages are more revealing. There, too, Odysseus, in disguise, tells an elaborate lie about a meeting with Odysseus, and like Laertes Penelope is struck with grief and weeps for Odysseus as if he were dead. And Odysseus feels great pain, pitying his wife, but "his eyes stood motionless in his eyelids, like horn or iron, and he hid his tears through his cunning" (19.211–12). It is Penelope here who is doing the testing (19.215) of the disguised Odysseus – openly and with good reason – whereas in Book 24 it is Odysseus who tests (24.216) his aged father. With Laertes, his deception in fact serves no real purpose – old habits die hard – but Odysseus at last kicks the addiction, at least in part. Still, as de Jong concludes (1994) 37, secrecy, dissimulation, and restraint are innate traits of Odysseus. Murnaghan (1987) 26–33 argues that Odysseus brings Laertes out of a state of weakness and grief that obscures his identity. This is true, but Odysseus' cruelty in torturing Laertes, as helpful as it may be for Odysseus' own independence from his father, is excessive by any measure. For a different interpretation of the scene but with a similar reading of the meaning of Odysseus' uncharacteristic reaction to the impact of his words, see Sultan (1999) 68–70. For bibliography on the parallels between Telemachus' journey and that of Odysseus, see Apthorp (1980) 12 n.53.

CHAPTER 3

Talking through the heroic code: Achilles learns to tell stories

Telemachus may become a speaker of words, but it is of course Achilles at whom Peleus directs his counsel to become both a "speaker of words and a doer of deeds." With the defeat of Hector, Achilles proves once again that he is a doer of deeds. But does the young hero ever become a true speaker of words, as his father had hoped? Does he mature *verbally* in some way by the end of the epic? Does he, in other words, go through some journey analogous to that of Telemachus? Does his speech reveal an "evolution of a hero"?[1]

Like Telemachus at the opening of the *Odyssey*, Achilles begins the Trojan War, according to Phoenix, as a *nêpios*: "On that day when Peleus sent you from Phthia to Agamemnon, you a *nêpios*, knowing nothing yet of leveling war, nothing of councils, where men are distinguished" (9.440–1). Achilles and Telemachus are the only characters in the epics to be described as "growing like a sapling (*ernei isos, Il.* 18.56 and 437 = *Od.* 14.175).[2] Each is a young man who has a mentor to guide him on his journey. And each begins his epic with an assembly scene in which he feels publicly humiliated and, in frustration at his ineffectuality, throws to the ground a scepter, the symbol that yokes speaking and authority (*poti de skêptron bale gaiêi, Il.* 1.245 = *Od.* 2.80, the only times the expression occurs in the epics).[3] Achilles' rhetorical

---

[1] Whitman's phrase; see his chapter by the title (1958) 181–220. Most scholars see some sort of shift in Achilles, but not necessarily a development into something different – Achilles may act more like his true character in the end; see Schein (1984) 159 on the "deepening" of a latent sympathy in Achilles by Book 24. Most radically, Redfield, following Fraenkel, has insisted that Homeric man in general is "incapable of development" (1975) 21–4, 211f. De Jong (1994) shows conclusively that Redfield is wrong to suggest that characters have no inner life; see also the arguments of Held (1987) 258–61 who out-Aristotles Redfield, although I doubt Aristotle's theories are necessary for our understanding of epic characters.

[2] Sinos (1980) 21–4. The stories of these two young heroes, as related by Thetis and Eumaeus, are nearly identical in outline: both are lamented while still alive; having been nurtured by the gods, they shoot up like saplings and are sent forth by the gods on voyages towards manhood, apart from their fathers, from where they may not or will not return to their ancestral homes.

[3] C. J. Mackie (1997) 4–5. In fact, Telemachus is here described for the only time in the epic as *chôomenos* (*Od.* 2.80), a word that has special connections to Achilles and is used only once elsewhere in the

deficiencies, whatever they are, also appear to be related to his youth. Nestor reminds Patroclus of Peleus' words: "Peleus told Achilles always to be the best and superior to others, but to you he said, 'Achilles is nobler in birth; you are older; he is much better in might, but you speak wise words and direct him and he will obey to his profit'" (*Il.* 11.786–9). Achilles himself is quick to concede that others are better at words and counsel (18.105–6).

But what could he mean? Recent studies of Achilles' language show him to be the most creative speaker in the poem. He utters more similes than any other character, invokes distant places and resounding names, and is uniquely given to speaking with directness, richness of detail, and emotive and violent expressions.[4] But despite these impressive linguistic skills, Achilles is in fact remarkably *unpersuasive* throughout the epic. His words rarely convince his audience to act as he is urging them.

If speech is a primary characteristic of humans in the early Greek mind, we would expect it to play a role in the development of Achilles' character as he swings from frustrated Achaean warrior to inhuman beast to tragic hero. Heroic life is about being successful, but it is this very definition of success that Homer holds up for scrutiny. Achilles discovers a use of language that departs from heroic norms and makes him, in the end, more fully human than anyone else in the poem. Authoritative speech is one of the defining characteristics of a heroic life, but Achilles transcends such conventional heroism by the end of the epic. In his journey to becoming something greater than a doer of deeds, he ultimately comes to redefine what it means to be a "speaker of words."

ACHILLES PLAYS THE GAME

Speaking is one of the primary agonistic arenas for the warriors at Troy, and Achilles is engaged in a competition for authority from the beginning

Odyssey of mortal anger (8.238, of Odysseus). On the frequent reference to Achilles' youth, especially at the beginning of the epic, see King (1987) 4–7. Martin (1989) 23, 124 argues that rhetorical skill at self-presentation must be acquired, as in the case of Diomedes; cf. Montiglio (2000) 58–9, who points out that Diomedes does not reply to Agamemnon's insults (4.401–2) until *after* he proves himself in his *aristeia*.

[4] Moulton (1977) 100; Friedrich and Redfield (1978); and especially Griffin (1986) 50–6, who concludes that Achilles is "the most impressive user of language in the *Iliad*" (51). Also good on Achilles' speech is Martin (1989) 148–96. I am not so concerned here with the actual language, that is, Greek, of Achilles, as in its effects; see the cautionary note in Messing (1981) about stylometric analyses of Homeric characterization. Much interesting work has been done on the language of Achilles; Mackie's (1996) extensive analysis of Achilles' "anomalous" and "incongruous" use of Hesiodic blame poetry is not pertinent to my discussion. For a critique of A. Parry's famous analysis of Achilles' language, see Lynn-George (1988) 93–8.

of the *Iliad*. He is acknowledged to be the greatest warrior at Troy, but his language surprisingly lacks authority when it should count most. If the mark of a successful speaker is to persuade someone of a course of action, particularly a wise course of action that leads to success, then Achilles is certainly not the "brilliant orator" he is sometimes claimed to be.[5] To speak powerfully, or at great length, is not the same as to make people obey. As Friedrich and Redfield have pointed out, there are different kinds of persuasion. Instead of persuading the person to whom he is speaking, Achilles far more often succeeds in persuading Homer's audience that he is what he says he is and means what he says.[6] Achilles *seems* to be an effective speaker, and his speech is memorable, but he nevertheless fails to convince his fellow warriors. Command of the nuances of language apparently does not necessarily translate into success. After the gifted speakers Odysseus and Phoenix fail to move Achilles in the embassy scene, the verbally less impressive Ajax nearly talks Achilles into relenting, at least keeping him on the shores of Troy. In this sense, Ajax is the "best" speaker of the three, even though his *muthos* is by far the shortest and least rhetorically embellished.

Achilles and Agamemnon are vying for control, and the latter's insecurity and the former's impetuosity make their speeches equally unproductive. The mere summoning of the assembly by the "junior" Achilles brings this competition to a head. Achilles' speech is notable for its rashness, just as Agamemnon's speech and actions are thoughtlessly precipitous. The first words of Achilles to Agamemnon address the king as "most greedy of all men" (*philokteanôtate pantôn*, 1.122), a tactic that does not bode well in an acquisitive society (*pace* Kirk ad loc.). Still, there is nothing in his speech that warrants Agamemnon's paranoid response: "Don't deceive me with your wit . . . since you will neither get around me nor persuade me" (1.131–2). Agamemnon believes that Achilles has an ulterior motive. But the charge of deception is groundless – Achilles speaks as straightforwardly as anyone in the epic. The real issue is marked in Agamemnon's choice of words: "you will not get around me" can also mean "you will not surpass me." Agamemnon reveals from the beginning that in his mind, to be persuaded is to be trumped in competition.[7] This attitude, another ugly appendage to the heroic culture, pervades the *Iliad*, and ultimately results in both

[5] Cramer (1976); Martin (1989) 86. Minchin (2001b) 204–5 observes that the function of stories within the *Iliad* is to persuade listeners to a certain course of action. An effective story results in the listener's adopting an action that is urged by the storyteller.
[6] Friedrich and Redfield (1978) 271.
[7] On this competition as part of Homer's general critique of the nature of Agamemnon's type of authority, see Hammer (1997) 4–11, who discusses the role of *peithô* in this struggle. He focuses more on Agamemnon's failures, noting that of the eight times the phrase "Do you also obey, since to be

Achilles' withdrawal and his refusal to return to battle. Agamemnon wants
to be obeyed, and so Achilles appropriately (if regrettably) wonders if any
of the Achaeans will obey the words of the king (150–1). Agamemnon ups
the ante by proclaiming that he will make an example of Achilles so that
Achilles might know how much more status the king possesses, so "another
too may shrink from declaring himself equal to me and likening himself to
me to my face" (1.186–7).[8]

So far, this has clearly been a battle of words. Achilles, feeling that he
must switch to the field of glory at which he excels, reaches for his sword.
But Athena immediately returns the warrior to the competition of words,
hoping to persuade him (207, 214) to use language alone (211) against
Agamemnon. Achilles agrees, complying with the word of the goddess
(216, 218), and the poet confirms both Achilles' obedience (220–1) and his
return to a battle of harsh words (223). Nestor leaps in, trying to convince
the leaders to listen to *him* (he uses *peithomai* three times in two verses,
273–4). But Agamemnon returns to his simple themes of refusing to be
persuaded (289) and criticizing Achilles' speech (291). Achilles concludes
the debate by insisting that he too will not yield or be persuaded (294–6). He
does not change through Book 9, but continues to insist that Agamemnon
will not persuade him with either words (9.315) or gifts (9.386). He feels he
has been deceived by words (9.376; cf. his famous words to Odysseus that
seem aimed at Agamemnon, 9.312–13), and announces that he will share in
neither the works nor the counsels of the king (9.374).

No one wins this "battle of contending words," as Homer calls it (1.304).[9]
Achilles fails to persuade, even though he has "right" on his side (as Athena
and Nestor, as well as the cries of the assembled Greeks, make clear). Even
more significant is his manner of speech. He cuts off Agamemnon to end
the quarrel: Homer describes the interruption with the word *hupoblêdên*
(292), the only time it appears in the epics. Speaking first is an honor
accorded Nestor for his wisdom and Agamemnon for his status. One way
the poet portrays the inherently flawed system of honor is by having Achilles
call the assembly in this book – he already seems to be appropriating
Agamemnon's prerogatives. But the interruption of a speaker is clearly

---

persuaded is better" is used in the *Iliad*, it is unsuccessful in only three, all spoken by Agamemnon. I
am more interested in *Achilles*' failures at persuasion. Haubold (2000) 52–68 examines Agamemnon's
"spectacular failure" as a "shepherd of the people." For links between Homer's political world and
the "historical" reality of the period, see the discussion of Raaflaub (2001) 73–89.

[8] See Pucci (1998) 183–9 for the significance of this expression and the translation of *phasthai*.

[9] Clark (2002) 113–14 notes that the word *antibios* is applied only two other times in the *Iliad* to
non-combat contexts (1.278, 2.377–8), both times with reference to the argument between Achilles
and Agamemnon. This really is a duel.

a sign of the breakdown in the normal speaking pattern, which ideally alternates and "circulates without ceasing."[10] Achilles refuses to wait his turn.

What is noteworthy about Achilles' use of language in the first book is not merely his inability to convince Agamemnon to relent – not even Nestor can accomplish that – but his approach. He does not even give Athena a chance to say a word before he starts speaking, an exceptional event in divine visitations.[11] Even Thersites is allowed to finish his harangue before he is thumped into humiliated silence. Achilles sees speaking as part of the system of authority, as it surely is. Its purpose is intricately linked to the exchange of honor that is always at stake in confrontations in the heroic society. But his anger forces him into patterns of linguistic conflict that, like his physical withdrawal, isolate him from community. It is this very place of language in the heroic system of honor that Achilles comes to see so differently by the end of the epic.

A remarkable scene provides insight into a side of Achilles that will become crucial to his journey through the *Iliad*. As the members of the embassy approach the huts and ships of the Myrmidons, they come upon Achilles "delighting his heart" by playing the lyre – a trophy won in battle – and singing of "the glorious deeds of men" (9.185–9). Nowhere else in the Homeric poems is a leading warrior depicted playing the lyre and singing like a bard.[12] Like Homer himself, Achilles is creating poetry, but for his own consolation (Patroclus seems to be his only audience). Significantly, his song about martial valor is sung with the help of a war prize. Achilles is thinking still of the honor that comes from glorious deeds (*klea*) of war. He is linguistically gifted, and a voluble speaker. His response to Odysseus (9.308–429) is the longest speech in the poem up to that point. But his speeches in the embassy scene are limited to the rejection of the three speakers. He makes no effort to persuade, or to make his words into

---

[10] Montiglio (2000) 90–2. Odysseus, understanding Achilles quite well, will comfort him in the underworld by reassuring him that his son, Neoptolemus, is always the first both to speak (*aiei prôtos ebaze*) and to fight at the front (*Od*. 11.510f.). This desire to be first runs in the family. Odysseus himself knows better. Antenor's description of the Ithacan's hesitation – the Trojan says Odysseus looked "senseless and churlish" before speaking *after* Menelaus – emphasizes Odysseus' patience and artful hesitation at the beginning of his speech (3.216f.). His most notorious intrusion, in the embassy scene (9.223–4), is singularly unsuccessful; *pace* Nagy (1996) 142 with n.124. To be *allowed* to speak first is surely the sign of authority, but it does not necessarily follow that listeners will be persuaded. In fact, first speakers are often trumped in councils (Thersites is only the most famous example).

[11] Edwards (1980) 14; cf. Beck (1998–9) 126 on Telemachus' "interruption" of Odysseus at *Od*. 16.1–11; Rabel (1997) 163–5, 180–1.

[12] See Hainsworth ad 9.189; King (1987) 10; Frontisi-Ducroux (1989) 12.

actions for the Greeks. We learn only of his disillusionment, contempt, and anger. Speech and song in this scene are a substitute for action, not a complementary pair.[13] He warns the speakers not to sit down next to him and croak like a frog one after another (*mê moi truzête*; see Hainsworth ad 9.311). He knows this is to be a battle of words, about who can persuade whom, and thus he tries to dismiss them as unworthy speakers, no better than animals. But in the end, even here Achilles is more persuaded than persuasive, and reveals his customary rashness. When nearly convinced by Ajax's direct and impatient appeal to the material heroic code, Achilles agrees in principle but cannot let his anger go, and utters fateful words: he will not enter battle until Hector comes to his own huts and ships (9.650f.).

In Book 16, these words come back to haunt him.[14] Persuaded by Patroclus to help the Greeks, and apparently ready to set aside his anger and take the gifts, he cannot enter battle because his own ships are not yet in danger (16.61–3). More importantly, he fails to induce Patroclus to follow his commands not to attack Troy (16.83f.). His words are consistently ineffectual. He later confesses to his mother – after angrily cutting her off in what is becoming a familiar pattern[15] – that he is the best of the Achaeans in war but there are others better at speaking and giving advice (18.105–6). He failed in both speech and action to keep Patroclus alive, and now sees that his word was "fruitless" (*halion epos*) when he told Patroclus' father that he would bring him back (18.324f.).

Books 19–22 present Achilles at his most bestial. His viciousness in battle, his rejection of social norms such as oaths and suppliants, his scavenging, and his similes reveal a man on the edge of humanity. We will examine this increasingly bestial behavior shortly. For now, it should be noted that Achilles' descent is marked by his language as well. From the death of Patroclus through that of Hector, Achilles speaks only to Agamemnon by name, and only to facilitate battle. He engages in no regular conversation with any other living human – his colleagues meet only silence, indifference, or rejection. In fact, his most frequent partners in speech are non-humans: gods, animals, ghosts, corpses, and enemies about to become corpses.[16]

Achilles' decision to enter battle – his suicidal dedication to vengeance and his first actual action of the epic – is carefully marked by his inhuman speech. To drive the Trojans away from Patroclus' body, Achilles stands

---

[13] Thalmann (1984) 175–9. Odysseus is the character who can engage fully in both peace and warfare, speech and action, at the proper time, as symbolized in the simile of the bow being strung like a lyre at *Od.* 21.406–11.

[14] As argued most persuasively by Scodel (1989) 94.   [15] Lohmann (1970) 145.

[16] Pelliccia (1995) 218 n.196.

at the ditch, a fire blazing above his head. Then, with Athena's aid, he shouts three times with such force that twelve Trojans immediately impale themselves (18.202–31). The hero's voice here is described as an *arizêlê phônê* (18.219–21), a "very clear" voice. The adjective is applied to a voice only here in Homer (twice in three verses). It is a portentous word, used elsewhere in the *Iliad* to describe flashes of Zeus' lightning (13.244) and the images of Athena and Ares in golden armor on Achilles' shield (18.519). There is something divine about Achilles' resonance, something superhuman and ominous to match the fire glowing about his head.[17]

Achilles' voice is further described by the poet as "of bronze" (*opa chalkeon*, 18.222). What does this mean? The adjective is not used by itself of voices anywhere else in the epics, although Stentor has a superhuman "voice of bronze" (*chalkeophônos*, 5.785; cf. Cerberus' bark in Hesiod, *Theog.* 311). Does it refer solely to the timbre of his shout, a "ringing" quality deriving from its comparison to the "very clear voice" of the trumpet (*salpinx*, 18.219)? Or is it borrowing from the metaphorical sense of "bronze," as is often found in the epics, a "hard" or "strong" shout (e.g. 2.490, 11.241)?[18] The adjective here more likely emphasizes Achilles' inhumanity: his voice is not that of a man, but of a weapon. The trumpet in the simile is used to sound the call of battle around a besieged city (18.219–20). More to the point, any reference to bronze must conjure up its major role in the epics as a modifier of heroic arms. Achilles' voice is now a superhuman vehicle that announces his reentry into battle, a symbolic precursor to the divinely created bronze armor he will soon don. His bronze voice functions as a weapon – men and horses alike are terrified, and twelve of the enemy perish in panicked confusion. His voice also accomplishes the task of warriors – Patroclus' body is recovered because of his otherworldly shout.

Jasper Griffin suggests, I think rightly, that behind this scene lies the idea of heroes dying from fright at the cry of great warriors, as in Irish legends.[19] In these tales, the hero is almost literally transformed into some kind of inhuman monster; here, Achilles is linked with the divine. But to the Greeks, to be too similar to the divine is the flip side of being bestial, a

[17] The only other certain appearance of the word, in fact, modifies the rays of the Dog Star, to which Achilles' gleam is compared as he approaches Troy. The MSS also use the adjective to describe the portent at Aulis (2.318), although this is a debated reading. The adverb *arizêlôs* is used by Odysseus to describe the fashion in which he told his amazing stories to the Phaeacians (*Od.* 12.453); see Kaimio (1977) 34–5. Shipp (1972) 50–3 adds that Herodotus used the word *aridêlos* of the portentous Eleusinian dust-cloud (8.65).

[18] Kaimio (1977) 35–6 discusses these choices, although she argues that the adjective has no connotations of a "metallic" quality; cf. West (1966) ad *Theog.* 311.

[19] Griffin (1980) 38–9; see also Miller (2000) 230–3. Edwards (1991) ad loc. calls this arming scene a kind of epiphany – the cry and fire make Achilles both bestial and divine, as so often in these books.

combination that is nicely represented by the symbol of Athena's aegis which Achilles wears at that very moment. The details of this famous accoutrement are variously described throughout the epic, but in every passage except for this one it is a weapon or tool of the gods.[20] Zeus, Apollo, and Athena all wield it, usually to terrify the enemy and drive them back in a panic (15.229, 308, 318, 17.593; *Od.* 22.297). The moment of Achilles' shout is the only time when this divine object, described in its first appearance in the poem with the divine epithets "ageless and immortal" (2.447), is donned by a mortal. Clearly, Achilles has left the human plane in some terrifying fashion. But Athena's aegis also has the head of Gorgon on it, the "dreadful monster" (5.741) that traditionally was part human and part snake, although Homer does not mention these details.[21] As he does so often in these final books, Achilles simultaneously transcends human nature and degrades it. One way Homer marks this transition is through his use of an inarticulate and terrifying cry that is at once bestial and divine.[22]

Similarly, the first action of Achilles after receiving his new armor is unparalleled in the epics – he lets out a terrible cry, the sheer power of which musters the Greeks in assembly. The phrase used to describe his shout, *smerdalea iachôn* (19.41), is found seven other places in the epic, always as part of an attack in battle. Achilles is so ready for battle and impatient in his rage that he can only give a war cry, and yet it brings his fellow Greeks together.[23] Only three other characters are described as shouting in this fashion in the *Iliad*, either Achilles' great enemies – Aeneas (who, as we will see, is the warm-up for Hector, and who may have had an important duel with Achilles in pre-Iliadic epics – they have certainly met in battle before; 5.302) and Hector (8.321), or his alter-ego Patroclus (16.785). Such shouting is limited to Achilles for the rest of the poem: he

---

[20] See Kirk (1985) ad 2.446–51; Janko (1992) ad 15.308–11. The aegis can also be a defensive weapon, impenetrable even by lightning bolts; see 21.400, and below on 24.20.

[21] See Gantz (1993) 20–2, 84–5. *Aspis* 229–37 contains the first reference to snakes, wrapped around waists (and possibly in their hair). Very early, at least by the middle of the seventh century, the sisters appear in art with snakes about their heads. Nevertheless, the Homeric Gorgon was a "terrible monster," the mere thought of which sends Odysseus scurrying out of the underworld (*Od.* 11.633–5).

[22] It is probably pushing etymological matters too far to suggest that Homer is pointing out the general speechlessness of terror by having Achilles shout, Athena yell, and a "wordless confusion" (*aspeton kudoimon*) rise among the Trojans (18.218; for the combination, see also 10.523). *Aspetos* refers to something that cannot be described adequately, rather than something that is without speech, but the concatenation of images of sound is noteworthy.

[23] When he had summoned the assembly at the opening of the *Iliad*, the verb used was the customary *kalessato* (1.54). The expression for the assembly itself in Book 19 is unformular; see Edwards (1991) ad 19.54. The entire assembly has something unprecedented about it, as everyone, even the pilots and waiters, come out from the ships. Tsagarakis (1982) 103 suggests the alteration in the type-scene reflects not so much the desperate plight of the Greeks as Achilles' emotional state.

ends Book 19 by entering battle with a shout (*iachôn*, 19.424), and then gives his terrible cry three more times in Book 20 (20.285, 382, 443).

The adjective *smerdaleos* itself has supernatural associations. Beyond its applications to sounds, the word is closely linked to inhuman objects such as serpents, lions, the heads of Scylla (cf. *smerdnos* of the Gorgon's head), Hades' house, Athena's aegis, and Heracles' belt.[24] Achilles' fury (cf. Hector's shaking of his head *smerdaleon* in battle madness, as he foams at the mouth, 15.609) is pushing him beyond the human realm into the worlds of both sub- and superhuman.

Although Achilles' speech at the assembly in Book 19 is generally courteous and well-composed, it also reveals his customary impatience and does not accomplish its immediate goal. Achilles' sole objective is to get back to war immediately, in order to kill Hector. He quickly acknowledges his own role in the quarrel with Agamemnon, "sets aside" his wrath, and urges preparations for battle. He seems no longer interested in competing with the Greeks for preeminence. In typical fashion, Agamemnon nearly ruins the moment by renewing his rivalry for control and hinting at Achilles' previous insults. Mark Edwards has clarified the dynamics of this passage.[25] When Agamemnon says, "It is good to listen to someone who is standing up," he means "as Achilles was just standing, whom you applauded; but I cannot stand, because of my wound." He reminds everyone, at a moment of supposed reconciliation, that he was wounded in battle while Achilles was sulking in his tent. When he immediately adds, "nor is it right to interrupt" (*oude eoiken / hubballein*, 19.79–80), he alludes to the interruption of his speech by Achilles at 1.292 (described by the poet with the hapax *hupoblêdên*) the last time these two met. The wounded king insists on explaining his own relative innocence in the matter and on demonstrating his graciousness by giving the gifts Achilles no longer desires. Achilles dismisses Agamemnon's offer: "Do whatever you want," he says brusquely, "this is no time to waste chattering" (19.149–50). Achilles even has a unique vocabulary for Agamemnon's useless prattle, the verb *klotopeuein* appearing nowhere else in Greek literature.

But Achilles once again does not get his wish. He loses his ensuing debate with Odysseus ("I far surpass you in thought," the wily Ithacan boasts without contradiction; 19.218–19), who insists that the men must eat before battle. Achilles wants to fight immediately, but ends up having to wait for gifts he does not want, an oath from Agamemnon he does not care about, and a meal for the troops he refuses to share. Once more, his

[24] Kaimio (1977) 62–3.   [25] (1991) ad 19.76–84.

language, though this time conciliatory, proves ineffective. He is forced to relent, brooding by himself and rejecting all attempts to bring him back into the community. Achilles has become such an outsider by the end of the book that he is ingesting the food of the gods (19.352–4) and speaking with his horse (19.400–17). The bestial and divine elements of his soul have begun to squeeze out his humanity.

Achilles' language in Books 20–22 becomes that of the warrior, comprised merely of competitive taunts and boasts. Here, the fruitless speech of children and women is contrasted with the actions of men in battle. This is the typical language of heroes. In Achilles' famous encounter with Aeneas, for example, Achilles suggests Aeneas is a *nêpios*, who will learn only by experience, rather than by words (20.198). Aeneas reverses the taunt, spending fifty-nine verses insisting that it is the sign of a *nêpution* (20.200; cf. *epeessi ge nêputioisin*, 211) and women (*gunaikas*, 20.252) to quarrel with words rather than deeds.[26] Similarly, Achilles rejects Hector's effort to extract an oath with the suggestion that the two of them are like animals (22.262–4), and he calls Hector a *nêpie* (22.333). Hector, in turn, fears that he will be killed "like a woman" (22.125) if he tries to talk to Achilles. Words ultimately have no place in battle, and Achilles finds his greatest heroic success – and falls furthest from his humanity – when he devotes himself solely to martial deeds.[27]

Achilles' commanding presence in Book 23, in his direction of Patroclus' funeral and masterly oversight of the games, indicates his reacquisition of status within the community and his own settlement with Agamemnon. This authority is marked now by his successful control of language in the conventional fashion of the culture: he tells Agamemnon to arrange a funeral pyre (23.49f.); he instructs Agamemnon to dismiss the army

[26] Cf. Hector's retort to Ajax's taunts at 7.235–6. Nagy (1979) 265–75 inaugurated the discussion of Aeneas as a master of praise and blame poetry. Mackie (1996) 71–4 has taken this kind of approach to the next level, arguing that Aeneas is typically Trojan in preferring words over warfare, displaying a Trojan versatility by shifting from genre to genre. This approach, while helpful in placing such "kiting" in some sort of generic context, has limitations. Aeneas may defend the Trojan "ethos" of poetic, quasi-philosophical narrative, but he does so while incorporating all the Greek "blame" techniques and insults by calling Achilles a woman and child. And if he is really just trying to stall, he fails miserably – Achilles would have dispatched him quickly after their exchange. Aeneas ironically puts down blame while blaming in much the same way that Socrates demonstrates a mastery of speech while claiming to be an inexperienced speaker.

[27] Perhaps this helps to explain the nature of the warrior vaunts – the brief speeches over the vanquished dead or dying opponent – that are peculiar to the *Iliad*. Kyriakou (2001) argues that they provide an opportunity for the hero to rework the past and connect with it, but notes that they have very little impact on the battle situation and overall image of the vaunting warrior. But they are more than elation and self-congratulation, more than efforts to shame enemies. The speech of victory reenacts and celebrates life over death, voice over silence. The last one standing – and speaking – wins.

(23.156f.); he orders Agamemnon and the other leaders to put out the fire (23.236f.). The king and the rest of the Achaeans do exactly as instructed, without uttering a word in response. At 23.257, Achilles arranges the funeral games, perhaps again encroaching on Agamemnon's turf.[28] His words, however, are readily obeyed. His authority is restored, at least in this public context of Patroclus' funeral. His status has been refurbished. His language is now accomplishing just what it is "supposed" to do in his culture – he speaks, others listen, and he both gains honor and dispenses it.

But despite this institutional restoration, his anger and alienation from human norms and life itself persist. In the midst of his return to Greek life he remains uniquely isolated as well. At the beginning of the final book of the *Iliad*, Achilles is still abusing Hector's corpse and refusing the feelings and routines that make human life meaningful. Apollo states plainly that Achilles has lost all pity and shame, and compares him to a lion who knows wild things and attacks a flock "to seize a meal." His *phrenes* are not fitting, his *noêma* implacable, his mourning beyond all reasonable measure (24.33–54). Interestingly, Apollo protects Hector's body from desecration by covering it with the aegis (24.20–1). Achilles, we will recall, wore Athena's aegis as he stood without armor, and made his reentry into war by shouting to scare the Trojans away from Patroclus' body. Now Hector's naked body is protected by the same device. Achilles' armor, a gift of the gods, has meant death to both Patroclus and Hector, the only people to wear it into battle in the *Iliad*.[29] The aegis, a piece of armor ageless and deathless like the very gods, is supplied by the Olympians to protect the corpse from defilement. The aegis is a tool in Zeus' plan, a symbol not merely of the panic of war (it has Rout, Strife, Valor, and Onset on it, as well as the head of the Gorgon, 5.738) but also of the tragic consequences of Achilles' wrath. Zeus tells Apollo to shake it over the Achaean warriors to frighten them (15.229, 308, 361), and he himself brandishes it to rout the Greeks shortly before Achilles returns to battle (17.593). Zeus, responding to Achilles' plea through his mother, favors the Trojans. The results are, of course, the death of Patroclus, Hector, and soon Achilles himself. The aegis represents Achilles' own madness of revenge, his animal responses and their consequences, a dreadful, divine monster (5.738) that does not belong in the human world.

---

[28] Postlethwaite (1995) 102. For the funeral games as "an enactment of political community," see the discussion of Hammer (2002a) 134–43. Taplin (1990) 77–8 observes that Agamemnon's last words of direct speech come (surprisingly) in Book 19 (258–66).

[29] See Heath (1992a) for the meaning of the gifts of the gods for mortals.

The remainder of Book 24 tells the story of Achilles' imposition of some kind of human order on the chaotic and destructive animal he has become, his "mysterious union of detachment and immediacy, of passion and order," as Whitman so nicely puts it.[30] He has been unable to stop acting like a beast, and he has shown no inclination to change. His mother notes that he is still rejecting sleep/sex and food, wondering how long he will mourn and "devour his own heart" (*sên edeai kradiên*, 24.129). In light of Achilles' expressed cannibalistic urges (see below), we cannot help feeling the literalness of this metaphor. Only animals devour human organs, and only the most insane would turn on himself.[31]

Homer's magnificent treatment of Achilles' confrontation with consequences of his actions, his exploration of the tragic necessities of the human condition in his meeting with Priam, has rightly been the subject of interminable discussion.[32] What is of special interest here is the manner in which Achilles explores a newly found understanding and pity. The Greek hero uses language for a purpose that transcends the heroic culture he has been struggling with throughout the epic. Achilles borrows from familiar narrative structures and patterns but puts his considerable linguistic skills to a novel use: the lyre-player now creates a story to console an adversary, to make a truly human connection possible. And this, his final attempt at persuasion, is successful. In this scene, several important motifs surrounding Achilles' journey come together. The hero's loss of humanity since the death of Patroclus is marked by his relation to animals in various ways, but especially in his diet. With the scene of Priam, language and food connect in a novel fashion to adumbrate Achilles' reemergence and development into a true speaker of words. So before turning to that crucial meeting, we must first take a necessary detour through Achilles' animal imagery. Before becoming a *homo loquens* in a profound sense, he must become more inhuman, more bestial than anyone else at Troy – the "be<a>st" of the Achaeans, as Katherine King has aptly named him.[33]

---

[30] (1958) 218.

[31] This is the only appearance of this expression in Homer, although Bellerophon (6.202) and Odysseus (*Od.* 10.379) and his men (*Od.* 9.75, 10.143) eat their *thumos*; cf. a "heart-biting" speech (*Od.* 8.185) and the expression "heart-gnawing strife" in the *Iliad* (7.210, 7.301, 16.476, 19.58, 20.253).

[32] Zanker (1994), esp. 127–54, provides an excellent overview of the basic issues in his analysis of Achilles' overcoming of the competitive model.

[33] King (1987) 13–28. Most studies of Achilles refer to this inhumanity, and my discussion of Achilles' bestial loss of humanity owes much to other scholars. None of the studies that I know of, however, pulls together all the various aspects of this depiction (similes, dietary images, levels of violence, etc.).

THE WIDE-JAWED DOLPHIN IN THE RIVER

Animals may play their most important cultural role in the epics as suppliers of the feast, one of the most familiar and thoroughly examined of Homeric cultural conventions.[34] Many studies have demonstrated the significance of the reception of guests – the ritually correct preparation and serving of food and appropriately negotiated exchange of information – as a sign of humanity and social reintegration. John Foley has recently shown that the breaking of bread not only creates essential bonds between humans, it also serves as a *sêma*, or sign, that "betokens *a ritualistic event leading from an obvious and preexisting problem to an effort at mediation of that problem.*"[35] It is, in other words, a quintessential human act that is idealized for thematic reasons, a cultural institution which beastly characters such as the suitors and Cyclopes – as well as Odysseus' own men on Thrinacia – invert and pervert at their own cost. This is one aspect of human morality which everyone (again, with such pointed exceptions as Polyphemus) can agree that the gods themselves sustain. To ignore or violate the feast is to deny one's humanity: vegetarianism and cannibalism are but two sides of the same uncivilized coin in the ancient world.[36]

Scenes of hospitality, the central feature of which is a shared meal, reveal the correct place for animals in the Homeric world. As much as agriculture is a sign of humanity and civilization in the epics – Greek man is a farmer – it is the slaughtering, cooking, distributing, and eating of domestic animals that marks most dramatically the legitimate relationship between the natural world and that of humans – and between humans themselves.[37] As

---

[34] For a recent structural analysis of type scenes, see Foley (1991) 175–89 and Reece (1993). On the significance of Homeric meals in general, especially as a symbol of community, see: Motto and Clark (1969) 118f.; Saïd (1979) 14–27; Griffin (1980) 14–21; Mueller (1984) 114–16; Nimis (1987) 25–73; Davies (1997). For the link between feasting and heroic politics, see Rundin (1996) 181–205. He notes the central role of the feast as a source of redistributive activity, as well as a place for the "equal" feast to articulate relations both among the politically powerful class and between council and king. He observes that man is a "feasting" animal (189). Bruns (1970) lays out the process of Homeric meal-making.

[35] Foley (1999) 169–87 (italics in the original). His larger point is that each reference to this ritual act conjures up the convention, so every instantiation should be read with and against the tradition.

[36] Vidal-Naquet (1986) 15–17; Cook (1995) 56–9, with further references. On vegetarianism in antiquity, see Haussleiter (1935); Dombrowski (1984a); Osborne (1995). Similarly, meat-eating can be used to distinguish classes – the elite warriors from the masses – as wells as genders; see Collins (1996) 24; Wickert-Micknat (1982) 54, with note 237, who argues that Homeric women appear to have a vegetarian diet!

[37] In its ritualistic aspect, of course, the slaughter of domestic animals for the ancient Greeks is the central act that articulates the relationship between humans with gods; see Chapter 4. Hesiod's Prometheus tale accounts for cooking and sacrifice as defining characteristics of man; see Vernant (1981a) and (1981b).

we have seen, meat-eating is serious business for the ancient Greeks. Not only is it connected to their central religious rite, but it serves as a sign (as it has done in most Western cultures) that the family and community are flourishing. Perhaps nothing has more eloquently heralded economic and political success than the carving of an animal on the table. In the Greek epics – where the word for feast, *dais*, etymologically refers to the division of the meat – better portions are given to higher-ranked individuals, and it remained true in classical times that the distribution of meat expressed social distinctions.[38] In one notorious account of what appears to be "beef-rage" (from the lost epic *Thebais, Fr. 3 PEG*), the sons of Oedipus send him the haunch rather than his preferred (and customary) portion of the sacrifice, the shoulder. Incensed at this insult – Oedipus is used to eating high on the hog – he prays to Zeus that his sons kill each other. And they do.

In a heroic context, the willingness and ability to provide a feast, more specifically meat for a feast, is the sign of leadership. Both Agamemnon and Achilles organize meals for other Greek leaders in the *Iliad* (e.g. 7.313–20, 9.70–2, 9.202–4). The communities at Ithaca, Pylos, Sparta, and Phaeacia are all shown to be flourishing, or not, by extensive pictures of meat-eating. Odysseus' disintegrating leadership is marked by his increasing difficulties in supplying meat for his men. First, they must hunt wild goats (*Od.* 9.152–60), obtaining nine for each ship. His success in providing meat is rewarded by the grant of a carcass of his own. Next, Odysseus bags a stag on Aeaea, apparently enough meat for his men, but nothing extra for him (*Od.* 10.156–84). Finally, on Thrinacia the men are forced to fish and catch birds, but since Odysseus cannot supply the necessary steaks they turn to the illicit beef of Helius' cattle (*Od.* 12.320–65).[39]

The mere fact that Odysseus is shown hunting signals a breakdown in the normal relations between leader and men, as well as between humans and animals (or culture and nature). Under normal conditions, human hunters in the epics are never described as trying to obtain meat, even the

---

[38] See references in Rundin (1998) 20–2; Jameson (1999) 326.

[39] Scodel (1994). A good general discussion of the symbolic value of cooking and eating meat as representing an attitude of power and domination over nature, women, and other men can be found in Fiddes (1991); the "sexual politics of meat" are discussed from a feminist viewpoint by Adams (1990). Beef-eating in particular has often conjured up feelings of superiority in status and strength. The Isthmian sculptor Euphranor boasted that his virile statue of Theseus ate meat, whereas the apparently feckless effort of Parrhasius must have been fed on roses (Plut. *De glor. Ath.* 346a; Pliny *HN* 35.129). Ritvo (1987) 47 notes in her study of the symbolic value of animals in Victorian England that, according to the British, "it was the consumption of red meat that distinguished brave and brawny English soldiers from puny, sniveling Frenchmen."

frequent deer, goat, or boar in the similes.[40] Hunting is a necessary means for survival on the edges of civilization, but it is sport in the heroic world. Wild beasts of any kind are rarely eaten in the epics. Ancient commentators noted the hesitance of heroes to ingest even the fish and fowl so abundant in and around the Mediterranean, although references to fishing and fowling (as well as milk and cheese) are frequently found in the similes.[41] This divergence between the diet of Homer's audience and that of the poet's heroes is surely intentional, functioning as a marker of the heroic world. Fish and birds are not suitable for either gods or heroes. For the heroes at Troy, it is what they eat, not how much, that distinguishes them. There is no sign in the *Iliad* of the excessive eating and drinking that are found in Norse epics or in other Greek myths, such as that of Heracles.[42] The suitors – and Polyphemus – come closest to displaying a drunken gluttony.

Domestic animals are to be sacrificed to the gods and eaten by the heroic community. They are central to civilization. Wild animals, on the other hand, represent the dangerous aspects of the natural world, including our own human natures. When viewed as part of a thematically significant dietary code, undomesticated animals serve an important symbolic role as both the antithesis of human culture and the representatives of what we could become – hunters for human flesh. Animals hunt for blood in the epics. While we eat cooked animals, they eat raw flesh. Homer applies the adjective "raw flesh eaters" (*ōmophagoi*, always in the plural) to jackals (11.479), wolves (16.157), and especially lions (5.782, 7.256, 15.592; for explicit eating, see 3.23, 11.172, 12.299, 15.629, 16.756, 17.61–7, 17.542, 17.657, 18.582–3, 24.41). Feral animals not only prey upon their fellow beasts, they will eat that supposedly most house-broken of all species, man himself.

But it is not just the ferocious creatures at the edge of the community that threaten this reversal. What strikes the Homeric Greek as most unsettling is that we can provide protein to the very animals we live with, the beasts that move easily in our midst, in particular birds and dogs. The "wild" beast is never safely extracted from animals, including the two most domesticated

---

[40] Scodel (1994) 532. Homeric hunting is examined in Buchholz et al. (1973) 1–130. For the political, social, and moral role of hunting in classical antiquity (as initiation, and a sport that reinforced the ideology of aristocratic masculinity), see: Anderson (1985); Schnapp (1997) 23–40, and (especially for the "iconology" of hunting depictions in vase-painting) Barringer (2001) 10–59.

[41] See Davies (1997) 98–9; Davidson (1997) 11–20. Fish-eating is found only in the *Odyssey*. The details of Homeric fishing can be found in Buchholz et al. (1973) 131–85. For the meaning of fish and fishing in antiquity, see Purcell (1995).

[42] Davies (1997) 98–9 with nn.9–10. For a classic description of the heroic appetite, see Murray (1934) 121.

species, dogs . . . and heroes. This unpleasant fact of nature, along with the Greek religious, social, and emotional concerns for proper burial, combine to form perhaps the single greatest terror for heroic culture of the *Iliad*: to have one's corpse left unburied to be torn and devoured by beasts in what Redfield has called the "antifuneral."[43] This motif is tied closely to the central themes of the epic, and to the wrath of Achilles in particular. The proem tells us – somewhat misleadingly but poignantly – that we are to hear of the "destructive wrath of Achilles which made heroes into spoil for dogs and birds."[44] The corpses of Patroclus and Hector are both threatened with just such treatment as the result of Achilles' anger, and through these images Homer creates one of his most vivid pictures of the hero's loss of humanity.

Hector is the first to dip seriously into the world of the beast. At one point in his *aristeia* he even threatens that any shirkers among his own men will be thrown to the dogs to be torn apart (15.348–51). He is at this point a veritable madman at war (cf. 15.605–10), foreshadowing the even crueler actions of Achilles directed at his own lifeless body. When he vaunts over the dying Patroclus, he promises that vultures will devour the dead man (16.836). The language is heroically direct: Hector wants to cut off Patroclus' head and toss it for the "bitches of Troy" to enjoy (17.125–7; cf. 17.272–3). The Greeks know full well his intentions (17.254–5). Iris prods Achilles into action by reporting that Hector desires to cut off Patroclus' head and fix it on stakes of the wall, the rest of his body presumably left to be "sport for Trojan dogs" (18.170–80; cf. Priam's wish that dogs and vultures would eat the unburied Achilles, 22.42–3). The brutality of decapitation of a corpse is in fact carried out only once in the poem, by the less-than-loved Ajax the Lesser. Hector's threat shows him to be a warrior who has stepped over the edge of acceptable behavior.[45]

Upon reentering the war, Achilles usurps Hector's violence and takes it to the next level in the climax of battle. In his madness, he moves beyond the desire to have animals abuse Hector's corpse, beyond even having others (including the narrator) imply that he is acting like a beast – he explicitly wishes to become one of those very animals.

---

[43] (1975) 183–6. He ties this threat to the role of the Keres, only on the shield in the *Iliad* 18.535–8, verses that are probably interpolated from the Hesiodic *Aspis* 248–57; see Edwards (1991) ad 18.535–8.

[44] For the theme of mutilation and its connections to Achilles, see Segal (1971) and Foley (1991) 163–8. See below for Zenodotus' reading of *daita* in the proem, and for the actual lack of such brutal treatment of corpses in the epic.

[45] Heads come off in battle, of course, and a few are even tossed back to the enemy, but only Ajax takes a stone-dead corpse and mistreats it in this fashion; see 10.456, 11.146, 11.261, 14.496, 14.65–8, 16.339–41, 20.486, with Segal (1971) 20–1.

Achilles matches and surpasses Hector by insisting that he will decapitate the Trojan and sacrifice – perhaps behead – twelve others on Patroclus' pyre (18.333–7; cf. 23.22–3).[46] In an ominous prelude to Hector's death, Achilles boasts over Lycaon's corpse that the fishes in the river shall lick up his blood and eat his white fat (21.121–7), something the eels and fish actually do with another body (21.203–4). In his final exchange with the stricken Hector, Achilles turns the tables on his best friend's killer. No fewer than three separate times he insists that Hector's body will be thrown to the birds and/or dogs (22.335–6, 348, 353) despite, or perhaps even partially because of, Hector's sole request that he not be left as carrion (22.339). Andromache (22.509–10), Hecuba (24.211–13), and Priam (24.408–9) all worry that their loved one's corpse will be eaten by dogs and/or worms. And Achilles has every intention of letting Hector rot (23.21, 23.182–3), although the gods protect the body from any corruption and eventually see to its burial (23.184–91, 24.23–137).

This particular image of nature's representatives overwhelming the "civilized" beast is so abhorrent to the Greeks and Trojans alike that the mere thought or threat of it – animals in fact only attack a dead body once in the epics, when the fish and eels attack a corpse in the river in Book 21 – evokes the most disturbing language in the poem. As Hecuba laments for the second time (cf. 22.89) that Fate has spun it so her son would glut dogs far from his parents, she adds that this horrific attack will happen "in the abode of a violent man whose heart I would like to fix my teeth into and devour" (24.212–13). Cannibalism represents the farthest one can be removed from humanity – only animals engage in such activity, and that, as Hesiod directly states (*Op.* 274–8), is what separates us from the beasts: eating one's own kind is the definition of a lack of *dikê*. Eating humans in particular is the marker for natural, uncivilized behavior at its most grue-some, associated only with monsters (e.g. Polyphemus, Laestrygonians, Scylla) and animals.[47] But Hecuba is responding in kind to the inhuman-ity of Hector's slayer, a man she dubbed *ômêstês*, "eater of raw flesh," just

---

[46] The verb Achilles uses to describe what he wishes to do to the other Trojans, *apodeirotomêsô*, is a "brutal" one (Edwards [1991] ad 18.336–7) and may imply decapitation, although it is used to mean "slit the throat" in animal sacrifices (e.g. *Od.* 11.35), and this is ultimately what Achilles does to the unfortunate youths (*dêioôn*, 23.174–6). Hector, Achilles, and Euphorbus, the cowardly killer of Patroclus (16.806–15) ultimately stabbed in the throat by Menelaus (17.38–40), are the only warriors to threaten someone with decapitation.

[47] For the ramifications of cannibalism, see Detienne (1979) 53–67. O'Brien (1993) 78–91 concludes that the epic's primary image of moral degeneration is the "raw-eater" to which she connects Hera's role in the epic (e.g. 4.34f.) as the central symbol for demonic appetite. Rawson (1984) suggests that Hecuba, as a foreigner, is more likely to act in such a way. Hecuba does, in fact, become a dog in later tradition. He also argues that there is no real cannibalism in the *Odyssey*, since the monsters

a few lines before (24.207). The word is used elsewhere in Homer only of animals (11.454, 22.67, 24.82), and especially of animals that eat corpses. Odysseus boasts that a slain enemy will not be buried but the *ômêstai* birds will tear him apart. This, he claims, is in explicit contrast to his own case, since he will be buried by his fellow Greeks (cf. Achilles' taunt to Hector about Patroclus, 22.335–6). Similarly, it is the *ômêstai* dogs of Priam who may turn on him at his death, tearing his body and drinking up his blood (22.66–76).[48]

Hecuba's application of the word to Achilles, however, strikes the reader as gruesomely apposite, since we have heard his inhuman remarks to Hector. Achilles had replied to the dying Trojan's final wish not to be thrown as food to the dogs with a famously grotesque rejoinder: "Don't supplicate me, you dog, by knees or parents. I wish that somehow my resolve would drive me to carve your meat and eat it raw (*ôma*), because of what you have done" (22.345–7). It is the ugly mixing of bestial and human that is especially discomfiting. The victor refers to Hector's body not as flesh (*chroa*, 321) but as meat (*krea*, 347).[49] Nowhere else in the epics is *krea* used by itself of human skin or flesh. It is meat that is to be eaten, both before and after it is cooked.[50] As we have seen, only animals and bestial creatures are raw-flesh-eaters. Hungry lions especially seek out *krea* (11.551 = 17.660, 12.300). When Polyphemus devours Odysseus' men, Odysseus cannot bring himself to say that the Cyclops ate merely "meat" – this might give a level of lexical legitimacy to the action – and so he modifies *krea* with "human" (*andromea*).

Achilles' placement of the word "raw" at the beginning of his statement is powerful. By referring to Hector's flesh as *krea*, he is trying to turn Hector into an animal. This is a standard tactic in pre-duel taunting, and

are not strictly human. The Polyphemus episode combines cannibalism with the inversion of all guest–host relations, supplication, and feasting.

[48] In the fourth use of the word, Iris is dispatched to fetch Thetis to Olympus, where she will be told to inform Achilles that he must return the body he has been abusing. As Iris plummets through the Ocean to Thetis' abode, she passes through the "raw-eating" (*ômêstêsin*) fishes (24.82). This seems to be an unnecessary detail – metrical filler – but its indirect connection with Hector's body may explain it: the word is tied to the abuse of corpses in all of its appearances, and this reminds us of Achilles' record of viciousness in the river. Fish, along with dogs and birds, are flesh-eaters in Homer; see Fraenkel (1921) 86–8, and especially Combellack (1953), who observes that one-third of the eighteen references to fish in the poems involve marine animals devouring humans. For fish and sea-monsters in early Greek art and poetry, see Vermeule (1979) 179–209.

[49] Lonsdale (1990) 100 sees the act as that of a scavenger, but it is more of a disgusting combination of scavenger and host.

[50] The *krea* of Helius' cattle bellows, both the bits that have been roasted (*optalea*) and those that are still raw (*ôma*), *Od.* 12.396. The word more often refers to meat that has been cooked, but see also *Od.* 24.364, where the *krea* is cut before it is roasted.

is underscored by his address to Hector, "You dog" (*kuon*, 22.345).[51] But Achilles' anger forces an escalation of animal imagery – he does not merely want to make Hector into a metaphorical animal, turning him into a subhuman through insulting language. By insisting that it is uncooked *krea*, he reveals his primary wish to *become* an animal himself, a hungry beast who, like a lion, sees the dying figure in front of him as a meal of pulsating flesh.[52]

Charles Segal noted the "striking" effect of separating the "raw" from the "flesh" with a long participle (*apotamnomenon*).[53] I would add that the participle, from a verb meaning "to cut off," cuts between the adjective and the noun, almost orally (visually to the modern reader) slicing off the raw flesh. When taken word by word, there is a careful building of meaning that delivers an increasing horror at what Achilles is saying: "I wish somehow me myself my anger and spirit compelled" (then the next verse begins) "raw" (raw what? never a good sign) "cutoff" (still not sure what, but this is butchery of some sort) "flesh" (flesh? but this is a human – is he really talking about Hector?) "to eat" (he *can't* be talking about Hector!), "for such things *you* have done" (he *is* talking about Hector!).

Who can blame Priam, then, when he tells Hermes of his fears that Achilles has cut up Hector "limb from limb" and tossed him to his dogs (24.409)? This may be a worse fate than even Achilles had directly promised,[54] but it is perfectly in line with his inhuman words to Hector. Achilles has violated most norms of humanity. Not only is he rejecting a suppliant, denying the possibility of oaths (human language as a means of mediating bestial impulses), threatening to violate the cultural necessity of burial, and wishing to collapse the gastronomic distinction between animal and human, he is projecting a complete inversion of the process of the feast. If the feast is a moment of reconciliation and reintegration, with the host serving meat to his guests, Achilles now envisions a world where he cuts up his suppliant and serves the "meat" to himself.

[51] "Dog" is also used in insults directed at those who are thought to be speaking out of turn or dealing out invective; see: Faust (1970) 24–9; Redfield (1975) 194–5; Lilja (1976) 21–5; Goldhill (1988) 15–17; Graver (1995) 43–53; Steiner (2001). On terms of animal abuse in general, Halverson's (1976) critique of Leach's famous article (1964) should be read: there is nothing particularly esoteric in the way animals' names are applied metaphorically to human beings.

[52] Lions hunt for food and their motivation is hunger (11.481, 20.164). The adjective *peinaôn*, "hungry," is theirs alone (3.25, 16.758, 18.161; the related noun and infinitive are used once each in the *Odyssey*). There is a late anecdote reported by Apollodorus (3.13.6) that Achilles' tutor, the half-bestial Chiron, fed him on lions, wild pigs, and bears.

[53] (1971) 40.

[54] Homer is not squeamish about depicting bizarre and horrific deaths, offering the reader a gruesome catalogue of butcheries in war; see compilations in Severyns (1948) 108–15 and Griffin (1980) 91–2.

The veneer of civilization has nearly worn off completely, the hero's violence driving him over the edge. As Michael Clarke has argued, the epic hero is always in danger of pushing, or being pushed, too far. Imposing culture on nature is a difficult task, and the Greeks never saw the job as securely finished. There is always the risk of falling back into a natural state.[55] Priam worries that with the loss of Hector, Troy will fall, and that he himself will become fodder for beasts. But unlike his son, who will feed Greek dogs, he will be torn and eaten by his *own* dogs, which he had reared at his table to guard his door. After they have filled themselves on his blood, they will return to their now-pointless duty, lying in the gateway (22.66–76). This, he concludes, is the most pitiable thing that can happen to wretched mortals. The dogs will be maddened (*alussontes*, 22.70). Whatever the actual etymology of the verb, it looks as if the poet related it to *lussa*, "martial rage," a condition that seems connected with wolves or rabid dogs (cf. 8.299) and would fit the context well.[56] Priam envisions the dogs returning to their undomesticated, feral state. Eumaeus' dogs, who fawn on Telemachus but nearly tear Odysseus to shreds, are described as acting "like wild beasts" (*Od.* 14.21). Nature unharnessed from civilization is rarely a pretty sight in the ancient Greek world, and the dog in some ways is most like man and his own "resistance to acculturation."[57] The noun *lussa* is applied to Achilles for the only time in the epic just 140 lines earlier (21.542; the word is otherwise reserved for Hector at 9.239, 9.305; cf. 8.299, 13.53). Achilles' "martial madness" there applies to his pursuit of Trojans into Troy, an attack that Priam personally witnesses and which scares him so deeply that he makes one of his rare intrusions into the war by ordering the gates opened to let the Trojans in as they retreat from the "monstrous" Achilles (21.527). Priam's maddened dogs are all too like Achilles. It is surely significant that what specifically prompts Priam's apocalyptic vision of his own fate is the sight of Achilles (Priam is "first" to see him) speeding across the plain towards the city, "shining like the Dog of Orion" (22.28).[58] Here are the two most dramatic images found in Achilles' similes – fire and animals – combined in brutally destructive fashion (cf. 22.317).

These similes themselves contribute greatly to our own image of Achilles' beastliness. As we have seen, comparisons between warriors and animals

[55] Clarke (1995).
[56] On the etymology of *lussa* from *lukos* (wolf), see Chantraine (1983/4), though Frisk (1960/70) is less sure; cf. Griffin (1980) 35; Hainsworth (1993) ad 9.239. For the "mad-dog" overtones of *lussa* in Greek tragedy, see Padel (1992) 163.
[57] Redfield (1975) 193–203. Mainoldi (1984) 105–9 also examines the "latent savagery" represented by dogs in the epics.
[58] Lonsdale (1990) 95–7.

are especially frequent in the combat episodes of the *Iliad*. But readers have noted that there is something different about the similes describing Achilles after he reenters the war. To begin with, there are a lot of them: over half of the similes in Books 18–22 (41/72) are his (he has only seven other comparisons in the entire epic).[59] Many of the most impressive of these involve fire or animals: the hero's inhuman wrath is described by images taken from the raw forces of nature.[60] But the animal imagery, especially that involving lions, differs in some important ways from other such comparisons in the epic. Here, highly anthropomorphic beasts are introduced that confuse the hero's nature with the animals involved, a conflation that will necessarily lead to disaster.[61] Clarke has even argued that the comparison with beasts, especially lions, carries an inherent danger, since such animals are symbols of the extremes of heroism – *menos, alkê, agênoriê* – that reveal a lack of restraint and a failure to acknowledge limitations. This embedded threat of self-destruction through excessive violence is the fatal flaw shared by beasts and heroes.[62] Patroclus possesses it (16.751–4), as does Hector (12.41–6) – both are doomed to perish from their own violence. But it is of course Achilles' self-destructive fury, his assimilation to the beast, that is the epic's major focus: "When Achilles likens himself to a lion, he is revelling not only in being a hero but in being a madman."[63]

Achilles has appropriated much of Hector's imagery in the final books in a reversal of animal motifs: the hunter now becomes the hunted.[64] The animal similes reflect this increasing removal from humanity. This is especially true of the lion similes (cf. 18.161f. of Hector), though it includes other beastly images as well. At 18.318–23, Achilles' groaning for Patroclus is compared to that of a lion whose cubs have been taken by a hunter. The grieving (*achnutai*) lion tracks down the man as his anger takes hold of him

---

[59] Moulton (1977) 100.

[60] For fire, see: Whitman (1958) 129–45; Moulton (1977) 106–10; King (1987) 18–19. For animals, see: Schnapp-Gourbeillon (1981); Lonsdale (1990); Clarke (1995).

[61] It should be noted that this merging of character with animal is quite different from the bird similes applied to the departure of gods, in which it is often difficult to determine if a comparison is being made or a metamorphosis is being described; see Edwards (1991) 29–30, with references. It is in the description of Achilles that Homer comes closest to the Indo-European tradition of the transformation of a warrior into a savage animal (bears and wolves, for example, in the Germanic lays); see Briquel (1995).

[62] Clarke (1995); especially good on the "predatory" Homeric hero and hunting imagery is Vermeule (1979) 83–116. For lions in the *Iliad*, see especially Lonsdale (1990). For lions in the *Odyssey*, see bibliography supplied by Glenn (1998), who demonstrates how sensitive we must be to each appearance of bestial images (here, the lion has erotic overtones!).

[63] Clarke (1995) 159. Clarke's provocative article does not explore what happens to Achilles in Book 24, which is what I believe is of most interest and will be examined below.

[64] Lonsdale (1990) 85–102.

(*cholos hairei*). This is the only application of *achnumai* to an animal in the epic, and its combination with the lion's anger – a reference to the major theme of the poem (cf. Achilles' anger at 18.337, *cholôtheis*) – personifies the lion in an especially vivid and personal way. The lion and Achilles are merging.[65]

Similarly, in Book 20 Achilles rushes at Aeneas like a ravenous (*sintês*) lion which sets upon the entire community (*pas dêmos*). Ignoring (*atizôn*) them at first, it is provoked into attack, its valiant heart (*êtor*) groaning, and it rushes on either to kill or be killed (20.164–75). Again, the personification and the suggestion that its *êtor* groans (nowhere else in Homer), combined with the level of destructive intent – the lion turns against the entire community, rather than the customary single attacker or mob of hunters and dogs – leads to a "closer identification beween man and lion than anywhere else in the *Iliad*."[66]

At the beginning of the next book, the Trojans in the river flee Achilles like fish who race from a huge-mouthed dolphin (21.22–6). Here, the simile of a wild animal meshes with the raw-flesh imagery discussed above. Achilles has crossed the boundaries of human nature in some fashion. In the next three verses, he catches the twelve Trojan youths doomed to human sacrifice and leads them off "like dazed fawns" (21.29; cf. 22.189–93, where Achilles closes in on Hector like a hound after a fawn). Achilles has become an animal, tracking down humans who are reduced to a predator's meal.

The great confrontation of Achilles and Hector swarms with animal comparisons: horse and chariot (22.22–4), Dog Star (21–32), snake (93–7), falcon and dove (139–44), race horses (at funeral games! 162–6), hound and fawn (189–93). Best known is Achilles' parable in response to Hector's pre-duel request that they swear the victor will treat the corpse honorably: "Don't talk to me of covenants, you wretch. As there are no oaths of faith between lions and men, neither do wolves and lambs share harmonious hearts but are always hostile minded towards each other, so it is impossible for you and me to be friends or to have any oaths between us" (22.261–6). Achilles applies the animal imagery to himself, rejecting human values such

---

[65] Perhaps the *hapax* for hunter, *elaphêbolos* (literally "deer shooter"), which is analogous in the simile for Hector, has some poignancy as well. The hunter, pursuing the most timid of animals, has picked on the young of the wrong animal. Hector, not prepared to tackle the "lion" of the Achaeans, has been killing the lesser ranks (he can hardly claim to have out-dueled even Patroclus). He has ventured too far, and will pay the consequences.

[66] King (1987) 24; cf. Moulton (1977) 113–14 on Achilles' temporary but absolute removal from society. Clarke (1995) 157 concludes that the psychological as well as visual assimilation of hero to beast – he analyzes the similar levels of *menos* – "is at its most evocative." Lonsdale (1990) 88 n.3 points out that *sintês* carries strong connotations of widespread, unlawful or sacrilegious destruction. In Homer it is used twice of lions (cf. 11.481) and once of wolves (16.353), always as an emphatic runover.

as supplication, burial, and oaths. Animals are simply enemies by nature –
they cannot speak, engage in reciprocal arrangements or share concerns
for their burial. His inclusion of men as one of the pairs of comparison
is significant in this regard. Even if one of the opponents is human and
therefore capable and desirous of making such arrangements (as is Hector),
the lion is by nature immune to such verbal entreaties and incapable of
responding in kind. In this duel, Achilles is proud to put himself in the
ranks of beasts, not only "glorifying in an extreme of heroism" with a suicidal
mania that indicates his abandonment of human values and society,[67] but
rejecting the value of speech itself that makes human community possible.
Achilles repudiates human language completely, telling Hector to shut up
and fight. Here, the customary pre-battle flouting that so often ends with
a "this is not the place for words, but deeds" takes a sinister turn. There
is no place for words at all, ever, in Achilles' vision of this confrontation.
This rejection of words is completely consistent with the animal imagery
Achilles takes on for himself – humans are a speaking species, and Achilles
wants none of it.

Achilles' removal from society is so complete at this point that even
Hector's martial similes render the Trojan impotent. As he rushes at Achilles,
he is compared to an eagle swooping on a hare or lamb. A similar image
was appropriate in the midst of Hector's *aristeia*, when he dashed at the
Greek ships like an eagle on fowl gathered on a riverbank (15.690–5). But
in Book 22 this comparison to an imminently successful animal attack is as
pathetically misleading as Hector's previous optimism. The poet switches
Achilles' imagery from the animal motif to the even more frequent fire
imagery. Achilles loses all connections with animal life of any kind in the
responding simile: "as a star gleams from the dark night, so did Achilles'
spear gleam in his hand . . ." (22.317–21). Here, the final animal simile of
battle, now applied to Hector, meets the final fire imagery as well (it is
the fourteenth and final time light/fire imagery is applied to Achilles in
Books 18–22[68]). Hector recovers his heroic animal imagery too late. He
had fled moments ago at the sight of the gleam of Achilles' armor (22.135),
and now, ready to fight like a bird of prey against a harmless waterbird,
he finds himself up against nothing more than a personified spear. Achilles

---

[67] Clarke (1995) 153; cf. Lonsdale (1990) 101, who connects this with the hunting imagery (see 21.251–
5, 21.573–80). Lonsdale (1989) 409 wonders if Hesiod's clarification of the moral of the hawk–
nightingale fable – that animals have no justice and so eat each other – is a reversal of the negation
of oaths by Achilles in this passage. Loraux (1995) 80–6 comments on the link between the animal
similes and the women in similes in the description of the meeting between the two heroes.

[68] Moulton (1977) 106–11.

has become just that, a weapon for vengeance. His shield and helmet had shone when he put them on (19.374–81), and his armor gleamed as he raced towards Troy (22.26, 22.135), but this is the first time his spear receives such a description. Achilles himself had raged with his spear (20.490) like fire, but now Homer focuses our attention solely on Achilles' weapon, a spear with a divine pedigree that will soon shatter Hector's neck. Achilles is beyond bestial venom and irrational animosity. He is vengeance itself, and not even animal images can fully capture this aspect of his inhumanity. Humans, after all, are animals in the Homeric world, and at the climax of his fighting Achilles shares little even with his speechless analogues.

Achilles' role in organizing and directing Patroclus' burial and funeral games partially reintegrates him socially, but only enough for the bestial imagery to become appropriate once again. He tells Patroclus' corpse that he has fulfilled his promise to drag Hector and give him "raw" (*ôma*) to the dogs to eat (*dasasthai*, 23.19–21). He still is treating Hector's body as animal flesh for other animals to ingest, although at least he no longer expresses a wish to be able to eat it himself. At the pyre, he slays four horses, two dogs, and twelve Trojans for the fire "to eat" (*esthiei*). Hector, however, will "be consumed" (*daptemen*) not by fire but by the dogs (23.181–3). Achilles himself is still consumed by eating metaphors – neither of these verbs is used elsewhere in the epics in this sense[69] – and he still stands outside human norms. Apparently, the "traditional" reintegration with his former world is insufficient to bring the epic, and thus Achilles' journey, to a close.

At the beginning of the final book, he is still rejecting most of the activities that make one human. In the eyes of the gods, his inhuman wrath has forced out all pity and shame. Apollo argues on Olympus that Achilles rages like a lion who attacks flocks in order to get a feast (*daita*, 24.41–5). As ancient commentators pointed out, this is the only use of *dais* for an animal's meal in the Homeric epics.[70] Achilles, at the beginning of the final

---

[69] Richardson (1993) ad 23.182–3. Morrison (1992) 83–92 shows that Homer, through thematic misdirection, has given the audience good reason to expect Achilles will in fact mutilate, rather than ransom, Hector's body. Hammer (1997) 13–21 argues that we see in Book 23 a new politics of mediation that reflects the incipient *polis* at Homer's time. There are connections between this vision of interdependency in the funeral games and the extension of it to the enemy in Book 24, but I think Book 24 is not so much about politics, and in several important ways is decidedly anti-*polis* in spirit; see below.

[70] Pfeiffer (1968) 111–13 argues that Zenodotus' famous reading of *daita* at *Il.* 1.5 (in Ath. 1.12e–13a) is "quite certain" for fifth-century MS, citing the parallels of Aesch. *Supp.* 800f., Soph. *Ant.* 29–30, and Eur. *Ion.* 504f. Whether he thinks it was an older reading or a later conjecture, Pfeiffer does not say. Redfield (1979) 104–10 argues persuasively (against the manuscript tradition) that we should accept Zenodotus' *daita* rather than *pasi* at 1.5. Thus, from the beginning of the epic we are informed of beasts doing a man-like thing, and so warned that the epic will explore the relations between man,

book of the poem, is still fully conflated with the beasts. He is a human acting like a beast (lion) who desires to engage in the human activity (feast) that is supposed to reaffirm the correct distance between men and animals (and gods as well). This conflation is extremely unusual in Homer, nearly Aeschylean in its complexity.

Apollo's words are carefully chosen. It is the "feast" that has been so perverted in Achilles' mind during the past few books, in his refusal to break bread with his comrades and his desire to leave Hector to be eaten by the animals, including his wish to become such a beast. The two worlds are still uncomfortably jumbled in the breast of the hero. The story of what happens to Achilles after this, in the opinion of most modern readers of the *Iliad*, forms the heart of the significance of the poem, the key to its greatness. Homer has brilliantly depicted Achilles' isolation by presenting him increasingly as wild animal and hungry scavenger, a potential cannibal living out his comparison to beasts in unique fashion. His new, more complex humanity emerges in the last book through the powerful combination of food and language. Achilles puts his linguistic skills to novel use, unwittingly yet profoundly transcending his culture's limitation of speech to public policy and status-seeking competitions.

INVITING PRIAM TO DINNER

The first unusual aspect of the encounter between Priam and Achilles is that the Greek hero not only listens carefully to Priam's brief autobiography, but he also obeys the king's request that he read himself into the story. Having suffered personal tragedy, Achilles weeps not only as a young man who has lost his closest friend, but also as a son who will never see his father again, and as a father-figure who only in death will share his life once more with Patroclus.[71] His response is to attempt to still the unavailing pain in Priam

---

beast, and god. This would be a powerful metaphor to find so early in the poem, especially in an unemphatic position in the verse. Fagles translates *daita*: cf. Rundin (1996) 188 n.19. West's recent Teubner edition (1998) has *pasi*, as does the text of Van Thiel (1996).

[71] On Priam as a surrogate father-figure, see Felson (2002) 46–50, with note 14 for references. Achilles' relationship with Patroclus is complex. Although Achilles is younger than Patroclus and in some way subject to his "fatherly" advice (11.786–9), in fact his feelings for his friend are more consistently described as paternal, in both his own words and thoughts (e.g. 9.323–7, 16.2–11) and the poet's (e.g. 18.318–23, 23.222–5); see: Lohmann (1970) 245–71; Moulton (1977) 101–6; Griffin (1980) 123–7 on the theme of the bereaved parent. Achilles has several more obvious parental figures, notably Phoenix. Finlay (1980) interprets Patroclus as something of a father-figure, and Mills (2000) sees an alternation between roles of protector and protected one; but see Held (1987) 246 n.9. Avery (1998) intriguingly makes Agamemnon the "third father" of both Achilles and Patroclus, for which relationship Austin (1999) 24–5 unnecessarily attaches "an oedipal component."

and in himself. And he does this in the only manner available, by trying to find a common humanity through the use of language. Achilles makes use of his uniquely powerful speech, applying the traditional genres of parable, autobiography, and mythological paradigm, but for a completely novel purpose. Ultimately, Achilles the lyre-player creates tales that attempt to understand and explain the apparent senselessness of life and stir in his enemy a similar acceptance of the universality of death and the necessity for endurance.

Achilles' speech to Priam, although falling into two separate conversations, can be divided into three thematically linked efforts at persuasion: parable, autobiography, and mythological exemplum. Autobiography is the standard stuff of Homeric speech, but parable and mythological exemplum are much less common. There are only three parables in all of Homer – Phoenix' account of the *Litai*, Agamemnon's tale of *Atê*, and Achilles' rendition of Zeus' jars (*pithoi*). Moreover, there are only four myths told by characters in the *Iliad* that are not personal, that is, that are not stories about the speaker or the person addressed (or a relation of one of them) or events witnessed by the speaker: Diomedes' tale of Lycurgus (6.130–40), Phoenix' account of Meleager, Agamemnon's story of Zeus and *Atê*, and Achilles' version of the myth of Niobe. Only those of Phoenix and Achilles are inversions of traditional myths. Only in the speeches of Phoenix and Achilles, then, do we encounter the combination of parable, mythological paradigm, and personal narrative. George Held has demonstrated the significance of the parallels between Phoenix's exhortation (9.434–605), Agamemnon's "concession" speech in Book 19 (19.78–144), and Achilles' conversation with Priam in the final book as the only three speeches in the epics to contain both a parable and a paradigm. This pattern is used, Held argues, to underscore Achilles' ethical and intellectual development.[72] It is not unreasonable to suggest that Achilles may have found his model for his speech – consciously or not – in his old mentor. The themes of Phoenix's personal narrative (the story of how he came to be at Peleus' court), parable (the Prayers), and mythological *paradeigma* (Meleager) all run parallel to the topics of Achilles' speech.[73] But in each case, Achilles alters the topics of Phoenix's narrative in significant ways that move his speech to another,

---

[72] Held (1987). At page 247 n.10, Held notes the threefold link between Phoenix's and Achilles, but he is most interested in the similarities between Phoenix and Priam. Achilles, in Held's words, develops into "a great speaker of words," the pupil becoming the teacher. I emphasize here rather the connections between Phoenix and Achilles, and differ slightly from Held on what exactly is myth and what personal narrative in Achilles' speech.

[73] Lohmann (1970) 121–4 points out the parallels between Priam's speech and that of Achilles, but admits that the tale of the two *pithoi* has no parallel in Priam's address. This is Achilles' spontaneous

more tragic and poignant level. He has been influenced by Phoenix, but he has learned from other speakers as well. And most importantly, he has his own tragic history on which to draw.

Phoenix's personal story, like that of Achilles, involves a variety of relations between father and son: Phoenix, who will never see his father again, is received by Peleus (Achilles' father) as a son, and in turn is cursed with childlessness. Consequently, he considers Achilles his own child. The differences between the autobiographies are even more revealing, however. Whereas Phoenix does not want to see his real father ever again, and worries that his "adopted" son will not gain glory in war, Achilles laments that he will never see his father again (he has often thought about his father, e.g. 18.330–2, 19.321f., 19.334f., 23.144f.) and grieves that Patroclus died while striving too hard for glory in war. In essence, Patroclus took Achilles' place, as Homeric sons are destined to do, and in dying failed to live up to his model and to obey his martial mentor.

Phoenix lives completely within the expectations of the heroic world. He sees honor through gifts given to a victor as the means to becoming a "doer of deeds." Achilles, however, now sees that the traditional means of gaining honor are ephemeral tidbits tossed out by the gods as they please. Priam's appearance with ransom for a dead son killed by Achilles is the perfect catalyst for Achilles' bitter realization of the universe's indifference which he so clearly expresses in the parable of the urns of Zeus.

While Phoenix's parable of the *Litai*, daughters of Zeus, emphasizes that the gods can be influenced by gifts, Achilles' tale of the urns of Zeus reveals man's helplessness in the face of an impenetrable system of divine "justice." Phoenix's parable lays out the sequence of events of the *Iliad* – wrath counteracted by supplication.[74] Achilles is trying not merely to

---

invention. For the thematic significance of the Meleager tale in the *Iliad*, see the thorough treatment of Alden (2000) 179–290. Sachs (1933) 24–5 sees parallels between Phoenix's use of autobiography, allegory, and paradigm and Achilles' tales, in that the autobiography is set against the paradigm. Deichgräber (1972) 69 finds parallels in the maxim, allegorical narrative, and *paradeigma*, and suggests that Achilles here has mastered Phoenix's technique, even becoming Phoenix symbolically; see also Andersen (1975) 192. Rosner (1976) presents a thorough list of parallels between Phoenix's life and that of Achilles, as well as between Meleager's tale and Achilles' situation, but does not examine the consequences for Book 24. Scodel (1982) applies, I think, an overly subtle interpretation of Phoenix's rhetoric. Yamagata (1991) provides a convenient summary of the connections between Meleager and Achilles in Book 9; see Zanker (1998) 82–4 on Phoenix as a model for Achilles' reconstitution of motives for cooperation. Noé (1940) 54–88 surveys the background of the story in an attempt to discover Homeric adaptations of a traditional tale; also Bremmer (1988). Now, on the Meleager tale in antiquity, see Grossardt (2001), especially 16–36 on Meleager's anger as a model for the anger of several heroes in the epic.

74 Still, the nature of this supplication in Book 24 could never have been predicted. Thus, Thornton (1984) 116–21 is only partially correct in finding a *direct* parallel between the two.

rationalize his own actions or prevent his anger from flaring up, but also to come to terms with the painful vicissitudes of life and the unpredictability of human affairs. And he does this in the unprecedented context of sharing his understanding with the father of his greatest enemy. He both connects this vision of divine apathy, or at least inscrutability, to the lives of Peleus and Priam, and embraces the truth that he himself is the cause of pain to both men. Achilles takes the burden of the human tragedy surrounding him onto his own shoulders. Having let Patroclus rush to his death, and as a past and future agent of the suffering of Priam and his sons, he will now fail to tend his father in old age. This heroic acceptance of responsibility contains the kernel of the tragic vision of life, matched in its power only by Achilles' insistence that they put an end to their lamentation. Nurturing one's misery accomplishes nothing. Life, with its attendant misery, must go on. This is ultimately the purpose of both the parable and the autobiography. There is no profit in grieving, he insists, emphasizing his point at both the beginning and end of his speech. Now they each are to let their sorrow lie quiet (24.522–4, 549–51).[75]

With the imminent release of Hector's body, Achilles suddenly comes to see the essential futility in overextending lamentation. How quickly he turns the gods' commands into a new personal philosophy! "Bear up. Don't lament endlessly in your heart. For you will accomplish nothing by grieving for your son, nor will you bring him back to life. Sooner you will suffer even some other evil" (549–51). His speech of consolation contains many of the *topoi* we later find in the genre. But what has given Achilles this insight? He is speaking as much to himself here as to his guest. The Greek hero is struggling to explain to himself the necessities of moving beyond his behavior of the past few weeks, to make the gods' command to return the body have some meaning. Unlike the pragmatic but in some ways too sensible Odysseus and Apollo, Achilles knows that there really is no end to lamentation. To suggest that one grieve for a day and then move on, as Odysseus does in Book 19 (a "mundane realism," as Davies calls it[76]), seems almost callous.

---

[75] I cannot accept interpretations, such as that of Scodel (2002) 211–12, that the urns of Zeus indicate that "Achilles completely ignores human responsibility." Humans often have little control over what actually happens to them – look at Peleus, who will suffer for no discernible reason. There seems to be no direct link between human behavior and how life turns out. This is plainly true. But Achilles does take full responsibility for his own actions and their consequences, for the deaths of Patroclus and Hector and the suffering these actions have caused. Achilles would not put it this way – although Aeschylus might – but he is in some vague way Zeus's agent, one of the lots tossed down for the two fathers.

[76] (1997) 108.

On the other hand, Achilles' excessive grief fueled by an inhuman anger brings no relief either, and his reaction has only brought more pain to others. What Achilles is coming to see is that the death of a loved one permanently alters the survivors. The *expression* of this grief, however, must have limits. As he explores these new ideas, he struggles also to find language that can adequately express his new understanding. As Richardson notes in his commentary (ad 527–33), the "language of the whole passage is untypical." In just seven verses, five words appear for the first time in Greek, along with one unique expression and a middle-form (*kuretai*, 530) that is found nowhere else in Greek literature. One of these new words, *boubrôstis* (532), does not appear again until Hellenistic literature, and has important connotations. When it does show up in later Greek, it means "ravenous appetite" or "famine." The scholiasts take it to be used metaphorically here as "great distress." Richardson notes that "ravening hunger" is possible, however, given the connections between hunger and the poverty of an outcast. I think it likely that Achilles is using the word in the context quite carefully. He is offering a chair to Priam and trying to get him to accept his hospitality in the form of a shared meal. In the course of this effort to understand, or at least accept, the ways of the gods and persuade Priam to eat with him, he observes that the fate of one upon whom the gods shower evil is to wander dishonored, driven by evil hunger. Here, he is subtly reminding the king of a worse fate that could have been his. For, as is clear from the narrative that follows, Priam and Peleus have received mixed blessings, gifts from both of Zeus's jars, not from the jar of evils only. In Achilles' mind, these are the only two options – no mortal is blessed with a completely happy life.[77]

We see here Achilles' first realization, or at least articulation, that eating is a sign of living life. The opposite, hunger, is associated with complete failure: loss of home, purpose (thus, a "wanderer"), and any honor from men or gods. Achilles realizes now, as his mother has just reminded him, that fasting is a sign of the rejection of life. Priam's continued refusal of hospitality, including eating (and sleeping), is exactly what Achilles has just been through and must now climb above. Achilles has already eaten. The food is not for sustenance – an empty table is present throughout the scene.[78]

It may seem that this reading is putting a great deal of emphasis on one odd word in the parable, and it is certainly unsound to suggest that any

---

[77] See Andersen (1975) 199–201 on Priam's mixed blessings.

[78] The Greek at 24.476 is explicit about this, a line that caused some problems in antiquity and was athetized (T).

passage with a number of stylistic or lexical oddities must reflect the poet's efforts to reveal a heightened and intentional use of language on the part of the speaker. There are many passages in Homer that have been singled out for some particular linguistic strangeness that do not seem to have any marked significance.[79] But the parable is part of a remarkable set of speeches, and I think it is worth our while to give the benefit of the doubt to both the hero and the poet.

One other "oddity" in the passage may help support this microscopic scrutiny. Achilles claims that the person on whom Zeus showers only gifts from the jar of griefs becomes *lôbêton* (24.531). What exactly does this *hapax* mean? This time we are better informed, because the word is related to several other words with the same root that appear twenty other times in the epics.[80] As Hainsworth (ad 9.387) observes, this is one of a number of locutions tied closely to the Homeric shame society that cares so much about the judgment and reactions of others (cf. *aischea, oneidea, elenchea*). The noun *lôbê*, he says, "expresses the construction put upon an action by one that suffers from it." On at least one occasion, it has a generic sense of humiliation at failure: Menelaus says that the Greek reluctance to answer Hector's challenge to one-on-one combat will surely be a *lôbê* (7.97).[81] More frequently, however, the word seems to connote the degradation that one feels when one is treated insultingly by the standards of the heroic code. Achilles calls his humiliation at the loss of Briseis a "heart-rending *lôbê*" (9.387) that Agamemnon must "pay back."[82] He also uses the verbal form to describe this shame Agamemnon has brought upon him (*lôbêsaio*, 1.232).[83] The word is thus linked with Achilles' initial reaction to his public abasement. His choice of its root in a novel form at the end of his epic journey is noteworthy in itself, especially given all the parallels between the first and last books of the epic scholars have remarked upon. But what has not been noted is that in every other reference to the root in Homer (sixteen times), the humiliation is limited to contexts of shattered hospitality or the failure to bury the dead. That the root shows up here at the climactic moment involving just these very themes warrants further investigation.

---

[79] To take just one example, the collection of linguistic oddities in Menelaus' speech in Book 13.622–39 has been considered grounds alone for excision from the text; see Shipp (1972) 282. Of course, this is part of the old analytical game that most scholars wisely tend to avoid these days.

[80] I leave out the two appearances of *lôbeuô* (*Od.* 23.15, 26), which means "to mock" or "to ridicule."

[81] Perhaps also *Od.* 24.433, where the parents of the dead suitors insist it would be a *lôbê* to leave the dead unavenged.

[82] On the meaning of this important phrase, see: Hainsworth (1993) ad loc.; Wilson (1999) 146.

[83] Thersites repeats Achilles' phrase (2.242) at the end of his attempt to humiliate Agamemnon, and in turn is called a "word-tossing humiliator" (*lôbêtêra epesbolon*) by the troops (2.275).

The root is most commonly associated with violations of hospitality, both the humiliation they bring on the assaulted individual and the consequent anger directed towards the violator. Menelaus, the paradigmatic victim of this kind of *lôbê*, uses both the verb and the noun to describe the injury done to him when his wife was stolen by the Trojans, men who had no fear of the wrath of Zeus *xenios* (13.620–39). The sons of Atreus are consequently sensitive to violations of hospitality of this kind. Agamemnon rejects the pleas for mercy from the sons of Antimachus by telling them that they must pay the price for their father's foul outrage (*aeikea tisete lôbên*). Antimachus had threatened to violate the guest–host relation by killing Menelaus and Odysseus when they visited Troy on an embassy (11.138–42). Agamemnon kills both of Antimachus' sons, slicing off the arms and head of one of them. Six of the seven appearances of the noun in the *Odyssey* refer explicitly to Odysseus' humiliation at the hands of the suitors or maids as they mistreat the newly arrived beggar (18.225, 347, 19.373, 20.169, 285, 24.326).

This specific connotation of the word also helps to explain its application to Paris in the *Iliad*. At 3.42, Hector is concerned not merely with his brother's failure to meet Menelaus in battle – the generic shame in a martial society – but that he is a *lôbê* for his role in stealing Helen. This insult comes after Hector has called him "most fair to look upon, mad after women, deceiver, how I wish you had never been born and had died unwed" (*agamos*, 3.39–42). Later, when Diomedes is wounded in the foot by one of Paris' arrows, he addresses the Trojan as "bowman, *lôbêtêr*, proud of your curling locks, ogler of girls" (11.385), conjuring up once again his role in the theft of Helen, as well as his unmanly fashion in fighting. This noun – an "agent of *lôbê*" – means one who shames others by violating some cultural norm, especially the guest–host relationship. The means by which he has done this to Menelaus and the Greeks is clear from the context.

The three remaining references to the root deal explicitly with burial, or more specifically, with the shame that comes from failing to protect a corpse. Iris tells Achilles that it will be *lôbê* to him if the body of Patroclus is mistreated (18.180). So Achilles is faced with a new source of humiliation that derives directly from his response to the original shame of losing Briseis. In the heated argument in Book 19 about reentering battle before or after eating, Achilles bids the Achaeans to do battle fasting and unfed – they can eat after "we have avenged the *lôbê*" (19.208). Achilles is specific about the source of this humiliation: now the dead that Hector had killed are lying mangled (*keatai dedaigmenoi*, 203–4), a situation he immediately links to the mangled body of Patroclus (*dedaigmenos . . . keitai*, 211–12).

The unburied dead are a horrific source of shame, particularly if their corpses are mistreated. Priam must now be suffering this same *lôbê*, then, since his son is unburied and, for all he knows and fears, terribly mangled. I think this sense of shame explains the strangely abusive tone Priam uses to address the mourning Trojans surrounding his palace. Although he is extraordinarily upset, impatient with those who are just sitting around as he has been doing, and no doubt frustrated with his own inaction and half-insane with inexpressible grief, this abuse of his own supporters is still unexpected.[84] As he leaves his palace, he drives his people from the portico with "words of reviling": "Get out, you disgraceful *lôbêtêres*. Haven't you enough to weep about at home, without coming to cause me misery?" (24.239–40). What does he mean here by *lôbêtêres*? The root has to do with shaming, with causing humiliation, especially with regards to the violation of guest–host relationships and the failure to bury the dead. The word was first applied in the *Iliad* by the Greek troops to Thersites (2.275). There, the generic sense of a "humiliator" is appropriate because he tried to shame Agamemnon in the assembly. He had in fact accused Agamemnon of shaming Achilles (repeating Achilles' use of *lôbêsaio*, 2.242; he closes his speech of blame by quoting Achilles exactly, 1.232). Thersites himself has violated the norms of council by reviling the leader so directly and from what appears to be a lower status than acceptable, and so he earns the label of *lôbêtêr*. Diomedes, we remember, called Paris a "humiliator" for violating the guest–host relationship and stealing a wife.

Now the Trojan king calls those grieving outside his door "humiliators" and accuses them of coming to cause him distress. His gibe is harsh, especially as the root of the word he uses to mean "to cause distress" (*kêdêsontes*) is the same one that so often means "mourning" in Homer.[85] How are the Trojans causing him shame? They obviously remind him of his own misfortunes, but in what specific way are they a source of reproach on him? Priam is noting that their mere presence, their obvious grief for Hector and the royal family, is a constant reminder that his son's body is not there to be tended to. That is why he refers to their own lamentation *in their houses* and it adds power to his odd question: "Do you take it lightly that . . . I have lost my son, the best one of all?" Of course they don't, but he sees them as a reminder of the further shame that he has not been

---

[84] Macleod (1982) ad 237–8 observes that Priam will in fact learn to share this grief with Achilles, the only person perhaps who can understand. Priam will have even more captious things to say to his surviving sons, those *kaka tekna* (24.253f.).

[85] Macleod (1982) ad 239–40. In classical Greek, the verb *kêdeuô* can mean to tend the corpse, that is, to bury; see Richardson (1993) ad loc.

able to bury his son.[86] So a translation for *lôbêtêres* such as Lattimore's, "failures," has the right connotation but the wrong application. It is Priam who feels like a failure, and the people whose presence reminds him of it.[87]

Priam, like Achilles, has felt shame and not merely grief at his inability to prevent what has happened to his loved one. One root for this feeling of humiliation is *lôb-*. When Achilles brings it up in a novel form in the parable, it has significance for both participants. Achilles suggests that the man on whom Zeus pours only griefs is one who is shamed. This root must conjure up the feelings of both men, since the word applies most directly to the man who has failed to bury the dead or to act hospitably. By returning Hector's corpse, which he has already announced he will do, Achilles is removing the shame from Priam. Priam's acceptance of Achilles' hospitality will restore Achilles as well. Achilles makes it clear immediately that only half of the parable need be relevant, since it applies to Peleus and Priam as analogues for the receivers of mixed blessings. Peleus, Priam, and Achilles need not be subject to the shame of failure any more. This realistic account of the way things are in an unsympathetic cosmos is meant to convince the king to see the need to accept his son's body, Achilles' hospitality, and the inherent tragedy of life.

Achilles is trying to use language to understand and express a new awareness of the way the world is constructed, but even more so to reach out and share this effort. In fact, these two elements are part of the same realization. Commiseration, sympathy, consolation, and courage to go on – these are our most human responses to our limitations, and they by definition require

---

[86] The phrase *ê onosasth'* ("do you take it lightly . . . ?") was Aristarchus' reading. The parallel at *Od.* 17.378, cited by Richardson, is helpful. There, Antinous asks Eumaeus if he "doesn't think it enough" (or "has made light of the fact") that while "they gather here and devour the property of your master, you invite this fellow [the disguised Odysseus] too." The phrase introduces a question that suggests the present behavior only aggravates a previous problem. So Priam sees the present public lamentation for the absent Hector as compounding his grief with shame.

[87] The word *lôbêtêres* has been treated by translators as a relatively neutral insult, apparently taking its meaning completely from the context. Looking at just four of the standard translations, we find the following range:

	Thersites (2.275)	Paris (11.385)	Trojans (24.239)
Lat.	braggart	foul fighter	failures
Fitz.	poisonous? clown?	(not translated)	craven fools? rubbish?
Lomb.	loudmouth	(not translated)	sorry excuses
Fagles	foulmouthed fool	big bravado	good for nothings

Applying a single term for each application violates the spirit of translation, of course. But by missing the connection with humiliation that seems central to the root of the word, these translations also slight the connection of the characters in these passages with the major themes of the poem.

a community that is larger than just oneself. It is all the more extraordinary that Achilles is reaching out to an enemy while exploring within. Priam's own suffering is directly relevant to Achilles and so forces him towards this effort. Their shared anguish for the moment links them in ways that outweigh their other differences.

Achilles' linguistic efforts to accomplish all this mark the turning-point in his journey from heroic warrior through berserk killer to the West's first reflector on a possible meaning of life greater than what is offered by the culture. But – and here's the rub – this magnificent piece of creative story-telling does not accomplish its goal! Achilles' speech has been unsuccessful once again. Priam immediately rejects his host's efforts at hospitality. The king's first words in response are "don't in any way me" (*mê pô m'*) – no verb is necessary to catch his impatience – and he asks for Hector's body in return for the ransom. He has missed Achilles' meaning and dismissed his effort. When he tells Achilles to accept the ransom so he can enjoy it and return to his land, he reveals grief-dulled insensitivity to what has just been said.[88] Achilles has been reflecting on the randomness of the gifts of the gods and the evanescence of both Peleus' and Priam's *aglaa dôra*. Moreover, the king has either ignored or misunderstood Achilles' parallels between Priam's fate and that of Peleus,[89] as well as his claim to have failed his father and to be *panaôrion* (24.540). Those of us who have watched and listened to Achilles throughout the epic will naturally want to translate this Homeric *hapax* as "doomed to die young." And correctly so, I think, but its meaning was contested even in antiquity. "Altogether despised" and "unlucky in all ways" would fit the context equally well,[90] and Priam has no way of knowing that Achilles is doomed to die within weeks. So Priam's response is understandable – his son is still unburied, "uncared for among the huts," and no one in the epic would think that mourning could end before burial. He is not in a position to reflect upon the meaning of his suffering as Achilles is, and he may simply not have the kind of heroic will to confront the abyss into which Achilles is now staring.

Achilles is incensed by this rejection. He "looks darkly" (*hupodra idôn*), a formula in speech introductions with a "decidedly minatory fervency" that indicates the speaker's anger at what he considers to be inappropriate words that somehow violate the rules of conduct between superiors and

---

[88] Aristarchus athetized 556–7 because of the apparent insincerity; see, however, Richardson's (1993) defense of the verses ad 556–8, especially as a parallel to the similar prayer of Chryses in Book 1. But my point is that it is poignantly insensitive here, quite intentionally so on the poet's part.
[89] Andersen (1975) 203.   [90] See Richardson (1993) ad 538–40.

inferiors.[91] The previous three appearances of the phrase all introduced Achilles' angry reponses to Hector: when he sees him for the first time on the battlefield (20.428–9); just before their duel, when Achilles rejects the possibility of any oath between them (22.254–9), and introducing his wish to hack off Hector's flesh (22.344). Its reappearance here signals his resentment for Priam, a startling return to the reality of the immediate disparity between suppliant and Achilles. He tells the king to avoid provoking him, repeating the same verb Agamemnon had used to his suppliant in Book 1 (1.32, 24.560). What in particular about the king's rejection of his offer of hospitality threatens to push Achilles into mistreating his suppliant?

Achilles' angry response has attracted much scholarly attention. Something seems to be going on here beyond the mere concern that his vengeful feelings might return upon thinking about what Priam's son had done to Patroclus. Typologically, the old man's refusal of a chair effectively rejects Achilles' hospitality, and thus the possibility of mediation this kind of scene implies.[92] Rejection of *xenia* of any kind is always a serious business. Commentators frequently suggest that Achilles seems upset that Priam has linked the return of Hector's corpse to the gifts, and the hero may want his decision to be viewed as independent of this incentive. If he is still playing the game of one-upmanship that some scholars have argued is central to gift-giving, then he is worried about the consequences of accepting the ransom and still remains very much interested in compensation. According to these readings, Achilles has really not shifted very much from his previous attitudes. He treats Priam with the same competitive spirit and pose of ethical superiority with which he handles Agamemnon.[93]

---

[91] Holoka (1983).

[92] Foley (1999) 171; see Minchin (1986) esp. 12–13 for a summary. Taplin (1992) 273 suggests that Achilles is saying it is better for Priam not to see the body or he might lose self-control; cf. 24.583–6.

[93] So, for example, Postlethwaite (1998), building on the work of Donlan (especially 1993) in gift-exchange. For a recent summary of the role of gifts in the *Iliad*, see Wilson (1999). Murnaghan (1997) 40–1 reaches a similar conclusion from a different approach: Achilles finds it necessary to deny that Priam's appeal inspired his own action, to admit that he gives in to paternal concerns, in order to stress what separates him from other mortals (as in his special connections to Zeus, rather than his commonality to other mortals). Van Wees (1992) 223–7 shows that there is no strong evidence, however, for Donlan's version of competitive gift-exchange. See also Thalmann (1998b) 259–71, although he agrees with the interpretation of the competition between Agamemnon and Achilles. Zanker (1998) makes a good case for Achilles' altruism as defined in the light of later discussions of the meaning and nature of altruism, even as the hero insists that his decision is independent of the incentive of gifts. More recently, Wilson (2002) 130–1 sees Achilles' acceptance of the *apoina* from Priam as an indication of his continued acceptance of "materially based *timê*" and thus a sign of his reintegration back into the community. I, however, do not see any "return to his *philoi*" depicted in Book 24. Instead, Achilles' comments consistently depict his heroic and isolated effort to make sense of the tragedy of existence as he has come to see it.

But the context suggests that Achilles is upset with Priam, although he may not understand the reasons clearly himself, because the king has rejected the effort Achilles took to find some closure through the creative use of speech. The "bestial" hero had made an attempt to reenter the human community through the most particular of human attributes, language. And this time his efforts were not to "defeat" an opponent, to taunt an enemy or prove himself superior in the assembly, but to persuade a suppliant and guest – and yes, the father of his greatest enemy – to set aside politics for the moment and be a partner in Achilles' effort to let their humanity reemerge. Achilles *needs* Priam in this sense more than vice versa. Priam's grief is great, but he knows what to do to address it: he must bury his son. It is Priam, however, not Achilles, who is still embedded in the traditional system of reciprocity. True, by insisting that Achilles take the ransom he deprives Achilles of some of the magnanimity of his gesture. But he also makes Achilles unsuccessful at persuasion one more time – an even more painful failure because this was a new, creative, and risky effort made for an unprecedented reason in an unparalleled context.[94]

So Homer tells us that at this specific moment, Achilles springs into action "like a lion," the final animal image associated with him in the epic. Lions have leapt before in the poem, always with death and a meal on their minds (e.g. 5.136–42, 5.161–2, 11.129–30, 15.630–6, 20.164). The exact phrasing of this particular leap, *leôn hôs alto*, is unique in Homer, but the two closest parallels (*ôrto leôn hôs*) are also the most inhuman: Agamemnon leaps on a suppliant and dismembers him in revenge for his father's outrage (*lôbê*, 11.129–30) – a nice reversal of the scene in Book 24 – and Achilles pounces on Aeneas (20.164). His anger forces him back to the edge of bestial violence, and the rejection of his efforts to become a "speaker of words" in some new sense nearly redirects him to become a savage doer of deeds once more.

Achilles' attendants take charge of Priam's horses and herald and then unload the ransom. This is a charged passage, as Homer informs us that Achilles is accompanied by two men whom Achilles honored above all others "after the dead Patroclus." They unyoke the horses and mules, an action that in reception scenes should come early on but must be postponed because of Priam's hurried supplication. Moreover, it leads nicely to the

---

[94] Hammer (2002b) 227–9 similarly argues for novelty in Achilles' actions in this scene, only from the perspective of promises. His promise to Priam is different from earlier ones because it does not rest on any possibility of getting something in return – he knows he will soon die.

unloading of the ransom "for Hector's head." But Achilles himself carries Hector's body out of the sight of Priam in order not to incite the old man, which could return Achilles to his bestial self by killing the suppliant. He would certainly be hated by the gods then, a *lôbêter* of the kind he is trying so hard to avoid becoming. The handmaids prepare the body; Achilles carries it to the bier, and it is lifted onto Priam's wagon. The emphasis throughout is on Achilles' unusual personal attention to details of the return of the body that are normally performed by attendants and members of the dead man's family.[95]

Now comes the unusual address of Achilles to Patroclus: don't be angry with me for returning the body, since I am getting gifts and I will see to it that you get your fair share (24.592–5). As Richardson notes in his commentary on this passage (ad 591–5), it is extremely rare to hear in the Homeric poems that the dead might require or even be aware of any offerings after burial. Moreover, what are we to make of Achilles' sudden interest in ransom (criticized even by Plato, *Resp.* 390e)? Are those readers correct who say that Achilles cared about the ransom all along but wanted to try to separate the gifts from the return of the body, so as not to be in Priam's debt? I don't think so, at least not completely. Achilles is explaining in traditional terms, within a system *Patroclus* would easily understand, why he is returning the body. He could simply note, of course, that Zeus has demanded the return. Perhaps that goes without saying. Ransom makes sense in its cultural context, but its strictly personal attachment to Achilles now seems insufficient. So Achilles adds the awkward clause about what it will do for Patroclus. The function of gifts, of course, has little to do with the dead after burial – such offerings are tangible sources of honor for the living, both to accumulate and to distribute as appropriate, even to the dead as they are interred. Achilles is clearly struggling. Why *is* he treating Priam in this way? Achilles here is talking to himself as much as to Patroclus – he is, after all, not at all sure the shade can hear him (592–3). Achilles finds himself acting in a fashion that even he does not quite understand. Zeus may require the return of the body, and Achilles may be interested in the ransom in some way, but there is absolutely no cultural or ritual mandate for Achilles to make extreme efforts to console the old man in his tent. Something new is happening within the hero. With the acceptance of the ransom and a final word to Patroclus, Achilles gives one last farewell to the past and steps firmly into his new world.

---

[95] See Richardson (1993) ad loc.

THE NIOBE OF ACHILLES

Reentering his tent and sitting down once again across from Priam, Achilles quite remarkably offers up yet one more tale, this time a mythological paradigm, to persuade the grieving father to accept his hospitality. This is a completely unnecessary step, at least as far as the gods' orders are concerned. The body has been returned. What happens now derives entirely from Achilles. And what he chooses to do is to speak, to create, to tell the famous and unusual version of the tragedy of Niobe that he (that is, Homer) has clearly adapted to fit the situation by emphasizing the seemingly inessential aspect of Niobe's eating. We can actually see Achilles at work here, manipulating a traditional tale for the sake of persuading his enemy to share a meal.[96] And, significantly, this new story works. Priam does not even reply. Achilles' invented narrative does the trick. A meal is prepared and shared, Priam's first since the death of Hector, and the first time since the death of Patroclus we actually see Achilles engaged in the ritual of preparing and eating a meal. The two enemies marvel at each other, Achilles now listening to the king attentively (*muthon akouôn*, 24.632) before sending him to bed.[97]

[96] For Homer's adaptation of traditional material, see: Kakridis (1949) 96–105; Willcock (1964); Gaisser (1969); Braswell (1971); Vivante (1971) 18–25; Austin (1978), and especially Alden (2000), who examines all secondary narratives in the *Iliad* and concludes that they all advance, or are related to, the main plot or an episode within it; see 292–6 for a brief summary of previous critical approaches to Homeric paradigms. On Homer's "contamination" of two versions of Niobe, see Pötscher (1985/6). Especially good on the uses of paradigm in general is Andersen (1987; 1998), with a cautionary note on suspected allusions to extra-textual matters in Homer. For attempts at advice or exhortation accompanied by an exemplum in the *Iliad*, see Howie (1995) 150–4. Nagy (1996) 113–46 argues against this critical consensus with his insistence that all mythological narrative already exists. The poet merely applies a particular extant variant to the present occasion; see also Lang (1983). But this is really not so significant a difference as it may seem. Even if the variant of the myth were available to the poet, the audience would still note the particular application of any specific variant, whether invented by the poet or merely applied. Finkelberg (2000) distinguishes between the written uniform text of the *Iliad* and the written multiform texts of other epics in the cycle, such as the *Cypria*; cf. Burgess (2001), who is excellent on invention and adaptation in the epic cycle, with Nagy (2001, 2002) in response to such criticisms. Edmunds (1997) 428–34 concludes that Homer presupposes his audience's knowledge of the entire myth. The audience in turn would note the speaker's application and find the implications extended beyond the speaker's intention. For the sensible suggestion of reverberation, that is, mutual attraction between tale and context, see Scully (1990) 144–7; similarly reasonable is the recent discussion by Scodel (2002) of "contextually bound" material (24–31) and "abbreviated narrative" (124–54).

[97] Lowenstam (1993) 131 notes that this is the first meal that appears to have meaning for Achilles, although we know he had eaten before (23.29–34, 23.55–6, 24.475–6). Seaford (1994) observes that Achilles' inconsistency, whereby he seems to end his abstinence on three separate occasions, arises out of Homer's desire to exploit the integrating power of feast with three different groups: the Myrmidons, Greek leaders, and Priam. Seaford places Homeric eating into its ritual context of the sacrificial meal as an effort to exclude potentially uncontrolled violence, especially in this case as it has been threatened against Priam.

How is Achilles successful? What does he do to persuade Priam to stay? One could argue that it was simply Priam's fear that kept him glued to his chair. Achilles' subdermally smoldering violence certainly reminds any listener that he is a doer of terrible deeds. But that possibility does not account for the positive reception of Achilles' message and hospitality that the poet so vividly recounts. What is Achilles after, and why is Priam's presence required?

Homer has drawn on different visit sequences in shaping this meeting. In the "typical" Homeric scene of the reception of the guest, the meal is served before any extended conversation takes place.[98] The only major exception to this rule is in the episode of Polyphemus in the *Odyssey*, a scene in which all the norms of Homeric hospitality are intentionally inverted and perverted as part of the overall theme of (in)hospitality and guest–host relations. In the final book of the *Iliad*, however, the apparent postponement of the meal is not a perversion of guest–host relations but is shaped by the sequence of elements found in supplication scenes, in which the suppliant naturally speaks first.[99] But even more importantly, the delay in eating is a dramatic necessity. The conversation, especially Achilles' speech, is absolutely required to come first, since his ostensible objective is to persuade Priam to share his hospitality. After the meal, the two men get down to the heart of their business, the determining of the truce for Hector's burial. Structurally, the scene focuses our attention on the hero's efforts to narrate a tale.

The hero told stories earlier in the epic, but for the most part they are relatively unimportant, applied allusively in a way that prevents Achilles from playing the role of storyteller.[100] In Book 1, he retells to his mother what has happened so far in the epic, adding the details of the acquisition of Chryseis after the sack of Thebe (1.365–92).[101] He then recounts his mother's aid to Zeus (1.393–412), his previously most persuasive speech in the *Iliad*, in that he convinces her to work on his behalf, thereby also supplying her with material to use in her own persuasion of Zeus. He briefly alludes to the parallel fate of Heracles (18.117–19) and his own heroic

---

[98] Macleod (1982) ad 596–620 observes that the scene requires the unusual postponement of the meal until after the conversation; see also Reece (1993) 12–39 for the sequence of events in hospitality scenes. He argues (123–64) that the two other possible exceptions, the reception of Odysseus and Telemachus by Eumaeus, are in fact special cases when an initial bit of dialogue takes place before the meal, after which the real tales are told.

[99] Arend (1933) 38; Edwards (1975).   [100] Friedrich and Redfield (1978) 278.

[101] Wyatt (1988) suggests that by hearing the story in Achilles' words, we sympathize and side with him. But the goal of his story is to bring destruction to his own comrades, not a particularly endearing ambition. Muellner (1996) 118–23 observes that Achilles reshapes the tale, but sees this in connection with the theme of *mênis* in the *Theogony*.

genealogy (21.187–9). These earlier attempts at storytelling thus do little to prepare us for the extraordinary creativity he exhibits in Book 24. He can tell stories, sing to the lyre, and is capable of finding mythological patterns to support his own actions, but he is much more likely to be persuaded by stories than to use them effectively.[102] Achilles, however, has learned to apply what he has observed about storytelling from others to a more profound vision of life. He in fact discovers how to create stories that are to be paradigmatic for himself, his enemy, and humanity in general.

Phoenix's long mythological tale of the battle of the Curetes and Aetolians was designed to prompt Achilles to accept the ransom and come back into battle, an effort at which Phoenix is unsuccessful, although Achilles does decide to think about leaving rather than departing straightway.[103] In the final book, however, Achilles uses a mythological tale for a completely different purpose. After Hector's body is placed on the wagon, Achilles returns to his tent and tells Priam that the next morning he can take his son away. "But now let us remember our meal, for even fair-haired Niobe remembered food." Clearly Achilles' choice to emphasize, of all things, Niobe's meal, is designed to persuade Priam to eat. But even more than this, the tale Achilles creates is a retelling of his own story, both for Priam's benefit and his own.[104] Here, too, is the story of a ruined family, the topic of their earlier speech and thoughts. Niobe lost all twelve of her children. Achilles responds to Priam's exaggerated lament that he has none of his fifty sons left, and that Hector was the last of 19 from Hecuba (24.490–506). Niobe in fact did lose all of her children, daughters

---

[102] Rabel (1997) 124–97 has argued that Achilles is uniquely persuaded by stories he hears, even the few he tells himself. He models his action in three separate phases of his wrath on three stories: his behavior in Book 1 on Chryses' story, in Book 9 on Meleager, and in Book 18 on Heracles. He lets these paradigms determine his conduct and shape his desires even when his emotions diverge from his self-chosen *exempla*, and the results are disastrous in each case. Only in Book 24, Rabel suggests, does he finally "act like himself," determining his actions according to his own inner character and personal conviction; see de Jong (2001b) for caveats on Rabel's approach. Pedrick (1983) makes the interesting argument that Nestor's paradigmatic speech to Patroclus in Book 11 is intended for Achilles but reaches the wrong audience, with calamitous consequences.

[103] On Achilles' "slippage," see Ebel (1972) 86–104, esp. 96. Whitman (1958) 191 suggests that Achilles decides to follow the Meleager parallels, to fight only at last and without gifts, in an ironic reversal of Phoenix's intentions; see also Rabel (1997) 133 and n.45. Or – worse – Alden (1983) 4–6 argues that Phoenix chooses the wrong paradigm and Achilles misinterprets it as well. For Phoenix's failure, see Brenk (1986).

[104] Segal (1994) 57: Niobe's tale is the "last great effort at self-understanding by this warrior . . ." Rabel (1997) 202–3 argues that Achilles unknowingly frames the completed story of his wrath with this tale, paralleling Book 1. For parallels between Chryses' supplication and Priam's as part of Achilles' attempt to interpret the events of Book 1 "as his own understanding of the events of the story grows and deepens," see: Macleod (1982a) 32–4; M. Clark (1998).

as well as sons, just as Peleus will lose his only son and as Achilles has lost Patroclus.[105]

Achilles specifies that the sons were killed by Apollo "in his wrath" (*chôomenos*, 606) at Niobe for making herself equal to Leto. This participle resonates with the main theme of the epic. It was Apollo *chôomenos* who brought destruction on the Greeks (1.44, 46) in answer to the prayer of the indignant (*chôomenos*) Chryses (1.380). The participial form is closely associated with divine anger, nearly half (14/31) of its appearances in the epics being applied to gods. The word is connected to the unrelenting anger of Achilles at key moments throughout the *Iliad* as well (1.429, 2.689, 9.107, 23.37). Phoenix uses the participle in both his personal tale of conflict with his father (9.463) and in his mythological exemplum to describe Meleager (9.555). Wrath contains the potential of becoming a hate that threatens to (and in Achilles' case does) go on hating too long. The last appearance of the participle comes in the chilling speech of Andromache towards the end of the epic. Holding the head of her dead husband, she laments that her son will follow her into servile attendance upon some ungentle master, or worse: with horrific prescience she wonders if some Achaean will seize him and hurl him from the wall, still angry (*chôomenos*, 24.736) that Hector had killed his brother or father or son.[106] Prideful anger in the epic ultimately destroys both enemies and loved ones in an endless cycle. Achilles' tale of Niobe reveals that he sees the waste in his own anger, even as he seems to accept that such human failures are tragically inevitable.

The unburied children "lay in their blood" for nine days, since Zeus had turned the people into stone. Apparently, Niobe could not perform the duties herself, for on the tenth day the gods themselves buried them. Here too, Achilles has included a detail in order to parallel the delay in Hector's burial and the role of the gods in assuring proper treatment of the bodies.[107] But the information about the transformation into rocks seems

[105] Andersen (1975) 215–16 suggests that another parallel here is that vengeful children (Apollo/Artemis, Achilles) kill children (of Niobe, Priam), the smaller number of children both times killing the greater number. While this is true, it puts Priam and Niobe in analogous positions, and I do not see any effort in Achilles' speech to vilify Priam. Andersen's treatment of the tale is the most complete, at least as an effort to place Niobe within the context of Achilles' journey (and, in particular, in the context of Achilles' understanding of the workings of the gods), although he sees little change in Achilles from Book 19.

[106] Macleod (1982a) ad 24.736–8 observes that this motive for Astyanax's death is not the one ever given in our extant texts. Homer is once again tying things together through the theme of wrath and its consequences.

[107] The sequence "for nine . . . then in/on the tenth" is a convention of oral tradition. It represents the pattern for the Trojan War itself (*Od.* 5.107, 14.241; cf. *Il.* 2.329, 12.15), and Homer balances the nine

unnecessary. Certainly, there could be other reasons for the delay in burial (in an alternate version, it was Niobe herself who was turned into stone from grief, a transformation that far better accounts for the unburied children). Yet Homer never explains what the people did to deserve this fate. In this analogy, which admittedly should not be pushed too far, Achilles and Priam are bound once again. Priam should have buried his son, but could not – this is the very source of shame (*lôbê*) Achilles is removing by returning the body.

But even more directly, Achilles finds his analogue in those petrified people who should have buried the dead but did not, thus necessitating the intervention of the gods. It is tempting to see their transformation into stone as Achilles' own reflection upon his inhuman transformation that caused him to treat Hector's body so shamefully. Perhaps in all this reflection upon his actions and his feelings, especially for Patroclus and his father, he recalls his friend's accusation of inhuman parentage when Achilles was so unmoved by the wounding and killing of his fellow Greeks: "Pitiless one, your father was not the horseman Peleus, nor was Thetis your mother, but the grey sea gave birth to you, and the steep rocks, for your heart is unbending" (16.33–5). Here, Achilles' birth is dehumanized, as his father's association with Mt. Pelion and his mother's with the sea are taken literally.[108] Now, in his attempt to assuage the intransigent Priam, he naturally thinks back to his dear friend's efforts to soften him. But it is worth noting that even the "gentle" Patroclus' intention was to incite Achilles back into battle, and failing that, to be allowed to lead the Myrmidons in his place. Patroclus' motivations, in other words, were perfectly consonant with the traditional concerns of speech in heroic society. Achilles, on the other hand, is now trying to find a place where human meaning can reside for a moment in the midst of the chaos surrounding him, for a great deal of which he is responsible.

days of plague and tenth of assembly at the beginning of the epic (*Il.* 1.54) with the burial of Hector on the tenth day (*Il.* 24.665, 785) at the end. Storytellers within the poems use the expression in their own tales. Odysseus applies it to four separate adventures (*Od.* 7.253 = 12.447; 9.83; 10.29; 14.314), the last of which is his invented autobiography. Even within the *Iliad*, the *topos* is applied to tales. Glaucus uses it in his account of Bellerophon (6.174–5), a story that Achilles does not hear. But he does listen attentively to Phoenix, who also uses the formula in his autobiography (9.470–4). Whether Achilles' application of the convention derives from Phoenix or not, the swift-footed warrior now shows himself to be a master of tale-telling technique.

[108] Andersen (1975) 218; cf. *Il.* 16.203f. Edwards (1987) 257 calls it "a kind of reversal of personification," and sees in it Achilles' confusion and eventual softening at Patroclus' bitter reproaches. Niobe's transformation into stone, with water flowing over the formation as her tears, has been compared to the image of crying with which Patroclus is introduced (16.3–4; cf. 9.14–15). Even in antiquity, the link between 16.3–4 and 16.35 was noted; see Janko (1992) ad 16.3–4.

After her children were buried, Niobe ate (*sitou mnêsat'*), for she was wearied with the shedding of tears (613). She needed sustenance, and her weeping was not over: even now as a rock she "digests the sorrows sent from the gods" (*theôn ek kêdea pessei*, 617).[109] The expression is used at only one other place in Homer, a mere twenty-two verses later. In Priam's first words to Achilles after their meal, he requests a bed to sleep in, for he had not slept or eaten or tasted wine since the death of Hector while he "digested countless sorrows" (*kêdea muria pessô*, 639). Homer chooses a gastronomical image to describe the grief that the two men can begin to come to terms with in their shared meal. Feasting and sorrowing, the cycle of life, are now to replace the previous Iliadic metaphor of digesting one's wrath. Calchas had introduced the image by asking Achilles for protection from a king who even if he can "swallow down his anger" (*cholon . . . katapepsêi*), will one day act upon it (1.81). Hector tells the Trojans not to give ground since Achilles is out of action, "digesting his heart-rending anger" by the ships (*cholon thumalgea pessei*, 4.513). Phoenix had used the same wording for Meleager, Achilles' paradigmatic double, as he "digested his anger" because of his mother's curses (*cholon thumalgea pesse*, 9.565). The idea behind *pessein* – bringing to maturity, cooking, digesting, and so "nursing" one's griefs or anger – is a slow percolation of an enduring object. Kirk (ad 4.513) observes that it implies absorption into the body.[110] Achilles' anger can be put away, perhaps, but the sorrows are eternal. Humans die, and Homer implies that there are two great advantages to this tragic truth:

1. Only in this way can life have any meaning (a topic that Odysseus' later adventures with Calypso bring home);
2. For most of us, unlike Niobe, our "eternity" is limited. Divine beings like Thetis and Achilles' horses face a literal eternity of sadness.[111]

The Niobe exemplum is a final reflection on this difference between gods and men, one that is subsequently played out in the rest of the scene. Even the verb Achilles chooses to describe the nymphs' dancing about Niobe's monolith poignantly demarcates the gods and mortals. When applied to

---

[109] Verses 614–17 were athetized by Aristophanes and Aristarchus for contextual and stylistic reasons, and some recent commentators agree (primarily because the lines intrude on a neat ring-structure). For a summary of these arguments, and their refutation as "groundless," see Richardson (1993) ad 599–620, 614–17; also Andersen (1975) 208–12, who unnecessarily sees Zeus as the unmentioned agent of Niobe's transformation; Schmitz (2001) 151–3. I hope my argument here adds further reasons for seeing the lines as thematically significant.

[110] I do not think the LSJ captures the correct connotations in translating it in these passages as "cool down." The only place that might be appropriate is at 1.81, with the compound *katapepsêi*, where it fits the context slightly better; see also Schmitz (2001) 152.

[111] Heath (1992a).

humans, *rhôomai* means to move swiftly, most often in the *Iliad* of warriors rushing forward (e.g. 11.50, 16.166). But when these nymphs move quickly, they dance (only here of the gods in Homer; cf. *Theog.* 8; *Hom. Hymn. Ven.* 261). Gods exist and play; humans live and die. Priam, in some ways, provides the means by which Achilles grapples with his awareness of this truth.

One might say that with the tale of Niobe Achilles demonstrates how much he has learned from others, and how radically he transforms that traditional purpose of speaking. He has watched the worst speakers at work, especially Agamemnon. In Book 19, Agamemnon had used a parable (*Ate*) with a mythological paradigm (the birth of Heracles) for the most selfish of reasons, to blame his behavior on divinely sent madness (19.91–136).[112] If Zeus could be blinded, how was he to be held accountable (he introduces the story by blaming Zeus, Fate, and the Erinyes, 19.87)?

Achilles has also watched the best speakers at work, Nestor and Odysseus, although neither had used a mythological paradigm.[113] Odysseus had spent a good deal of rhetorical effort in Book 19 in persuading Achilles that food was necessary, Achilles' task now with Priam. But Odysseus' efforts are completely pragmatic, as are all of Nestor's. Odysseus wants time for his men to eat so they can be strong and courageous in battle (19.155–72).[114] When Achilles replies that he wants the Achaeans to fight, "fasting and unfed" until they are avenged (19.203–8), Odysseus famously replies that it is not possible for the Achaeans to mourn a corpse with their bellies (19.225). And he criticizes Achilles' excessive grief: "But we must bury whoever dies and hold a pitiless heart, weeping for a day. And all who remain for hateful war must remember drink and food, so still more we can fight against our enemies, unceasingly" (19.228–32). Achilles now comes to see eating in a more profound way than Odysseus does, and he uses his skills at language for a more significant purpose than to persuade one to fight in what must now appear to him to be a senseless war.

It is hard also not to find here a deeper reflection upon the meaning of life and death, one final word on his new perception of the human condition.

---

[112] See especially Taplin (1990) 76–7, in whose eyes Agamemnon throughout the epic is a "nasty piece of work."

[113] Besides Phoenix, Agamemnon, and Achilles, only Diomedes narrates a non-personal mythological event (6.130–40), when he cites the story of Lycurgus' punishment for fighting with a god as the only reason he would not fight Glaucus. His *exemplum* is poorly chosen: he has in fact just finished jousting with two gods (albeit with Athena's permission and aid), and he will not end up fighting Glaucus at all.

[114] For Odysseus' speeches in Book 19, see Worman (1999) 35–9. Postlethwaite (1998) 98–9 sees Achilles' adoption of Odysseus' role as a recollection of Achilles' disregard for Agamemnon in that scene.

Odysseus, ever practical, sees that one must bury the dead, have a pitiless heart (*nêlea thumon*), weep for a day and move back to war. Achilles has clearly descended too far into his anger and pain, but his experience has taught him that one does not recover from life's tragedies so easily. In his tale of Niobe, the bereaved mother laments forever. This thematic detail helps to explain the oddity of Niobe's own transformation into stone in Achilles' tale.[115] The poet has most likely transferred the traditional petrifaction of Niobe and her children to the people of the town in order to make this version fit the new context: Niobe must live so that she can eat, and there must be some reason the children were left unburied (so there would be a parallel with the treatment of Hector's body). But the other variant of the tale seems to sneak back in when we learn that Niobe (for no obvious reason) has at some later time also been turned into stone in the mountains, where she can apparently still be seen "digesting her sorrows." Achilles, however, knows what he is doing. The grief is not over – it is never really over. Priam is to eat, and then when he gets home he can lament (*klaioistha*, 619) more for his son, a source of many tears (620). Food for Priam, for Achilles, for us all, is a break between lamentations. Thus, Achilles says that the king will suffer "some other evil" rather than bring Hector back to life (24.550–1). Food is sustenance for endurance, an opportunity for moments of reintegration and renewal between life's inevitable tragedies. The war will go on (this is their next topic of conversation). Achilles and Priam will die without having fully recovered from their losses, and their loved ones will be left to grieve. The *Iliad* ends amidst Trojan mourning and feasting. This lamentation reminds us not merely of the sorrows of the past, but of the ravages of the future, the fates of the "survivors" so well-displayed in Greek tragedy and outlined in the mourning of Helen, Hecuba, and Andromache that fills the rest of Book 24. The final image of the *Iliad* is the funeral feast of Hector. After that, there will be more war, more death, more lamentation.

All of this will take place while the gods continue to "dance" in their limited and timeless condition. Niobe is eternalized only in death and only in sorrow, placed quite intentionally (and uniquely) in Achilles' version amidst the "beds" (*eunas*) of the nymphs (614–16). The gods one last time

---

[115] See especially Seaford (1994) 174–5. He places this scene in the context of the integrative power of lamentation and death ritual. For Homer's manipulation of the tale to fit the scene, see Kakridis (1949) 101. He suggests, wrongly I think, that Homer transfers the traditional petrifaction of Niobe to the people so Achilles might be able to justify his cruel abuse of Hector's body, since the gods allowed the corpses of Niobe's children to remain unburied for the same number of days. But here the gods step in because Niobe does *not* bury her children, and no one else can – this hardly exculpates Achilles; see next footnote.

form a foil for Homer's – and now Achilles' – vision of life. When the gods quarrel, they face no consequences. At the end of Book 1, Zeus and Hera are asleep in their bed. The "bed" (as well as food), as Thetis reminds her son the last time she speaks with him in the epic, is good (24.128–31). The bed is a place for sleep and sex, two wonderful if potentially dangerous necessities of human life: joy, respite from the toils of existence, and the potential for immortality through offspring. The final image we have of Achilles, we are often reminded, is in his bed alongside Briseis (24.675–6). But this picture remains full of ambiguity, in sharp contrast to the unnecessary rest and fickle sex of the immortals. Homer tells us that Achilles sleeps in his tent, lying with "fair-cheeked" Briseis (24.675–6). Verse 675 is repeated from the end of the failed embassy scene (9.663), where Achilles goes to sleep in his tent next to "fair-cheeked" Diomede. So the poet reminds us here at the end of Achilles' journey of the quarrel that began it all – he is back with Briseis, ready once again to fight against Troy. Achilles' loss, though, still hovers over the scene. In Book 9, the very next sentence after the reference to Diomede had emphasized the closeness of the hero with his best friend: "Patroclus lay down on the other side." Patroclus' absence in the tent in Book 24 is felt in the missing three words.[116]

Some scholars see the last book of the epic as a "salvation" of the gods, who appear here "as what they are throughout the *Odyssey*, the guarantors of justice and kindness among mortals."[117] But these are not really "gods who care" and Homer does *not* focus on the power of "Priam's supplicating prayer" that "bends even fierce Achilles."[118] The gods care about their honor (Achilles always listens to them), their privileges (Hector honored them with sacrifices), appropriate ritual (the treatment of Hector's corpse, which Apollo refers to as "mute earth" 24.54), a measured (e.g. human) response to tragedy (Achilles must relent), and avenging their own petty humiliations (Hera's unrelenting hatred of Troy, e.g. 4.31f.). They do not pass judgment on whether something is "just" in any large sense in human life. Zeus has a vested interest in guests and oaths in general, but even this divine concern

---

[116] Richardson (1993) ad loc. Taplin (1986) 17–18 notes the significance here of Diomedes' replacement by Briseis, and her similarities with Chryseis, Andromache, and Helen. This also ties in nicely with the discussion by Clarke (2001) of the meaning of the participle *epikertomeneôn* (24.649) describing Achilles' tone in telling Priam to sleep outside: these "heart-cutting" words reveal the unresolved psychological tension and dark, half-hidden emotional current still running through the angry hero.

[117] Macleod (1982a) 15; cf. Richardson's approval (1993) 22–4; Lloyd-Jones (1983b) 1–27; the critique of Griffin's (1980) fairly positive conclusions about the gods by Rose (1997) 190–1, although I do not see Homer's picture of the gods as a critique of the "ideological [e.g. aristocratic] bias of the epic form." Again, I believe the ending of the *Iliad* transcends the political (at least as Rose means it).

[118] Lateiner (1997) 268.

is not emphasized by the poet as it is in the *Odyssey*. In the *Iliad*, even supplication operates strictly on the human level and depends upon custom and human sanctions, not the divine, as opposed to in the *Odyssey*, where Zeus may appear as an upholder of a suppliant's appeals.[119] Achilles shows no confidence in the gods at all by the end of the poem. His tales of Zeus' jars and Niobe's eternal grief make that clear. We do not have here a celebration of just gods, at least as developed in the main action of the epic. True, we learn in one simile that Zeus punishes those who give crooked judgments and "drive out justice" by wiping out their crops (*Il.* 16.384–92), but this possibility is left out of the epic's main moral themes.[120]

But neither is Niobe's petrification "an eternal indictment of the injustice of the gods."[121] Both these extreme readings are too easy, too comforting, one nurturing the Judeo-Christian yearning for a theology that somehow justifies the misery of life, the other reading a modern sense of alienation into a very different sense of religion found in the poems. The *Iliad* emphasizes the tension and inherent ambiguity in the real world, an ambiguity that the *Odyssey* ultimately does not countenance.[122] The gods reveal an indifference

---

[119] Pedrick (1982).

[120] Yamagata (1994) 22–7, 61–92 analyzes the significance of this simile in detail. Her study of justice in Homer, including the *Odyssey*, reveals that Homeric men know for certain only that the gods will take action against those mortals who injure their honor. The characters believe, however wrongly, that the gods reward the righteous and punish bad ones. Winterbottom (1989) arrives at a similar conclusion, that even in the *Odyssey* Zeus is less active in the punishment of wrongdoing or in aiding the good than humans fear or hope. My study of Achilles in Book 24 suggests that his attitude is closer to that of Homer than other characters. The simile at *Il.* 21.522–4, which is sometimes used to support the view of just gods, does not do so. We are not told the reason for the angry gods' destruction of the city; see Janko (1992) ad 16.384–93 on the inappropriateness of the passage.

[121] Rose (1997) 190. Similarly, I find it hard to accept Gould (1990) 90–103, the interpretation of justice in the *Iliad* (and elsewhere) as a view summarized by "life is unfair." Gould thinks this dismissal enables the characters to avoid self-blame. Thus, Achilles, for example, is not responsible for his own unhappiness, and can earn our sympathy. But Achilles does see himself as responsible, both for his own and for Priam's unhappiness. And the vision of justice is not that "life is unfair," but that "life is neither unfair nor fair." The universe is not hostile; it is indifferent. A huge difference, that. Edwards (1987) 320 finds a brilliant parallel in a poem of Stephen Crane:

> A man said to the universe:
> "Sir, I exist!"
> "However," replied the universe,
> "The fact has not created in me
> A sense of obligation."

[122] Cook (1995) 38–46 nicely distinguishes the connection between justice and the gods in the *Iliad* from that of the *Odyssey*. He suggests that the *Iliad* suppresses part of a common thematic stock that is picked up by the *Odyssey*, especially that divinity absolves itself from responsibility for evil and hence from suffering. Kullmann (1985) believes that the concepts of justice in the two poems are so incompatible religiously that the epics cannot be by the same poet, but he too rejects the familiar argument that the concept of justice progresses over the two epics. Instead, we have two contradictory traditions that are drawn upon for different thematic purposes.

to the very issues we humans take so seriously. If the gods do care, then there is all the more a mystery, for it seems like so many rolls of the dice, or lots shaken from a jar or two.

Achilles' masterful piece of storytelling not only depicts these differences, but this very act of creation makes him more human than anyone else in the epic. His has exercised our unique gift, speech, in an act of consolation while simultaneously exploring what it means to be human. In this, Achilles supersedes all speakers in the *Iliad*. His new technique of persuasion is successful at accomplishing a task he could never have dreamed of when Peleus handed him over to Phoenix to learn to be a doer of deeds and a speaker of words. He has done his tutor proud, although his success in speech has shown him exercising a penetrating vision of humanity rather than persuading his colleagues to a course of action and exercising quotidian authority.[123] And in accepting the suppliant before him, Achilles does in fact fulfill Phoenix's request in Book 9 to yield, albeit in a very different context.[124] He is maturing quite conventionally by stepping into the shoes of his father, who accepted both Phoenix (9.478f.) and Patroclus (23.85f; cf. 11.765f.) as suppliants.[125] In the course of his honest confrontation with mortality, Achilles reveals a compassion that makes him the most tragic of dramatic heroes. A part of that journey is his learning to apply the most human of characteristics, language, to something larger than himself and the glories of war of which he once sang. Achilles' verbal art transcends the boasting, taunting, and tactical advising of his compatriots. By becoming a storyteller, affirming life while discovering sympathy for suffering, Achilles aligns himself with humanizing power of the poet himself. And vice versa, of course.

What keeps man from constantly devolving into the bestial? The *Iliad* suggests that heroic nature itself brings with it the risks of losing touch with the human, especially in the madness of anger and battle. Community

---

[123] Hammer (1997) 22 has summarized the movement of persuasion in the epic as "from an Achilles whom, as Agamemnon confidently proclaims, no one will obey, to an Achilles who is listened to and obeyed." I think that this is more significant in terms of Achilles' tragic understanding and less about the institutions and formal procedures of the human political animal. Achilles is beyond that, in both the good and bad senses. Howie (1995) 165–6 draws a more poignant comparison, it seems to me, by suggesting that the interview with Priam raises Achilles to the level of a speaker in a piece of wisdom literature.

[124] Kim (2000) 150–1 suggests that Achilles' pity for Priam corresponds to Phoenix's appeal to pity his *philoi*, except that his definition of *philoi* has been redefined to include all humans, bound as we are by death and suffering.

[125] Peleus is one of the few in the epics to be called *agorêtês* (7.126); see Crotty (1994) 24–41, who argues that Peleus inculcates values through maxims and thus reveals the importance of the father's imparting of the warrior ethos; cf. Schlunk (1976). All three father-figures in Phthia – Peleus, Phoenix, and Patroclus (who is father, brother, and son) – are linked here at the end.

standards play a role in trying to keep any individual from gaining so much glory or confidence that the barriers between species collapse. At the same time, it is just this individual glory that the community demands. Homer is critiquing the very system he has designed in his poem. His "shame" society leads inherently to the possibility of losing one's humanity. But it is also the greatness, the sheer magnitude of Achilles, that both pushes him over the edge and also restores him. By creating a new purpose for his ability with language and exercising it so powerfully, he not only brings Priam back to humanity but explores the hollowness of life without giving in to it. It is, after all, a heroic act of human will, not the gods, that salvages Achilles in the end. Poetry, Homer ultimately implies, may be our most human act.

The *Odyssey* seems more classical in its emphasis on the importance of culture in its various manifestations, one of which is language. Odysseus is reintegrated into human life by learning how to control his speech, and Telemachus grows into a fully human life by doing the same. Here, language finds its place in the community. But the community, not quite yet a polis, does not in itself make humanity possible. The focus is still on the hero, the single individual maintaining a position of authority through the correct manipulation of his language. Speech is not yet the tool of society that makes humanity possible – or that monitors status in the city-state. It is to that world we must now turn.

PART II

Listening for the Other in classical Greece

CHAPTER 4

Making a difference: The silence of Otherness

In Part One I argued that in our earliest evidence for Greek thinking about the nature of man, the ability to speak is what makes us human. Oral mastery and control of language are the essential features that define humanity. This linguistic differentiation is literal in the case of animals – they don't talk and we do. This simple fact of nature is then used metaphorically to distinguish other categories of human status: men and women, humans and gods, the living and the dead, Greek and non-Greek, the young and the old, the heroic and the rest of us.

In Part Three we will take a close look at two classical authors for further reflections upon the connection of bestial silence with human speech and status. But first we need to make a more general survey of what happens to this connection in Greece after Homer. We will find that the basic differentiations uncovered in the epics are not entirely *invented* in the classical period, but are more carefully and systematically *applied*, especially in Athens. This review will necessarily lead us through some familiar terrain. Although the Other may have been muzzled in classical antiquity, recent scholarship on the topic certainly has not been. My analysis differs from most previous studies, however, in its two primary theses:

1. Control of speech is central to *all* Greek hierarchical thought about status;
2. This emphasis on speech as the primary criterion of differentiation between groups supplied the very tool by which the status of "muted" members has been so drastically improved in modern Western culture.

SILENCE

Although many studies have examined the classical Other from various points of view, none has seen the speechlessness of animals as a primary metaphor that defines and sustains the various polarities. An excellent recent study of the cultural significance of silence in Athens, "the land of *logos*," makes no mention of animals in this context.[1] The most thorough surveys of women's language and silence in Greece include not a word about this connection with animals.[2] The best account of the development of the Greek concept of the barbarian is likewise wholly without a reference to the link between barbarians, animals, and language.[3] And a recent examination of the relationship between women, children, slaves, and barbarians in Greek anthropological thought makes no mention of animal silence.[4] But the various categories of Other are intimately linked by their cultural definition as non-speaking beings. Once they are perceived as being deficient in *logos*, in its basic sense of speech, they can be assumed to be lacking rationality as well. (This is, after all, why many people still feel certain that all non-human animals are *alogoi*.) They are associated, that is, with the basic category of bestial Other.

This is by no means to suggest that these categories were always kept distinct in the Greek mind, or that the silencing of an individual or group was consciously felt to be a demotion to the realm of the animal. What was really at stake was a reduction of human status – the silence of animals supplied the original metaphor that continued to fuel Greek ideas of difference. There was a fluidity and overlap between categories, a protean structure that could be applied variously in different contexts. Otherness is, if nothing else, dynamic and flexible. After being bitten in a wrestling match by Alcibiades, an opponent scornfully accused him of biting "like a woman." Quickly redefining the category to his own advantage, Alcibiades replied, "No, like a lion" (Plut. *Alc.* 2.2).

The various groups usually discussed under the rubric of Other are consistently linked in the classical sources. Women, slaves, children, and barbarians are often associated in Thucydides.[5] In the ethnographical descriptions of Herodotus, women are frequently connected to barbarians.[6] Slaves and women, as well as foreigners, are also connected in their exclusion from the

---

[1] Montiglio (2000).   [2] McClure (1999); Lardinois and McClure (2001).

[3] Hall (1989). However see Buxton (1982) 61–3, who makes the following useful analogy: Greeks : barbarians :: mankind : beasts :: *peitho* : *bia*.

[4] Sassi (2001). A partial exception is Nye (1990) 58–9, who observes in passing that in Aristotle the rationality of natural rulers is continually defined in opposition to unacceptable speech of women, slaves, barbarians, and those who perform manual labor; still, animals somehow seem to slip out of the actual analysis.

[5] See Wiedemann (1983) and the list in Harvey (1985) 73–8. Browning (2002) surveys the general approach taken by Greeks to Others from antiquity to the Renaissance.

[6] For example, Greeks record that in despotic Asia women are subjugated, and in Libya and Northern Europe women are promiscuous and have intercourse in public "like cattle"; see Rosellini and Saïd (1978); Walcot (1978b) 145–7. Dewald (1981) argues that barbarian women in Herodotus observe and transmit cultural values, and limits, that the Persians habitually violate; cf., though, Loraux (1995) 226–48.

Athenian "men's club."[7] Women, Persians, and catamites even *walked* the same way, as far as the Greeks were concerned.[8] Plato consistently links children with women, slaves, and animals. Aristotle – beyond his infamous denial of full rational capacity or authority (*logistikon*) to women, slaves, and children in the *Politics* (1254b, 1260a) – frequently lumps together these various groups of Other with animals as well.[9] Metics, as resident aliens, were often foreigners and of servile origin.[10] One of the cultural functions of such mythological hybrids as satyrs, Centaurs, and Amazons – creatures at the edge of the known world, where the sexual, cultural, and species poles collapse – was to articulate some general vision of Otherness in an effort to explore what it meant to be a Greek, or sometimes even more specifically, an Athenian citizen.[11] And critics of Greek rationalism, like Euripides, virtually made a living out of pointing out how fluid the boundaries were, and how easily they could disappear.[12]

What has made the various groups of the Other of particular interest to modern scholars is their status: they were not considered to be – or treated

---

[7] Vidal-Naquet (1986) 206–17.   [8] Bremmer (1991) 20–1.

[9] For Plato, see: *Clit.* 409d–e; *Ep.* 8.355c; *Leg.* 4.710a; 7.808d–e; 12.963e; *Resp.* 4.431c; 441a–b; *Tht.* 171e, and Wender (1973). Socrates never denied the polarities, but argued that most people had made sloppy divisions (e.g. *Polit.* 262d–e); see Rist (1982) 26–32; Thesleff (1984) especially 25–29. One of Plato's greatest contributions was an additional duality, that between philosophical life and all others (that is, experts and non-experts; see Chapter 6). There is no need to rehearse here the hierarchical aspects of Aristotelian biology. On women and biological differences (e.g. women as inferior by nature, mutilated males, errors of nature, monsters, infants, unfinished males, etc.), see: Clark (1975) 206–11; (1982) 189; Horowitz (1976); Lloyd (1983) 58–111; Saïd (1983b); Spelman (1983), who challenges Fortenbaugh's argument (1977) 137–9. On differences between man and animals, see: Introduction and Fortenbaugh (1971); Clark (1975); Lloyd (1983) 18–57. On animals and Others, see Baldry (1965) 88–101; Vegetti (1979); Sassi (2001) 82–139. Hughes (1975) 119–22 argues that Aristotle built on a Greek attitude toward nature as a theater of reason. The natural world operates according to rational principles in a dependable manner, and the human rational mind can come to understand it. Hughes suggests that the view can be traced back to Presocratics, but Aristotle gave it an anthropocentric and utilitarian spin.

[10] In addition, they suffered from the low reputation of all laborers (*banausoi*); see Whitehead (1977) 109–24. Németh (2001), however, notes that metics were socially stratified, of diverse origins (although most were Greeks) and occupations. Still, they could not own property, and were excluded from most aspects of civic life.

[11] The Amazons were even considered to be flesh-eaters, and had a language so difficult that no man could learn it (Herodotus 4.114.1–2; Aesch. *Supp.* 287; cf. Diod. Sic. 3.53.5); see: duBois (1982); Tyrrell (1984), and especially Hardwick (1990). On the other hand, they never managed to master the Scythian language (Herod. 4.117). For Centaurs as hybrids, see Auger (1996).

[12] Segal (1978) points out how the threatening aspects of Dionysus represent the ambiguous place between human and bestial realms where there is a dissolution and confusion of basic polarities. Dionysus is both god and beast, Greek and foreign, male and female, neither child nor man. Medea is similarly Greek and non-Greek, female and male, animal and human, human and divine; see McDermott (1989). Thus, although I agree with Sourvinou-Inwood (2003) 297 that Euripides is articulating criticisms and fears felt in real life, I do not see the playwright giving "positive, reassuring, albeit complex, answers."

as – the political, social, psychological, or physiological equals of free male citizens in the polis. Scholarship on each group has tended to evolve from an interest in recovering what can be known about a particular group to a more overtly political agenda. Here, the Greeks, classical scholars, and subsequent Western culture may be reprimanded or even condemned for creating and perpetuating this subordination.[13]

But this subordination is endemic in the ancient world where women, slaves, and foreigners were universally treated as outsiders in some fashion. I am curious about the ideas and images that were used to connect these groups, what concepts bound the various categories in the Greek mind that could define and nurture the subordination. Linking *all* marginal groups in Greece was the lack or deprivation of authoritative speech. All except animals of course *could* speak, but they were each thought to have a language disability of some sort.[14] There was something wrong with their speech, either their grasp of Greek itself, or their control of it, or their ability to use it rationally or truthfully. In return, cultural norms prevented them from speaking in any public, autonomous, and authoritative way. As Montiglio concludes in her study of the meaning of silence in Athens, the Greeks identified reduced speech with silence. A partial, timid, or ineffective use of language was identical to possessing no language at all.[15] Thus, the traditional attitudes reinforced what was felt to be a natural deficiency, and vice versa. At this point, we cannot unravel the origins of Otherness, but we can see how the system reinforced itself. Women, for example, were politically silent because they were not allowed to speak publicly; they were publicly silent because they had no political role. I am not interested in which is the chicken and which the egg, but rather why both are eaten.

PROGRESS

By placing speech at the top of an admittedly long list of abilities and characteristics that differentiate humans from animals, and thus humans from other humans, the Greeks actually made it possible to challenge this very differentiation. *All* ancient civilizations had various ideological and institutionalized processes of inclusion and exclusion. Otherness studies frequently cite a late anecdote – variously associated with Thales or Socrates –

---

[13] Such criticisms are often couched in a heavily encoded patois of words like "carnophallogocentrism," e.g. Wood (1999) 33.

[14] For dumbness as a physical disability (e.g. Croesus' famous son in Herodotus 1.34, 85), see Garland (1995) 96–7.

[15] Montiglio (2000) 84–5.

as an aphorism of Greek hierarchical thinking. The philosopher used to say that he was thankful to Fortune for three blessings: that he was born a human and not a beast (*thêrion*), a man and not a woman, and a Greek and not a barbarian.[16] (The first of these godsends – what actually turns out to be the most crucial – is rarely commented upon in modern scholarship, no doubt because it is deemed to be both obvious and inoffensive.[17]) But what man from any ancient Mediterranean society would *not* have wished to be born a male and a member of his own culture? Solomon? Khufu? Cyrus?

The important thing about the Greek Other was that this Hellenic form of categorical thinking was part of a larger, more open-ended effort at self-definition than found anywhere else, and it focused on the effective use of reason and language:

> This activity of judging and choosing, and the very idea of it, is a Greco-Western activity and idea – it has been created within this world and nowhere else. The idea would not and could not occur to a Hindu, to a classical Hebrew, to a true Christian, or to a Moslem.[18]

The consequences of this Hellenic self-exploration were and continue to be revolutionary. In Athens, as we will see, the ability and opportunity to express one's opinions – freedom of speech – became the equivalent of freedom itself. Disagreement – that is, *difference* – is built into the Western paradigm provided by the Greeks. The centrality of speaking – even when it includes saying something that goes against the majority opinion – in the definition of what it means to be human, has two conflicting consequences. First, status can be determined and maintained by granting or denying individuals or groups access to speech. But it also means that speech can be used to argue against the second-class status of any particular group traditionally denied speech and full humanity:

> For the mass of [Athenian] citizens who listened, judged, and voted, *parrhêsia* [the right to speak freely] fostered a critical attitude and a sense of intellectual autonomy, and so became the frontline defense against flattery, bullying, corruption, deception, or incompetence on the part of the speakers. *Parrhêsia* also allowed any member of the demos, be he as inconsequential as Thersites, publicly to expose

---

[16] Diog. Laert. 1.33. Plutarch (*Mar.* 46) says that Plato on his deathbed praised his *daimôn* and Fortune that he was born a man and Greek, rather than an *alogon* beast or barbarian; he adds that he is grateful to have been born while Socrates was living.

[17] Sassi (2001) 34–53 with note 1 is an exception, although she explores the links with animals only through the Greek interest in physiognomics, the "science" of deducing character from physical characteristics.

[18] Castoriadis (1991) 87; cf. Kennedy (1998) 138: "As in non-literate societies, rhetoric in the ancient Near East was primarily a tool of transmitting and defending traditional political, social, and religious values."

the misbehavior, dishonesty, bad counsel, or incompetence of anyone, however powerful, who threatened the integrity or well-being of the community.[19]

This was the ideal, of course. Much of Greek literature examines the sub-tleties, paradoxes, and perversions of this ideal. Free speech can just as easily be used to hide the truth as pursue it (as Achilles tells Odysseus), not for the good of the community but for personal power (ask Aristophanes), for expediency and empire rather than justice (so the Athenians admitted to the Melians), to entice to slaughter rather than to unravel wrongs (consult almost anyone in Euripides), for unfounded opinion rather than criti-cal inquiry (so Plato repeatedly demonstrates); in other words, to oppress rather than liberate. Yet the ideal remained the stick by which actions were measured.

So although the Other was deprived of a public, authoritative voice in ancient Greece, in a Western culture that inherited some expectation of dissent and critique, both iconoclastic male and bold female voices could be raised in protest. In the modern Western world, women are approach-ing political and economic equality; slavery has virtually been abolished; children and animals are increasingly protected by (some) law. These steps have been made not directly by sit-ins, bra-burnings, and marches, although such activities have often drawn needed attention to perceived injustices. Progress has come primarily as the result of passionate but ulti-mately cogent arguments made to the public, legislators, and courts against unwarranted discrimination. As we shall see, Aeschylus was not misguided in using the origin of trial by jury of one's peers as a symbol of human progress.

Compare this Hellenic Other with one created without the benefit of free speech or any of the other cultural protocols handed down to the West by the Greeks.[20] When "difference" is interpreted and implemented by a community that does not have a tradition of open dissent, where free speech is not a defining criterion, social progress may not happen at all. The entire blueprint of the culture, not just who has access to certain parts of it, must be altered for change to occur. "Wherever it is not possible to speak with freedom what is best, and the worse is victorious in the polis," insists one of Sophocles' characters, "then mistakes (*hamartiai*) throw down its preservation" (*Fr.* 192P).

I am suggesting, then – without irony – that the very nature of Greek Otherness has helped, indeed has been and will continue to be required to mitigate the evil consequences of dogmatism. The Hellenic foundation of

[19] Henderson (1998) 256–7.   [20] Hanson and Heath (2001) 28–74.

difference was such that it is bringing about the collapse of the hierarchical structure it helped to build. By focusing on the development of speech and its rational application, the Greeks established a pattern for the West that has resulted in the dramatic improvement in the status of the Other. This beast is slowly disappearing, a victim of its own success.

FREEDOM OF SPEECH: *ISÊGORIA* AND *PARRHÊSIA*

The Athenians took the equation of speech with humanity directly into the political realm: to be a participant in one's own political future, to be a complete member of the polis, one had to have the "right" to speak.[21] The Athenians were noted for their loquaciousness, but more than anything they prided themselves on their openness. As Socrates lamented (himself a critic of the practice), there was more freedom of speech in Athens than anywhere else in Greece (*Grg.* 461e2; cf. Isoc. *Antid.* 295–6, *Paneg.* 47–8; Chariton 1.11.6–7). Athenians saw themselves – rightly – as the first city to institute equality of speech for all citizens as a political ideal (Eupolis *Fr.* 291K). Over half of all the appearances of the adverb *eleutherôs*, "freely," "without restraint," in the fifth century occur with verbs of speaking.[22]

For the Athenians in particular, to be able to speak freely in public, especially in the assembly, was the primary definition – "perhaps the most striking characteristic"[23] – of citizenship in their democracy. They even had two different words (and several other expressions) describing free speech that could overlap in meaning to suggest freedom in general. *Isêgoria*, "equality of speech," applied literally to the equal opportunity for speaking in political assemblies. Any citizen could ascend the speaker's rostrum, the *bêma*, and say what he wanted upon the herald's cry of "Who wishes to speak?" This concept was intimately connected with *isonomia*, equality under the law. Every citizen's opinion, at least in theory, carried the same weight.[24]

Parrhêsia was freedom of speech in general – the "right to say all" – whether speaking one's own mind in conversation, on stage, or in political

---

[21] There is much debate about the existence of rights in Athens; see the summary in Wallace (1996). I use the word loosely, therefore, but I believe it would make sense in this way to an Athenian in the middle of the fifth century.

[22] Edmunds and Martin (1977) 189–90.   [23] Sinclair (1988) 32.

[24] For a classic statement of this procedure of speaking in the assembly, see Dem. *De Corona* 169–73, as well as Eur. *Supp.* 438–42 with Collard's comments (1975) ad loc. There is some (debated) evidence for a Solonian law that gave priority in speaking to those over fifty. But even those scholars who accept the existence of this law concede that it was not observed by 462, probably even much earlier; see the summary in Kapparis (1998).

deliberations. This word was also closely associated with the democratic liberties afforded to Athenian citizens. There is a recent trend to translate it as "frank speech" in order to differentiate it from *isêgoria*, but in fact the two tended to overlap.[25] By the fifth century, Athenian citizens felt they had the right to address fellow countrymen. Herodotus, equating free speech with democracy and Athens' military victories (5.78), suggests that *isêgoria* was institutionalized as early as the democratic reforms at the end of the sixth century. For our purposes, it matters not whether Herodotus is right or, as is more likely, the word took on special political meaning only as the century moved on, perhaps around the time of new democratic reforms after 462.[26] Nor of immediate concern are the significant shifts in the way *logos* was manipulated as a medium of political power throughout Athens' history.[27] From at least the time of Aeschylus (e.g. *Pers.* 592–4; *Supp.* 948–9; cf. *Prom.* 180) we have evidence that speech was a primary determinant of the boundary between citizen and non-citizen for defining the very nature of democracy. For the rest of Athenian history, free speech of every kind remained the password for freedom. "Free men have free tongues," says a character in a lost play of Sophocles (*Fr.* 927aR). Only in Athens can children live as free men, with free speech (*parrhêsia*; Eur. *Hipp.* 421–3). The Athenians alone, observes Thucydides' Pericles, consider debate (*logous*) not as an obstruction to action (*ergois*); rather, harm comes from not having been taught beforehand by speech (*logôi*, 2.40.2–3). The same sentiment is expressed over and over in every genre: tragedy (e.g. Soph. *OT* 408; *Aj.* 1257–61; Eur. *Ion* 670–5; *Supp.* 438–42; *Fr.* 737N); comedy (e.g. Ar. *Thesm.* 541); philosophy (e.g. Democ. 226D; Plato *Resp.* 557a2–b6; Arist. *Eth. Nic.* 1124b28–30; cf. Diogenes' remark in Diog. Laert. 6.69); oratory (e.g. Dem. 21.124, 45.79, 60.26), and historiography (Herodotus 5.78). Aristophanes has Euripides boast that his tragedies made Athens more democratic by creating a wide variety of prolix (*lalein*) characters, including women and slaves (*Ra.* 948–54). The Athenians even had a trireme called *Parrhêsia* (IG II² 1624.81).

The yoke – a symbol from animal domestication – is one of the most frequent images in Greek literature of servitude. Aeschylus' *Persians* gains

---

[25] See Monoson (2000) 52 with n.5. Monoson's chapter (51–63) provides a recent survey of the importance of free speech in Athens; see also Henderson (1998) 255–60. Ahl (1984) examines the role of "figured speech," that is, speech by indirection, in ancient Greece and Rome.

[26] See Woodhead (1967) agreeing with Griffith (1966). Raaflaub (1980), (2004) 222–5 argues that *parrhêsia* became especially important in the last third of the fifth century; the word first appears in Euripides' *Hippolytus*; see also Momigliano (1971).

[27] O'Regan (1992) 9–21 summarizes the changing role of rhetoric in fifth-century Athens; see also Yunis (1998). For the context of a changing fifth-century Athens, see Raaflaub (1998).

much of its thematic power, for example, from harnassing the metaphor of yoking to the loss of free speech. Most remarkable, perhaps, is the fearfully unsubtle dream of Atossa about Xerxes' failed efforts to bridle Athens (*Pers.* 176–99). In this premonition, two women appear, one dressed as a Persian, the other in "Dorian" attire. The latter is from Hellas, the former from a "barbarian" land. Xerxes tries to yoke them both to his chariot. The barbarian accepts the harnassing and keeps her mouth (*stoma*) "easy to manage in the reins." Greece rebels and tears herself free, breaking the yoke in half. Later, after hearing the news of the disaster at Salamis, the chorus concludes that with the loss of the king's power, a dangerous freedom will emerge in the Persian Empire: "Men's tongues (*stoma*) will no longer be guarded, for the people have been let loose to speak freely (*eleuthera bazein*), since the yoke (*zugon*) of strength was loosed" (*Pers.* 591–4; I translate with the rather awkward "loose(d)" here to indicate that the same verb is used twice, a verb that can also be translated "unyoked").

This is not to say that the mere opportunity to speak guaranteed that one would be successful, or even be allowed to finish – we hear of unpopular speakers who were shouted down or even dragged off the speaker's platform (e.g. Xen. *Mem.* 3.6.1; Plato *Prt.* 319c).[28] The challenge, as we are reminded so frequently in classical literature, was to avoid the dichotomy of word and deed (*logos/ergon*) and make one's words become flesh.[29] As Eteocles says of one the defenders of Thebes, he will not allow a "tongue without deeds" (*glôssan ergmatôn ater*) to break into the city (*Sept.* 556). But to be a citizen was to be able to talk in public, and to be a leader was to be able to talk persuasively. Many of the Greek terms for what we would call politicians (when we're being nice) reflect their primary role as addressers of the public, e.g. *hoi legontes*, "the speakers," or *rhêtores*, "public speakers."[30] Oedipus asks an Attic stranger whether there is one leader there, or if the people have the *logos* ('*pi tôi plêthei logos*, *OC* 66). Attic judicial curse tablets designed to bind an opponent's tongue not only aimed at suppressing an enemy's speech but at reducing his power and status even before a verdict was delivered.[31]

---

[28] See Wallace (1996) 106. Some have argued that few could actually have spoken in the assembly, but see Raaflaub (1996) 155 with references. Hansen (1984) has calculated that between 700 and 1,400 speakers made proposals in the assembly just in the years 355–322. Ober (1989) 105 notes that a plurality of extant orations (59/132) were delivered by individuals who "as far as we know, did not have great political ambitions."

[29] A convenient summary of this division between words and things, thought and actuality, remains Parry (1981) 15–61; for Plato, see Wallach (2001).

[30] See Ober (1989) 104–12.

[31] All of the Attic judicial curse tablets that have been discovered to date belong to the classical era, the oldest dates back to the end of the fifth century. It may be significant that these curses fall into

Enforced silence in the public arena was the equivalent of non-citizenship. This official muting naturally applied to slaves, children, women, and aliens of all sorts, but it was also synonymous with *atimia*, the civic exclusion of former citizens. *Atimia* denotes the loss of some or all of the protections and privileges accorded to citizens. But on the political side, it practically amounted to the prohibition of making oneself heard in public.[32] A diminution in status meant a loss of authoritative speech, a reduction from fully human to something akin to female and slave – dangerously close to the realm of the animals. Thus, Aeschines insists that his rival Demosthenes, a brute beast (*thêrion*), uttered such a "dead" proem to his speech to Philip that the speaker was turned silent, "completely at a loss," and finally lost (literally, "was banished from") his entire oration. His ultimate silence forced the herald to order them all to withdraw in humil-iation (*On the Embassy* 34–5). Demosthenes, in turn, says that his own speaking the truth silences Aeschines, as the awareness of guilt cripples tongues, closes lips, and stifles all utterances (*On the Embassy* 208–9).

Free speech was one of the principal losses associated with exile. A char-acter in Euripides bemoans that exile means loss of *parrhêsia*, a slave's lot to be unable to say what you are thinking (*Phoen.* 385–92; cf. Pl. *Cri.* 53c–e; *Ap.* 37c–e). But one could also lose the right to speak as a consequence of *atimia* resulting from being found guilty of various crimes, such as mistreat-ing parents, failing in military duty, prostituting oneself, or squandering a patrimony (see Aeschin. *In Tim.* 3, 14, 28–32; cf. Andoc. 1.74). Similarly, one of the consequences of religious pollution was enforced silence, a type of excommunication from the community. Socially silenced, the polluted individual (like Orestes, with his mother's blood on his hands) had to be purified to be ritually reintegrated. Thus, Oedipus calls down the curse of exile and silence (apparently he is neither to be spoken to nor speak himself) on whoever has killed King Laius (*OT* 236–43, 350–3, 813–19, 1436–7).

Loss of civic rights meant silence, the worst thing a citizen could suffer (Dem. 21.92–5; cf. 59.28; 68.68–9). As a character in a lost comedy of Nicostratus says, "Surely you know that freedom of speech (*parrhêsia*) is a weapon (*hoplon*) against poverty? If someone should lose it, he will have thrown away the shield (*aspida*) of life" (*Fr.* 29K).

Free speech means free speech, however, and there was no small group of Athenian critics of open expression. Plato may be the most famous censor

disuse in Attica when the civil courts cease to be areas of real political competition; see Faraone (1985); (1991) 15–19; Gager (1992) 117f.; McClure (1997).

[32] See Montiglio (2000) 116–57; Allen (2000) 230–2. On Ober (1996) 100–6 and the distinction between the honor of the elites and the ordinary citizen, see Chapter 6.

of the dangerous chemistry of the demagogues and the ignorant mob in the assembly (e.g. *Prt.* 319b–320a; *Grg.* 455a–456; *Resp.* 557b, 560–1), but others before and after considered equality and freedom of speech – usually given its pejorative connotation of "license" – to be the greatest weakness of the political system.[33] Isocrates states boldly in the assembly (with no apparent irony) that there is no *parrhêsia* in the democracy for those who oppose the masses, but free speech exists only for reckless orators in the assembly and comic poets (8.14). Aristophanes was famous for ridiculing both demagogues and the Athenians who listened to them. And there could be consequences. According to a scholiast on Aristophanes' *Acharnians* 67, a decree was passed in 440 limiting the right to deride individuals in comedies. It was repealed just three years later, however, and we have no evidence that a comic poet was ever prosecuted in Athens for slander. The scholiast on *Acharnians* 376–82 informs us that Cleon, ridiculed in the *Babylonians*, brought Aristophanes before the 500 and accused him of having made fun of magistrates in the presence of foreigners.[34] Comedy, like oratory, was a primary outlet of free speech – but it seems to have had its limits: "all speech was allowed as long as it did not threaten the democracy or impede its processes."[35]

The incessant Athenian insistence on their openness was not a mere "discourse of power." We have no evidence for anything like this kind of freedom of speech in any contemporary Mediterranean community. Aeschylus and Herodotus are not simply manufacturing stereotypes when they suggest that under Persian despotism there was little tolerance for free speech even among the elites, and none at all for the vast majority of the population. Plato's idealized Cyrus listens only to his counselors (*Leg.* 694b; cf. Xen. *Cyr.* 1.3.10 for the equation of *isêgoria* with drunken shouting), and Herodotus' kings have little patience even with their senior (and related) advisers (7.8–11, 7.135, 9.42). The historian tells us that those who spoke

---

[33] Especially the Old Oligarch (*Ath. pol.* 1.2, 1.6–12) and Isocrates (2.28, 7.20, 12.12); cf. Thucydides' portrayal of Cleon 3.36–7; see: Roberts (1994) 48–92; Montiglio (2000) 151–7; Thornton (2000) 180–1; Rhodes (2000) for criticisms by Greeks of democracy.

[34] At *Ach.* 497–508, Aristophanes insists that he will not shut up (he's safe at the Lenaea in any case, since no foreigners are present!), even though Cleon had slandered him on charges that he defied the state. On the connections between comic invective and laws against public defamation, and for other (primarily scholiastic) evidence for attempts to curtail comic freedom of speech, see: Halliwell (1991a); Hansen (1995) 21 n.96; Henderson (1998) 262–3; Sidwell (2000) 254–5. The Old Oligarch's comments (*Ath. pol.* 2.18) about restrictions on old comedy need to be read in his derisive spirit of Athenian liberty; see Frisch (1942) ad loc.

[35] Henderson (1998) 272. Halliwell (1991a) shows that comedy does present satirical topics which fell under the definition of slander, but as a genre seems to have been granted a virtual (thought not legally defined) immunity to the law of slander that was probably in effect in the classical period.

their honest opinions to Xerxes would be and were in fact killed (e.g. 8.65; cf. 8.90 for Phoenician generals executed after battle for speaking out to the king against the Ionians). As we have seen, Aeschylus' Persians realize that with the fall of Xerxes, the subjugated Asians will stop paying tribute and prostrating themselves, no longer curbing their tongues "for people are set free to utter their thoughts at will" (*Pers.* 584–97). The historian and playwright are not creating Persian despotism *ex nihilo*. What the Greeks tell us about the lack of freedom in the Persian Empire is completely in line with the evidence from the Achaemenids themselves.[36] The first sign of tyrannical behavior in Athenian tragic presentations of kings is the repression of *parrhêsia*, as any number of messengers will testify.[37] Dio Chrysostom (32.6; cf. 33.9–10) remonstrates with the Alexandrians about their lack of *parrhêsia* on the classical Athenian model: the poets could reprove not only individuals but the polis, whereas the Alexandrians lack either a chorus or poet who will "reproach them in goodwill" (*oneidiei met' eunoias*).

The choice of language is the significant issue here – free speech defines a culture, a political system, a mentality. What is remarkable is not that the Athenians criticized others for not being like them, but that they invented the concept of freedom itself. Not only is there no word for "free speech" in any other culture in the ancient Mediterranean (remember, the Greeks had *two*), there does not appear to be any term for the broad concept of freedom.[38] This freedom was manifested in economics (e.g. proto-capitalism, inheritance) and politics (e.g. democracy, trial by jury), but these developments were dependent upon the free speech of its citizenry.

The other side of this Athenian self-image as a people of free, contentious, and fluent speech is the Spartan pride in laconic responses: "All Greeks understand that our city [of Athens] is fond of words (*philologos*) and full of words (*polulogos*), but Lacedaemon . . . is a place of few words (*brachulogos*)" (Plato *Leg.* 641e). This "brachylogy," particularly of Sparta but also Argos, is mentioned throughout the sources, by writers both friendly and hostile to Sparta. For the perfect Dorian Other, one could hardly do better than the chorus in Aeschylus' *Supplices*, who state that their word will be "brief and clear." They are, after all, female, Argive,

---

[36] Hanson (2001) 32–9.
[37] E.g. Soph. *Ant. 293–331.* The messenger in Euripides' *Bacchae* (668–71) wonders if he can speak with *parrhêsia*, given the "too kingly" (*to basilikon lian*) temper of Pentheus. Tiresias protests to Oedipus that he has equal right to reply to the king – he is a slave to no one but Apollo (*OT* 408–10).
[38] Thornton (2000) 162–87 and Hanson (2001) 46–54 conveniently survey the Greek vision of freedom; Raaflaub (2004) offers the most complete recent analysis.

and (as they themselves note) derived from a cow (*Supp.* 274–6; cf. Soph. *Frs.* 64, 462P)![39] Herodotus (3.6) relates the quintessential Spartan tale. The Samians, expelled by Polycrates, came to Sparta and gave a long speech to show the depth of their desperation. The Spartans answered that they had forgotten the beginning of the speech and could not understand the end. The Samians came a second time with a sack and said simply, "The sack is lacking meal." The Spartans replied that they had not needed to use the subject "sack." Sparta, as Ion of Chios observed, was not a polis built by words (*TGF Fr.* 63).

Such stories sometimes seem intended to paint the Spartans as rather doltish, a bellicose bunch who have little command over either speaking or listening (cf. Thuc. 4.84.2). But it is more likely that the classical Spartans themselves cultivated the image of tough, brusque, anti-intellectual thugs as part of a very conscious self-presentation.[40] Xenophon says boys educated under the system of Lycurgus – himself a man of "brief and sententious speech" (Plut. *Lyc.* 19.6) – were taught to be silent: you were more likely to hear a stone speak than one of them (*Lac. Pol.* 3.4; cf. Plut. *Lyc.* 12.6; *Mor.* 237d10). Aristotle believed that the Spartan educational system made boys "animal" in nature (*Pol.* 1338b).[41] But Spartan silence was very different to that of the "barbarians," whose relationship with speech was not self-projected but labeled by the Greeks. The Scythians, for example, were known for short and brutally frank speech – thus, the proverbial "Scythian speech" applied to crude language and savage address – but this was how the Greeks viewed them. We do not know if the Scythians saw themselves in this fashion, much less if they took some sort of cultural pride in it. The conversion of sources indicates that the Spartans prided themselves on an elaborate and sophisticated manipulation of silence in service to the state, what one scholar has deemed a *sigocracy*: Spartans had an "exceptionally developed awareness of the multidimensional power condensed in silence: its integrative, authoritarian, conservative, intimidating, suppressive, disciplinary, derisive, ostracizing, mediating, conspirative, deceptive and other manipulative capacities."[42]

---

[39] The Danaids are an intriguing weave of Greek and Egyptized barbarian; see Turner (2001) 41–8.
[40] Powell (1989) 175–6 suggests that the Spartans' alleged simplicity, in language as well as other things (e.g. military), was an essential part of their own effort to separate themselves from their enemies. Their superiority came from an austerity and discipline that no one else could match; cf. Thuc. 8.96.5 for the traditional differences in the Lacedaemonian and Athenian character.
[41] For Spartan education, see Kennell (1995) and Ducat (1999).
[42] See the thorough study of the Spartan's "restricted code" by David (1999) with full references; quote is from page 135. He identifies seven areas in Spartan life in which silence functions pervasively: education; deferential silences and gerontocracy; socio-ritual silences; cryptic-deceptive xenophobic

But if speech is so central to the Greek concept of humanity, how does this Spartan terseness fit in? Very well, in fact, since the important issues are:

1. Having the ability to speak;
2. Controlling speech.

The crux is control. For the Athenians, governing speech primarily meant persuading the public assembly through the dexterous and voluble use of language. For the Spartans – and perhaps the two cultures exaggerated natural differences as they became politically polarized – control meant limiting language to its minimum to accomplish their goals.[43] When the Spartan Demaratus was asked if he was silent because he was a fool or lacked words, he replied that a fool would not be able to be silent (Plut. *Mor.* 220b). Success meant having command over one's mouth, as well as the power to support words with action.[44] A Spartan, upon plucking a nightingale and finding almost no meat, said, "You're all voice and nothing else" (Plut. *Mor.* 233a; cf. 212e, 213e, 223f.). Thucydides has a Spartan envoy tell the Athenians that it is their fashion not to use many words when few will suffice, but to speak at length when it is necessary to accomplish the end they have in view (4.17.1–2; cf. 1.86.1–3). Plato makes Socrates claim that even the lowest of Spartans, although weak in conversation at first, will eventually hit the bull's-eye with a "short and concise" remark (*Prt.* 342d–e). Plutarch's collection of *Sayings of the Spartans* is filled with their pride in knowing when to speak and how much to say, especially as compared to other Greeks (e.g. *Mor.* 209e, 215f, 218b, 235b, 235e, 208c, 224c, 239c, 232e;

silences; political silences; emotional silences, and cultural-religious silences. Rawson (1969) traces the idea of "Laconism" in Western thought, but does not suggest it is merely a "construct." For Scythian speech, see Diog. Laert. 1.101 of Anacharsis the Scythian; cf. Ath. 12.524c; Ael. *Ep.* 14; Demetr. *Eloc.* 216; Aristaenet. *Ep.* 2.20; Lucian *Dial. meret.* 10.4. Diodorus (5.31) refers to the Celts as *brachulogoi.*

43 Debnar (2001) makes the interesting argument that one can observe in Thucydides a progressive transformation of Spartan attitudes towards, and performance of, speech. As the history moves along, there is a gradual collapse of the antithesis between the Spartans and Athenians. The Spartans sound and respond more and more like Athenians. For Thucydides' characterization of individual Spartans, at least to some degree, through their speech, see Tompkins (1993) and especially Francis (1991–3).

44 Spartan "silence" might be compared, with some major caveats, to the Japanese distrust of many words and beautiful speech. For the Japanese, however, silence is an active silence, a form of social discretion that can help one avoid humiliation; see Lebra (1987). Sajavaara and Lehtonen (1997) review the evidence for the stereotype of the "silent Finn" (an image accepted by both Europeans and the Finns themselves) and conclude that "a good speaker for a Finn is one who can give expression to what he or she wants to say briefly and efficiently without talking too much and too profusely" (quote on p. 271). They compare North-American Indians. Suspicion of smooth-talkers goes back to the beginnings of Greek literature as well, with Achilles' famous dismissal of Odysseus (and Agamemnon) in Book 9 of the *Iliad*; cf. the remarks of Pittacus (Diog. Laert. 1.78) and Thales (Diog. Laert. 1.34).

cf. *De garr.* 510e–11a). Agesilaus puts his finger on the matter. When a sophist said speech is the most important thing of all, he replied caustically that such a claim would mean that if you were silent, you were of no worth at all (*Mor.* 215e).

The power of speech comes from knowing when and how to use it, not merely in articulation itself. Silence can be a potent weapon. But silence as power is only available to those who can, or are allowed, to speak. Being silenced is absolutely different from choosing not to speak. For the Greek Other, enforced silence means one has little more control over destiny than the mute animals slaughtered on the altar or laboring in the fields.

WOMEN AND LANGUAGE

Of all the Others, women have been the most thoroughly scrutinized over the past thirty years. The connection between their status and speech has recently been surveyed by Laura McClure.[45] She demonstrates the "strategy of containment" of women's voices, how female uncontrolled speech was thought to disrupt the male-governed household and city. Women's voices were to be heard in lamentation, and were acceptable only in very limited contexts (usually religious). Otherwise, they were likely to be subversive. Pandora serves as the model of the association of female language with deception.[46] This archetypal woman is given a human voice (*Op.* 61), a shameless (literally "doglike") mind and deceitful nature (67) together with lies and wily words (78).[47] And by opening the jar of evils, Pandora releases "countless diseases" that steal upon us "in silence," since Zeus "took away their voice (*phônên*)" (102–4). Pandora's dangerous voice is analogous to the speechless illness – both are plagues for humans.

The key point once again is not that women could not speak, or did not speak – a free woman had the right to speak her mind.[48] Ideally, however,

---

[45] McClure (1999) 8–31. For women's "tricky" and "alluring" language, see also Bergren (1983) 69–71. McClure (1999) 32–8 provides a recent synopsis, with references, of modern theories about women's speech differences; see also McClure (2001) 6–11. For a more thorough, but now slightly dated, review of feminist models of language, see Cameron (1985) 91–133. Gal (1991) critiques feminist approaches to linguistic issues. The limitations of linguistics research based on the dichotomy of gender has recently been recognized; see the articles in Bergvall, Bing, and Freed (1996); Bucholtz, Liang, and Sutton (1999).

[46] For the well-documented association of women's speech with deceit, see also the references in Hesk (2000) 11 n.34; for Pandora as model for woman in general, see Brown (1997).

[47] Lincoln (1997) shows that in Homer and Hesiod *logos* is strongly associated with lies, masquerade, and dissimulation, and is used to mark the speech of women, as well as the weak, young, and shrewd. *Logos*, like a woman, is soft, delightful, charming, and alluring, but also can deceive and mislead.

[48] Schaps (1998) 171–3.

women should not speak in most public environments. Their language was denied authority – and they were not supposed to speak as if they had authority. No one doubted that women could speak and often did.[49] Too much, even.[50] Woman's speech was considered to be prolix, slippery, and untrustworthy. Hesiod advises: "Don't let some *pugostolos* ("lewd," but literally "butt-decorating") woman deceive you, beguiling you with wily words" (373–5). The word translated here as "beguiling" (*kôtillousa*) seems to have associations with the ceaseless chatter of women and birds, applied by Anacreon and Simonides to the swallow.[51] Theocritus (15.87–8) portrays a man, tired of women's gossip, telling them to "stop babbling (*kôtillousai*), you turtledoves." There was, according to a Greek proverb, nothing more chattering (*lalisteros*) than a turtledove.[52] Creon triply insults his son, Haemon, by associating him with women, slaves, and animals when he commands him to "stop wheedling (*kôtille*) me, you slave of a woman" (Soph. *Ant.* 756).[53] Sophocles' Electra has 655 lines filled with such emotion that her brother wisely keeps insisting she quiet down a bit, so they might actually be able to carry out their secret plans of revenge. Yet more than three-quarters of the way through the play she insists, much to our surprise, that until now she had kept her anger "speechless" (*anaudon*, 1281–4).

Old women in particular were known for their rambling, combining the garrulity of old age (think Nestor) with the lack of control associated with all females. Even in Homer we hear the beggar Irus compare the "glib" speech of the disguised Odysseus to that of an old kitchen maid (*Od.* 18.26–7).[54] For Plato, mothers, nurses, and especially old women

---

[49] For the Greek views of the qualities of women's speech as tending towards archaizing, unique forms of address, and fondness for diminutives and certain oaths, see: Gilleland (1980); McClure (1995); Sommerstein (1995). The lack of female voices from antiquity makes a study of women's language virtually impossible. Skinner (1993) 133 concludes that Sappho's language is in fact different from that of males, especially in her modes of subjectivity; see summary with references in McClure (2001) 6.

[50] As Loraux (1995) 240–4 puts it, women are associated with silence as well as with uproar (*thorubos*). On the recurring stereotype of women as "overtalkative," see Graddol and Swann (1989) 70–1; Romaine (1999) 160–5. Kramer (1975) 47–8 suggests that a woman is still considered "talkative" if she talks as much as a man. Lakoff (1995), esp. 27–30, surveys the study of woman's silence and emphasizes that men have exercised "interpretive control" to determine just what silence is to mean.

[51] Anac. *Fr.*154; Simon. *Fr.* 243. Tzetzes on Hes. 374 says the word was applied to the swallow because it chattered endlessly; cf. Callim. *Fr.* 194.81. The word could be used of a man who would not shut up as well (e.g. Thgn. 295–8); see McClure (1999) 62. For foreign language and the chatter of birds, see below.

[52] *Paroemiogr.* II.183; cf. Thphr. *Char.* 7.7; Men. *Fr.* 416; Alciphr. 2.26 Sch.; Ael. *NA* 12.10; Zen. 6.8, with Gow (1950) on Theocritus 15.87.

[53] For the animal imagery in the play, in connection with slaves, gods, and men, see Goheen (1951) 26–35 and 136 n.36.

[54] The adverb *epitrochadên*, derived from "run," seems to mean something like "fluent" or "running easily." It is not necessarily pejorative. At *Il.* 3.213, Antenor uses the word to describe Menelaus'

were proverbially associated with senseless prattling and "old wives' tales."[55] Aristotle says a woman would be known as a chatterer (*lalos*) if she had the same virtue as a man (*Pol.* 1277b21–3). Semonides' infamous women all share some particular "animal" characteristics – mostly unrestrained sexual and gastronomical appetites – but the Bitch also can't keep her mouth shut, barking ceaselessly (7.12–20). The lone blameless female, the Bee, takes no delight in sitting with women and sharing amorous tales (*aphrodisious logous*, 7.90–1). Euripides' Hippolytus insists that wives should not have access to any humans at all, not even slaves, but just wild and mute (*aphthonga*) beasts, so they can neither speak nor be spoken to (*Hipp.* 465–50). In this extreme case, even the private female voice is suspicious, a potential disruption to the *oikos*.[56]

Publicly, the ideal was complete silence, a condition, as Hippolytus reminds us, that associates women with beasts. The aphorisms are numerous and well rehearsed throughout Greek literature: silence – or the briefest speech possible – was the proper condition, the true "adornment" (*kosmos*) of a woman.[57] The one primary exception was in sacred and ritual activities, where a female presence was often required. In this case, the Greeks were well "ahead" of many of their contemporary cultures, not to mention several major religions in the current millennium. But again, it should be noted that even in these cultic environments women infrequently had independent voices. They raised laments, screamed at the appropriate moments,

speech in a favorable fashion (but in contrast to the even more eloquent Odysseus); see Kirk (1985) ad 3.213–14. I think Russo (1992) ad *Od.* 18.26 places too much emphasis on linguistic history and not enough on cultural context when he suggests that the negative connotations in the *Odyssey* passage can be explained by the fact that meanings of words often evolve in a pejorative direction, and so this may be an example of the relative lateness of Odyssean diction compared to Iliadic. Rather, volubility is much more likely to be seen as a defect in a woman than in a man at *any* period in Greek history.

[55] See Plato *Tht.* 176b; *Resp.* 350e, 377a; *Hp. mai.* 286a; *Leg.* 887d; *Grg.* 527a; *Lys.* 205c–d, and Buxton (1994) 18–21. The same sorts of tales categorized as "old women's" are also said to be those of children (*Ti.* 23b). For these *aniles fabulae*, see: Massaro (1977); Scobie (1983) 15–22; cf. Plaut. *Aul.* 123–6: "As the proverb goes, women are never silent." Houston and Kramarae point out (1991) 389 that ridiculing and trivializing women's language as "chattering, gossiping, nagging" is an obvious method of denying them effectual speech.

[56] On Semonides' poem, see Loraux (1993) 94–106; for women as animals, see North (1977). Women as witches, with their magical incantations, are an exaggerated case of the same mismanagement of language, of authority usurped dangerously. This remains a forceful accusation for much of Western history; see Belsey (1985) and Baron (1986).

[57] Most often cited from Aristotle's quotation (*Pol.* 1260a30) of Ajax's proverbial words to Tecmessa (*Aj.* 292–3). Nearly identical phrasing can be found in Democr. 274DK; Soph. *Fr.* 64P; Eur. *Heracl.* 474–6; *Fr.* 219; cf. Aesch. *Sept.* 230–2; Ar. *Lys.* 514–38; Eur. *El.* 945–6; *Tro.* 654–5; *Fr.* 953.1–3. The idea was common enough in the later classical period as part of the appropriate subordination of woman to husband; e.g. I Timothy 2:11–15 and I Corinthians 14:34–5 (a Greek context, where a woman is to address her husband at home only, and not to speak in public); cf. Plaut. *Rud.* 1114. For the various roles of silence in post-classical Europe, see Burke (1993) 123–41.

sang in festivals, or chanted (perhaps) incoherently, but their individual articulate speech was not to be heard outdoors in the presence of men on matters personal or public.[58]

This public silence is all the more noteworthy because, as recent scholarship has shown, Greek women did not live lives of Eastern seclusion.[59] They simply, ideally, were not to be heard. Greek women were not invisible; they were inaudible, at least in any place their words could be recorded. Since to be a public person required the ability and opportunity to speak, women's deprivation of speech rendered them *de facto* non-citizens. The mere title of Aristophanes' *Ecclesiazusae*, "Women at the Assembly," locates the play in the fantastical never-never world of comedy.[60] Women could not vote, of course, but perhaps more fundamentally they could not speak in the assembly. They could not even give evidence in person in a court of law. If challenged to testify, they could do so only extrajudicially, in the form of a sworn oath and with permission of their guardian.[61] In Greek myth, women's voices frequently emerge primarily in the one skill they are

---

[58] Gould (1980) 50, and now especially Dillon (2002). For the Pythia's language – her mouth moved, but the words were not considered her own – see Sissa (1990) 9–36; though cf. Fontenrose (1978) 204–19 for the lack of good evidence for the Pythia's ecstasy and incoherence. Schmitt Pantel (1992b) 473 summarizes: "To be sure, the gods gave Pandora, the first woman, a voice, and from the day of her creation the ancient world resounded with female voices. Women screamed when animals were put to death in blood sacrifices; they cried as they accompanied the body of a dead household member to the cemetery; they chanted in choruses during festivals; they gossiped at home behind closed doors; according to comic poets, they spoke in hectoring tones in imitation of citizens in the assembly; and those who called themselves Amazons made inarticulate and therefore incomprehensible sounds. But did women speak?" Some scholars have concluded that women did not function in religion as the sacrificers of animals, and so were excluded from the primary symbol of active civic and political life (see Bruit Zaidman [1992] 338–9, following the conclusions of Detienne). But see the evidence for such cultic roles assembled by Dillon (2002) 245–6 and Osborne's argument (1993) for women's regular sharing in the sacrificial meal. For recent discussions of the limited semi-public opportunities for and "genres" of female speech, see Blok (2001) and Lardinois (2001).

[59] Cohen (1989) warns us, for example, that the social "ideal" of female, especially her seclusion, need not correspond to reality of separation; cf. Murnaghan (1988) for Xenophon's idealized treatment of women. Llewellyn-Jones (2003) has recently argued that Greek women were veiled in a fashion that can be compared to modern Muslim veiling, but until the Hellenistic period there is little evidence for the specific covering of the entire female form – women were visible, at least literally.

[60] See the analysis of Saxonhouse (1992) 1–19. One myth even accounts for the exclusion of women's voices from the assembly: Athenian women once had a part in public deliberations until they voted for Athena over Poseidon. They were punished with the loss of their vote (among other things); Varro in Aug. *De civ. D.* 18.9.

[61] Harrison (1968) 79; Just (1989) 26–39; Gould (1980) 46 n.57. Hunter (1994) 89–90 points out that the procedure was analogous to that devised for slaves, also under a *kurios*. A challenge was necessary to pave the way for both (an oath for women, torture for slaves). Sissa (1990) 53–9 notes the correspondence in Hippocratic corpus between mouth (*stoma*) and mouth (*stoma*) of the uterus – these female mouths required explicit legislation as the greatest two chinks in the armor of the polis, where women were concerned.

taught and allowed to practice: the "messages" embedded in their spinning and weaving.[62]

The silence of women extended beyond their muted voices. Pericles' famous pronouncement on the virtue of women as being "least mentioned among males" (Thuc. 2.45.2) is but one aspect of this culturally imposed silence: one was not supposed to hear *about* women, or even their names.[63] For men, such silence meant social death – fame, public honor, and eternal speech about one's accomplishments meant a successful life. The eulogist Bacchylides, whose job was to immortalize rich men in song, understandably remarked that silence does not bring adornment to one who has succeeded (3.94–6).[64] Even Spartan women of the ruling class, whom other Greeks like Aristotle often found to have been granted too much license (*Pol.* 1269b30–1270a16; though cf. Plato *Prt.* 342d) and who may have had a greater public role than most other Greek women through their economic power, were supposed to be unspoken of outside the family (e.g. Plut. *Mor.* 217f.; 220d).[65]

[62] One thinks of Penelope's shroud, Helen's tapestry, the robe of Clytemnestra, and Philomela's severed tongue; see most recently Ferrari (2002) 11–86, especially for artistic evidence.

[63] On Thucydides, see Rusten (1989) ad loc. who rejects the efforts of Gomme, Walcot, Dover, and Lacey to turn Pericles' words into a sort of compliment or advice merely to avoid excessive or deficient grief; see also Eide (1981) 40–2. Rusten in turn has recently been criticized by Tyrrell and Bennett (1999), who argue that Pericles is urging women to mourn but in moderation – for his own political agenda, Pericles needs the laments ("always dangerous") – while desiring to mute their voices. Kallet-Marx (1993) argues that Pericles coopts the war widows partly into the public sphere by offering them public esteem. For a complete list of women in Thucydides, and their significance, see Harvey (1985) 67–77. Cartledge (1993b) observes that Thucydides' "earsplitting" silence about women, especially Aspasia, shows the historian following Pericles' advice; cf. Crane (1996) 75–92. There certainly was an extreme reluctance to mention respectable living citizen women by name in public. Those women whose names are spoken in court seem to be primarily those of shady reputation, connected with the speaker's opponent, or dead. Slaves, freed women, foreigners, and "bad" women are much more likely to be named than "good" Athenian females; see: Schaps (1977); Sommerstein (1980); Bremmer (1981); Harvey (1984).

[64] In Pindar (*Ol.* 2.95f.), envy attacks praise, wishing to babble (or "chirp," *lalagêsai*) and throw a cloud over the noble deeds of good men. In epitaphs, another form of idealized praise, men are lauded for speech and action, for what they say and do. Women are praised for their physical appearance and for their virtue, that is, for what they abstain from doing and saying; see Vérilhac (1985). On modern Crete, men who are *caught* stealing are considered to have lost their manhood and may not speak, since this is a male activity. On the other hand, maintaining secrecy indicates the self-restraint of a powerful man in control; Herzfeld (1985) 182, 207.

[65] See, for example, Aristides' interpretation (*On Rhetoric* 2.40) of the Spartan Alcman's verse (27E): "the man's name is 'Talk A Lot,' the woman's 'Delight In It All.'" On Spartan women and speech, see Cartledge (1981) 92; Millender (1999); David (1999) 120; Powell (1999) for the Hellenistic period; Pomeroy (2002) 92–3, 135. Thommen (1999) has recently challenged the popular perception of free and influential women in Sparta. Different cultures have different expectations of "appropriate" speech for women, but in this respect the Spartans were still quite like the Athenians and, from what we can tell, the rest of Greece and the Mediterranean.

The perfect symbol for *sophrosune* as a female virtue became the tortoise, at least according to Plutarch: both had to keep at home and remain silent. He seems to be thinking of the tortoise in its posthumous role as a musical instrument. Silent on its own, in the hands of others, it gains its voice. "For a woman ought to talk either to her husband or through her husband, and should not be aggrieved if, like a flute-player, she makes more impressive sound through a tongue not her own."[66]

Scholars frequently observe a network of imagery and metaphor that associates women with animals. We are told especially of images of domestication, such as taming, yoking, and breaking.[67] Women are wild, "natural" creatures who must be acculturated – and, as with all domesticated creatures, at any moment an eruption of irrational, bestial appetites can threaten to undermine the family and community. But often ignored is that one of the most fundamental links between the two is their lack of language. Women are assimilated to the world of the beast by being denied a voice. Once this step is taken, all the other connections can be made, and women can be denied access to, or control over, *logos* of every sort.

Women do speak publicly in drama, of course, loudly and frequently (although respectable women do not seem to have appeared in Old Comedy

[66] Plut. *Conj. Praecept.* 142d; *De Is. et Os.* 381e. Plutarch is describing a statue made by Pheidias for the Eleans of Aphrodite, with one foot on a tortoise. Pausanias mentions the same statue, but leaves it to the reader to interpret its meaning (6.25.1). As Griffiths (1970) ad 381e.10 notes, Plutarch's interpretation says more about Greek thoughts on the place of women than about the statue, the actual meaning of which is still the subject of debate. Tortoises do seem to be connected in some fashion with correct female behavior. Polemon (in Ath. 13.589a) reports that Lais, a notorious beauty, was beaten to death with wooden tortoises (sometimes translated as footstools) by jealous women, the precinct thereafter called that of "Sinful" (*anosias*) Aphrodite; see also Sissa (1990) 53–9, and Arthur (1980–81) 58–9 for the links between the tortoise, women, and children. Llewellyn-Jones (2003) 190 observes that the "Greeks had a popular assumption that the tortoise was a mute creature, and, moreover, that all tortoises were female." On assimilation of women to pigs, based on female sexuality (*choiros* = young pig and vagina), see Golden (1988a). On women's sexual organs named for animals, see Henderson (1991) 131–2.

[67] E.g. Gould (1980) 53; Just (1989) 231f. with references; Reeder (1995) 299–371. These bestial metaphors for women are often connected to agriculture as well; see Mirón Pérez (2000) 156–62. On similarities in language and imagery between marriage and animal sacrifice, see Burkert (1983) 58–72; Rabinowitz (1993) 31–66. Women are perhaps most commonly compared to animals in references to their sexuality; see Forbes Irving (1990) 64–79, and Loraux (1990) 30–3 for female appetites. Since cattle were an early measuring-stick of wealth (e.g. *Il.* 23.700–5) – primitive money – and cattle were exchanged in dowry, girls were often given cow names to encourage prospective husbands, e.g. Euboea, Phereboea, Polyboea, Stheneboea (i.e. rich in cattle, bringing cattle, worth many cattle, strong in cattle); Lonsdale (1979) 147; also Lyons (2003) on the "gendered nature of the gift-economy." For the equation of women and food, especially meat (including an unappetizing anecdote anticipating Portnoy), in Athenaeus, see Henry (1992) 255–60. The feminist scholar Carol Adams (1990) 46 criticizes "radical feminist discourse" for ignoring animals as the truly oppressed "Other": we have "failed to integrate the literal oppression of animals into our analysis of patriarchal culture." Gruen (1993), on the other hand, in her analysis of the connection between women and animals, rejects most forms of feminism for creating more dualisms.

until the third quarter of the fifth century[68]): over one-third of the speaking roles in extant tragedies belong to female characters; only one extant tragedy (the *Philoctetes*) contains no women.[69] The challenges of determining the significance of this form of female voice, written and performed by and probably for male citizens, have been the subject of much recent literary criticism. As Victoria Pedrick recently wrote in her review of McClure's book: "Fifteen years into the study of alterity as the grid for mapping the aims and ideology of Athenian drama, the landscape looks pretty familiar: all roads, however twisted, lead back to the male political self."[70] Indeed, the target of gender studies has increasingly become the "performative" construction of the male rather than the female, the ideology that supports masculine self-presentation. This "technology of masculinity," as it has been called (without apparent reference to power tools or barbecues), is part of a larger debate about the construction of gender, both ancient and modern.[71]

This is not the place to enter into this controversy, in which *nomos* seems to have trumped *phusis* once again.[72] To understand what is going on in Greek literature, however, I would return to what the dramatic movements of the plays themselves suggest. Women in Greek tragedy are presented the same way women are depicted in the rest of our evidence, but drama places these characterizations under the microscope. Yes, the appropriation of male language by females often leads to disaster; but far more often it is the speech of men, or the failure of men to understand speech, that brings about catastrophe. And true, by the end of some tragedies either women's voices have been silenced in apparent support of the status quo, or they are let loose to symbolize the collapse of order. Ajax makes what appears to be a proverbial statement: "Woman, for a woman silence carries adornment" (*Aj.* 292–3),[73] and Tecmessa may be muted by the end of the play, aligned as

---

[68] Henderson (1987). Henderson (2000) 136 notes that the same taboos that applied in oratory to the naming of respectable women applied to comedy; see 144–9 for a checklist of comedies with speaking women.

[69] E. Hall (1997) 105 (excellent on the presentation of the Other in terms of gender, class, and citizenship in Athenian tragedy); Griffith (2001) 117 for a survey of women's roles in tragedy, from which he concludes that there is no simple dramatic category of "tragic female"; also Shaw (1975); Bouvrie (1990) 24–31. Perhaps the best analysis of the relations between women in Greek drama and cultural norms is Foley (2001).

[70] Pedrick (2001) 283; see Zeitlin (1996) 341–74, especially 346 and n.13, for the kind of approach critiqued by Pedrick.

[71] A veritable primer for the uninitiated can be found in Parker (2001), which has my favorite title in the bibliography: "The myth of the heterosexual: anthropology and sexuality for classicists."

[72] Schaps (1998) 180–3 seems to me to approach the matter sensibly when he concludes that gender is neither perfectly arbitrary nor perfectly natural.

[73] That the sentiment is proverbial is suggested by Tecmessa's introducing it with *aie humnoumena*; see Stanford (1963); Kamerbeek (1953) ad loc.; Pearson (1963) ad Soph. *Fr.*64. But as Stanford notes, Tecmessa may also be suggesting that Ajax has used the aphorism more than once.

a legitimate wife in dutiful silence.[74] Alcestis' perfection may be also found in her mute final scene.[75]

But the context of this silence and subjection is crucial. Neither Ajax nor Admetus looks good, to us or to the chorus. Hippolytus is perversely immature, his misogynistic diatribe juxtaposed with the hunter's strange and freakishly anti-social vegetarianism (as I read the passage). Creon's suffocation of Antigone in a battle of the sexes is not intended to make him look kingly. Even Medea's duplicitous language against her despicably wimpish husband is tolerable until she acts. Eteocles' misogyny is not rewarded. No one much likes Agamemnon – his misinterpretation and brusque rejection of Clytemnestra's reception speech suggest that he is little more than the insensitive dolt we met at the beginning of the *Iliad*. Cassandra is much more sympathetic than either her captor or his wife. Lysistrata may be a comic heroine but heroine she is. Told to keep silent by her husband, she did, but to the detriment of the entire polis. Tragedy and comedy both frequently emphasize the wisdom of listening to the Other – women, as well as slaves and young adults – who may have surprisingly good advice that is ignored at great cost.

The cultural expectations of female silence came into play almost by definition in Greek drama, where impressive women took front stage. The point was neither simply to reinforce cultural codes nor to overturn them, but to take advantage of them, even thematize them, to make good theater. Women were publicly silent in Athens, but Athenians also started us on the long road to equality of voice: ". . . tragedy does not simply aim to prove that all the negative stereotypes are true or to enforce cultural ideals. Here as elsewhere Greek male writers are using fictional women to think in a challenging fashion."[76]

BARBARIANS

Otherness studies love the barbarian: he is, we are told, everything that the Greeks are not. He is characterized by tyranny, immoderate luxuriousness,

---

[74] See, for example, the interpretation of Ormand (1996).

[75] See, for example, O'Higgins (1993). On female silence in tragedy, see Loraux (1987) 221–3; for female characters' failure to speak in general, see Griffith (2001) 123.

[76] Foley (2001) 116. Similarly, Hall (1997) 118–26 contrasts tragedy with the culture that produced it: "Greek tragedy does its thinking in a form which is vastly more politically advanced than the society which produced Greek tragedy." But can the tragic competition be so easily excised from the "historical conditions of its own production"? Athens provided a publicly funded arena for the community to reflect upon its own traditions. Saïd (1998) 284 concludes that different tragedians – indeed, different tragedies – may both endorse and criticize civic ideology; cf. Lefkowitz (1986) 38–40; Saxonhouse (1992) 52–3, 54–89; Mossman (2001) 384; Wohl (1998) xiv; Pelling (2000) 189–96.

unrestrained emotionalism, effeminacy, cruelty, timidity, irrationality, and servility. Many scholars, rightly suspicious of this emotional profile, have consequently tossed out the cultural analysis of the non-Greek foreigner as well. We can now readily recognize the "ideological construct" of this warped "mirror image" of the Greeks. He lives in a "funny" (i.e. *unGreek*) place on the margins of the civilized world (perhaps even an island); his abode is funny, not a house but a tent, wagon, or cave; he dresses funny – maybe he has no clothes at all; he eats funny things, dining not on wine, bread, and cooked meat but on milk and raw flesh (possibly with a little human tossed in); he is a pastoralist, unaware of or consciously rejecting Hellenic sedentary agrarianism; his daily life has something seriously anti-Hellenic, backwards or inverted about it – maybe he practices incest or polygamy, has sex in public or is ruled by women.[77]

Whether northern Scythians, southern Libyans, one-eyed Cyclopes or dwellers on the imaginary Isle of Thule, the exotic Other, we are told, often represents a breakdown in and reversal of Greek Otherness itself: women act like men; men act like animals and/or live like gods. Like the description of utopias, they are extremely useful ethical *paradeigmata*.[78] Occasionally, barbarians live in a golden age; more often, their uncivilized world is distinctly bestial. As we saw in the case of Polyphemus, combinations of both are not hard to find.[79]

What can be helpful about this approach is that it focuses our attention on what I take to be a central facet of Greek intellectual history: their fascination with who they are through the exploration of what they are not. Such studies run the risk, however, of overemphasizing the nature and import of this barbarian "construct" when they primarily censure the Greeks for this behavior or *a priori* dismiss what a Greek says about a foreign culture as pure invention.[80] And they miss the actual complexity – and ultimate

---

[77] For a catalogue of barbarian attributes in post-classical antiquity, especially those derived from Pliny, see Friedman (1981) 9–29. Wiedemann (1986) 189–92 also has a nice list, but he makes no reference to the language of the barbarian. For food as a marker of divergence, see Garnsey (1999) 62–72. Walbank (1951) remains an excellent discussion of the challenges of the "problem of Greek nationality."

[78] See especially Dawson (1992) 13–43; Romm (1992); also the recent discussion of the "utopian novels" of Euhemerus and Iambulus in Holzberg (1996) 621–8.

[79] The Cynics advocated a life of Otherness, an intentional challenge to Greek concepts of culture, a "back to the natural world" of incest, cannibalism, public and community sex, aggressive women, eating of dead bodies (including one's parents), community property, in short a life so "natural" and "shameless" that they "live like dogs"; see Dawson (1992) 135–239. For the natural life viewed as closer to the golden age, see Saïd (1985).

[80] The Greek (and Roman) vision of the "barbarian" has remained a powerful image throughout history, at times leading to the misunderstanding of foreign cultures and the imperious butchering of the indigenous civilizations; on the connection of classical visions of the barbarian and monster

value – of a distinctively Western approach to the "barbarian."[81] When studying the alien Other "created" by the Greeks, three things should be kept in mind.

First, virtually *all* ancient cultures viewed their neighbors, both nearby and distant, with great suspicion and frequent hostility. One need only glance at the presentation of Pharaohs smiting the lowly Asiatic in Egyptian monuments and documents, or read of the moral waywardness of Philistines in the Hebrew Bible, to see that the Greeks were hardly unique in constructing an ethnocentric picture of the Other.[82]

But far more importantly, the Greeks *were* unique in the degree to which they were genuinely interested in – and influenced by – other cultures. There is nothing comparable in any ancient Mediterranean culture to the Hellenic curiosity about other places and peoples, an interest by no means always fueled by the desire for exploitation or self-congratulation.[83] When Cartledge, following Hartog, focuses his attention in Herodotus' account of the Egyptians on the familiar Greek "binary opposition," he fails to mention the more important point: in over three thousand years of documented history, the Egyptians produced no extended ethnography of any other

---

in the middle ages, see Friedman (1981); for the sixteenth and seventeenth centuries, see Hodgen (1964), and for (mis)interpretations of American Indians, Pagden (1982). Nippel (1990) provides a general survey of the use of the "barbarian" in the West; see also Bras-Chopard (2000) 287–327. But some scholars have now either banished the barbarian as a *complete* fabrication or reconstructed him as a genuine golden age figure. Nowhere is this more true than in the debased Romanticism through which Native Americans have been depicted lately as ecological titans inhabiting an antediluvian paradise despoiled by crude Westerners; see the criticisms by Coates (1998) 84–95; Thornton (1999) 131–76.

[81] Some recent studies of Greek concepts of ethnicity refreshingly call for a "more nuanced picture of Greek ethnicity than the bipolar discourse that insists on dichotomies of Greeks and Others, center and periphery" (Malkin [2001b] 12–15) and caution us against the danger of becoming oversimplified (Thomas [2001] 213–14); see also Thomas (2000) 75–167 for Herodotus' refusal to follow standard ethnographic grids "slavishly." Hall (2002) 175–89, after outlining the "barbarian antitype," warns us that there are differences of degree between barbarians and "ourselves" and criticizes the "simplistic core-periphery model" (121–4). Even Munson's rather turgid "metanarrative" analysis (2001) finds room for a Herodotus who "subverts his own antitheses" and "redistributes the criteria of otherness" (phrases from p. 32).

[82] On subjectivity and ethnocentricity in all classical ethnography, not just Western, see Karttunen (1992). Hall (1997) 32–3 concludes that ethnic identity is likely to become salient *only* in opposition to other ethnic identities. The articles in Poliakov (1975) reveal that Greeks were only one of many ancient civilizations (e.g. Babylon, Israel, the Christian Middle Ages) to see other cultures and races as beastly.

[83] This limited appreciation of Western curiosity is found especially in those who follow the Foucault/Saïd model; see, for example, the self-confessed foundations of Vasunia's recent examination (2001) of the Greek representation of Egypt: ". . . the European study of non-European cultures has led to colonial hegemony and political control," an "othering mechanism [!], which is couched in an idiom of grandeur, [that] ultimately turns on an obsessive domination of the other's space and time" (quote on p. 12).

culture whatsoever.[84] Egypt produced no Herodotus, whose interest in foreigners caused Plutarch to label him "a barbarian lover" (*philobarbaros, Mor.* 857a). Even the improbable tales told in the *Persica* of Ctesias were probably engendered by experiences at the court of Artaxerxes II.[85] J. P. Arnason rightly concludes that "the diversity and reflexivity of references to otherness set Greek culture apart from contemporaries and predecessors."[86]

Nor did Greeks always or automatically present alien cultures as inferior. They were equally capable of crediting foreign cultures with a golden age existence, of projecting paradise onto its distant contemporaneous acquaintances. With the possible exception of Old Comedy, almost all authors and genres of Greek writing temper a generally negative presentation of the barbarian with positive and sympathetic portrayals.[87] Where else in the fifth-century Mediterranean can be found the insistence that "by nature we are all the same in every way, both barbarians and Greeks"?[88]

The Greeks did not steal their culture from Semitic civilizations or Egypt, but the opening for such an interpretation was available because of the consistent Greek fascination with exotic lands. An interesting comparison can be made with the ancient Jews' story of migration into Canaan. Many scholars now argue that as the Jews emerged as a distinct people they developed a mythology that quite intentionally emphasized an original – and historically dubious – Otherness from their neighbors. In contrast, the Greeks were unusually prone to recognizing – and even exaggerating – their debts to other cultures.[89]

Second, certainly, the crude psychological profile of the barbarian should be dismissed. But what about the cultural profile of the barbarian outlined at the beginning of this section? An entire industry of scholarship has been built, for example, on the premise that Herodotus' barbarians exist

[84] (1993a) 56–9. This absence is unexpected because in another publication Cartledge goes out of his way to defend Herodotus' program: "Compare and contrast his historiography with, say, the triumphalist annals of the Pharaohs and the Assyrian monarchs, or with the 'manifest destiny' ideology of the Hebrew Bible's book of *Kings*, and one cannot fail to be struck by the relative disinterestedness and impartiality of the Greek historian towards Greek and non-Greeks, friend and foe, alike" (1995) 79. Similarly, Harrison's (1998) argument that the Greeks "lacked interest" in foreign languages loses much of its force when viewed in comparison with contemporary Mediterranean cultures.

[85] See the brief discussion, with references, in Holzberg (1996) 629–32.

[86] (2001) 181. He goes on to conclude that "far too much has been made of the so-called stereotype of the 'barbarian.'"

[87] See Long (1986) 145–7; Losemann (2003). Even Hall (2002) 180–1 admits that barbarians are not always shown in an unremittingly negative light.

[88] Antiphon *Fr.* 44 B2 DK; see other similar references in Trédé (1991) 74.

[89] For critiques of the various theories regarding the origins of the Israelites, see Isserlin (1998) 53–64; Stager (1998); Callaway and Miller (1999). I owe this last point to one of the anonymous readers. For a thorough cataloguing of possible Eastern links with Greece, see Burkert (1992); West (1997).

primarily, if not exclusively, for ideological purposes. The assumption here is that Herodotus doesn't know, or isn't telling, or is not interested in reporting, or is culturally constrained from seeing the truth – usually referred to as the "truth" – about these cultures. The problem is that almost every time we find out something new about a people or place Herodotus discusses, he turns out to be right. One of the most devastating – and delightfully ornery – books in the last decade is Kendrick Pritchett's dismantling of what he terms the "liar school of Herodotus." Time and time again what we discover about these barbarians independent of the historian supports rather than conflicts with his account.[90]

Clearly what is needed here is some balance. The Greeks were human, and they made assumptions and exaggerations about foreign cultures they did not immediately understand. They had the usual prejudicial and presumptive ideas about Otherness, and were very capable of projecting them onto distant peoples. And they were constrained, as everyone is, by their own notions of culture and history. But not every tale of cannibalism is a fabrication, not every difference between the Occident and the Orient part of an expansionist conspiracy.[91] We must be careful before we reject Greek writing about foreign cultures because of some postmodern prejudice *against* the existence and significance of difference.[92]

---

[90]   Pritchett (1993). He aims (191f.) at Hartog's work (1988) in particular, but covers the entire field. Fowler (1996) debunks Fehling's thesis (1990) that most of Herodotus' citations are fictive: "[Herodotus] did not invent his sources; he discovered the *problem* of sources" (page 86). Pembroke (1967) argues for distortion and reversal in Herodotus, although not all invention; cf. Rosellini and Saïd (1978).

[91]   Arens' (1979) belief that there is no evidence for cannibalism as an accepted practice at any time or place, for example, has now been rejected, if reluctantly, even by many anthropologist apologists (if not Arens himself) like Goldman (1999) 3, who "regard questions about the historical incidence of cannibalism as *passé*[!]"; see the bibliography in Gardner (2000) 142. For a neo-evolutionary account of survival cannibalism, and a good critique of the weaknesses of the social-science method, see Petrinovich (2000) 147–67. As for "Orientalism," Saïd's questionable thesis (1994) must now be supplemented by an "Occidentalism" and the lethally parochial "constructions" the East has put on the West; see, for example, the works of Lewis (1995; 2002; 2003).

[92]   David Castriota's recent attempt (2000) to smooth over the differences between Greek and Persian cultures, for example, in fact reveals the large gaps between them. He concludes that "the acceptance of Persian monarchy by its subjects was not slavish and blasphemous obedience to an overblown mortal, as the Greeks liked to portray it. Quite the contrary, it was an act of piety due beyond question to God's anointed earthly surrogate" (quotation from page 453). But surely that notion of piety is the crucial point, and this "definitional" issue is the reason Greek literature, philosophy, and history are filled with examinations of the nature of such concepts as piety. The Persian definition of piety was very different from that of the archaic and classical Greeks, who could never tolerate a "God's anointed." That both cultures acted "piously" or "legally" and desired "justice" by their own standards does not make them similar. Harrison is the latest to deny the Athenians any true understanding of the Persians (or any other contemporary culture), concluding that the Greeks had "a relative ignorance of, and indifference towards, the people in question" (2002b) 10–11; cf. (2000a) passim. He reads Aeschylus' *Persians* as an antiliberal, completely unsympathetic portrayal of the

Third, often lost or quickly passed over in all this ideological wrangling is the most frequent and obvious connection made by the Greeks between all "foreigners," indeed the very definition of barbarian: they speak a different language. The Greeks were not the only culture to divide the world by speech. Herodotus (2.158) observes that the Egyptians call all men of languages not similar to their own barbarians. But, as the author of one of the most thorough discussions of the Greek encounter with the barbarian concludes, "No other ancient people privileged language to such an extent in defining its own ethnicity."[93] A barbarian first and foremost does not speak Greek.

Herodotus famously includes similarity of language (*homoglôssa*, 8.144) as a central aspect in his definition of Hellenic culture.[94] Elsewhere (1.57–8) he boasts that Hellenic stock has used the same language since its beginning, a crucial factor in the culture's successful expansion: "Greek was always Greek and the Greeks always spoke Greek: these are Herodotus' priorities."[95] Philoctetes, abandoned on a deserted island for nine years, associates the sound of the Greek language, not just a voice, with humanity and civilization (Soph. *Phil.* 225, 234–5). Typically, then, Thucydides suggests the very name of "Hellenes" may have come about as Greek cities

enemy. He seems to suggest that the contrast in the play between democracy and monarchy is merely part of an ideological invention tied to the chorus' (historically inaccurate) belief in the divinity of Persian royalty (2000a) 76–91. But in fact the Persian king was much more closely associated with the divine than any Athenian leader would claim to be. The Athenians may not have seriously reflected upon the actual workings of Persian tyranny as "objective" inquiry would now require, but they did know that democracy is qualitatively different from monarchy. That most (but certainly not all) citizens felt democracy to be superior to despotism is, in my opinion, to their credit. Pelling (1997b) offers a more subtle reading of Herodotus' "national stereotypes." Rather than a contrast between the free-speaking Athenians and the muted Persian court, for example, Herodotus reveals both the intimidated silence of the Persians and the ineffective but articulate wiliness of the Greeks. Miller (1997) shows that through the battlefield, trade, visitors, and embassies the Athenians were familiar enough with Achaemenid culture to appropriate and reshape it for their own needs; cf. Briant (2002). Of the many foreign animal species known to the fifth-century Greeks, only the Persian peacock acquired a reputation for being "exotic"; Bodson (1998) 78–80. For the accuracy of Greek interpretations of Persian cultural values, see Hanson (2001) 32–9.

93 Hall (1989) 5; see also the conclusions of Nippel (2002) 281. Colvin (1999) 50–89 provides an excellent review of the language of foreigners in Greek literature between Homer and Aristophanes. Hall (1989) suggests that the Greeks focused on language because of their geographical dispersal and their consequent exposure to different worlds. This is no doubt true. But I think the Greeks were also predisposed to think about language as a division maker because of the connection with animals. This is mere speculation, of course, but it is language – or lack of it – that connects *all* the Others. Werner (1992) provides an overview of antique thought about foreign language. On Egyptian ideas, see Donadoni (1986) 193–206.

94 He includes as markers of Greekness, along with language, being of the same blood, religion, and way of life; cf. Thuc. 7.63.3 for pride in Greek language. Harrison (1998) gives a thoroughly documented review of Herodotus' conception of foreign languages.

95 Harrison (1998) with notes 102–5.

began to understand one another's speech (1.3.2–4). To "speak Greek," *hellênizô*, is the same verb (in the passive) as "to become Greek," and is contrasted with *barbarizein*, "to speak like a foreigner," that is, "not to speak Greek."[96] So when Thucydides notes that some of the Amphilocians became Hellenes when they learned Greek, he naturally concludes that the rest of them are still "barbarians" (2.68.2–6).

This sense of identity through language does lead to some marvelous descriptions of the speech of the imaginary barbarian. The dogheaded folk of India, according to Ctesias' *Indika* (in Photius' epitome, 21–3), speak no language but bark, make hand signals, and understand the speech of the Indians. In Iambulus' tale (Diod. Sic. 2.55–60) of a golden age island, we find men with double tongues who can speak every language on earth, both human and avian. They also possess the ability to speak to more than one person at the same time! Five of Pliny's races (in Book 7 of his *Natural History*) are monstrous because they lack human speech entirely (sometimes they do not even have mouths).

The Greeks, in other words, first defined the alien "other" as a non-Greek speaker, even for cultures primarily of their own creation. Language once again was the major criterion for differentiation. The Greeks were proud of their language and quite parochial, rarely developing any true bilingualism (beyond being familiar with varying Greek dialects). Although there was no unified Greek language, there was an abstract notion of Greek as a common language from at least the fifth century.[97] An Athenian could divide the Mediterranean world between the "barbarians" on the one hand and on the other themselves and those "speaking the same language" (e.g. Plato *Menex.* 242a). The Greek language, like certain core values, was not up for renegotiation in the Mediterranean context:

The special place of language in Greek self-definition in the archaic and classical period is signalled by the fact that, while Greeks of this time borrowed extensively from the older cultures of Egypt and the Near East in the sciences and arts, even

---

[96] See Casevitz (1991) 14–16.

[97] Davies (2002). Colvin's review (1999) 50–6 of Greek attitudes towards language in archaic poetry shows that language is used as indicator of ethnicity, or subdivisions among Greeks, but there is not yet any Greek/barbarian antithesis. Themistocles was unusual in taking the time – out of necessity, it might be added – to try to learn a foreign language (Thuc. 1.138.1; but cf. Plut. *Them.* 28–9). Greeks primarily relied on interpreters, usually Hellenized foreigners (e.g. Xen. *An.* 1.2.17); see: Mosley (1971); Baslez (1984) 185–6; Harrison (1998). Even educated Romans, many of whom learned Greek, were suspicious of bilingualism, often associating it with Carthage, slavery, and duplicity (Plaut. *Poen.* 1032–4; *Per.* 299; *Truc.* 780–1; Verg. *Aen.* 1.661).

recognizing the technical apparatus of the alphabet as a Phoenicial import, in the one area of language they were remarkably exclusive.[98]

The word *barbaros*, we perhaps do not need to be reminded, originally merely described the incomprehensible speech of any foreign tongue. It is an adjective, a "reduplicative onomatopoeia" that captures how an exotic language sounds.[99] A modern American creation would be something like "blah-blah-ous."[100] Before the fifth century, *barbaros* is tied to language,[101] and even after the Persian Wars, when the word becomes increasingly pejorative by encompassing the negative stereotypes of the "barbarian" (particularly from the East), the word remains closely connected with speech. It continues to mean "unintelligible," but now also comes to mean "unGreek" (the world can be said to be composed of Hellenes and barbarians), and

[98] Swain (1996) 17–18; cf. Cartledge (1995) 79: ". . . for the Greeks language was (to use Weberian terminology) a criterion not a mere indicium of ethnicity."

[99] So most scholars (after Strabo 14.2.28); but see Hall (2002) 112. The Latin adjective *balbus* is similarly onomatopoeic for a defect in speech, a lisp or stammer or babble. On language as the most important characteristic of the barbarian, and the origins of the word, see: Jüthner (1923) 5 with references; Lévy (1984) 5–10; Hall (1989) 4. As the cultural circle drew tighter, *barbaros* was eventually applied to non-Attic Greek, e.g. Aesch. *Sept.* 170; Ar. *Av.* 1700; Plato *Prt.* 341c; *Ath. pol.* 2.8. Thucydides (3.94.5) says that the speech of the Eurytanians, the largest group of Aetolians, was even more unintelligible than that of other Aetolians – and they were eaters of raw meat to boot. On dialects and ethnicity within Greece, see Hall (1997) 170–81. He downplays language as a defining criterion of ethnicity, as he does in (1999) and (2002) 111–17, and this may be true for dialects – though cf. Colvin (1999) – but he engages in much special pleading in trying to minimize (or rather, ignore) the Greek/non-Greek polarity. Ideologically, the Greeks made language their first criterion in defining the barbarian, even the Hellenic "barbarian." Pindar can refer to a polis as *barbaros*, for example, when he claims that no polis is so *barbaros* or backward in speech (*palinglôssos*) that it has not heard of the fame of Peleus (*Isthm.* 6.2–6). Dorian, to the Athenians, said something more about the Spartans than mere dialectical difference – the Laconian accent even "smelled" different (Soph. *Fr.* 176R). The Greeks may have defined the pre-Greek inhabitants of the Balkans by their inability to speak the language. One of the terms they used for these people was Leleges (Pelasgoi is the other frequent term), which functions like *barbaros*, an onomatopoeic word to describe those who speak unintelligibly; see Dowden (1992) 81. Herodotus (1.57) claims that the Pelasgians did not speak Greek.

[100] Cf. the Latin American "Gringo," which means "gibberish." It may also be a typical, if late, example of a Roman-based culture thumbing its nose at the Greeks, if the word does in fact derive from "griego." Harrison (1998) compares the Arabic root *ae-ja-ma*, which can mean "speaking incorrect Arabic, dumb, speechless, barbarian, non-Arab, foreigner, alien, Persian."

[101] *Pace* Hall (2002) 112. Anacreon *Fr.* 423 directly refers to language: *mê pôs barbara bakseis*, "so you don't in any way speak a barbarian language" (or "like a barbarian"). The connection between language and *barbaros* is so familiar that Hecataeus *Fr.* 107 can use it slightly metaphorically: "Bad witnesses are the ears and eyes for men if they have barbarian souls (*barbarous psuchas*)." Every commentator I have found takes this as a reference to language. Barbarian souls are those that do not understand the language spoken by "that which is wise," or the language of the senses, or both; see the summary of interpretations by Robinson (1987). Hecetaeus (*FGrH* 1.119) simply says that before the Greeks the Peloponnesus was inhabited by barbarians (*barbaroi*); whether he means those who did not speak Greek, or those not from Greece originally, or both, is unclear. Strabo, who cites Hecataeus (7.7.1), is referring to non-indigenous and thus non-Greek speaking groups, and thus their "barbarian" origin is revealed by their names.

frequently carries implications of the "stereotypical" foreigner. The Egyptianized chorus in Aeschylus' *Suppliants* speak a barbarous language (*karbana audan*, 118–19) and note that the whole world is prepared to cast reproaches at speakers of foreign tongues (*allothroois*, 972–4; cf. Eur. *Fr.* 139N). The hysterical women in besieged Thebes see the threat against them from an Argive army as so terrifying that they refer to the enemy as if it were speaking another language (*heterophônôï stratôi*, *Sept.* 170).[102] In Sophocles' *Women of Trachis*, Heracles can describe the entire world as either Hellas or where there is "no tongue" at all (*aglôssos*, 1060; cf. Soph. *Aj.* 1262–3). A glance at the LSJ reveals that related words continue to emphasize language: *barbarizô* means "to speak like a foreigner, to speak gibberish, to use barbarisms in speech"; *barbarismos* signifies the "use of a foreign tongue, or even one's own tongue, wrongly" (Xenophon can use it to mean "siding with the barbarians"); *barbaristi* connotes "in a foreign tongue or barbarian fashion"; and *bebarbaromenô*, from *barbaroô*, means "to become barbarous, unintelligible," and is used of birds in Soph. *Ant.* 1002.[103]

This last example is revealing. Barbarian language, like that of women, is frequently compared to the chattering of birds. Herodotus (2.54–7) says that the "talking doves" of Dodona were really just Egyptian priestesses whose barbarian language sounded like that of birds. The Ethiopian cave-dwellers, he notes, squeak like bats (4.183). The chirp of the swallow (*chelidôn*) in particular apparently sounded like barbarian babble. The verb *chelidonizein*, to twitter like a swallow, is attributed to Aeschylus (*Fr.* 450) and said by a scholiast on Aristophanes (*Birds* 1680) to be the equivalent of *barbarizein*.[104] Clytemnestra assumes that Cassandra's "barbarous voice" is like that of a swallow (Aesch. *Ag.* 1050–1). In Aristophanes' *Frogs*, the living playwrights are said to chatter in a chorus of swallows (93), and Cleophon's "barbarous tongue" is compared to a Thracian swallow (678f.). It is especially amusing, then, at *Birds* 196–200 when the hoopoe says that Peisthetairus can

---

[102] This reference is often taken to be limited to a dialect difference, but I think the point is that the chorus exaggerates the danger of attack. Polynices wants to be king, not to enslave the women, but the women wail as if they are to become war captives like the Trojan women; see Colvin (1999) 75 for the dialect interpretation, and the athetizing of v. 72.
[103] On the development of the concept of barbarian, with references to primary sources, see Bacon (1961) 6–17; Baldry (1965) 20f.; especially Hall (1989) 2–20; de Romilly (1993); J. M. Hall (1997) 34–51. See the often quoted lines from Euripides' *Philoctetes* on the shame of allowing barbarians to speak while remaining silent about Greeks (Eur. *Fr.* 796N, with Nauck's note on Aristotle's adaptation of the phrase).
[104] See Dunbar (1995) on *Birds* 1681; cf. Rochette (1997) 37. Thus, the disparaging references to one's poetic rivals as boisterously chattering crows (e.g. Pi. *Ol.* 2.86f.) assign the inferior authors to the realm of barbarian, female, and beast.

now speak with the birds because he has taught them language and thereby "debarbarized" them. Although there is no direct representation of dialect or foreign language in Athenian tragedy or historiography,[105] ancient comedy did not share our modern sensitivities to difference. Putting foreign "gibberish" on stage could be counted on to raise a good laugh: "We can now establish that there is no example in extant Old Comedy of a non-Athenian Greek or barbarian whose speech is not marked in some foreign way."[106] Yet by the mid-fourth century, even the references to old dialectical divisions within the Greek language tended to disappear, leaving just the two worlds of Greek and non-Greek.[107]

The barbarian Other, then, is also first and primarily language deficient. As Edith Hall observes, the close connection between speech and reason made it easy in the fifth century to assume that *barbaroi* – like slaves (and animals, I would add) – lacked both.[108] With the loss of speech and reason, foreigners were in danger of losing all of their humanity. Pliny is entirely classical when he notes that the national languages, dialects, and varieties of speech are so numerous that a foreigner scarcely counts as a human in the eyes of a member of a different race (*HN* 7.1.7). It became only natural for *logos*-deficient barbarians to be associated with animal imagery as in, for example, Aeschylus' *Suppliants*. There, the pseudo-Greek chorus describes the race of Aegyptus as a crow (751), dog (758), monster (762), spider (887), and snake (995). To the more complete significance of animal imagery and speech in Aeschylus we shall return in the next chapter.

[105] Colvin (1999) 57–87; see also his analysis (54–6) of the portions of Timotheus' lyric piece *Persians* in which a Phrygian speaks some sort of pidgin Greek.

[106] Colvin (1999) 294; see 287–95 for a review of strange and barbarian language in Old Comedy. He argues (302–8) that the use of Greek dialect, on the other hand, is not solely for humorous purposes. Still, this is comedy. Barbarian language and dialect differences must both have been potentially amusing, since Old Comedy did not focus on vocal disparities between Attic characters of different ages, social status, or cultural level. Slaves, for example, many of whom must have been non-Athenian or barbarian, do not speak in any marked fashion; see: Halliwell (1990a); Dover (1997); Long (1986) 136: "So, in comedy, language is the first point of attack with foreigners" and 133–37 for barbarian language in Greek comedy, 129–56 for the barbarian-Hellene antithesis in general. Silk (2000) 99 with note 6 aptly refers to *Tractatus Coislinianus* XIVb = page 38 of Janko (1984): "The comic poet must endow his characters with their own native idiom, and (use) the local (idiom) himself"; see his comments ad loc. (223–5). Brixhe (1988) provides a technical analysis of the Scythians' lengthy babbling in the *Thesmophoriazusae* and the barbarian gods gibbering "like Illyrians" in the *Birds*; see Sier (1992); cf. *Ach.* 100, 104 and Morenilla-Talens (1989) on the sounds of foreigners and the different use made of them by Aeschylus and Aristophanes; further references in Harrison (1998) n.48; cf. Plautus *Poen.* 930f. with Dauge (1981) 648–53 on the different Roman conception of barbarian language. Harrison's conclusion (1998) n.76 that barbarian speech is characterized as "verbose" is not supported by the sources he cites.

[107] Saïd (2001); see also Hall (2002) 205–20 for the nature of "Panhellenism" in the late fifth and fourth centuries.

[108] Hall (1989) 198; also Buxton (1982) 58–9, 64, 161–3; Baslez (1984) 186; Rosivach (1999) 152–4.

SLAVES AND LANGUAGE

Much has been written about slavery in ancient Greece, both its day-to-day workings and the ideology that supported it. Whether one believes that Greek civilization was built on the backs of slaves, or that the institution was perhaps even necessary for the development of the concept of freedom itself, we now are rightfully forbidden to forget the hundreds of thousands of "human tools" working in the fields, houses, shops, and mines.[109] We should also not forget that Aristotle introduces his infamous defense of "natural slavery" by observing that others believe for one human to be master over another is contrary to nature (*Pol.* 1253b20–3). Later, the philosopher concedes he is arguing against "many" who hold that slavery by custom – servitude through force – is "monstrous" (*deinon*; *Pol.* 1255a8–12). That is, once again we have testimony that the nature of slavery, if not the existence of the institution itself, was up for debate in Greece. There is little such testimony in any other ancient society.[110] That Aristotle's conclusions, rather than the debate, became embedded in much of Western culture is an unfortunate truth. Much the same, I would add, could be said about the current treatment of animals. But that the West eventually abolished slavery must also, however, be credited in great part to the Greek legacy of open inquiry.

For this study, however, slaves are perhaps the most obvious of the voiceless Others because their voices clearly lack authority.[111] For Aristotle, slaves are living tools that are consistently compared to animals: they work with their bodies and lack reason (*logos*; e.g. *Pol.* 1253b–1254a; 1254b16–26). The animal and slave are interchangeable – the poor must use an ox instead of

---

[109] For the argument of the complementary nature of slavery and the development of freedom, see Patterson (1991).

[110] See Garnsey's excellent recent collection of sources (1996) especially 53–76. He concludes that despite criticisms of the practice of slavery, the Greeks never contemplated abolition. But he also observes that these criticisms were "progressive utterances" that "might have led to a campaign against the institution in a different historical context" (64), which indeed is what happened two millennia later. To point out faults in a system is to open up the possibility that it is simply wrong. Greek golden ages and utopias occasionally were slave-free, another sign that there was an awareness of the troubling nature of servitude; see: Vogt (1975) 26–38; Garlan (1988) 126–38. Athenian drama offered many opportunities to explore the nature of slavery. Gregory (2002) 151–61, for example, reviews the presentation of slavery in Euripides and concludes that he goes out of his way to question received ideas (including those about women), but is "far less interested in emending the actual position of these marginalized members of society."

[111] Vidal-Naquet (1986) 205–23 suggests that the distinction between free men and slaves was simply not a "problem" of self-definition in Athens (unlike in Argos and Sparta), since the distinction was so absolute. Just (1985), on the other hand, argues that the freedom–slavery distinction was the dominant metaphor in Athens, applied secondarily to women and barbarians.

a slave (*Pol.* 1252b12).[112] A Roman definition of a slave was *instrumentum vocale*, a tool with a voice. What this unhappy phrase denotes is that slaves *can* speak, as opposed to a plow or an ox. Again, we see that voice is the distinguishing criterion of being human – it is the *only* thing to distinguish a slave from an ox or plow.[113] But it certainly does not mean that slaves *should* speak, and in ancient Greece the distinction in status was even more severe than in Rome, where manumission was more common, and the sons of freedmen could become citizens and important public figures. One of the many Greek words for a slave was *andrapodon*, a "man-footed thing" analogous to the *tetrapoda* "four-footed thing," a common expression for cattle.[114] War against those barbarians who are by nature fit to be ruled and made slaves is the exact equivalent of hunting animals: both are "arts of acquisition" (Arist. *Pol.* 1256b23–6). Xenophon insists that the identical training used on wild animals is most suitable for slaves (*Oec.* 13.9). A slave had no rights beyond those relating to his master. He simply had no public voice (and those of foreign origin were likely to speak little or no Greek at all, in any case).

The Greeks knew, of course, that slaves were human and had voices. One of their important roles, after all, was to raise and teach the children of citizens. Deianira asks her son to listen to her nurse, "for though this woman is a slave, she has spoken a word worthy of the free" (*eleutheron logon, Trach.* 62–3). Aristotle refers to Simonides' "long story" (*makros logos*), the kind of lengthy, rambling account produced by a slave when he says nothing sound (*Metaph.* 1091a7–10; cf. Alex. of Aphrod. ad loc., who concludes this behavior probably derives from slaves' foreign origin – *barbaron* – and lack of education). Critics of Athenian democracy frequently believed that slaves there had far too much freedom. The Old Oligarch complains that servants won't even move aside for a free man, and he claims that slaves possess *isêgoria* (*Ath. pol.* 1.10–12). At best, he has insidiously conflated *isêgoria* with *parrhêsia*, but his (legitimate?) point is that the practice of slavery has slipped from its ideology. Isocrates, perhaps reflecting upon his own city, puts into the mouth of the Spartan Archidamus a more explicit report of this slippage: "It is disgraceful that we, who in former times would not allow even free men the right of equal speech (*isêgoria*), now openly tolerate the frankness (*parrhêsia*) of slaves" (6.97).[115] Plato's Socrates

---

[112] Smith (1991) 150–4.
[113] Skydsgaard (1980) 68 warns against taking offense at the term "instrumentum vocale," since Varro applied it not only to slaves but to *all* human laborers.
[114] Cartledge (1993a) 136 notes that the word was more precisely applied to slaves captured in war.
[115] Sparta was usually thought by critics of Athenian democracy to have a better system of dealing with slaves as communal property; e.g. Arist. *Pol.* 1263a35; Xen. *Lac.* 6.3.

is even more direct – and revealing – in his disapproval of the breakdown
in hierarchy in a city like Athens:

The extreme of freedom of the people occurs in such a city when the purchased
slaves, both male and female, are no less free than those who purchased them. And
I nearly forgot to mention how great are the equal rights and freedom between the
sexes . . . How much freer are the beasts controlled by men in that city than in any
other – no one would believe it if they hadn't seen it with their own eyes. For the
dogs are just like their mistresses, as the proverb goes. Similarly the horses and asses
are accustomed to carry themselves with total freedom and pride, ramming into
anyone along the roads who meets them and does not stand aside. (*Resp.* 563b–c;
cf. Lycurg. *Leoc.* 41 for the horror of Athenians voting to expand the circle.)

Plato's animals – like the Old Oligarch's slaves – with almost rational
calculation refuse to acknowledge their superiors in *logos* by moving aside.
Indeed, the lesson seems to be that if you treat a being as if it possesses *logos*
(even if it supposedly doesn't), it will become as arrogant as those few who
rightfully can claim full access to *logos*.

So how was it that people could be treated as animals? The fact that
they were often foreign must have made it easier to ignore their claims to
being treated as fully human.[116] Plato (*Leg.* 777c–e) observes that slaves are
difficult chattels, especially dangerous when they speak the same language.
Consequently, he recommends finding slaves from different nations.

Slaves had even less opportunity to speak authoritatively than did
women, and thus they too got their shot at public speech primarily on
the stage. In the intentionally inverted world of comedy, slaves could act
like gods and gods like slaves, even swapping punches to "prove" who is
which (e.g. in Aristophanes' *Frogs*)! But one does not need to read Aristotle's bizarre justification of "natural slavery" to understand that only a good
deal of mental gymnastics could justify human bondage. Slaves were said
to lack *logos*.[117] The easiest way to reinforce the system was to deny slaves
speech, to denigrate their language in some fashion that kept them near the
bestial level. And in fact the Athenian treatment of slaves' public speech –
a fairly bizarre system rarely (if ever) even applied – supports the thesis that
language is a primary factor in Greek self-definition.

---

[116] Rosivach (1999) 129–30 argues that there is "not one Athenian slave in either the literary or epi-
graphical record who can be securely identified as of Greek origin," and shows that except for
women and children there is surprisingly little evidence for Greeks enslaved by other Greeks.

[117] Plato agrees with Aristotle in seeing the slave's condition as deficiency of reason, and in fact seems
to go one step further in denying slaves any *logos* and suggesting they have only a possession of
belief (*Leg.* 720; 773e; 966b). A slave can have true belief, but not know why his belief is true; he
can neither give nor follow a rational account, and is therefore susceptible to persuasion; see Vlastos
(1981) 147–63. For Aristotle's account, see Garnsey (1996) 35–8.

One of the most peculiar aspects of the Athenian legal system was that the evidence of slaves *had* to be extracted under torture, and was limited to answers of either yes or no.[118] Like women and children, slaves had no public personhood and had to be represented by a *kurios*. They could not appear in court as witnesses. Women could give an oath, but slaves could not volunteer evidence under most circumstances. In fact, a master could not freely offer evidence of his slave, even if the owner was not directly involved in the case. Athenian speakers in court often claimed that testimony extracted from slaves under torture was more reliable than that given by free men of their own volition.[119] Although orators sometimes argued that torture produced only lies,[120] Demosthenes agrees with what he takes to be the jurors' unanimous opinion that "torture is the most certain of all methods of proof" and states, without apparent fear of contradiction, that not one slave put to torture has ever been convicted of giving false testimony (30.37). Lycurgus calls it "most just and democratic" to examine slaves of either sex by torture, since this way they will tell the whole truth (*Leoc.* 29–31).[121]

It is hard to imagine that such *basanoi* – inquiries by torture – developed out of any philosophical explorations of the presumed irrationality of slaves. There is no obvious reason to think rationality is involved at all. The issue here is primarily the unreliability of the word from beings that are viewed as corporeal rather than fully human. Slaves, like animals, were primarily bodies. Demosthenes argues that the greatest difference between slave and free is that the former is answerable with his body for all offenses

---

[118] The standard work is Thür (1977). Hunter (1994) 70–1, 90–4 with references has a good discussion of judicial torture of slaves. She notes that there were exceptions, such as when slaves were encouraged by the promise of freedom to inform against their master, who was charged with treason, sacrilege, or theft of public moneys. She provides appendices with references to known incidents; also duBois (1991) 24–35.

[119] Harrison (1971) 147–50; Hunter (1994) 90 n.42 for primary sources.

[120] See Allen (2000) 104–5 and notes for references.

[121] There is an oddity in our evidence. A slave owner had to challenge his opponent to accept the evidence of his slave, or agree to accept his opponent's challenge. Yet despite the nearly universal approbation of judicial torture, in every extant reference to the procedure one side or the other refused the challenge (in two cases, the litigants apparently could not agree upon the preferred form of torture). That is, no case with evidence extracted by torture is known to have made it to trial (though cf. Thür [1977]). This has caused historians problems, with various solutions proposed. Hunter (1994) 93 accepts the suggestion that judicial torture was intended to serve as an alternative to jury trial – like the oath challenge – and so none reached the courts; see also Mirhady (1991; 1996). Johnstone (1999) places these judicial proceedings under the category of "dares": the mere acceptance of the "dare" of having a slave tortured effectively produced a settlement. If this is true, then the words of a slave in court are a complete mirage, since they were never to be heard in any case.

(22.55) – "proof" is to be taken "from his body" (49.56).[122] The speech of slaves could be assumed to be untrustworthy simply by nature of the individual and the institution. Plutarch insists that it is most important to accustom children to speaking the truth, for lying is fit only for slaves (*De Liberis educ.* 11c). Oaths might work to obtain the truth from the free, but for the enslaved one must use "other devices" (Antiph. 6.25). The word *basanos* itself means a touchstone, the means of testing (and consequently the test itself) "to try whether a thing be genuine or not" (LSJ). Slaves were not fully human, deprived of speech and eventually conceived of lacking rationality as well. Speech in Greece is the power of self-identification. To lose that truly was, as a once noble man reduced to servitude says, to lose half of his worth (*aretê, Od.* 17.322–3).

LANGUAGE AND AGE

This is a category often ignored in Otherness studies, since boys can grow up into citizens, that is, complete humans, and old men still possess their privileged citizen status. But in fact the Greeks considered children to be incomplete adults, and they also held deeply ambivalent attitudes toward the elderly. One of the most popular Greek proverbs was that old men are children again – it was not meant to be a compliment to either.

The status of children, especially in Athens, has been thoroughly studied by Mark Golden.[123] Children are consistently described by the Greeks as inferior adults, weaker in physical fitness, moral development, and especially intelligence. The most frequently noted characteristic of children is their intellectual incapacity – they are not fully rational, often linked in this inadequacy with women, slaves, and animals, especially by philosophers. Plato, with his philosophical twist to *logos*, even states that some children never gain *logos* at all (*Resp.* 441a–b). *Pais* is a common word for both a child and a slave (as well as pathics) of any age.[124] Golden sees the commonality in statuses. That is, the cultural subordination came first, and only later did the identity of certain similar characteristics appear.[125] This may well be true, but of concern here is what characteristic the Greeks decided should count, the one that linked the subordinated groups. Once again, it was

---

[122] See Finley (1998) 161–90; Fisher (1995) 59–62. Slaves *owed* their bodies, both in work and sex, to their owners. It is interesting, and understandable, that the word *kloios*, a dog collar, was also applied to the device secured around the neck of slaves under torture (as well as of criminals as punishment); Eur. *Cyc.* 235; Xen. *Hell.* 3.3.11; Lucian *Tox.* 32; Pollux 10.177; see Hunter (1994) 157.

[123] Golden (1990), especially 1–22 for summary and references.

[124] Golden (1985); Garland (1990) 127.　　[125] Golden (1985).

logos. And once again, I think, underlying rationality, or lack of it, was language.

As we have seen, the most common early word for small child was *nêpios*, frequent in Homer but rare later in Attic prose, which may well refer to a deficiency in speech. I would suggest that any interpretation of a small child's rationality, like that of animals, must ultimately be linked to his lack of speech. Infants' wailing is referred to by the verbs *blêchaomai* and *bruchaomai*, the former otherwise used of sheep and goats, and the latter usually applied to the bellowing of beasts and raging of storms.[126]

After children learned to speak, they still shared in the world of slaves and women, in that they were said to be unable to control their speech effectively and were instructed to remain silent. As Plato says, no young creature can govern his speech or is capable of keeping the body or tongue quiet, nor able yet of grasping the rational (*Leg.* 653a–e). Thus, the cultural burden on children, as on women and slaves, was to remain silent. The Better Argument in Aristophanes' *Clouds* remembers the good old days when not a sound was heard from boys (961f.). Socrates comments on the appropriate silence of the younger in face of the older (*Resp.* 425a–b). In a fragment of an oration "On the Constitution" by Thrasymachus, the sophist laments that the time has passed when young men stayed silent in public and older men supervised the city.[127] Isocrates (*Aereop.* 48–9) adds that in the olden days young men did not contradict their elders. We will recall that Spartan boys were trained to be more mute than a stone. Long after children could speak – and presumably show some elements of rationality – they were still not supposed to utter a word.[128]

Of course, some moment came when a boy became a man, and with this maturation came the sudden demand (if he was a citizen) that he not only speak but speak persuasively and effectively. This capability, as we have seen, made him a citizen and leader. But what happened when one got old?[129] On the one hand, such senior citizens were sure to be the repositories of wisdom and honored speech, as we have seen in the case of Nestor. A character in a play by the comic poet Pherecrates repeats a common Greek sentiment

---

[126] Golden (1990) 9. Golden (1995) 12 notes that the word uttered by the children in Herodotus' famous story of the "earliest" language – *bekos* (said to be the Phrygian word for "bread") – was later interpreted to be the sound of the bleating of goats (Sch. Ap. Rhod. 4.262, Suda β 229).

[127] DK B1; see the discussion of White (1995), and cf. Eupolis *Fr.* 310E. For the depiction of youth in Aristophanes, see Bryant (1907).

[128] Herodotus (2.80) suggests that the Spartans were unusually strict in their expectations of deference of the younger to their seniors; see David (1991) 64–9 for Spartan deferential silence towards elders. Some Stoics argued that children acquire rationality only between the ages of 7 and 14, and until then they have no more than animals; see Inwood (1985) 72–3.

[129] See Reinhold (1976) 31–7.

in remarking that youth is impulsive, whereas elders deliberate (*Fr.* 146; cf. Eurip. *Fr.* 115.5N). In Solon's catalogue of the ten ages of man, on the other hand, the peak of intellect and power of speech comes in what we would call middle age, not until the seventh and eighth periods (e.g. 43–56 years old – this seems about right to me; cf. Hes. *Fr.* 321M–W).

A cultural tension exists here as well. Speech must be connected with some kind of action to be effective. What counts is authoritative speech, not mere articulation. As we saw in Homer's world, that most famous aged counselor, Nestor, must tie his words to his past actions to have authority. Greek literature is filled with proverbs that suggest speech is merely the "shadow" of action. At some point, one leaves the world of action just as quickly as one had entered it, and speech is once again challenged. We may think of the aged senators of Rome running the Republic, but in fact Sparta's Council of Elders of men over sixty was the exception rather than the rule in Greece, and even there the elderly could find it tougher, especially if poor, than at Athens.[130] Another Greek proverb ran "never do good to an old man (*gerôn*) or to a child (*pais*)."[131] The connection is that neither can do anything good for you in return – they are powerless. *Leschai* – a term used for public places for conversation as well as the conversations themselves – are linked specifically with old men.[132] Feeble geezers make good comedy because of their impotence (the *double entendre* here is rarely left unexplored). Of the eleven extant comedies of Aristophanes, only the *Frogs* does not include any geriatrics.[133] Euripides, too, enjoys the dilemma of the voluble but anemic elderly character: all but two of his extant plays have at least one.[134] Members of tragic choruses are frequently old. Indeed, the ideal chorus, which most of the time must stand fretfully and helplessly, uttering inefficacious words as horrible things happen around them, is comprised of two or more categories of Otherness. The chorus can thus be doubly or even triply "marginal."[135]

---

[130] David (1991) 87–93. True, prophets, seers, and soothsayers are old men, but as Finley (1981) 162–3 points out, they are also normally irascible and unpleasant, blind and unheeded.

[131] Garland (1990) 11.   [132] Buxton (1994) 42–3.

[133] Henderson (1987) 128–9 argues that before 411 we find only disreputable women in Attic comedy; after that, older women could be used to express safely "what was thought" in the city. For old men in Aristophanes, see Hubbard (1989). Bremmer (1987) 203 notes that of the terrifying female monstrosities in the Greek imagination (Empousa, Erinyes, Harpies, etc.), many are old as well: Moirae, Empousa, Lamia, Graiae, Erinyes.

[134] Falkner (1995) 169.

[135] Gouldner (1965) 110–11. Oddly, although one can find combinations of the elderly, slaves, and foreigners – and plenty of females – tragedy does not depend upon the choruses of old women that are found in comedy; see Gould (1996).

Greeks were not unaware of the mental debilitation that often comes with old age, thus rendering language fruitless. Nestor – and Jung – aside, the wise old man is not a regular feature of Greek mythology.[136] The stereotyped profile of old men connotes weakness, lack of control, and helplessness. Thomas Falkner concludes his study of the "poetics of old age" by observing that "in Hesiod and the *Homeric Hymns*, in lyric and elegiac tradition, and in Greek tragedy, the picture [of old age] ranges with few exceptions from bleak to horrid."[137] Although some of the aged are wise but powerless, others are childish in their loss of sense (e.g. Soph. *OC* 930–1; Eur. *Fr.* 25N). Xenophon argues that Socrates committed a type of public suicide in his speech of defense at least in part because he wished to avoid the inevitable diminution of his mental powers (*Mem.* 4.8.1). Solon notes that by the ninth septad (57–63) speech and discrimination have begun to slip. In this sense, old age as a second childhood refers to diminished mental skills and the concomitant lack of status. The old can speak, but once again without authority. There was even a term *kronolêros*, "old babbler," probably coined by a comic writer (*Com. Adesp.* 860; cf. Plut. *De Lib. Educ.* 13b). Old men may easily become ineffectual prattlers (cf. Ar. *Ach.* 679–89; *Nub.* 129–30; Democr. 104DK). In this sense, Tithonus stands as an excellent example of the perils of old age. In the *Homeric Hymn to Aphrodite*, the goddess relates how Tithonus, granted immortality but not eternal youth, is pressed by "hateful" old age. Locked in a room, he has lost the strength in his limbs, and can only ramble unceasingly (literally in a "voice that is no voice," *phônê . . . aspetos*, 236–8). By the fifth century, his non-human voice has earned him a full transformation into a grasshopper or cicada.[138] The cycle is complete: born wailing and irrational, even those who possess *logos* are eventually reduced to bestial incomprehensibility once again.

THE GODS

As we have seen, language is a distinguishing criterion in the conception of the divine in the Homeric poems. The language and voice of the gods separate them not only from animals but from humans as well. By classical times, however, the gods were not conversing much with humans, at least

---

[136] Kirk (1971) 128–31.
[137] (1995) 262; Falkner notes that Homer's picture of the elderly is ambivalent, and Sophocles' *Oedipus at Colonus* is iconoclastic; see also Richardson (1969) 3–23; Silk (1995) 188f.
[138] Hellanicus (4F140); see the discussion of King (1989), although Silk (1995) 205 n.46 rightly corrects her interpretation of *aspetos* in the *Homeric Hymn* as "strong-voiced"; see also Falkner (1995) 125 with 289 n.43.

directly. Not that the divine could not be seen at work in human affairs: retribution for past sins, mysterious events in battle, oracular pronounce-ments, and otherwise inexplicable portents all signaled the interest of the gods in the Greeks' lives. But the gods no longer were thought to share our world in the way they had in the glorious days of epic heroes. Athena did not chat with Pericles; Apollo did not stroll with Themistocles. Socrates' claim that a little divine voice – he never said it was a god – often warned him to avoid certain actions was considered bizarre, perhaps even sacrilegious (see Chapter 6). Even at Delphi, the god may have revealed the future through the garbled oracles of the female priestess, gibberish that required expert exegesis.[139] One of the most attractive elements of mystery cults seems to have been that they put the individual into more direct contact with the divine than was regularly possible.[140]

Yet the gods did share space with humans, and Greeks did communi-cate with the gods. The vehicles for most of this "conversation" were, in addition to inanimate votive offerings, the voiceless animals themselves.[141] One thinks of augury – the clattering birds Tiresias tells Creon about in the *Antigone*, for example, and the close association often made between animals and prophecy (e.g. Xanthus, Achilles' horse). A seer was usually present at sacrifices to inspect the lobes of the animal liver. Many oracles and portents involved animals, as even a quick reading of Herodotus reveals (e.g. 5.56, 5.92, 6.131, 7.57, 9.20). Sometimes animal "language" is learned by legendary prophets. Seers such as Melampus (as well as Helenus and Cassandra) got their powers of prophecy from snakes licking their ears. Melampus could converse with birds, and even saved himself when he heard worms commenting that the beam in the ceiling was almost eaten through (Pherecydes in scholion to *Nekuia*, 3F33; Apollod. 1.9.11–12).

But of course animals' primary role in the mediation between gods and humans was as sacrificial victims.[142] The ritual slaughter of domesticated

[139] Fontenrose (1978) 204–19, however, notes the lack of good evidence for the Pythia's incoherency.
[140] See Burkert (1987). Herodotus' account (1.60) of Pisistratus' duping of the Athenians by dressing up a tall Paeanian woman as Athena may describe a pageant rather than an actual deception. Still, the historian's logic suggests that the gods were enough present that a Greek could believe, even if just for a moment, that they were riding a chariot into town. But Herodotus can hardly give credence to the story himself, noting with a shake of his head that Greeks are distinguished from barbarians by their cleverness, and the Athenians are the cleverest of Greeks; see Harrison (2000b) 82–92 for Herodotus' "non-committal" treatment of divine epiphanies.
[141] See Prieur (1988) for the role of animals in religion in the ancient Mediterranean, and especially Bodson (1978) for animals in Greek religion.
[142] Much has been written about the origin and function of sacrifice, but most scholars still build on the seminal work of Burkert (1983) esp. 1–58; see the critical survey in Katz (1990) and the summary of Jameson (1988b). Detienne and Vernant (1989) is a collection of essays from the French school

animals was the primary cultic act of the Greeks, and served as a means of both connecting and separating the human and the divine. Sacrificial killing is the basic experience of the sacred, and, combined with the sharing of victim's flesh, the shedding of animal blood supplies the ritual basis for community through a festival of guilt and reparation, death and renewal.

The ritual itself then is a kind of language, similar though not identical to myth. The bloodshed, slaughter, and eating of domesticated animals links them with humans, creating a vehicle for communication with the gods while also creating a polarity between the mortal and the divine: "Through the death which it dies, it confirms *e contrario* the superior power of the wholly other, deathless, everlasting god."[143] It was essential, then, that animals did not speak. In a kind of game that redirected guilt and made the animal acceptable to the gods, the victim was thought to go willingly to its death. This sacred farce was best accomplished by dousing its head with water, the subsequent shaking taken to be acquiescence in its role.[144]

Animals, through their silent and central place in ritual, became the language for communication with the gods. The gods used animals as tools to reveal their wills and intentions, and humans used animals to communicate their piety in return. Yet once again, even this most crucial event did not go unchallenged. Cults likes those of the Orphics and Pythagoreans, as well as religious nuts like Empedocles, found the killing of ensouled beings objectionable. Philosophers too, especially Theophrastus (but also Varro and Seneca), argued against the necessity of shedding ritual blood.[145] The mythic origins of sacrifice through the deception of Zeus by Prometheus reveal an interest from the beginning of the archaic age in understanding and justifying at least the obviously self-serving distribution of the dead animal.[146] Once again, the Greeks started us on a road that 2,500 years later

---

(with a good bibliography). For animals in Greek religion, see Bodson (1978). The gods own their own animals in both mythology (e.g. Helius' infamously slaughtered herd) and various historical communities; see Parker (1983) 176; Isager and Skydsgaard (1992) 191–8.

[143] Burkert (1985) 66.

[144] References in Burkert (1983) 4 n.13. This becomes problematic in myth where women are substituted for the sacrificial animal – they must go bravely (e.g. Polyxena and Iphigenia in Euripides) or be gagged (e.g. Iphigenia in Aeschylus). It is interesting that at the very moment the deathblow was delivered to the silent beast, the ordinarily muted women in the gathering let out a piercing cry, the "Greek custom of the sacrificial scream" (Aesch. *Sept.* 269). Female inarticulate voices fill the air in place of the animal's.

[145] See references in Burkert (1983) 7–8, and the Epilogue to this study.

[146] Vernant (1989); see Mason (1987) for connections between Prometheus, women, the golden age, and animals.

we are still traveling. Of major world religions, only Islam retains animal slaughter as a central cultic rite.

The classical Other, then, is bestial in its silence. If our goal is to live fully human lives, then we must find ways to use our language that will evoke and develop our humanity. Part Three explores in detail two very different visions of the significance of speech for living a meaningful life. For Aeschylus, only through speech applied correctly can we disentangle ourselves from the bestial world. The rise of the polis, the development of persuasive speech, and the differentiation of human, animal, and divine simultaneously signal the necessary condition for human flourishing. For Plato, on the other hand, this political definition of human success is a mistake. Socrates has a different interpretation of meaningful language – philosophy alone qualifies as our goal. In his efforts to exercise his humanity, and to get others to exercise theirs, he reduced his fellow citizens to aporetic silence. And silence, as we have seen, is political death in Athens. The Athenians may have gotten even by silencing Socrates, but Plato got the last laugh by eternalizing Socrates' speech.

PART III

Speech, Animals, and Human Status in Classical Athens

CHAPTER 5

Disentangling the beast: Humans and other animals in the Oresteia

The Greeks of the polis knew a thin line separated their own humanity from the life of the beast. Hesiod provides the first explicit testimony to the difference between the two worlds:

But you, Perses, deliberate on this in your heart and listen now to right (*dikê*), forgetting violence altogether. For the son of Cronus drew up this law for men, that fish and beasts and flying birds eat one another, since right is not in them. But to mankind he gave right which is by far the best. For if anyone knows the right and is willing to speak it (*agoreusai*), to him far-seeing Zeus gives prosperity. (*Op.* 274–81)

Man alone has access to justice, whereas animals are condemned to live by violence, turning on one another. But in an agrarian world where words are to be matched by deeds, justice is not a passive entitlement but must be "spoken aloud" and acted upon. For, as Hesiod continues, there is no prosperity for those whose words betray their humanity, for those who lie (*pseusetai*, 283) and swear falsely, who know one thing and speak forth another. Justice requires the correct use of language. As the poet notes in his other epic, speech is intimately linked with justice and the just community:

All the people look towards him [the Muse-favored king] as he decides cases with just judgements. Speaking out unerringly he quickly brings even a great dispute to a wise end. For this is why the wise are kings, since in the agora they easily accomplish restitution for those who have been wronged, persuading them with gentle words. (*Theog.* 84–90)[1]

This connection between humanity, justice, and speech – and its contrast with the lives of "dumb" beasts – is central to early Greek thought, as we have seen in the previous chapters. Nowhere is it found with greater force, however, than in Aeschylus' *Oresteia*. The trilogy depicts, as we are so often told, the birth of a more democratic community, the evolution of

---

[1] For some of these issues in Hesiod, see Leclerc (1993).

justice from a morally primordial desire for blood vengeance to a civic system of trial by jury.[2] The "beast" in this process is more than a mere foil for the human action, more even than a representative of the violence of retribution that must be caged and locked away if civilization is to progress.

Animals in the pre-polis arena erected by Aeschylus are insidious creatures, refusing to accept simple metaphorical, that is, stylistically ornamental roles. When Agamemnon becomes an eagle, it is no simple figure of speech – the bird and king merge before our eyes. The boundaries of humanity itself are too porous, allowing the beast to slip in and out with discomforting ease. The poet's powerfully metaphorical language creates an anarchic world where man and beast are muddled, where human and non-human species share a single soul. The *Oresteia* presents an undifferentiated and untenable world that finally, under the force of humanity's unique endowment of speech, gives way to mankind's unique political structure, the polis. Only here can *dikê* exist at all. By the end of the three plays, the bestial, human, and divine elements have been separated and channeled into their proper places in the polis, an institution that not only represents this proper arrangement, but also makes such an essential differentiation possible.[3] And language – persuasive speech – is the central feature of the newly fashioned community, the only place where we can become fully human.

---

[2] As Goldhill has observed (1997) 138, the "teleology of this account has been extensively and rightly challenged and redefined," but it still holds as a useful outline of some of the larger themes; see also Decreus (2000) for a survey of the critical and artistic responses to the "Eurocentrism, foundation of democracy, and position of women" evoked by the trilogy over the past few centuries.

[3] Peradotto (1969) 246 n.32, in an illuminating note not directly linked to his main argument, refers to the "assimilation" of man to beast and its connection to the development of *dikê* in *Oresteia*. My ideas in this chapter are in several ways an amplification of that suggestion. Also similar in approach is Rosenmeyer (1982) 138–41, who sees animals as representatives of the repulsive world which exists prior to the advent of civilization. A detailed study of this imagery and the theme of violence is Moreau (1985) esp. 61–99, 267–91. The introductory chapters of Segal (1981) on the man/beast and man/god polarities in Greek are still a good starting-place for these issues, although Aeschylus does not maintain the "in-betweenness" to the end and thus defies most structuralist approaches. Segal himself in a later study (1986) 60 seems to note that Aeschylus must be treated differently; cf. Vidal-Naquet (1981). A brief but important treatment of the birds in the *parodos* of the *Agamemnon* is Easterling (1987) 54–9. Aeschylus' style and structure result not merely in a tension between polarities but in a mingling that can and must be – and *is* – brought to an end by the conclusion of the trilogy. The polis itself is in some ways the heroic figure in the *Oresteia*. The term polis in this chapter refers to the mature polis, the functioning, democratic institutions that a contemporary of Aeschylus would associate with Athens. The word itself is used in the *Oresteia* to describe Troy (25x), Argos (19x), a city in general (9x), and finally Athens (30x). Troy is a polis that becomes *apolin* (*Eum.* 457) at its destruction. Argos is a dysfunctional polis, with Delphi as the transitional point to Athens, which is referred to twenty-one times as a polis in the final three hundred verses of the trilogy. Here alone can the beast be coopted into civilization.

In this chapter, I will explore the various ways Aeschylus presents this jumbled world, how it is finally resolved, and the thematic significance of this resolution. Most previous approaches to Aeschylean animals have taken one of two routes. Some do not treat the creatures as primary symbols but as subsidiary to what are considered broader motifs, such as the ubiquitous expressions of entanglement, the hunt, sacrifice, corrupted fertility, spilled blood, etc. I believe, however, that the human/beast conflation is one of the primary images in the *Oresteia*, from which most of the other famous polarities ultimately derive.[4] Other scholars have concentrated on individual species – lions bagged this time, a viper and eagle trapped another, hounds collared in still another. But my interest is in the kind of world created when animals – any animals – are so easily blurred and confused with the human characters. I make no attempt here to analyze all of the animal imagery in the trilogy, much less all of its potential meaning – I fully acknowledge the importance of animals in these other thematic roles. Rather, by examining certain episodes in detail in the order in which they occur in the text (the few exceptions to this sensible rule will, I hope, clarify rather than confuse the argument), we will uncover the intimate connections of Aeschylus' style and structure with the moral and political themes of the text – how the complexities of his style embody the thematic problems. Ultimately, the trilogy suggests that by developing our uniquely human facility of speech we have the chance to isolate and manage the beast within.

VULTURES AND KINGS

We can best begin by examining the first extensive use of animal imagery in the *Agamemnon* and the kind of critical response it has elicited. The extended simile towards the beginning of the *parodos* ostensibly compares

[4] Surprisingly, the animal/human dichotomy does not make it onto the list of twenty-six antitheses compiled by Zeitlin (1978) 171–2. It does appear in the shorter list of Greek (not necessarily Aeschylean) polarities of Buxton (1982) 62. Of course, one scholar's "primary" metaphor may be another critic's derivative. Fowler (1969) 39 suggests that the animal imagery derives from other figures of compulsion, an issue which itself is primarily related to gender. Rosenmeyer (1982) 130 considers eating as the primary metaphor of which animals are a subset. An especially thorough treatment of imagery is Petrounias (1976) 129f., who divides his chapters into a "leitmotiv" – usually animals – and secondary images. Less analytical but similarly arranged is Dumortier (1975); Bernand (1986) 242–9 surveys the moral significance of animals in Aeschylus. We often take for granted that animal imagery is pervasive throughout the entire Aeschylean corpus. Earp's catalogue (1948) 104 is revealing: there are more animal metaphors in the *Agamemnon* (33) than in the *Libation Bearers* (18) and *Eumenides* (13) together, more than in the other four plays combined. But even the *Eumenides* contains more than any Aeschylean play outside the trilogy. Earp counts only patent allusions, not all the allusions and twists of language.

the war cry of the Atreidae (48) evoked by the theft of Helen (60f.) to the screeching of vultures robbed of their young (49).[5] But the comparison involves a subtle shift, as Fraenkel and others have pointed out.[6] The simile begins as a comparison between two different sets of cries, but it slips quietly into a deeper, more thematically significant level of thought. The poetic movement goes prosaically (and thus awkwardly) something like this: the sons of Atreus raise a cry like bereaved vultures whose lament is heard by a god who sends an avenging Fury – so does Zeus send the sons of Atreus to exact punishment on Paris for this theft. Even a straightforward reading of the simile, then, involves a fairly elaborate system of analogies. Few critics in the last forty years, however, have been content to walk away from such rich imagery. The vultures and their lost children are commonly viewed as representing Thyestes and his children, or Clytemnestra and Iphigenia, as well as Menelaus, Agamemnon, and Helen. A brief review of the arguments for these interpretations will provide a necessary background for the slightly different interpretation offered here of the meaning of Aeschylus' animal imagery throughout the *Oresteia*.[7]

The Atreidae cry out war like vultures "who, off their usual tracks in grief for their children, very high above their beds, wheel in circles, sped on by the strokes of their wings, having lost the labor they put into watching over the beds of their young."[8] The pain felt by the vultures for the missing chicks (*algesi paidôn*, 50) is brought into the human world by the anthropomorphism of *paidôn* and seems to demand explication. Moreover, if this is an analogy for the theft of Helen, critics have wondered at the significance of the plural (and indeed why "children" at all, instead

---

[5] The text is that of Page's OCT unless otherwise noted. I retain the traditional translation of *aigupioi* as vultures, despite the arguments of Whallon (1980) 12–16 that they would better be called "erens." As he notes, some commentators and translators have also rendered the word as "eagles," thus implying the birds of the simile are identical to those of the famous omen; see below.

[6] Ad 59. Daube (1939) 99 maintains that the cry of the Atreidae is a combination of lament (*goos*) and call to war (*boê*).

[7] Almost alone among recent scholars in rejecting any multi-layered symbolism for the vultures in the simile is van Erp Taalman Kip (1996) 122–3 and 136 n.11; cf. (1990) 49–51, for the (misguided, I believe) concern that spectators will not endure ambiguity and so must either know the references beforehand or have them spelled out immediately. Similarly, Van Dijk (1997) 171–6 denies the polyvalence of the lion image in the fable at *Ag.* 717–36 on the grounds that this kind of reading is not compatible with drama that is meant to be understood in performance. He suggests the lion may conjure up a dominant image but not a person; I think the two cannot be so easily separated. Still, it is good to be cautioned about pushing ambiguity to the point of denying any possible meaning. Many of the following observations can be found in the critical literature; I have added a few that I think strengthen the argument, especially for the identification of the birds with Clytemnestra and Iphigenia.

[8] This translation uses an interpretation of *ekpatiois* proposed by Goldhill (1989); see discussion below. I have nothing new to add to the debate over the meaning of *hupatoi*, and simply repeat the standard rendition.

of, perhaps, a spouse). One answer has been that buried here is a subtle allusion to Thyestes' children, lost to their father in beastly fashion. On the other hand, the individual most associated in the trilogy with grief for a lost child is Clytemnestra. Thus, the plural chicks become Iphigenia, and the plural vultures Clytemnestra, or (in an ironic coupling) Clytemnestra and Agamemnon.

The rare use of *lecheôn* for nests has also drawn understandable attention. It is unquestionably appropriate for the immediate context – Menelaus' bed has been fouled by an Eastern interloper – but how does it apply to the other possible referents? Thyestes' bed may have been an issue, as he seduced Atreus' wife – they were "away from their usual tracks," to be sure. Agamemnon's bed has also entertained an adulterous affair for several years when the old men of the chorus chant these verses, but this has nothing to do with the causes of the war. From Clytemnestra's point of view, however, her marriage bed has been betrayed in the most brutal manner. The queen's anger derives from the slaughter of her daughter, Iphigenia, the child of her marriage, the product of her bed. Perhaps this interpretation of *lecheôn* can be connected with the rare adjective used of the labor the vultures wasted over the young – "careful-watching-over-the-bed" (*demniotêrê / ponon*, 53–4). The care and painful effort in raising children is not a central element in the life of Agamemnon or Menelaus. Thyestes could be accused by structuralists of becoming too close to his children,[9] and whatever effort he did take in watching his sons grow was certainly wasted. The extant tales of his family, however, do not suggest that he was any more involved in the rearing of his sons than any other mythological father.

It is Clytemnestra, of course, who fits this picture most closely. She laments the loss of her child in quite similar terms when she contrasts her feelings towards Iphigenia with those of her husband who "sacrificed his own child, my dearest child" (literally, "one born through labor pains," 1417–18). The "careful-watching-over-the-bed" effort may implicate Clytemnestra in the vulture simile.[10] Perhaps it is no coincidence that the only other appearance of this adjective in all of extant Greek literature

---

[9] Goldhill (1984) 14 n.11, for example, believes that in Lévi-Straussian terms such substitutions can be made, noting that Helen as the *paidôn* can also be child, "both child and not child." Well, yes and not yes.

[10] Clytemnestra had earlier (1392) rejoiced in the shower of Agamemnon's blood no less than a crop "during the birth-pangs" (*en locheumasin*) of the buds. Although there is no careful distinction between *teknon* and *pais* in the *Oresteia*, it is interesting that Clytemnestra uses only *pais* of her daughter (cf. *Ag.* 1432). She calls Orestes both *teknon* (*Cho.* 896, 910, 912, 920, 922; cf. 829) and *pais* (*Cho.* 896). At *Ag.* 877, she refers to Orestes as *pais*, but in a context that at first could easily, and with painful irony, refer to Iphigenia. Agamemnon, according to the chorus, called his daughter *teknon* (208). Clytemnestra resented being treated like a *pais* (277), no doubt at least in part because

appears just thirty lines after Clytemnestra's reference to her fruitless labor pains (1448–54). The chorus asks for a quick death, rather than a painful and "careful-watching-over-the-bed" fate, now that Agamemnon has been struck down (literally "tamed," *damentos*, 1451; cf. 1495) by a woman. The lingering labor wasted over the (presumed dead) young in the vulture simile now becomes the lingering death of the (still alive) old, and Clytemnestra is the figure lurking behind both passages. Sex (cf. *koinolektros* of Cassandra, 1441), birth, and death are all linked by images of the bed, and – as we shall see – Clytemnestra is lying comfortably in the middle of it.

This survey of possible readings of the simile – by no means exhaustive[11] – indicates what most critics have long suggested, that Aeschylus' images are multivalent, that sets of meaningful analogies can be legitimate without being mutually exclusive. The simile conjures up for different readers Agamemnon, Menelaus, Helen, and Clytemnestra, Iphigenia, Thyestes and his children. To what end, though? Why the multiple layers of correspondence? The reasonable answer usually provided by studies of imagery is that the symbolism foreshadows incidents and subtly evokes important themes – such as parental loss, corrupted sacrifice, and perverted fertility – that eventually become central to the tragedies. While I don't disagree with this approach, my suggestion is that the equally important point here for understanding the trilogy is the fact of the ambiguity itself, the blurring of distinctions between human and animal in particular, that produces the desire for critical analysis and systematizing of the resulting disorder. Scholars for some time have pointed out that one of the constants in Aeschylean poetry is the movement from ambiguity to clarity, from multiple and muddled readings to a comparatively univocal resolution.[12] What is thematically significant, then, about this simile – and other animal images with similar linguistic richness – is not so much any exact analogy for the vultures and their young but the troubling fusion of human and bestial identities the poetic ambiguity creates. The poet's language mirrors the thematic conflation of the various polarities – and their ultimate resolution – so often recounted in the scholarship. The audience, in other

she had witnessed how lightly a woman's life and speech could be valued. Rabel (1982) 325 notes the frequent use of *paides* for the children, but places these references in the context of Apollo's role as protector of young.

[11] Rabel (1984), for example, suggests that the *paidôn* here become the *Atreôs paidas* in v. 60 and are to be numbered among the "lost children" of the trilogy. Fowler's detailed study of the Furies (1991) finds them in the vultures – indeed, in most of the animals and characters in the three plays – but for reasons discussed later, I remain skeptical.

[12] Fowler's lengthy article (1969) and Lebeck's book (1971) formed the basis for this kind of reading of images, and these two studies touch on most categories of symbolism. A nice summary of the Aeschylean progression from ambiguity to clarity can be found in Herington (1986) 67.

words, becomes lost at times in the menagerie of images from which we are slowly extricated over the course of the dramas.

What is dangerous about the pre-polis world represented by the action of the plays is that these two categories of living beings can be, and consistently are, confused, and the results are predictably disastrous. We are by nature beastly, and it is – as Aristotle will later set out more systematically – the polis that keeps us from devolving to our uglier sides. The city-state makes it possible for us to live fully human lives. Humans are speaking, law-needing animals.[13] Aeschylus tells us that without the polis we live in moral chaos. And the single most important part of the development of culture is the isolation of the beast in us, the differentiation of our separate parts into their proper places.

The *Oresteia* traces just such a progression, from a world where animals and humans are inextricably and ruinously woven together to the rise of a differentiated polis with animals, humans, and gods in their respective places. This balance, or order, is one of the various meanings of *dikê* articulated in the text. Studies tracing the development of images throughout the three plays tend to emphasize the subordination of one side of a polarity to another by the trilogy's end – women to men, family to state, etc. – or speak of a harmonizing or shift in the meaning of the symbolism (sacrifice, wind, wrestling, etc.). But a better description of this movement for the animal imagery might be from mingled to separated, conflated to segregated. We can return to the opening lines of the *parodos* to discover just how perilously fluid this world is at the beginning of the trilogy.

PROTEAN LANGUAGE

Before the simile even begins, the chorus of elders combines a metaphor from the human polis with one appropriate to animals. The first image used to describe Menelaus and Agamemnon comes from the world of the Athenian courts – *megas antidokos* (41) – avenger, to be sure, but with connotations of an adversary at law.[14] But in the same sentence they are also called the "firm pair of Atreidae" (*ochuron zeugos Atreidan*, 44), the word for "pair" really meaning a pair of yoked animals.[15] Here is an immediate

---

[13] See the discussion of Macleod (1982b) 135. He compares Plato's *Laws* 937e1, where the law itself is said to civilize or tame all human life. We will see this image again at the beginning of the *Eumenides*.

[14] See Fraenkel (1950) ad loc.; cf. *stratiôtin arôgên*, 47.

[15] The term is less likely here to allude to the vehicle pulled by a pair of animals. Thomson (1938) ad loc. remarks that the image "anticipates the image of the eagles which follows" in that it could be used of a pair of birds.

conflation of what will later in the trilogy come to represent the most human/civic of institutions, the court of law, with the animal world. The sons of Atreus are harnessed by Zeus (43) to seek justice. So the polis, justice, Zeus, and the human agents are bound together in the first five verses of the *parodos* through a metaphor taken from the domestication of animals.

This important thematic imagery of entanglement, binding, and control so frequently observed in the *Oresteia* – nets, yokes, snares, robes, traps, coils, webs, bits, etc. – derives its power, I would suggest, from the connection with animals. Animals are to be trapped and domesticated for the good of the community – agriculture and sacrifice will provide the images of a just polis at the end of the trilogy. By its very definition, the yoking of men – an activity for animals brought into the human sphere – reveals an unhealthy and chaotic world. It is not merely uncivilized or inverted; it is confused. To be coupled with Zeus in the pursuit of justice must appear at first to be the most appropriate of images for kings seeking vengeance for a direct violation of divinely-sanctioned hospitality. Subsequent events, however, will prove that something is seriously wrong with the fusion suggested in the metaphor, with Agamemnon's putting on the "harness of necessity" (218). Human and animal must not be bound so closely, so tightly "yoked" that their worlds are indistinguishable.

The Atreidae share in the animal kingdom again just as the simile is introduced. The participle used to describe their war cry is *klazontes* (48), a word borrowed from Homer that resonates with both the shouting of men in war and the screeching of birds.[16] In fact, in one of the similes frequently pointed to as a source for the Aeschylean passage, *Iliad* 16.428–30, *klazô* depicts both the warriors' shouts (*keklêgontes*, 430) and the cries of the vultures (*klazonte*, 429) to whom they are compared.[17] Aeschylus chooses a word to describe the human shouts of the Atreidae that already has connections with the animal world. It is the perfect pivotal point from which to dangle the human on one side and the animal on the other. In Homer, the point is merely a comparison of the martial screams of different sets of fighters – the word is repeated for each pair. In Homeric similes, often wonderfully complex in their own right with multiple analogies to both past and future action, the two objects of comparison usually remain

---

[16] Vultures, cranes, a heron and an eagle, as well as various warriors, are subjects of the verbal idea in Homer; the root also modifies the screech of dogs, arrows, and the wind. At *Scutum* 442, Ares himself shouts. Aeschylus uses the word elsewhere six times of persons, once of bells and once of axles on a chariot. For *klazô* of men and animals in other early Greek authors, see Silk (1974) 18 n.2.

[17] The parallels between the Homeric and Aeschylean passages, as M. L. West observes (1979) 1 n.1, do not demand Page's change from *megan* to the Homeric *megal'*; so also Bollack and Judet de La Combe ad loc. For Aeschylus' borrowing from Homer here, see Easterling (1987) and Heath (1999a).

distinct. As we saw in Chapter 3, it is only in the extreme cases of bestial behavior such as Achilles' that the language in one part of the simile is allowed to spill over into the other.[18] For Aeschylus, however, the cries belong to the same world where human and animal overlap. The sons of Atreus metaphorically share in the world of the birds *before* they are compared to them in the simile. The boundaries are already insecure.

The adjective modifying the vultures' grief, *ekpatiois* (49), a *hapax*, has most often been translated "extreme" or "immense." Simon Goldhill has argued for "off their usual tracks," returning to the definition given by the scholion in M and Tr, and in Hesychius, and compatible with the Homeric expression *ek patou*.[19] If this interpretation is right, we are presented with a particularly vivid picture of the birds' "distraught circling," and, as Goldhill observes, another element of comparison between the Atreids and the vultures in the suggestion that they both turn away from their homes as a result of their loss.[20] This interweaving of human and animals is part of the preparation for the more complex hybridization of the brothers to come.

Verse 50 contains two well-known examples of anthropomorphism mentioned above. The Atreidae give the war cry like vultures "in grief for their children (*paidôn*), very high above their nests (*lecheôn*)." The use of the noun *paidôn* for animal offspring is extremely unusual, its only previous application to non-humans coming in a fable of Archilochus (179W). Clearly, this brings the vultures' lives into the human sphere, almost demanding the kind of exegesis so frequently undertaken. Who is the human counterpart to the "children"? Helen hardly fits the part, so we naturally (despite Denniston–Page's hesitation) turn to other lost children in the myth.[21]

---

[18] Cf. *Il.* 17.755–9 for the repetition of *keklêgontes* with each pair. As Segal (1981) 7 asserts, in the Homeric epic the limits between human and bestial, though threatened, are relatively stable. I find in the Homeric language of the Aeschylean passage little of what Ewans (1975) 19 calls "epic confidence."

[19] (1989); see his complete review of the history of this issue.

[20] The main verb of which the vultures are the subject is also a hapax, *strophodinountai* (51). We have no way of being certain that the verb was unknown at the time, but its filling up the entire verse – as *demniotêrê*, another word unique to Aeschylean verse (used twice, as we have seen), will shortly do (53) – suggests poetic pride. Fraenkel (1950) dryly reminds us of Aristophanes' *rhêma boeion*. Perhaps an astute listener would have heard Homer's *strephedinêthen* (*Il.* 16.792), the subject of which are Patroclus' eyes after his Apolline crack on the back; see Bollack and Judet de La Combe ad 51. If so, the tragic and very human context of fated loss and suffering might also bring the vulture's pain into the human arena.

[21] On *paides* in Archilochus as a probable reference to animals, see M. L. West (1979). Bollack and Judet de La Combe ad loc. compare the use of *inin* at *Ag.* 717–18 of the lion cub and think *paidôn* gives the passage an allegorical rather than Homeric twist. Whallon (1961b) 82 concludes that "the vocabulary in which the symbolism is couched conveys the lack of distinction between human and bestial lives," but he does not follow up on this insight.

As is often noted, *lechos* is also borrowed from the human world. Aeschylus is the first to apply the word to animals.[22] It appears in only two other places in the *Oresteia*, both of which are in the *Agamemnon*. At 410–11, the chorus laments for the house and the Atreidae (*promoi*), as well as for the bed (*lechos*) and the "husband-loving tracks."[23] No matter how we read this last expression, clearly the reference is to the violated bed of Menelaus and Helen, the cause of the Trojan War and thus of the action of the play.

The other appearance of *lechos* is equally portentous, as it refers to the betrayed bed of the elder son of Atreus. Cassandra tells the chorus that there is someone – an impotent lion tumbling in bed (*en lechei*), a stay-at-home – plotting vengeance against the master on his return (1223–6). Fraenkel (ad 1224) comes to the odd conclusion that strictly "it is only the indolence of Aegisthus which is here denoted, not his adultery." This interpretation ignores the obvious significance of the tumbling in bed (Clytemnestra will not be shy about her strange sexual thrill at the death of her husband, 1388f., esp. 1446–7), as well as the consistent use in pre-Aeschylean Greek of *lechos* as a bed of cohabitation.[24] It is also frequently used in Homer of a funeral bier – that of (or planned for) Patroclus, Lycaon, Hector, Achilles, and Odysseus. For Andromache, it is both empty marriage bed and bier for her husband (*Il.* 24.743). That is, *lechos* is polyvalent and ambiguous by nature, a place of love and life, treachery and deceit, death and burial. Its appearance as a vultures' nest, now empty of offspring, a site of mourning and the source of war, should make us take notice.[25]

Although slightly off the beaten track as well, a more detailed examination of the Aegisthus-as-lion passage would be useful at this point. Here, we find the conflation of human and animal used in particularly vivid fashion, and the lessons we can learn from its examination can better illuminate the nature of Aeschylean imagery.

---

[22] He uses the adjective *lechaiôn* to modify the *teknôn* of a dove at *Sept.* 291–2; cf. Sophocles' *Ant.* 422–5.

[23] So Denniston–Page (1957) and Fraenkel (1950) take *stiboi philanores*, although some other commentators read it as a reference to the tracks left on the bed by Helen and Paris.

[24] In Homer and the *Homeric Hymns*, for example, *lechos* is used of the bed of Zeus and Hera, Aphrodite and Anchises, Helen and Paris, Nestor and his wife, Alcinous and Arete, Hephaestus and Aphrodite, Odysseus and Penelope, Hades and Persephone, Dawn and Tithonus, Aeolus' sons and daughters, and Circe and Odysseus. Perhaps most interestingly, Agamemnon refers to his *lechos* at home in Mycenae (*Il.* 1.31), where he imagines a captive slave girl, "whom I prefer to Clytemnestra," tending his needs. Cassandra has taken Chryseis' place. Fraenkel (1950) is a bit squeamish about such matters. He believes, for example, that Clytemnestra's reference to her bed at 1447 is unqueenly and out of character, and so sides with critics who believe *eunês* to be corrupt.

[25] The verb *pateô* is applied with similar double-sidedness to Atreus' marriage bed, Paris' abduction of Helen, and the slaying of Agememnon by Clytemnestra and Aegisthus; see Rehm (1994) 48.

A strengthless lion tumbles in Agamemnon's bed. The mixing goes further than the mere comparison of a man to a lion. A man – unnamed but whom we know to be Aegisthus – becomes a lion that in turn romps in a human bed. Here, as with the two vultures, the poet wants the blending of the two worlds to be felt, and so he chooses a word that had never before (as far we know) been shared by both. Aeschylus could have used a more familiar synonym, *eunê*, which in fact he does use eight times in the *Oresteia* (six in the *Agamemnon*, three times for Clytemnestra's bed – 27, 1447, 1626 – and once for Atreus' violated bed, 1193). This word (and others with the same root) had a long tradition of metaphorical application to the animal world. Homer uses it six times of animal beds, including once of a nest.[26] Instead, Aeschylus opts for a more severe metaphor, similar to his choice of *paidôn* instead of the well-established *teknôn* for animal young. The poet thus manages to blur the dividing lines between the human and bestial, even to the point of pushing the language to the breaking-point.

In this same passage, the reference to Aegisthus as a *leont' analkin*, an impotent lion, has raised some objections by editors. Denniston–Page, for example, insist that Aegisthus as lion "is most unexpected, particularly since the same metaphor is applied to Agamemnon in 1259; and the phrase as a whole, 'a cowardly lion,' is so unlikely that corruption of the text may well be supposed here . . ." Fraenkel goes further, claiming that the phrase is "hard to swallow . . . it would be for a Greek one might say an offence against the laws of nature to call a lion – of all creatures – *analkis*." Since Bernard Knox's pathbreaking article on the lion imagery nearly half a century ago (not, it seems, considered by Denniston–Page), we have learned to be more appreciative of the subtlety and flexibility of Aeschylus' handling of his animals.[27] Still, Knox's and most other analyses aim to unveil the meaning of specific species – lions, serpents, dogs, etc. We can, I think, add to the many important insights these studies have supplied by considering the lion image as another example of the conflation of animals with humans.

To begin with, it seems clear (as Fraenkel notes) that these lines about Aegisthus should be read with the similar words about Clytemnestra's lover later snarled by the chorus at the usurper himself:

Woman, did you lie in wait for those returning from battle, a housekeeper defiling a man's bed, plotting his death, the chief of the army? (1625–7)

---

[26] *Od.* 5.65; it is used especially of a deer's lair: *Il.* 11.115, 15.580, 22.190; also a pigpen (*Od.* 14.14); cf. *Od.* 4.438, where the places for ambush of Menelaus and his men disguised as seals are called *eunas*.
[27] (1952).

The parallels are obvious on both the verbal and the thematic level: *poinas* (1223) / *moron* (1627); *bouleuein* (1223) / *ebouleusas* (1627); *lechei* (1224) / *eunên* (1626); *oikouron* (1225) / *oikouros* (1626); *tôi molonti* (1225) / *tous hêkontas* (1625); *despotêï* (1225) / *stratêgôï* (1627). I would suggest that another parallel is to be found in the two words *leont'* (1224) and *gunai* (1625). Aegisthus is compared to an animal in one passage and a woman in the other. We are conditioned from Homeric usage to accept the former as a natural description of martial prowess – particularly in the case of a lion[28] – and the latter as an insult. But Aeschylus differs from Homer in the underlying meaning of his bestial images. The lion, as Knox showed us, does not stand for any single character (*pace* Fraenkel) but for the ever-renewed process of evil that moves from generation to generation. Aegisthus is a lion here, a wolf to Agamemnon's lion thirty-five verses later. But the larger point is that none of these animal images is meant to be flattering or positive (except, perhaps, in the misguided minds of the characters). Humans should not confuse themselves with the beast that lives in us all. Agamemnon may be a "better" lion, that is, more courageous than the feeble Aegisthus, but his conflation with the beast bodes no better – indeed, his actions are more savage than anyone else's in the play. Rosenmeyer concluded that most animal imagery in Aeschylus has a negative value,[29] and here is the reason why that must be so. Fraenkel's reference to a cowardly lion's being an "offence against the laws of nature" is to the point, but not as he means it. Aegisthus is not fully human, but is too like a beast. Indeed, he is triply unnatural – a human who is a beast, a man who is a woman, a "king" who knows nothing of war.[30] These oxymorons are at the heart of Aeschylean imagery, with the human/animal dichotomy supporting most of the others.

We return now to the conflation in the opening simile, which grows increasingly labyrinthine in verse 52. The vultures circle, very high above their nest, rowed by the oarage of their wings (*pterugôn eretmoisin eressomenoi*). That is, the sons of Atreus are sailors – itself an unusual depiction of the leaders in the literary tradition (cf. 114–15, 184–5) – who are like

---

[28] See especially Lonsdale (1990) and Schnapp-Gourbeillon (1981) 38–63.　　[29] (1982) 138, 140.

[30] The adjective *analkis* is exactly the right word for Aegisthus, as Fraenkel (1950) concedes. Homer had already used it to describe Aegisthus (*Od.* 3.310; cf. 3.263–75). The suitors are also described as *analkides*, wishing to be in the bed of Odysseus, another Trojan hero not yet back from the war (*Od.* 4.333–40). All twenty appearances of the adjective in Homer refer to those who avoid, flee from, or are unfamiliar with war. The suitors, of course, did not fight, but stayed home like Aegisthus. See Edwards (1991) 33 for a discussion of this passage, including an interesting suggestion that Homer employs a pun on the word for bed in his use of *xulochôï* at *Od.* 4.335.

birds who are like sailors.[31] Animals and humans stumble over each other in the final four verses of the sentence as well. The vultures have lost the "watching-over-the-bed" (*demniotêrê*, 53) labor for their chicks. The noun buried in this word, another of Aeschylus' trademark compounds, is *demnion* (usually found in the plural), "bed," used thirteen times in Homer (it is not otherwise found in Aeschylus), only of human or divine sleeping-places. The compound adjective, a word from the human world (its only other appearance in Greek literature, as we saw above, is in an explicitly human context), is applied to the effort of the vultures to raise their *ortalichôn* (54), a word specifically limited to the young of animals, particularly birds.

With *ortalichôn*, we find ourselves back in the animal world of the simile, but the metaphorical ground remains shaky. Some god on high hears the "shrill-screaming, bird-crying lament of these metics" (56–7) and sends a late-avenging Fury. The lament (*goon*), so often associated with death (especially in Aeschylus; see Fraenkel ad loc.), suggests that the missing chicks can be presumed dead, an implication that fits the underlying Thyestes' children/Iphigenia readings better than the Helen interpretation. But the modifiers of the wailing complicate the imagery, again confounding species. The funereal weeping is labeled a bird cry (*oiônothroon*), but the vultures have suddenly been transformed into metics (*metoikôn*), a word taken directly from the very human, civic world of fifth-century Athens. The usual explanation for this description – the high-flying birds are temporary residents of the gods' polis – is acceptable but hardly sufficient (on the Erinyes/Semnai Theai as metics, see below). Once again, the human and animal have been integrated in startling fashion, and this time in the context of a major theme of the trilogy, the pursuit of justice and the role of the divinely sanctioned human polis. The god hears the birds and sends an avenging Erinys. As Rose notes (ad 59), the chorus is still humanizing the birds, for we would not expect the gods to be concerned with justice within the animal kingdom, much less to send a Fury to avenge them. Indeed, one might suspect that the main reason a god conjures an Erinys here is so that the chorus can shift to the central theme of vengeance.

After this elaborate (nearly eighty-word) simile that began by comparing the cries of the Atreidae to those of vultures, the old men change the point of

---

[31] Rosenbloom (1995) 106–7 suggests that Aeschylus emphasizes the maritime nature of the Atreidae's leadership as part of his growing concern over Athens' naval hegemony and imperial dreams. For the reversal here of the typical imagery (a boat has wings, rather than birds have oars), see Nes (1963) 109–10. Goldhill (1984) 14 observes that there is a "slide between subject and object as the structure of the simile (*x* is like *y*) becomes self-referential (*x* is like *y* in that *y* is like *x*) – and thus subverted away from the function of generating new meaning." But my argument is that this slide itself does carry meaning and does not merely represent the slipperiness and unreliability of language.

similitude: "so Zeus sends the sons of Atreus after Alexander . . ." (60f.) The thought is intricate and carefully executed: the Atreidae cry out like vultures whose lament upon discovering their chicks missing is heard by god, who sends (*pempei*, 59) a punishing Fury; so does Zeus send (*pempei*, 61) the Atreidae to wring justice from the Trojans. The Atreids are both victims and punishers, both vultures and Fury.[32] This is an important mixture, since we shall discover in the *Eumenides* that the Furies are the embodiment of the conflated world we have been witnessing in this simile. They will eventually be differentiated and brought into the community as metics. And here at the beginning of the trilogy, the Atreids are found both in birds who have become metics and also in an avenging Fury itself.

The opening simile of the *parodos* introduces the central theme of the fusion of human and animal. The language and imagery blend the two worlds in a difficult and complex fashion, creating a poetic environment in which little is secure. This is a more thematically significant system than is usually discussed under the rubric of "fusion" or "intrusion,"[33] stylistic terms used to describe the tendency in similes for elements of one part of the comparison to slip into the other. This sort of thing happens in Homer's similes as well, although not to the same degree as in Aeschylus. It is not merely a stylistic device, however, but a thematic issue of corrupted boundaries and unworkable blending. It can make for disconcerting and difficult reading, and it is intentional.[34] The dangers of this intermingling

---

[32] Zeitlin (1965) 482–3 compares this to the lion parable, arguing that the animals "transcend" their immediate context, moving from victim to avenger to murderous impulse.

[33] Smith (1965) 52–65 calls it fusion when parts of a simile coalesce and the poet does not distinguish strictly between the "illustrans" and the "illustrandum," terms invented by Friis Johansen (1959). Oddly, Johansen (17–18) himself concludes that the vulture simile is purely ornamental or descriptive, not argumentative or reflective, and that it adds "clearness" to the description of the action. Silk (1974) 138f. labels this "intrusion." He comments, for example, on the "faint and slightly surreal proleptic" evocation of Iphigenia and concludes that "there is certainly a remarkable amount of intrusion of one sort or another in the play" (146–7), but does not link it directly with the themes of the *Oresteia*. Rosenmeyer (1982) 121f. calls it a transference from the "vehicle" to the "tenor." I think he goes too far in suggesting that Helen and Troy are forgotten, replaced by thoughts of Iphigenia (125–7). The referents are fully integrated – one does not exist without the other – and it is this integration that is of importance. Long ago, Headlam (1902) 436 put it simply: "no one has his [Aeschylus'] habitual practice of pursuing a similitude, of carrying a figure through."

[34] Whallon (1993) 496 made the imaginative proposal that the confusion between the simile (and the later omen) and the events themselves is the result of the chorus' incipient senility: they "truly think like old men." In a similar if less extreme vein, Owen (1952) 65–6 states that the old men's "words turn against them and defeat their purpose." I agree rather with the majority of critics who see the chorus as speaking under severe conditions, cryptically and cautiously, and occasionally saying more than it knows. As Winnington-Ingram puts it (1983) 363, the *Oresteia* reveals a "polysemous circle of reference [that] shows Aeschylus' brilliance in the art of suggestion: by the disposition of parallels and analogies he indicates connections we could never have dreamt of, opens up perspectives which give added meaning to each other."

are presented in the rest of the *parodos*, then acted out with increasing clarity until the end of the final play.

METAPHORICAL INSTABILITY

Just forty verses after the conclusion of the simile begins the notorious omen of the eagles devouring the hare and her unborn young (109f.). At the heart of this passage lies Artemis' anger, the obscure motivation for which has launched much of the analysis of the nature of justice in the trilogy. But from the perspective of this study, once again the pursuit of exact analogies for the animal actors is not as important as the amalgamation of human and bestial in general, culminating in the "corrupted" sacrifice of Iphigenia.[35] Key words and images from the simile appear in the first few verses of the omen: *dithronon* (109) / *dithronou* (43); *pempei* (111) / *pempei* (59, 61); *thourios ornis* (112) / *aigupiôn hoit'* . . . *strophodinountai* (49–51); *basileusi neôn* (114–15) / *stolon Argeiôn chilionautên* (45). And a familiar connection between birds and humans begins immediately with the order of words: *oiônôn basileus basileusi ne-* / *ôn* (114–15). The eagles and Atreidae are juxtaposed before Calchas utters a word about the omen and its relation to the capture of Troy (126). The kings, victimized vultures in the first part of the simile, now become the punishing Erinyes sent against Troy (*Teukrid' ep' aian*, 112) promised in the second part (*ep' Alexandrôi*, 61). The city of Troy is viewed as prey to be hunted down – *agrei* (126) is a rare verb in tragedy, its root again taking us outside the polis to the wild.[36]

---

[35] Reviews of the standard interpretations of the imagery can be found in Lawrence (1976) and Conacher (1987) 76–83. For bibliography, see Fowler (1991) 87 n.11. Conacher disapproves of Lebeck's understanding of the omen because she sees in it *both* the sack of Troy *and* the sacrifice of Iphigenia. Similarly, Lloyd-Jones (1983a) 87–8 disagrees with the Page/Conington interpretation that Artemis is angry with the eagles themselves and not what they symbolize, because this "confuses" the world of the portent with reality. As is clear by now, I think it is exactly this confusion that is significant. Clinton (1988) 11 answers Lloyd-Jones, but only by separating Artemis' reaction to the event (unsymbolic) from the other characters' response to the symbolism. But to us, the audience, it is the combination of event and symbolism that is so striking – Artemis is just another one of the characters.

[36] Cf. *polin neaireton*, 1065, juxtaposed with Cassandra as a *thêros neairetou*, 1063. There is perhaps some inter-species confusion built into the scene. The vultures have become eagles – is there a suggestion here that these eagles are the exact same birds who lost their young and so wreak vengeance by destroying the unborn? Have they, like the sons of Atreus, become their own Furies? This interpretation may seem far-fetched, since the first pair of birds exists only in the imaginations of the chorus, and besides, they were *aigupioi* and the second pair are *aietoi* (137). But in fact the two names were often confused in antiquity – they were considered by many to refer to the same bird; see the passages cited by Thompson (1936) in articles under both names: "The Vultures were, and are, frequently confused under the name *aetos*," and he suggests that this passage is one of the confused references (5). Zeitlin (1965) 481, Thomson (1938) 1, 21, and Finley (1955) 9–10 consider both sets

The sons of Atreus have once more become birds of prey. Human and animal are less and less distinguishable, leading us to the terrible climax in the sacrifice of a human being. Again, Aeschylus carefully crafts powerfully ambiguous language. The most famous example is verse 136, *autotokon pro lochou mogeran ptaka thuomenoisin*, which Stanford long ago noted could be translated "slaying a trembling hare and its young before their birth," but also "sacrificing a trembling, cowering woman, his own child, on behalf of the army."[37] Less frequently commented upon is the conflation that leads to this blending of hare with innocent young girl. Artemis in pity bears a grudge against the hounds of her father (*ptanoisin kusi patros*, 135) who "sacrifice" (*thuomenoisin*) – a purely human activity – the hare. These flying hounds of Zeus are the eagles, of course, so the chain of poetic images runs like this: "Artemis is angered with dogs (who are really eagles who are the Atreidae) who sacrifice a hare and her fetuses who stand for . . ." what? Iphigenia, or Troy, or Thyestes' feast again? Or all three? There is no easy way to resist analogy hunting.[38]

Calchas concludes his interpretation with a terrifying presentiment, praying that Artemis will not bind the ships by winds and thus bring about a *thusian heteran anomon tin' adaiton* (150), a second sacrifice, unholy and not to be eaten. The adjective *adaiton* is strange and evocative. Why a sacrifice that can't be eaten? Why emphasize the ingestion of the prey by the eagles at all? Clearly, Iphigenia's sacrifice is the immediate point, since there will be no customary eating of the flesh of the victim after her death. But there is more. The eagles, in the chorus' words, fed on a family (*boskomenô . . . gennan*, 119), a feast which is later referred to as a *dais* (*lagodaitas*, 124) and a meal (*deipnon*, 137) hated by Artemis. These words again are borrowed from the human world – the eagles take part in a feast that elicits a prayer that there may not be a second sacrifice that is *not* a feast.[39] The animal and

---

of birds to be eagles. English-only readers of Lattimore's translation (Chicago 1953) would scarcely come to any other conclusion. D. R. Slavitt's recent version (Philadelphia 1998) labels the first pair of birds "eagles" and does not specify the species of the second pair at all. The most complete study of these birds is that of Whallon (1980) 9–23, who, for very different reasons, suggests that the two sets of birds may have been intentionally confused. He prefers to believe that Aeschylus leaves the issue indeterminate – we cannot tell to what degree the birds are the same. Interestingly, vultures had a reputation in antiquity for inordinate affection for their young – and the young of other species; see Pollard (1948) 116–17, and Petrounias (1976) 130 with n.496.

[37] Stanford (1939) 143–4, citing Lawson's 1932 edition on *Agamemnon* 137. See (with patience) Degener's (2001) somewhat similar efforts to relate the ambiguities at 109–13 to the "guilt" of Calchas.

[38] Fraenkel (1950), citing Wilamowitz, sees the hounds as servants. That is, the Atreids (human) are eagles (animal) who are dogs (animal) who are servants (human). Birds and dogs dominate the zoology of the *Agamemnon*, combined here in the canine eagles.

[39] The word *dais* is used of animal meals at *Il.* 24.43, *deipnon* at *Il.* 2.383, Hes. *Op.* 209, and Archil. 179W; see Pelliccia (1995) 79 n.130 and above, Chapter 3, for *Iliad* 1.5.

human worlds are completely collapsing, for we are now seemingly plunged into the realm of threatened cannibalism as well. The one human meal that is an issue in the *Oresteia*, the one unholy substitution of a human for an animal at a feast, is that of Thyestes (*daita*, 1242; cf. the lion parable, where the lion cub enjoys a home-made *daita*, 731). We are back in the same complex series of multivalent analogies of the simile. The chorus and the seer, after all, are capable of telling us their interpretation of the symbolism: the Atreidae are the eagles. All the rest, the other analogies that have been found by readers and are suggested above, are the result of the basic conflation of human and animal. Aeschylus mixes the worlds into a chaotic jumble that even Calchas' foresight cannot disentangle – and we have spent the past 2,500 years trying to understand the exact homologies. It is not that there is no meaning here, but that there are too many possibilities.[40]

The obvious admixture of Iphigenia and a beast that forms the emotional climax to the *parodos* has so often been noted that we can merely review the images in passing. She is first presented as a hare in Calchas' prophecy; then she is said to have been tossed on the altar like a goat (232).[41] Within a few verses she becomes equine, gagged into silence by a bit (238). The chorus contrasts the pitiful picture of her last, silent pleas to the songs sung by the "chaste" – so LSJ for *ataurôtos* (245) – maiden at her father's table at home. The adjective seems to mean literally the "unbulled" girl – it is, as Denniston–Page suggest, a brutal word, and connects the young girl with yet another species. Clytemnestra later notes angrily that Agamemnon sacrificed his own daughter, thinking no more of it than of the death of a beast (*botou moron*, 1415). There is further irony here in that young women were supposed to be "yoked" and "tamed" in Greek culture, as the terms frequently used of marriage and wife reveal.[42] Iphigenia is to be denied her

---

[40] The deconstructionist leanings of the 1980s reached their nadir in such nihilistic readings as that of Elata-Alster (1985) 27, who faulted critics for sharing the (apparently nutty) "presupposition that Calchas is making some sort of statement"; cf. the mantic evocations of Degener (2001). Goldhill (1984) 20–3 insists that the "unbounded metaphoricity" and "literalization of metaphor" – terms that I can agree with – "challenges that process of production of meaning by challenging the produced level of referentiality" (69), going too far in this direction, I think; see also his (1997) 136–41 discussion of Vernant's theory of polysemy of terms. Seaford (1995) 202–4 rightly warns of the "fetishization" of ambiguity and the fuzziness of the critical terminology.

[41] My colleague Helen Moritz has pointed out to me that the choice of the word *chimaira* for goat, instead of one of the other more common words for goat, must have evoked images of the mythological creature as well as the domestic animal sacrificed before battle. Iphigenia is not merely confused with an animal, but is described as a mixed-species creature to be killed by a grotesquely mock-epic Bellerophon.

[42] Loraux (1987) 32–7 notes that sacrificial victims should be untouched by the yoke. Iphigenia's unwillingness as presented in the *Agamemnon* is the exception (contrast her response in Eur. *IA* 1417–19, 1560, 1564, or Polyxena's in *Hec.* 530). Her gagging is a scandalous effort to maintain

place in the community – and her life itself – and this tragedy is marked by a word that simultaneously connects her to and isolates her from the world of animals. She is both human and animal, culture and nature, simultaneously: clothed, she sheds her garments;[43] filled with voice, she is without words; unyoked, she is bridled; she is like a figure frozen in art, the old men say, but her death is so real that they cannot speak of it even ten years later. Iphigenia is not merely a corrupted sacrifice – a woman substituted for an animal – but a hybridized creature. Her father, too, is both breaker of animals and subjugated beast. Bound to Zeus's justice (see above), he puts on the harness of necessity (*lepadnon*, 218) and will eventually yoke Troy (*Troiai peribalôn zeuktêrion*, 529). But it does not matter on which side of the analogy characters find themselves, agent or victim, yoker or yokee, for it is the melding with animals through poetic language that is the main issue. The *parodos* reveals with painful clarity that the world of the *Agamemnon* mixes the human and animal with far too much ease. No good can come of this conflation, and none does.

One of the telling expressions in the eagle and hare omen is the description of the eagles as Zeus's hounds. The sons of Atreus become birds who become dogs. This instability even within the animal imagery marks the *Agamemnon*, a play in which birds and dogs dominate the landscape.[44] The watchman's appearance at the opening of the play, lying or crouching like a dog (*kunos dikên*, 3), sets the stage: humanity stands only moments

---

euphêmia. For the ritual of self-sacrifice, usually a young woman as a substitute for an animal, see Wilkins (1990) 182 and Hughes (1991) 73–81. Observe also the gender reversal implied by the chorus' application of *damentos* (1451) and *dameis* (1495 = 1519) to Agamemnon when slaughtered by his wife. Enger inserts *damartos* into 1495, a suggestion Fraenkel (1950) finds attractive.

43 Tarkow (1981) 156 proposes that the shedding of clothing, especially by Iphigenia and Cassandra, reduces them to the level of animals by separating them from an aspect of culture that distinguishes humans. Even more intriguing is Sourvinou's suggestion (1971) that the *arktoi* of the Brauronia festival shed the *krokotos* during the ritual as a mark of their successful fulfillment of a "bear's" career. Thus, the description of Iphigenia's final actions may have conjured up this crucial moment from the ceremony for the Athenian audience and so produced complex associations of animal and beast: Iphigenia is presented as a "bear" who is becoming human just as she is sacrificed, a near inversion of the myth in which she is replaced at the last moment by a deer or even a bear (Schol Ar. *Lys.* 645, cited in Sourviniou 340 n.5).

44 The conflation of dogs and birds, as seen in Zeus' eagles, may help make some sense of one difficult passage. Clytemnestra tells her husband that she fell asleep each night watching for the beacons, sleeping so fitfully that she could be awakened from her dreams by the light flight (*rhipaisi*) of a *thôussontos kônôpos* (892–3). What exactly is the noise made by this gnat? The LSJ, under both *thôussô* and *rhipê*, defines it as the "buzz of a gnat's wing." Fraenkel (1950) argues that this translation cannot be right because *thôussein* always indicates a loud shout, cry, etc. He suggests "trumpeting," seeing in it Clytemnestra's supposed agony at such moments, and accepts Barrett's argument for something like a loud rush through the room (*Addenda* III, 830). But might not the participle conjure up a bark (cf. Hom. *Fr.* 25, cited in LSJ), so the gnat keeps Clytemnestra awake like a dog barking next door? This would be in keeping with the conflation of winged creatures and dogs.

away at any time from collapse into its bestial state. Since a major thematic point is the chaotic fluctuation between human and animal, there is no consistent characterization of a character as any one particular animal.[45] Different species dominate our attention at different times, adding to the impression of instability. Thus, Agamemnon is a vulture (49), eagle (112–37), hound (135, 896), horse (218), bull (1126), and lion (1259; cf. 824f.). Casssandra becomes a sparrow (1050), horse (1066), nightingale (1140–5), cow (1297–8), and swan (1444). Clytemnestra, as one might expect, displays tremendous versatility: a watchdog and bitch (607, 1093, 1228; cf. *Cho.* 420), cow (1125), serpent (1233), lioness (1258), crow (1472–4), spider (1492), and hen (1671).[46] Even a minor character like Aegisthus changes from lion (1224) to wolf (1259) to cock (1671) only to end up a decapitated serpent (*Cho.* 1046–7). Homer's similes also compare individual animals to many different characters: Hector, Ajax, Diomedes, Sarpedon, Patroclus, Menelaus, Achilles, Aeneas, Agamemnon, Automedon, Odysseus, Artemis, the Trojans, the Achaeans, Polyphemus – even Penelope – are all compared to lions, for example. But as important as these comparisons are to the texture of the epic poems, they do not approach the level of conflation of the *Oresteia*.

A BATTLE OF SERPENTS

The *Agamemnon* presents a morally unworkable world, a place where humans have not yet progressed beyond violent, instinctual impulses. The gods themselves are implicated in this moral and political disorder, and it will take another generation of suffering to attain the necessary discrimination between human and animal. The insidious blending continues in the *Libation Bearers*, not as pervasive and diffuse as before, yet more focused and hostile.[47] The language becomes less ambiguous, the vocabulary of human and beast less directly mixed, but only because the characters themselves now make no effort at all to distinguish themselves from beasts. The

[45] Saayman (1993) esp. 11 notes the shifting of positive to unfavorable meaning of the dog images, arguing that they are positive when associated with war against Troy, but perverted when functioning in the context of the family. Goldhill (1984) 204–5 again feels that the difficulty in limiting the inter-references of the dog image is meant to be a challenge to meaning itself; cf. his similar discussion of serpent imagery, 201–2.

[46] While the "demonization" of Clytemnestra may grow stronger over the course of time, her characterization is consistently bestial, and until the very end of the trilogy, no beast is a good beast. For the gradual devolvement of Clytemnestra, see Goheen (1955) 130 and Betensky (1978). The detailed examination of *Ag.* 1223–38 by Campbell (1935) reveals the complex level of animal imagery at work in the depiction of Agamemnon's wife, a proverbial "Cerberus."

[47] Excellent on the violence inherent in the confusion between man and beast is Moreau (1985) 71.

first play creates a world in which species are conflated; the second play shows more directly what happens in this kind of world. Whereas before, Agamemnon had become a vulture or eagle primarily through the verbal dexterity of other actors (especially the chorus), in the *Libation Bearers* Orestes transforms himself into a snake, victim of a snake, and snake-killer all at once, and we watch it happen.

If the *Agamemnon* is a text of species confusion centering on birds and dogs, the second play concentrates on the enmity inherent in the image of the serpent. The transition is neatly marked by Orestes' rereading of the *parodos*. At *Cho.* 246f., Orestes compares himself and Electra to abandoned chicks (*neossous*, 256), the orphaned offspring of an eagle father (247) killed in the twisted coils of a terrible viper.[48] He thus ties the entanglement imagery so prevalent in the description of Agamemnon's death to a specific animal allusion (cf. *Ag.* 1164, 1232–6). His words carefully evoke the initial three events of conflation in the *parodos*. The helpless young birds now lament the loss of their parent, an inversion of the vulture simile. The omen of the eagle and hare is echoed in Orestes' insistence that for Zeus to allow the eagle brood to be wiped out would make it impossible for him to send (*pempein*, 259; cf. *pempei* in *Ag.* 59, 61, 111) easily persuading signs to mortals (*sêmat' eupithê brotois, Cho.* 259; cf. *morsim' ap' ornithôn hodiôn, Ag.* 157). The hare, allusively called *laginan . . . gennan* at *Ag.* 119, may be evoked as well in the reference to the destruction of the family/race (*gennan*, 247; cf. *genethl'*, 258) of the eagle. And Iphigenia's sacrifice must surely be felt in Orestes' reference to his father as *thutêr* (255), a word used in the extant plays of Aeschylus only of the killers of Agamemnon's daughter (*Ag.* 224, 240–1).[49] And even here, as the *parodos* is being reconfigured, we find

[48] Electra repeats the image by referring to herself and Orestes as *neossous* sitting by the tomb (*Cho.* 501). Belfiore (1983) traces the death of the hare back to the destruction of Troy by the Trojan horse (*hippou neossos, Ag.* 825) through the imagery of inverted parent/child relationships. See also Janko (1980) for the reversal of the vulture image. On the traditional enmity between eagles and snakes, see references in Garvie (1986) ad *Cho.* 247–9. Goldhill (1990) 106–8 notes that in folklore the female viper was said to destroy the male in copulation, and that the children eat their way out of the womb in revenge! Perhaps we are also asked to look back at the initial simile of the trilogy in a new light. What happened to those missing chicks? Did a snake take them? Has there been a serpent lurking in the trilogy from the beginning? It was well known that eagles ate snakes – see *Il.* 12. 200–7, Arist. *Hist. an.* 609a 4–5, and the fable of the eagle and the snake eventually transformed into the eagle and the fox (Adrados (1964)) – but snakes were also known for stealing into birds' nests and devouring both eggs and fledglings; see Nicander *Ther.* 451–2 and especially *Il.* 2.308–19 for the famous omen of the serpent and the sparrows at Aulis, with Sancassano (1997) 28–37. If Aeschylus modeled much of the *parodos* on this Homeric passage – see Heath (1999a) – then we are indeed warranted in wondering about the unmentioned fate of the missing chicks. If we are to imagine that they may have been eaten by a hungry serpent, then the serpentine Erinyes are sent to avenge the eagles in a further ironic – and ominous – conflation of species.

[49] See Moreau (1985) 93.

the disquieting combination of human and animal. Agamemnon, a father eagle of young birds, is a human sacrificer who brings sumptuous gifts with a very human hand (*cheiros*, 257).

Although other species do not disappear from the *Libation Bearers*, it is of course the serpent that dominates the play.[50] The intriguing aspect of the snake imagery is the competition between Orestes and Clytemnestra: who is going to be the snake? Clytemnestra is first characterized as a viper by Orestes in the passage discussed above.[51] We next hear of Clytemnestra's famous dream of suckling a snake (527–34), and then witness Orestes' remarkable linguistic contortion into a serpent to kill his mother (*ekdrakontôtheis*, 549). The metamorphosis implied in this "powerful *hapax*" (Garvie ad loc.) is exactly the problem posed in the trilogy: the lack of boundaries between human and animal, so thoroughly embedded in the father and now passed on to the next generation, will inevitably lead to more chaos.

The chorus, however, seems to prefer the initial imagery, for it encourages Orestes to become Perseus for the unstated but clear purpose of hunting down the serpentine Clytemnestra (831–7). Clytemnestra is thus a monstrous Medusa, a mixture of beast and woman that must be destroyed.[52] And which is Orestes to be – lethal snake or dragon slayer, chthonic beast or civilizing hero? The two possibilities should be mutually exclusive, yet in the world of the *Libation Bearers* they have become one. Clytemnestra never envisions herself in this play as reptilian and so consistently (if too late) sees in her son the snake of her dream (928). Orestes, however, counters with his original insistence that she is a *muraina* or *echidna* (994), defiling everything by her mere presence. This is the triumphant image of the duel, as the chorus concludes that Orestes has fulfilled his role of Perseus, liberating Argos by decapitating the two snakes (*drakontoin*) of Clytemnestra and Aegisthus with one stroke (1046–7).

---

[50] The animal imagery remains complex. At one point in the play, Electra announces somewhat cryptically, "Let her (Clytemnestra) fawn – these things are not charmed away. For like a savage-minded wolf (our) *thumos* – derived from our mother – is not susceptible to fawning" (*Cho.* 420–2). Clytemnestra is thus imagined as a dog whose feral nature is revealed in her lupine offspring. Where are the humans in this scenario?

[51] Rabinowitz (1981) has much to say about Clytemnestra's serpentine characteristics, seeing her in the "mythic role of dragonness." Although Rabinowitz seems to me to make too much out of the mythic parallels, her comments on the cosmogonic movement from mixed and undifferentiated matter to an ordered world fit in well with my argument. It is not a battle merely with a dragon but with all similar images as well; see also Zeitlin (1978) 164. On the snake in the trilogy, see: Whallon (1958); Petrounias (1976) 162–73; Dumortier (1975) 88–100; Sancassano (1997) 159–84.

[52] Burnett (1998) 109–10 with n.41 adds that the Gorgon was also androgynous, so Clytemnestra continues to represent an untenable mixture of genders and species.

Like the lion imagery, the snakes represent the entanglement and cease-less coils of the cursed house, of the old system of vengeful justice. They also reveal the dangerous complexity of the intertwining of beast and human in the royal household. Mother and son see each other as serpents who have turned on loved ones, and each tries to make that interpretation into reality. Orestes wins the battle of images, but the war is not over so easily. Cer-tainly, it is striking that immediately after the chorus congratulates him for destroying the two serpents, he spies the snake-wreathed Furies (1048–50). We now take it for granted that the Furies are somehow serpentine, but it should be noted that the only direct allusion in the *Oresteia* to this aspect of their appearance occurs in these lines (1049–50). Orestes quickly con-cludes that they are the hounds of his mother (1054; cf. 924), thus blending animal species as had Zeus' eagles earlier. The Furies are the last – and best – representations of the unacceptable conflation of animal and human (as anthropomorphic deities), as well as the divine. The resolution of this entanglement – the necessary and difficult isolation of the human, bestial, and divine – is the story of the *Eumenides*. As with so many Aeschylean themes, we see the verbal images of the first two plays now acted out on stage by the Furies in the final movement of the trilogy.[53]

DIVINE BEASTS

The *Eumenides* begins, as has been frequently observed, on a falsely peace-ful note. Aeschylus substitutes a non-violent inheritance tale of Delphi for the more common version of Apollo's subjugation of a chthonic power.[54] The forces of civilization are emphasized, the present world thus cast in an unreal image of harmony, with nature gently tamed rather than force-fully overthrown – there is, for example, no suggestion of the killing of the serpentine Python. The shrine, so the Pythia informs us, was handed down through succeeding generations willingly rather than by force (5) and even as a birthday present (7). A version of the foundation legend that takes Apollo through Attica rather than Boeotia on his way to Delphi puts Athens in a favorable light. Apollo lands in Attica, greeted by the "road-building children of Hephaestus" (13). These civilizing agents escort him

[53] The first important steps towards demonstrating this movement from verbal to visual are found in Lebeck (1971) 131f. Roberts (1985) 291 n.18 avers that Aeschylean images move easily from metaphor or simile to verbal description to actual representation on stage. For the reconciliation of images in the *Oresteia* through the transformation of the Furies, see Moreau (1985) 267–91.

[54] Sourvinou-Inwood (1986) demonstrates how the myth is structured to express this progression, homologous to Zeus' own succession myth and reign of justice; see also Vidal-Naquet (1981) 162 and Loraux (1995) 183–7.

to Delphi, making an untamed land tame (*chthona / anêmeron tithentes hêmerômenên*, 13–14).[55] Thus this initial scene-setting connects – or better, contrasts – Delphi and Athens, foreshadowing the reconciliation of powers and offering a momentary vision of harmony towards which the entire play moves.[56] Delphi is the place of archaic conflation, Athens of progressive differentiation. This optimistic opening also serves as a foil for the dramatic demonstration of just how thin is this veneer of civilization, how thoroughly mixed the world remains.

There are hints even before the second entrance of the priestess that all is not as orderly as she would have us believe. The Pythia is still part of a world, so familiar from the first two plays, where animal and human mix too effortlessly. She says that she worships the nymphs on a rock loved by birds, the haunt of gods (22–3). Here, humans live with wild animals in peace, with an additional element so important to the play: gods also share in this idyllic existence. The next allusion broadens the crack in this picture, intimating the violent reality of such an undifferentiated existence. Bromius too holds sway at Delphi, from where the god led his Bacchants in war against Pentheus. Dionysus "devised a death for Pentheus like a hare" (*lagô dikên Penthei katarrhapsas moron*, 26). There is no immediately obvious reason to recount a Theban tale that reveals the power of the god, a part-time tenant at Delphi, except to remind us of the destruction inherent in the mingling of beast and human that Dionysus represents so well. Delphi, where order meets disorder and control meets instinct, provides the ideal symbolic backdrop for the major themes of the trilogy. After all, even in classical times Apollo took an extended leave whenever Dionysus came to town. Both the rational and irrational, order and flux, may need to be incorporated into life, but they do not and cannot share the same space at the same time. This brief allusion links the earlier omen at Aulis, where the eagles/Furies hunt the hare (*laginan gennan*), with the imminent hunting of Orestes *qua* hare (*ptôka, Eum.* 326; cf. *kataptakôn*, 252) by the Furies who will call themselves maenads (499–500). Dionysus is a logically symbolic home for the familiar imagery of binding ("stitched tight" is the literal translation of *katarrhapsas*) and the deadly intermingling of human, animal, and divine, as well as the lethal conflation of the hunt and the sacrifice.

[55] See the explanation of Ephorus (*FGrHist* 70 F 31b), cited in Sommerstein (1989) ad 10. A scholion adds that when a sacred delegation was sent to Delphi, it was led by men with axes, as if they would "tame the land."
[56] On parallels between the opening and close of the play, see Roth (1993) 16 and Saïd (1983a) 99–104. On the significance of Delphi, see Bowie (1993) 14–16. Zeitlin (1990) establishes the centrality of Athens as an image in Greek tragedy, with Thebes as the "anti-Athens."

This ominous imagery bursts onto stage when the Pythia returns after catching a glimpse of the blood-stained suppliant and the ooze-dripping creatures snoring around him. This same woman, who just a few moments ago so calmly and confidently recounted the orderly establishment of Delphi, now crawls out of the shrine on her hands and knees, an old woman suddenly turned child (*antipais*, 38). Her undignified posture casts her as an animal as well, like the watchman on all fours at the beginning of the *Agamemnon*.[57] In one swift moment, the self-possessed priestess has lost her grip on her Apolline disposition, descending rapidly to the level of animals. This conflation forms the heart of the first half of the play, acted out in the physical presence of the horrific Furies, presented anthropomorphically here perhaps for the first time.[58] They must undergo the reverse process of the priestess of Apollo, whose thin shell of humanity is cracked so quickly. The Furies are to shed their bestial aspects and so become the symbols – and guardians – of a fundamental shift in the nature of human existence.

The animal characteristics of the Furies are frequently observed in the critical literature, but upon close inspection their beastlike qualities are left rather vague. The ancient goddesses are difficult to describe, amorphous, not anything seen by human or god. They are most commonly referred to as dogs, usually in connection with hunting imagery as they smell blood and track down the mother's killer (e.g. *Eum.* 131–2, 230, 244–53; cf. *Cho.* 924, 1054). Oddly, their inherent serpentine qualities are never commented upon directly in the *Eumenides*.[59] The Pythia notes their similarity to the Gorgons without explanation, but no doubt their snakelike appearance is the point (48; cf. *Cho.* 1048–50). Clytemnestra tries to rouse her slumbering avengers with the rebuke that sleep and toil have sapped the strength of the terrible she-dragon (*deinês drakainês*, 128). Although the use of the singular, and her frequent earlier characterization by others as a serpent, may suggest that this is a self-reference by the dead queen, the image applies more directly to the sleeping deities. Still, this is a surprisingly limited number of direct references to the two animals most commonly associated with the Furies. They also compare themselves to goaded horses at one point (155–9; cf. 136). The priestess claims they snore or snort – *rhenkousi*, 53 – a word used only once elsewhere in tragedy where it refers to the sound of horses (Eur.

---

57 Taplin (1977) 363 contrasts the Pythia's humbling posture with her previous "quiet dignity" and compares Euripides' Polymestor (*Hec.* 1056f.), who similarly enters on all fours and is explicitly compared to a four-footed mountain beast.

58 See the discussion in Sommerstein's commentary (1989) 2–12.

59 Padel (1992) 168–72 suggests that the "pervasive" snake imagery of the *Oresteia* does not mean that the goddesses were originally snakes. Her conclusion is certainly correct, but in fact the snake imagery in the *Eumenides* is slight.

Rh. 785). Clytemnestra herself describes the sound of the sleeping Furies as bestial moaning (*muzoit*', 118).[60] Apollo, who has few nice things to say about them at any point in the play, insists that they should dwell in the cave of a blood-drinking lion. The lion imagery of the *Oresteia* thus ends on a particularly dark note.[61] Resenting their independence and wanting to emphasize their isolation and lack of honor, Apollo compares them to a herd of goats (196) with no goatherd. In Athens, they slyly rejoin that all the land "has been shepherded" (*pepoimantai*, 249), that is, "traversed by our flock" – they need no help from the Olympians.

In general, then, the Furies are beastlike but not like any particular beast. They are closely tied to the image of the hunt that pervades the first half of the play, but even here we should pay close attention to their character-ization. At 110–13, for example, Clytemnestra tells the Furies that Orestes has escaped from the middle of their nets (*ek mesôn arkustatôn*, 112) like a fawn. Even so astute a critic as Sommerstein (ad 111) is slightly mislead-ing, commenting that "the Erinyes are hounds, Orestes their quarry." This equation is true in other places (e.g. *Eum.* 131–2, 230, 244–53), but not here. The nets surely must belong to human (or at least relatively anthropomor-phic) hunters – whose nets could they be, other than those of the Furies? Similarly, at 147 the chorus wakes up to discover that the beast has escaped its nets (*ex arkuôn peptôken, oichetai d' ho thêr*). The Furies are human hunters ready to sacrifice (again, a purely human activity) their prey (328; cf. Powell's emendation of *kakkunêgesô* at 231, accepted by Sommerstein).

My point is that the Furies are much more rarely depicted as particular species of animals in the text than is usually assumed. They are the ultimate representatives of the indeterminacy of species, as they are now depicted as hounds on the scent, now as hunters driving on the dogs and holding nets.[62] The dominant picture of the Furies is in fact that of a disgusting conflation, a combination of elements that makes them part beast, part human, certainly divine but excluded from the ranks of all three categories. They embody Aeschylus' thematic concern with the unhealthy fusion of

---

[60] Cf. 189. The verb is used of dolphins, fish, and wounded men and dogs. Taplin (1978) 106–7 argues that the stage instructions transmitted with the text are probably not Aeschylean. Montiglio (2000) 44 sees a connection with the Furies' pollution, *musos* (*Eum.* 40, 195, 378, 445, 839). Rose (1957–8) ad 53 compares *Scutum* 267, where Achlys has a running nose and blood drips from her cheeks; I think, rather, that Aeschylus' point is the bestial sound, not the swollen sinuses.

[61] At 106 Clytemnestra tells the Furies that they have lapped up (*eleixate*) many of her sacrifices. The verb is used of a flesh-eating lion at *Ag.* 828 which feasts on the blood of Trojan kings, though it could describe the drinking of any number of animals.

[62] Compare the *labe labe labe labe* in 130 shouted by the Furies in their sleep. Are these the shouts of hunters to their dogs or the "vocalization of hounds on the trail" as Sommerstein (1989) suggests ad loc.?

disparate elements, and it is only by separating these – a "rite of passage from savagery to civilization," Stanford and Fagles call it[63] – that civilization itself can progress to the differentiated and differentiating world of the polis.

From the very first description of the Furies by the Pythia (46–59), it is clear that they do not belong to any world at all. They are women but not women, Gorgons but not Gorgons, Harpies but not Harpies (they have no wings). Aeschylus here almost goes out of his way to dissociate the Erinyes from any particular species. Wings would make them birdlike and familiar, if monstrous.[64] Even their dress is unfitting for both gods and humans to observe, much less to wear. The Pythia concludes that she has never seen the tribe to which this company belongs, nor a land that could boast without pain that it had brought them forth. They are unique and nearly indescribable.

Apollo, with a large axe to grind, goes one step further in his first words of the play. He calls them old women who are still children (69), thus conflating the old/young dichotomy that is stressed in the confrontation between the Olympians and the chthonic deities. The young god goes on to claim that they are repulsive maidens with whom "no god or man or beast (*ou . . . | theôn tis oud' anthrôpos oude thêr*) ever holds any intercourse" (69–73). They fit into none of the traditional categories of being. They are outcasts from the Olympians, hated and avoided by them, as both Apollo (196–7, 644, 721–2) and the Furies themselves (350–1, 365–6, 385–6) frequently acknowledge. Even the magnanimous Athena is puzzled at first sight (406–14). She says that they are "like no seed of begotten beings" (410), neither goddesses nor in human form. They are like nothing else in this world, on earth or on Olympus. Athena, not wishing to insult her guests, has to stop herself from gushing on about their unclassifiable appearance.

The Furies, then, are deities who are not welcome among deities; they are intimately connected to human actions – their sheer existence depends on mortals – but they are not humans; they are beasts – Apollo calls them

---

[63] (1977) 19.

[64] Cf. 250–1, where the Furies have just arrived in Athens across the water: *apterois potêmasin /êlthon.* Sommerstein (1989) ad 51 points out that they do have wings in later tragedies (e.g. Eur. *IT* 289, *Or.* 317) and some post-*Oresteia* vase paintings. At 424, Athena asks them if they *epirroizeis* Orestes into flight. It is not clear to what kind of inarticulate noise this refers. Podlecki (1989) ad loc. notes that it is used by Theophrastus of a croaking raven; the LSJ cites the Aeschylus passage and translates "shriek flight at him." But Sommerstein (1989) senses the rushing noise of a pack of hounds in full cry, and Thomson (1938) hears the cries or whistles of the hunters urging on the pack, comparing Eur. *H.F.* 860. In no other place does Aeschylus use bird imagery of the Erinyes, which in my mind greatly weakens the central thesis of the detailed examination by Fowler (1991) of the animal imagery associated with the Furies.

knôdala (644) – but they do not belong completely to that realm either.[65] Their most memorable and appalling aspect, the ingestion of human blood, defies all definition. If they were simply animals, then they would be merely the equivalent of the blood-sucking lions or serpents we have seen before. But since they are divine, and presented anthropomorphically, such scenes are nearly cannibalistic. Orestes is to supply blood for them to drink, fodder for them to eat, and even a live sacrifice (183–4, 264–6, 302, 305; cf. *Ag.* 1188–90, *Cho.* 577–8). This version of vampire Erinyes is almost unknown in Greek literature, and seems designed to accentuate the distance of the goddesses from both human and animal.[66] The blood and gore dripping from their eyes (54) sets them apart from any animal species familiar to man.

The Furies are the ultimate representatives of the old world where human and beast are undifferentiated, where deity is mixed up in the ugly convolutions of human suffering without end. The first part of the *Eumenides* emphasizes the composite nature of the goddesses and the hideous consequences of empowering such anomalies.[67] They are ostracized from the rest of the cosmos (with the possible exception of a few other "older" gods), hated by Olympians and men, dedicated to the dead rather than attached to the living, grotesquely consumed with hatred and wounded pride. Apollo's spite is little better, however, and it must be through Athena that the Erinyes are given a chance to separate the various aspects of their nature and so become integrated in the community. Athena's positive use of speech becomes the turning post for the entire movement of the trilogy. The hunting imagery dissipates, barely noticeable after Orestes' final reference to Clytemnestra's trap (*agreumasin*, 460), and the animal imagery itself is rarely evident after the trial.[68] The members of the chorus may not realize it, but they have already begun to fall under the power of Athena's rhetoric when they tell Orestes that his confidence will disappear when the verdict "catches" him (*marpsei*, 597). As Sommerstein notes (ad 583–4), the use of *diôkein* and other terms connected with pursuit and capture common to Attic forensic vocabulary transforms the metaphor. First, there is the pursuit of Orestes in the trial, then the hunt of the Furies by Athena. These will now be hunts with words as the human element associated with

---

[65] Sommerstein (1989) ad 644 notes that nowhere else in tragedy are humans, let alone deities, addressed as beasts. Aeschylus uses *knôdalôn* at *Cho.* 587 to refer to beasts of the sea, and contrasts them at 601 with mortal men.

[66] See Brown (1983) 26.

[67] They are, perhaps, the tragic equivalent of the comic satyrs as composites of bestial and divine used to explore the boundaries of human life; see: Lissarrague (1990); Griffith (2002) 195–236.

[68] Petrounias (1976) 178; see also Rosenmeyer (1982) 141.

logos rises and the animal imagery subsides. The remaining references to animals increasingly point to the necessary separation of beast and man – and god – with each playing its separate and crucial role in the rise of the polis.

The tale of the incorporation of the Furies into the community is a familiar one in the critical literature, but what needs to be seen more clearly is that the process is really one of a successful differentiation of the divine, bestial, and human in the social and political development suggested by the trilogy. External integration requires internal disintegration. Athena is the supreme example of this careful demarcation of elements and thus the appropriate figure to bring about the Furies' own individuation.[69] Female yet masculine, divine yet always closely associated with the welfare of men and the polis, anthropomorphic yet regularly linked in cult and myth to birds and snakes, she manages to keep her various elements distinct. The development of the Furies under Athena's guidance is to tell us something about human nature itself, its reliance on speech, and about the function of the polis as both representative of and necessary for our own humanity.

DISENTANGLING THE FURIES

Athena is gracious from the start to the older goddesses.[70] She concentrates on the goddesses' immediate and most consistent complaint, that they are dishonored deities, attacked especially by the younger gods. They repeatedly bewail their loss of privileges, first in Apollo's usurpation and then in the jury's verdict (209, 227, 323–7, 385–8, 419, 622–4, 747, 780, 792), reproaches which they frequently couch in the equine expression of being "ridden down" by the other gods (150, 731, 779 = 809). And so Athena promises them a home in the city where they will be honored as resident deities by the citizens (804–7), but they return to their lament (808–22). The goddess insists once more that they are not dishonored (824) and then, as if to act on her promises, immediately addresses them as *theai* (825). The carefully controlled use of the word *theos/thea* in the *Eumenides* is worth noting. Clytemnestra calls on them as *kata chthonos theai* at the beginning of the play (115) – that honorable label, along with the name of Clytemnestra

---

[69] See Moreau (1985) 276–8 with bibliography.

[70] Athena's role in this differentiation may help to explain her seemingly unnecessary and odd statement on arrival in Athens that she came "without wings" (*pterôn ater*, 404). She is suggesting to the Furies that she does in fact share something with these strange creatures who also came to Athens *apterois potêmasin*, 250. If this is her motivation, then this interpretation supplies further argument for retaining 404 and excising 405; Sommerstein (1989) ad loc. summarizes the issues.

herself, may be the reason the proud deities are finally roused a bit from their sleep – but they are never called "goddesses" again until Athena's words at 825.[71] Athena's task is to get them to set aside certain parts of their nature – those that are antithetical to a role as tutelary deities of a civic community – without their having to give up any of their essential powers.

Athena cleverly juxtaposes the vocative *theai* with a grammatically unconnected *brotôn* to focus on their separate and elevated status, as well as to suggest the new responsibilities to mortals that come with this promised role. She wants them to protect rather than destroy the land and its citizens. They will reside near Athena herself, she promises, and most importantly, get first fruits as sacrifices from citizens before marriage and childbirth (834–5). Not only is this a reminder of what will be impossible should the Furies vent their anger on the land and destroy everything bearing fruit (*karpon*, 831), but it provides the first subtle suggestion of the correct relation between the parts of the world that Athena is trying to establish. The goddesses will preside over a community that flourishes in the areas commonly associated with a just community: fertility of crops, flocks, and citizens.[72] Athena first refers to crops and citizens – it is too soon to hope for the de-beasting of the goddesses – but even this limited appeal is quickly rejected by the enraged Furies.

The Erinyes persist in their complaint about the loss of honors (845–6), and Athena counters with promises that they will be honored by the citizens as nowhere else (853–4). But she ties her rosy vision to words of warning (858–66): the goddesses are not to spoil her territory with bloodshed, not to plant in her citizens a heart like that of fighting cocks (*alektorôn*). She adds, "I take no account of a bird that fights at home" (*enoikiou d' ornithos*).[73] Civil war – she explicitly condones foreign war – is not to be transplanted from the beast into her citizens. The Furies are to excise their natural propensity for inspiring internecine strife, not to clone their own hybrid ethos into the community.

---

[71] Most of the references to gods in the play are either to individual deities (especially Apollo and Athena) or to the Olympians in general, with whom the Furies are consistently contrasted, even in the speech of the Furies themselves. At 411, Athena blurts out that they are not among goddesses seen by the Olympian gods, if we follow the manuscript and read *horômenais*. Page emends to *horômenai*, which would then suggest even more strongly that the Furies were not seen as goddesses by the gods.

[72] For classical references (beginning with *Od.* 19.109f. and Hes. *Op.* 220f.), see Segal (1963) 29f. Vidal-Naquet (1981) 164 notes the shift in vocabulary from the hunt to agriculture and husbandry. Peradotto (1964) esp. 379–83 examines the development of nature and vegetation metaphors in the trilogy and finds a resounding harmony at the end. I think that the order established with the close of the *Eumenides* can always fall back into chaos; see below.

[73] On the cock as a symbol of civil war and tyranny (cf. the chorus' jibe at Aegisthus, discussed below) and the Erinyes' association with *stasis*, see Saïd (1983a) 109–11.

The bird imagery has already undergone an important transformation under Athena's guidance. Always representative throughout the trilogy of the bestial within human nature – which until now has exploded within the family – this imagery now represents the potential within man for civil strife. This transformation of the significance of imagery corresponds to the shift in the play's movement from family justice to civic justice, from concern over individuals (i.e. Orestes) to the community at large now threatened by the irate deities. As the Furies gain recognition from the polis, its citizens, and its gods, they must abandon their mingled nature. The beast within must be isolated and relegated to its proper role in the state. Should they accomplish this task, they will gain the divine honors (868) by sharing in a land beloved by the gods (869).

The Furies remain immune to Athena's rhetoric, however, and repeat their lament (870–80 = 837–47). Athena now makes one final, ultimately fruitful verbal assault. She insists that the Erinyes will never be able to say that an aged divinity (*theos palaia*) was dishonored by a younger deity and the people of the city (881–4). The goddess thus amicably acknowledges not just their divinity (*theos*) a second time but the respect due to the elder generation (she uses the root *tim*- two more times in her final eight lines). She promises them landowner status (890) and oversight of the *oikos* (895) as their honor (*timê* once more, 894). As the Furies relent under the onslaught of proffered respect, they wonder what prayers they should ask for, and Athena's answer puts the bestial in its proper place:

> [Invoke upon the land that] the abundant fruits of the earth and grazing beasts, flourishing, not fail our citizens over time, and preserve the seed of man ... (907–9)

They are to pray that the fruit of the land and flocks – the *karpon* now includes the animal world – flourish for citizens, and that human generation be protected. Crops, flocks, and humans are to be fertile, overseen by divinities now separated from their previous bestiality. Athena herself will look after all three, setting the paradigm. She says that like a *phitupoimenos* – a shepherd of plants – she will look over the just race of men (911–12). This image is carefully chosen by Athena, combining the agricultural, pastoral, and human. The gods are not to be bestial themselves but to be shepherds of flocks and gardeners of fruits; in other words, to tend to mankind. From shepherdless herd, the Furies are to emerge as protectors of the flock.[74]

Athena concludes by insisting that she will honor the city (*timân polin*, 915) by bringing victory in war. The Furies seem convinced, echoing that

[74] Petrounias (1976) 179–83 traces the images of shepherd, watchdog, and protector.

they will not dishonor the polis (*oud' atimasô polin*, 917), and they accept co-residency with Athena. They have moved from concern over their own honor to a new position of honoring the city, from thinking of destroying the land with their poison (478–9, 729–30, 780–7, 810–17) to vouching for its fertility. Their subsequent prayer responds directly to Athena's suggestions: they pray that trees be free from blight, buds from heat, crops from sterility, and that Pan rear flocks and make them flourish with offspring at the appointed time (943–5). Animals are now in their proper position, not residing destructively within man or god but on the land for their benefit.

More specifically, the *bota* (907) and *mêla* (943), whose increase was hoped for by Athena and the Furies, are now merely that: animals in the fields. They have no more composite, metaphorical meaning – no learned articles have been written about *these* humble grazers. Almost all the generic references to beasts before this in the trilogy carried broader, more sinister ramifications as indicators of the bestial conflation with the human. The term *dakos*, for example, referred to the men in the Trojan horse (*Ag.* 824), Clytemnestra (*Ag.* 1232), and Orestes (*Cho.* 530; he calls himself a *teras* a few lines later, 548). The single appearance of *ktênê* indicated the flocks or cattle in front of Troy, a passage which is usually interpreted to refer to the people themselves who will perish in the Achaean pursuit of justice (*Ag.* 129).[75] The most memorable use of *mêlon* is in the famous parable of the lion cub, a beast that stands for all the principal human figures and the entire destructive inheritance of the house.[76] There we are told that the lion turns on its "parent" with "ruinous slaughter of flocks" (*mêlophonoisi sun atais, Ag.* 730). And *thêr* usually applies to humans in ominous circumstances, e.g. Cassandra (*Ag.* 1063), Agamemnon (*Cho.* 251, 998), Orestes (*Eum.* 131, 147), as well as the wild beasts that Artemis cares for (*Ag.* 142–3) that set off the destruction of innocent human life. Now, at the end of the trilogy and for the first time, beasts may simply be domestic animals firmly ensconced in the polis.

With the acknowledgment of this necessary segregation of elements, the Furies are ready to be enrolled among the deities of the polis. Athena puts her stamp of approval on their acquiescence, granting them great power among the immortals both above and below the earth, and among humans

---

[75] This interpretation requires *prosthe ta* rather than Page's *prostheta*. Lloyd-Jones (1960) 77–8 gives the best explanation for this reading, that in oracular language humans are referred to as animals. But the mixture of animal and human extends far beyond prophetic *topoi*.

[76] Knox (1952) 18, 20. Nappa (1994) 82–7 replaces Helen with Paris as the primary referent. *Mêlon* also surfaces in several sacrificial contexts discussed below.

as well (950–3). The Furies, having prayed for the fertility of the earth and animals, now move to the third characteristic area of fertility in a just city, that of men and women (956–60). To mark this transformation, the Furies call on their sister Fates to see to it that their prayers are answered. Previously in the play, the Furies had held up the Fates as examples of the dishonor given older deities by the younger generation (169–73; 723–4, 727–8). Now, these other dark powers have been coopted into the city as most honored of gods (*pantai timiôtatai theôn*, 967) through the agency of the Furies. Not only are the Erinyes committing themselves to their new cause, they are recruiting for it.

The chorus also responds to Athena's animal imagery, praying that *stasis* never "roar" (*bremein*) in the polis (976–8). They bury their former vampirical selves, asking that the dust not drink up the black blood of the citizens (980). Athena rewards their rejection of the past by immediately labeling them "kindly ones," the same appellation given to the citizens themselves (*euphronas euphrones*, 992). There is an identity between the Furies and the just citizenry. Most revealingly, the Furies now display their own manipulation of animal imagery. Having cut themselves free of the bestial, they create the last direct animal allusion of the trilogy. As they bid farewell, they observe that the people of the city, "having grown wise in time" (like themselves), are now *objects* of reverence: "the father respects them as they are under Pallas' wings" (1001–2). Zeus is calmly now accepted as father (*patêr*), marking the new position of the "kindly ones" among the gods who once scorned them. And Zeus reveres (*hazetai*) the Athenians, a remarkable inversion that places the city of Athens and its citizens close to divine status. To emphasize this new importance of the polis, the Furies suggest that the Athenians are nestlings "under Athena's wings" (*Pallados d' hupo pterois*). The goddesses now hand over the animal conflation to Athena in a final reversal of the repeated bird images of the trilogy. Instead of brutal visions of stolen chicks, murderous eagles, orphaned eaglets, and bellicose cocks, the corrupted fertility and wasted nurturing so central to the trilogy find their resolution in a picture of comforting, political custody. The only bestial element allowed in the polis is the protection afforded the population under the aegis of Athena. And so, in their final words, the chorus bids farewell to all the *daimones te kai brotoi* throughout the city (1014–20).[77]

---

77 Thus Sommerstein's remark (1989) ad 1016 that the "unity of the Athenian polis transcends the gulf between mortals and immortals" is only partially correct. The larger issue is that each section of the polis is in its rightful place – animals exist as a means to establish communication between men and the divine (not really "transcendence") and so are now excluded from the list. There is no pathetic fallacy here, no farewell to birds, sheep, fields or trees that are part of the wild, not of the polis.

This moment of closure also marks another shift in the concept of deity: Zeus' justice, perhaps Zeus himself, has changed; the Furies have been transformed, and the virginal, male-oriented, and martial goddess assumes a maternal (at least parental) role.[78]

These dramatic metamorphoses are signaled by visual cues. Commentators frequently note the new political status of the Erinyes as metics (1011, 1018), presented quite theatrically by the donning of purple robes (1028–9). The vultures in the *parodos* had been metics too, but abstractly and temporarily, animal resident aliens of divine Olympus. Now, the gods are invited into the human polis. At the beginning of the trilogy, the reference to metics marked an inappropriate conflation of human, animal, and divine; at the end, the gods, having put the bestial part of their characters in its proper place, are to share in and aid the city.[79] The Furies do not lose their bite – they retain their ability to punish, and their blessings are conditional upon the good behavior of the citizens. But their psyches now are similar to that of Athena, with the controlled differentiation of divine, human, and beastly elements supported by and in service to Athens.[80]

But there is an even more striking theatrical effect indicating the Furies' transition. As they prepare to march off, the escorts enter with torches – and with animals for sacrifice to the Furies (*sphagiôn tônd' . . . semnôn*, 1007). These sacrificial beasts bear the Furies' own adjective, *semnôn*, as if to note their connection with the goddesses' development into their more positive manifestation.[81] This connection between the deities and sacrifice

[78] The "development" of deities – or any characters at all, for that matter – within a tragic work is still a controversial claim, but clearly at least what the gods stand for has been altered; see Sommerstein (1989) 19–25. Athena, ironically, evolves into the parental figure that Agamemnon and Clytemnestra fail so wretchedly to become. The polis becomes Athena's "family." The virgin goddess is many things to Odysseus and his royal house in Homer's epic – and she even seems to transform herself into a bird to watch his final act of vengeance – but it is hard to imagine the hero tucked metaphorically under her wings.

[79] On the Furies as metics, and on the associations with the Panathenaia, see Headlam (1906), with Bowie's detailed discussion and bibliography (1993) 27–30. On the technical status of the Furies as metics, with a review of the issue, see Vidal-Naquet (1997) 111. Whitehead (1977) 38 interprets this reference as outside the semantic norm in Aeschylus because of its apparent positive associations. But this may be Athena's greatest trick, to keep the Furies as an essential part of the polis without overwhelming it in some destructive fashion. As Whitehead concludes (38f.), there is a duality about the *metoikia*: to *have* metics in the city was advantageous; to *be* a metic was not. Athena manages to play up the positive aspects of this situation by manipulating the Furies into looking at the role from the outside. Perhaps it should not be forgotten that a central rite of the Panathenaic Festival was giving Athena a veil/robe illustrating the battle of the Olympians with the giants. The procession itself marks the successful suppression of the hybrid creature that is so dangerous.

[80] Chiasson (1999–2000) emphasizes the golden age harmony found in the unity of gods and Athenians elevated to heroic status, but the segregation makes this harmony possible.

[81] The adjective *semnos* is applied by Clytemnestra to the feast of the Furies (*Eum.* 108), thus ironically anticipating the metamorphosis of the deities (see Henrichs [1994] 44). The Furies also describe

is of great significance. As Albert Henrichs has demonstrated, the Erinyes and the Eumenides/Semnai Theai represent polar identities – opposite, yet mutually reinforcing aspects – of the same chthonic beings, one sinister, the other benign.[82] The Erinyes *qua* Erinyes received no cult anywhere in Greece, the Eumenides/Semnai Theai no myth. The mere appearance of sacrificial animals at this point, then, carefully marks the transition of this group of deities into its more benevolent nature, from Erinyes into Eumenides.

On the same stage, then, are the Furies, the animals, and the citizens, separate and distinct but sharing space, as it should be in a flourishing community.[83] The animals have now taken on their most important role in the classical world as mediators between man and the gods. The ritual shedding of blood distinguishes the separate spheres of men, gods, and beasts, since animals provide access by men to the divine. Here may be the first legitimate sacrifice in the trilogy.[84] So it is most appropriate that the final reference to the honors so coveted throughout the play by the Furies is connected with sacrificial victims: *timais kai thusiais* (1037). The goddesses are now fully part of the polis and human life, receiving divine honors in the form of sacrifices. Sacrifice itself has been redeemed from its corrupted state, but this redemption is possible only because the animal victims are no longer overlapping with either human or divinity. Sacrifice stands at the heart of the Dionysian tragic festival, both in the possible connection with the sacrifice of a *tragos* and in the constant visual reminder of the *thumelê* erected in the heart of the orchestra.[85] These rites at the end of the *Oresteia* represent initiation, overcoming of crisis, succession of young to old, and the reintegration of community that form the central function of sacrifice in the Greek polis. And so as the goddesses earn their

---

themselves with this adjective (383), but it is only at the very end of the play (1041) that they are officially recognized as Semnai Theai, as most commentators now accept Hartung's supplement <*theai*>.

[82] (1994) 27–58; see also Lloyd-Jones (1990), esp. 208–11.

[83] Taplin (1977) 412 observes that the text even implies that sacrifices were carried out on stage. Henrichs (1994) 47 and n.98 reminds us that *sphagia* can refer to both slaughtered animals and victims still in the process of being sacrificed. Sourvinou-Inwood (2003) 238–9 suggests the final procession may reflect the actual ritual out of which tragedy originally emerged.

[84] Even when mentioned earlier in the context of sacrifice, animals rarely remained simply animals. Clytemnestra angrily insists that there were many flocks (*mêlôn*) available when Iphigenia was slaughtered like a beast (*Ag.* 1415–17). Clytemnestra grows impatient with Cassandra, declaring that the flocks (*mêla*) stand ready for sacrifice (*Ag.* 1057). Cassandra comments on her father's useless sacrifices (*Ag.* 1169). A transition is made at *Eum.* 450 and 452, where Orestes claims he was purified by the animal sacrifice (*botou/botoisi*), marking the beginning of the change in imagery. Good on the role of sacrifice in tragedy in general is Segal (1986) 50f.

[85] Burkert (1966).

proper Athenian cult-title, *Semnai <Theai>* (1041), and their baneful side subsides, animals and humans take their appropriate place in the polis. The transformed deities fulfill what appears to us to be the new purpose of Zeus, a new concept of the balance, order and reciprocity referred to as *dikê*. As Heraclitus observed, Helios will not overstep his bounds (*metra*); otherwise, the Furies – guardians (hired thugs?) of Justice, will find him out.[86] Once the representatives of political disorder through their own hybrid natures and in the pursuit of a personal justice, they now become the powers that exact punishment and restore order when the limits of *dikê* are transgressed within the community.

CIVILIZATION SPEAKS UP

It is no wonder that the sign on the weaving that designates Orestes an Atreid and proves his identity to his sister is a *thêreion graphên* (*Cho.* 232). The house has been stigmatized by a constant confusion of human and animal since Thyestes' feast on kindred rather than animal flesh (the Pelops episode does not appear in the trilogy). The "beastly figure" is left intentionally vague – there is no need to attempt to identify what animal is enmeshed in the fabric.[87] At the end of the trilogy, we have moved away from the family tragedy in kingly Argos to the rise of the Athenian polis. Here, the correct model for dealing with the beast residing in us all has been played out before our eyes – the polis simply cannot tolerate this kind of conflation. The beast must be given its own place – in the fields and as victims to maintain harmony between man and god, community and cosmos. For Sophocles, these issues and tensions create a civic background from which the heroic character is increasingly isolated. In Plato, they will provide images for the battle in and for the soul. In Euripides, they will provide a metaphor for human psychological perversity. But for Aeschylus,

---

[86] *Fr.* 94; see the discussion of Henrichs (1994) 27 n.4. Palmer (1950) ties the Greek idea of justice to an Indo-European concept of order in human affairs. This order is the result of an elemental "act of apportionment whereby each component of the universe, gods, men, and natural objects had its allotted portion, the boundaries of which might not be transgressed without grave results" (quote on p. 168). The necessary boundaries between animals and other beings would thus be built into a Greek vision of justice. For *dikê* in this larger sense of order and balance, and a discussion of all its various meanings in the trilogy, see Gagarin (1976) 66–8 and Thalman (1985) 104–5. Sourvinou-Inwood (2003) 243 puts it nicely: ". . . the Greek perception of Zeus was not that of a scrupulously fair kindergarten supervisor; it is the ultimate order that he safeguards, and the ultimate order that matters." Brown (1983) 27 notices that the Furies had been associated with the justice of Zeus in the first two plays, and thus the closure in the *Eumenides* represents a return to the former harmony under a new dispensation.

[87] Knox (1952) 20, for example, welcomes Headlam's guess that it must be a lion, as the badge of the dynasty of Pelops; see also Garvie (1986) ad loc.

the emphasis is on the religious and especially the political nature of the problem and its solution.[88]

Athena's weapon in her engagement with the Furies is, as is often observed, persuasion, the tool of the polis. Her victory with words over the Furies is homologous to the triumph of civilizing mortal heroes over similar but irredeemable hybrid monsters like the Minotaur, Medusa, and the Centaurs. It also parallels the Olympians' defeat of the composite giants, another succession myth that featured Athena – the tale was represented on the Parthenon, inside the shield of Athena Parthenos, and on the *peplos* brought to her at the Panathenaia (when the metics donned purple robes).[89] This civilizing aspect of the goddess at least in part explains the puzzling reference by Orestes in his prayer that Athena come to his aid whether in Libya or "reviewing the Phlegraean plain like a man who is a bold commander" (*Eum.* 295–6). Phlegra was the traditional site of the battle between the Olympians and the Gigantes,[90] and Orestes summons the goddess to wage another war against dangerously composite agents of chaos, this battle directly connected with human as well as cosmic order. Similarly, Aeschylus' peculiar etiology for the Areopagus (681–93) – taking its name when a threatening encampment of Amazons there sacrificed to Ares – can be read as another reference to Athena's refounding of Athens by removing the taint of conflation. The Amazons, attacking Theseus, were nomadic, foreign, masculine women who tried in vain to establish a "newly

---

[88] My use here of "politics" is much less specific than that found in much of the recent work that attempts to place Greek tragedy into its political context; see the survey of Saïd (1998) 277–84. Aeschylus' trilogy is no longer merely mined for contemporary allusions to Argos or the reforms of the Areopagus – see Pelling (2000) 167–77 – but for information on the tensions within the democracy. Good reviews can be found in Sommerstein (1996) 288–95 and Goldhill (2000) 42–56. No matter which side of the liberal/conservative debate scholars come down on, there is general agreement on my central assumption that "the polis is always implied here as being part of the route from chaos to order," Meier (1993) 131–2; see also: Schaps (1993); Zak (1995); M. Griffith (1995); Rocco (1997). Griffith (64) concludes that "by any account the ending of the *Eumenides* represents a ringing endorsement of Athens and its political system. Such, I take it, is the prevailing view of Aeschylus' masterpiece." This does not mean, of course, that most critics find a simplistic, comfortable closure to the trilogy – many issues remain unresolved. Goldhill (1984) 280, 283 in particular sees a "profound ambiguity in the reconciliation . . . achieved through language, *peitho*", and so the "telos of closure is resisted in the continuing play of difference." But even he agrees (1990) 114 that the city's order – the polis itself – is never seriously questioned as the necessary basis of civilization. Since he sees the "difference" as a matter inherent in the nature of language, there can be no avoidance of "slipping." My approach is less subtle, suggesting difference is species-bound, and the slippage between species, or between genders or age groups etc., can be and is stopped through divine guidance. Language can ultimately be used by humans to organize and reflect upon reasonably sensible lives within a community.

[89] See Moreau (1985) 271. A convenient survey of the Gigantes and Athena can be found in Gantz (1993) 445–54.

[90] See Sommerstein (1989) ad loc. for references.

founded polis" *(polin neoptolin)*.[91] This is just what Athena accomplishes in the *Eumenides*.

Athena's victory through language goes deeper than representing mere forensic power over physical force and archaic religious obligations. Athena uses a distinctly human quality, speech, to civilize the Furies – she is the mouthpiece for a new vision of humanity, a vision represented in the victory of Zeus of the Agora (*Zeus agoraios*, 973). The oft-noted development of *Peitho* across the three plays is significant here,[92] and has become the subject of much study in connection with the shifting place of women in the trilogy:[93] the deceptive speech of women (especially Clytemnestra) gives way to the divinely sanctioned, judicial speech of men in the *Eumenides*. But it is also useful, I think, to recall from our study so far that language is frequently cited by the Greeks as the main feature distinguishing humans from animals. We should remember that when Achilles' horses begin to speak, the carefully differentiated worlds of human and beast are intolerably mixed, and so the Erinyes as guardians of the natural order put the cosmos back in order by silencing the animals.

But we really do not have to move outside the *Oresteia* itself to learn that speech is a human characteristic, and to lose it is to become mingled with the world of the beast. Athena's speech may be a victory for *Peitho*, but her success is only one part of a larger theme of the triumph of speech over silence, of human articulation over bestial howls.[94] From the opening lines of the fearful watchman with an ox on his tongue to Iphigenia's gagging, Cassandra's first inarticulate screams, Orestes' polluted muteness, and the final alternation between holy silence and religious cry that brings the trilogy to a close, the *Oresteia* can be read as a battle for who can speak, who is silenced, who controls the conversation, who is persuaded. The entire final drama has even been interpreted as a debate on whether Orestes, ritually

---

[91] Bremer (2000) 58–9.

[92] Especially good on the "politically redemptive role" of persuasion in the *Oresteia* is Kane (1986). Edwards (1977) esp. 25f. examines the close link between persuasion, temptation, and infatuation. *Peitho* is not always a matter of logical persuasion; cf. Gagarin (1976) 85f.; Buxton (1982) 105–14; and the bibliography in Rabinowitz (1981) n.80. On the place of rhetoric in Aeschylus' world, see Halliwell (1997).

[93] For recent summary, see McClure (1999) 70–111, and for Clytemnestra's persuasive power of speech, Foley (2001) 208–11 with references.

[94] See Segal (1981) 52–8 for the disruption of *logos* in tragedy. Thalmann (1985) 225 makes the important argument that the effective use of, or a failure to master, speech and silence can represent the workings of *dikē* and is finally one with the moral issues. He discovers a concern with speech and silence pervading the entire trilogy. His article concentrates on the inner psychic entities that make up human activity as central to the major themes, whereas I am here more interested in the external, political links; for a thorough discussion of *logos* as a psychic/intellectual activity in Aeschylus, see Sansone (1975) 79–92.

polluted and officially purified, should be allowed to speak.[95] Our interest here is in the connection with who is bestial – or who can be categorized and thus treated as such – and who is not. A child is like a beast (*boton*), the nurse in the *Libation Bearers* reminds us – it is not wise and cannot speak (753, 755). And so Athena marks the conversion, the realignment of the bestial in the Erinyes who had been introduced to us in the play by their inhuman howling (53, 118), by noting their new wisdom in connection with speech: "Do they intend to discover the path of good speech?" (*glôssês agathês | hodon, Eum.* 988–9). This emphasis on "good speech" that leads to justice is the final image of a war of tongues in the trilogy.[96] In fact, Athena had just insisted (970–2) that she loves the eyes of *Peitho* because they guide her tongue and mouth (*glôssan kai stom'*) in her dealings with the Furies, who were rejecting her like an animal (*agriôs*). Here too is the last appearance of that root for the wild (*agr-*) used to describe snares (*Ag.* 1048; *Cho.* 998; *Eum.* 460), capture (*Ag.* 126), and quarry (*Eum.* 148). The Furies are no longer associated with the untamed world of animals. The "good tongues" have replaced their earlier "savage teeth" (*agriais gnathois, Cho.* 280).[97] The inhuman tongue, notoriously wielded by Clytemnestra against Agamemnon (Cassandra refers to the "tongue of the cursed bitch," *glôssa misêtês kunos, Ag.* 1228; cf. 1399), synonymous with the reciprocal vengeance in the next generation ("let hostile words be paid for with hostile words," *echthras glôssês echthra | glôssa, Cho.* 309–10) – the weapon (*glôssês mataias*) that just moments ago threatened to destroy the land of Athens (*Eum.* 830) – now becomes the tool for civilization in the mouth not just of Athena, but of the Furies as well.

At this point, there is no need to review all the ramifications of the thematic connection between speech/silence and human/animal that pervades the *Oresteia*. Two dramatic clusters of allusions in the *Agamemnon* can serve as examples of the significance of language to the human or bestial status of the characters. Aegisthus and the chorus exchange insults that revolve around these issues. Aegisthus refers to the chorus as old (1619), slaves (1618), and animals: they are told not to kick against the goads (1624); they will be broken and tamed beasts (1632), and eventually become yoked horses (1640). These threats are interspersed with denigration of the chorus' speech: their words (*tapê*) will become cries (*klaumatôn*); their tongues (*glôssan*) will be silenced (*apo phthongês*) to be replaced by childish barking

[95] Sidwell (1996) 53–5.   [96] Cf. Hes. *Op.* 216–17.

[97] *Peitho* is connected by Athena with the *glôssês emês meiligma kai thelktêrion* (886). There is no doubt that words can cast spells, and this "magical" aspect of language has become the subject of much discussion; see McClure (1997).

(*nêpiois hulagmasin*); in short, their words are empty (*mataian glôssan*). The chorus, referring at least partially to themselves, had earlier claimed that "some barked silently" (*siga tis baü- / zei*, 449–50) at the Atreidae for the loss of life at Troy. Now they are barking at their new leader, and are up to the challenge. Their most direct hit, as we saw before, is their accusation that Aegisthus has taken on the role of woman (1625), and we learn early in the play what value the old men put on a woman's words (483–7). They reject the role of animal, refusing to "fawn" (1665), instead calling their new tyrant a boasting cock next to his hen (1671).[98] Clytemnestra, the master speaker herself, who now only hopes that men will listen to the words of woman (*logos gunaikos*, 1661), persuades her lover to stop fighting by repeating his own words: don't pay attention to this empty barking (*mataiôn tônd' hulagmatôn*, 1672). And they are portrayed as the victors in this competition for effective speech – there is no exit song for the chorus. The new royal couple enter the palace, and the old men must desert the stage in silence, politically disenfranchised and dehumanized, reduced not just to the role of women but to beasts.[99]

But the scene that displays the connections between silence and the beast most clearly is Cassandra's long-awaited outburst in the *Agamemnon*. The prophetess – an unruly conflation of divine (at least when possessed by Apollo), beast, and mortal that foreshadows the Furies – cannot make herself understood and dies the brutal death of an animal.[100] Athena's verbal victory presents the mirror image, as through language she compels the Furies to subordinate the bestial to the good of the city and themselves.

Clytemnestra orders long-silent Cassandra to take her place with the other slaves near the domestic altar (*ktêsiou bômou*, 1038). The adjective reveals the status of the captured princess, now an acquisition or piece of property – the word is related etymologically to the *ktênê* prophesied by Calchas to be destroyed in front of Troy (see above; Cassandra later says these flocks were victims slain in vain by her father, 1168–9). The chorus notes that Clytemnestra has spoken "clearly" (1047), and we have already witnessed her masterly verbal manipulation of Agamemnon. Cassandra,

---

[98] The old men also say to Aegisthus, "Go ahead, fatten up, staining justice" (1669). This is usually taken as a response to Aegisthus' threat to starve them (1621, 1642). But the verb (*piainou*) is also the word used of fattening animals, so the chorus may well be encouraging Aegisthus to prepare himself to become a sacrifice, since they have just thought of Orestes' return (1667).

[99] Taplin (1978) 35–40. Scott (1984) 76–7 shows that the chorus' silence is the culmination of a musical pattern as well. The metrical rhythms of the chorus are disjointed after the death of Agamemnon: "Its weak and irregular exit is a fitting culmination of the progressive disability."

[100] Schein (1982) 15 aptly observes that Cassandra is a victim, like Iphigenia, the vultures robbed of the nest, the unborn in the hare's womb – and also a Fury, like Helen and Clytemnestra.

caught in "fatal nets" (1048), should obey – the root *peith-* is used three times in one verse (1049). Cassandra's continued silence is met by the queen's suggestion that unless her captive possesses some incomprehensible barbarian speech, like a swallow, "speaking within her *phrenes* I persuade her with my speech" (*legousa peithô nin logôi*, 1052).[101] Cassandra is in fact caught in the nets of fate, her own bind. She had come to an agreement with Apollo, but she had lied, misused her language (1208), and so is doomed for her crime never to persuade anyone of anything (1212). A slave now, her words are meaningless anyway; but she is also cursed – her power to shape her world with speech has been taken away. She has been reduced to the level of beast even before setting foot in Argos. We are to witness the final stages of that degradation. Her direct silent defiance, her only option other than immediate capitulation, marks her as human – our species alone can choose whether to speak or not. Yet this silencing also ironically makes her all the more bestial – animals do not speak, as Clytemnestra snipes – and thus all the more an appropriate victim. And she does eventually march off to her sacrifice like the perfect, willing victim (*theêlatou | boos dikên pros bômon*, 1297–8).

Clytemnestra, on the other hand, has been shown, especially in the carpet scene, to be a master of persuasive rhetoric. She prides herself on her speech – there will be no girlish or womanly impotence in her words or thoughts, she has insisted (277, 348, 592). Still, it is a losing battle – it is not merely the chorus of elders who dismiss a "woman's rumor," but her husband's first words of greeting after ten years remind her that it is not her place to speak (914–17). She kills him. Good riddance, we mutter with our modern sensibilities, but her fellow conspirator and lover will say the same thing about her (*Cho.* 845–6). She will fail to humble Cassandra, to talk her into submission. She wields the axe (or sword) effectively, but her final failure at persuasion – Orestes carries the weapon this time – will silence her serpentine tongue just as swiftly. Both women are presented as beasts as language fails them.[102]

---

[101] On the connection between *phrên* and speech, see Sullivan (1997) 30–2 and Sansone (1975). Animals don't have *phrenes* in Aeschylus, making it impossible for them to have or understand speech. Clytemnestra may be hinting that if Cassandra does not understand, she really is no different than a swallow. Ahl (1984) 183 points out several other interesting implications of the swallow: augurally, swallows nesting in a general's tent were a bad sign; the reference may ominously conjure up the fate of Philomela – the chorus in fact later compares her to a nightingale; see below.

[102] McCoskey (1998) 44–6 briefly examines Clytemnestra's "justification" of her slaughter of Cassandra by emphasizing this aspect of "otherness" and notes that Clytemnestra is similarly endowed with a certain "foreignness" of expression. The two women may also be linked by their initial long silence on stage. Cassandra is certainly mute for many minutes after entering. The moment of

The chorus continues to juxtapose the two crucial roots (*legei.* | *peithou*, 1053–4), but Cassandra does not budge from the chariot. Clytemnestra then impatiently insists that the flocks are standing by the fire, ready for sacrifice. There were slaves standing before the altar a minute before; now there are animals to be slaughtered. We can understand Cassandra's hesitation. The queen stoops to absurd lengths as she suggests that Cassandra gesture with a "barbarian hand" instead of using her voice if she does not understand her speech (*logon*, 1060–1). The chorus says the stranger (*xenê*) needs an interpreter, since she is like a newly captured animal (*thêros*, 1062–3). Clytemnestra will have no more of this – the young girl is obviously possessed, not yet knowing how to bear the bit (1066). The chorus reinforces the image, telling Cassandra to take up the yoke for the first time (*zugon*, 1071; Cassandra herself will later refer to her *doulion zugon*, 1226).

In this introductory exchange, then, the silence of Cassandra labels her a slave, female, stranger, barbarian, madman, and animal – a nice list of Athenian Others who were defined, as we have seen, at least partially by their lack of legitimate speech. Only the very old and very young are missing from this catalogue of those excluded from full participation in the community, and the chorus represents the silenced elders (548) who compare themselves to children (75). Most of these characteristics will be found again in the Furies.

Cassandra now speaks, but the chorus never completely understands her. This constant confusion (1105, 1112–13, 1177, 1245, 1253) renders Cassandra unheard as well.[103] The old men catch glimpses of what she is saying, enough to be amazed at her accuracy, especially since she was raised in a foreign (speaking) city (*allothroun polin*, 1200; cf. 1162). Although sympathetic to the young woman, they apply animal imagery with surprising vigor: she is a keen-scented dog (1093–4; cf. 1184–5), a nightingale (1140–5), a cow marching to sacrifice (1297–8). She even attacks them metaphorically when they insist that her fate strikes them with a bloody fang/deadly bite

Clytemnestra's first entrance is still debated. If she does appear at 83, as many scholars suggest, even if she departs again at 103 her prolonged speechlessness makes her a sister in silence to Cassandra; see both Taplin (1977) 280–5, who argues strongly against an early entrance, and the rebuttal by Pool (1983). The jury is still out: see March (1987) 81–2 with n.7, for example, for agreement with Pool, and Ewans (1995) 132 n.17 for agreement with Taplin on the basis of the pragmatics of a modern production.

103 Being unheard is the equivalent of being outside of moral consideration. The gods do not hear the wicked man (*Ag.* 396; cf. *Eum.* 558–9). The herald's appearance is contrasted with Clytemnestra's womanly faith in torch signals – he is *out' anaudos* (496; cf. Iphigenia at 238). Clytemnestra prays that Agamemnon's speech in Hades not be loud (*Ag.* 1528–9) – he can't be too dead.

(1164).[104] Cassandra herself says that she is no bird fluttering at a bush; rather, she asks the chorus to bear witness to her dying prophecy (1316–20). Indeed, Clytemnestra later refers to this final lament of Cassandra as the song of a swan (1444–5). The disgusted chorus responds by asserting that Clytemnestra boasts over the corpse like a crow singing a hymn out of tune (unlawfully? *eknomôs*, 1472–4). Once again, the conflation of human and animal, this time with respect to human voice and bestial inarticulateness, leads only to destruction.

So this study of animal imagery in the *Oresteia* draws to a close with the cackling of crows, having begun long ago with the screaming of vultures. Birds were known for their voices, the screeches often compared with human voices, especially those of barbarians and females.[105] The morally debased persuasion of Clytemnestra, the silence of beasts and the inarticulate cries of the birds in the *Agamemnon* give way to the morally responsible rhetoric of Athena, to the repeated demand for holy silence for well-omened words (*euphameite, Eum.* 1035, 1042) and echoed call for the cries of ritual terror and joy (*ololuxate*, 1043, 1047). The trilogy ends with the sounds of sacrifice, with animals and speech juxtaposed in civic harmony at last. This cry had throughout the three plays been associated with the cycle of vengeance, the slaughter within the house of Atreus. News of Troy's defeat is met by shrieks of joy from Clytemnestra (*anôloluxa, Ag.* 587) and the entire town, or so she herself insists (*ololugmon . . . elaskon euphêmountes*, 595–6; cf. *ololugmon euphêmounta*, 28).[106] Cassandra can't stand the hypocrisy of the "monstrous woman" seeming to cry out in rejoicing (*epôloluxato*, 1236), having herself summoned the spirit of discord to "shriek over" the "sacrifice" of Agamemnon (*katololuxatô thumatos*, 1118). The chorus rightly believes that Cassandra is calling upon a Fury (1119–20). The chorus in the *Libation Bearers* wishes to chant the *ololugmos* at the death of Clytemnestra and Aegisthus (*Cho.* 387) and in fact do so right after Clytemnestra is dragged offstage to her death (*epololuxat'*, 942).

This ritual cry is tied to the theme of the corrupted sacrifice,[107] but the sound itself is of significance. Associated throughout the trilogy with the old

---

[104] See Padel (1992) 119–20 for biting and eating associated with the "assault" of passion – the passions themselves are bestial.

[105] See Chapter 4.

[106] Sheppard (1922) compares Clytemnestra's shriek with that of the vultures: "it was a mother's cry for vengeance;" cf. Moreau (1985) 95.

[107] Zeitlin (1965) 507 observes the restoration of the *ololugmos* to its proper function. She also notes the contrast between the previous blasphemy of spilled blood and the truce (that is, poured offerings, *spondai*, 1044). On *euphêmia* as the silencing of ill-omened words in order to lead to well-omened speech, see Montiglio (2000) 16–17.

system, it is now to welcome in the new. No doubt we should be heartened at the metamorphosis – the howl is to be at the heart of a community ceremony, not to celebrate a personal vendetta. But we are also reminded that the polis is a compromise, a place where *under the right conditions* we can live fully human lives. It is a difficult balancing act to keep the beast around and yet not let it overwhelm us. We cannot eliminate the beast from inside or around us, so we must shackle it in its proper place. The Furies even at the end of the trilogy are metics, not citizens. They too reside on the margins, not aliens, not Aristophanes' Triballians, yet not Olympian either. Although they have agreed that their actions will no longer be based on an automatically triggered anger, they retain elements of their former anger in their new role.[108] We should also recall that the Athenian Semnai Theai were strongly and unusually associated with silence, worshipped in complete silence in a cult presided over by the Athenian *genos* of Hesychidae, named after Hesychus, "the silent one" – that is, there remains something different, something beastly about them, even in their most sympathetic guise.[109]

We rely on speech, persuasion, and reason, yet we cannot eliminate the irrational howl. To live well requires the blessings of the gods, blessings that can only be gained through the shedding of animate blood. Success in this new community depends upon a broad-based commitment to speech – even the god Apollo makes a uniquely silent and unremarked-upon departure from the play.[110] His efforts at silencing the Erinyes are too extreme for a polis that requires cooptation and cooperation of its citizens and protectors.

The *Oresteia* ends on an unusually positive note, but it is an optimism in the *potential* we have to live ordered lives.[111] The structure is in place and

---

[108] Allen (2000) 18–24.

[109] See Henrichs (1994) 43–4; also Henrichs (1991) 162–9 and Montiglio (2000) 38–45. Bacon (2001) 58 observes that the Furies retain their Gorgon face, having changed their status but not their fundamental identity.

[110] Taplin (1978) 38–9 notes that there is nothing like it in all surviving Greek tragedy.

[111] As Griffith (2002) 237–54 has recently reminded us, the *Eumenides* was not in fact the end of the dramatic moment. The *Proteus* brought the tetralogy to a close. But to what kind of conclusion? Griffith makes a detailed argument that the satyr play included (or even featured) Stesichorus' virtuous Helen re-uniting with Menelaus in Egypt. In some way, at least, the tragic trilogy receives a romantic and depoliticized revision. Without a shred of evidence (which is only slightly less than what is available for Griffith's thesis), I like to think the very issues discussed in this chapter are brought up for review in a more rowdy rendering. Rather than mitigating "the level of misogynistic fervor that dominated parts of the first three plays," what we might have seen in the final play was a similar (if parodic, as in Euripides' presentation of Polyphemus in the *Cyclops*) failure of the conflation of the divine, human, and beast in the person of Proteus himself. Helping to carry the theme would be the chorus of satyrs, those grotesquely childish, equine mixtures of human and divine who leap freely about the stage dramatizing the beast in us all that the celebration of Dionysus evokes; see Easterling (1997b).

came about with great suffering; that is another way to say that it is a daily, difficult struggle to keep the chaos away. Aeschylus was too Greek, too much a student of human nature to believe that the bestial could be either hunted to extinction or allowed to run unchecked.[112] Instead, restrained by the reins of tradition, law, and shame, it must serve the needs of the community even at the expense of the individual. Heraclitus (44D) insisted that we must fight for our law as though for the city wall. One keeps us free from the beast within, the other from the enemy without. Contrary to modern romantic and therapeutic visions of human nature, the Greeks knew that culture, not nature, provides our salvation – it is our one chance to limit the damage we do and to live meaningful lives by managing the beast with the bits, curbs, and spurs – all the accouterments of entanglement – of duties and obligations to something larger than ourselves. Thucydides' tragic accounts of Corcyra and Melos, Euripides' ruined heroines, Plato's unworkable utopia, and Aristotle's degenerative constitutions all suggest that Aeschylus had reason to celebrate – and worry about – the Athenian polis. He, like Aristotle, knew that:

Just as man, when he has been perfected, is the best of animals (*beltiston tôn zôiôn*), so too when he has been severed from law and justice (*nomou kai dikês*) he is the worst of all. For injustice is most dangerous when it possesses weapons, and man is born possessing weapons in wisdom and virtue, which it is possible to use for exactly opposite purposes. (*Politics* 1253a32–6)

Man is born with speech, and should he use it to pursue justice, to form a partnership with others in this search, he exercises that part which most distances him from the beast. But, without virtue, man is the most unholy and savage (*agriôtaton*) animal of all (*Pol.* 1253a36–7; cf. Plato *Leg.* 765d–766a). As Thucydides knew full well, horrible things happen, and always will happen, as long as human nature is the same and circumstances allow (3.82.2f.). Like Nessus' blood, the beast in all of us is never completely gone. It waits, usually for a sunny day, to remind us – too late – of our tragic destinies.

---

[112] It is somewhat surprising to me, then, to find Palladini (2001) 442–6 arguing that Aeschylus' "cynical" view of human inconsistency, weakness, baseness, and hypocrisy is a "departure from common or traditional viewpoints."

CHAPTER 6

Socratic silence: The shame of the Athenians

Aeschylus' hope that the polis could keep the beast in place was, of course, doomed. The great Athenian writers after him, confronted with challenges to the city from outside its walls, increasingly found that the creature within presented the greater danger. Authors on all sides of the intellectual and political controversies of the day could agree that the animal in human nature was out of the cage and unlikely to be enticed back in. Sophocles' riddle-solving Oedipus, an apparent master of language, discovers that the rational control of his destiny is an illusion. His heroic and horrifying search for himself finally leads to a blinding vision of our human limitations. The wasps, frogs, and birds of Aristophanes' fantastic choruses recite – and croak – both direct and indirect commentaries on the attitudes and politics of war-torn Athens. Thucydides tells us that the internecine bloodbath in Corcyra led to such savage revolutions throughout Greece that language itself, our most human attribute, became fluid and the ordinary meanings of words changed as men tried to justify their butchery (3.82.4f.). Euripidean characters like Medea, Hippolytus, Heracles, and Hecuba abuse *logos* and lose their humanity before our eyes, becoming gods or beasts – or both. The hyper-rationality of the repressed Pentheus in the *Bacchae* ultimately leads to civic disruption and a bestial death. Dressed as a bacchant, wearing animal skins, the king becomes the feral prey of the women of Thebes, now symbolically metamorphosed through their madness into hunting dogs. Pentheus' ability to communicate, to identify himself as human, is obliterated. His cries to his frenzied mother – "No, no, I am your own son Pentheus!" – fall on inhuman ears as she rips his arm out of its socket. The play closes out Euripides' career and fifth-century drama with the image of a polis in chaos, its founders marched off to become serpentine testaments to the inability to isolate the beast.

Plato, writing after the disastrous ending of the Peloponnesian War and the death of his mentor at the hands of the restored democracy, is standing on familiar ground when he has his characters use bestial imagery for anything hostile to reason (e.g. the desires and appetites, *Resp.* 439b, 571c, 572b, 573a,e, 586a–b, 591c; *Leg.* 831d, *Ti.* 70e).[1] He was neither the first nor the last Greek to compare the unphilosophic *dêmos* and unjust citizens to a wild animal (e.g. *Resp.* 493a–d, 496d, 535e, 559d, 590b; *Plt.* 309e; *Phlb.* 67b2, 5; *Leg.* 906b, 909a–b).[2] Socrates' belief that the divinely rational part of us must – and *can* – tame the irrational beast within the soul and the polis expresses an exceptional optimism, but even he must admit that few humans or communities are likely to accomplish the task.

The Platonic political and moral zoology is in fact rather complex and contradictory, as we briefly saw in the introductory chapter. The dialogues are filled with animals, and not just in Socrates' famous analogies drawn from horse-racing: king-shepherds become sheep, civil society turns into a pig, tyrants emerge as lions, wolves, and hawks, while dialecticians prove to be as destructive as puppies, and philosophers as inspired as cicadas.[3] I intend here to leave the specific philosophical uses of animals in Plato for philosophers to track down, and instead in this final chapter to continue exploring the connection between animals, silence, and status that is so firmly embedded in the Greek view of the world. Although animals do not speak in the Platonic dialogues, people must if they are to live meaningful lives. If speech is central to the definition of being human, if the practice of philosophy must involve conversation, if Socrates wants us all to live philosophic, that is, fully human lives – what are we make of the awkward fact that Plato's Socrates silences so many of his interlocutors and leaves them apparently even more bestial in their anger and confusion?

My answer in this chapter is that the negative consequences of Socratic dialectic as displayed in the dialogues are especially thematically significant when viewed in light of the cultural meanings of animalization and silence. Although an extraordinary amount of scholarly attention has been directed to the debate over the "development" in Platonic thought and the chronology of the dialogues, Plato's presentation of the *dangers* of dialectic remains unchanged throughout his work. He may have changed his mind about its efficacy – a topic much discussed – but from beginning to end, Plato realizes that philosophy as practiced by Socrates in Athens is an isolated and hazardous profession, and this risk derives from the personal nature of elenctic confrontation.

---

[1] See Blondell (2000) 128.
[2] Saxonhouse (1978) 892–8 suggests that by metaphorically turning humans into animals as they participate in politics, Socrates takes away from them their humanity.
[3] De Fontenay (1998) 72–3 summarizes Plato's bestiary.

This examination of the hazards of dialectic cuts to the heart of the Platonic agenda in at least one important way. Plato is using his depiction of Socrates to show just how different the philosopher and his values are from ordinary citizens and theirs. As William Prior has recently written, "[t]he dialogues are *unhappy encounters* between the philosopher and non-philosophers, and the point of the encounters is to show the incompatibility between the life of philosophy and that lived by non-philosophers."[4] The misunderstandings provoked by these incompatible visions of life are part of the reason Plato's Socrates is "singularly unpersuasive," as another recent commentator has observed.[5] What we find are arguments from such different points of view that Socrates' interlocutors can rarely understand or appreciate his objectives. This Socratic moral and intellectual revolution has many components, but the key element under scrutiny here is shame: under what circumstances is a person to feel humiliation, and what is the appropriate response? Plato's Socrates, I believe, was primarily sent to his death because he shamed fellow citizens into bestial silence in his efforts to create a radical reorientation of the traditionally external system of values based on reputation and political service.

I am, of course, not the first to suggest that Socrates was done in by democratic bullies primarily seeking vengeance for years of humiliation at the hands of a master of dialectic. Already fifty years ago, Eric Havelock had apparently had enough of what struck him as insulting and sentimental defenses of Socrates:

Students of elementary Greek who consult the prefaces to any of a score of editions and translations of Plato's *Apology* or *Crito* or *Phaedo* will read that Socrates was a kind of saint, perhaps not too good for us in our enlightened condition, but certainly too good for Athenian democrats of 400 B.C.; a saint, however, with

---

[4] Prior (1997) 117; see also: Carter (1986) 186; Kahn (1996) 90, and Nightingale (1995) 43, the explicit discussion of Plato's efforts to define the philosopher against the traditional views of excellence. Kahn (1996a) also suggests that the Socratic dialogue was developed by Plato in order to replace the heroes of rival literary forms (e.g. Achilles, Oedipus, and Pericles) with his own hero, Socrates; cf. Hobbs' extended argument (2000) that Plato attempts to establish Socrates as a new ideal; Blondell (2002) 84–8.

[5] Beversluis (2000) passim defends Socratic interlocutors, noting that Socrates silences the opposition without persuading it, and that scholars too seldom pause to ask what is so unconvincing and infuriating. I agree with Beversluis that in fact the interlocutors often do have better arguments than they are credited with, but disagree about why this is so. He ultimately cannot explain why Plato would do this except by suggesting that he "greatly overestimates the arguments he puts into the mouth of Socrates, and greatly underestimates the objections he puts into the mouths of the interlocutors" (13). Instead, I tend to think Plato knew exactly what he was doing, and Socrates' failure to convince his interlocutors is thematically significant. See also Seeskin (1987), who reads Socrates' failure to convince anyone, including readers, to alter their lives, as a tragic tale. Scott (2000) sets out to explain why Plato's Socrates is less successful than the historical Socrates "must have been."

the irritating habit of exposing the ignorance of his fellow citizens, on a generous scale, and in public, till they could take it no longer, so that they put him to death. This explanation of the reasons for one of history's most famous trials is patently absurd. Such ordeals, with their inevitable trouble and cost, requiring as they do the intervention of the state, are not provoked by personal habits (provided these are not criminal) nor by personal conversations (however painful). . . . The reasons must lie deeper, and historians have probed them without achieving anything like agreement as to what they may have been.[6]

Havelock's summary of "saint" Socrates, however, is in fact completely fair neither to the argument he summarily dismisses nor to the editions he names without citation. Surely by 1952 the primary editions for the *Apology, Crito*, and *Phaedo* were those of Burnet, who makes it clear throughout his work that he believes the real ground of the prosecution of Socrates was political.[7] Most commentators from Xenophon to the present have argued that the primary indictment of Socrates was political and/or religious in nature. After all, the indictment brought by Meletus et al. in the *Apology* specifically charges Socrates with "impiety."[8] Anytus' connections with the restored democracy have suggested that there may have been a political motive as well, one that could not be explicitly mentioned because of the amnesty of 404/3.[9] Socrates was perceived by fellow citizens, rightly or wrongly, as a threat to the political and/or religious traditions of Athens. Ancient commentators in fact introduce and/or refute a variety of charges[10]: he undermined democratic institutions, distrusting the

---

[6] Havelock (1952) 95. His own answer is that Socrates represented a revolutionary challenge to the traditional educational system. His argument has been taken up more recently by Robb (1993). This was certainly part of the prejudice against Socrates, in that it aligned him with the sophists even though he did not take money for his "teaching"; see below. For a similar insistence that the Athenians' anger must come from "something more than wounded pride," see Allen (1980) 20.

[7] Burnet (1924) e.g. ad *Apology* 24b9, 32e1.

[8] The formal charges as mentioned in Plato match almost exactly the indictment as listed in Xenophon (*Mem.* 1.1.1) and Diogenes Laertius (2.40); see Brickhouse and Smith (1989) 30–7. Many commentators believe that Meletus is the same man who brought a charge of impiety against Andocides that same year, and who also arrested Leon of Salamis; Strycker–Slings (1994) agree with Burnet and Dover on this; so also Connor (1991) 51, although see *Euthyphro* 2b7–8 for Socrates' unfamiliarity with his accuser.

[9] On the amnesty of 403, see: Atkinson (1999); Carawan (2002), and especially Loening (1987). Loening observes (116) that many accusers may have claimed public interest in their prosecutions in order to mask their personal enmity against those suspected of helping the oligarchy. Hansen (1995) 11–15 argues that these political charges were brought up by the prosecution and in fact addressed in (non-extant) speeches by Socrates' advocates. On the backgrounds of the prosecutors, see Brickhouse and Smith (1989) 27–30 and Reeve (1989) 97–107.

[10] I make no effort to be comprehensive here, but merely lay out the main charges made against Socrates over the past 2,400 years and refer the reader to some major scholarship on these ideas, pro or con. For convenient summaries, particularly associated with Polycrates' pamphlet against Socrates, see: Hackforth (1933) 71; Chroust (1957) 69–100; Hansen (1995). As Burnyeat (1997) 3 reminds us, jurors

opinion of "the many," especially in such radical constitutional elements as election by lot;[11] he educated and associated with dangerous men like Critias and Alcibiades;[12] he taught children to treat fathers and all relatives with contempt; he used passages from the poets selectively and perversely to teach immorality; he counseled idleness and indifference towards the social life of the city;[13] and, most famously, he was a religious iconoclast,[14]

will not have voted guilty for exactly the same reasons. I would agree with Hyperides, a younger contemporary of Plato, who said that "our ancestors punished Socrates for what he said" (*epi logois*, Fr. 55 Kenyon), if this means how people *responded* to what he said to them and not the specific content of his philosophy.

[11] Plato (?) *Ep.* 7.325b–c says that the prosecution was at least partially politically motivated, since it was the democrats who acted immoderately in a cycle of vengeance in bringing Socrates to trial on impiety. Vlastos (1994) 87–108 argues that Socrates was wrongly perceived as anti-democratic; Wood and Wood (1996) argue Vlastos is wrong and that Socrates was not demophilic. Monoson (1994) 187 concludes that Plato's Socrates affirms the value of free speech while denying that known institutions of democracy can actually deliver it; see also her more complete argument (2000) 113–238. Roberts (1994) 71–86 concludes that Socrates' relationship with democracy is complex; she goes on to differentiate between "early" and "late," a distinction I am wary of. Rowe (1998), on the other hand, argues that the Laws are *Plato's* ideal community and show him advocating a better kind of democracy. For the political ramifications of Socrates' opposing philosophy to rhetoric, see Lhuillier (1995). Kraut (1983) 194–244 still provides a good survey of the issues. He concludes that Socrates thinks democracy is inevitably a bad form of government but is pessimistic about the chances of there ever being a better form. Irwin (1986b) 410–15 agrees with Kraut but for different reasons; a more recent review can be found in Wallach (2001) 116–99. Hansen (1995) 26 completes his study of the issue by arguing that Socrates must have been a loyal democrat. Stone's book (1988) is famous for its undemocratic Socrates. T. G. West (1979) finds Socrates guilty of almost everything; see the rebuttal of Umphrey (1982). An overview can be found in Ober (1998) 156–247.

[12] For the "unsavory" – that is, anti-democratic and irreligious – reputation of Socrates' associates, see Brickhouse and Smith (1989) 19–26, 70–87, who however conclude that the political motive was not a substantial feature in the prejudice Socrates faced. For the "oddness" of these associates of Socrates, see also Carter (1986) 52–75. Aristophanes associates the verb *sôkratein* with a pro-Spartan sentiment (*Birds* 1280–3), along with certain physical characteristics.

[13] Ehrenberg (1947) 60 suggests that it was Socrates' strange mixture of being politically removed (his *apragmosunê*) in the traditional sense and yet still being meddlesome on the private level that caused suspicion and hatred among fellow citizens. For Socrates as a problematic "quiet Athenian," see also Carter (1986) 183–6 and below.

[14] As is frequently pointed out, the charge of *asebeia* appears to have been quite vague, and would be subject to much individual interpretation; see Steinberger (1997) 23–4 with n.13 for a recent discussion with bibliography of the wide range of activities that could be covered by the indictment, and the suggestion that heterodoxy was punishable in Athens. Burnet (1924) ad 24b9 notes that in the very few cases of prosecution for impiety about which we know anything (e.g. Aspasia in Plut. *Per.* 32), other charges were tacked on to the main charge. Jackson (1971) 34–5 concludes (against the portrait of Xenophon) that Socrates is pious but not always in a customary way. Similarly, Connor (1991) believes that this element of unorthodoxy in Socrates, converging with his claim to have a private voice, was taken to be a form of civic disloyalty; so also Garland (1992) 144, who finds the charges "fully justified"; cf. Kraut (2000). On Socrates' *daimonion*, see Strycker–Slings (1994) 96–100, and for the appropriation of Greek ecstatic ritual in Plato's works, Morgan (1992). Burnyeat's recent (1997) defense of the jury's verdict is based primarily on Socrates' refusal to rebut the specific charge that he does not believe in the gods of the city (as opposed to other gods), and the fact that he does not mention specific gods often enough(!). Hansen (1995) 24–6 admits that it is difficult to see how Socrates committed acts of impiety, but takes him to be charged with being a "proselytizer"

disbelieving either in the gods or in the gods of the city, perhaps not per-forming rituals in orthodox fashion,[15] and instead introducing new gods and corrupting the youth.[16]

There have been few recent scholars, then, who have been content to contend that Socrates was executed because he threatened the individual status of powerful Athenians. Most discussions of Plato's *Apology*, for exam-ple, mention briefly that Socrates confronted and embarrassed important members of the community. The philosophical analyses, however, quickly move on to ferret out the arguments, whereas historians dig into the reli-gious charges dismissed by Socrates, or even the less overt political issues not explicitly referred to in his speech of defense.[17] Perhaps it is folly to attempt to resuscitate an interpretation of Socrates' fate, pronounced dead without need of autopsy over half a century ago. But Havelock's dismissal of the "personal" reveals a basic underestimation of both the political and social nature of Socratic conversations, as well as the different conception of the function of legal institutions in ancient Greece. Simply put, *nothing* that took place between any two citizens in Athens was without some polit-ical and potentially public consequences. And as I have argued throughout this book, the control of language and conversation was one of the most important means of establishing one's political and social identity, one's very humanity, in ancient Greece.

Socrates was brought to trial for misusing language, although in his defense he calls it "leading the philosophical life": examining himself and others (28e5–6), exhorting and explaining (29d5–6), questioning, examin-ing, cross-examining, and reproaching (29e5–30), awakening, persuading, and reproaching (30e7–31).[18] In other words, to Socrates, a good life must be a verbal life. I would argue that Socrates was killed as much for depriving

---

of a new cult. Hansen, Burnyeat, and Steinberger all conclude that the jury cannot be blamed for its decision, given Athenian law and practice. For a kind of Athenian "religious crisis" in the second half of the fifth century, especially concerning the "atheistic scientists" such as Anaxagoras, see Parker (1996) 199–217. Gocer (2000) concludes that given the available historical evidence, no confident conclusion is possible.

[15] There is some agreement now that the expression *oude theous nomizein* may have primary reference to – but is not restricted to – participation in cult acts, and thus also involves questions of belief; see the arguments, with references, in Connor (1991) 50 with n.10 and Strycker–Slings (1994) ad 18c3. Reeve (2000) 27–9 nicely combines belief and performance by defining the positive expression as *all* behavior that shows proper acknowledgment of the existence of the gods.

[16] Burnet (1924) ad 24b9 admits that there is no conclusive evidence that *diaphthora tôn neôn* was a legal offense, but thinks it likely. No doubt corrupting the youth could be conceived of as part of the impiety charge, as Socrates implies; see *Ap.* 26b and *Euthphr.* 3a–b, and Reeve (1989) 75.

[17] E.g. Robinson (1953) 10; Brickhouse and Smith (1989) 198–9; Reeve (1989) 14; Hansen (1995).

[18] On the terms Socrates uses for philosophizing, see Guthrie (1971) 129; Vlastos (1994) 2; Brickhouse and Smith (1994) 5. On philosophy as a duty, see McPherran (1986).

men of their voices, for driving them dialectically into humiliated silence, as for any particular anti-democratic sentiments, heterodoxical religious activities, or undermining of traditional education. Athenian citizens resented being demoted to the level of animals, women, children and slaves, and they got even by silencing his dangerous voice.[19]

The guiding text for my analysis of Socratic shame is the first book of the *Republic*. I use the descriptor "guiding" because the contest between Socrates and Thrasymachus will primarily serve as a springboard into an examination of the entire Platonic corpus. I am not so much interested in the philosophical issues of the dialogue as I am in placing the extensive animal imagery used in this book into its larger, cultural, and specifically agonistic context. Thrasymachus serves as a model of the unhappy consequences of dialectic. Many scholars have previously pointed out that even Socrates – that is, Plato – grows impatient with and abandons dialectic after failing to make progress in the pursuit of justice in Book I.[20] But under examination here is the wider issue of the effect of Socratic dialectic on the interlocutors. The animalization of Thrasymachus – there are more beasts per square inch of Stephanus' page in this episode than almost anywhere else in Plato – becomes a paradigm for the numerous other silenced and humiliated victims of Socratic elenchus. By comparing similar passages from the dialogues, we can see the full force of Plato's depiction of Socratic conversation: Socrates' intentions were at such odds with those of his community that the philosopher – as a model of the philosophic life – was doomed to be misinterpreted to death.[21]

---

[19] Dio Chrys. 33.9–10 similarly argues that Socrates shamed the Athenians and was punished for it, whereas the comic poets got away with it. The silence I focus on in this chapter is that imposed on Socrates' interlocutors. Other scholars have examined Socrates' own silence in the later dialogues (e.g. Eades [1996]) and his temporary *aporia* or indirect representation through Plato's words (e.g. Nehamas [1992b] 158). Susanetti (1991) discusses the significance of Socrates' silent contemplation. The "modernist" or "dialogic" school has come to argue that the significant (and overlooked) silence is that of Plato, since we cannot trust that any of the characters in a dialogue acts as a "mouthpiece" of the author; see: Kosman (1992); the collection of analyses in Press (1993a with especially 1993b) and (2000); Gonzalez (1995a); Hart and Tejera (1997) with references; and Wallach (2001) 86–92 for a recent survey.

[20] E.g. Ryle (1966) 119; Annas (1981) 56–8; Reeve (1985) 262–3; Vlastos (1991) 248–51; see especially Reeve (1988), a book-length argument for the thematic connection between the first book and the rest of the *Republic*; also Kahn (1993). Matthews (1997) sees the shift with the *Meno*, Schofield (1992) 132–3 with the *Protagoras*. Nehamas (1990) 12–14 is less specific, but also believes that in Plato's eyes the elenctic method was insufficient. Kahn (1996a) finds a change in literary *form* after the *Phaedrus*, but sees the dialogues as providing various points of entry into a complete Platonic thought from the start, a thought that finds its fullest expression in the *Republic*. It is thus a case of progressive disclosure in the terminology for dialectic.

[21] It is customary in an examination such as this to make an explicit statement about one's stand on the "Socratic Question." My approach here avoids some of the more contentious issues by making

SHAME

Before we turn to Thrasymachus, it will be helpful to review quickly just how significant public performance was in the shame society of ancient Greece. One of the few things scholars agree about regarding ancient Greek

the patent objective to understand what Plato is saying about the fate of Socrates as depicted in his writing. By looking at the Platonic dialogues, we can get a fair picture of what *Plato* wants us to think about the meaning of Socrates' life and death. Was this Socrates the "real" Socrates? For a summary of opinions on the relation between Plato's Socrates and the historical figure, see: Patzer (1987); Rutherford (1995) 39–62; Sayre (1995) 1–32; for extensive extracts from scholarly opinion on the issue over the past three centuries, see Montuori (1992). Nehamas (1998) and Kofman (1998) examine important readings of Socrates by modern philosophers. A majority of contemporary philosophers seem to accept the basic historical accuracy of Plato's portrait, but this position has recently begun to meet resistance; see especially Morrison (2000) and Prior (2001). Morrison observes that the *Apology* has been used as evidence for: a) certain events in Socrates' life; b) certain features of Socrates' character and activities; c) Socrates' "philosophy." He believes that the *Apology* can be used, with care, as evidence for (a) and (b) but not (c). Prior sets out three different levels of what he terms "historicism": a) Plato's Socrates is inspired by the historical figure; b) Plato's portrait presents an accurate account of the real Socrates' philosophical views and arguments; c) certain Platonic dialogues provide an accurate transcription of what Socrates actually said on a given occasion. In these terms, I would accept "a" only, as does Prior (who does not reject the other levels but argues that one cannot know). It should be noted that neither of these articles is primarily concerned with the historicity of Socrates' trial *per se* but with the ideas and beliefs of the historical Socrates. Lefkowitz's (1981) study of ancient biography should make us extremely wary of uncritically accepting anything said about a classical figure. No matter how exactly Plato may have wanted to "set the record straight," he is surely giving us his own take on his mentor, and it is that interpretation that is of interest. Kahn (1996a) 35 likens the dialogues to a good historical novel. He has little confidence in ever determining anything about the real Socrates, arguing that his philosophy, as distinct from his impact on his followers, does not even fall within the reach of historical scholarship (161–2 with n.10); cf. Kosman (1987). It may be that Socrates is primarily a vehicle for Plato's idealized vision of the philosophical life, and that he has been created as a character in an effort to invent and define the genre of philosophical discourse. This is not to deny that Plato's Socrates shares certain characteristics with other representations of the historical figure in Aristophanes and Xenophon. For attempts to reconcile the accounts of Xenophon with Plato, see Navia (1984) and Morrison (1996); but on Xenophon's muddled understanding of dialectic, see Kahn (1996a) 76–9 and Vlastos (1971b) 1–3; (1991) 99–106, 288–300. For the connections between Xenophon's *Apology* and the actual charges of the trial, see Chroust's speculative account (1957) 69–100 and Hansen (1995) 6. The most extensive attempt to reconstruct Socrates' ideas through "source-criticism" is that of Döring (1987), on which see Morrison (2000) 247–61. I find it interesting that later anecdotes about the dialogues naturally assume that it is Plato who is making fun of the interlocutors, not Socrates; see Gorgias' (probably apocryphal) comment on the dialogue in his name: "how well *Plato* knows how to lampoon" (*iambizein*, DK 82A.15a), and his reported reference to *Plato* as a "new Archilochus" (Ath. 505d). But my aim is to analyze *Plato's* Socrates, and so when I occasionally draw on what we know of Socrates outside of the dialogues it will not necessarily be because I think we are getting closer to the historical figure. Although I will be looking at the dialogues from a literary and social-historical perspective, I do not claim to be doing philosophy here, so the analytic/dialogic split in contemporary philosophical approaches is for the most part irrelevant. Few scholars would deny that the author Plato created dialogues in which he described his characters as acting in certain ways that were somehow connected with his larger intellectual concerns. This is the extent of my claims here.

society is that it was consumed with a concern for honor.[22] From Homer to Aristotle, the striving for public recognition, and the concomitant fear of public humiliation and reproach, remained undiminished. In this competitive system, what mattered was a good reputation. There was little if anything to separate who a person was from what others thought of him. Attic Greek often uses "to be regarded" where we would use "to be." War, athletics, politics, civic liturgies, even the arts were constructed and viewed as battles for public esteem. Disgrace came from failure, whether one deserved it or not. Results counted, intentions much less so. Xenophon even suggests that the primary difference between humans and other animals is our craving for honor and praise.[23] For our study of Plato, three aspects of this shame culture are of particular interest.

[22] Almost any study of Greek culture or literature will discuss this aspect of their society. Dodds (1951) 28–63 was one of the first to speak explicitly of "shame" cultures, although the sharp distinction between "shame" and "guilt" cultures can no longer be maintained; see the thorough critique by Cairns (1993) 14–21. Adkins (1960) lays out the "competitive virtues" very thoroughly. His insistence that these always override cooperation has rightly been challenged – see the early responses by Long (1970) 122–6, Creed (1973), and Dover (1983) – but no one doubts his basic outline of the competitive system. For other references, see: Gouldner (1965) 45–74, 81–98; Walcot (1978a) 15–21; Strauss (1986) 31–6; Cohen (1995) 62–8, and especially Dover (1974) 217–42. Cohen (1991) 54–69 places the Greek sense of honor and shame, the "politics of reputation," into its broader Mediterranean context. Carter's first chapter (1986) 1–25 provides a convenient survey of the relatively unchanging nature of Greek shame society from Homer to Aristotle. This continuity is now the dominant view among scholars, *contra* the argument of Dodds and Adkins that the honor–shame opposition was restricted primarily to the archaic period. Herman (1995; 1996; 1998) has tried to demonstrate that fourth-century Athenians uniquely subordinated the desire to retaliate to the ideal civic standards of self-restraint and compromise. His evidence is drawn almost exclusively from forensic speeches (used by Dover to reach the opposite conclusion). I think he misses the main rhetorical point of this insistence by some speakers on their remarkable patience before bringing their opponent to trial. Each speaker is demonstrating that the present case is not trivial. The cataloguing of a long history of abuse by his opponent, which he supposedly endured without retaliation, is the speaker's way of marking the severity of the present charges (whether or not this is actually the case). These are wonderfully effective *praeteritiones*. Moreover, in this fashion the speakers acknowledge the importance of the jury in settling the dispute (rather than having taken matters into their own hand), never a bad strategy in such a politically charged environment. Herman has shown, I think, that Athens had a different way of working out its agonistic ethos than the more direct *lex talionis* often found in other Mediterranean countries. He has also drawn attention (although indirectly) to the need of Athenians to tie their own desire for revenge into the larger good of the polis, to regain honor through punishment while at the same time respecting the honor of others as determined by the city and its institutions; excellent on this is Allen (2000) 127–8. But Herman miscalculates the personal stakes involved in a trial in the very public world of Athens. On trials as arenas for competition for status, see below. In fact, Herman's argument that Plato got his inspiration for a "purging revenge from punishment" (1995) 59–60 from the "popular notion" of self-restraint is countered by Plato's depiction of Socrates' disagreement with the community on the nature of shame and punishment, as I will show.

[23] *Hiero* 7.3. The Greeks were well aware of the challenges to a community such a competitive ethos entailed – witness the *Iliad*. Many authors examined the negative sides of *philotimia, philonikia*, and *nemesis*. For Xenophon's own attempts to mitigate the dangers that rivalry for distinction might engender, see Johnstone (1994) 224–5.

First, what is important to most Greeks is looking good, "winning" at whatever competition is at hand. From victory comes honor, an aphorism that applies as much to verbal disputation as fighting in the phalanx. Shame comes from being stumped in a discussion about justice, just as much as it does from failing to persuade the assembly or coming up short in the discus. In Greece, there is first place and everybody else. And, as Bernard Williams has shown, this sense of shame need not be evoked in front of huge numbers of people. Indeed, just imagining that others have witnessed a failure is enough.[24] The basic feeling of shame is of being seen by the wrong people in the wrong condition. The humiliation is a reaction to the awareness of a sense of loss in which one's whole being seems diminished or lessened.

Secondly, one of the primary signals of this dreaded "loss of face" is the haughty laughter of one's opponent, who is usually considered to be an "enemy." As Athena herself asks in the *Ajax*, "Is not laughing at one's enemies the most delightful kind of laughter?" (79). Stephen Halliwell observes that this kind of laughter is especially potent "in a society with a strong sense of shame and social position, for the laughter of denigration and scorn is a powerful means of conveying dishonour and of damaging the status inherent in reputation."[25] This "natural" desire to exult in victory and to fear and expect such treatment upon defeat permeates all genres and periods of Greek literature, from the first book of the *Iliad*, with Nestor's concern that the strife in the Achaean camp will give Priam and his sons cause for rejoicing (*Il.* 1.255–8).[26] This nearly pathological aversion to ridicule can be seen particularly clearly in Sophoclean heroes.[27] Angry and struggling to maintain loyalty to their self-conception, they feel they have been disrespected, especially in the "extreme" expression of mockery and laughter.[28] Isolated and filled with fierce resentment, they appeal for vengeance. Finally, they wish for and often choose self-destruction over a shameful life not worth living. The archetypal hero here is Ajax. His eponymous play contains at least a dozen references to the expected laughter

---

[24] Williams (1993) especially 78–101, 220–1. His suggestion that by the later fifth century the Greeks distinguished between a shame that merely followed public opinion and shame that expressed inner personal conviction – his example is Hippolytus – is supported by my analysis of Plato's Socrates.

[25] Halliwell (1991b) 285.

[26] Athena boasts and laughs in Homer as well over Ares' discomfiture (*Il.* 21.408–23; cf. 16.829); other familiar examples in Homer include *Il.* 3.43–51, 6.82, 12.390–1, 13.413–16, 17.537; cf. Hes. *Op.* 701; Aesch. *Ag.* 885, 1394; Aeschin. 2.182; Thuc. 3.67.4; Xen. *An.* 1.9.11–13; *Cyr.* 5.5.9.

[27] Knox (1964) 15–52 for references. He considers Achilles to be the ultimate model; see *passim* for a discussion of individual tragic heroes, and also Blundell (1989); Burnett (1998).

[28] Stanford (1963) ad *Ajax* 79 notes that *gelôs, epengelan*, and *gelan* are used four times more often in Sophocles of mocking than merry laughter.

of the victor mocking his enemy (including his own mistaken delight at having wreaked vengeance on those who had shamed him).[29] When we spot such laughter in Plato, we should be aware of its implications.

Thirdly, such shaming elicits a very predictable response: the desire to get even. The famous Greek concept of *hubris* – which was a punishable crime in Athens – refers primarily to an assault on someone's honor (often but not necessarily with violence) that is likely to cause shame and evoke anger and attempts at revenge.[30] Central to this demand for vengeance is the familiar traditional Greek morality that requires one to help one's friends and hurt one's enemies, to punish the "winners" and have them suffer in return.[31] Although the difficulties that arise from such a morality are frequently alluded to – one need only remember Achilles' unsatisfying anger in the *Iliad* – it is not until Socrates that this morality is rationally challenged with his famous insistence that it is always wrong to cause harm.[32] Yet even Socrates sees vengeance as a legitimate means of "avoiding shame" if it involves punishing a wrongdoer and not doing wrong in return. He applauds Achilles' willingness to accept death if he should be able to "avenge his friends" by killing Hector (*Ap.* 28b9–d5; cf. *Symp.* 179e–180b).[33] There is hardly a major piece of Greek literature that does

---

[29] For shame and fear of an enemy's mockery, see: 79, 198, 303, 367, 382–4, 454, 473–9, 479, 955–71, 988–9, 1042–3, 1092, 1348, and Pearson (1922) 125; Knox (1961); Burnett (1998) 80–98; cf. *Phil.* 257–8, 1019, 1125; *OC* 1339, 1422–3; *Fr.* 210.47 (*Eurypylus*); *El.* 277, 807, 1153–4, 1293–5; *OT* 1422; Euripides *HF* 284–6; *Bacch.* 842, 1080; *Med.* 797, 807–10, 1049–52 with McDermott (1989) 54–6. Ajax' own deranged laughter at his apparent success in taking vengeance upon his enemies (303) became proverbial; see Grossmann (1968).

[30] The standard work is now Fisher (1992). Note the subtitle to his book: *Hybris: A Study in the Values of Honour and Shame in Ancient Greece.* Cairns (1996) refines Fisher's definition by demonstrating that *hubris* can also be purely dispositional; that is, it need not involve a *conscious* intention to insult someone, and it may define a *victimless* form of self-assertion or "thinking big"; see also Cairns (1993) 14–21, 370–92. But both Fisher and Cairns agree that *hubris* must be construed in terms of shame and honor.

[31] Dover (1974) 180–4; Blundell (1989) 26–59; see especially the recent discussions of Burnett (1998) and Belfiore (1998). For classic formulations of the sentiment (this is just a sampling), see Homer *Od.* 6.182–5; Aesch. *Cho.* 121–3, 144, 274, 3006–14, 438; Ar. *Av.* 417–20; Pind. *Pyth.* 2.83–5; Solon 13.5–6; Thuc. 7.68.1–3; cf. 3.67.4, 6.89.2–3; Xen. *Hier.* 1.34, 2.2; *Mem.* 2.6.35; 4.5.10; *An.* 1.9.11–13; *Cyr.* 1.4.25; Soph. *Aj.* 1348; *Ant.* 641–7; *Phil.* 315–16, 791–2, 1040–4, 1113–15; Eur. *HF* 731–3; *Or.* 1163; *Bacch.* 1080; *Ion* 1045–7; *El.* 281; *Med.* 807–10, 1040–8, 1049–52; Thgn. 363–4, 869–72; cf. 1032–3, 1087–90; and Pl. *Men.* 71e.

[32] E.g. *Ap.* 25d–e; *Cri.* 49a–d; *Grg.* 475e–481b, 508c; *Resp.* 331e–336a; cf. *Leg.* 862b–c; see: Vlastos (1991) 179–91; Burnett (1998) 7; Allen (2000) 245–58.

[33] For the different presentations of Achilles in Plato, especially the thematic implications of the Achilles of the *Apology* versus the Achilles of the *Republic*, see Hobbs (2000) 179–86, 199–209. Oddly, our modern reading of Achilles' revenge on Hector suggests that his actions are held up by the poet as a much more complex issue than, say, Odysseus' revenge upon the suitors. Michelakis (2002) examines Achilles' characterization in Greek tragedy but does not focus on the reception of Homer's Achilles. The *Oresteia*, as we have seen, examines some of these questions, but revenge itself is never

not involve revenge in some manner. A successful retaliation is a delight, and failure to pursue revenge is always a matter of increased humiliation. Aristotle, as he so often does, captures typical Athenian attitudes. Anne Pippin Burnett neatly summarizes his position on the appropriateness of revenge:

By Aristotle's definition, revenge is a self-engaged and retrospective action taken privately against an equal who has injured one's honor. Its purpose is not to get rid of someone who is in the way, or to harm someone who succeeds where the avenger has failed, for it is not a mode of advancement or even of self-defense. Its intention is rather to restore the broken outline of self suffered in an unprovoked attack from a member of one's own class or group. It occurs in cases where an instantaneous and open return of blow for blow is impossible, so that a debt of hatred remains to be covertly repaid to him who has unfairly injured you or someone close to you. Such vengeance is the correction of an imbalance rooted in the past, a calculated harm returned for an intentional, shameful injury or insult gratuitously given by an unrepentant equal. This return is wrought in time, by the disciplined will of an angered individual, and according to its own rules it is good when it is appropriate and timely.[34]

Vengeance, then, was not only expected but demanded of a "manly" man, and the motivations of "manly" women such as Clytemnestra and Medea are understandable, if simultaneously inappropriate. Getting even was praiseworthy and necessary when aimed at restoring personal honor. "To take vengeance on one's enemies is more noble than to reconcile with them; for to get revenge is just and the just is noble, and it is the mark of manliness not to be worsted by another" (Arist. *Rh.* 1367a).

Most importantly, vengeance was an acceptable incentive for bringing someone to trial. Enmity could be declared, or even taken for granted by a defendant, as a prosecutor's motive.[35] A trial was referred to as a hunt, a competition (*agôn*) with "pursuers" (prosecutors) and "those in flight" (defendants). Demosthenes has a prosecutor admit he is an "avenger," paying back the defendant for starting the animosity. Indeed, others would call him "most unmanly" if he did not get even (59.1, 8, 12). Elsewhere, Demosthenes proudly claims that he believes his duty is to avenge himself and that "it is sufficient to have taken vengeance" (53.2, 15; cf. 18 and 57.8).

really questioned as an appropriate motive, just upon whom, by whom, and for what. Odysseus in Sophocles' *Ajax* may be the first character to question the need to gloat openly over a fallen enemy (Stanford ad 79), but even he admits that he "hated Ajax when it was honorable to hate" (1347). Socrates is still Greek, seeing nothing "wrong or envious" in rejoicing in the misfortunes of our enemies (*Phlb.* 49d); his concern is with the *doing* of injustice; cf., however, the words of Protagoras on the correct function of punishment in *Prt.* 324a–c.
[34] Burnett (1998) 2 with references; cf. 8.   [35] Dover (1974) 180–4.

Those who bring charges often add that the desire for personal revenge on an enemy is combined with the opportunity to do the state a service; vengeance is both a moral and civic obligation (Dem. 24.8–9; cf. Lycurg. *Leoc.* 42–6; Lys. 7.20, 39, 9.20, 13.3, 14.2, 15.12, 32.22; Isae. 7.29, 32).

The significance here is that the desire to prosecute someone could be primarily, if not completely, motivated by a personal wish to see one's enemy suffer. The judicial system was one more venue in which to earn honor and to inflict or recover from shame. Athenian law courts often "were a public stage upon which private enmities were played out."[36] Recent analyses of the interconnectedness of law and society in ancient Greece emphasize the "open texture" of Athenian law.[37] The Athenians' notorious litigiousness was not merely an offshoot of their competitiveness, but was embedded "in the broader context of agonistic social practices and a field of values organized around notions of honor, competition, hierarchy, and equality."[38] There were many different ways to prosecute someone, each with a different kind of trial, with different possible penalties and rewards. For example, Demosthenes tells us that in the case of impiety (*graphê asebeias*), the charge under which Socrates was brought to court, one could use any of several different actions: *apagôgê*, *graphê*, a *dikê* to the Eumolpidae, or a *phasis* to the *basileus* (22.25f.). The choice of kinds of prosecution was likely determined by a wide variety of agendas. *Graphai*, for example, were open trials of strength, perfectly designed to bring the prosecutor to public attention as a champion of the community's interests, not merely his own. The legal system was a crucial arena for adjusting or clarifying social and political relationships. Once an enemy did something that could be interpreted as prosecutable – "impiety," for example, provided a wonderfully fuzzy catch-all for an indictment[39] – the injured party could wreak personal vengeance and regain status by performing "good works" for the state in a successful prosecution: "When punishment stripped a convicted wrongdoer of honor, it simultaneously gave honor back to his victim, honor that the act of wrongdoing had taken away."[40]

The potentially lethal consequences of Greek shame society are obviously relevant to an understanding of Plato's Socrates. This was a culture, after all, in which fellow citizen-soldiers looked at Socrates angrily (*hupeblepon*) because they thought he was trying to show them up (*kataphronounta*) by walking out shoeless into the cold with just a coat (*Symp.* 220b1–c1). Even a cursory glance at the dialogues reveals that Socratic "conversations"

[36] Osborne (1985) 52.
[37] Especially Osborne (1985); Todd and Millett (1990); Cohen (1995).
[38] Cohen (1995) 181.   [39] Sullivan (1997) 147–8.   [40] Allen (2000) 61.

are viewed by all concerned as competitions.[41] Protagoras, famous for his "contests of *logoi*," sees Socrates as an opponent (*antilegôn, Prt.* 335a–336e). Socrates in turn says that to let Protagoras establish the rules of discussion would create a handicapped foot-race. This "complicity in competitive ideology" in his conduct of elenchus (cf. 329c–333c) confirms to those so inclined that it was competitive in motivation.[42] Adimantus compares the participants in dialectic to contestants in draughts (*Resp.* 487b–c). These competitions must produce winners and losers, and Alcibiades concedes that Socrates "defeats everyone in words" (*Symp.* 213e). These are battles of *logoi* in which rivals "make raids" on each other's arguments (*Resp.* 472a). Socrates admits his verbal assaults are battles (*diemachometha, Phd.* 106c; cf. *Phlb.* 15d, 58; *Resp.* 534b–c; *Phd.* 89–91) and readily agrees with Theodorus' charge that he does not "let anyone who approaches you go until you have forced him to strip and wrestle with you in argument" (*Tht.* 169a–b). Metaphors from athletics and war abound in reference to Socratic conversations. Whether "friendly" or not, they are viewed as public contests with winners and losers, and are therefore deadly serious in the competitive environment of classical Greece.[43]

Let me clarify what I mean by "public" failure or success. Socrates admits in the *Apology* that he is a "busybody" (*polupragmonô*, 31c5) in "private," intruding personally in people's lives but avoiding public office at the caution of the divine voice (cf. 36c). Private here means outside of formal office, the assembly, and the lawcourts, but certainly not outside of the public eye. Socrates is always with people, talking to small groups in the agora, or gymnasia, or in their homes. Public humiliation in the Athenian setting requires no more than an individual's feeling that he has been attacked and his status diminished. As we learned from Williams' definition of shame, it really does not take a crowd to create dishonor in a shame society – just

---

[41] Although this point is frequently conceded by most scholars, few choose to focus on Plato's depiction of the competitive nature of the philosophical life as depicted in the dialogues; see below. One exception is Gouldner (1965) 57–65, who sees the Platonic dialogues as fitting into the "zero sum" game of the Greek contest system; see below. As Allen (2000) 353 n.58 observes, the system was not necessarily zero sum, but was definitely relational: when someone gained *timê* (honor), someone else may not have lost any, but was still relatively further behind. Ross (1989) 71 notes, with only slight exaggeration, that "without exception the dialogues dramatize competitive, agonistic discourse, nearly always resolving inconclusively, and manifest consensus only where a weaker interlocutor has been overcome by a stronger." Also excellent on the combative model for Socratic dialogue is Blondell (2002) 121–7.

[42] Schofield (1992) 129.

[43] For wrestling metaphors, among others, see Herrmann (1995). Greene's suggestion (1920) 72 that the unpopularity of Socrates arises from the fact that the public has no sense of humor is thus true, in the sense that leading members of the community find it difficult to laugh at their own expense.

ask Euthyphro.[44] Throughout the *Apology*, Socrates repeatedly reminds the jury that his inquisitions took place publicly, in the presence of many people "in the market and elsewhere" (17 c7–9). They not only heard what he said but witnessed the humiliation of the silenced interlocutors. He calls upon "many of you" in the jury as witnesses to his conversations (19d1, 19d3), and he assumes that the jury ("you") have "often" heard him speaking of the divine voice (31c7–d1). His explicit mission is to philosophize with whomever he meets (29d6), whether young or old, citizen or foreigner (30a2–4) – anyone who wishes can answer and hear what he says. He has never said anything to anyone privately that others did not hear in public (33a6–b8). Most of Athens – and this quite pointedly includes the jury – have seen Socrates' dialectic in action, or know some friend or relative who has.[45] There were other people present (*hoi parontes*) when he examined the leading figures of Athens (23a4) who were not necessarily part of the specific elenchus. He later observes that through his dialectic an enmity arose "among many" (28a5), the prejudice and envy "of the many" (28a7–8). The attack on men's status, especially men with good reputations (*hoi men malista eudokimountes*, 22a3), is the source of the anger. It's not just business, Sonny; it's also personal.

Worse still, Socrates reports that many people enjoy following him around in order to witness the humiliation of fellow citizens, rejoicing at the examination of those who believe themselves to be wise but are not. "It's not unpleasant," he adds as final explanation (33c2–4).[46] The young especially enjoy watching their elders brought down a notch or two – then, as now. In his insistence that many have seen him in

---

44 Moreover, the events in a Platonic dialogue occur only in the dialogue (they are fictional), and that dialogue was promulgated. Interlocutors will be shamed as long as we read Plato. On the meaning of Socrates' "private" conversations as one-on-one meetings to gain understanding rather than formal gatherings to effect a public decision, see Ober (1998) 174–5 n.37, who cites also Diog. Laert. 2.21: Socrates philosophized at workshops and in the agora.

45 Nehamas (1990) 15–16 with n.19 challenges the idea of Socrates as a "street philosopher" (Vlastos' term), suggesting that Socrates' practice as depicted in the dialogues differs from what Socrates says here in the *Apology*. Instead, Nehamas sees Socrates addressing a very small class of people limited to those who thought themselves wise and therefore who were in need of elenchus; cf. Ober (1989) 31–5 for a rejection of Finley's face-to-face model of Athenian society. But here I am discussing Plato's depiction of Socrates in the *Apology*, and there is no doubt about this picture. Moreover, one spectator is crowd enough for shame to work, and even that one extra person is not necessary for shame to take hold. The interlocutors do come from a single class for the most part, but their connection is not the need of elenchus – we *all* need that, including Socrates – but their position as leading or potentially leading citizens. Beversluis is closer to the truth, I think, when he refers to Socrates as a street fighter and philosophy as a spectator sport (2000) 8.

46 The expression "not unpleasant" is used twice in the *Apology*, both times referring to the emotions evoked by those *performing* dialectic. Only the few "converted," such as Nicias (*La.* 188b5–6) and Glaucon (*Resp.* 529c3–4), see anything "pleasant" in being tested by Socrates.

action, and can thereby refute the prosecutors' charges that he is irreligious and a teacher of sophistic, Socrates supplies the context for the
real charges against him. No one has seen him do what he is said to
have done, but all these people have witnessed the humiliation of neighbors, leaders, family members – and perhaps suffered such public shame
themselves.

Finally, we should remember that Socrates' interlocutors are for the most
part not just "ordinary citizens" but individuals who move in the higher
echelons of society, Athenian and otherwise, the people most likely to be
concerned about how they are perceived by others.[47] Thrasymachus, as
depicted in the *Republic*,[48] is in this respect an archetypal victim of Socratic
dialectic. Very much wanting to "defeat" Socrates in a "contest of honor,"
he is instead transformed into a mute beast.

THRASYMACHUS

Thrasymachus is perhaps Plato's most famous bad boy, depicted from first
to last as a brutish and intemperate thug, the very embodiment of the "thumoeidic" lion Socrates later describes in the *Republic*.[49] But Thrasymachus
also makes as great an impact on the course of the discussion as any other
figure in the dialogue. His challenges to Socrates' method, in particular
the use of elenchus and crafts analogy, must be linked in some fashion
to the fact that these familiar techniques are abandoned for the remaining

---

[47] Beversluis (2000) 30, who notes their similar aspirations and class despite differences in age, background, and education. Ober (1996) 100–6 argues that at least for fourth-century Athens we should
distinguish between the personal honor (*timê*) of the elite – primarily a matter of aristocratic competition among wealthy individuals or families – and the *timê* of the ordinary Athenian, "citizen
dignity" – the "basket" of privileges, immunities, duties and responsibilities accorded full citizens.
Even if we should make the strong ideological distinctions between a mass and an elite that forms
the basis for Ober's work, I follow Williams and others in viewing the effects of shame as similar
throughout Athenian culture. What happens to elite or ordinary citizen alike is that his worth is
challenged. The emotional effects are identical. Any person in the community whose value has been
diminished in some fashion feels humiliation and a desire for vengeance. The shame may come in
different contexts, only one of which (official *atimia*) involves the literal loss of citizen privileges.
The question is, does my voice have influence? In all cases, shame involves the silencing, or potential
silencing, of that voice.

[48] See Beversluis (2000) 221–2 for references to discussions of the connection between the character
and the historical Thrasymachus (irrelevant here, although I will refer to him as a "sophist" for
convenience). Quincey's insightful suggestion (1981) that Plato's message is as likely to be conveyed
in the dramatic presentation as in the philosophical arguments is attenuated, I think, by his efforts
to tie the character to the historical figure.

[49] Wilson (1995); Hobbs (2000) 164–74; Blondell (2002) 188, with 180–1 on Platonic beast imagery
used for anything hostile to reason. See: Tarrant (1946) 27–8; Saxonhouse (1978) 892–8; Frère (1997)
for other uses of animal imagery in the *Republic*.

nine books, whereas Thrasymachus' ideas are taken up throughout.[50] Many commentators have argued that Socrates' refutation of the sophist is at times heavy-handed and rhetorical, rather than logically legitimate; the philosopher's arguments against Thrasymachus may not hold up under scrutiny as well as has usually been thought.[51] Socrates himself, after all, is disappointed with the results of the conversation, and feels they must make a fresh start in Book 2. But for our purposes, the scene provides a perfect stage on which Socrates' real "crime" is played out. Indeed, the dramatic movement of this scene would be obvious even if it were staged in classical Greek to a non-Greek speaking audience: Thrasymachus is flattened into silence by a steamrolling Socrates. In any normal cultural sense, Socrates is the victor in the competition. But Socrates is not out to win for the sake of winning, and realizes that his "victory" is no real victory at all. He insists on pursuing the discussion about justice for nine more books. In the meantime, however, he has shamed another proud member of the community, taking one more step towards his prosecution and death. In this episode, as in so many others, Plato dramatizes Socrates' "failure in victory," which illuminates the difference between Socrates' vision of life and that of others.[52]

ERISTIC AND DIALECTIC

Cephalus dashes out of the first philosophical conversation of the *Republic* once his attempts to discuss the nature of justice meet a Socratic dead end. His son Polemarchus "inherits" his father's argument, breaking in quickly when his father admits he is wrong (331d). His own efforts to define justice along traditional lines – first with a general "to render back what is due" and finally with the more specific and familiar "to do good to friends and evil to enemies" – soon meet the same fate. Driven to *aporia*, he must confess that "I no longer know what I meant." But he still insists that justice is to

---

[50] See especially Reeve (1985) 259–62 and Reeve (1988). As was noted earlier, the apparent abandonment of elenchus is often tied to a belief that Plato himself lost confidence in its efficacy.

[51] Argued most recently and extensively by Beversluis (2000) 221–44 (with references) and Hobbs (2000) 170–4, but many others have found Socrates' attacks on Thrasymachus' position to be defective; see, for example: Henderson (1970); Annas (1981) 50; Reeve (1985; 1988) 9–24; Ross (1989) 72; Jang (1997).

[52] Blondell (2000) acutely interprets the scene as a presentation of Thrasymachus' dialectical failings. Patterson (1987) 344–5 argues that Thrasymachus is intended to be an example of failures in all four areas of a philosophic character: gentleness, anger, shame, and competitiveness. In other words, he is the model of the anti-philosophic life. Allen (2000) 259–63 sees the depiction of Thrasymachus' aggressiveness as an exaggerated portrayal of Athenian competitiveness that must be banished.

help friends and harm enemies (334), and that a man ought to adopt this morality (335b). Socrates swiftly corners him again, and they agree that in no case would harming anyone be just.

At this point, Socrates must suddenly deflect the aggressive intrusion of Thrasymachus. His very name ("Bold Fighter") reveals the animus that has been building in the impatient witness. Socrates has sensed that previously Thrasymachus had often rushed in to take hold of the discussion only to be restrained by those eager to hear out the conversation. Unable to keep silent (*hêsuchian êgen*) any longer, Thrasymachus hurls himself "like a wild beast (*hôsper thêrion*) about to tear us to pieces" upon the two speakers, who are frozen in fear (336b).

Thrasymachus has grown frustrated with the direction and method of the discussion, a method that has excluded his own participation and led to conclusions he cannot agree with. So he breaks his enforced silence and stakes his claim. Plato pointedly depicts this self-assertion as the act of a beast, thereby ironically introducing the eager speaker with a phrase that challenges his very ability to speak. If the comparison is born out – that is, if the simile becomes flesh – it will result in Thrasymachus' demotion from the circle of articulate (and thus worthy) beings, to the world of the silenced Other.

As if in response to his bestial introduction, Thrasymachus bursts in verbally to reclaim his status.[53] He accuses the group of talking nonsense, playing the fool and giving in to one another (*hupokataklinomenoi*, 336c). The image is one of submission, a wrestler throwing a match, or a humbled guest being seated at the lower end of the table. There is no question in Thrasymachus' mind that this is a contest and he must win it. He views the process that Socrates has developed in his dialectic as a competition for honor, and tells Socrates to stop asking questions and finding glory in refuting the answers (*mêde philotimou elenchôn*). Instead, Socrates is to state simply what he believes justice is and leave off the nonsense. The battle lines have been clearly drawn. Thrasymachus has entered the fray to challenge Socrates' command of the conversation.

Socrates in turn clarifies who is the beast in this passage of the *Republic*. He notes that he was afraid of Thrasymachus, and claims that "if I had not looked at him before he looked at me I would have lost my voice" (*aphônos*, 336d), an allusion to the well-known bit of folk-wisdom that one became

---

[53] *Phthenxamenos*. The word is frequent in Plato to express articulation. In the *Republic*, it is also contrasted with silence (515b8; cf. Xen. *Mem.* 4.2.6) and used of the sounds of the masses as a beast (493b4, twice).

mute if seen by a wolf before seeing the beast oneself.[54] Thrasymachus has been transformed from a generic beast crashing the conversation into a wolf capable of silencing his victim. The wolf in the *Republic* comes to represent the savage tyrant, a leader or guardian who is transformed from watchdog (374e–376c) into a lupine despot (416a–b, 565d–566a).[55] But Socrates retained his voice, as the philosopher is quick to clarify, since he glanced at the angry beast first and so was capable of responding. Indeed, by this clever twist he has managed to turn Thrasymachus into the inarticulate animal. This becomes explicit when he notes that Thrasymachus was "beginning to be made savage" by the argument itself (*hupo tou logou êrcheto exagriainesthai*, 336de). His exclusion from and frustration with the discussion were transforming him into a beast, and now he is to act out his metaphorical metamorphosis.

Plato's careful framing of the conversations that comprise the *Republic* is put to excellent use here. Socrates is relating the events to an unknown audience. This second-hand reporting allows him to set up the scene thematically. Socrates introduces Thrasymachus in such a way as to suggest the sophist wants to silence him, but in fact Thrasymachus will increasingly take on the role of the mute beast. In terms of the larger philosophical argument, this life devoted to honor, success, and ambition without regard to reason that Thrasymachus seems to represent may well portray the "thumoeidic" life that derives from the lion's part of the soul (*Resp.* 440d, 586c–590b). But in his introduction to his "opponent," before the actual exchange of views has even begun, Socrates has already asserted the nature of the "competition" as seen by the sophist, and thus established the public risks in this agonistic conversation. As so often in the dialogues, Socrates' efforts at philosophical dialectic are misconstrued by the interlocutor as a hostile engagement in eristic.

The truth is, when viewed from a cultural rather than philosophical perspective, there really *is* little difference between sophistic eristic and Socratic elenctic as presented by Plato. This is not to say that Plato did not see important differences, or perhaps even change his opinion over time concerning the value of Socratic dialectic. Students of philosophy from Aristotle to the present have argued about the nature of these differences: eristic pursues merely verbal oppositions, neglects to distinguish and divide

---

[54] Cf. *Prt.* 339e for Socrates' mock stunning and silencing by a speech; also *Euthd.* 303a *ekeimên aphônos*; *Symp.* 198a. For the belief in the silencing power of the wolf, see the collection of material in Eckels (1937); Gow (1950) on Theoc. 14.22; Coleman (1977) on Verg. *Ecl.* 9.53–4.

[55] Mainoldi (1984) 187–93.

(e.g. hypothesis from its consequences), concentrates on verbal consistency or inconsistency, is only about winning instead of the pursuit of truth, etc.[56] What are more to Plato's point, I think, are not the differences but the similarities. Most readers of Plato have agreed that the rather subtle distinctions between dialectic and eristic that can be detected in the dialogues would have been – and in fact are – lost on Socrates' audience. As Nehamas concludes in his discussion of the difference between philosophy and sophistry, "we should also concede that it might easily have failed to impress – as it patently did not on the whole impress – those of his contemporaries who had been reduced to embarrassing and humiliating perplexity by him or by one of his followers."[57] Plato consistently depicts throughout the dialogues the negative effects of Socrates' dialectic. Interlocutors and bystanders frequently accuse him of playing unfairly in his conversational tactics (as will Thrasymachus), and many scholars have noted his "cheating" and lapses into spurious argumentation.[58] For my argument, it does not matter whether he does or does not stoop to tricks; what *does* matter is that those he speaks to are portrayed by Plato as believing that he does. That is, they assume his objective is primarily to win the argument, and when they find themselves at a dialectical loss they feel anger and shame at their defeat and little enlightenment. Plato regularly depicts the *negative effects* of elenctic on interlocutors and bystanders. This orchestration of the drama is very much part of Plato's presentation of the differences in the philosophic life that "the many" just don't apprehend.

The word that best describes these effects of the Socratic elenchus – seen as negative by "victims" but as essential by the philosopher – is *aporia*. Socrates is attempting to redefine the function of *aporia*. Socrates' own

[56] For the various "types" of dialectic (particularly as dissected by Aristotle into didascalic, peirastic, gymnastic) and various attempts to distinguish antilogic, eristic, agonistic, etc. see: Ryle (1966) 102–45; Kerferd (1981) 32–4; Nehamas (1990); Frede (1992) 211–13; Blank (1993) 429–31; Watson (1995) 197–200; Gonzalez (1998) 94–128; Notomi (1999) 100–19; Beversluis (2000) 39 with note 8 for bibliography on differences, "real or alleged," between dialectic and eristic. For a convenient outline of the Socratic approach to inquiry, see Brickhouse and Smith (1989) 3–29; they deny (1994) 3–10 any specific "method" can be attributed to Socrates.

[57] Nehamas (1990) 11. Indeed, it is almost a cliché in scholarly attempts at distinguishing Socrates' methods from those of other intellectuals to conclude with something similar; cf. Ryle (1966) 131; Guthrie (1971) 129; Skousgaard (1979) 379–80; Reeve (1989) 160–9; Watson (1995) 197; Wallach (1996) 70–1; Gonzalez (1998) 94–128; Beversluis (2000) 39.

[58] Even Vlastos (1991) 132–56 famously asks "does Socrates cheat?" and answers "yes," but for the interlocutors' own good (cf. Rossetti [1993]) and not when "arguing seriously," a subjective category that really does not stand up to scrutiny; see Beversluis (1996) 212–16 and (2000) 40 with note 13 for bibliography of over twenty other scholars who have accused Socrates of dialectical aberrations, eristic, and deliberate sophistry. Not everyone agrees; see, for example, Irwin (1986a) and Nehamas (1998) 57.

aporia is a "difficulty," a point of ignorance that in fact spurs him from potential silence into speech. *Aporia* for him is a starting-point, a catalyst for dialectic. When he claims that he is, or would be, "utterly at a loss" as to how to speak in front of a court, just like a doctor tried by children on charges brought by a cook (*Grg.* 521e–522b), he may be referring to the kind of speech that would be expected. Or he may just be waxing ironic. But his *aporia* does not result in silence, as the *Apology* itself so convincingly demonstrates. We should not forget that the first example of *aporia* in the dialogue is that of Socrates himself, not one of his interlocutors, as he puzzles over the riddle of the Delphic oracle.[59] His entire philosophic life, in fact, can be viewed as an attempt to address his own aporetic response to the oracle's reply that no one was wiser than he (*Ap.* 21b). Socrates is trying to recreate in others his own experience. When initially confronted with the oracle, he was at a loss (*ēporoun*) for a long time, and then, only with great reluctance, he proceeded with his investigation. And at the end of the *Apology*, Socrates' *aporia* is as different as ever:

"Perhaps you think, gentlemen, that I have been convicted for being at a loss (*aporiai*) for the kinds of words that would have persuaded you, if I had thought it right to do and say everything to gain my acquittal. Far from it. But I have been convicted through being at a loss (*aporiai*) – not for words, however, but for a lack of recklessness and shamelessness (*anaischuntias*), and of wishing to say to you the kinds of things that would have been sweetest for you to hear." (38d2–8)

When Protagoras knocks him "dizzy" with his argument, Socrates immediately launches into his customary question-and-answer session with Prodicus (*Prt.* 339e). The entire conversation of the *Hippias Minor* is prompted by Eudicus' opening query (363a) as to why Socrates has fallen silent after listening to Hippias. In the *Symposium*, Socrates ironically puns on Gorgias' name, suggesting that he feared the Gorgon's head would "turn me dumbfounded (*aphôniai*) into stone," defeated and frozen by the bestial lolling

---

[59] Socrates cross-examines the oracle by cross-examining others. Hackforth (1933) rejects this parallelism of *aporia*, but with no argument. As Rappe (1995) 6–7 concludes, *aporia* in the Delphi story is a kind of miniature representation of the Socratic method. Stokes (1992) 69–70 sees Socrates' public refutation of the oracle before fully understanding it as evidence for his theory that Plato made up the oracle as a shorthand explanation of Socrates' career. As Strycker–Slings (1994) note, the oracle is not really of paramount importance in Socrates' life beyond the trial. On the historicity of the Delphic oracle, see Beversluis (2000) 3 with note 3. For a good discussion of the function of *aporia*, see Kahn (1996a) 95–100. Erler's study (1987) does not focus on the emotional or cultural ramifications. A majority, perhaps all of the early or transitional dialogues may be termed aporetic, with the discussants in a state of confusion or perplexity. Brickhouse and Smith (1994) 3–4 think eight of fifteen; Press (1995) 136 n.15 sees only five of the twenty dialogues in which Socrates leads the discussion as non-aporetic or conclusive. Benson (1990b) 141–4 treats all these dialogues as aporetic.

tongue, silenced forever (*Symp.* 198b–c). Socrates is never really at a loss for words.

For Socrates, true *aporia* is a failure to know, to follow through in his pursuit for truth. It is an incentive. Socrates claims to be happy to be proved wrong, for it is a greater benefit to him to be rebuked than to refute others. It is the mark of a friend to deliver him from false opinion and "foolery" (e.g. *Grg.* 458a; cf. 470c, 486d–488b), and he openly affirms his own *aporia* (e.g. *Chrm.* 165b8–10, 166c7ff., 169c).[60] There is every reason to take Socrates at his word when, at the end of the *Apology*, he asks that his sons be censured just as Athenians have been reproached by him, if they care about things they should not and think they are something when they are not (*Ap.* 41e1–42a2).

For interlocutors like Thrasymachus, however, *aporia* is an "impasse," a helplessness, a loss for words at the *end* of a conversation. It is a public defeat, a failure to persuade and thus maintain or gain status. *Aporia* for Socrates' victims is a climax in silence. As Adimantus summarizes (*Resp.* 487b), Socrates' interlocutors and listeners often feel defeated: owing to their inexperience in dialectic, they are led astray under his questioning by the argument until finally, at the end of the discussion, they meet with a great contradiction and failure. Their words are blocked, and they are unable to answer (cf. *Chrm.* 169c3ff.; *Lach.* 196b2).

Socratic interlocutors are embarrassed at being shown publicly to be ignorant of what they claimed to know. There is no place to hide, and in desperation they sometimes even try to concede defeat. "Let it be just as you say," gasps Agathon, after having to admit in front of his friends: "It is very likely, Socrates, that I didn't know what I was talking about at that time" (*Symp.* 201b–c; cf. Protarchus' efforts to squirm out of the conversation at *Phlb.* 58). Laches observes that Nicias is unwilling to admit honestly that he has no meaning at all but dodges this way and that, hoping to conceal his own *aporia* (*Lach.* 196b). For everyone but Socrates, *aporia* leads to shame, anger, embarrassment, and resentment.

---

[60] See McAvoy (1996) 29–30, who rightly notes that only Socrates takes kindly to this unmasking of pretensions to knowledge; cf. Patterson (1987) 343–5 for the inability of most to adopt this kind of "ego-detachment" required of the philosophic character. West (1995) 55–60 goes so far as to suggest that Socrates' *aporia* leads to our own response of asking questions of the text. Blank (1993) similarly sees the process of arousing emotion in interlocutors and readers as a catharsis that leads to the desire to participate; see also Yonezawa (1995–6) 65. This, as we have seen, is certainly the "ideal" Socrates discusses, but the dialogues concentrate on his failures. Nehamas (1998) 41–8 gives this a neat twist by arguing that Platonic irony manipulates readers into becoming characters, like those in the dialogue, who do not alter their way of life. Gordon (1999) 43–61 applies reader-response theory to the dialogues. Morrison (2000) 261 observes that "no sensible person will find this response [that Socrates finds the passing on of his conviction of ignorance to be beneficial] very comforting."

Note also that Socrates' interlocutors care little if his elenchus has only negative results in exposing ignorance, or also yields certain positive results that ameliorate or even eliminate ignorance, or elicit from the interlocutor/reader an understanding of a positive philosophical position. Modern scholars have debated the purpose of elenchus and Plato's view of it throughout the dialogues.[61] Interlocutors do occasionally bring up Socrates' apparent ignorance or refusal to share his wisdom (e.g. *Resp. 338b*; *Clit.* 410a–b). Plato is often viewed today as having lost faith in the Socratic method, abandoning elenchus and/or the elenctic dialogue at some point. But from the perspective of the reaction of interlocutors to Socratic conversations, we need not speak of development at all but of a consistent view of Socratic practices as dangerous. It may, of course, be true that the historical Socrates was an "agonist,"[62] and that his practice of elenchus was something much more personal and unsystematic than is found in Plato's dialogues[63] – this explanation would go some way, I think, toward explaining the animosity aimed at the man sentenced to death in 399 B.C. But Plato chooses to depict Socrates consistently evoking anger through his conversations, and this is as far as we need to take the matter when analyzing the dialogues. The real consequence of Socrates' frequent failure to "have the answers" is that it increased the impression that his objectives were hostile, that he was in fact out merely to humiliate his interlocutors. Socrates appeared either to be withholding the answers or to be using the "knife-thrusts of his syllogisms" (as Nietzsche referred to dialectic) to slice his opponents into pieces. In either case, his actions would much sooner be seen as an effort to belittle an "opponent" than as a step towards improving a peer. Plato takes great pains to show the difference between Socrates' objectives and how they were interpreted by the rest of his society.

---

[61] One can start, as often, with Vlastos (1994) 1–37. I have found the most helpful contributions to the discussion to be those of Benson (1987; 1989; 1990a; 1990b), and many of the articles in Scott (2002); see also Rappe (1995) and May (1997) for succinct outlines of the debate, and Gonzalez (1995b; 1998) 3–18 for a history of the constructivist/non-constructivist controversy. He argues for a constructionist view that involves non-propositional knowledge gained in the aporetic dialogues (especially 19–93). Nehamas (1998) 83–4 believes that Socrates' elenchus of the oracle is a demonstration that the process is capable of establishing truth.

[62] Watson (1995) 197. This matches *some* of the characterization of Socrates in Aristophanes, for example; against the traditional view (e.g. of Dover [1968] xxxv–lvii) that the character of Socrates in the *Clouds* primarily represents some sort of composite intellectual, see the arguments of Clay (1994); Vander Waerdt (1994b); Nussbaum (1996). Especially interesting, if necessarily inconclusive, is the suggestion that distinctive Socratic question-and-answer is to be found in the comedy; see Philippson (1932); Clay (1994) 37–40; Vander Waerdt (1994b) 59; Nussbaum (1996) 93–4.

[63] Kahn (1996a) 302, which seems an unnecessary supposition from a scholar who more rigorously than most attempts to downplay the connection between Plato's literary creation (the only one open to scholarly study, as he insists) and the historical figure.

MOCKERY AND THE OTHER

Socrates tells Thrasymachus that the speakers certainly have not erred intentionally, but should be pitied by clever men such as him, rather than reproached. The sarcasm is not lost on Thrasymachus, who gives a bitter laugh (*anekanchase te mala sardanion*, 337a). The appropriation of laughter, as we shall see, is one of the key elements of Socrates' agenda. The entire *Republic* can in fact be read in part as Socrates' attempt to redefine what is truly and meaningfully laughable.[64] Socrates appears "deserving of laughter" for his ideas and proposals (e.g. 392d, 398c, 432d, 445a, 473c, 499c, 504d, 506d, 536b; cf. Glaucon's concerns at 526d–527a, 527d, 528d–529c, 529e–530a). He acknowledges that his novel concepts, such as a philosopher as ruler or the equation of women to men or men to animals, opposed as they often are to convention, make him appear a laughing-stock (especially 452–7). Nevertheless, he argues that the laughable must be defined by the criterion of good and bad, not mere opinion (452c–e). Thrasymachus here, as throughout this first book, represents familiar patterns of behavior that run directly counter to the philosophic life.

The sophist accuses Socrates of avoiding a response in typically ironic fashion (337a). And indeed, Socrates' mock-humility is annoyingly smug and might easily be interpreted as part of an agonistic effort to establish his superiority.[65] Socrates attempts to explain that, given Thrasymachus' guidelines, he cannot answer – he has been silenced by the methodological constraints of the sophist, a momentary victory for the speech-maker who is dying to supply his own superior definition of justice. He thinks it appropriate for Socrates to pay a penalty, a fine for his defeat in this discussion (*apotison argurion*, 337d; cf. *Ap.* 36b5, 37c4, 38b1–9). Socrates says he does not have any money, but Glaucon guarantees it for the group. Here, in miniature, is the very case of Socrates' life and death in the *Apology*. If found guilty of incorrect speech – speech which deprives others of their full humanity (for this is his real crime) – he is expected to pay a fine which others guarantee. He is no doubt serious when he suggests that the learning itself is reward – or penalty – enough. But Thrasymachus is still suspicious that Socrates will contrive as always to avoid answering, and instead will seize the argument and refute him (*lambanêi logon kai elenchêi*, 337e). Each of the contestants in this battle is accusing the other of grabbing the

[64] See Saxonhouse (1978) 889–90, 895–6.
[65] See Nehamas (1998) 49–69 for a discussion of irony and Thrasymachus' understanding of Socrates' remark.

conversation. They are wrestling for the *logos* like two *pancratiasts* struggling for their very lives.

Socrates knows what is at stake from his interlocutor's point of view. He tells us that Thrasymachus was eager to speak "in order to be highly esteemed" (*eudokimêseien*), believing that he had an excellent answer (338a; cf. Critias' similarly emotionally charged interruption as he is "burning to distinguish himself" at *Chrm.* 162e). Thrasymachus at first pretends he wants Socrates to answer, but finally and proudly announces that the just is nothing other than the advantage of the stronger. The exact nature of Thrasymachus' claim(s) has been the subject of much debate,[66] but in its immediate context, Thrasymachus is also hinting that the superior individual will do as he pleases. This is exactly what he hopes to prove in his speech and his actions – as the superior man, he will be able to impose his definition, his methodology, his voice upon the rest of the company.[67] The conversation – or the battle of words, for he does not subscribe to Socrates' methods – is to prove who is the fully successful human. He asks to be praised but does not expect Socrates to give him the satisfaction. Socrates instead twists both terms of the definition and asks what must be an intentionally misguided question. This sets off Thrasymachus, who calls Socrates a beastly wretch (*bdeluros*) and accuses him of taking hold of his *logos* in such a way as to injure it (338d).[68] Perhaps by flinging bestial sobriquets at his opponent he can regain control of the argument. Socrates, fully convinced that his dialectic is the best means of pursuing the truth, quickly reverts to his customary role of inquisitorial and unenlightened (*agnoô*) guide.

Thrasymachus, however, is on the lookout for Socrates' syllogistic tricks, and greets the first sign of refutation with a terse reply (*ti legeis su*, 339d). Thrasymachus' suspicions are confirmed when Socrates concludes his demonstration of Thrasymachus' self-contradiction with the smugly ironic "O most brilliant Thrasymachus" (339e).[69] The sophist rejects Cleitophon's attempt to help him and turns on Socrates directly. He calls him a

---

[66] See the summary of interpretations of the propositional content of Thrasymachus' various pronouncements provided by Chappell (1993) 1–4.

[67] Ophir (1991) 107–9 observes that Thrasymachus tries to be a "tyrant of discourse," and that his abuse of power and violation of space boundaries bring him to the level of beast.

[68] For the violently adverse reaction implied in *bdeluros*, see Ar. *Ran.* 465; *Eq.* 304; *Ach.* 287; Theophr. *Char.* 11; it is a common form of abuse in the orators; e.g Aeschin. 1.31, 189; Dem. 25.27.

[69] On the use of vocatives in the "battle" between Thrasymachus and Socrates, see Halliwell (1995) 92, 105–6, and especially Dickey (1996) 109–19. Dickey concludes that these "friendship terms" are used in the dialogues by the person in the "dominant position" at any time, or by another person when he feels he has won the upper hand in debate.

sukophantês . . . en logois, a quibbler in words, and accuses him of being a tightwad in speech (*su akribologei*). The charge is a serious one, for a sycophant could mean an informer or a dishonest prosecutor, and "accurate speaking" had a strongly pejorative side as well. This charge against Socrates is a familiar one. Here, he feigns concern with the growing hostility and misunderstanding and addresses his opponent directly:

> Thrasymachus, do I seem to be quibbling with you?
> You certainly do.
> So you think that I treacherously used unfair arguments against you in asking the question as I did?
> Indeed, I *know* you did, and you won't get anything from it, for you won't do me injury without my noticing it, and you will not overpower me in argument (*biasasthai tôi logôi*).
> I wouldn't dream of it! (341a–b)

Thrasymachus dares Socrates to try his old tricks (*kakourgei kai sukophantei*), defiantly challenging Socrates to prove him wrong, convinced he will win the duel: "I ask no quarter." Socrates artfully claims that he could not play the quibbler with Thrasymachus, for who is so mad as to "try to shave a lion" (341c)? This rare proverb again puts Thrasymachus into the role of the beast, a fitting introduction to his inevitable downfall in the quickly ensuing elenchus. The animal allusion introduces the typical Socratic dialectic that will shortly demote Thrasymachus to the dreaded position of silenced victim. This is all the more embarrassing, for Thrasymachus plays the role of audience dupe in a magic show or hypnotism demonstration. Prepared for every trick, he is humiliated all the more – the roaring lion de-clawed, de-fanged, and muzzled.

We can trace this descent away from the fully human rather quickly. As the force of Socrates' arguments mounts, Thrasymachus is limited in customary Socratic fashion to one- or two-word answers (341d–342c). When the discussion begins to take an increasingly uncomfortable turn, however, Thrasymachus can only agree reluctantly (*sunechôrêsen entautha kai mala mogis*). Significantly, this is the first time Socrates gives his victim's response in reported speech rather than as a direct quotation. As Thrasymachus grows less voluble in the dialogue, he begins to lose his voice in the text as well. Similarly, he is reported to have fought in vain before assenting to Socrates' next point (342d). His further admissions are glossed by Socrates (*xunephê . . . hômologêtai*), along with his doomed struggle to maintain his independence (*xunephêse mogis*, 342d–e). Socrates now has brought the discussion to such a point that it is painfully obvious to everyone – at least as far as Socrates can see – that Thrasymachus' definition of justice has suffered a complete reversal.

No longer able or willing to reply to Socrates' leading questions, Thrasymachus launches into a speech designed to clarify his argument, but also intended to reestablish the "correct" relation between Socrates and himself. He has been nearly silenced, his status threatened, his humanity challenged, and he now attempts to gain through sheer insult the upper hand gained by Socrates through pointed dialectic:

> Tell me, Socrates, do you have a nurse?
> Why do you ask that? Shouldn't you answer me rather than ask such a thing?
> Because your nurse overlooks the snot running down your face and doesn't wipe it up, though you need it, you who have not learned from her to distinguish the sheep from the shepherds. (343a)

Having been shoved too close to the bestial, Thrasymachus is attempting to push Socrates into another of the sub-human categories, that of a little child who has no full access to the *logos* and can only drivel.

This mixing of various Others can be put into its full agonistic context by comparing other passages in Plato where the status of children is evoked in similar contexts. In the *Protagoras*, for example, we learn that even the basest of the Spartans will appear dull in conversation until at some crucial point he will drive home a short and compressed remark, a deadly shot "that makes his interlocutor appear no better than a child" (342d–e).[70] Socrates draws the direct connection between being portrayed as a child and public humiliation when he notes that "you will probably mock (*katagelasei*) me if I, an old man, seem to you still to be playing like a child" (*paizein*; *Menex.* 236c). Socrates' "victims" believe that philosophizing itself reduces one's status. Callicles (*Grg.* 485a–d) snarls that "philosophy, like speaking inarticulately and playing the child, is tolerable in the young. But for a grown man to partake of any of these is humiliating (*katagelaston*) and unmanly and deserving of a whipping" (that is, slavish).[71] Here, the nexus of inarticulateness, being a child, and becoming a slave is associated with

---

[70] Cf. *Tht.* 177b: "Their brilliant rhetoric withers away, so that they seem no better than children"; also *Cri.* 49b.
[71] Cf. Euthydemus in Xenophon *Mem.* 4.2.39–40, who remonstrates with himself after an embarrassing encounter with Socrates: "I am inclined to think that I had better hold my tongue, or I shall know nothing at all presently." Xenophon concludes, "And so he went away very dejected, disgusted with himself and convinced that he was indeed a slave."

the laughable and unmanly activity of the philosopher.[72] Socrates, however, defines the laughable very differently than his peers.

Everyone in the dialogues agrees that a laughter-producing loss in dialectic makes one a fool (*lian anoêtos*), ashamed (*aischuntheis, Prt.* 348b–c), and embarrassed (*ethorubêsa, Phlb.* 28b–c). Theodorus, desperately trying to avoid such shame, begs Socrates to pick on one of the younger members in the crowd, for if they slip up they would be less disgraced (*aschêmonêsei, Tht.* 165a–b). For Socrates' "opponents" – usually public men with a reputation at stake – this is a concern that fits in closely with the old heroic code. But the concern of Socrates and his faithful acolytes is based on a different premise from that of his detractors. He worries that he will appear ridiculous for failing in his quest for the truth. For him, the fear is not of being laughed at for "losing" an argument to his "opponent," but of falling further into ignorance and failing his friends and city (cf. *Resp.* 450e–451a). What is shameful, he tells Polus, is not to have knowledge of who is happy and who is not (*Grg.* 472c). Socrates feels shame not because he has failed in front of other men, but because he has failed to succeed in his own determined search for the truth. His concern is not with maintaining his political or social status, but in his (and others') metaphysical health. One of Plato's important themes is the contrast between this kind of semi-internalized shame based on personal conviction and the conventional cultural protocols of the community.

Whereas most interlocutors, like Thrasymachus, fear being mocked for losing in debate or failing publicly, the philosopher feels such humiliation only when failing at pursuing dialectic.[73] At one point in the *Gorgias*, the philosopher even accuses Polus of introducing a new form of elenchus, mockery itself; laughter here becomes a substitute for refutation (*Grg.* 473e). The most frequent way of contrasting the philosophical and non-philosophical lives is to imagine the truth-seeking philosopher stuck in the courtroom of opinion, struggling for a forensic victory just as Socrates finds himself in the *Apology*. In the *Theaetetus* (172c–175e), for example, Socrates concedes that the philosopher can get lost in the mundane world, hardly knowing whether he is a human or some other creature. Instead, working on quite a different level, he inquires what a human

---

[72] Cf. *Resp.* 487c–d, where Adimantus notes that even those who lose their arguments to Socrates still feel that people pursuing philosophy past youth (*neoi*) mostly become quite strange (*allokotous*), if not utterly depraved (*pamponêrous*) and ultimately useless to the city.

[73] Socrates thus is attempting to redefine a series of ideas associated with conventional Greek morality: shame, mockery, and revenge. This matches well with Fisher's analysis of *hubris* in the dialogues (1992) 453–92. Plato alone has a different definition, internalizing the concept by applying it to one who has given too much rule to the passions.

being is and what he should do. As a result, when he must converse in private or in court about "the things at his feet and before his eyes," he is a laughing-stock (*gelôta*) to everyone, and feels at a loss (*aporia*). This perplexity (*aporôn*) makes him look laughable (*geloios*; cf. *Resp.* 517d). The philosopher laughs at eulogies of rulers, the wealthy, or blue-bloods, finding human vanity completely ridiculous. The philosopher in turn is laughed at (*kategelatai*) by the multitude (*hupo tôn pollôn*), considered ignorant of the things at his feet and at a loss (*aporôn*) in everything. Interested only in truth, philosophers do not know how to wheedle with words and gain favor with their master (*Tht.* 172c–173b; cf. *Resp.* 498c–499a; *Euthd.* 271c–272c, 275d–e). To the uninitiated, all philosophers appear ridiculous (*Euthd.* 305a8–9) and are likely to be considered mad (*Phdr.* 249; *Soph.* 216d).

On the other hand, when a philosopher draws someone into an investigation of philosophical issues, the tables are turned: the small-minded "everyman" is at a loss (*aporôn*), stammers (*Tht.* 175d), and becomes ridiculous (*gelôta*). Note again the nexus of failure at language and shame. Socrates is redefining what should be the source of ridicule. For most Athenians, laughter and shame come from failing to impress one's peers, from an inability to use language for the "fawning speech" (*thôpas logous, Tht.* 175e) of persuasion. One must defeat one's opponent in conversation and gain the approbation of the crowd. Socrates, however, tells Polus that the only person he must convince is Socrates – otherwise, even if Polus' "courtroom elenchus" persuades everyone else, it is in reality a failure (*Grg.* 470d–472). The "art of speeches," he declares elsewhere, is laughable and not in fact an art at all, as it aims at opinion and not truth (*Phdr.* 262b–c).

Similar contrasts are found throughout the Platonic corpus. Crito, for example, is ashamed (*aischunomai*), and fears that he will look like a coward for failing to save Socrates by letting the trial go on so ridiculously (*katagelôs, Cri.* 45e). Socrates, however, worries he will look ridiculous if he violates his agreements by leaving the city. Socrates is concerned about being consistent with his philosophical principles; Crito worries what others will say about him when viewed through the lenses of the conventional morality of helping friends. Euthyphro says he is laughed at for his opinions about the divine, while Socrates suggests that this kind of laughter may not be of such great consequence (*Euthphr.* 3c2, 6, d10). When the philosopher proposes that a man would laugh at Hippias' entirely conventional attempt to define the beautiful – wealth, health, long life and splendid burial by dutiful children – Hippias replies that the philosopher will be laughed at by all those present.

Socrates agrees, adding that the man would not only be likely to laugh but also to beat him, and with justice, since he has failed at finding a definition (*Hp. mai.* 291d–292b)!

A glance at the appearances of the family of compounds connected with *katagelos* brings the point home quickly.[74] Socrates feels "ridiculous" when he fails to pursue dialectic. Failure to arrive at a definition (e.g. *Ly.* 223b5), to make or see the right argument (e.g. *Thg.* 130b8; *Ly.* 211c1–2; *Euthd.* 279d1, 4; *Men.* 96e2; *Resp.* 432d8–9, 493d9, 499c4–5), and to avoid self-contradiction (e.g. *Soph.* 241e5; *Phlb.* 14e3) result in humiliation for the philosopher. A deceitful argument threatens to make the speakers look ridiculous (*Lg.* 892d4), and the end of the unresolved argument itself mocks Socrates and Protagoras (*Prt.* 361a4–5). The subject of the discussion may even ridicule the speakers if their inquiry comes up short (e.g. *Lach.* 194a1–5). The perfect irony of it all is that Socrates alone believes that this process is ultimately beneficial, since it forces one to see an argument through and to start over when it leads to a dead end.

This entire Platonic vision is neatly outlined, and the *Apology* brilliantly adumbrated, in the celebrated give-and-take between Callicles and Socrates in the *Gorgias* (484c–486d, 521b–522d). The sophist lays out the familiar contrast between the philosophic and practical life. Philosophy provides a fine little pool for the young to dip their toes in, but brings men to ruin should they dive into it too deeply or for too long (cf. *Resp.* 487c–d; *Euthd.* 306e; *Prt.* 346a; *Soph.* 216c). Philosophizing into adulthood renders one useless in the very things that mark a real man. Philosophers are ridiculous (*katagelastoi*) when they attempt to enter any business, just as public men are ridiculous (*katagelastoi*) when they fall into Socrates' conversations. He repeats: for a man to pursue philosophy into adulthood is ridiculous (*katagelaston*). He feels the same way towards an elderly pursuer of philosophy as towards those who "lisp like children" – he is ridiculous (*katagelaston*), unmanly (*anandrian*), and deserving of a good whipping. Note here the familiar concatenation of characteristics of the Other: slavish, childish, feminine, and lacking efficacious language. To be an effective citizen, that is, fully human, Callicles insists that one must exercise speech in the "centers and *fora* of the city where 'men get note and glory'" (quoting Homer *Il.* 9.441). "Doesn't it seem disgraceful (*aischron*) to you to be in such a state?" Callicles wonders prophetically. For should someone accuse Socrates of a crime, no matter how unjustly, Socrates would be at a loss,

---

[74] Similar results are found in an examination of the more frequent uncompounded *gel-* roots. *Katagel-*, however, has more consistently pejorative connotations; see Aristophanes' fears not so much that he will say something *geloia* – this is his muse – as something *katagelasta* (*Symp.*189b).

dizzy, and agape. He would not have anything to say, and end up punished with death.

Socrates replies that he knows all too well that he could be hauled off to death. Since he is the only man who attempts the true art of statesmanship and makes speeches not aimed at gratification but at what is best, he will in fact not have a word to say. Like a doctor tried by a jury of children on charges brought by a cook, he will be in complete perplexity (*aporia*). "If anyone claims that I either corrupt the younger men by reducing them to perplexity (*aporein*), or abuse the older men by saying bitter words either in private or in public," Socrates concedes, he is in trouble. He will be unable either to tell the truth that he does all this for the citizens' interest (for there will be an outcry) – or to say anything else for that matter. When Callicles asks if such a powerless man makes himself a fine figure in the city, Socrates answers yes, by avoiding any unjust word or deed. And only if convicted – by one or many – of failing to protect himself or others from avoiding injustice would he feel ashamed and vexed.

Here, of course, is Socrates' review (or preview) of his trial (cf. *Resp.* 517a–c). Note, however, how Socrates sees the indictment. He suggests that the charges against him will be corrupting the youth by reducing them to *aporia*, or by speaking ill (*kakêgorein*) of the elder citizens when they are not living correctly. Certainly, it is no coincidence that Socrates uses the same verb in describing what his future prosecutor Anytus feels has been done to the "gentlemen" of Athens (*Men.* 95a3–4).[75] In other words, Socrates sees exactly the nature of his prosecutors' motives: Athenians have been chastised and rendered silent for failing to care about those things they should most care about. The conversation here is more about who has the power to speak than what the conversations accomplish. Callicles thinks philosophers are unable to talk where citizens should most hold sway; Socrates notes that his conversations with citizens drive them into perplexity and anger. Thrasymachus would agree with both.

As did, apparently, much of Athens. From the beginning to the end of the *Apology*, Socrates never wavers from his conviction that he is found guilty because of his dialectic, that he is delivered to death because of his conversations with individuals, in which he argued that they should care about more important things than money and politics (36b6–d1). He has been convicted, he insists, not on the charges but because Athenians could

---

[75] Socrates does not intend to "slander" the elderly any more than he believes he is corrupting the young. Slander, revealingly linked with ridicule, is forbidden in the *Laws* because it turns the users into beasts while starting hatreds and feuds (934e–935e).

not endure his discourses and words (*diatribas kai logous*)[76] which jury members (as Athenians) have found burdensome and odiously humiliating, and from which they now want release (37c5–d2). The jurors who voted against him did so in the (false) hopes that they could avoid conversing with Socrates and giving an account of their lives (39c6–7).[77] And so most of the defense is in fact a return to addressing these underlying misconceptions about Socrates. What should be noted here is the effort to redefine "shame." Since the humiliation felt by Socrates' interlocutors is the issue, Plato demonstrates how Socrates sees the world so differently from "the many."

Socrates brings up a hypothetical accusation: "Then aren't you ashamed (*aischunê*), Socrates, of having pursued the kind of activity that now puts you in danger of being put to death?" (28b3–5). His response – what I take to be the heart of Plato's image of the philosophical life as presented in the *Apology* – is that one must only consider whether one acts justly or not, whether one's deeds are those of a good or bad man. In other words, the public consequences of one's actions, what other people think of them and may do to you for them, are not important. He is, in effect, redefining shame.[78] He uses a mythological exemplum to bring out his new definition. Achilles despised death so much in comparison with suffering shame (*to aischron*) that he was willing to race to his death provided only that he could get justice from the evil doer (*adikounti*), lest "I remain here a mockery (*katagelastos*) besides the curved ships, a burden on the earth." (28b9–d5). In his paraphrase of this passage from *Iliad* 18, Socrates has added the word *katagelastos* (it is not found in the Homeric passage).[79]

Shame, according to Socrates, arises from not doing what is right.[80] To "be a mockery" is to put any concern, including one's own life, before

---

[76] Burnet (1924) ad loc. notes that this is the first appearance in Greek of *diatribas* used in this way. Socrates' discussion literally becomes his "occupation."

[77] Even the well-argued section (33c7–34b5) where he suggests that if he did corrupt the youth their families would object, but they don't and Meletus can produce none, is not primarily about the present charges. These facts are introduced not to prove directly that he does not corrupt the youth but as proof that the god has sent him on this task and that it therefore could do no harm, as proved by the absence of witnesses.

[78] Woodruff (2000) felicitously calls this effort "Socrates' rehabilitation of shame," and observes that it comes very close to what moderns mean by "conscience."

[79] Observed by Knox (1964) 175 n.89, who says it is perfectly in keeping with the Sophoclean spirit of tragedy.

[80] Strycker–Slings (1994) ad 28d3 suggest that at the very moment Socrates is replacing shame with radically different standards, he "does not discard it altogether." Socrates is in fact redefining it, understanding that shame is the strongest form of morality. He wants to use an old tool for a different job.

doing what a good man must do. The philosopher agrees with the traditional Greek notion that nothing must be considered more important than avoiding disgrace (*tou aischrou*), but he simply sees shame quite differently: one of the things that Socrates does seem to know is that doing wrong and disobeying a better, either god or man (29b6–7), is bad and shameful (*aischron*).[81] And god has stationed Socrates to philosophize. His causing shame through dialectic, then, can be neither a source of shame to him nor – and here's the rub – a cause of humiliation to the interlocutors. Instead, their present concern with incorrectly defined matters of honor and reputation should be the cause of their humiliation. Socrates famously asks: "Best of men, you are from Athens, a city that is the greatest and most famous for wisdom and strength. Are you not ashamed (*aischunê*) that you care for acquiring as much wealth as possible, and for reputation and honor, but you neither care about nor consider wisdom and truth and how your soul will be the best possible?" (29d7–e3). He summarizes his mission, and the source of his troubles, quite clearly: if he finds someone who under cross-examination is shown not to possess virtue while claiming to, Socrates will rebuke him (*oneidiô*, 29e3–30a2). There is a close semantic link, often lost in translation, between *oneid-* ("rebuke") and *aischun-* ("shame").[82]

Socrates' final remarks in defense also conclude his redefinition of shame. He suggests that some of the jury may grow angry (*aganaktêseien, orgistheis, met' orgês*) that he did not beg tearfully for his life and produce his family in pathetic squalor. He refuses not out of stubbornness, but out of concern for reputation – his, the jurors', and the city's. Such behavior is shameful (*aischron*) and hangs the label of shame (*aischunê*) around the city's neck. The city leaders behaving like this would appear no better than women, and the jurors should condemn anyone making the city into a mockery (*katagelaston*, 35b8). Socrates here emphasizes that "reputation" (*doxês*; cf. 35b3–5) can be defined so as to be associated with what is right rather than what is successful, as he quickly adds that it does not seem right to beg for acquittal; one must teach and persuade. This is pure Socrates, dependent to the end on reason over emotion, still hoping that someone else in Athens will act on the basis of an ordered examination of life, rather than on prejudice, passion, and opinion. He is, of course, condemned.

---

[81] There is no need in this context to enter the troubled waters of the meaning of Socrates' avowal of ignorance; see the bibliography in Brickhouse and Smith (1989) 100 with n.85.

[82] Strycker–Slings (1994) ad 30a1; cf. *Resp.* 347b1–3.

SAYING WHAT YOU MEAN

Thrasymachus, having been pushed towards the level of the beast, has now attempted to gain a bit of ground on Socrates by dragging him down to the level of a child. His example of the shepherd and the sheep also implies that Socrates has confused essential categories by placing the rulers (and Thrasymachus would no doubt like to include himself in their company) in the animal category. Socrates will clarify this image later by explaining the true nature of the relationship between ruler and ruled, but for Thrasymachus the tactic is part of a painfully belated attempt to resist Socrates' argument and regain his superior position in the conversational competition. He refers to his rival in their battle of superlatives as "most simpleminded" (343d), and delivers a lengthy speech as if to mark his territory.

After concluding his lecture, Thrasymachus intends to depart, having "poured like a bathman a torrent of words over our ears" (344d). The company demands that he give an account of what he said, complaining that he merely hurled his speech at them. But Thrasymachus doubts he can persuade them if he has not convinced them already: "Am I to take my argument and stuff it inside you?" (345b). Socrates quickly seizes control of the conversation again, picking up the distinction between shepherd and his flock to point out a further inconsistency. Thrasymachus' inevitable journey from fully-fledged partner in this pursuit to ventriloquist's dummy is perfectly predictable. At first happy to supply his simple one or two words of agreement (345e–346c), he again senses that things are slipping from his control, and Socrates reports his reluctant assent (*xunephê mogis*, 346c). At a similar point earlier in the dialogue, Thrasymachus broke in rudely with his insulting remarks about Socrates' childish naiveté. This time, however, he manages to get in only four more words before he is cut off by the intrusion of Glaucon. This interlude serves to review the discussion, reconfirm the misguided direction of Thrasymachus' argument, and most importantly reaffirm the methodology. Thrasymachus is not to be allowed another speech, nor is Socrates or Glaucon to reply to his points in a speech – the dialogue is to be reengaged.

When Thrasymachus is invited back into the discussion, he is not happy, and supplies sarcastic and short-tempered responses (348b ff.). Socrates latches onto Thrasymachus' mood, insisting that he believes that the sophist is not mocking the company but offering his honest opinions about the truth. Thrasymachus himself is on the line – he had wagered he would win. His response then is completely understandable: "What difference is it to you whether I believe it or not? Why don't you examine the argument (*logon*)?" (349a). The sophist is trying to separate himself from his argument because he sees he is crashing to defeat. The matter is not so simple, however, for the entire conversation has been a competition for control of *logos*, and with surrender he must lose his standing as well. When Socrates replies that "it makes no difference to me" if Thrasymachus answers only what he believes, it appears, as Beversluis points out, that he does not really care whether the sophist replies honestly.[83] The personal nature of the inquisition, however, is unchanged. Thrasymachus does try to answer in non-committal fashion (e.g. *isôs, phêmi, eoiken, phainetai, kinduneuei*), but Socrates keeps reminding him of what he has said before and forcing personal replies (*egôge, nai, hômologoumen*).

What we can see here is that Socratic dialectic is in some important ways more personal than sophistic eristic.[84] Thrasymachus is desperately attempting to avoid the shameful acknowledgment that he has been shown to be wrong. Similarly, Gorgias is driven by dialectic to a feeling of shame that prevents him from saying what he thinks without incurring public hostility and risk to reputation.[85] He takes his "loss" in the sophistic sense – Socrates won the debate. Later, he tells the recalcitrant Callicles to let Socrates test him: "What's it matter to you? It's not your honor (*timê*) at stake" (*Grg.* 497b). But of course to the status-conscious Callicles, that is exactly what is at stake. The extremely personal nature of the elenchus makes it appear even more hostile than the more typical sophistic gamesmanship. Any debate in Athens was competitive – the very root of the word elenchus, found first in Greek in a verb and neuter noun, conveyed the idea of shame, reproach and disgrace, and was consistently linked with failure in contests.[86] The verb and masculine noun in Plato connote some sort of

---

[83] Beversluis (2000) 242–4. Scott (1999) 24 believes that Thrasymachus agrees "only in order to please Socrates and the rest of them," but I see no genuine concern for Socrates in anything the sophist says. Reeve (1988) 21–2 argues that this gap between Thrasymachus' theory and himself makes him an unsuitable candidate for elenctic examination, but just because he cannot defend his theory in the face of an elenchus does not mean that his theory is wrong. I would agree, and suggest that this very frustration and embarrassment are at the heart of the animosity aimed at Socrates.

[84] Some have even argued – rightly, I think – that the primary distinction between eristic and dialectic is the difference between establishing only the consistency or inconsistency of what the interlocutor says (eristic), rather than the consistency or inconsistency of what the interlocutor believes (dialectic); see especially Benson (1989) 592–7. Among others who see the difference primarily in intent are Rankin (1983) 22; Nehamas (1990) 11; Gonzalez (1998) 105.

[85] See the excellent analysis by Kahn (1983). McKim (1988) argues that Socrates' chief weapon in psychological warfare is shame as he maneuvers respondents into acknowledging that, deep down, they have not been honest.

[86] Lesher (2002) 22–8; also Beversluis (2000) 4 n.4. As Strycker–Slings point out (1994) 102, Aristotle discusses *to geloion* right after he examines question and answer (*Rh.* 3.18, 1419b3–9; cf. Quint. 6.3/6.4.10).

"testing," "questioning," or "refutation" which in Athenian culture were likely to result in dishonor for those who appeared to come up short. Socrates would look no different than Euthydemus (*Euthd.* 304cff.) – not a good thing in itself for one's reputation among the democratic elite. But Socrates' arguments were viewed as even more invidious because he insisted that interlocutors put their own ideas, their own status, on the line. Humiliation from failure to defend one's own position would be worse than a loss in debate about some abstract and impersonal theory.[87]

Gregory Vlastos termed this aspect of Socratic dialogue the "say what you mean" criterion (it is also frequently referred to as "sincere assent").[88] Although several scholars have recently claimed that this requirement has been greatly exaggerated,[89] I believe that when seen in its cultural context, it is even more compelling and serious than Vlastos argued, as we can see in the case of Thrasymachus. Vlastos suggested, for example, that Socrates was willing to waive the rule to allow an opponent to save face, and uses Protagoras (especially *Prt.* 333b–c, 353e) as his example.[90] According to this interpretation, Protagoras is coopted into Socrates' argument, joining him in a cross-examination of popular views about pleasure and knowledge in an indirect elenchus. But this reading misses the dramatic presentation of

[87] For the personal nature of the Socratic conversation, see Robinson (1953) 15; indeed, Robinson's entire approach to elenchus can best be understood as an examination of its effects; also Seeskin (1987) 2. Kahn (1983) shows how all three refutations of Gorgias, Polus, and Callicles are in a deep sense *ad hominem*; also Teloh (1986) and Annas (1992) 44–61, who contends that Socrates always argues from what the other person accepts. Kahn (1996a) 95–100 sees Plato transforming the Socratic elenchus into the method of hypothesis, starting with the *Meno*, as the testing of persons (as in the *Apology*) becomes the refutation of theses (propositions) in the *Gorgias*. But he notes that the "arguments are still *ad hominem*, and in this sense it is not only the thesis but the man as well who is tested and refuted"; cf. Blondell (2000) 130, and Blondell (2002) 113 with note 3, 125. Beversluis (2000) 37 n.2 presents a concise recent review with further bibliography.

[88] Stated most concisely in Vlastos (1994) 7–8; see also Benson (1987) 75–7. Nehamas (1990) 10–11 acknowledges that Socrates' insistence on receiving answers his interlocutors truly accept reflects a crucial difference between him and the sophists. Important passages are *Cri.* 49c–d; *Euthd.* 286d; *Prt.* 331c–d; *Grg.* 458a–b, 495a–b, 500b; *Men.* 83d1–3; cf. *Tht.* 167a; *Men.* 75c–d; *Phd.* 91c; *Euthd.* 275c–e.

[89] See: Stemmer (1992) 101–7; Brickhouse and Smith (2002) 148, and especially Beversluis (2000) 37–58, with whom I agree that assent is a complex phenomenon with varying degrees, and that Socrates himself appears on at least one occasion to "violate" the rule. But my point here is not so much about assent as it is about the personal nature of the argumentation. The *demand* for assent from interlocutors is important for my argument, not whether the interlocutors actually give in to it all the time, and not whether Socrates himself always plays by his own rules (although his *apparent* violations would increase the hostility of the "defeated" interlocutor; see below). As Frede (1992) 208–14 argues, the respondent is supposed to answer questions truthfully, to speak his mind, but he does not always do so. See below on Thrasymachus' apparent avoidance – with Socrates' permission – of having to give answers from the heart.

[90] Vlastos (1994) 10–11, 29–33; see also Schofield (1992) 132–3. Irwin (1993) 5–8 notes that Vlastos elsewhere (1991) 113 n.29 gives a second reason for relaxing the requirement: an insincere interlocutor is better than nothing.

how the dialogue actually unfolds. Socrates has led Protagoras to admit "much against his will" that he has argued for two propositions that cannot both be true (*Prt.* 333b). When cornered, Protagoras says he would be "ashamed" to admit a particular proposition "in spite of what many men say." When Socrates asks if he should address the argument "to them or to you," Protagoras suggests that Socrates debate first against the popular theory.

Socrates here says something that may appear to violate the "say what you mean" canon, but in fact the scene proves just the opposite. "It makes no difference to me as long as you answer, whether it is your own opinion or not. For it is the argument that I most of all am examining, however it may happen that both I who question and you who answer are examined" (333c). Note now what happens. Protagoras is upset, at first coy and ill-tempered (333d). When he finally agrees to answer, Socrates proceeds as if Protagoras is answering for himself rather than "the many," and in fact he clearly is (he moves from the impersonal answer "so be it" [*estô*] to "I say so" [*legô*] in five brief questions). Protagoras feels angry, provoked, and harassed, and sets his face against answering. Socrates goes "gently" with his questions (333e) but Protagoras still wants out of the conversation (335a–b), is reluctant to join (348a–c), and only when shamed into it reluctantly asks to have questions put to him. Socrates and Protagoras do agree on some issues, but the sophist has certainly not "saved face." By the end of the conversation, he can only nod in assent, and even then agrees extremely reluctantly (360d). Finally, he can no longer even bring himself to nod in agreement, and remains silent. When prodded by Socrates, he blurts out "finish it yourself." Socrates wants to go on, but Protagoras has had enough, gives a half-hearted compliment, and bows out.[91]

Plato shows us the personal and humiliating consequences for defeated interlocutors in the competitive world. The other participants and witnesses are supposed to believe Socrates' insistence that his objectives are

---

[91] Cf. the weird presentation of Protagoras, or at least his head, in *Theaetetus* 169a–171d, with Bemelmans (2002). Similar arguments can be made, I believe, in defense of Socrates' personal interrogation and "sincere assent" in the few other passages occasionally cited as exceptions. At *Grg.* 505c f., Callicles does desperately want out in order to save face, but he actually keeps reentering the argument with his own opinions intact – Socrates has found a way to goad him into continuing the debate, even against his will. Thus, when he is forced by logic to see that Socrates is "right," he still cannot accept the conclusions (513c). *Grg.* 474c f. is not a valid example, *pace* Scott (1999) 17–18. Polus never claims to abandon his own opinions. In all these cases, the point I am emphasizing is not "sincere assent" in any case, but just how personally each interlocutor takes his failure to "win" the argument. The interlocutors try to distance themselves, but Socrates keeps reminding them, and us, that they cannot. This explains Scott's correct perception of the "impersonal way in which he [Polus] refers to the argument – as having nothing to do with him" (18).

different, that he is after truth and not merely victory at any cost. But that is the very catch: if they believe this, Socrates has already won the game. To accept that this is not a debate in which the winners gain "face" but instead a conversation about how to live one's life – this is already to have changed one's direction towards that of becoming a philosopher. Thus, the constant misconceptions and rejection of Socrates' agenda are naturally and necessarily accompanied by the shame of silence.

Athenians had every reason to think Socrates' conversations were even more personal and antagonistic than those of the sophists, since what separated his approach from the rest was its *ad hominem* style. Socrates' efforts to depersonalize the results of his method, even if unironic, would only increase the shame. When he says, for example, that it is not he whom Agathon cannot contradict, but truth itself (*Symp.* 201b–c), there can be little doubt who stands on the side of truth and who just had the shallowness of his views hung out for public display (cf. his advice to "give little thought to Socrates and much more to truth," *Phd.* 91a–c). And, of course, Socrates *is* after victory of this kind, although his idiosyncratic concepts of shame and honor make him vastly different from his fellow citizens.[92] This crucial distinction is understandably lost on Thrasymachus as well.

CAN ANIMALS BLUSH? THE SILENCE OF LOSING

Socrates continues his relentless questioning (349b–350c) until we arrive at the inevitable "proof" that Thrasymachus has been quite wrong, indeed, 180 degrees wrong. At this point, Socrates stops to tell his audience that his account of the previous discussion had omitted Thrasymachus' physiological reactions to his humiliation:

Thrasymachus agreed to all these things, not easily as I now relate them, but after it was dragged out of him and with difficulty, and with an amazing amount of sweat, in as much as it was summer. Then too I saw something I had never seen before – that Thrasymachus was blushing. (350d)

Thrasymachus' humiliation is now manifested physically, invisible to no one. His defeat in the competition has led to the "destroying of his self-image, and with it his sense of his own identity"[93] – the very force of shame. This risk to his status is accompanied and marked by his increasing silence.

---

[92] Craig (1994) 75–80 argues that the clear distinction between the timocrat and the philosopher is that the philosopher still endorses victory, but not honor as traditionally defined.

[93] Blondell (2000) 129. Blushing is associated with shame throughout the dialogues; *Euthd.* 297a8, 275d6, *Ly.* 213d3; *Prt.* 312a2; cf. *Prt.* 312a3, 5; see Lateiner (1998) and Gooch (1988), although the latter's attempt to argue that most of these occasions reflect "self-conscious embarrassment" rather

He replies to Socrates' continued prompting by insisting that he could answer the apparent contradiction if he were allowed to speak at length.[94] If this is not permitted, and Socrates insists on asking questions, then he will respond to Socrates "just as to old women telling their stories, [. . .] say 'Fine' and nod in agreement and disagreement" (350e). This final, feeble effort to reverse the dynamic and put Socrates into the position of the verbally insignificant Other goes nowhere. Socrates pretends to object that Thrasymachus must answer as he believes, but Thrasymachus insists that he will answer to please Socrates, since "you do not allow me to speak." Socrates agrees and drives ahead, Thrasymachus bobbing his head in agreement for the rest of his appearance.

Clearly, at this point Socrates makes no effort to force Thrasymachus to "say what he believes." But there is not a more personal, humiliating conversation in all of Plato.[95] With each answer, Thrasymachus is essentially admitting that there is no way to beat Socrates' method, even if he remains completely convinced that he is right. This is Thrasymachus' last desperate strategy to maintain some control of the *logos* and to avoid complete submission to Socrates in discourse. His suggestion and subsequent behavior attempt to reduce Socrates to the role of another category of the sub-human, an old woman who has no full access to *logos* but can only hand down tales (*muthous*) to children. Thrasymachus feels that he has been deprived of the ability to speak. This means he has lost his competition with Socrates and been demoted below the ranks of men. He has been embarrassed in front of other members of the community. Socrates grabs his "victory" and runs with it, continuing with his questions. Thrasymachus goes along with all that Socrates has to say, even inviting him to feast on his own discourse (*euôchou tou logou*) without fear of his opposition (352).

Socrates himself finally notes that this has been no victory at all: the discussion has been unsuccessful (354a), for they have set out to find something without first defining it. But what has indisputably taken place is the silencing of a brutish interlocutor with a competing concept of justice. Although he continues to utter responses, his will is beaten down and his own voice is lost. He fades from the dialogue, not speaking again until

---

than shame errs both in the interpretation of the individual scenes and in an understanding of the public nature of such "embarrassment"; he may be right about Hippothales in *Lysis* (204b5, c3). Nichols (1987) 52–3 notes that after the blush Thrasymachus is "tamed."

[94] A common reaction in the dialogues; cf. *Tht.* 162d; *Prt.* 336b; *Grg.* 461d, 482c, 494d, 513a, 519d.

[95] Thus when Blondell (2000) 129 says that he abandons both his intellectual integrity and consistency rather than face defeat, she is right in that Thrasymachus acknowledges he cannot win at Socrates' "game." However, his ever-increasing silence is defeat in itself.

Book 5, and then in only brief sentences.[96] Socrates himself views Thrasymachus' defeat as a "giving up of speech" (*apeipon*, 337c8; *aporrêssin*, 357a4). Significantly, and perhaps with a glance at Thrasymachus, he calls Glaucon "most manly" (357a) for not accepting Thrasymachus' abandonment of the subject and taking up the battle.

Thrasymachus' metaphorical exit from the dialogue, then, represents the ultimate silencing, the final humiliation of a Socratic victim. Glaucon criticizes his precursor directly and in most revealing terms: "For Thrasymachus, like some snake, seems to me to have been charmed by you sooner than was necessary" (358b).[97] This is the effect Socrates has on his opponents: he charms them into acquiescence but not agreement, stunning them into silence. Having avoided Thrasymachus' lupine effort to silence his dialectic, Socrates has become the snake-charmer, muting the slithering sophist with his argument.

Thrasymachus is just one of many humiliated quitters in the dialogues. In fact, he is not even the first silenced failure in the *Republic*. The dramatic point about Cephalus' appearance as the first interlocutor is his quick disappearance. Caught looking foolish by Socrates' dialectic, he abruptly recalls that he has sacrifices to attend. Yet just minutes before, the old man welcomed Socrates into his home, claiming that he was no longer able to get around much and enjoyed conversation (*Resp.* 328c–d). It only takes a few exchanges with Socrates for his definition of justice to be discarded, however, and he gladly hands the discussion over to his son Polemarchus – his heir in argument, as in all else – apparently finding his aged limbs rejuvenated.[98]

Such discomfited and muted interlocutors abound. Callicles repeatedly tells Socrates to "ask someone else," drop the discussion, talk on, or answer

---

[96] Rutherford (1995) 214 suggests that Thrasymachus is "won over" as the conversation goes on. But the sophist's brief insistence (450a–b) that Socrates not be allowed to side-step a difficult discussion serves dramatically to emphasize his otherwise completely silent attendance. Surely most readers have almost completely forgotten he was still there. Similarly, Socrates' remark (498c–d) that he and Thrasymachus "have just become friends" – although they weren't enemies (*echthrous*) before – reminds us of the ugliness of the failed elenchus of Book 1 that has since been abandoned.

[97] Wilson (1995) 59 and Hobbs (2000) 25 note that at *Resp.* 590b the *thumos* is (for the first and only time) compared to a dragon or serpent, thus again linking Thrasymachus with a certain type of human behavior central to the larger issues of the *Republic*.

[98] *Pace* Zyskind (1992) 209, who believes that this refutation bothers Cephalus "not at all," and Donohue (1997) 243, who describes Cephalus as departing "cheerfully" and "amiably"; better is Reeve (1988) 5–7, who observes that Cephalus leaves "before he can become grist for the elenctic mill." True, Cephalus "laughingly" (*gelasas*, 331d9) agrees to let Polemarchus take over his argument, but this is the laugh of relief at Socrates' joking reference to Polemarchus' being the "heir to all his affairs." Cephalus is already (*hama*) heading out the door; for the sinister side of laughter, see above. Blondell (2002) 169 suggests that the old man's bodily feebleness is analogous to his moral and intellectual inadequacy.

his own questions, anything but continue so overbearingly (*Grg.* 505c, 505d, 506c, 510a, 515b, 516b, 522e). Previously in that same dialogue, Polus called Socrates' discussion extremely boorish and finally disappeared from the scene with no apparent explanation (480e). None is needed. Humiliated at his dialectical defeat, he is silenced and invisible. At the very beginning of his eponymous dialogue, the hedonist Philebus retires (*apeirêken*), acquitting himself (*aphosioumai*) of the entire conversation (*Phlb.* 11c–12b; cf. Cleitophon's claim that he gave up – *apeirêka* – after repeated questions of Socrates, *Clit.* 410a–b[99]). When he is finally compelled to give a response, he is quickly stumped and snaps at Protarchus, "Didn't you decide to reply in my place?" He never opens his mouth again (*Phlb.* 27e–28c). Euthyphro is an eager instigator of his conversation with Socrates but eventually races off the stage: "Some other time, Socrates. Now I am in a hurry and it is time for me to go" (*Euthphr.* 15e). Apparently having had plenty of time to begin his discussion, he suddenly remembers that he has left the iron on at home and dashes off to escape further humiliation.[100]

The ultimate fate of many of Socrates' interlocutors, both friendly and hostile, is silence. Euthydemus (*esigêsen, Euthd.* 299 c–d), Glaucon (*diesôpêsen*, Xen. *Mem.* 3.6.3–4), Lysis (*esigêsen, Ly.* 222a), and even the solicitous Crito (*ouk echô legein, Cri.* 54d) are made speechless. The great sophist Protagoras, as we have seen, fares no better.[101] The only way to avoid such results, we are warned, is to refuse to talk with him when he asks such questions (*Hp. mai.* 291a). But the characters in Plato's dialogues learn this too late. Beversluis neatly comments that "the Socratic interlocutor has no idea of what he is in for. Entering into disputation with Socrates is like inadvertently strolling into a minefield."[102]

The appearance of Anytus – one of Socrates' accusers – as one of the philosopher's humiliated victims in the *Meno* (90a–95a) is hardly a coincidence.[103] Anytus sits down next to Socrates and Meno, and is coopted into

---

[99] See also Clitophon's brief appearance at *Resp.* 340a–b. On his silence here, and on Socrates' muting in the *Clitophon*, see Roochnik (1990) 98–107.

[100] Nehamas (1998) 38–40 suggests that Euthyphro may have lost the argument, but in his conceit and stupidity he departs "undaunted and unchanged." This is probably true as concerns his commitment to self-examination, but he certainly would have a changed opinion of Socrates. How likely would he be in the future to expect Socrates to sympathize with his vision of piety? Would he even care to engage in conversation with him?

[101] Gower (1992) 11 suggests that the sophists' conversations with Socrates invariably end in defeat, although the speakers are usually "allowed to withdraw with some dignity and grace." But this is certainly not the case with Protagoras and Thrasymachus.

[102] Beversluis (2000) 31.

[103] Allen (1996) 10–11 observes that the nature of Socrates' offense is exhibited here in the very intensity of Anytus' emotions.

their discussion of whether or not virtue can be taught. When Socrates asks if the sophists could perform this task, Anytus explodes. Although never having had anything to with them, he is absolutely convinced that they are a plague on and corruption of the body politic. Rather, any noble Athenian (*kalôn kagathôn*) can teach virtue. Socrates quickly leads Anytus through the anticipated elenchus to face the conclusion that noble fathers have not in fact been able to pass virtue on to their sons.

Anytus' response to this refutation is predictable and paradigmatic: he can say no more on the topic. Finding himself effectively silenced in the conversation, he grows angry, threatens Socrates, and leaves. He snorts that Socrates seems to speak ill of people too easily, and warns him that especially in Athens it is easier to do people harm than good. This passage on the one hand can be interpreted as indicating that Anytus finds in Socrates an enemy of democracy and is making a veiled threat about the power of a jury to punish him. To be sure, the traditionalist democrat Anytus would be most unhappy with Socrates' conclusion about virtue and the value of conventional political and social associations (*sunousia*) in educating the young.[104] But what Plato also shows us is a man humiliated for claiming to know things without having examined them. He calls Anytus a "prophet" for "knowing" (*oistha*) the evil effects of sophists without ever having any experience of them. Anytus is, in other words, the perfect Socratic "victim" as described in the *Apology*. He has been shown publicly – in front of Meno, a family friend – to claim to know something when in fact he does not, a crushing blow to the ego of any public figure.[105]

Anytus responds to his humiliation by becoming angry with Socrates and thinking of revenge. And Socrates' sees that Anytus' anger is personal as well as political. Anytus is upset, Socrates concludes, because he thinks Socrates is speaking ill of the class of men to which Anytus believes he belongs. Socrates is convinced, however, that the real issue is that Anytus does not know what "speaking" ill really means. The larger point here is that disentangling Anytus' disagreement over politics from his humiliation in conversation is extremely difficult, if not impossible. Socrates not only angered politicians over politics but all sorts of people about all sorts of topics by the *way* he conversed, as he is at pains to show in his defense.[106]

---

[104] See Robb (1993).

[105] Gonzalez (1998) 123 argues that eristic needs crowds and Socrates does not, and he includes the *Meno* as an example. But as we have just seen, in fact Meno himself provides an audience.

[106] Meno notes that Anytus was angry (*achthetai*, 99e). The same root is used throughout the *Apology* to explain the emotional source of the prosecution (e.g. 21e2, 21e4, 23a1, 23e5, 28a5, 31a4, 31e1). Socrates hopes that they will continue their conversation with Anytus "later" and make him "more gentle"

Nowhere is the connection between the silencing of Socrates' method and his prosecution more clear than in the interrogation in the *Apology* of Meletus, another of his accusers. Most scholarship has understandably concentrated on the disputed connection between Socrates' performance and the letter of the indictment: does Socrates attempt to refute the formal charges against him, or does he merely attempt to discredit Meletus? Many have been disappointed by the rhetorical "tricks," unhappy with the philosopher's twisting Meletus into knots around the possibly irrelevant issue of atheism. Why does he never just say that he believes in the state gods? Some scholars have jumped in to defend Socrates' efforts by trying to uncover the philosopher's genuine efforts to clear himself of damaging charges.[107] But the interrogation of Meletus is really no more directed at the formal charges than any other part of the speech. This cross-examination primarily serves as a demonstration of Socrates' claims in the first part. It does not directly address the terms of the indictment because, as Socrates has already stated, these charges are merely the reflections of ancient prejudices brought about by his shaming of public figures. The *erotêsis* is an example of just how Socrates' method works, and how its results – the public humiliation of the interlocutor through *aporia*, or enforced silence – are what have really brought Socrates to trial.[108]

The repeated dramatic point of the interrogation is the reluctance of Meletus to answer Socrates.[109] Even his single-word reply "*egôge*"

(*Men.* 100b). Xenophon (*Ap.* 29), in typically less subtle fashion, has Socrates taunting Anytus from his jail cell for his "servile" profession of tanner. He prophesies that Anytus' son will become a degenerate because there is no good man to guide him. Xenophon understands the personal nature of Socrates' approach but is not interested in Socrates' method.

[107] For a review of the *erotêsis*, see Smith (1995) 372. Brickhouse and Smith (1989) 30–7, 109–12 dispute the traditional reading of Socrates' "entrapment," instead concluding that the charge is specifically that Socrates is an atheist, and so his interrogation is not a sly misdirection but directly applicable to the case. Reeve (1989) 79–96 suggests that there was a law under which atheists could be charged. Steinberger (1997) 19–23 agrees that Meletus was not entrapped, but also notes that Socrates' interrogation is more like an old-fashioned cross-examination in the courts than the innocent pursuit of truth suggested by Brickhouse–Smith and Reeve.

[108] Steinberger captures the approach of most scholars when he suggests that "our understanding of the *Apology* . . . depends in large part on whether we think Socrates, in confronting Meletus, has directly refuted the formal charges" (1997) 14. But I think Strycker–Slings (1994) 70, 124–6 are more accurate when they suggest that Socrates' approach deprives Meletus' indictment of any substantial power by demonstrating that the formal charges were derived from the *diabolê*. The *erotesis* shows the ignorance and superficiality of the new accusers, but also gives full illustration of how the dialectical method appeared to people who did not truly understand it. The issue of the historicity of the interrogation is moot, since this is Plato's attempt to explain the philosophical life through a depiction of Socrates' life. For what it's worth, Xenophon includes a similar scene in his *Apology*; see Guthrie (1971) 19–20. Those who think Plato invented the entire scene include Hackforth (1933) 112 and Ryle (1966) 177–8.

[109] Burnet (1924) ad 24c9 supplies examples from other court cases that show that the interrogated party could not refuse to answer.

("I certainly do") to Socrates' first question is confrontational, the sign of a man who wants to be forceful but who expects to be tricked.[110] After only the second question, in which Socrates asks him who makes the young better, Meletus is rendered silent: "Do you see, Meletus, that you are silent and have nothing to say? Doesn't this seem shameful (*aischron*) to you and sufficient proof of what I say, that you have not cared at all about these things?" (24d7–9). Significantly, Socrates ties this inability to speak to the issue to shame. Here, once again, is one of the key differences between Socrates and the "many" that Plato is pointing out in the *Apology*. Meletus should be ashamed because he claims to know who makes the young worse – Socrates – but cannot say who makes them better. He has no knowledge about the issue that he claims to care so much about.[111] His case, then, is nearly identical to that of Anytus in the *Meno*. Can it be coincidence that the one thing we know for certain about two of Socrates' prosecutors, at least as Plato presents them, is that they both engaged Socrates in public "conversations" about who makes citizens better, and "lost"?

For Socrates, shame comes from failing to pursue the philosophical life; for the rest of the Athenians, shame comes from failing to achieve status by making one's public statements influential. That Meletus cares most about looking good is revealed by his next answer: the very jury now considering Socrates' fate makes the young better. Meletus is forced into the role of demagogue – and sophist – by pandering to the crowd.[112]

Soon after this exchange, Socrates falls into his customary dialectical analogies from crafts, comparing the rearing of children with the training of horses. Meletus, apparently sensing his doom early on, refuses to answer any of a series of questions (25a12–b7).[113] Socrates finally answers for him, saying: "Of course this is the case, whether you and Anytus agree or disagree." Meletus refuses or is hesitant to answer Socrates' questions again (25c6–7), and again (25d1–2), and again (27b7–8), and again (27c9–10).

---

[110] Smith (1995) 375–80. He argues that Meletus' responses are dictated by the common logic of sophistry. Socrates turns the tables by putting Meletus on trial for being a sophist. If Smith's argument is correct, and I think it may be, we see once again that the *erotêsis* is really about the old accusations, not the indictment. Of course, Socrates is also taking advantage of a standard forensic tactic of asking an opponent a question that he could not answer: silence means refutation and a momentary victory for the interrogator; see Ausland (2002) 37–46.

[111] See Burnet (1924) throughout this section on Socrates' punning on Meletus' name and "caring" (*melô*).

[112] Burnet (1924) notes ad 26d4 that Meletus uses the traditional formula *ô andres dikastai* that Socrates intentionally refuses to apply to the entire jury (40a2).

[113] The appearance of analogies indicated that the hostile interlocutor was in for a tough time; see especially the amusing exchange between Callicles and Socrates on this incessant repetition of cobblers, fullers, doctors, etc. (*Grg.* 489e).

He replies only when humiliated ("I'm not asking you anything difficult"), threatened ("the law commands you to answer"), compelled by the jury ("thank you for answering with difficulty when forced by these men"), or with words put into his mouth ("I'll assume you agree since you aren't answering").

Meletus, then, also stands at this dramatic moment in Socrates' defense for the many interlocutors who have been silenced and shamed by Socrates.[114] He has joined the ranks of those who have been publicly shown to think they know something but in fact do not. And like them, he has sought revenge but found himself not knowing what exactly to accuse Socrates of: "But, Meletus, you can only have brought this suit either to test me or because you were at a loss (*aporôn*) to find any wrongdoing to accuse me of" (27e3–5). This is exactly the charge Socrates had made earlier about those who threw at him the stock accusations made against all philosophers in order not to admit their *aporia* (23d2–9).[115]

Meletus' silence serves as a dramatic portrayal of just what Socrates did to anger Athenians. The philosopher's dominating command of *logos* on this occasion must have suggested sophistry to the jury, and his mastery must have confirmed in their minds what many already believed. The jury become the witnesses who surround the victims of a Socratic elenchus, some enjoying the spectacle, others appalled, but few understanding what is really going on.[116]

The *Apology* gives us Plato's version of the philosophical life, the only life worth living. Socrates is killed because his vision of verbal competition

---

[114] Stokes (1992) 40 observes that there are two elenchi in the *Apology*, a successful one of Meletus and the unsuccessful testing of the oracle, and wonders whether Plato wanted to show both the "hostile" and "friendly" forms. But, as Stokes himself notes, Socrates does not in fact refute the god but the citizens who claim to know something. The results of the elenchi are the same: both are viewed by citizens as hostile. Similarly, Woodruff (1987) 81–9 argues that the elenchus in the *Apology* is presented as serving three separate purposes: an exhortation to virtue (29e4–30a2, 30e7); an aid in interpretation (21b3–23c1, 22a6), and as a means of disproving knowledge (21e3–23c1). He suggests that only the last is a primary source of antagonism. But in fact all three evoke irritation: Socrates' exhortations derive from his interpretation of the oracle, which leads to his disproof of knowledge. Citizens who encounter Socrates would not easily distinguish his motives but would certainly note the similar results – they look foolish. Similarly, Reeve's acute attempt (1989) 26–46, 122–4 to separate three stages of Socrates' elenctic activities and to distinguish positive from negative aspects is unnecessary from my perspective, since all three stages elicited hostile responses.

[115] Xenophon (*Mem.* 1.2.31–8) makes an interesting connection between the general charges, personal hostility, and public policy. Socrates, he says, compared Critias' attempts to seduce Euthydemus to a piglet's efforts to scratch himself on a stone. As a result, when Critias became one of the Thirty, he introduced a law against teaching the "art of debate" and eventually Socrates was summoned for "conversing with the young."

[116] Allen (1996) 9 observes that Socrates' entire approach in Plato's *Apology* violates Aristotle's prime recommendation that one make the dicasts feel "friendly and placable" (*Rh.* 11.1377b3).

varies so markedly from that of the rest of the community.[117] In this speech, even if not a "typical" dialogue, we see him once more engage in a battle with his fellow citizens. He believes he is "teaching and persuading"; most of them, as usual, think he is being difficult, humiliating a rival, and remaining unrepentant. Six different times, Socrates refers to actual or potential interruptions of his speech by those listening (17d1, 20e4, 21a5, 27a9–b2, 27b4–6, 30c2–6). His words seem to evoke the constant threat of an uproar, *thorubos*. Burnet (ad 17d1) notes that the word means something like a "noisy demonstration," and thus may mean "applause" as well as "interruption." But a closer look at the use of the root in Plato reveals that the word never has a positive connotation in the dialogues.[118] It most often refers to a disturbance of some kind: of the soul (e.g. *Phd.* 66d6; *Phdr.* 245a4, 248b1; *Resp.* 518a5, 561b1, 571e2; *Ti.* 70e7), of the universe (e.g. *Plt.* 273a5), of someone's confidence (e.g. *Symp.* 194a6, b5;), by revellers (e.g. *Symp.* 223b5; *Lg.* 700d2), of a train of thought (e.g. *Phdr.* 245b3; *Resp.* 438a1). It can mark a loud commotion (e.g. *Resp.* 413d9; *Criti.* 117e7) and general chaos (e.g. *Ti.* 42d1, 43b6; *Leg.* 640b3), and is also applied to someone confused by an argument (*Phlb.* 28c3; *Euthd.* 283d4). The four times it is used of applause it appears in a dubious context: of the uproar from Gorgias' fans for his continued participation with Socrates (*Grg.* 458c3), and especially of the applause given to the clever sophistry of Euthydemus and Dionysodorus (*Euthd.* 276d1, 303b4, 6). Sophists are associated with the word in the *Republic* as well. Socrates observes that the multitude in assemblies, theaters, camps, and gatherings with a great uproar (*thorubôi*) censures and approves with shouts and clapping, the area echoing with a double *thorubon* of blame and praise (492a–c; cf. *Prt.* 319c5). In fact, *thorubos* in Plato generally implies the opposite of Socratic conversation. It is the sign of truly expert judges of music that they do not yield to the "uproar of the many" (*Leg.* 659a5; cf. 700d2, where the populace is said formerly to

[117] Wallach (2001) 101–9 argues that Socrates' elenchus did not just discomfit the Athenians but posed an alternative way of life that insisted on private deliberation over public debate.

[118] Similarly, Strycker–Slings (1994) ad 17d1 note that the root always refers to indignant reactions of the audience, arguing that all but one request of the jury (30c2–3) excuse potentially shocking language Socrates is about to use. At 27b5, Meletus is in fact shouting as well; see, however, Renehan (1993), who argues that this very oddity (Meletus throughout the scene does not "interrupt" but refuses to speak) suggests a corruption in the text, and the subject of the imperative should be the audience (e.g. *mê . . . thorubeite*), as elsewhere, and not Meletus (indirectly) as the text currently stands (*mê . . . thorubeitô*). Strycker–Slings do not look at Plato's use of the word, but survey other authors and note that in Aristotle *thorubos* can stand for applause only in the case of rhetorical exercises or of theatrical performances. For *thorubos* in general as a frequent phenomenon of the courts, see Bers (1985). Tacon (2001) has recently argued that *thorubos* in the assemblies – this does not obviously apply to the courts, however – was an essential (and not necessarily negative) part of the Athenian people's ability to communicate its collective views.

have refrained from judging music by making a *thorubos*). The Athenian in the *Laws* argues that in worse states the courts are either silent (*aphôna*) and secret or, even more dangerous, make decisions with a *thorubos* (876b3; cf. 949b), as in theaters, filled with praise and blame.

So when Socrates seeks to quell or forestall the jury's uproar, he is insisting that the mob not slip to its worst form but rather rise to Socrates' dialectical challenge. He will not be silenced, outvoiced by the beastly crowd.[119] Seen in this light, the entire *Apology* is Plato's drama of Socrates' life, Socrates' final attempt to teach the Athenians as a whole. The jury and onlookers have become the typical audience of Socrates' dialectic, watching someone (here, Meletus) humbled into silence. And they too have been silenced, as Socrates has forced them to stop their customary uproar.[120] They have the last word – or so they think – and vote to condemn the philosopher, thus providing the most poignant example of the incompatibility of the philosophical and political lives. Still, death itself may not silence the philosopher. The gods have stationed him to use his voice for the good of all, and only the divine can shut his mouth. The divine voice alone can redirect his mission by stopping him in mid-sentence, as he insists it has frequently done (40a8–c3).[121]

Socrates himself dies rather than suffer his own peculiar sense of shame at being silenced. Athenian citizens, the jury, and probably the prosecutors would have been happy for Socrates to skip town.[122] Socrates is quite clear about what they really are after: they want him to shut up and leave them alone. He imagines the jury suggesting that they would let him go if he would give up his life in examining and philosophizing (29c–d). In the penalty phase, he wonders what he deserves for not keeping silent in life (36b5–6). But exile would be worse because his words would be even less tolerated in an alien polis (37d6–e2). Besides, Socrates cannot be silent (*sigôn de kai hêsuchian agôn; hêsuchian agein*) because his divine mission is to spend each day conversing about and examining virtue: the unexamined

---

[119] Montiglio (2000) 144–8 concludes that the relationship between any speaker and audience in antiquity was conceived as a struggle between two utterances striving to be heard. If a speaker's voice fails, shouts rise to silence him completely. Plato may be playing on this traditional challenge to a public speaker. Socrates wants not to win a speaking match but to teach the Athenians, and to do this he must speak. Once again, Socrates and his audience are at cross-purposes.

[120] Vasiliou (2002) 227 also sees Socrates' efforts here as an attempt to "generate perplexity *en masse*," and therefore to produce something positive and educative.

[121] Interestingly, this statement is not borne out in the rest of the Platonic dialogues. The voice elsewhere (e.g. *Ap.* 40a6, *Phdr.* 242b8–c4) prevents actions, not words. Gooch (1996) 81–108 discusses Socrates' speech in terms of "an act of obedience" and compares it to Jesus' silence.

[122] Few commentators quarrel with this interpretation of the purpose of the trial; see Burnet (1924) ad 37e4.

life – that is, the life that neither inquires nor is inquired about – is not a human life (37e3–38a6).[123] Speech is essential to lead a human life. Any Greek would agree with this, but Socrates means something rather different: this distinctly human possession must be used in philosophizing, and not for the temporal goals of politics and power. Speech in and of itself is of little use, and hardly makes one fully human. Scholars debate whether the historical Socrates would really have been given the opportunity to speak after his death sentence was announced. One thing, however, is clear: Plato's Socrates converses (*dialechtheiên*) to the very end.

THE SIGNIFICANCE OF THRASYMACHUS' SILENCE: NUMBED BY A STINGRAY

Thrasymachus, on the other hand – like so many other Platonic interlocutors – does *not* converse to the very end. Although present for the remainder of the conversation, his two brief sentences midway through the long dialogue serve primarily to remind us of his muting in Book 1. His silence, I believe, is just as thematically significant as his argument. The whole episode is somehow unsatisfying. Cephalus has disappeared, Polemarchus is refuted, and Thrasymachus is silenced, but no workable definition of justice has emerged. Socrates realizes this, and Glaucon admits that he still is left at a loss (*aporô*, 358c7) when subjected to the endless discourses of Thrasymachus and innumerable others like him. And this *aporia* seems to be an intentional and crucial point. So central are the unhappy *consequences* of dialectic in the hands of Socrates that Plato rarely misses a chance to make them thematically significant. The *Republic* is different in that Socrates continues his discussion with more amenable interlocutors and in a less hostile fashion – no doubt, this shift is an important aspect of the dialogue. But the destructive nature of dialectic – not just to Thrasymachus, but to the reputation of Socrates – matches what we find throughout the dialogues. Socrates (or his representatives) even occasionally suggests that it is the *misuse* of dialectic, especially by the young, that causes such resentment and gives both Socrates and philosophy a bad name (e.g. *Phlb.* 15e; *Tht.* 150e; 167d–168; *Resp.* 500b; especially *Resp.* 537d–539, where young imitators delight "like puppies" in pulling and tearing the words of all who approach).[124] We hear that ideally the interlocutors should grow angry only

---

[123] *Anexetastos* means both "without being examined" and "without examining"; see Strycker–Slings (1994) ad 38a5 for parallels.

[124] Reeve (1989) 160–9 especially argues that Socrates thinks opponents are mad at the deflationary effects of dialectic in young hands on their reputations for wisdom. While this is definitely part of

with themselves and gentle towards others; they gain lasting benefit while bystanders get pleasure from watching this "purgation" (*Soph.* 230b–e). Correctly performed, dialectic will cause those who debate to cast blame for their confusion and *aporia* on themselves, not on the philosopher.[125] They will hate themselves and run away from themselves, taking refuge in philosophy (*Tht.* 167d–168b; cf. *Lach.* 188a–b; cf. *Hp. mai.* 286d2–4, 292a2–d8). When someone without proper knowledge is forced to see he is wrong, he should blame himself or his own lack of skill, and not the arguments (*Phd.* 89d–90). Careful attention must be paid, we are told, to the distinction between dialectic and wrangling (*erizein, Resp.* 454a), between conversing (*dialegomenos*) and competing (*agonizomenos, Tht.* 167e): "We are not competitors (*agonistai*) but lovers of wisdom" (*philosophoi, Tht.* 164c). Prodicus calls on Protagoras and Socrates to dispute as friends do with friends – from good feelings – not wrangle as enemies do (*echthroi, Prt.* 337a–b; cf. *Resp.* 498c–d). The language is revealing: Socrates risks looking like, and thus becoming, an enemy every time he engages in conversation. But he insists that, unlike competitors in eristic and agonistic, friends converse together and such conversations require a more mild, "more dialectical" response (*Men.* 75c–d). Theatetus listens to the Stranger's description of the man practicing elenchus and remarks how very similar he is to the sophists. "Yes, in the way a wolf is like a dog," replies the Stranger. The cautious man must be especially on his guard in the matter of resemblances, for they are very slippery things (*Soph.* 231a).

Plato, however, has filled his dialogues with just these "mistaken" resemblances.[126] The "ideal" result is rarely found. Instead, we are confronted time and time again with confused, angry, shamed and silenced interlocutors who are even farther from becoming philosophers and closer to the bestial multitude than before, just as Socrates feared.[127] After all, he concedes, it is not easy for people to make good definitions, and when

Socrates' problem, the dialogues reveal a clear hostility towards Socrates for what he himself brings about in his conversations.

[125] The seventh letter notes that the elenchus must be "kindly" and the questions and answers made "without envy" (344b).

[126] Kahn (1981) 317 points out that even the verb *dialegesthai* is co-opted to describe the sophists' art at *Euthd.* 295e2; on the use of the word and its cognates in Plato, see Kahn (1996a) 303–28.

[127] Thus, Gordon's analysis (1999) 22–8 of the function of shame in Plato mistakenly confuses Socrates' goals with the actual results depicted in the dialogues. She suggests that shame works on a personal, existential level to compel interlocutors to reflect more deeply about who they are, what they believe, and how they choose to live their lives. In fact, the dialogues show the consistent failure of dialectic to produce this effect on *any* interlocutor, shamed or not. Nehamas (1992a) 295 catalogues Socrates' failures; see also Schmid (1998) 68–78 for the inability of interlocutors to learn from their refutation.

some point is disputed, they think the criticism comes from jealousy and rivalry (*philonikountas*) rather than inquiry, thus causing a nasty scene (*Grg.* 457c–e; cf. *Prt.* 333e; Xen. *Mem.* 4.2.39–40). Callicles, for example, calls Socrates' silencing of his victims "vulgar" and "popular clap-trap" (*phortika kai dêmêgorika, Grg.* 482c–e), and accuses him of sophistic (*Grg.* 497a) and of being an unscrupulous debater (*Grg.* 489b–c; cf. 494d) and contentious (*philonikos, Grg.* 515b).[128] Meno calls Socrates' power to bind his opponents with words "spells" and "incantations" (*goêteueis . . . pharmatteis . . . katepaïdes*), only half-jokingly cautioning the philosopher that he is wise not to leave Athens, for as a stranger in another city he would quickly be arrested as a sorcerer (*goês*). But the accusation of magic cuts both ways. Socrates tells Euthydemus and Dionysidorus that "in truth you actually sew up people's mouths, just as you say you do; as for your sewing up not only the mouths of others but seeming to sew up your own as well, this is a most graceful maneuver that removes the offense from your words" (*Euthd.* 303d–e). Although Plato may be presenting philosophy's "magic" as a counter to sophistic legerdemain, in fact the results for those who stumble across practitioners of either are identical.[129] Socrates himself confesses, if only ironically, that he found himself "speechless (*aphônos*) as if knocked out by their argument" (303a; cf. *Symp.* 198c; *Resp.* 336d7–9). Little difference does it make to those who find their mouths sewn up whether it happened as a result of sophistic tricks aimed at victory or a Socratic elenchus. Euthyphro is befuddled by Socrates, and finds himself not knowing "how to say what I mean" (cf. *Alc.* 1 127d). No matter what statement is advanced, it keeps moving about and won't stay put (*Euthphr.* 11b). When Socrates suggests that Euthyphro's statements are the culprits, moving on their own like the works of Daedalus, Euthyphro will have none of it: he is not the one who makes the statements move about. Socrates himself is Daedalus, for the statements otherwise "would have stayed put, as far as I am concerned." Socrates' insistence that he too would prefer to have the words stay still, and that he is clever "against his will," hardly appeases the unsettled interlocutor.

---

[128] Cf. Polus' challenge to Socrates' methods (*Grg.* 461b–c), Hippias' complaints about Socrates' "picky arguments" (*Hp. mi.* 369b–c), or Charmides' belief that Socrates refutes without troubling to follow the subject of discussion (*Chrm.* 166c; cf. *Euthd.* 295c–d).

[129] Both the sophists and Socrates are accused of using magic. According to Belfiore (1980), philosophical magic drives out false opinion (the aim of magic and sophistic), enables us to resist the power of pleasure and fear, and does not compel us the same way that magic does. For Socrates' magic as the destruction of illusion, see also de Romilly (1975) 25–43. For *logos* as a drug, especially in the works of Gorgias, see Segal (1962). Gellrich (1994) looks at the broader issues of Socratic magic.

Socrates, of course, claims throughout the dialogues that his objective is not to freeze others into silence but to goad them into thought. He admits that he is like a bee intent to sting, worried only that he will be unsuccessful in cross-examining Phaedo, thereby leaving his stinger in him (*Phd.* 91c). But try as he may to insist that he is a gadfly rousing his sluggish horse of a city to virtue (*Ap.* 30e), his victims have quite a different animal image of him.[130] Alcibiades drunkenly acknowledges that Socrates has struck and bitten more painfully and tenaciously with his words on philosophy than any viper (*Symp.* 217e–218b; cf. *Euthd.* 294d, where the interlocutors are compared to "boars driven up to face the spears"). Similarly, Callicles protests that Polus had been bound and *bridled* by Socrates' words (*hupo sou sumpodistheis en tois logois epestomisthê, Grg.* 482d–e). Broken by Socrates' dialectic, Polus has been turned into a mute horse. The philosopher's method necessarily requires removing the false knowledge of his interlocutors, but his is a dangerous task. By refuting their arguments, he in effect – and often literally – leaves them without words, thus driving them into the category of the silenced Other.[131]

We have seen throughout this book that in the Greek world *silencing* is an especially effective representation and enforcement of diminution of status, as it reduces one to the sub-human level of slaves, women, children, and especially animals. We can see the effects of this process quite clearly in Meno's charge that Socrates stuns his victims into silence:

If I can speak in jest, I think that in both outward appearance and in other respects you are entirely like the flat stingray in the sea. For it always makes numb whoever approaches and touches it, and you seem to have done just this sort of thing to me now. For truly my mind and my mouth are numb, and I do not have anything to reply to you. (*Men.* 80a–b).

Meno, who has previously always found himself to be especially brilliant and articulate when discussing virtue, has suddenly had his soul/mind and mouth completely numbed (cf. *Resp.* 503d). Socrates does not deny Meno's charge, but adds that he is like the stingray only if it numbs itself (which it does not). He also agrees with Meno's initial indictment, that he himself is "at a loss" (*aporeis*) and makes others "at a loss" (*poieis aporein*) as well: "It isn't from my own knowledge (*euporôn*) that I put others at a loss (*aporein*); rather, I myself being at a greater loss (*aporôn*) put others also at a loss

---

[130] Compton (1990) 338–42 draws parallels between Aesop's trial and death and that of Socrates, noting along the way that both defendants tell animal parables in their defense.

[131] Blondell (2002) 123–4 draws similar conclusions: these Socratic "victories are often – and rightly – experienced as displays of power by the losers, who are humiliated by a refutation or silencing that makes them feel ashamed, emasculated or infantalized."

(*aporein*)" (80c–d; for this admission, cf. *Tht.* 149a; *Lach.* 194c, 200e; *Ly.* 216c). And, most importantly, Socrates insists that Meno's *aporia* is better than his previous false knowledge (80d), and that his "stingray" attack on the slave had improved him by pushing him towards *wanting* to find the truth (84a–c7).[132]

But Plato's Socrates consistently fails to recreate his own intellectually ambitious experience of *aporia* in his interlocutors. Rarely does he make a dent in the bedrock of his audience's traditional definitions. By being silenced, losers like Thrasymachus in the dialectical contest feel reduced from the ranks of superior beings to the lower level of beast, a category shared at least in part by women, children, and slaves. The dialogues reveal a competition for status that Socrates inevitably wins. His opponents are frozen, muted, and finally limp home like scolded puppies, but puppies that will grow and return to bite the lover of wisdom who would not let them be careless. Socrates insists that the soul is maimed that is not distressed when convicted of lack of knowledge and instead wallows in the mud of ignorance as insensitively as a pig (*Resp.* 535d–e). Socrates means that we should be upset when we discover we have not found the truth, but his audience is worried more about being exposed publicly than as being on the same level as insensate barnyard animals.

Even his so-called friends often want Socrates to disappear. Alcibiades' inebriated laudation shows how uncomfortable the philosopher could make life for those who tried to listen to him with an open mind (*Symp.* 215a–216c). Alcibiades compares Socrates to Marsyas, a pied piper who entrances people with his discourses in place of the satyr's pipes. When Alcibiades hears Socrates speak, he is overwhelmed; his heart leaps, and his tears gush forth – and many others react the same way. He is forced to reconsider his choices, finding his life "not worth living" upon examination, since he attends the affairs of Athens rather than his own. To avoid following further, he blocks his ears as if from the Sirens and takes off as fast as he can. Socrates has become a singer of truth whose voice can lure the ambitious politician onto the rocks of philosophy. As a result, Alcibiades has one experience that no one else can produce and no one would expect: he is ashamed. Nevertheless, as soon as he leaves Socrates' presence he comes under the influence of "the many" once again. So he flees, ashamed anew when he sees Socrates and remembers their conversation. "And often," he has to admit, "I would gladly see him no longer

---

[132] Mackenzie (1988) 333–4. Belfiore (1980) 133 compares Meno's reaction to magical *katadesis*. And as Plato himself suggests in the *Laws* (909f.), such magical practices are to be suppressed by the state.

among men." With friends like this, who needs to go about making enemies?

Finally, we should observe the distinctly political consequences of Socrates' conversations. S. Sara Monoson has recently argued that Plato appropriates open speech (*parrhêsia*) – a central ideal of Athenian democracy, as we saw in Chapter 4 – for his practice of philosophy.[133] But what *parrhêsia* is there if interlocutors ultimately cannot speak at all? Frank speech in Athens never meant one was guaranteed a hearing. Such a "right" had to be earned through personal influence and persuasive speech – it has no real meaning outside of the competitive environment of Athens. Socrates may reorient *parrhêsia* as part of philosophical discourse, but he then is viewed as denying it to his conversational partners. Socrates appears to "win" the competition, silencing other citizens. The dangers of being perceived in this light are obvious: "To deny to a person as a matter of principle the right to compete means denying them a full social identity as an Athenian citizen, as women, slaves, foreigners, and certain social outcasts were excluded."[134] To drive a citizen through dialectic into silence was to reduce his social identity. An apparent "loser" would, at least for the humiliating moment, be no better than any dumb beast.

We should not be surprised, then, if Socrates' accusers were after good old-fashioned Greek revenge of the purest kind. They were trying to harm their enemy by silencing his humiliating voice.[135] Socrates clearly sees his fate in this way in the *Apology*, as he lays out the connection between his elenchus and the charges of his accusers. Whenever they are asked what exactly it is that Socrates does or teaches that is so corrupting:

They have nothing to say, since they do not know. And in order not to seem to be at a loss (*aporein*), they say these things that are trotted out against all who philosophize: 'the things in heaven and under the earth' and 'not believing in gods' and 'making the weaker argument the stronger.' For I do not think they would wish to speak the truth, that they are clearly revealed to pretend to know, but know nothing. (23d)

Since these are public men, worried about how they look – "lovers of honor" (*philotimoi*) – they have constructed lies to protect their reputations. Athenians (and influential non-Athenians) grow angry at being humiliated,

---

[133] Monoson (2000) 154–80.   [134] Cohen (1995) 64.

[135] Strycker–Slings (1994) ad 18a–b2 is one of few studies to state this motive as boldly as I think it should be understood: the victims of Socrates' cross-examination wish to avenge themselves and spread accusations, fill the ears of Athenians with slander, and as a result the three prosecutors bring the lawsuit. I would suggest that the slander is secondary, and that the real source of animosity is the personal humiliation suffered at the hands of Socrates. The slander does add to the hostile environment that Socrates must attempt to explain in the course of his trial.

at having their pretensions (*prospoioumenoi*) to wisdom "made very clear" (*katadêloi*). To avoid future humiliations, take vengeance for past "defeats," and protect their reputations – Socrates will later say, as we have seen, that they are trying to avoid giving an account of their lives – they have brought charges against him in order to silence him. The silencer will be silenced forever – the very definition of the traditional justice. Vengeance – a successful prosecution – will restore their tarnished honor. Socrates concludes that his accusers, and those who voted against him, should be blamed not for their decision but for their motive – they believed they would harm him (*oiomenoi blaptein*, 41d7–e1). Plato's Socrates is famous for arguing against this traditional definition of justice, as well as for his unfamiliar claim that others cannot harm the just man. Those whose desire to punish arises from the passions and past injustices rather than for the sake of education act "irrationally like a beast" (*ôsper thêrion alogistôs*, *Prt.* 323d–324b). In fact, vengeance itself (*timôria*) is a beast, associated with wild animals and *alogistoi*. On the other hand, correctly administered punishment tames the bestial element (*to thêriôdes*) of the miscreant (*Resp.* 588c–591b; cf. *Grg.* 472e ff.).[136] In the *Apology*, Socrates turns the tables on his accusers by redefining revenge. A different kind of vengeance (*timôrian*) will strike those who voted against him, his killers: a whole new crop of interrogators (*hoi elenchonteis*) will arise, younger and harsher, who will vex Athenians even more by forcing them to give an account of their lives (39c3–d8). In their efforts to silence him, Athenians have merely cut off the hydra's head, from whose corpse will spring a dialectical progeny of monstrously energized inquisitors to continue questioning. Death for individual dialectic will be avenged by dialectic *en masse*, a wonderfully Socratic twist on the *lex talionis*.

For no one is silencing more deadly and speaking more closely identified with living than for Socrates. To leave Athens would mean to give up meaningful life, for he would be deprived of his *logos* (*Cri.* 53c). The *logos* is life, and if it should die, then one must mourn (*Phd.* 89b–c). No worse evil can happen to a man than to become separated from argument, to hate the *logos* (*misologoi*, *Phd.* 89d; cf. *Phdr.* 228b–c for Socrates as a "lover of *logos*"). Indeed, the spoken word, not writing (which is silent), is a form of immortality, the speaker's only legitimate offspring (*Phdr.* 275–8). The *Apology*, the defense of Socrates' life, is a defense of *logos* as Socrates sees it. The roots of speaking, *log/leg*, are used over twenty times in the opening paragraph alone. It is speaking, not silence, that makes Socrates who he is (cf. *Alc.* 1. 106a).

---

[136] Allen (2000) 248, 256–7.

Crito, visiting Socrates for the last time, repeats the executioner's words about the need for the condemned to speak as little as possible: "He says people get too warm when they talk and you should not do anything like this to the poison. Otherwise sometimes those who talk are forced to drink twice or even three times" (*Phd.* 63d–e). For Plato's Socrates, to engage in conversation is to live a fully human life, the only life worth living. So as death approaches, Socrates appropriately demands silence (*hêsuchian*) from the friends who surround him, for he has heard that one must die in silence (117d–e). With his silence comes death, rather than the other way around.[137]

[137] Not surprisingly, Socrates gets the last, if enigmatic, words: "Crito, we owe a cock to Asclepius. Pay what we owe and don't forget" (*Phd.* 118a). Madison (2002) 430–6 reminds us that the words usually translated "don't forget," *mê amelêsête*, can also mean "don't be careless." Her conclusion that the final words of Socrates reveal his thankfulness that "his friends have been healed from their carelessness," that is, that they should give thanks for their conversion to philosophy, is contradicted by Crito's immediate response to Socrates' death. Certainly, the suggested gesture of piety itself ironically reminds us that Socrates was ostensibly condemned for religious unorthodoxy. Ahrensdorf (1995) 9–16 notes that the *Phaedo* itself is Socrates' last apology, the final defense of the philosophical life and a counter to the impiety charges. The traditional interpretation (or even a modern variant, such as that of Cropsey [1986] 173–4), that Socrates thanks Asclepius for healing him of the sickness of life by the cure of death, has been successfully refuted. As Stern (1993) 178 concludes, Socrates does not succumb to a tragic view of life; see: the thorough review of Most (1993). Most's solution is that Plato is depicting Socrates' clairvoyant thankfulness for Plato's own recovery from illness (thus crowning Plato as Socrates' successor); see the recent review of the issue by McPherran (2003). For the historical accuracy of the description of Socrates' death, see: Gill (1973); Hansen (1995) 32–3. Most efforts at teasing out further meanings in this sentence have focused on the deity – why Asclepius? – but perhaps it is the sacrifice itself that is of significance. Several commentators have found significance in the appearance of a cock in a Pythagorean context. Mitscherling (1985) sees an ironic tweaking of the Pythagoreans by reference to the sacrifice of an animal that had particular significance for that cult; see also Crooks (1998) for "Socratism" as an "antidote to the *pathos* of Pythagorean discourse." Socrates may be continuing his efforts right to his last breath to convince his friends that he has made the right choice, to attempt (although probably once more without success) to teach them how to be lovers of wisdom. Part of his argument for the immortality of soul involved a discussion of the transmigration of souls between humans and animals. One of the basic themes of the dialogue is that the philosopher alone can avoid such metempsychoses. Crito, however, as usual has not been able to grasp Socrates' argument. He remains worried about his traditional role as friend, asking Socrates how he would like to be buried (115c–d). Socrates realizes Crito is still confusing his body with his "real" self, and answers "however you please – if you can catch me." The request for the sacrifice of a cock to Asclepius is a reminder of the difference between animals and humans in both Socratic and traditional terms. Socrates hopes that by reminding Crito to undertake the traditional rites by which humans are both linked and separated from the divine – animal sacrifice – Crito will also remember that the job of humans is to explore together the nature of the soul and disregard the concerns of the body (associated with animals throughout Plato). Crito's performance of traditional rites at the death of his mentor also reminds us of how difficult were Socrates' demands. Crito shuts his mouth and eyes (*Phd.* 118). The shutting of the mouth – "fixing of the jaws" – was entirely traditional, with antecedents back to Homer and perhaps beyond; see Vermeule (1979) 14 and Garland (1985) 23–4 for lip bands perhaps back to the Mycenaean period. The basic idea behind it is that the body appears in the afterlife as it left the upper world, a concept about the link between body and soul that Socrates has just been arguing against at great length. Crito, one of Socrates' closest associates, never does understand the

Plato in his dialogues depicts the life of a philosopher at almost total odds with his community. Misunderstood and unsuccessful at changing the priorities of his community, Socrates is finally silenced. But, of course, the story of this struggle is really what matters, and the written dialogues have never been muted. The biggest irony of all may be that Plato, through the voluble portrait of his mentor's "failure," changed Western culture forever.

demands of the philosophical life that Socrates has spent his life trying to articulate and model. Thus, Plato depicts Socratic failures even after his mentor's death.

Epilogue

> *Man*, n. An animal so lost in rapturous contemplation of what he thinks he is as to overlook what he indubitably ought to be. His chief occupation is the extermination of other animals and his own species, which, however, multiplies with such insistent rapidity as to infest the whole habitable earth and Canada.[1]

"In the beginning was the *Logos*," intones the fourth Gospel. The Christian God did not merely use *logos* to create the universe, as suggested in Genesis and some other ancient Mediterranean traditions.[2] The Word (as it is usually translated) was with God, the Word *was* God, and eventually "the Word became flesh" (John 1.1, 1.14). The history of the West can be read as the development of the social, political, moral, and ultimately metaphysical significance of *logos*. Animals, conspicuously lacking the word, have suffered accordingly, although not always in silence.

Yet the Greeks bequeathed to us not just an attitude towards non-human animals, but also a debate and – most crucially – the cultural demand for debate. The long centuries it took for us to mount a serious effort to eliminate slavery and women's second-class status should not obscure the Hellenic blueprint bequeathed to the West for challenging its other less attractive traditions. Animals, who have often provided the fundamental metaphor of Otherness, are merely the most recent group to have their case reevaluated in good Hellenic fashion.

Philosophers have long considered it a fallacy to connect directly how we should behave with the way things are, to derive "ought" from "is." But the history of the moral consideration of the Other – women, slaves, different races or classes – is the story of deriving "ought" from false definitions of "is." The Other can and *should* be treated as something less

---

[1] Ambrose Bierce, cited in Dunayer (2001) 11.
[2] See, for example, the Egyptian myth of creation through the god Atum's "creative utterance" (*hu*); Allen (1997) 124–5. There were competing concepts: Atum is also credited with generation by masturbation (Pyramid Text 527) – a nice example of creation by the hand of god.

than full persons, it has often been argued, because they are *in fact* more irrational, infantile, "soulless," and uncivilized than we are. Treating them as subhuman is ultimately for their own good, as well as that of the larger community.[3]

Arguing from facts to values is not only legitimate, however, but necessary as *part* of the process of aligning a moral compass: morality has both objective and subjective components. As Mary Midgley has shown (and as the examples of racism and sexism reveal), the trick is getting the facts and values right.[4] Ethical theories are based upon interpretations of who can and should be moral agents and beneficiaries. These interpretations in turn depend upon our perception of the intellectual, emotional, and physical endowments and abilities (and sometimes potential abilities) of the actors and recipients. Our understanding of these endowments has changed dramatically as we have followed our Greek instincts to explore who we are. Over the past 150 years, our knowledge of the mental and psychological capabilities of both humans and animals – and our awareness of just how bestial we humans are in origin – has greatly expanded.[5] We know now that behaviorally and neurologically we are very much like the beasts, especially – but not only – other mammals.

[3] It is no coincidence that nineteenth-century feminists were often anti-vivisectionists, abolitionists, and pro-labor (even though trade unions and the working class in general were not usually supporters of women's votes). For example, the Parisian pet cemetery was founded in 1899 by Marguerite Durand, editor of the feminist journal *La Fronde*; see: Kete (1994) 33; Lansbury (1985); Ferguson (1998). Some feminist scholars have argued that much prejudice against women may have been based not so much on male pride or lust for power as on a philosophical conception of the distinction between human beings and animals, between reason and emotions; see, for example, McMillan (1982) 23. For the (mis)treatment of women affirmed by animal imagery, see: Adams (1990); Regan (1991) 83–103; Donovan and Adams (1996). The comparison of animals with slaves was made by Darwin himself: "Animals whom we have made our slaves, we do not like to consider our equals"; see Rachels (1990) 132 and especially Spiegel (1988); for women, slavery, and the Other, see Regan (2001) 106–38. Classicist Raphael Sealey (1990) 41, 159 notes that modern society has put an end to two of Aristotle's domestic relationships of authority, slavery and inequality of sexes, but preserves the "third type" unimpaired: the improvement in status of women has been accomplished at the expense of the status of *children*; see also Golden (1988b), who argues that children and slaves are similar in that both are liable in law and custom to physical violence. But what both scholars are missing is the primary Other upon which the rest were built. The imagery of physical violence, submission, and domestication were applied interchangeably to categories of human subordinates, but it derived from the treatment of animals; see Arluke and Sanders (1996) 132–66 and Patterson (2002) for a chilling account of this linkage in the Nazi mind. For more recent connections, see Adams (1994) 144–61; Ascone and Arkow (1999).

[4] See the discussion of Hume's dictum and G. E. Moore's "naturalistic fallacy" in Midgley (1995) 177–200; Dombrowski (1997) 76–9; Rachels (1990) 66–70, along with Rachels' entire argument for the relevance of the facts of evolution to ethics. Interestingly, it was also Hume who wrote that "no truth appears to me more self-evident, than that beasts are endow'd with thought and reason as well as men"; cited in Jamieson (2002) 52.

[5] Thomas (1983) shows that this process had in fact already begun by 1800 A.D., but it has rapidly accelerated, especially in the last thirty years.

Philosophical approaches have arisen that incorporate this new knowledge and question the dogmatic "wisdom" of tradition, but most of us are only vaguely aware of this scientific evidence and moral debate. We are busy people in the twenty-first century. Few of us have the time or talent to absorb the developments in fields as diverse and complex as Western cultural history, moral philosophy, physical anthropology, linguistics, genetics, psychology, cognitive ethology, evolutionary biology, and primatology. (As a classicist, I do not pretend to be able to read even the 300-some publications each year on Homer, my favorite author.) Moreover, the process of ideological change is bound to be slow, especially given the increasing specialization and isolation of academic research. As Peter Singer has wryly noted, "If the foundations of an ideological position are knocked out from under it, new foundations will be found, or else the ideological position will just hang there, defying the logical equivalent of the law of gravity."[6]

Yet someplace in the crossroads of this research and philosophical inquiry lie the past, present, and future of animals. What becomes clear from even a cursory review of the relevant fields is just how thin is the support for what we have been doing to many non-human animals for so long. In the remaining pages of this brief Epilogue, I coarsely summarize a handful of the questions that have been raised concerning the place of animals in our moral world. It is my hope that my analysis of the importance of language in the archaic and classical Greek efforts at self-definition helps to explain some of the tenacity of the attitudes so thoroughly embedded in our culture. I also hope, as should by now be obvious, that we will continue to learn from the Greek spirit of ethical dynamism that was so deeply embedded in their love of the word.

THE UNIQUENESS OF HUMAN LANGUAGE?

Is language in fact unique to humans, as the Greek texts we have examined seem to take for granted? Many contemporary anthropologists and most linguists continue to consider language to be the primary characteristic that

---

[6] Cited in Rachels (1990) 222. Disciplinary specialization has its benefits, of course, but we all have our limits. For example, Tom Regan, an important philosopher, who has raised so many of the crucial questions concerning the treatment of animals, steps into a giant historical hole when he reports (much to the surprise of any classicist) that Cicero, Epicurus, Herodotus, Horace, Ovid, Plutarch, Seneca, and Virgil were "ethical vegetarians all" (1991) 105. Classicists will be even more startled to read Franklin (1999) 32: "In this chapter we have traced the development of human–animal relations from the very earliest period of recorded history until the end of the twentieth century." Her survey begins in 1500 A.D.

has distinguished *homo sapiens* from other species.[7] On the other hand, even some ancient Greek philosophers took issue with this prevailing view of animals. Some granted animals some form of external *logos* but not internal; others allowed them internal without external, and some even ascribed both kinds of *logos* to animals.[8] Few modern linguists, philosophers, zoologists, or ethologists deny that animals communicate, but to what extent this communication can be called language is a matter of definition.[9] In fact there *is* no universally accepted barrier above or below which communication must or must not be termed "language." These discussions have often devolved to the question of whether humans are the only species with syntactical abilities. Frustrated efforts to teach chimps and gorillas to speak have revealed just what common sense would suggest – even those species most closely related to us cannot learn to carry on profound conversations at the breakfast table. Human vocal tracts are unique, although infants do not have the right vocal equipment in the right place for speaking until they are three to six months old. We are *all* born *alogoi*.

Modern studies of a wide variety of species in their native habitats, as well as efforts to teach animals in captivity to understand and employ different kinds of symbolic communication, reveal that while there is probably little if any grammatical complexity in most animal "language," animals do

---

[7] See, for example, the works of linguists Lieberman (e.g. 1998) and Pinker (e.g. 1994), who otherwise disagree as to the origins and nature of human language. This is a bitterly contested topic among researchers. Not only is there a substantial list of different "unique" properties that may have made modern man successful, but the time (two million years ago? fifty thousand years ago?) and role of speech itself in the evolutionary tree (could Neanderthal man speak?) are still quite unsettled; see the convenient discussion in Allen and Saidel (1998) 184–7. There is no consensus on the origins and evolution of language itself; see the contrasting arguments in Hurford et al. (1998), for example. Konner (2002) 145–71 provides an up-to-date review of many of the issues surrounding that nature of human speech. The issue becomes even more complicated in light of the discovery of a human gene that appears to have some direct relevance for language ability; Lai et al. (2001). More recently, this so-called "speech gene" (*FOXP2*) has been determined to date back no more than two hundred thousand years – about the time anatomically modern humans emerged; Enard et al. (2002). One geneticist has even concluded that "this is the best candidate yet for a gene that enabled us to become human" (*Science* 297 August 16 2002:1105). Other geneticists and linguists are understandably more cautious about making such claims for a single gene, much less a single species-specific characteristic. Marks (2002), especially 159–97, uses a "molecular anthropological" approach to attempt (not always successfully) to deny the significance of genetic similarity across species. Many researchers point to the evolutionary continuity of language as a social behavior; see, for example, the fascinating theory of Dunbar (1996) linking grooming and gossip, and (from different perspectives) the work of Tomasello (1999) and Stanford (2001) 151–62. Kennedy (1998) 1–45 argues for the continuity between animal communication and human language in an interesting account of "rhetoric among social animals."

[8] See Sorabji (1993) 80–6 for references, especially his account of Porphyry's discussion.

[9] See the very detailed summary of research on the evolution of communication by Hauser (1997), who uses a multi-species, comparative approach; also the survey of definitions of "communication" in Rogers and Kaplan (2000) 1–25, and for distinctions between intentional and unintentional signaling, pp. 48–69.

communicate with each other in fairly sophisticated ways.[10] Experiments in teaching apes to speak through sign language and the manipulation of other symbols have demonstrated that these animals at least are able to tell us what they want, desire, prefer, and fear. They can and do create new words for novel objects. Moreover, the receptive competencies of animals appear to be more highly developed than are their productive competencies.[11] Studies reveal the symbolic abilities of great apes, providing "independent confirmation of abilities in other cognitive domains."[12]

Intuitively, we remain fixated on language as the key marker of a morally significant being. The non-pet beasts whose mistreatment has gained the most media attention are the very ones who have appeared to demonstrate complex forms of communication: apes, dolphins, and whales. Other animals who do not seem to have a "language" but are quite high on the animal "intelligence scale" – pigs, for example – have remained below our moral radar. We are just more impressed with creatures who do not grunt or roll in mud (and on whom we do not habitually snack).

The more we learn about animal communication, the more we are directed towards three conclusions:

1. Syntactically sophisticated communication is probably peculiar to humans and is, in fact, a central part of our unique biological make-up and ultimately of our mental and cultural superiority to other animals;

2. Animal communication – vocal, symbolic, and gestural – often reveals a complex mental, social, and emotional life that cannot be dismissed by casual appeals to "instinctive" or "reflexive" behavior with any more success than behaviorists' attempts to excise cognition from humanity.[13] Indeed, the irony is that the more we discover about animal communication and its apparent grammatical deficiencies, the harder it is to deny animals consciousness;

---

[10] One bonobo (Kanzi), a couple dolphins, and an African grey parrot named Alexis seem to have acquired an understanding of human syntax; see DeGrazia (1996) 193–4 and Hauser (2000) 205–8 for a summary, and especially Pepperberg (1999). Discussions of the "uniqueness" of human language (or not) that I have found helpful include: Noske (1989) 128–32; Wallman (1992); Pinker (1994) 332–69; various articles in Cavalieri and Singer (1993) and King (1999a); Kiriazis and Slobodchikoff (1997); Seyfarth and Cheney (1997); Schusterman and Gisiner (1997); Deacon (1997) 47–68; and especially Miles (1997) and Parker and McKinney (1999) 162–89 on the comparison of ape language to that of children, and the survey of King (1999b). Shettleworth (1998) 523–65 provides an unusually objective survey of current research on animal communication and language; in general, her book can be profitably consulted for a current overview of the various topics raised in this Epilogue concerning non-human abilities; see also the articles in Matsuzawa (2001) for human links with primates.

[11] Herman and Morrel-Samuels (1996).   [12] Parker and McKinney (1999) 189.

[13] Especially good on this are Rudd (1992) and Rollin (1998).

3. The lack of syntax in non-humans has no ethical consequences (see below).

The modern animal-rights movement, and scholars who write about the relations between man and beast, have been accused of being sentimental bunny-huggers, concerned much more about defining humanity – and feeling smugly superior – than about acting morally.[14] And some popular and anecdotal accounts of brilliant poodles and compassionate elephants are understandably viewed with some suspicion by those who demand scientific "proof." One postmodern critic even charges that those who write about animals prefer their subjects to remain silent so we can inscribe our own meaning on them.[15] This accusation is decidedly unfair to much of the work I have read on the subject, but the connection between thinking about animals and thinking with animals is important. Like the Greek investigations, these modern discussions are central to exploring who we are and how we are to live. And it turns out that this kind of exploration offers a challenge to how we treat beings of all kinds, not just those that can speak.

THE UNIQUENESS OF HUMAN RATIONALITY?

The major impetus behind most of the philosophical discussions about language uniqueness in *homo sapiens* is this effort to examine how we are to live ethical lives. The conventional argument is not that language itself provides a morally relevant difference between animals and humans, but that external *logos* provides proof of, and/or the necessary materials for, the processes of the kind of mental life (we are *homines sapientes*, after all), especially rationality (internal *logos*), that make a being a moral beneficiary. Many of us in the West continue to bow rather unreflectively to a religious heritage based upon little knowledge of animal – or human – physiology or psychology. Language and its connection to reason and thus morality are embedded in the Western religious, social, philosophical, and political tradition.[16] Plato hints at the connection; Aristotle draws on the parallels,

---

[14] Some American neurologists have even labelled animal advocates "incurably insane" and suffering from "zoophil-psychosis"! Sources in Regan (2001) 133.

[15] Tester (1991). He seems to me to read his own nihilism into others' more earnest efforts. It is worth noticing that modern arguments against animal rights often rely on the antique and circular insistence that pro-animal arguments obscure "the differences between creatures like ourselves, who use language, and those that do not"; Leahy (1991) 220. A more comprehensive and open-minded study of the animal-rights movement is that of Guither (1998).

[16] See the convenient surveys in Dombrowski (1984a) 5–17; Singer (1990) 185–212; Sorabji (1993) 195–201; Preece and Chamberlain (1995) 5–43. De Fontenay (1998) presents a veritable history of

and the Stoics cement it. The criterion of rationality, divorced from its original connection with language, is picked up in turn by Augustine, according to whom animals have no rational soul and so cannot share in our community (e.g. *De moribus Manichaeorum* 2.17, 59; *De civ. D.* 1.20). And what are Augustine's authorities for his understanding of the relationship of human, animal, and divine? Aristotle and the Bible. Aquinas adopts this same line of reasoning, citing Augustine and Aristotle (e.g *S.T.* 2.2, q.64 a1), and concluding that the difference is between a mortal and an immortal soul. Aquinas in fact simplifies the Aristotelian concept of irrational animals (Aristotle, as we saw in the Introduction, is not quite as clear about this as he is sometimes thought to be). Aquinas then combines the Greek philosopher's teleological theory (animals' function in the *scala naturae* is to serve humans) with an appeal to scripture. That reason formed the absolute boundary between animals and humans was not the only early Christian doctrine, but it became the central tenet of medieval Catholicism and the West, and went virtually unchallenged until the eighteenth century.[17]

Interestingly, when pressed for proof that animals are not rational, many influential thinkers have retreated to animals' lack of human language. Descartes, for example, famously supported his belief in animals' complete absence of mind and even sentience – animals are soulless automata – on the slim thread of their lack of "real speech."[18] Even Thomas Huxley, the eloquent promoter of Darwinism, mollified concerned listeners by insisting that language still separates us from the gorilla and leaves us superior.[19]

Given the importance of rationality in the Western tradition, the next logical question then becomes this: is language really necessary for a morally

philosophy as seen through ideas about animals. A full treatment of the history of speciesism, especially in Britain, can be found in Ryder (1989); see also Kean (1998) for the place of animal rights in the context of social change over the past two centuries in Britain. Preece (2002) offers up a "chronicle of sensibility to animals" over the past 2,500 years.

[17] See: Linzey (1995) 13; G. Clark (1998); Yamamoto (1998); Ickert (1998). The belief that God has given animals for our use can be traced back to the fifth century B.C.; see Sorabji (1993) 199 and Osborne (1990), who however unnecessarily dismisses the connections between Greek ideas and those of Christianity. For Paul's dismissal of God's concern for animals, see Grant (1999) 7–13. Note again that before Augustine, as Sorabji shows (1993) 202, "the linkages between animals, reason and immortality were by no means settled." He cites Lactantius, for example, who argues that animals have reason, can converse, laugh, and exercise foresight, differing from humans only through their lack of knowledge of god (*Div. inst.* 3.10, 7.79.10; *Epitome* 65.4).

[18] The passages are conveniently collected in Linzey and Regan (1990) 47–52; see also: Gunderson (1964); Malcolm (1977) 40–57; the extensive discussion of both Descartes and Montaigne in Gontier (1998).

[19] Cited in Rachels (1990) 82–3. Huxley's version of Darwinian ethics has been criticized; see de Waal (2001) 348–9.

relevant mental life? The Greeks themselves provided a far greater range of conjecture on this topic than the Western tradition has generally acknowledged. "Reason" had a variety of definitions, and some Greek philosophers found plenty of evidence in animal behavior, as well as through their own speculations, for attributing rational thought to animals.[20] Capacities other than speech, such as perception, memory, preparation, emotion, skills, virtues and vices were adduced as proof of animal reason. Empedocles, Anaxagoras, Diogenes of Apollonia, even Theophrastus and Strato (Aristotle's own successors) believed that animals could reason. Many Platonists, especially Plutarch (see in particular his anti-Stoic dialogues *On the Cleverness of Animals* and *Beasts Are Rational*) and Porphyry, argued that animals were rational to various degrees.[21]

Current research by linguists, philosophers, and cognitive scientists reaches similarly diverse conclusions. Some believe that morally relevant mentation – "rationality" is no longer a term much favored in the scientific or philosophical literature – is impossible without language. Just what exactly *is* a relevant mental quality, and how it is to be defined and measured, varies greatly from scholar to scholar. Is it consciousness? Cognition? Desires? Beliefs? Intentions? Self-awareness? And what is *consciousness* anyway? Are these all-or-nothing qualities? Some scholars still insist that only the most clever and verbal species, *homo sapiens*, can hit these (moving) targets.

Many other researchers, however, contend that some, or all, of these endowments are not reliant upon language. For some scholars, language is only the product, not the producer, of consciousness, at best "the bastard child and obedient slave of awareness, ever at its beck and call."[22] The linguist Steven Pinker has argued persuasively against the common idea

---

[20] Dickerman (1911); Sorabji (1993) 65–77. Newmyer (1999) discusses Plutarch's response to the Stoics, highlighting the relevance of the ancient discussion to the modern debate.

[21] Brink (1956) 124–31; Guthrie (1957) 32–59; Preus (1983) 153–7; Preus (1990) 88–99; Sorabji (1993) 78–96. Excellent on Plutarch's reaction to the Stoics is Newmyer (1992). Preus (1990) 72 concludes that the general trend of many of the Presocratic philosophers can be summarized in DK Parmenides A45: "Parmenides, Empedocles, and Democritus thought that νοῦς and ψυχή were the same, so they thought that no animal would be completely ἄλογον." Plato, according to Preus (73–4), seems to have concluded that the difference between humans and animals was one of degree, not kind. Both he and Pythagoras were said to hold that "the souls of the so-called irrational creatures are rational (*logikai*) but do not actually function rationally because they do not have the power of speech (*to phrastikon*). Thus, monkeys and dogs think (*noousi*) but do not speak (*phrazousi*); see Plass (1973) 35–46. An excellent study of Empedocles' vegetarianism and the various meanings of sacrifice in its cultural context is that of Rundin (1998). For Theophrastus, see especially Cole (1992) 52–61.

[22] Donald (2001) 20, 46–91. He presents a concise summary of the definitional issues of consciousness, and discusses those animals that might possess various aspects of consciousness (the "consciousness club"), 117–48.

that thought is the same as language. Thinking without language, what he terms "mentalese," is exactly what babies and monkeys do.[23]

Pinker – a strong advocate of the uniqueness of human language as a hard-wired, biological "instinct" – nevertheless dismisses the unscientific, "fruitless and boring debate over what qualifies as true language." He decries the fallacy that there is some line to be drawn across the ladder, the species on the rungs above it being credited with some glorious trait, those below lacking it. Pinker thus rejects the "brouhaha raised by the spectacle of humans trying to ennoble animals by forcing them to mimic human forms of communication. Why should language be considered such a big deal? Other creatures have unique features."[24] But of course this brouhaha is at the heart of the ethical debate about why we can experiment upon chimpanzees and not upon one-month old infants or severely retarded, irreparably senile, or brain-damaged humans. Brains and grammar, not wings (or the capacity to suffer), seem to matter. As far as I know, no one has yet argued that we may eat philosophers because they cannot fly.

Our untested beliefs about animal mental abilities – whether or not these abilities are linked to any linguistic skills – have had tremendous ethical implications. The conventional religious assumption and philosophical argument that *no* non-human animals are capable of cognition, consciousness, desires, beliefs, etc., however, can no longer be easily supported by the facts. Animal ethologists have shown that many animals reveal a mental level equivalent to two to three year-old humans in a wide variety of categories. For example, Marc Houser of Harvard University, in a recent and balanced account of the state of research on animal cognition, concludes:

"We share the planet with thinking animals. Each species, with its uniquely sculpted mind, endowed by nature and shaped by evolution, is capable of meeting the most fundamental challenges that the physical and psychological world presents. Although the human mind leaves a characteristically different imprint on the planet, we are certainly not alone in this process."[25]

---

[23] Pinker (1994) 55–82; see also: Ehrlich (2000) 145–9; Damasio (1999) 107–112; Bloom (1998) has a good discussion of the debate. Waldron (1985) examines those writers who make thought (or possession of a "mind") completely dependent upon, or inseparable from, language, a very common view even now; see, e.g. Torey (1999) 103–9; Budiansky (1998) 193; Noble and Davidson (1997), with a survey of other views. For philosophical discussions of the weakness of the traditional link between language, rationality, and morality, see: Rollin (1981) 10–28; Regan (1983) 1–81; Clark (1984a) 26–32; Midgley (1983) 53–61, especially on the centrality of language in Wittgenstein's thought; Midgley (1995) 203–51; DeGrazia (1996) 183–98; Rollin (1998).

[24] Pinker (1994) 347, 369. Similarly, Stanford (2001) 151–2 entitles a chapter that discusses the controversy over animal language "The Silliest Debate."

[25] Hauser (2000) 257. Many other researchers recently have reached similar positive (or potentially positive) conclusions about animal consciousness; see: Dawkins (1993); Vauclair (1996); Rogers

Although he is a healthily skeptical scientist who throughout the book rejects animals' mental capabilities unless verifiable, Hauser also must draw the following conclusions as he surveys our current state of knowledge: "With respect to numerical abilities, adult rhesus monkeys and tamarins are at least as talented as one-year-old infants when it comes to summing objects" (61). Language, he observes, is not necessary for spatial knowledge: "For both rats and human children, accurate navigation following disorientation is based on a mental tool that references stable geometric cues (e.g., the shape of an enclosure) and ignores or, more precisely, is blind to nongeometric cues such as landmarks" (83). On the possession of self-recognition and self-consciousness, he summarizes that at least some animals pass the tests far better than young children (109): "There is little evidence that children at this age [under two years old] recognize themselves in the mirror" (97). Whereas "three-year-olds and autistics think that what they know, everyone knows" (165), "conceptually, some animals have the capacity to detect mismatches between a signal's common function and the way it is currently being used. These animals can therefore detect cheaters, liars, and other self-interested observers" (156).

The point here is not that animal cognition or consciousness is necessarily similar to that of humans – the truth is that we do not know (although the research on cognition is especially impressive) – but that scientific evidence reveals complex mental abilities in many animals that are superior to those in many human beings. Much more research is necessary to know what animals are thinking – we may never know for sure. Wittgenstein's apothegm is often quoted in these studies: If a lion could talk, we could not understand him.[26] But the scientific study of animals is undermining any confidence in the traditional conclusions drawn from such philosophically comforting statements. As Hauser concludes:

(1997); Allen and Bekoff (1999); Griffin (2001); Bekoff (2002) 84–99. Shettleworth (1998) and Schulkin (2000) 29–57 present open-ended summaries of current research into animal cognition and self-awareness. Budiansky (1998) attempts to refute the "anthropomorphism" of such studies while maintaining a respect for the many (non-human) kinds of intelligence of animals. An excellent summary of animal cognition and its significance for animal legal rights is Wise (2002). There are still researchers, however, who argue that animals do not even feel pain; see the discussion of Rollin (1998) 273–92. Compare the distinctions between pain and suffering designated by Dennett (1991, 448–53; 1996, 161–8): suffering requires a certain level of cognition (which Dennett concedes to "many, but not all, animals"). At what point, however, does the unnecessary infliction of pain itself become morally significant? And at what point does uncomprehended pain cause more suffering than pain that can be prepared for and understood?

[26] (1958) 223; see Bavidge and Ground (1994) 107–22, and especially Wolfe (2003) 44–94. Wolfe unnecessarily throws out all humanistic approaches in favor of poststructuralist philosophy, but he does demonstrate how difficult it is for thinkers embedded in traditional approaches, even those who favor better treatment of animals, to remove themselves from anthropocentric points of view.

Most animals are like the unfortunate Gregor Samsa after metamorphosis. They are Kafka-creatures, organisms with rich thoughts and emotions but no system for translating what they think into something that they can express to others. By making this claim I do not mean that animals, lacking a human language, have the kinds of thoughts that Samsa-as-beetle has. Without a doubt, our thoughts are different, and language has contributed to this difference, though I am not convinced we know exactly how."[27]

In other words, it is likely that animals think without human language, but to what degree, about what, and by what process is still unknown. And as some researchers observe, the human/other species comparison is a distraction to pursuing more important questions. Animals develop and use their abilities to survive in their distinctive environments. How "useful" is it to claim a chimpanzee can reach the intellectual level of a young child?[28] What is scientifically interesting is the study of how chimpanzees have evolved in many ways (including mentally) to meet their own distinctive ecological challenges.

But the evidence of *any* significant cognition or consciousness in non-human animals *is* extremely consequential when placed in the history of ethical argumentation. Since our treatment of animals is frequently based upon the historical certainty of the insurmountable mental gap between humans and other animals, this conclusion should cause any thoughtful being considerable discomfort. Before we act – *especially* before killing, or causing what may very well be unnecessary suffering – should we not be reasonably convinced that we are doing so ethically? Voltaire, pondering the nature of right and wrong, quoted the following "wise" maxim from the *Sadder* (an abridgement of the laws of Zoroaster): "'When it is uncertain whether an action you are asked to take is right or wrong, abstain.' Who has ever proposed a more admirable rule? What legislator has spoken better?"[29]

THE PLACE OF RATIONALITY IN MORAL THEORY?

But suppose we were to discover (unlikely as it now appears) that rationality, or consciousness, or self-consciousness, or some other highly specialized mental capacity is in fact entirely limited to humans. Is the possession of this kind of intellectual attribute really the best criterion for determining a moral beneficiary?[30]

[27] Hauser (2000) 209.   [28] Bekoff (2002) 86.   [29] (1972) 273.
[30] I focus here on the moral consequences of a mental life. In the American legal world, as Wise clearly shows (2002) 33–4, cognition remains a crucial endowment for access to basic rights; see also Francione (1995) and Wise (2001).

Unfortunately, those who insist that only psychologically sophisticated beings can be granted full moral concern[31] must logically eliminate many humans from their list. Innumerable unlucky humans do not actually possess the requisite mental endowments. These "marginal cases," as they are often labelled, are the mentally defective or deficient, and may include the brain-dead or damaged, severely retarded, senile, comatose, as well as the addicted or sociopathic, and even healthy infants. The philosophical Argument from Marginal Cases, as it is termed, has not been successfully avoided, undermined, or dismissed. Evelyn Pluhar and Daniel Dombrowski have recently surveyed the philosophical discussions both for and against this argument, and have demonstrated that no one has yet been able to counter its logic.[32] This is a complicated issue that cannot be adequately examined here – I especially recommend Dombrowski's book-length study – but the implications are extraordinary. Here, I borrow from Dombrowski's summary made by Lawrence Becker (an opponent of the argument):

1. It is undeniable that many species other than our own have "interests" – at least in the minimal sense that they feel and try to avoid pain, and feel and seek various sorts of pleasure and satisfaction.
2. It is equally undeniable that human infants and some of the profoundly retarded have interests in only the sense that members of these other species have them – and not in the sense that normal adult humans have them. That is, human infants and some of the profoundly retarded (i.e., the marginal cases of humanity) lack the normal adult qualities of purposiveness, self-consciousness, memory, imagination, and anticipation to the same extent that some other species of animals lack those qualities.
3. Thus, in terms of the morally relevant characteristic of having interests, some humans must be equated with members of other species rather than with normal adult human beings.
4. Yet predominant moral judgments about conduct toward these humans are dramatically different from judgments about conduct toward the comparable animals. It is customary to raise the animals for food, to

---

[31] This includes most major philosophical approaches developed over the past 200 years, especially the various schools of reciprocity or social contract theory and Kantian rationalism, since they either directly or indirectly require the beneficiary of full moral concern to be rational, autonomous members of the community. These theories are all very Hesiodic: animals cannot expect to be treated with *dikê* since they do not act with *dikê*. Most animal-rights philosophers discuss the inadequacy of rationality as a relevant moral criterion, even if they do not use the argument from marginal cases; see Sapontzis (1987).

[32] Pluhar (1995); Dombrowski (1997). One philosopher to fail recently to avoid falling into self-contradictory statements in an extended effort to reject the argument from marginal cases is Cohen in Cohen and Regan (2001).

subject them to lethal scientific experiments, to treat them as chattels, and so forth. It is not customary – indeed it is abhorrent to most people even to consider – the same practices for human infants and the retarded.

5. But absent a finding of some morally relevant characteristic (other than having interests) that distinguishes these humans and animals, we must conclude that the predominant moral judgments about them are inconsistent. To be consistent, and to that extent rational, we must either treat the humans the same way we now treat the animals, or treat the animals the same way we now treat the humans.

6. And there does not seem to be a morally relevant characteristic that distinguishes all humans from all other animals. Sentience, rationality, personhood, and so forth all fail. The relevant theological doctrines are correctly regarded as unverifiable and hence unacceptable as a basis for a philosophical morality. The assertion that the difference lies in the *potential* to develop interests analogous to those of normal adult humans is also correctly dismissed. After all, it is easily shown that some humans – whom we nonetheless refuse to treat as animals – lack the relevant potential. In short, the standard candidates for a morally relevant differentiating characteristic can be rejected.

7. The conclusion is, therefore, that we cannot give a reasoned justification for the differences in ordinary conduct toward some humans as against some animals.[33]

The Argument from Marginal Cases shatters any ethical complacency. When we experiment on adult chimpanzees but not on anencephalic babies, or eat pigs and not the incurably senile, we are not acting from any rationally consistent position. Brain-dead babies will never speak, will never be rational or self-conscious or have beliefs, will never possess any morally relevant distinction that separates them from the most humble non-human animal. They do not even have the potential to develop these abilities. For that matter, no plausible case has yet been made for the moral relevance of potential itself, an awkward gap that poses a problem even for granting orphaned but healthy infants (and all fetuses), who can neither think nor communicate as efficiently as many adult non-human animals, the safeguards of full moral personhood unless these same safeguards are given to many other animals.[34] Under most normal circumstances, membership in

---

[33] Cited in Dombrowski (1997) 1–2.

[34] See Feinberg (1984) on the illogicality of the "strict potentiality criterion"; Pluhar (1995) 107–13, 146–50. Perhaps it is helpful to recall that Aristotle, who laid the foundations for this discussion, argued that the human fetus does not really become a human until some time after birth; Preus (1990) 75.

a species – even a species as potentially chatty and bright as our own – turns out to be no more ethically relevant for determining a moral beneficiary than membership in a particular race or gender. Every attempt to find a morally relevant distinction that would "save" the severely retarded infant and not the chicken he is fed comes up short. There will always be some humans who come out below many animals in whatever psychological test is conjured up. And the Greeks – we are no longer surprised – were there long before us on this topic as well: Porphyry used this argument (*Abst.* 3.19) to defend sentience as the only appropriate criterion for moral consideration.[35]

A few modern philosophers have even been driven by the logic of this argument to exclude some marginalized humans from the moral community. To be consistent, we will have to eat and experiment upon the severely mentally defective.[36] Many other thinkers have attempted to develop theories based on concepts such as inherent value, equal consideration of interests, and moral individualism that avoid the inconsistencies of the traditional views while also bringing both marginalized humans and many animals within the scope of full moral concern. Some focus on consciousness and sentiency, assigning full moral significance to any being who is able to care about what happens to him or her. Having an interest in avoiding pain or continuing to experience life are given primary consideration in making moral decisions under ordinary circumstances. Phrases such as "consciously purposive sentient beings," "practical autonomy," and "experiencing subjects of a life" and the distinctions between a "biological life" and a "biographical life" are becoming more common in the literature.

It should be noted that all of these theories have been challenged as well. The important point, however, is not that we have no universally accepted grounds for treating animals better, but that our current treatment of animals does not seem to rest upon a rationally defensible ethical position. Neither the arguments from antiquity about the moral status of animals nor those developed over the past two centuries allow us to treat differently beings that have no different capabilities that are morally relevant to the action under consideration. The failure of these arguments results in part from their dependence upon an ill-informed distinction between humans and other animals.

---

[35] Dombrowski (1984b). Porphyry based his argument on animal sentiency, but also argued, as noted above, for the rationality of animals.

[36] For example, the utilitarians Singer (1986) 369 and Frey (1983) 115–16, although Singer includes many animals within his moral circle.

Not that many of us consciously act on the basis of this distinction, of course. For the most part, it seems to me that we treat animals the way we do because we always have treated them that way. When asked why, we have often relied on precarious philosophical theories, religious dogma, and psychological conjectures – as we have with all groups of the Other – to support the status quo. We rightly scoff now at previous and similar efforts to deny full moral consideration to women and African-Americans – they were once considered by the majority to lack the requisite mental and linguistic abilities to be granted full moral and legal personhood.[37] But the case for animals, the ultimate Other, is not much less compelling logically. "Deprived of the gift of language, animals are the ideal disenfranchised group."[38]

Much of human behavior is not grounded on specific rational choices, nor can it always be. Studies have even shown that we reason better when emotion plays a role.[39] We often do what we have grown accustomed to doing, what our families, religions, and communities have taught us – no less a speciesist than Aristotle made this point. We eat animals because we always have (when we could), because it is easy, because they taste good, because it puts animals and other humans in their "right places," and because it is profitable for producers and appears to be cheap for consumers (at least in the affluent West).[40] When pressed, a few will say something about animals having no soul. This is unarguable and therefore irrelevant – and not unchallenged by many religious leaders and thinkers.[41] Most

[37] Not to mention the barbarian Other, whose different language still reveals his subordinate status. As Hegel infamously suggested, that the Chinese do not understand us proves them inferior, and that we do not understand them proves us superior; cited in Clark (1984a) 95.
[38] Savage-Rumbaugh (1997) 48.
[39] E.g. Damasio (1994) on the "emotional" brain.
[40] I say "appears to be" because the health and environmental consequences of factory farming (such as cardiovascular disease, cancer, deforestation, topsoil erosion, desertification, aquifer depletion, and water pollution) are not part of the price producers must usually pay for raising meat. (We should remember that for most of the history of the West, eating meat has been a wonderfully conspicuous sign of wealth and status.) Other common uses of animals, from the trivial (e.g. for sport, clothing, product testing, psychological experimentation) to the potentially more significant (e.g. medical research) are subject to the same ethical challenges.
[41] See, for example, Linzey (1987; 1995); Webb (1998) offers a thoughtful if slightly odd Christianity-meets-postmodernism defense of animals. The Catholic Church, for example, still accepts Aquinas' view that animals have mortal, sentient "souls" whereas humans have immortal, rational ("substantive") souls. Pope John Paul II was on familiar (indeed antique) ground, then, when he recently justified human "domination" of other animals by insisting that what "makes man like God is the fact that – unlike the whole world of other living creatures, including those endowed with senses (*animalia*) – man is also a rational being (*rationale*)"; "*Mulieris Dignitatem*," Apostolic Letter "On the Dignity and Vocation of Women," *Origins*, vol. 18., No. 17 (October 6, 1988), #6, pp. 265–6, and #10, p. 268, cited in Hilkert (2002) 4. See Badham (1998) for a defense of this position, and

importantly, it ignores the crucial demand of the Greeks that we critically reexamine everything, including these very protocols and their consequences. The philosopher Stephen R. L. Clark – an Aristotelian sounding much like Socrates – summarizes the issue in this way: "People who won't do this [engage in philosophical inquiry] are usually, though they fail to realise it, acting out the theories of some earlier philosopher: the sort of self-styled 'practical person' who is ignorant of the principles upon which she acts and careless of the long-term consequences of what she does."[42]

But in the last 150 years many people have struggled to expose their intuitions to the light of reason. They have attempted to find a philosophy of life that addresses a subconscious discomfort with the disjunction between how we feel about animals as companions and what we actually do with them in the rest of our lives – even Descartes is said to have treated his dog humanely.[43] And so once again we run headlong into the Greek method, not just one side of their debate.

RETURNING TO THE GREEKS

The Greeks were right, I believe, to insist that human nature, bestial at heart, requires a series of cultural protocols to keep it in check. Culture separates us from our natural, potentially savage selves. For the Greeks, natural impulse unchecked by the constricting bridles of law, tradition, and civic order leads not to liberation, self-fulfillment, and full humanity (as is often supposed by both the modern liberal and libertarian agendas), but more likely to holocaust.[44]

This belief that we are all animals was what prompted the Greek search for difference. The quest for criteria that might separate us from other animals,

---

(and less cogently) Reichman (2000), who argues against both the significance of evolution and the possibility of a true Christian even becoming a vegetarian since it "renders impossible a coherent understanding of the central mystery of Christian belief, namely, the Incarnation" (372).

[42] Clark (1989) 5.

[43] Dombrowski (1997) 174 puts it nicely: "What most people now find to be counterintuitive is the Kantian view that only rational and linguistic beings fall into the scope of moral concern, for most believe that infants, the mentally retarded, the insane, the senile, the autistic, the comatose, and animals are within the scope of moral concern. Moreover, most people have intuitions that the capacity for suffering is a sufficient condition for being morally considerable, even if it does not usually concern them that their everyday (speciesist) practices contradict these intuitions." For the immense linguistic efforts we make both to palliate our inconsistent behavior, see Dunayer (2001).

[44] This is not to conclude that humans alone possess culture, but merely to accept that there is (to say the least) a large difference in degree between the social learning exhibited by other animals and the enormous human cultural capacity. For the continuity between primate species, a "Darwistotelian view" that blends nature and culture, see especially de Waal (2001). He seems to me to make many excellent points about apes; his confidence in the inherent kindness in human nature is less convincing.

and the search for cultural protocols that might keep us from behaving like animals, were core aspects of Hellenic thought. What makes us distinct as a species should perhaps be what we nurture, support, develop; it could help tell us how to organize a community, construct an education, design a government; it might indicate the relative importance of family, friends, and state, and even suggest how we are to treat each other, animals, and the natural world. In short, what makes us distinctly human can lead us towards the answers of how to *be* fully human.

In this post-Darwinian age, we are back to the Greeks, this time with evidence: we *are* all animals, different in degree, to be sure, but how exactly in kind?[45] The modern world, both liberal and conservative, has rejected the most crucial inheritance of the Greeks. We Westerners are overwhelmingly theistic and increasingly therapeutic – often at the same time – apparently convinced (or at least hopeful) that we can bargain or buy our way out of our tragic limitations. Part of our self-satisfaction has derived from our denying the bestial side of our human natures. We believe we are uniquely rational and (simultaneously) uniquely "spiritual" beings, who, with a little therapy from shrink, guru, priest, psychic, lawyer, or TV infomercial, will find a long, healthy, happy, and affluent life on earth and an everlasting paradise in the hereafter (or perhaps another even more prosperous round here on earth).[46]

We ignore, then, our most important inheritance. The Greeks sensed humanity's bestial, ephemeral, circumscribed nature that forms the necessary background for the awesome (*deinos*) dignity we can attain only through the daily confrontation with our limitations. Our only hope of living lives different from other animals is to apply our talents to create communities that constrain our worse natures and encourage the pursuit of lives worth living. The Greeks insisted that human speech and reason *be exercised*, not merely possessed, that without the use of our "unique" endowments we are the worst kind of beast. We are to apply our gifts; we are to examine everything, including the grounds for treating the various

---

45 James Rachels (1990) has pointed out that Darwin and evolutionary theory have dismantled "human dignity" as a moral category. The doctrine of human dignity, at least as traditionally defined, rests on two untenable premises: 1) that man is made in God's image; 2) that man is a uniquely rational being. See, however, Petrinovich (1999) for different conclusions from a neo-Darwinian bio-ethical approach.

46 Kaminer (1999) offers a refreshingly non-ideological examination of the common denominators of new-age irrationalism and "traditional" religion. As she notes (20), we Americans are especially in denial: three-quarters of us rate our chances of going to heaven as excellent or good; only 4 percent expect to go to hell. There are few links to be found between Augustine's quite classical vision of human nature, as ugly as his vision of Original Sin may be, and the Catholicism I see at the Jesuit university at which I teach.

members of our households and communities – and this always included animals – in such completely different ways.

I am not saying that there are no good arguments for eating or experimenting on all non-human animals. Nor would I deny that human beings are often and in important ways of greater value than many non-humans. Language and rationality unquestionably make life richer and far more complex, and the two make human culture possible. The question remains, however: are these attributes *morally* relevant? If so, when and how? Linguistic competence and a rational demeanor would certainly be relevant criteria (or should be) in choosing between babysitters or applicants to college, but they are immaterial when the issue is whether a being should be tortured, worn, or eaten. One often runs across such *reductiones* – "So chimps have a right to go to school?" – when defenders of the traditional morality find themselves backed into an intellectual corner. The Stoics, for example, seem to have worried that if rationality were rejected as the essential moral criterion, then not only animals but plants would warrant full moral consideration. This half-serious concern was repeated by Augustine (and I have heard it from dinner companions), although it was ably answered long ago by the Greeks themselves. As Stephen R. L. Clark observes, "It is remarkable how sympathetic the orthodox become to tomatoes when asked how they excuse torments to which we put a veal-calf."[47]

What is clear to me, at least, is that there are no easy arguments for most of us in the West for harming or killing many different kinds of animals, and that there are some very good arguments for not eating, wearing, hunting, or experimenting upon them under most circumstances. These ideas are creeping out beyond the crypts of academic journals and the newsletters of vegetarian groupies into low-level public awareness. And occasionally they sink in a bit deeper: even McDonald's, a *bête noire* of many animal-rights groups, has recently demanded that all its suppliers of chickens and eggs improve (a bit) the treatment of their animals. It is unlikely that a very sophisticated corporation – that happens to be the largest purchaser of eggs and second largest purchaser of chicken in the United States[48] – would alter its policy if it did not sense that it would be good for business. McDonald's must surely have discovered that enough of the fast-food public was bothered by the media-covered protests against the company's alleged support of animal cruelty that it was more profitable to change (a bit).

[47] (1984a) 17 with references; see DeGrazia (1996) 37–74 for what "equal consideration of interests" really does and does not mean.
[48] Zwerdling (2002); Schlosser (2001) 140, who reports that McDonald's is also the country's largest purchaser of beef and pork (136, 4).

When Aristotle writes, "None of the other animals speaks except man" (*Probl.* 899a2–3), who would object? Yet so much has derived from that simple observation. Rationalizations, religious dogma, profit, a sense of power, a bit of pleasure, and simple convenience have ridden lazily on the back of ignorance and prejudice for centuries and are due for, and have started to receive, a thorough review. To understand that our attitudes about animals are as old as Western culture itself – and our justifications for these attitudes ultimately based on the observation that we talk and they do not – should make us all the more eager to use the tools the Greeks handed down to us to scrutinize those very attitudes.[49] And finally, most Greek of all, we are called to make our deeds match our words.

[49] The linguist Derek Bickerton, who accepts the centrality of language for our species, expresses a similar concern: "For although language made our species and made the world we inhabit, the powers it unleashed drove us to understand and control our environment, rather than to explore the mainspring of our own being. We have followed that path of control and domination until even the most daring among us have begun to fear where it may lead" (1990) 257. I think we have followed both roads, but we need constantly to be reminded that they meet. The public impotence of philosophy is not *always* a good thing.

Bibliography

COMMENTARIES AND EDITIONS

Bollack, J. and Judet de La Combe, P. (1981–) *L'Agamemnon d'Eschyle*. Lille.

Burnet, J. (1924) *Plato's Euthyphro, Apology of Socrates and Crito*. Oxford.

Chantraine, P. (1983/4) *Dictionnaire étymologique de la langue grecque*. Paris.

Collard, C. (1975) *Euripides' Supplices*. Groningen.

Conacher, D. J. (1987) *Aeschylus' Oresteia: A Literary Commentary*. Toronto.

Denniston, J. D. and Page, D. (1957) *Aeschylus: Agamemnon*. Oxford.

Dover, K. J. (1968) *Clouds*. Oxford.

Dunbar, N. (1995) *Aristophanes: Birds*. Oxford.

Edwards, M. W. (1991) *The Iliad: A Commentary. Volume V: Books 17–20*. Cambridge.

Fraenkel, E. (1950) *Aeschylus: Agamemnon*. Oxford.

Frisk, H. (1960/70) *Griechisches etymologisches Wörterbuch I–II*. Heidelberg.

Garvie, A. F. (1986) *Choephori: Aeschylus*. Oxford.

Gow, A. S. F. (1950) *Theocritus*. Cambridge.

Hainsworth, B. (1988) *A Commentary on Homer's Odyssey. Volume I. Books I–VIII*. Oxford.

　(1993) *The Iliad: A Commentary. Volume III: Books 9–12*. Cambridge.

Heubeck, A. (1989) *A Commentary on Homer's Odyssey. Volume II. Books IX–XVI*. Oxford.

　(1992) *A Commentary on Homer's Odyssey. Volume III. Books XVII–XXIV*. Oxford.

Hoekstra, A. (1989) *A Commentary on Homer's Odyssey. Volume II. Books IX–XVI*. Oxford.

Janko, R. (1992.) *The Iliad: A Commentary. Volume IV: Books 13–16*. Cambridge.

Kamerbeek, J. C. (1953) *The Ajax*. H. Schreuder, tr. Leiden.

Kirk, G. S. (1985) *The Iliad: A Commentary. Volume I: Books 1–4*. Cambridge.

　(1990) *The Iliad: A Commentary. Volume II: Books 5–8*. Cambridge.

Long, A. A. and Sedley, D. N. (1990) *The Hellenistic Philosophers*. Vol. II. Cambridge.

Macleod, C. W. (1982a) *Homer: Iliad Book XXIV*. Cambridge.

Pearson, A. C. (1963) *The Fragments of Sophocles*. Amsterdam.

Pease, A. S. (1955) *M. Tulli Ciceronis De Natura Deorum I*. Cambridge, MA.

Podlecki, A. J. (1989) *Eumenides: Aeschylus*. Warminster.

Richardson, N. (1993) *The Iliad: A Commentary. Volume VI: books 21–4.* Cambridge.

Rose, H. J. (1957–8) *A Commentary on the Surviving Plays of Aeschylus.* Amsterdam.

Russo, J. (1992) *A Commentary on Homer's Odyssey. Volume III. Books XVII–XXIV.* Oxford.

Rusten, J. S. (1989) *Thucydides: The Peloponnesian War, Book II.* Cambridge.

Sommerstein, A. H. (1989) *Eumenides: Aeschylus.* Cambridge.

Stanford, W. B. (1959) *The Odyssey of Homer.* London/Basingstoke.

(1963) *Sophocles: Ajax.* London/New York.

Strycker, E. de and Slings, S. R. (1994) *Plato's Apology of Socrates. Mnemosyne* Suppl. 137. Leiden.

Thomson, G. (1938) *The Oresteia of Aeschylus.* Cambridge.

West, M. L. (1966) *Hesiod: Theogony.* Oxford.

West, S. (1988) *A Commentary on Homer's Odyssey. Volume I. Books I–VIII.* Oxford.

BOOKS AND ARTICLES

Adams, C. J. (1990) *The Sexual Politics of Meat: A Feminist–Vegetarian Critical Theory.* New York.

(1994) *Neither Man Nor Beast: Feminism and the Defense of Animals.* New York.

Adkins, A. W. H. (1960) *Merit and Responsibility: A Study in Greek Values.* Oxford.

(1972) "Truth, KOSMOS, and ARETH in the Homeric poems," *CQ* 22: 5–18.

(1983) "Orality and philosophy," in Robb (1983) 201–27.

Adrados, F. R. (1964) "El tema del aguila, de la epica Acadia a Esquilo," *Emerita* 32: 267–82.

(1999) *History of the Graeco-Latin Fable. Mnemosyne* Suppl. 20. L. A. Ray, tr. Leiden.

Ahl, F. (1984) "The art of safe criticism in Greece and Rome," *AJP* 105: 174–208.

Ahl, F. and Roisman, H. M. (1996) *The Odyssey Re-formed.* Ithaca/London.

Ahrensdorf, P. J. (1995) *The Death of Socrates and the Life of Philosophy.* Albany.

Alden, M. (1983) "When did Achilles come back?" in *Mélanges Edouard Delebecque.* Intr. C. Froidefond. Aix-en-Provence: 3–9.

(2000) *Homer Beside Himself: Para-Narratives in the Iliad.* Oxford.

Allen, C. and Bekoff, M. (1999) *Species of Mind: The Philosophy and Biology of Cognitive Ethology.* Cambridge, MA.

Allen, C. and Saidel, E. (1998) "The evolution of reference," in Cummins and Allen (1998) 183–203.

Allen, D. S. (2000) *The World of Prometheus: The Politics of Punishing in Democratic Athens.* Princeton.

Allen, J. P. (1997) "The celestial realm," in *Ancient Egypt*, ed. D. P. Silverman. New York: 114–31.

Allen, R. E. (1980) *Socrates and Legal Obligation.* Minneapolis.

(1996) "The trial of Socrates: a study in the morality of the criminal process," in Prior (1996) vol. II: 1–17.

Amouretti, M. C. (2000) "Paysage et alimentation dans le monde grec antique: conclusion," *Pallas* 52: 221–8.

Andersen, Ø. (1975) *Paradeigmata: Beiträge zum Verständnis der Ilias.* Oslo.

(1977) "Odysseus and the wooden horse," *Sym. Osl.* 52: 5–18.

(1987) "Myth, paradigm and spatial form in the *Iliad*," in *Homer: Beyond Oral Poetry*, eds. J. M. Bremer et al. Amsterdam: 1–13.

(1990) "The making of the past in the *Iliad*," *HSCPh* 93: 25–45.

(1998) "Allusion and the audience of Homer," in Paisi-Apostolopoulou (1998) 137–49.

Anderson, J. K. (1961) *Ancient Greek Horsemanship*. Berkeley/LA.

(1985) *Hunting in the Ancient World*. Berkeley/LA/London.

Anderson, W. S. (1958) "Calypso and Elysium," *CJ* 54: 2–11.

Anhalt, E. K. (1995) "Barrier and transcendence: the door and the eagle in *Iliad* 24.314–21," *CQ* 45: 280–95.

(2001–2) "A Matter of perspective: Penelope and the nightingale in *Odyssey* 19.512–34," *CJ* 97: 145–59.

Annas, J. (1981) *An Introduction to Plato's Republic*. Oxford.

(1992) "Plato the sceptic," in Klagge and Smith (1992) 43–72.

Apthorp, M. P. (1980) "The obstacles to Telemachus' return," *CQ* 30: 1–22.

Arend, W. (1933) *Die typischen Scenen bei Homer*. Berlin.

Arens, W. (1979) *The Man-Eating Myth: Anthropology and Anthropophagy*. Oxford.

Arluke, A. and Sanders, C. R. (1996) *Regarding Animals*. Philadelphia.

Arnason, J. P. (2001) "Autonomy and axiality: comparative perspectives in the Greek breakthrough," in Arnason and Murphy (2001a) 155–206.

Arnason, J. P. and Murphy, P. (eds.) (2001a) *Agon, Logos, Polis: The Greek Achievement and its Aftermath*. Stuttgart.

(2001b) "Introduction," in Arnason and Murphy (2001a) 7–14.

Arnott, P. D. (1989) *Public Performance in the Greek Theatre*. London.

Arthur, M. B. (1980–81) "The tortoise and the mirror: Erinna *PSI* 1090," *CW* 74: 53–65.

Ascone, F. R. and Arkow, P. (1999) *Child Abuse, Domestic Violence, and Animal Abuse: Linking the Circles of Compassion for Prevention and Intervention*. West Lafayette, IN.

Atkinson, J. (1999) "Truth and reconciliation the Athenian way," *AC* 42: 5–13.

Auger, D. (1996) "Variations sur l'hybride: le mythe des centaures, Pindare et Sophocle," *Uranie* 6: 61–79.

Ausland, H. W. (2002) "Forensic characteristics of Socratic argumentation," in Scott (2002) 36–60.

Austin, N. (1960) "Telemachos polymechanos," *CSCA* 2: 45–63.

(1975) *Archery at the Dark Side of the Moon*. Berkeley.

(1978) "The function of the Digressions in the *Iliad*," in *Essays on the Iliad*, ed. J. Wright. Bloomington: 70–84.

(1983) "Odysseus and the Cyclops: who is who?" in *Approaches to Homer*, eds. C. A. Rubino and C. W. Shelmerdine. Austin: 3–37.

(1999) "Anger and disease in Homer's *Iliad*," in Kazazis and Rengakos (1999) 11–49.

Avery, H. C. (1998) "Achilles' third father," *Hermes* 126: 389–97.

Bacon, H. H. (1961) *Barbarians in Greek Tragedy*. New Haven.

(2001) "The Furies' homecoming," *CP* 96: 48–59.

Badham, P. (1998) "Do animals have immortal souls?" in Linzey and Yamamoto (1998) 181–9.

Baker, S. (1993) *Picturing the Beast: Animals, Identity and Representation.* Manchester/New York.

Bakker, E. J. (1995) "Noun-Epithet formulas, Milman Parry, and the grammar of poetry," in Crielaard (1995) 97–125.

(1997) *Poetry in Speech: Orality in Homeric Discourse.* Ithaca/London.

Baldry, H. C. (1952) "Who invented the golden age?" *CQ* 2: 83–92.

(1965) *The Unity of Mankind in Greek Thought.* Cambridge.

Barck, C. (1976) *Wort und Tat bei Homer.* Hildesheim/New York.

Baron, D. (1986) *Grammar and Gender.* New Haven/London.

Barringer, J. M. (2001) *The Hunt in Ancient Greece.* Baltimore/London.

Baslez, M.-F. (1984) *L' etranger dans la Grèce antique.* Paris.

Battegazzore, A. M. (1995) "La dicotomia greci-barbari nella grecia classica: reflessioni su cause ed effetti di una visione etnocentrica," *Sandalion* 18: 5–34.

Bavidge, M. and Ground, I. (1994) *Can We Understand Animal Minds?* New York.

Beck, D. (1998–9) "Speech introductions and the character development of Telemachus," *CJ* 94: 121–41.

Beck, W. (1991) "Dogs, dwellings, and masters: ensemble and symbol in the Odyssey," *Hermes* 119: 158–67.

Beekes, R. S. P. (1998) "*Hades* and *Elysion*," in *Mír Curad: Studies in Honor of Calvert Watkins*, eds. J. Jasonoff, H. C. Melchert, L. Oliver. Innsbruck: 17–28.

Bekoff, M. (2002) *Minding Animals: Awareness, Emotions, and Heart.* Oxford.

Belfiore, E. (1980) "Elenchus, epode, and magic: Socrates as Silenus," *Phoenix* 34: 128–37.

(1983) "The Eagles' feast and the Trojan horse: corrupted fertility in the *Agamemnon*," *Maia* 35: 3–12.

(1998) "Harming friends: problematic reciprocity in Greek tragedy," in Gill, Postlethwaite, and Seaford (1998) 139–58.

Belmont, D. E. (1967) "Telemachos and Nausicaa: a study of youth," *CJ* 63: 1–9.

Belsey, C. (1985) *The Subject of Tragedy: Identity and Difference in Renaissance Drama.* London/New York.

Bemelmans, R. (2002) "Why does Protagoras rush off? Self-refutation and haste in Plato, *Theaetetus* 169a–171d," *Anc. Phil.* 22: 75–86.

Benardete, S. (1963) "Achilles and the *Iliad*," *Hermes* 91: 1–16.

(1997) "Plato's Theaetetus on the way of the logos," *Rmeta* 51: 25–53.

Benson, H. H. (1987) "The problem of the elenchos reconsidered," *AncPhil* 7: 67–85.

(1989) "A note on eristic and the Socratic elenchus," *JHPh* 27: 591–9.

(1990a) "The priority of definition and the Socratic elenchus," *OSAPh* 8: 19–65.

(1990b) "Meno, the slave boy and the elenchos," *Phronesis* 35: 128–58.

Bergren, A. L. T. (1981) "Helen's 'good drug': *Odyssey* IV 1–305," in *Contemporary Literary Hermeneutics and the Interpretation of Classical Texts*, ed. S. Kresic. Ottawa: 201–14.

(1983) "Language and the female in early Greek thought," *Arethusa* 16: 69–95.

Bergvall, V. L., J. M. Bing, A. F. Freed (eds.) (1996) *Rethinking Language and Gender Research: Theory and Practice*. London.

Bernand, A. (1986) "Les animaux dans la tragédie grecque," *DHA* 12: 241–69.

Bers, V. (1985) "Dikastic *Thorubos*," in Cartledge and Harvey (1985). 1–15.

Berthiaume, G. (1982) *Les rôles du mágeiros. Mnemosyne* Suppl. 170. Leiden.

Besslich, S. (1966) *Schweigen-Verschweigen-Übergehen: Die Darstellung des Unausgesprochenen in der Odyssee*. Heidelberg.

Betensky, A. (1978) "Aeschylus' *Oresteia*: the power of Clytemnestra," *Ramus* 7: 11–25.

Beversluis, J. (1996) "Vlastos's quest for the historical Socrates," in Prior (1996) vol. I: 202–23.

(2000) *Cross-Examining Socrates: A Defense of the Interlocutors in Plato's Early Dialogues*. Cambridge.

Bickerton, D. (1990) *Language and Species*. Chicago/London.

Birge, D. (1993) "Ambiguity and the stag in *Odyssey* 10," *Helios* 20: 17–28.

Blank, D. L. (1993) "The arousal of emotion in Plato's dialogues," *CQ* 43: 428–39.

Blok, J. H. (2001) "Virtual voices: toward a choreography of women's speech in classical Athens," in Lardinois and McClure (2001) 95–116.

Blok, J. and Mason, P. (eds.) (1987) *Sexual Asymmetry: Studies in Ancient Society*. Amsterdam.

Blondell, R. (2000) "Letting Plato speak for himself: character and method in the *Republic*," in Press (2000) 127–46.

(2002) *The Play of Character in Plato's Dialogues*. Cambridge.

Bloom, P. (1998) "Some issues in the evolution of language and thought," in Cummins and Allen (1998) 204–23.

Blundell, M. W. (1989) *Helping Friends and Harming Enemies: A Study in Sophocles and Greek Ethics*. Cambridge.

Blundell, S. (1986) *The Origins of Civilization in Greek and Roman Thought*. London.

(1995) *Women in Ancient Greece*. London.

Bodson, L. (1978) *Hiera Zôa*. Brussels.

(1983) "Attitudes toward animals in Greco-Roman antiquity," *Int. J. Stud. Anim. Prob.* 4: 312–19.

(1998) "Ancient Greek views on the exotic animal," *Arctos* 32: 61–85.

Boedeker, D. (1984) *Descent from Heaven: Images of Dew in Greek Poetry and Religion*. Chico.

Boedeker, D. and Raaflaub, K. A. (eds.) (1998) *Democracy, Empire, and the Arts in Fifth-Century Athens*. Cambridge, MA/London.

Boeder, H. (1959) "Der frühgriechische Wortgebrauch von Logos und Aletheia," *Archiv für Begriffsgeschichte* 4: 82–112.

Bolmarcich, S. (2001) "ΟΜΟΦΡΟΣΥΝΗ in the *Odyssey*," *CP* 96: 205–13.

Bologna, C. (1978) "Il linguaggio del silenzio," *Studi Storico Religiosi* 2: 305–42.

Bömer, F. (1957) "Interpretationen zu den Fasti des Ovid," *Gymnasium* 64: 112–35.

Bonnafé, A. (1984) *Poési, nature et sacré*, vol. I. Lyon.

Bonnefoy, Y. (ed.) (1991) *Mythologies*. W. Doniger, tr. Chicago and London.

Bonnet, C., Jourdain-Annequin, C. and Pirenne-Delforge, V. (eds.) (1998) *Le bestiaire d' Héraclès. Kernos* Suppl. 7. Liège.

Bouvrie, S. des. (1990) *Women in Greek Tragedy: An Anthropological Approach*. Oslo.

Bowie, A. M. (1993) "Religion and politics in Aeschylus' *Oresteia*," *CQ* 43: 10–31.

Bras-Chopard, A. le. (2000) *Le zoo des Philosophes: de la bestialisation à l'exclusion*. Plon.

Braswell, B. K. (1971) "Mythological innovation in the *Iliad*," *CQ* 21: 16–26.

Bremer, J. M. (2000) "The Amazons in the imagination of the Greeks," *Acta Ant. Hung*. 40: 51–9.

Bremmer, J. N. (1981) "Plutarch and the naming of Greek women," *AJP* 102: 425–6.

(1983) *The Early Greek Concept of the Soul*. Princeton.

(1987) "The old women of ancient Greece," in Blok and Mason (1987). 191–215.

(1988) "La plasticité du mythe: Méléagre dans la poésie homérique," in *Métamorphoses du mythe en Grèce antique*, ed. C. Calame. Genève: 37–56.

(1991) "Walking, standing, and sitting in ancient Greek culture," in *A Cultural History of Gesture*, eds. J. Bremmer and H. Roodenburg. Ithaca: 15–35.

(1994) "The soul, death and afterlife in early and classical Greece," in *Hidden Futures: Death and Immortality in Ancient Egypt, Anatolia, the Classical, Biblical and Arabic-Islamic World*, eds. J. M. Bremmer, Th. P. J. van den Hout, and R. Peters. Leiden: 91–106.

(2002) *The Rise and Fall of the Afterlife*. London/New York.

Brenk, F. E. (1986) "Dear child: the speech of Phoenix and the tragedy of Achilleus in the ninth book of the *Iliad*," *Eranos* 84: 77–86.

Briant, P. (2002) "History and ideology: the Greeks and 'Persian decadence'," A. Nevill, tr., in Harrison (2002a) 193–210.

Brickhouse, T. C. and Smith, N. D. (1989) *Socrates on Trial*. Princeton.

(1994) *Plato's Socrates*. New York/Oxford.

(2002) "The Socratic *elenchos*?" in Scott (2002) 145–57.

Brink, C. O. (1956) "Οἰκείωσις and οἰκειότης: Theophrastus and Zeno on nature in moral theory," *Phronesis* 1: 123–45.

Briquel, D. (1995) "Des comparaisons animales homériques aux fauves indo-européens," *Kernos* 8: 31–9.

Brixhe, C. (1988) "La langue de l'étranger non grec chez Aristophane," in *L'Etranger dans le monde grec*, ed. R. Lonis. Nancy: 113–38.

Brock, R. and Hodkinson, S. (eds.) (2000a) *Alternatives to Athens*. Oxford.

(2000b) "Introduction: alternatives to the democratic polis," in Brock and Hodkinson (2000a) 1–31.

Brown, A. L. (1983) "The Erinyes in the *Oresteia*: real life, the supernatural, and the stage," *JHS* 103: 13–34.

Brown, A. S. (1997) "Aphrodite and the Pandora complex," *CQ* 47: 26–47.

Brown, C. G. (1996) "In the Cyclops' cave: revenge and justice in *Odyssey* 9," *Mnem*. 49: 1–29.

Brown, C. S. (1966) "Odysseus and Polyphemus: the name and the curse," *Comp. Lit.* 18: 193–202.

Browning, R. (2002) "Greeks and others: from antiquity to the Renaissance," in Harrison (2002a) 257–77.

Bruit Zaidman, L. (1992) "Pandora's daughters and rituals in Grecian cities," in Schmitt Pantel (1992a) 338–76.

Bruns, G. (1970) *Küchenwesen und Mahlzeiten.* Archaeologia Homerica IIQ. Göttingen.

Bryant, A. A. (1907) "Boyhood and youth in the days of Aristophanes," *HSCPh* 18: 73–122.

Buchheit, V. (1986) "Tierfriede in der Antike," *WJA* 12: 143–67.

Buchholz, H.-G., Jöhrens, G., and Maull, I. (1973) *Jagd und Fischfang.* Archaeologia Homerica IIJ. Göttingen.

Bucholz, M., Liang, A. C., and Sutton, L. A. (eds.) (1999) *Reinventing Identities: The Gendered Self in Discourse.* Oxford.

Budiansky, S. (1998) *If a Lion Could Talk: Animal Intelligence and the Evolution of Consiousness.* New York.

Burckhardt, J. (1998) *The Greeks and Greek Civilization.* S. Stern, tr. London.

Burford, A. (1993) *Land and Labor in the Greek World.* Baltimore/London.

Burgess, J. S. (1995) "Achilles' heel: the death of Achilles in ancient myth," *CA* 14: 217–43.

(2001) *The Tradition of the Trojan War in Homer and the Epic Cycle.* Baltimore/London.

Burke, P. (1993) *The Art of Conversation.* Ithaca.

Burkert, W. (1966) "Greek tragedy and sacrifical ritual," *GRBS* 7: 87–121.

(1972) *Lore and Science in Ancient Pythagoreanism.* E. L. Minar, Jr., tr. Cambridge, MA.

(1979) *Structure and History in Greek Mythology and Ritual.* Berkeley/London/LA.

(1983) *Homo Necans: The Anthropology of Ancient Greek Sacrificial Ritual and Myth.* P. Bing, tr. Berkeley/LA/London.

(1985) *Greek Religion.* J. Raffan, tr. Cambridge, MA.

(1987) *Ancient Mystery Cults.* Cambridge, MA.

(1992) *The Orientalizing Revolution.* Cambridge, MA.

Burnett, A. P. (1998) *Revenge in Attic and Later Tragedy.* Berkeley/LA/London.

Burnyeat, M. (1997) "The impiety of Socrates," *AncPhil* 17: 1–12.

Burton, J. (1998) "Women's commensality in the ancient Greek world," *G&R* 45: 143–65.

Bushnell, R. W. (1982) "Reading "winged words": Homeric bird signs, similes, and epiphanies," *Helios* 9: 1–13.

Buxton, R. G. A. (1982) *Peitho. A Study of Persuasion in Greek Tragedy.* Cambridge.

(1994) *Imaginary Greece: The Contexts of Mythology.* Cambridge.

(ed.) (1999) *From Myth to Reason? Studies in the Development of Greek Thought.* Oxford.

Byl, S. (1976) "Lamentations sur la vieillesse chez Homère et les poètes lyriques des VIIe et VIe siècles," *LEC* 44: 234–44.

Cairns, D. L. (1993) *Aidôs: the Psychology and Ethics of Honour and Shame in Ancient Greek Literature*. Oxford.

(1996) "*Hybris*, dishonour, and thinking big," *JHS* 116: 1–32.

Callaway, J. A. and Miller, J. M. (1999) "The settlement in Canaan: the period of the judges," in *Ancient Israel: From Abraham to the Roman Destruction of the Temple*, ed. H. Shanks. Washington, D.C.: 55–89.

Cameron, D. (1985) *Feminism and Linguistic Theory*. New York.

Campbell, A. Y. (1935) "Aeschylus' *Agamemnon* 1223–38 and treacherous monsters," *CQ* 29: 25–36.

Carawan, E. (2002) "The Athenian amnesty and the 'scrutiny of the laws'," *JHS* 122: 1–23.

Carter, L. B. (1986) *The Quiet Athenian*. Oxford.

Cartledge, P. (1981) "Spartan wives: liberation or license?" *CQ* 31: 84–105, reprinted in *Spartan Reflections* (2001), Berkeley/LA: 106–26.

(1993a) *The Greeks: A Portrait of Self and Others*. Oxford/New York. (2nd edition, 2002)

(1993b) "The silent women of Thucydides: 2.45.2 re-viewed," in Rosen and Farrell (1993) 125–32.

(1995) "'We are all Greeks'? Ancient (especially Herodotean) and modern contestations of Hellenism," *BICS* 40: 75–82.

Cartledge, P. A. and Harvey, F. D. (eds.) (1985) *Crux: Essays in Greek History presented to G.E.M. de Ste Croix on his 75th birthday*. Exeter and London.

Casel, O. (1919) *De Philosophorum Graecorum Silentio Mystico*. Giessen.

Casevitz, M. (1991) "*Hellenismos*: formation et fonction des verbes en -ίζω et de leurs dérivés," in Saïd (1991) 9–16.

(1998) "Vieillesse grecque, vieillesse troyenne," in Isebaert and Lebrun (1998) 55–69.

Cassin, B. and Labarrière, J.-L. (eds.) (1997) *L'animal dans l'antiquité*. Paris.

Castoriadis, C. (1991) *Philosophy, Politics, Autonomy*. New York/Oxford.

(2001) "Aeschylean anthropology and Sophoclean self-creation of *anthropos*," in Arnason and Murphy (2001a) 138–54.

Castriota, D. (2000) "Justice, kingship, and imperialism: rhetoric and reality in fifth-century B.C. representations following the Persian wars," in Cohen (2000b) 443–79.

Cavalieri, P. and Singer, P. (eds.) (1993) *The Great Ape Project: Equality beyond Humanity*. New York.

Ceccarelli, P. (2000) "Life among the savages and escape from the city," in Harvey and Wilkins (2000) 453–71.

Chappell, T. D. J. (1993) "The virtues of Thrasymachus," *Phronesis* 38: 1–17.

Chaston, C. (2002) "Three models of authority in the *Odyssey*," *CW* 96: 3–19.

Cheyns, A. (1985) "Recherche sur l'emploi des synonymes ἦτορ, κῆρ et κραδίη dans l'*Iliade* et l'*Odyssée*," *Rev. Belge Philol. Hist.* 63: 15–73.

Chiasson, C. C. (1999–2000) "Σωφρονοῦντες ἐν χρόνωι: the Athenians and time in Aeschylus' *Eumenides*," *CJ* 95: 139–61.

Chroust, A. H. (1957) *Socrates, Man and Myth: The Two Socratic Apologies of Xenophon*. Notre Dame.

Clark, G. (1998) "The fathers and the animals: the rule of reason?" in Linzey and Yamamoto (1998) 67–79.

(2000) "Animal passions," *G&R* 47: 88–93.

Clark, M. (1998) "Chryses' supplication: speech act and mythological allusion," *CA* 17: 5–24.

(2001) "Was Telemachus rude to his mother? *Odyssey* 1.356–9," *CP* 96: 335–54.

(2002) "Fighting words: how heroes argue," *Arethusa* 35: 99–115.

Clark, S. R. L. (1975) *Aristotle's Man: Speculations upon Aristotelian Anthropology*. Oxford.

(1982) "Aristotle's woman," *Hist. Pol. Thought* 3: 177–91.

(1984a) *The Moral Status of Animals*. Oxford/New York.

(1989) "Ethical problems in animal welfare," in *The Status of Animals: Ethics, Education and Welfare*, eds. D. Paterson and M. Palmer. Wallingford: 5–14.

Clarke, H. W. (1967) *The Art of the Odyssey*. Englewood Cliffs, NJ.

Clarke, M. (1995) "Between lions and men: images of the hero in the *Iliad*," *GRBS* 36: 137–59.

(1999) *Flesh and Spirit in the Songs of Homer*. Oxford.

(2001) "'Heart-cutting talk': Homeric κερτομέω and related words," *CQ* 51: 329–38.

Claus, D. B. (1981) *Toward the Soul: An Inquiry into the Meaning of Ψυχή before Plato*. New Haven.

Clay, D. (1994) "The origins of the Socratic dialogue," in Vander Waerdt (1994a) 23–47.

Clay, J. S. (1972) "The planktai and moly: divine naming and knowing in Homer," *Hermes* 100: 127–31.

(1974) "Demas and aude: the nature of divine transformation in Homer," *Hermes* 102: 129–36.

(1981–2) "Immortal and ageless forever," *CJ* 77: 112–17.

(1983) *The Wrath of Athena. Gods and Men in the Odyssey*. Princeton.

Clinton, K. (1988) "Artemis and the sacrifice of Iphigenia in Aeschylus' *Agamemnon*," in *Language and the Tragic Hero*, ed. P. Pucci. Atlanta: 1–24.

Coates, P. (1998) *Nature: Western Attitudes since Ancient Times*. Berkeley/LA/London.

Cohen, B. (2000a) "Introduction," in Cohen (2000b) 3–20.

(ed.) (2000b) *Not the Classical Ideal: Athens and the Construction of the Other in Greek Art*. Leiden/Boston/Köln.

Cohen, C. and Regan, T. (2001) *The Animal Rights Debate*. Lanham, MD.

Cohen, D. (1989) "Seclusion, separation, and the status of women in classical Athens," *G&R* 36: 3–15.

(1991) *Law, Sexuality, and Society: The Enforcement of Morals in Classical Athens*. Cambridge.

(1995) *Law, Violence, and Community in Classical Athens*. Cambridge.

Cole, E. B. (1991) "Plato on the souls of beasts," circulated for Studies in Ancient Greek Philosophy Central, Chicago, 26 April 1991.

(1992) "Theophrastus and Aristotle on animal intelligence," in *Theophrastus: His Psychological, Doxographical, and Scientific Writings*. Rutgers University Studies in Classical Humanities, vol. V, eds. W. W. Fortenbaugh and D. Gutas. New Brunswick/London: 44–62.

Cole, T. (1967) *Democritus and the Sources of Greek Anthropology*. Atlanta.

Coleman, R. (1977) *Vergil: Eclogues*. Cambridge.

Collins, B. J. (ed.) (2002) *A History of the Animal World in the Ancient Near East*. Leiden/Boston/Köln.

Collins, C. (1996) *Authority Figures*. Lanham.

Collins, D. (1998) *Immortal Armor: The Concept of Alkê in Archaic Greek Poetry*. Lanham.

Colvin, S. (1999) *Dialect in Aristophanes and the Politics of Language in Ancient Greek Literature*. Oxford.

Combellack, F. M. (1953) "Homer's savage fish," *CJ* 48: 257–61.

(1987) "The λύσις ἐκ τῆς λέξεως," *AJP* 108: 202–19.

Compton, T. (1990) "The trial of Socrates: poetic *vitae* (Aesop, Archilochus, Homer) as background for Plato's *Apology*," *AJP* 111: 330–47.

Conacher, D. J. (1977) "Prometheus as founder of the arts," *GRBS* 18: 189–206.

Connor, W. R. 1991. "The other 399: religion and the trial of Socrates," in *Georgica. Greek Studies in Honour of George Cawkwell*. Institute of Classical Studies Bulletin Supplement 58, eds. M. A. Flower and M. Toher. London: 49–56.

Cook, A. B. (1895) "The bee in Greek mythology," *JHS* 15: 1–24.

Cook, E. F. (1995) *The Odyssey in Athens: Myths of Cultural Origins*. Ithaca/London.

(1999) "'Active' and 'passive' heroics in the *Odyssey*," *CW* 93: 149–67.

Cosset, E. (1983) "Choix formulaire ou choix semantique? La désignation d'Ulysse et de la lance (ἔγχος) dan l'*Iliade*," *REA* 85: 191–8.

(1985) "Esthétique et système formulaire dans l'*Iliade*," *LEC* 53: 331–40.

Craig, L. H. (1994) *The War Lover: A Study of Plato's Republic*. Toronto/Buffalo/London.

Craik, E. M. (ed.) (1990) *"Owls to Athens," Essays on Classical Subjects Presented to Sir Kenneth Dover*. Oxford.

Cramer, O. C. (1976) "Speech and silence in the *Iliad*," *CJ* 71: 300–4.

Crane, G. (1996) *The Blinded Eye: Thucydides and the New Written Word*. Lanham.

Creed, J. L. (1973) "Moral values in the age of Thucydides," *CQ* 23: 213–31.

Crielaard, J. P. (ed.) (1995) *Homeric Questions*. Amsterdam.

Crooks, J. (1998) "Socrates' last words: another look at an ancient riddle," *CQ* 48: 117–25.

Cropsey, J. (1986) "The dramatic end of Plato's Socrates," *Interpretation* 14: 155–75.

Crotty, K. (1994) *The Poetics of Exile*. London.

Csapo, E. (1993) "Deep ambivalence: notes on a Greek cockfight," *Phoenix* 47: 1–28; 115–24.

Cummins, D. D. and Allen, C. (eds.) (1998) *The Evolution of the Mind.* New York/Oxford.

Dahlmann, J. H. (1928) *De philosophorum graecorum sententiis ad loquellae originem pertinentibus capita duo.* Diss. Leipzig.

Dalby, A. (1995) *Siren Feasts: A History of Food and Gastronomy in Greece.* London/New York.

Dale, A. T. (1982) "Homeric ἐπητής/ἐπητύς: meaning and etymology," *Glotta* 60: 205–14.

Damasio, A. R. (1994) *Descartes' Error: Emotion, Reason, and the Human Brain.* New York.

  (1999) *The Feeling of What Happens: Body and Emotion in the Making of Consciousness.* New York/San Diego/London.

Darmon, J.-P. (1991) "The semantic value of animals in Greek mythology," in Bonnefoy (1991) 428.

Daube, B. (1939) *Zu den Rechtsproblemen in Aischylos' Agamemnon.* Zürich/Leipzig.

Dauenhauer, B. P. (1980) *Silence: The Phenomenon and its Ontological Significance.* Bloomington.

Dauge, Y. A. (1981) *Le barbare.* Collection Latomus 176. Bruxelles.

David, E. (1991) *Old Age in Sparta.* Amsterdam.

  (1999) "Sparta's *kosmos* of silence," in Hodkinson and Powell (1999). 117–46.

Davidson, J. (1997) *Courtesans and Fishcakes.* London.

Davies, A. M. (2002) "The Greek notion of dialect," in Harrison (2002a). 153–71.

Davies, M. (1987a) "Description by negation: history of a thought-pattern in ancient accounts of blissful life," *Prometheus* 13: 265–84.

  (1987b) "The ancient Greeks on why mankind does not live forever," *MH* 44: 65–75.

  (1988) "'Ere the world began to be': description by negation in cosmogonic literature," *Prometheus* 14: 15–24.

  (1994) "*Odyssey* 24.474–7: murder or mutilation?" *CQ* 44: 534–6.

  (1997) "Feasting and food in Homer: realism and stylisation," *Prometheus* 23: 97–107.

Dawkins, M. S. (1993) *Through Our Eyes Only? The search for animal consciousness.* Oxford/New York/Heidelberg.

Dawson, D. (1992) *Cities of the Gods: Communist Utopias in Greek Thought.* New York.

Deacon, T. W. (1997) *The Symbolic Species.* New York/London.

Debnar, P. (2001) *Speaking the Same Language: Speech and Audience in Thucydides' Spartan Debates.* Ann Arbor.

Decreus, F. (2000) "The *Oresteia*, or the myth of the western metropolis between Habermas and Foucault," *Graz. Beitr.* 23: 1–21.

DeForest, M. (ed.) (1993) *Woman's Power, Man's Game. Essays on Classical Antiquity in Honor of Joy K. King.* Waucanda, IL.

Degener, J. M. (2001) "The *caesura* of the *symbolon* in Aeschylus' *Agamemnon*," *Arethusa* 34: 61–95.

DeGrazia, D. (1996) *Taking Animals Seriously: Mental Life and Moral Status.* New York.

Deichgräber, K. (1972) *Der letzte Gesang der Ilias.* Mainz.

De Lacy, P. H. (1939) "The Epicurean analysis of language," *AJP* 60: 85–92.

Delebecque, E. (1951) *Le cheval dans l'Iliade.* Paris.

De Luce, J. (1993) "'O for a thousand tongues to sing': a footnote on metamorphoses, silence, and power," in DeForest (1993) 305–21.

Dennett, D. C. (1991) *Consciousness Explained.* Boston/New York.

(1995) *Darwin's Dangerous Idea: Evolution and the Meanings of Life.* New York.

(1996) *Kinds of Minds: Toward an Understanding of Consciousness.* New York.

Depew, D. J. (1995) "Humans and other political animals in Aristotle's *History of Animals*," *Phronesis* 40: 156–81.

Desclos, M.-L. (1997) "'Le renard dit au lion . . .' (*Alcibiade Majeur*, 123A) ou Socrate à la manière d'Ésope," in Cassin and Labarrière (1997) 395–417.

Detienne, M. (1979) *Dionysus Slain.* M. and L. Muellner, trs. Baltimore.

(1981) "Between beasts and gods," in Gordon (1981) 215–28.

(1989) "Culinary practices and the spirit of sacrifice," in Detienne and Vernant (1989) 1–20.

Detienne, M. and Vernant, J.-P. (1989) *The Cuisine of Sacrifice among the Greeks.* P. Wissing, tr. Chicago/London.

(1991) *Cunning Intelligence in Greek Culture and Society.* J. Lloyd, tr. Chicago/London.

Dewald, C. (1981) "Women and culture in Herodotus' histories," in *Reflections of Women in Antiquity*, ed. H. P. Foley. New York: 91–125.

Dickerman, S. O. (1911) "Some stock illustrations of animal intelligence in Greek psychology," *TAPA* 42: 123–30.

Dickey, E. (1996) *Greek Forms of Address: From Herodotus to Lucian.* Oxford.

Dickson, K. (1990) "A typology of mediation in Homer," *Oral Tradition* 5: 37–71.

(1995) *Nestor: Poetic Memory in Greek Epic.* New York.

Dierauer, U. (1977) *Tier und Mensch im Denken der Antike.* Studien zur antiken Philosophie 6. Amsterdam.

(1997) "Raison ou instinct? Le développement de la zoopsychologie antique," in Cassin and Labarrière (1997) 3–30.

Dietrich, B. C. (1965) *Death, Fate, and the Gods.* London.

(1983) "Divine epiphanies in Homer," *Numen* 30: 53–79.

Dietz, G. (2000) *Menschenwürde bei Homer: Vorträge und Aufsätze.* Heidelberg.

Dihle, A. (1994) *Die Griechen und die Fremden.* München.

Dijk, G. J. van. (1997) *AINOI, LOGOI, MUTHOI: Fables in Archaic, Classical, and Hellenistic Greek Literature. Mnemosyne* Suppl. 166. Leiden.

Dillon, J. (1992) "Plato and the golden age," *Hermathena* 153: 21–36.

Dillon, M. (2002) *Girls and Women in Classical Greek Religion.* London/New York.

Dimock, G. E. (1962) "The name of Odysseus," in *Homer: A Collection of Critical Essays*, eds. G. Steiner and R. Fagles. Englewood Cliffs, NJ: 106–21.

Dinzelbacher, P. (ed.) (2000) *Mensch und Tier in der Geschichte Europas.* Stuttgart.

Dirlmeier, F. (1967) "Die 'schreckliche' Kalypso," in *Lebende Antike: Symposium für R. Suehnel*, eds. H. Meller and H.-J. Zimmermann. Berlin: 20–6.

Dobrov, G. W. (ed.) (1997) *The City as Comedy: Society and Representation in Athenian Drama*. Chapel Hill/London.

Dodds, E. R. (1951) *The Greeks and the Irrational*. Berkeley/LA/London.

(1973) *The Ancient Concept of Progress and other Essays on Greek Literature and Belief*. Oxford.

Doherty, L. E. (1995) *Siren Songs. Gender, Audiences, and Narrators in the Odyssey*. Ann Arbor.

Dombrowski, D. A. (1984a) *The Philosophy of Vegetarianism*. Amherst.

(1984b) "Vegetarianism and the argument from marginal cases in Porphyry," *JHI* 45: 141–3.

(1997) *Babies and Beasts: The Argument from Marginal Cases*. Urbana/Chicago.

Donadoni, S. F. (1986) *Cultura dell' Antico Egitto*. Rome.

Donald, M. (2001) *A Mind So Rare: The Evolution of Human Consciousness*. New York/London.

Donlan, W. (1993) "Duelling with gifts in the *Iliad*; as the audience saw it," *Colby Quarterly* 29: 155–72.

Donohue, B. (1997) "The dramatic significance of Cephalus in Plato's *Republic*," *Teaching Philosophy* 20: 239–49.

Donovan, J. and Adams, C. J. (eds.) (1996) *Beyond Animal Rights: A Feminist Caring Ethic for the Treatment of Animals*. New York.

Döring, K. (1987) "Der Sokrates der Platonischen Apologie und die Frage nach dem historischen Sokrates," *Würzburger Jahrbücher für die Altertumswissenschaft* 14: 75–94.

Dougherty, C. (2001) *The Raft of Odysseus: The Ethnographic Imagination of Homer's Odyssey*. Oxford.

Douglas, M. (1966) *Purity and Danger*. London.

(1990) "The pangolin revisited: a new approach to animal symbolism," in Willis (1990) 25–36.

Dover, K. J. (1974) *Greek Popular Morality in the Time of Plato and Aristotle*. Berkeley/LA.

(1983) "The portrayal of moral evaluation in Greek poetry," *JHS* 103: 35–48.

(1997) "Language and character in Aristophanes," in *Greek and the Greeks: Collected Papers Volume I: Language, Poetry, Drama*. Oxford: 237–48.

Dowden, K. (1992) *The Uses of Greek Mythology*. London/New York.

duBois, P. (1991) *Torture and Truth*. New York/London.

(2001) *Trojan Horses: Saving Classics from the Conservatives*. New York/London.

Ducat, J. (1999) "Perspectives on Spartan education in the classical period," in Hodkinson and Powell (1999) 43–66.

Duchemin, J. (1960) "Aspects pastoraux de la poésie Homérique: les comparaisons dans l'*Iliade*," *REG* 73: 362–415.

Due, O. S. (1965) "The meaning of the Homeric formula χρυσηλάκατος κελαδεινή," *C&M* 26: 1–9.

Dumont, J. (2001) *Les animaux dans l'antiquité grecque*. Paris et al.

Dumortier, J. (1975) *Les Images dans la Poésie d'Eschyle*. Paris.

Dunayer, J. (2001) *Animal Equality: Language and Liberation*. Derwood, MD.

Dunbar, N. (1997) "Aristophane, ornithophile et ornithophage," in *Aristophane: la langue, la scène, la cité*, eds. P. Thiercy and M. Menu. Bari: 113–29.

Dunbar, R. I. M. (1996) *Grooming, Gossip, and the Evolution of Language*. Cambridge, MA.

Dunkle, R. (1997) "Swift-Footed Achilles," *CW* 90: 227–34.

Dupont-Roc, R. and Le Bouluec, A. (1976) "Le charme du récit (*Odyssée*, IV, 219–89)," in *Écriture et théorie poétiques: lectures d'Homère, Eschyle, Platon, Aristote*. Paris: 30–9.

Durand, J.-L. (1989) "Greek animals: toward a topology of edible bodies," in Detienne and Vernant (1989) 87–118.

Duzer, A. van. (1996) *Duality and Structure in the Iliad and Odyssey*. New York.

Eades, T. (1996) "Plato, rhetoric, and silence," *Ph&Rh* 29: 244–58.

Earp, F. R. (1948) *The Style of Aeschylus*. Cambridge.

Easterling, P. E. (1987) "Notes on tragedy and epic," in *Papers Given at a Colloquium in Honour of R. R. Winnington-Ingram*. Society for the Promotion of Hellenic Studies, Supplementary Paper 15, ed. L. Rodley. London: 52–62.

(1991) "Men's κλέος and women's γόος: female voices in the *Iliad*." *Journal of Modern Greek Studies* 9: 145–51.

(ed.) (1997a) *The Cambridge Companion to Greek Tragedy*. Cambridge. 1997.

(1997b) "A show for Dionysus," in Easterling (1997a) 36–53.

Ebel, H. (1972) *After Dionysus*. Rutherford.

Eckels, R. P. (1937) *Greek Wolf-Lore*. Philadelphia.

Edelstein, L. (1967) *The Idea of Progress in Classical Antiquity*. Baltimore.

Edmunds, L. (1997) "Myth in Homer," in Morris and Powell (1997) 413–41.

Edmunds, L. and Martin, R. (1977) "Thucydides 2.65.8: ΕΛΕΥΘΕΡѠΣ," *HSCP* 81: 187–93.

Edmunds, S. T. (1990) *Homeric Nêpios*. New York.

Edwards, M. W. (1966) "Some features of Homeric craftsmanship," *TAPA* 97: 115–79.

(1970) "Homeric speech introductions," *HSCPh* 74: 1–36.

(1975) "Type-scenes and Homeric hospitality," *TAPA* 105: 51–72.

(1977) "Agamemnon's decision: freedom and folly in Aeschylus," *CSCA* 10: 17–38.

(1980) "Convention and individuality in *Iliad* I," *HSCPh* 85: 1–28.

(1987) *Homer: Poet of the Iliad*. Baltimore and London.

(1997) "Homeric style and oral poetics," in Morris and Powell (1997) 261–83.

Ehrenberg, V. (1947) "*Polypragmosyne*: a study in Greek politics," *JHS* 67: 46–67.

Ehrlich, P. R. (2000) *Human Natures*. Washington, D.C.

Eide, T. (1981) "Thucydides' λόγος παραμυθητικός·. Thuc. II, 44–5," *Sym. Osl.* 56: 33–45.

Eilberg-Schwartz, H. (1990) *The Savage in Judaism*. Bloomington/Indianapolis.

Elata-Alster, G. (1985) "The king's double bind: paradoxical communication in the parodos of Aeschylus' *Agamemnon*," *Arethusa* 18: 23–46.

Enard, W. et al. (2002) "Molecular evolution of *FOXP2*, a gene involved in speech and language," *Nature* 418 (August 22): 869–72.

Engels, D. (1999) *Classical Cats: The Rise and Fall of the Sacred Cat.* London/New York.

Erler, M. (1987) *Der Sinn der Aporien in den Dialogen Platons: Übungsstücke zur Anleitung im philosophischen Denken.* Untersuchungen zur antiken Literatur und Geschichte 25. Berlin/New York.

Erp Taalman Kip, A. M. van. (1990) *Reader and Spectator: Problems in the Interpretation of Greek Tragedy.* Amsterdam.

(1996) "The unity of the *Oresteia*," in *Tragedy and the Tragic: Greek Theatre and Beyond*, ed. M. S. Silk. Oxford: 119–48.

Euben, J. P., Wallach, J. R. and Ober, J. (eds.) (1994) *Athenian Political Thought and the Reconstruction of American Democracy.* Ithaca/London.

Everson, S. (ed.) (1991) *Psychology.* Cambridge.

(ed.) (1994a) *Language.* Cambridge.

(1994b) "Introduction," in Everson (1994a) 1–9.

Ewans, M. (1975) "Agamemnon at Aulis: a study in the *Oresteia*," *Ramus* 4: 17–32.

(1995) *Aischylos: The Oresteia.* London.

Fagles, R. and Stanford, W. B. (1977) "A reading of the Oresteia," in *Aeschylus: The Oresteia.* New York: 13–97.

Falkner, T. M. (1989) " Ἐπὶ γήραος οὐδῷ: Homeric heroism, old age and the end of the *Odyssey*," in Falkner and de Luce (1989) 21–67.

(1995) *The Poetics of Old Age in Greek Epic, Lyric, and Tragedy.* Norman.

Falkner, T. M. and De Luce, J. (eds.) (1989) *Old Age in Greek and Latin Literature.* Albany.

Faraone, C. A. (1985) "Aeschylus' ὕμνος δέσμιος (*Eum.* 306) and attic judicial curse tablets," *JHS* 105: 150–4.

(1987) "Hephaestus the magician and near eastern parallels for Alcinous' watchdogs," *GRBS* 28: 257–80.

(1991) "The agonistic context of early Greek binding spells," in *Magika Hiera: Ancient Greek Magic and Religion*, eds. C. A. Faraone and D. Obbink. New York: 1–32.

Farron, S. (1979) "The portrayal of women in the *Iliad*," *A Class* 22: 15–31.

Faust, M. (1970) "Die künstlerische Verwendung von κύων 'Hund' in den homerischen Epen," *Glotta* 48: 8–31.

Fauth, W. (1973) "Kulinarisches und Utopisches in der griechischen Komödie," *WS* 7: 39–62.

Fehling, D. (1990) *Herodotus and his "sources".* J. G. Howie, tr. Leeds.

Feinberg, J. (1984) "Potentiality, development, and rights," in *The Problem of Abortion*, 2nd edition, ed. J. Feinberg. Belmont, CA: 145–50.

Felson, N. (1999) "Paradigms of paternity: fathers, sons, and athletic/sexual prowess in Homer's *Odyssey*," in Kazazis and Rengakos (1999) 89–98.

(2002) "*Threpta* and invincible hands: the father–son relationship in *Iliad* 24," *Arethusa* 35: 35–50.

Felson-Rubin, N. (1994) *Regarding Penelope. From Character to Poetics.* Princeton.

Fenik, B. (1974) *Studies in the Odyssey. Hermes* Einzelschriften 20. Wiesbaden.

Ferguson, M. (1998) *Animal Advocacy and Englishwomen, 1780–1900: Patriots, Nation, and Empire.* Ann Arbor.

Ferrari, G. (2002) *Figures of Speech: Men and Maidens in Ancient Greece.* Chicago/London.

Festugière, A. J. (1949) "À propos des arétalogies d'Isis," *Harv. Theol. Rev.* 42: 209–34.

Fiddes, N. (1991) *Meat: A Natural Symbol.* London/New York.

Finkelberg, M. (1995) "Odysseus and the genus 'hero,'" *G&R* 42: 1–14.

(1998) *The Birth of Literary Fiction in Ancient Greece.* Oxford.

(2000) "The *Cypria*, the *Iliad*, and the problem of multiformity in oral and written tradition," *CP* 95: 1–11.

Finlay, R. (1980) "Patroklos, Achilleus, and Peleus: fathers and sons in the *Iliad*," *CW* 73: 267–73.

Finley, J. H., Jr. (1955) *Pindar and Aeschylus.* Cambridge, MA.

Finley, M. I. (1975) "Utopianism Ancient and Modern," in *The Use and Abuse of History.* New York: 178–92.

(1981) "The elderly in classical antiquity," *G&R* 28: 156–71.

(1998) *Ancient Slavery and Modern Ideology.* Expanded edition, ed. B. D. Shaw. Princeton.

Fisher, N. R. E. (1992) *Hybris: A Study in the Values of Honour and Shame in Ancient Greece.* Warminster.

(1995) *Slavery in Classical Greece.* London.

Fitzgerald, R. (1963) *Homer: The Odyssey.* New York.

Foley, H. P. (1995) "Penelope as moral agent," in *The Distaff Side*, ed. B. Cohen. New York/Oxford: 93–115.

(2001) *Female Acts in Greek Tragedy.* Princeton/Oxford.

Foley, J. M. (1991) *Immanent Art: From Structure to Meaning in Traditional Oral Epic.* Bloomington.

(1999) *Homer's Traditional Art.* University Park, PA.

Foley, R. (1995) *Humans before Humanity.* Oxford/Cambridge, MA.

Fontenay, E. de. (1998) *Le Silence des Bêtes: La philosophie à l'épreuve de l'animalité.* France.

Fontenrose, J. (1978) *The Delphic Oracle.* Berkeley/LA/London.

Forbes Irving, P. M. C. (1990) *Metamorphosis in Greek Myths.* Oxford.

Ford, A. (1992) *Homer. The Poetry of the Past.* Ithaca/London.

(1999) "Performing interpretation: early allegorical exegesis of Homer," in *Epic Traditions in the Contemporary World*, eds. M. Beissinger, J. Tylus, and S. Wofford. Berkeley/LA/London: 33–53.

Fortenbaugh, W. W. (1971) "Aristotle: animals, emotion, and moral Virtue," *Arethusa* 4: 137–65.

(1975) *Aristotle on Emotion.* New York.

(1977) "Aristotle on slaves and women," in *Articles on Aristotle I*, eds. I. J. Barnes, M. Schofield, and R. Sorabji. London: 135–9.

Fowler, B. H. (1969) "Aeschylus' imagery," *C&M* 28: 1–74.

(1991) "The creatures and the blood," *ICS* 16: 85–100.

Fowler, R. L. (1988) "ΑΙΓ – in early Greek language and myth," *Phoenix* 42: 95–113.

(1996) "Herodotus and his contemporaries," *JHS* 116: 62–87.

Foxhall, L. and Forbes, H. A. (1982) "*Sitometreia*: the role of grain as a staple food in classical antiquity," *Chiron* 12: 41–90.

Fraenkel, H. (1921) *Die homerische Gleichnisse*. Göttingen.

(1975) *Early Greek Poetry and Philosophy*. M. Hadas and J. Willis, trs. New York/London.

Frame, D. (1978) *The Myth of Return in Early Greek Epic*. New Haven.

Francione, G. L. (1995) *Animals, Property, and the Law*. Philadelphia.

Francis, E. D. (1991–3) "Brachylogia laconica: Spartan speeches in Thucydides," *BICS* 38: 198–212.

Franklin, A. (1999) *Animals and Modern Cultures*. London.

Frede, M. (1992) "Plato's arguments and the dialogue form," in Klagge and Smith (1992) 201–19.

French, R. K. (1994) *Ancient Natural History: Histories of Nature*. London/New York.

Frenzel, C. (2001) "Tier, Mensch und Seele bei den Vorsokratikern," in Niewöhner and Sebon (2001) 59–92.

Frère, J. (1997) "Les métaphores animales de la vaillance dans l'oeuvre de Platon," in Cassin and Labarrière (1997) 423–34.

Frey, R. G. (1983) *Rights, Killing, & Suffering*. Oxford.

Friedman, J. B. (1981) *The Monstrous Races in Medieval Art and Thought*. Cambridge, MA.

Friedrich, P. and Redfield, J. M. (1978) "Speech as personality symbol: the case of Achilles," *Language* 54: 263–88.

Friedrich, R. (1987) "Heroic man and *polymetis*: Odysseus in the Cyclopeia," *GRBS* 28: 121–33.

(1991) "The hybris of Odysseus," *JHS* 111: 16–28.

Friis Johansen, H. (1959) *General Reflection in Tragic Rhesis. A Study of Form*. Copenhagen.

Frisch, H. (1942) *The Constitution of the Athenians*. Copenhagen.

Fritz, K. von. (1943) "ΝΟΟΣ and ΝΟΕΙΝ in the Homeric poems," *CP* 38: 79–93.

Frontisi-Ducroux, F. (1989) *La cithare d'Achille*. Rome.

Frost, F. (2001) "Sausage and meat preservation in antiquity," *GRBS* 40: 241–52.

Fudge, E. (2002) "A left-handed blow: writing the history of animals," in *Representing Animals*, ed. N. Rothfels. Bloomington/Indianapolis: 3–18.

Fulkerson, L. (2002) "Epic ways of killing a woman: gender and transgression in *Odyssey* 22.465–72," *CJ* 97: 335–50.

Furley, D. J. (1956) "The early history of the concept of soul," *BICS* 3: 1–18.

Gagarin, M. (1976) *Aeschylean Drama*. Berkeley.

Gager, J. (1992) *Curse Tablets and Binding Spells from the Ancient World*. New York.

Gaisser, J. H. (1969) "Adaptation of traditional material in the Glaucus–Diomedes episode," *TAPA* 100: 165–76.

Gal, S. (1991) "Between speech and silence: the problematics of research on language and gender," in *Gender at the Crossroads of Knowledge: Feminist Anthropology in the Postmodern Era*, ed. M. di Leonardo. Berkeley/LA/Oxford: 175–203.

(1995) "Language, gender, and power: an anthropological review," in *Gender Articulated: Language and the Socially Constructed Self*, eds. K. Hall and M. Bucholtz. New York/London: 169–82.

Gallant, T. W. (1991) *Risk and Survival in Ancient Greece: Reconstructing the Rural Domestic Economy*. Cambridge.

Gambarara, D. (1984) *Alle Fonti della Filosofia del Linguaggio*. Rome.

Gantz, T. (1993) *Early Greek Myth: A Guide to Literary and Artistic Sources*. Baltimore.

Gardner, M. (2000) *Did Adam and Eve Have Navels? Debunking Pseudo-Science*. New York.

Garlan, Y. (1988) *Slavery in Ancient Greece*. J. Lloyd, tr. Revised edition. Ithaca and London.

Garland, R. (1981) "The causation of death in the *Iliad*: a theological and biological investigation," *BICS* 28: 43–60.

(1985) *The Greek Way of Death*. London.

(1990) *The Greek Way of Life: From Conception to Old Age*. Ithaca.

(1992) *Introducing New Gods*. Ithaca.

(1995) *The Eye of the Beholder: Deformity and Disability in the Graeco-Roman World*. Ithaca.

Garnsey, P. (1988) *Famine and Food Supply in the Graeco-Roman World*. Cambridge.

(1992) "Yield of the land," in Wells (1992) 147–53.

(1996) *Ideas of Slavery from Aristotle to Augustine*. Cambridge.

(1999) *Food and Society in Classical Antiquity*. Cambridge.

Gatz, B. (1967) *Weltalter, goldene Zeite und sinnverwandte Vorstellungen*. Hildesheim.

Gellrich, M. (1994) "Socratic magic: enchantment, irony, and persuasion in Plato's dialogues," *CW* 87: 275–307.

Gentili, B. (1988) *Poetry and its Public in Ancient Greece from Homer to the Fifth Century*. A. T. Cole, tr. Baltimore/London.

Georges, P. (1994) *Barbarian Asia and the Greek Experience*. Baltimore/London.

Gill, C. (1973) "The death of Socrates," *CQ* 23: 25–8.

(1991) "Is there a concept of person in Greek philosophy?" in Everson (1991) 166–93.

Gill, C., Postlethwaite, N. and Seaford, R. (eds.) (1998) *Reciprocity in Ancient Greece*. Oxford.

Gill, J. E. (1969) "Theriophily in antiquity: a supplementary account," *JHI* 30: 401–12.

Gilleland, M. E. (1980) "Female speech in Greek and Latin," *AJP* 101: 180–3.

Glenn, J. (1971) "The Polyphemos folktale and Homer's KYKLÔPEIA," *TAPA* 102: 133–81.

(1978) "The Polyphemus myth: its origin and interpretation," *G&R* 25: 141–55.

(1998) "Odysseus confronts Nausicaa: the lion simile of *Odyssey* 6.130–6," *CW* 92: 107–16.

Glidden, D. K. (1994) "Parrots, pyrrhonists and native speakers," in Everson (1994a) 129–48.

Gocer, A. (2000) "A new assessment of Socratic philosophy of religion," in Smith and Woodruff (2000) 115–29.

Goff, B. (ed.) (1995) *History, Tragedy, Theory. Dialogues on Athenian Drama*. Austin.

Goheen, R. F. (1951) *The Imagery of Sophocles' Antigone*. Princeton.

(1955) "Aspects of dramatic symbolism: three studies in the *Oresteia*," *AJP* 76: 113–37.

Golden, M. (1985) "Pais, 'child' and 'slave,'" *AC* 54: 91–104.

(1988a) "Male chauvinists and pigs," *EMC* 32: 1–12.

(1988b) "The effects of slavery on citizen households and children: Aeschylus, Aristophanes and Athens," *Historical Reflections* 15: 455–75.

(1990) *Children and Childhood in Classical Athens*. Baltimore/London.

(1995) "Baby talk and child language in Ancient Greece," in Martino and Sommerstein (1995) 11–34.

Goldhill, S. (1984) *Language, Sexuality, Narrative: The Oresteia*. Cambridge.

(1986) *Reading Greek Tragedy*. Cambridge.

(1988) "Reading differences: the *Odyssey* and juxtaposition," *Ramus* 17: 1–31.

(1989) "The sense of ἐκπάτιος at Aeschylus' *Agamemnon* 49," *Eranos* 87: 65–9.

(1990) "Character and action, representation and reading: Greek tragedy and its critics," in Pelling (1990) 100–27.

(1997) "The language of tragedy: rhetoric and communication," in Easterling (1997a) 127–50.

(2000) "Civic ideology and the problem of difference: the politics of Aeschylean tragedy, once again," *JHS* 120: 34–56.

Goldman, L. R. (1999) "From pot to polemic: uses and abuses of cannibalism," in *The Anthropology of Cannibalism*, ed. L. R. Goldman. Westport, CT: 1–26.

Gontier, T. (1998) *De l'homme à l'animal*. Paris.

Gonzalez, F. J. (ed.) (1995a) *The Third Way: New Directions in Platonic Studies*. Lanham.

(1995b) "A short history of Platonic interpretation and the 'third way,'" in Gonzalez (1995a) 1–22.

(1998) *Dialectic and Dialogue: Plato's Practice of Philosophical Inquiry*. Evanston.

Gooch, P. W. (1988) "Red faces in Plato," *CJ* 83: 124–7.

(1996) *Reflections on Jesus and Socrates: Word and Silence*. New Haven/London.

Gordon, J. (1999) *Turning Toward Philosophy: Literary Device and Dramatic Structure in Plato's Dialogues*. University Park, PA.

Gordon, R. L. (ed.) (1981) *Myth, Religion and Society: Structuralist Essays by M. Detienne, L. Gernet, J.-P. Vernant, and P. Vidal-Naquet*. Cambridge.

Gould, J. (1980) "Law, custom and myth: aspects of the social position of women in classical Athens," *JHS* 100: 38–59.

(1996) "Tragedy and collective experience," in *Tragedy and the Tragic*, ed. M. S. Silk. Oxford: 217–43.

Gould, T. (1990) *The Ancient Quarrel Between Poetry and Philosophy*. Princeton.

Gouldner, A. W. (1965) *The Hellenic World: A Sociological Analysis*. New York.

Gower, B. S. (1992) "Introduction," in Gower and Stokes (1992) 1–25.

Gower, B. S. and Stokes, M. C. (1992) *Socratic Questions: New Essays on the Philosophy of Socrates and its Significance*. London/New York.

Graddol, D. and Swann, J. (1989) *Gender Voices*. Cambridge, MA.

Grant, R. M. (1999) *Early Christians and Animals*. London/New York.

Graver, M. (1995) "Dog-Helen and Homeric insult," *CA* 14: 41–61.

Green, M. (1992) *Animals in Celtic Life and Myth*. London/New York.

Greene, W. C. (1920) "The spirit of comedy in Plato," *HSCPh* 31: 63–123.

Gregory, J. (2002) "Euripides as social critic," *G&R* 49: 145–62.

Griffin, D. R. (2001) *Animal Minds: Beyond Cognition to Consciousness*. Chicago/London.

Griffin, J. (1980) *Homer on Life and Death*. Oxford.

  (1986) "Homeric words and speakers," *JHS* 106: 36–57.

  (1998) "The social function of Attic tragedy," *CQ* 48: 39–61.

  (1999) "Sophocles and the democratic city," in *Sophocles Revisited: Essays Presented to Sir Hugh Lloyd-Jones*, ed. J. Griffin. Oxford: 73–94.

Griffith, G. T. (1966) "*Isêgoria* in the assembly at Athens," in *Ancient Society and Institutions: Studies Presented to Victor Ehrenberg*, ed. E. Badian. Oxford/New York: 115–38.

Griffith, M. (1995) "Brilliant dynasts: power and politics in the *Oresteia*," *CA* 14: 62–129.

  (2001) "Antigone and her sister(s): embodying women in Greek tragedy," in Lardinois and McClure (2001) 117–36.

  (2002) "Slaves of Dionysos: satyrs, audience, and the ends of the *Oresteia*," *CA* 21: 195–258.

Griffith, R. D. (1995) "A Homeric metaphor cluster describing teeth, tongue, and words," *AJP* 116: 1–5.

  (1997) "The voice of the dead in Homer's *Odyssey* and in the Egyptian funerary texts," *SMEA* 39: 219–40.

Griffiths, J. G. (1970) *Plutarch's De Iside et Osiride*. Cambridge.

Grossardt, P. (2001) *Die Erzählung von Meleagros. Mnemosyne* Suppl. 215. Leiden.

Grossmann, G. (1968) "Das Lachen des Aias," *MH* 25: 65–85.

Gruen, L. (1993) "Dismantling oppression: an analysis of the connection between women and animals," in *Ecofeminism: Women, Animals, Nature*, ed. G. Gaard. Philadelphia: 60–90.

Guither, H. D. (1998) *Animal Rights: History and Scope of a Radical Social Movement*. Carbondale/Edwardsville.

Gumpert, M. (2001) *Grafting Helen: The Abduction of the Classical Past*. Madison.

Gunderson, K. (1964) "Descartes, La Mettrie, language, and machines," *Philosophy* 39: 193–222.

Güntert, H. (1921) *Von der Sprache der Götter und Geister*. Halle.

Guthrie, W. K. C. (1957) *In The Beginning*. Ithaca.

  (1962) *History of Greek Philosophy I*. Cambridge.

(1969) *History of Greek Philosophy III*. Cambridge.

(1971) *Socrates*. Cambridge.

Hackforth, R. M. (1933) *The Composition of Plato's Apology*. Cambridge.

Hall, E. (1989) *Inventing the Barbarian: Greek Self-Definition through Tragedy*. Oxford.

(1997) "The sociology of Athenian tragedy," in Easterling (1997a) 93–126.

Hall, J. M. (1997) *Ethnic Identity in Greek Antiquity*. Cambridge.

(1999) "The role of language in Greek ethnicities," *PCPhS* 41: 83–100.

(2002) *Hellenicity: Between Ethnicity and Culture*. Chicago/London.

Halliwell, S. (1990a) "The sounds of the voice in old comedy," in Craik (1990) 69–79.

(1990b) "Traditional Greek conceptions of character," in Pelling (1990) 32–59.

(1991a) "Comic satire and the freedom of speech in classical Athens," *JHS* 111: 48–70.

(1991b) "The uses of laughter in Greek literature," *CQ* 41: 279–96.

(1995) "Forms of address: Socratic vocatives in Plato," in Martino and Sommerstein (1995) 82–121.

(1997) "Between public and private: tragedy and the Athenian experience of rhetoric," in Pelling (1997a) 121–41.

Halverson, J. (1976) "Animal categories and terms of abuse," *Man* 11: 505–616.

(1985) "Social order in the *Odyssey*," *Hermes* 113: 129–45.

Hammer, D. C. (1997) "'Who shall readily obey?': Authority and politics in the *Iliad*," *Phoenix* 51: 1–24.

(2002a) *The Iliad as Politics: The Performance of Political Thought*. Norman.

(2002b) "The *Iliad* as ethical thinking: politics, pity, and the operation of esteem," *Arethusa* 35: 203–35.

Hansen, M. H. (1984) "The number of rhetores in the Athenian ekklesia, 355–322," *GRBS* 25: 123–55.

(1995) *The Trial of Sokrates: From the Athenian Point of View*. Historisk-filosofiske Meddelelser 71. Copenhagen.

Hanson, V. D. (1989) *The Western Way of War*. London.

(1995) *The Other Greeks: The Family Farm and the Agrarian Roots of Western Civilization*. New York.

(1996) *Fields Without Dreams*. New York.

(2001) *Carnage and Culture: Landmark Battles in the Rise of Western Power*. New York.

Hanson, V. D. and Heath, J. (2001) *Who Killed Homer?* Revised edition. San Francisco.

Hardwick, L. (1990) "Ancient Amazons – heroes, outsiders or women?" *G&R* 37: 14–36.

Harriott, R. M. (1982) "The Argive elders, the discerning shepherd and the fawning dog: misleading communication in the *Agamemnon*," *CQ* 32: 9–17.

Harris, W. V. (1989) *Ancient Literacy*. Cambridge, MA/London.

Harrison, A. R. W. (1968) *The Law of Athens. Family and Property*. Vol. I. Oxford.

(1971) *The Law of Athens. Procedure*. Vol. 2. Oxford.

Harrison, T. (1998) "Herodotus' conception of foreign languages," *Histos* 2: online
(www.dur.ac.uk/Classics/histos/1998/harrison.html)
  (2000a) *The Emptiness of Asia*. London.
  (2000b) *Divinity and History: The Religion of Herodotus*. Oxford.
  (2002a) (ed.) *Greeks and Barbarians*. Edinburgh.
  (2002b) "General introduction," in Harrison (2002a) 1–14.
Hart, R. and Tejera, V. (eds.) (1997) *Plato's Dialogues – The Dialogical Approach*.
Studies in the History of Philosophy 46. Lewiston.
Hartigan, K. V. (1973) "'He rose like a lion . . .': animal similes in Homer and
Virgil," *Acta Antiqua Academicae Scientiarum Hungaricae* 21: 223–44.
Hartog, F. (1988) *The Mirror of Herodotus: The Representation of the Other in the
Writing of History*. J. Lloyd, tr. Berkeley/LA/London.
Harvey, D. (1985) "Women in Thucydides," *Arethusa* 18: 67–90.
Harvey, D. and Wilkins, J. (eds.) (2000) *The Rivals of Aristophanes: Studies in
Athenian Old Comedy*. London.
Harvey, F. D. (1984) "The wicked wife of Ischomachos," *EMC* 28: 68–70.
Haubold, J. (2000) *Homer's People: Epic Poetry and Social Formation*. Cambridge.
Hauser, M. D. (1997) *The Evolution of Communication*. Cambridge, MA/London.
  (2000) *Wild Minds: What Animals Really Think*. New York.
Haussleiter, J. (1935) *Der Vegetarismus in der Antike*. Berlin.
Havelock, E. A. (1952) "Why was Socrates tried?" in *Studies in Honour of Gilbert
Norwood*. Phoenix Supp. vol. 1, ed. M. E. White. Toronto: 95–109.
  (1957) *The Liberal Temper in Greek Politics*. London.
  (1982) *The Literate Revolution and its Cultural Consequences*. Princeton.
Headlam, W. (1902) "Metaphor, with a note on transference of epithets," *CR* 16:
434–42.
  (1906) "The last scene of the *Eumenides*," *JHS* 26: 268–77.
Heath, J. (1992a) "The legacy of Peleus: Death and divine gifts in the *Iliad*," *Hermes*
120: 387–400.
  (1992b) *Actaeon, the Unmannerly Intruder*. New York.
  (1999a) "The serpent and the sparrows: Homer and the parodos of Aeschylus'
Agamemnon," *CQ* 49: 396–407.
  (1999b) "Disentangling the beast: Humans and other animals in Aeschylus'
Oresteia," *JHS* 119: 17–47.
  (2001) "*Telemachus pepnumenos*: Growing into an epithet," *Mnemosyne* 54: 129–
57.
Hedrick, C. W., Jr. (2000) *History and Silence*. Austin.
Heichelheim, F. M. and Elliott, T. (1967) "Das Tier in der Vorstellungswelt der
Griechen," *Studium General* 29: 85–9.
Helck, W. (1964) "Die Ägypter und die Fremden," *Saeculum* 15: 103–14.
Held, G. F. (1987) "Phoinix, Agamemnon and Achilleus: parables and
paradeigmata," *CQ* 37: 245–61.
Helleman, W. E. (1995) "Homer's Penelope: a tale of feminine *aretê*," *EMC/CV* 14:
227–50.
Henderson, J. (1987) "Older women in Attic comedy," *TAPA* 117: 105–29.

(1991) *The Maculate Muse*. 2nd edition. New York/Oxford.

(1998) "Attic old comedy, frank speech, and democracy," in Boedeker and Raaflaub (1998) 255–73.

(2000) "Pherekrates and the women of old comedy," in Harvey and Wilkins (2000) 135–50.

Henderson, T. Y. (1970) "In defense of Thrasymachus," *Am. Phil. Q.* 7: 218–28.

Henrichs, A. (1991) "Namenlosigkeit und Euphemismus: Zur Ambivalenz der chthonischen Mächte im attischen Drama," in *Fragmenta Dramatica*, eds. A. Harder and H. Hofmann. Göttingen: 61–201.

(1994) "Anonymity and polarity: unknown gods and nameless altars in the Areopagos," *ICS* 19: 27–58.

Henry, M. M. (1992) "The edible woman: Athenaeus's concept of the pornographic," in *Pornography and Representation in Greece and Rome*, ed. A. Richlin. New York/Oxford: 250–68.

Herington, J. (1986) *Aeschylus*. New Haven.

Herman, G. (1995) "Honour, revenge and the state in fourth-century Athens," in *Die athenische Demokratie im 4. Jahrhundert v. Chr.*, ed. W. Eder. Stuttgart: 43–60.

(1996) "Ancient Athens and the values of Mediterranean society," *Med. Hist. Review* 11: 5–36.

(1998) "Reciprocity, altruism, and the prisoner's dilemma: the special case of classical Athens," in Gill, Postlethwaite, and Seaford (1998) 199–225.

Herman, L. M. and Morrel-Samuels, P. (1996) "Knowledge acquisition and asymmetry between language comprehension and production: dolphins and apes as general models for animals," in *Readings in Animal Cognition*, eds. M. Bekoff and D. Jamieson. Cambridge, MA/London.

Herrmann, F. G. (1995) "Wrestling metaphors in Plato's Theaetetus," *Nikephoros* 8: 77–109.

Herzfeld, M. (1985) *The Poetics of Manhood*. Princeton.

Hesk, J. (2000) *Deception and Democracy in Classical Athens*. Cambridge.

Heubeck, A. (1949–50) "Die homerische Göttersprache," *Würzburger Jahrbücher* 4: 197–218.

(1970) "Griechisch-Mykenische Etymologien," *Studi Micenei ed Egeo-Anatolici* 11: 63–72.

Hilkert, M. C. (2002) "*Imago Dei*: does the symbol have a future?" *The Santa Clara Lectures* 8.3 (14 April 2002). Santa Clara, CA.

Hobbs, A. (2000) *Plato and the Hero: Courage, Manliness and the Impersonal Good.* Cambridge.

Hodgen, M. T. (1964) *Early Anthropology in the Sixteenth and Seventeenth Centuries*. Philadelphia.

Hodkinson, S. (1988) "Animal husbandry in the Greek polis," in Whittaker (1988) 35–74.

Hodkinson, S. and Powell, A. (eds.) (1999) *Sparta: New Perspectives*. London.

Hoffer, S. E. (1995) "Telemachus' 'laugh' (*Odyssey* 21.105): Deceit, authority, and communication in the bow contest," *AJP* 116: 514–31.

Holoka, J. P. (1983) "'Looking darkly' (ΥΠΟΔΡΑ ΙΔѠΝ): reflections on status and decorum in Homer," *TAPA* 113: 1–16.

Holzberg, N. (1996) "Novel-like works of extended prose fiction II," in *The Novel in the Ancient World. Mnemosyne* Suppl. 159, ed. G. Schmeling. Leiden/New York/Köln: 621–53.

(2002) *The Ancient Fable: An Introduction.* C. Jackson-Holzberg, tr. Bloomington/Indianapolis.

Horowitz, M. C. (1976) "Aristotle and woman," *JHB* 9: 183–213.

Houlihan, P. F. (1996) *The Animal World of the Pharaohs.* London.

Houston, M. and Kramarae, C. (1991) "Speaking from silence: Methods of silencing and of resistance," *Discourse and Society 2.2. Special Issue: Women Speaking from Silence*, eds. M. Houston and C. Kramarae. 387–99.

Howe, N. (1999) "Fabling beasts: traces in memory," in *Humans and Other Animals*, ed. A. Mack. Columbus, OH: 229–47.

Howie, J. G. (1995) "The *Iliad* as exemplum," in *Homer's World. Fiction, Tradition, Reality*, eds. Ø. Andersen and M. W. Dickie. Bergen: 141–73.

Hubbard, T. K. (1981) "Antithetical simile pairs in Homer," *GB* 10: 59–67.

(1989) "Old men in the youthful plays of Aristophanes," in Falkner and de Luce (1989) 90–113.

(1997) "Utopianism and the sophistic city in Aristophanes," in Dobrov (1997) 23–50.

Hughes, D. D. (1991) *Human Sacrifice in Ancient Greece.* London/New York.

Hughes, J. D. (1975) "Ecology in ancient Greece," *Inquiry* 18: 115–25.

Hunter, V. (1994) *Policing Athens: Social Control in the Attic Lawsuits, 420–320 B.C.* Princeton.

Hurford, J. R., Studdert-Kennedy, M., and Knight, C. (eds.) (1998) *Approaches to the Evolution of Language: Social and Cognitive Bases.* Cambridge.

Ickert, S. (1998) "Luther and animals: subject to Adam's fall?" in Linzey and Yamamoto (1998) 90–9.

Ingalls, W. B. (1998) "Attitudes towards children in the *Iliad*," *EMC/CV* 42: 13–34.

Inwood, B. (1985) *Ethics and Human Action in Early Stoicism.* Oxford.

Irwin, T. H. (1986a) "Coercion and objectivity in Plato's dialectic," *Revue Internationale de Philosophie* 40: 49–74.

(1986b) "Socratic inquiry and politics," *Ethics* 96: 400–15.

(1993) "Say what you believe," *Apeiron* 36: 1–16.

Isager, S. and Skydsgaard, E. (1992) *Ancient Greek Agriculture: An Introduction.* London/New York.

Isebaert, L. and Lebrun, R. (eds.) (1998) *Quaestiones Homericae.* Collection d' Études Classiques 9. Bruxelles.

Isserlin, B. S. J. (1998) *The Israelites.* London.

Jackson, B. D. (1971) "The prayers of Socrates," *Phronesis* 16: 14–37.

Jahn, T. (1987) *Zum Wortfeld "Seele-Geist" in der Sprache Homers*. Zetemata 83. München.

Jameson, M. H. (1983) "Famine in the Greek world," in *Trade and Famine in Classical Antiquity*. Proceedings of the Cambridge Philological Society, Supp. vol. 8, eds. P. Garnsey and C. R. Whittaker. Cambridge: 6–16.

(1988a) "Sacrifice and animal husbandry in classical Greece," in Whittaker (1988) 87–119.

(1988b) "Sacrifice and ritual: Greece," in *Civilization of the Ancient Mediterranean: Greece and Rome*. Vol. II, eds. M. Grant and R. Kitzinger. New York: 959–79.

(1999) "The spectacular and the obscure in Athenian religion," in *Performance Culture and Athenian Democracy*, eds. S. Goldhill and R. Osborne. Cambridge: 321–40.

Jamieson, D. (2002) *Morality's Progress: Essays on Humans, Other Animals, and the Rest of Nature*. Oxford.

Jang, I. H. (1997) "Socrates' refutation of Thrasymachus," *HPTh* 18.2: 189–206.

Janko, R. (1980) "Aeschylus' *Oresteia* and Archilochus," *CQ* 30: 291–3.

(1984) *Aristotle on Comedy: Towards a Reconstruction of Poetics II*. Berkeley/LA.

Jaworski, A. (1993) *The Power of Silence*. Newbury Park.

(1997) (ed.) *Silence: Interdisciplinary Perspectives*. Berlin/New York.

Jeanmaire, H. (1975) *Couroi et Courètes*. New York.

Johnston, S. I. (1992) "Xanthus, Hera, and Erinyes. (*Iliad* 19.400–418)," *TAPA* 122: 85–98.

(1999) *Restless Dead: Encounters Between the Living and the Dead in Ancient Greece*. Berkeley.

Johnstone, S. (1994) "Virtuous toil, vicious work: Xenophon on aristocratic style," *CP* 89: 219–40.

(1999) *Disputes and Democracy*. Austin.

Jones, P. V. (1988) "The KLEOS of Telemachos: *Odyssey* 1.95," *AJP* 109: 496–506.

(1996) "The independent heroes of the *Iliad*," *JHS* 116: 108–18.

Jong, I. J. F. de. (1987a) "Silent characters in the *Iliad*," in *Homer: Beyond Oral Poetry*, ed. J. M. Bremmer. Amsterdam: 105–21.

(1987b) *Narrators and Focalizers: The Presentation of the Story in the Iliad*. Amsterdam.

(1994) "Between word and deed: Hidden thoughts in the *Odyssey*," in *Modern Critical Theory and Classical Literature*. Mnemosyne Suppl. 130, eds. I. J. F. de Jong and J. P. Sullivan. Leiden: 27–50.

(1995) "Homer as literature: Some current areas of research," in Crielaard (1995) 127–46.

(2001a) *A Narratological Commentary on the Odyssey*. Cambridge.

(2001b) Review of Rabel (1997), *Mnemosyne* 44: 221–3.

Joshel, S. R. and Murnaghan, S. (eds.) (1998) *Women and Slaves in Greco-Roman Culture*. Ithaca/London.

Just, R. (1985) "Freedom, slavery, and the female psyche," in Cartledge and Harvey (1985) 169–88.

(1989) *Women in Athenian Law and Life*. London and New York.

Jüthner, J. (1923) *Hellenen und Barbaren: Aus der Geschichte des Nationalbewusssteins*. Leipzig.

Kahn, C. H. (1981) "Why did Plato write Socratic dialogues?" *CQ* 31: 305–20.

(1983) "Drama and dialectic in Plato's Gorgias," *OSAPh* 1: 75–121.

(1993) "Proleptic composition in the *Republic*, or why book I was never a separate dialogue," *CQ* 43: 131–42.

(1996) *Plato and the Socratic Dialogue*. Cambridge.

Kaimio, M. (1977) *Characterization of Sound in Early Greek Literature*. Commentationes Humanarum Litterarum 53. Helsinki.

Kajanto, I. (ed.) (1984) *Equality and Inequality of Man in Ancient Thought*. Commentationes Humanarum Litterarum 75. Helsinki.

Kakridis, J. (1949) *Homeric Researches*. Lund.

(1971) *Homer Revisited*. Lund.

Kallet-Marx, L. (1993) "Thucydides 2.45.2 and the status of war widows in Periclean Athens," in Rosen and Farrell (1993) 133–43.

Kaminer, W. (1999) *Sleeping with Extra-Terrestrials*. New York.

Kane, F. I. (1986) "Peitho and the polis," *Ph&Rh* 19: 99–124.

Kapparis, K. (1998) "The law on the age of the speakers in the Athenian assembly," *RhM* 141: 255–9.

Karttunen, K. (1992) "Distant lands in classical ethnography," *GB* 18: 195–204.

Karydas, H. P. (1998) *Eurykleia and Her Successors*. Lanham.

Katz, M. A. (1990) "Problems of sacrifice in ancient cultures," in *The Bible in the Light of Cuneiform Literature*, eds. W. W. Hallo, B. W. Jones, G. L. Mattingly. Lewiston/Queenston/Lampeter: 89–201.

(1991) *Penelope's Renown. Meaning and Indeterminacy in the Odyssey*. Princeton.

(1993) "Buphonia and goring ox: Homicide, animal sacrifice, and judicial process," in Rosen and Farrell (1993) 155–78.

Kazazis, J. N. and Rengakos, A. (eds.) (1999) *Euphrosyne: Studies in Ancient Epic and its Legacy in Honor of Dimitris N. Maronitis*. Stuttgart.

Kean, H. (1998) *Animal Rights: Political and Social Change in Britain since 1800*. London.

Kearns, E. (1982) "The return of Odysseus: a Homeric theoxeny," *CQ* 32: 2–8.

Keller, O. (1963) *Die Antike Tierwelt, Vol. I–II*. Hildesheim.

Kelly, E. (ed.) (1984) *New Essays on Socrates*. Lanham.

Kelly, S. T. (1990) *Homeric Correption and the Metrical Distinctions Between Speech and Narrative*. New York and London.

Kennedy, G. A. (1998) *Comparative Rhetoric: An Historical and Cross-Cultural Introduction*. New York/Oxford.

Kennell, N. M. (1995) *The Gymnasium of Virtue*. Chapel Hill/London.

Kerferd, G. B. (1981) *The Sophistic Movement*. Cambridge.

Kete, K. (1994) *The Beast in the Boudoir: Pet-keeping in Nineteenth-Century Paris*. Berkeley/LA/London.

Kim, J. (2000) *The Pity of Achilles: Oral Style and the Unity of the Iliad*. Lanham. 2000.

King, B. J. (ed.) (1999a.) *The Origins of Language: What Nonhuman Primates Can Tell Us*. Santa Fe, N. M.

(1999b) "Introduction: Primatological perspectives on language," in King (1999a) 3–19.

King, H. (1989) "Tithonos and the tettix," in Falkner and de Luce (1989). 68–89.

King, K. C. (1987) *Achilles: Paradigm of the War Hero from Homer to the Middle Ages*. Berkeley.

Kiriazis, J. and Slobodchikoff, C. N. (1997) "Anthropomorphism and the study of animal language," in Mitchell et al. (1997) 365–9.

Kirk, G. S. (1970) *Myth, its Meaning and Functions in Ancient and Other Cultures*. Cambridge/Berkeley.

(1971) "Old age and maturity in ancient Greece," *Eranos-Jahrbuch* 40: 123–58.

(1974) *The Nature of Greek Myths*. New York.

Klagge, J. C. and Smith, N. D. (eds.) (1992) *Methods of Interpreting Plato and his Dialogues*. OSAPh supplementary vol. Oxford.

Kleingünther, A. (1933) *ΠΡΩΤΟΣ ΕΥΡΕΤΗΣ: Untersuchungen zur Geschichte einer Fragestellung*. Philologus suppl. 26.1. Leipzig.

Klingender, F. (1971) *Animals in Art and Thought to the End of the Middle Ages*. Cambridge, MA.

Knox, B. M. W. (1952) "The lion in the house (*Agamemnon* 717–36)," *CP* 47: 17–25.

(1961) "The *Ajax* of Sophocles," *HSCPh* 65: 1–37.

(1964) *The Heroic Temper: Studies in Sophoclean Tragedy*. Berkeley/LA.

Kofman, S. (1998) *Socrates: Fictions of a Philosopher*. C. Porter, tr. London.

Kokolakis, K. (1981) "Homeric animism," *Museum philologum Londiniense* 4: 89–113.

Konner, M. (2002) *The Tangled Wing: Biological Constraints on the Human Spirit*. 2nd edition. New York.

Konstan, D. (1995) *Greek Comedy and Ideology*. New York/Oxford.

Körner, O. (1930) *Die homerische Tierwelt*. München.

Kosman, A. (1987) "Commentary on Teloh," *BACAP* 2: 39–43.

Kosman, L. A. (1992) "Silence and imitation in the Platonic dialogues," in Klagge and Smith (1992) 73–92.

Kouklanakis, A. (1999) "Thersites, Odysseus, and the social order," in *Nine Essays on Homer*, eds. M. Carlisle and O. Levanioiuk. Lanham: 35–53.

Kramer, C. (1975) "Women's speech: Separate but unequal?" in *Language and Sex: Difference and Dominance*, eds. B. Thorne and N. Henley. Rowley, MA: 43–56.

Krapp, H. J. (1964) *Die akustischen Phänomene in der Ilias*. München.

Kraut, R. (1983) *Socrates and the State*. Princeton.

(2000) "Socrates, politics, and religion," in Smith and Woodruff (2000). 13–23.

Kullmann, W. (1985) "Gods and men in the *Iliad* and *Odyssey*," *HSCPh* 89: 1–23.

(1991) "Man as a political animal," in *A Companion to Aristotle's Politics*, eds. D. Keyt and F. R. Miller, Jr. Cambridge, MA: 94–117.

(1999) "Homer and historical memory," in Mackay (1999) 95–113.

Kurzon, D. (1998) *Discourse of Silence*. Amsterdam/Philadelphia.

Kyriakou, P. (2001) "Warrior vaunts in the *Iliad*," *RhM* 144: 250–77.

Labarrière, J. (1984) "Imagination humaine et imagination animale chez Aristote," *Phronesis* 29: 17–49.

Lai, C. S. L. et al. (2001) "A forkhead-domain gene is mutated in severe speech and language disorder," *Nature* 413 (4 October): 518–23.

Laín Entralgo, P. (1970) *The Therapy of the Word in Classical Antiquity*, eds. and trs. L. J. Rather and J. M. Sharp. New Haven/London.

Laird, A. (1999) *Powers of Expression, Expressions of Power: Speech Presentation and Latin Literature*. Oxford.

Lakoff, R. T. (1995) "Cries and whispers: the shattering of silence," in *Gender Articulated: Language and the Socially Constructed Self*, eds. K. Hall and M. Bucholtz. New York/London: 25–50.

Lane Fox, R. (1988) *Pagans and Christians*. London and San Francisco.

Lang, M. L. (1983) "Reverberation and mythology in the *Iliad*," in *Approaches to Homer*, eds. C. A. Rubino and C. W. Shelmerdine. Austin: 140–64.

Lansbury, C. (1985) *The Old Brown Dog: Women, Workers, and Vivisection in Edwardian England*. Madison, WI.

Lardinois, A. (2001) "Keening Sappho: female speech genres in Sappho's poetry," in Lardinois and McClure (2001) 75–92.

Lardinois, A. and McClure, L. (eds.) (2001) *Making Silence Speak: Women's Voices in Greek Literature and Society*. Princeton.

Latacz, J. (1968) "ἄπτερος αὖθος-ἄπτερος φάτις: 'ungeflügelte Worte'," *Glotta* 46: 27–47.

Lateiner, D. (1995) *Sardonic Smile*. Ann Arbor.

(1997) "Homeric prayer," *Arethusa* 30: 241–72.

(1998) "Blushes and pallor in ancient fictions," *Helios* 25: 163–89.

(2003) "'Is teaching classics inherently colonialist?': a response," *CW* 96: 427–33.

Lau, D. (2000) *Der Mensch als Mittelpunkt der Welt*. Aachen.

Lawrence, S. E. (1976) "Artemis in the *Agamemnon*," *AJP* 97: 97–110.

Leach, E. R. (1964) "Anthropological aspects of language: Animal categories and verbal abuse," in *New Directions in the Study of Language*, ed. E. H. Lenneberg. Cambridge, MA: 23–63.

Leahy, M. P. T. (1991) *Against Liberation*. New York.

Lebeck, A. (1971) *The Oresteia: A Study in Language and Structure*. Washington.

Lebra, T. S. (1987) "The cultural significance of silence in Japanese communication," *Multilingua* 6: 343–57.

Leclerc, M. C. (1993) *La parole chez Hésiode*. Paris.

Lee, D. J. N. (1964) *The Similes of the Iliad and Odyssey Compared*. Sydney.

Lefkowitz, M. R. (1981) *The Lives of the Greek Poets*. Baltimore.

(1986) *Women in Greek Myth*. Baltimore.

Leinieks, V. (1986) "The similes of Iliad Two," *C&M* 37: 5–20.

Lesher, J. H. (2002) "Parmenidean elenchos," in Scott (2002) 19–35.

Lévi-Strauss, C. (1969) *Totemism*. R. Needham, tr. London.

Lévy, E. (1984) "Naissance du concept de barbare," *Ktèma* 9: 5–14.

(1991) "Apparition des notions de Grèce et de Grecs," in Saïd (1991) 49–69.

Lewis, B. (1995) *The Middle East*. New York.

(2002) *What Went Wrong? Western Impact and Middle Eastern Response*. Oxford/New York.

(2003) *The Crisis of Islam: Holy War and Unholy Terror*. New York.

Lhuillier, V. (1995) "Le procès de Socrate," *AphD* 39: 47–71.

Lieberman, P. (1998) *Eve Spoke: Human Language and Human Evolution*. New York/London.

Lilja, S. (1974) "Theriophily in Homer," *Arctos* 8: 71–8.

(1976) *Dogs in Ancient Greek Poetry*. Commentationes Humanarum Litterarum 56. Helsinki.

Lincoln, B. (1997) "Competing discourses: Rethinking the prehistory of *mythos* and *logos*," *Arethusa* 30: 341–67.

Linzey, A. (1987) *Christianity and the Rights of Animals*. New York.

(1995) *Animal Theology*. Urbana/Chicago.

Linzey, A. and Regan, D. (eds.) (1990) *Animals and Christianity: A Book of Readings*. New York.

Linzey, A. and Yamamoto, D. (eds.) (1998) *Animals on the Agenda: Questions About Animals for Theology and Ethics*. Urbana/Chicago.

Lissarrague, F. (1990) "Why satyrs are good to represent," in Winkler and Zeitlin (1990) 228–36.

(2000) "Aesop, between man and beast: ancient portraits and ilustrations," J. C. Gage, tr. in Cohen (2000b) 132–49.

Llewellyn-Jones, L. (2003) *The Veiled Woman of Ancient Greece*. Wales.

Lloyd, G. E. R. (1966) *Polarity and Analogy*. Cambridge.

(1983) *Science, Folklore, and Ideology*. Cambridge/New York.

(2002) *The Ambitions of Curiosity: Understanding the World in Ancient Greece and China*. Cambridge.

Lloyd, G. and Sivin, N. (2002) *The Way and the Word: Science and Medicine in Early China and Greece*. New Haven/London.

Lloyd-Jones, H. (1960) "Three notes on Aeschylus' *Agamemnon*," *RhM* 103: 76–80.

(1983a) "Artemis and Iphigenia," *JHS* 103: 87–102.

(1983b) *The Justice of Zeus*. 2nd edition. Berkeley/LA.

(1990) "Erinyes, Semnai Theai, Eumenides," in Craik (1990) 203–11.

Loening, T. C. (1987) *The Reconciliation Agreement of 403/2 BC in Athens*. Hermes Einzelschriften 53. Stuttgart.

Lohmann, D. (1970) *Die Komposition der Reden in der Ilias*. Berlin.

(1988) *Die Andromache-Szenen der Ilias*. Spudasmata 42. Hildesheim.

Long, A. A. (1970) "Morals and values in Homer," *JHS* 90: 121–39.

(1971) "Language and thought in Stoicism," in *Problems in Stoicism*, ed. A. A. Long. London: 75–113.

Long, T. (1986) *Barbarians in Greek Comedy*. Carbondale/Edwardsville.

Longo, O. (2000) "La mano dell'uomo da Aristotele a Galeno," *QUCC* 66: 7–27.

Lonsdale, S. H. (1979) "Attitudes towards animals in ancient Greece," *G&R* 26: 146–59.

(1989) "Hesiod's hawk and nightingale (*Op.* 202–12): fable or omen," *Hermes* 117: 403–12.

(1990) *Creatures of Speech. Hunting, Herding, and Hunting Similes in the Iliad.* Beiträge zur Altertumskunde 5. Stuttgart.

Loraux, N. (1986) "Le corps vulnérable d' Arès," in *Le temps de la réflexion VII. Corps des Dieux*, eds. C. Malamoud and J.-P. Vernant. Paris: 335–54.

(1987) *Tragic Ways of Killing a Woman.* A. Forster, tr. Cambridge, MA.

(1990) "Herakles: The super-males and the feminine," in *Before Sexuality*, eds. D. M. Halperin, J. J. Winkler, and F. I. Zeitlin. Princeton: 21–52.

(1992) "What is a goddess?" in Schmitt Pantel (1992a) 11–44.

(1993) *The Children of Athena.* C. Levine, tr. Princeton.

(1995) *The Experiences of Tiresias.* P. Wissing, tr. Princeton.

(2000) *Born of the Earth: Myth and Politics in Athens.* S. Steward, tr. Ithaca/London.

Lorenz, G. (2000) *Tiere im Leben der alten Kulturen.* Wien.

Losemann, V. (2003) "Barbarians," in *Brill's New Pauly*, eds. H. Cancik and H. Schneider. Leiden/Boston: 500–4.

Louden, B. (1999) *The Odyssey: Structure, Narration, and Meaning.* Baltimore.

Lovejoy, A. O. and Boas, G. (1965) *Primitivism and Related Ideas in Antiquity.* New York.

Lowenstam, S. (1993) *The Scepter and the Spear.* Lanham.

Luce, J.-M. (2000) "De l'ers ou du bonheur chez les boeufs," *Pallas* 52: 109–14.

Lynn-George, M. (1988) *Epos. Word, Narrative and the Iliad.* Atlantic Highlands, NJ.

Lyons, D. (2003) "Dangerous gifts: Ideologies of marriage and exchange in ancient Greece," *CA* 22: 93–134.

MacCary, W. T. (1982) *Childlike Achilles.* New York.

Mackay, E. A. (ed.) (1999) *Signs of Orality: The Oral Tradition and its Influence in the Greek and Roman World. Mnemosyne* Suppl. 188. Leiden.

Mackenzie, M. M. (1988) "The virtues of Socratic ignorance," *CQ* 38: 331–50.

Mackie, C. J. (1997) "Achilles' teachers: Chiron and Phoenix in the *Iliad*," *G&R* 44: 1–10.

Mackie, H. (1996) *Talking Trojan: Speech and Community in the Iliad.* Lanham.

(1997) "Song and storytelling: An Odyssean perspective," *TAPA* 127: 77–95.

Macleod, C. W. (1982b) "Politics and the *Oresteia*," *JHS* 102: 124–44.

Madison, L. A. (2002) "Have we been careless with Socrates' last words? A rereading of the *Phaedo*," *JHist. Ph.* 40: 421–36.

Mainoldi, C. (1984) *L'Image du loup et du chien dans la Grèce ancienne d'Homère à Platon.* Paris.

Malcolm, N. (1977) *Thought and Knowledge.* Ithaca/London.

Malkin, I. (ed.) (2001a) *Ancient Perceptions of Greek Ethnicity.* Washington, DC.

(2001b) "Introduction," in Malkin (2001a) 1–28.

Malten, L. (1914) "Das Pferd im Totenglauben," *JDt. Arch. Inst.* 29: 179–225.

March, J. R. (1987) *The Creative Poet. BICS* Supplement 49. London.

Margolis, J. (1983) "The emergence of philosophy," in Robb (1983) 228–43.

Marinatos, N. (1987) "An offering of saffron to the Minoan goddess of nature," in *Gifts to the Gods: Proceedings of the Uppsala Symposium 1985*, eds. T. Linders and G. Nordquist. Uppsala: 123–32.

Marks, J. (2002) *What It Means to Be 98% Chimpanzee*. Berkeley/LA/London.

Marquardt, P. A. (1993) "Penelope as weaver of words," in DeForest (1993) 149–58.

Mars, G. and Mars, V. (eds.) (1993) *Food Culture and History*. Vol. 1. London.

Martin, R. P. (1989) *The Language of Heroes: Speech and Performance in the Iliad*. Ithaca.

   (1993) "Telemachus and the last hero song," *Colby Quarterly* 29: 222–40.

Martino, F. D. and Sommerstein, A. H. (eds.) (1995) *Lo spettaculo delle voci*. Bari.

Mason, P. (1987) "Third person/second sex: Patterns of sexual asymmetry in the *Theogony* of Hesiodos," in Blok and Mason (1987) 147–89.

Massaro, M. (1977) "Aniles fabellae," *Studi Italiani di Filologia Classica* 49: 104–35.

Matsuzawa, T. (ed.) (2001) *Primate Origins of Human Cognition and Behavior*. Tokyo.

Matthews, G. B. (1997) "Perplexity in Plato, Aristotle, and Tarski," *Philosophical Studies* 85: 213–28.

May, H. (1997) "Socratic ignorance and the therapeutic aim of the elenchos," *Apeiron* 30: 37–50.

McAvoy, M. (1996) "The profession of ignorance, with constant reference to Socrates," *Prudentia* 28: 16–34.

McClure, L. (1995) "Female speech and characterization in Euripides," in Martino and Sommerstein (1995) 35–60.

   (1997) "Clytemnestra's binding spell (*Agamemnon* 958–74)," *CJ* 92: 123–40.

   (1999) *Spoken Like a Woman: Speech and Gender in Athenian Drama*. Princeton.

   (2001) "Introduction," in Lardinois and McClure (2001) 3–16.

McCoskey, D. E. (1998) "'I, whom she detested so bitterly': slavery and the violent division of women in Aeschylus' *Oresteia*," in Joshel and Murnaghan (1998) 35–55.

McDermott, E. A. (1989) *Euripides' Medea: Incarnation of Disorder*. University Park/London.

McDermott, W. C. (1938) *The Ape in Antiquity*. Baltimore.

McGlew, J. F. (2002) *Citizens on Stage: Comedy and Political Culture in the Athenian Democracy*. Ann Arbor.

McKay, K. J. (1958) "Stentor and Hesiod," *AJP* 80: 383–8.

McKim, R. (1988) "Shame and truth in Plato's *Gorgias*," in *Platonic Writings, Platonic Readings*, ed. C. L. Griswold, Jr. New York: 34–48.

McMillan, C. (1982) *Women, Reason and Nature: Some Philosophical Problems with Feminism*. Princeton.

McPherran, M. (1986) "Socrates and the duty to philosophize," *SoJP* 24: 541–60.

   (2003) "Socrates, Crito, and their debt to Asclepius," *Anc. Phil*. 23: 71–92.

Meier, C. (1993) *The Political Art of Greek Tragedy*. A. Webber, tr. Baltimore.

   (2001) "The Greeks: The political revolution in world history," in Arnason and Murphy (2001a) 56–71.

Mensching, G. (1926) *Das Heilige Schweigen*. Giessen.

Messing, G. M. (1981) "On weighing Achilles' winged words," *Language* 57: 888–900.

Michelakis, P. (2002) *Achilles in Greek Tragedy*. Cambridge.

Midgley, M. (1983) *Animals and Why They Matter*. Athens, GA.

(1995) *Beast and Man: The Roots and Human Nature*. Revised edition London/New York.

Miles, H. L. (1997) "Anthropomorphism, apes, and language," in Mitchell et al. (1997) 383–404.

Millar, C. M. H. and Carmichael, J. W. S. (1954) "The growth of Telemachus," *G&R* 1: 58–64.

Millender, E. (1999) "Athenian ideology and the empowered Spartan woman," in Hodkinson and Powell (1999) 355–91.

Miller, D. A. (2000) *The Epic Hero*. Baltimore/London.

Miller, M. C. (1997). *Athens and Persia in the fifth century BC: A Study in cultural receptivity*. Cambridge.

Mills, S. (2000) "Achilles, Patroclus and parental care in some Homeric similes," *G&R* 47: 3–18.

Minchin, E. (1986) "The interpretation of a theme in oral epic: *Iliad* 24.559–70," *G&R* 33: 11–19.

(1995) "Ring patterns and ring-composition: Some observations on the framing of stories in Homer," *Helios* 22: 23–35.

(2001a) "Similes in Homer: Image, mind's eye, and memory," in Watson (2001) 25–52.

(2001b) *Homer and the Resources of Memory*. Oxford.

(2002) "Verbal behaviour in its social context: Three question strategies in Homer's *Odyssey*," *CQ* 52: 15–32.

Mirhady, D. C. (1991) "The oath-challenge in Athens," *CQ* 41: 78–83.

(1996) "Torture and rhetoric in Athens," *JHS* 116: 119–31.

Mirón Pérez, M. D. (2000) "Las mujeres, la tierra y los animales: naturaleza femenina y cultura política en Grecia antigua," *FlorIlib* 11: 151–69.

Mitchell, R. W., Thompson, N. S. and Miles, H. L. (eds.) (1997) *Anthropomorphism, Anecdotes, and Animals*. Albany, NY.

Mitscherling, J. (1985) "*Phaedo* 118: The last words," *Apeiron* 19: 161–5.

Momigliano, A. (1971) "La libertà di parola nel mondo antico," *Rivista Storica Italiana* 83: 499–524.

Mondi, R. (1983) "The Homeric Cyclopes: Folktale, tradition, and theme," *TAPA* 113: 17–38.

Monoson, S. S. (1994) "Frank speech, democracy, and philosophy: Plato's debt to a democratic strategy of civic discourse," in Euben et al. (1994). 172–97.

(2000) *Plato's Democratic Entanglements*. Princeton.

Montiglio, S. (1993) "La ménace du silence pour le héros de l' *Iliade*," *Métis* 8: 161–86.

(2000) *Silence in the Land of Logos*. Princeton.

Montuori, M. (1992) *The Socratic Problem: The History – The Solutions*. Amsterdam.

Moreau, A. M. (1985) *Eschyle: la violence et le chaos*. Paris.

Morenilla-Talens, C. (1989) "Die Charakterisierung der Ausländer durch lautliche Ausdrucksmittel in den *Persern* des Aischylos sowie den *Acharnern* und *Vögeln* des Aristophanes," *IF* 94: 158–76.

Morgan, M. L. (1992) "Plato and Greek religion," in *The Cambridge Companion to Plato*, ed. R. Kraut. Cambridge: 227–47.

Morris, I. (1989) "Attitudes toward death in archaic Greece," *CA* 8: 296–320.

Morris, I. and Powell, B. (eds.) (1997) *A New Companion to Homer. Mnemosyne* Suppl. 163. Leiden.

Morrison, D. (1996) "On professor Vlastos' Xenophon," in Prior (1996) vol. I. 119–35.

(2000) "On the alleged historical reliability of Plato's *Apology*," *Archiv für Geschichte der Philosophie* 82: 235–65.

Morrison, J. V. (1992) *Homeric Misdirection*. Ann Arbor.

(1997) "*Kerostasia*, the dictates of fate, and the will of Zeus in the *Iliad*," *Arethusa* 30: 273–96.

(1999) "Homeric darkness: Patterns and manipulation of death scenes in the *Iliad*," *Hermes* 127: 129–144.

Mortley, R. (1986) *From Word to Silence: The Rise and Fall of Logos*. Bonn.

Mosley, D. J. (1971) "Greeks, barbarians, language and contact," *Ancient Society* 2: 1–6.

Mossman, J. (2001) "Women's speech in Greek tragedy: The case of Electra and Clytemnestra in Euripides' *Electra*," *CQ* 51: 374–84.

Most, G. W. (1993) "A cock for Asclepius," *CQ* 43: 96–111.

Motto, A. L. and Clark, J. R. (1969) "*Ise dais*: The honor of Achilles," *Arethusa* 2: 109–20.

Moulton, C. (1977) *Similes in the Homeric Poems*. Hypomnemata 49. Göttingen.

Mueller, M. (1984) *The Iliad*. London.

Muellner, L. (1990) "The simile of the cranes and pygmies: A study of Homeric metaphor," *HSCPh* 93: 59–101.

(1996) *The Anger of Achilles*. Ithaca.

Müller, C. W., Sier, K. and Werner, J. (eds.) (1992) *Zum Umgang mit fremden Sprachen in der Griechisch-Römischen Antike*. Palingenesia 36. Stuttgart.

Müller, R. (1980) *Menschenbild und Humanismus der Antike*. Leipzig.

Münch, P. and Walz, R. (eds.) (1998) *Tiere und Menschen: Geschichte und Aktualität eines prekären Verhältnisses*. Paderborn.

Munson, R. V. (2001) *Telling Wonders: Ethnographic and Political Discourse in the Work of Herodotus*. Ann Arbor.

Murnaghan, S. (1987) *Disguise and Recognition in the Odyssey*. Princeton.

(1988) "How a woman can be more like a man: The dialogue between Ischomachus and his wife in Xenophon's *Oeconomicus*," *Helios* 15: 9–22.

(1992) "Maternity and mortality in Homeric poetry," *CA* 11: 242–64.

(1997) "Equal honor and future glory: The plan of Zeus in the *Iliad*," In *Classical Closure: Reading the End in Greek and Latin Literature*, eds. D. H. Roberts, F. M. Dunn, and D. Fowler. Princeton: 23–42.

(2002) "The trials of Telemachus: Who was the *Odyssey* meant for?" *Arethusa* 35: 133–53.

Murray, G. (1934) *The Rise of the Greek Epic.* 4th edition. London.

Murray, O. (1991) "War and the symposium," in *Dining in a Classical Context*, ed. W. J. Slater. Ann Arbor: 83–103.

Naas, M. (1995) *Turning: From Persuasion to Philosophy. A Reading of Homer's Iliad.* New Jersey.

Naerebout, F. G. (1987) "Male–female relationships in the Homeric Epics," in Blok and Mason (1987) 109–46.

Nagler, M. N. (1974) *Spontaneity and Tradition.* Berkeley.

(1993) "Penelope's male hand: Gender and violence in the *Odyssey*," *Colby Quarterly* 29: 241–57.

(1996) "Dread goddess revisited," in *Reading the Odyssey*, ed. S. L. Schein. Princeton: 141–61.

Nagy, G. (1979) *The Best of the Achaeans.* 2nd edition (1999). Baltimore/London.

(1983) "Sema and noesis: Some illustrations," *Arethusa* 16: 36–55.

(1990a) *Greek Mythology and Poetics.* Ithaca/London.

(1990b) *Pindar's Homer: The Lyric Possession of an Epic Past.* Baltimore/London.

(1996) *Homeric Questions.* Austin.

(2001) "Homeric poetry and problems of multiformity: The 'panathenaic bottleneck.'" *CP* 96: 109–19.

(2002) *Plato's Rhapsody and Homer's Music: The Poetics of the Panathenaic Festival in Classical Athens.* Cambridge, MA/London.

Nails, D. (1995) *Agora, Academy, and the Conduct of Philosophy.* Dordrecht/Boston/London.

Nappa, C. (1994) "*Agamemnon* 717–36: The parable of the lion cub," *Mnemosyne* 47: 82–87.

Navia, L. E. (1984) "A reappraisal of Xenophon's *Apology*," in Kelly (1984) 47–65.

Nehamas, A. (1990) "Eristic, antilogic, sophistic, dialectic: Plato's demarcation of philosophy from sophistry," *Hist. Phil Quart.* 7: 3–16.

(1992a) "What did Socrates teach and to whom did he teach it?" *RMeta* 46: 279–306.

(1992b) "Voices of silence: on Gregory Vlastos' Socrates," *Arion* 2: 157–86.

(1998) *The Art of Living: Socratic Reflections from Plato to Foucault.* Berkeley/LA/London.

Németh, G. (2001) "Metics in Athens," *Acta Ant. Hung.* 41: 331–48.

Néraudau, J.-P. (1984) *Être enfant à Rome.* Paris.

Nes, D. van. (1963) *Die maritime Bildersprache des Aischylos.* Groningen.

Newmyer, S. T. (1992) "Plutarch on justice towards animals: Ancient insights on a modern debate," *Scholia* 1: 38–54.

(1999) "Speaking of beasts: The Stoics and Plutarch on animal reason and the modern case against animals," *QUCC* 63: 99–110.

Newton, R. M. (1983). "Poor Polyphemus: Emotional ambivalence in *Odyssey* 9 and 17," *CW* 76: 137–42.

(1997) "Odysseus and Melanthius," *GRBS* 38: 5–18.

Nichols, M. P. (1987) *Socrates and the Political Community: An Ancient Debate.* Albany.

Nicolay, E. (2001) "Homère et l'âme des bêtes," in Niewöhner and Sebon (2001) 51–8.

Niewöhner, F. and Sebon, J.-L. (eds.) (2001) *Die Seele der Tiere.* Wiesbaden.

Nightingale, A. W. (1995) *Genres in Dialogue: Plato and the Construct of Philosophy.* Cambridge.

Nimis, S. A. (1987) *Narrative Semiotics in the Epic Tradition: The Simile.* Bloomington.

(1999) "Ring-composition and linearity in Homer," in Mackay (1999) 65–78.

Nippel, W. (1990) *Griechen, Barbaren und "Wilde,"* Frankfurt-am-Main.

(2002) "The construction of the 'Other,'" in Harrison (2002a) 278–310.

Noble, W. and Davidson, I. (1997) *Human Evolution, Language and Mind.* Cambridge.

Noé, M. (1940) *Phoinix, Ilias und Homer. Untersuchungen zum neunten Gesang der Ilias.* Leipzig.

North, H. F. (1977) "The mare, the vixen, and the bee: *Sophrosyne* as the virtue of women in antiquity," *ICS* 2: 335–48.

Noske, B. (1989) *Humans and Other Animals.* London.

Notomi, N. (1999) *The Unity of Plato's Sophist: Between the Sophist and the Philosopher.* Cambridge.

Nussbaum, M. C. (1996) "Aristophanes and Socrates on learning practical wisdom," in Prior (1996) vol. I: 74–118.

(2001) *The Fragility of Goodness.* Cambridge.

Nye, A. (1990) *Words of Power.* New York/London.

Ober, J. (1989) *Mass and Elite in Democratic Athens: Rhetoric, Ideology, and the Power of the People.* Princeton.

(1996) *The Athenian Revolution.* Princeton.

(1998) *Political Dissent in Democratic Athens.* Princeton.

Ober, J. and Hedrick, C. (eds.) (1996) *Dêmokratia: A Conversation on Democracies, Ancient and Modern.* Princeton.

O'Brien, J. V. (1993) *The Transformation of Hera.* Lanham.

O'Brien, M. J. (1985) "Xenophanes, Aeschylus, and the doctrine of primeval brutishness," *CQ* 35: 264–77.

O'Higgins, D. (1993) "Above rubies: Admetus' perfect wife," *Arethusa* 26: 77–97.

Olson, S. D. (1989) "The stories of Helen and Menelaus (*Odyssey* 4.240–89) and the return of Odysseus," *AJP* 110: 387–94.

(1991) "Women's names and the reception of Odysseus in Scheria," *EMC* 36: 1–6.

(1991–2) "Servants' suggestions in Homer's *Odyssey*," *CJ* 87: 219–27.

(1995) *Blood and Iron: Stories and Storytelling in Homer's Odyssey. Mnemosyne* Suppl. 148. Leiden.

Ophir, A. (1991) *Plato's Invisible Cities: Discourse and Power in the Republic.* London.

O'Regan, D. E. (1992) *Rhetoric, Comedy, and the Violence of Language in Aristophanes' Clouds.* New York/Oxford.

Ormand, K. (1996) "Silent by convention? Sophocles' Tekmessa," *AJP* 117: 37–64.

Ornstein, R. (1997) *The Right Mind: Making Sense of the Hemispheres.* New York.

Osborne, C. (1990) "Boundaries in nature: Eating with animals in the fifth century B.C.," *BICS* 37: 15–29.

(1995) "Ancient vegetarianism," in *Food in Antiquity*, eds. J. Wilkins, D. Harvey, and M. Dobson. Exeter: 214–24.

Osborne, R. (1985) "Law in action in classical Athens," *JHS* 105: 40–58.

(1993) "Women and sacrifice in classical Greece," *CQ* 43: 392–405.

(2000) "An other view: An essay in political history," in Cohen (2000b) 23–42.

O'Sullivan, J. N. (1990) "Nature and culture in *Odyssey* 9?" *Sym. Osl.* 65: 7–17.

Owen, E. T. (1952) *The Harmony of Aeschylus.* Toronto.

Padel, R. (1992) *In and Out of the Mind: Greek Images of the Tragic Self.* Princeton.

Padilla, M. W. (1998) *The Myths of Herakles in Ancient Greece: Survey and Profile.* Lanham, MD.

Pagden, A. (1982) *The Fall of Natural Man: The American Indian and the Origins of Comparative Ethnology.* Cambridge.

Page, D. (1955) *The Homeric Odyssey.* Oxford.

Paisi-Apostolopoulou. (ed.) (1998) *Homerica. Proceedings of the 8th International Symposium on the Odyssey (1–5 September 1996).* Ithaca.

Palladini, L. P. (2001) "Traces of 'intellectualism' in Aeschylus," *Hermes* 129: 441–58.

Palmer, L. R. 1950. "The Indo-European origins of Greek justice," *TPhS* (no #): 149–68.

Parker, H. N. (2001) "The myth of the heterosexual: Anthropology and sexuality for classicists," *Arethusa* 34: 313–62.

Parker, R. (1983) *Miasma: Pollution and Purification in early Greek Religion.* Oxford.

(1984) "Sex, women, and ambiguous animals," *Phronesis* 39: 174–87.

(1996) *Athenian Religion: A History.* Oxford.

Parker, S. T. and McKinney, M. L. (1999) *The Origins of Intelligence: The Evolution of Cognitive Development in Monkeys, Apes, and Humans.* Baltimore/London.

Parry, A. M. (1981) *Logos and Ergon in Thucydides.* New York. (1957 Harvard dissertation).

(1989) *The Language of Achilles and Other Papers.* Oxford.

Patterson, C. (2002) *Eternal Treblinka: Our Treatment of Animals and the Holocaust.* New York.

Patterson, O. (1991) *Freedom in the Making of Western Culture.* London.

Patterson, R. (1987) "Plato on philosophic character," *JHPh* 25: 326–50.

Patzer, A. (1987) "Einleitung," in *Der historische Sokrates.* Wege der Forschung 585, ed. A. Patzer. Darmstadt: 1–40.

Payne, S. (1985) "Zoo-archaeology in Greece: A reader's guide," in *Contributions to Aegean Archaeology. Studies in honor of William A. McDonald*, eds. N. C. Wilkie and W. D. E. Coulson. Minneapolis: 211–44.

Pearson, A. C. (1922) "Sophocles, *Ajax*, 961–73," *CQ* 16: 124–36.

Pedrick, V. (1982) "Supplication in the *Iliad* and *Odyssey*," *TAPA* 112: 125–40.

(1983) "The paradigmatic nature of Nestor's Speech in *Iliad* 11," *TAPA* 113: 55–68.

(1988) "The hospitality of noble women in the *Odyssey*," *Helios* 15: 85–101.

(1994) "Eurycleia and Eurynome as Penelope's confidantes," in *Epic and Epoch: Essays on the Interpretation and History of a Genre*. Studies in Comparative Literature 24, ed. S. M. Oberhelman et al. Lubbock: 97–116.

(2001) Review of McClure (1999). *CW* 94: 282–3.

Pelliccia, H. (1995) *Mind, Body, and Speech in Homer and Pindar*. Hypomnemata 107. Göttingen.

Pelling, C. (ed.) (1990) *Characterization and Individuality in Greek Literature*. Oxford.

(1997a) (ed.) *Greek Tragedy and the Historian*. Oxford.

(1997b) "East is east and west is west – or are they? National stereotypes in Herodotus. *Histos* 1: (online) (www.dur.ac.uk/Classics/histos/1997/pelling.html).

(2000) *Literary Texts and the Greek Historian*. London/New York.

Pembroke, S. (1967) "Women in charge: the function of alternatives in early Greek tradition and the ancient idea of matriarchy," *Journal of the Warburg and Courtauld Institutes* 30: 1–35.

Pepperberg, I. M. (1999) *The Alex Studies: Cognitive and Communicative Abilities of Grey Parrots*. Cambridge, MA.

Peradotto, J. J. (1964) "Some patterns of nature imagery in the *Oresteia*," *AJP* 85: 378–93.

(1969) "The omen of the eagles and the ΗΘΟΣ of Agamemnon," *Phoenix* 23: 237–63.

Person, R. F., Jr. (1995) "The 'became silent to silence' formula in Homer," *GRBS* 36: 327–39.

Petrinovich, L. (1999) *Darwinian Dominion: Animal Welfare and Human Interests*. Cambridge, MA/London.

(2000) *The Cannibal Within*. New York.

Petrounias, E. (1976) *Funktion und Thematik der Bilder bei Aischylos*. Hypomnemata 48. Göttingen.

Pfeiffer, R. (1968) *History of Classical Scholarship*. Oxford.

Philippson, R. (1932) "Sokrates' Dialektik in Aristophanes' Wolken," *RM* 81: 30–8.

Pinker, S. (1994) *The Language Instinct*. New York.

(2002) *The Blank Slate: The Modern Denial of Human Nature*. New York.

Pinotti, P. (1994) "Gli animali in Platone: metafore e tassonomie," in *Filosofi Animali nel Mondo Antico*, eds. S. Castignone and G. Lanata. Pisa: 101–22.

Pinsent, J. (1984) "The Trojans in the *Iliad*," in *The Trojan War: Its Historicity and Context*, eds. L. Foxhall and J. K. Davies. Bristol: 141–62.

Plass, P. (1973) "A fragment of Plato in Diogenes Laertius," *Modern Schoolman* 51: 29–46.

Pluhar, E. B. (1995) *Beyond Prejudice*. Durham.

Podlecki, A. J. (1961) "Guest-gifts and nobodies in *Odyssey* 9," *Phoenix* 15: 125–33.

(1967) "Omens in the *Odyssey*," *G&R* 14: 12–23.

Poliakov, L. (ed.) (1975) *Homme et bêtes: entretiens sur le racisme*. Paris.

Pollard, J. R. T. (1948) "Birds in Aeschylus," *G&R* 17: 116–27.

Pomeroy, S. B. (2002) *Spartan Women*. New York.

Pool, E. H. (1983) "Clytemnestra's first entrance in Aeschylus' *Agamemnon*: Analysis of a controversy," *Mnemosyne* 36: 71–116.

Postlethwaite, N. (1988) "Thersites in the *Iliad*," *G&R* 35: 123–36.

(1995) "Agamemnon best of spearmen," *Phoenix* 49: 95–103.

(1998) "Akhilleus and Agamemnon: Generalized reciprocity," in Gill, Postlethwaite, and Seaford (1998) 93–101.

Pötscher, W. (1985/6) "Homer, *Ilias* 24, 601ff. und die Niobe-Gestalt," *GB* 12: 21–35.

Poulakos, T. (1997) *Speaking for the Polis: Isocrates' Rhetorical Education*. Columbia, SC.

Powell, A. (1989) "Mendacity and Sparta's use of the visual," in *Classical Sparta: Techniques Behind Her Success*, ed. A. Powell. Norman/London: 173–92.

(1999) "Spartan women assertive in politics? Plutarch's lives of Agis and Kleomenes," in Hodkinson and Powell (1999) 393–419.

Powell, B. B. (1991) *Homer and the Origins of the Greek Alphabet*. Cambridge.

(2002) *Writing and the Origins of Greek Literature*. Cambridge.

Pratt, L. H. (1993) *Lying and Poetry from Homer to Pindar*. Ann Arbor.

Preece, R. (2002) *Awe for the Tiger, Love for the Lamb: A Chronicle of Sensibility to Animals*. Vancouver/Toronto.

Preece, R. and Chamberlain, L. (1995) *Animal Welfare and Human Values*. Waterloo, Canada.

Press, G. A. (ed.) (1993a) *Plato's Dialogues: New Studies and Interpretations*. Lanham, MD.

(1993b) "Principles of dramatic and non-dogmatic Plato interpretation," in Press (1993a) 107–27.

(1995) "Plato's Dialogues as Enactments," in Gonzalez (1995a). 133–52.

(2000) (ed.) *Who Speaks for Plato? Studies in Platonic Anonymity*. Lanham, MD.

Preus, A. (1983) "Biological theory in Porphyry's *De abstinentia*," *Ancient Philosophy* 3: 149–59.

(1990) "Animal and human souls in the peripatetic school," *Skepsis* 1: 67–99.

Prier, R. A. (1989) *Thauma Idesthai: The Phenomenology of Sight and Appearance in Archaic Greek*. Tallahassee.

Prieur, J. (1988) *Les animaux sacrés dans l'antiquité*. Rennes.

Prior, W. J. (ed.) (1996) *Socrates: Critical Assessments*. 4 vols. London/New York.

(1997) "Why did Plato write Socratic dialogues?" *Apeiron* 30: 109–23.

(2001) "The historicity of Plato's *Apology*," *Polis* 18: 41–57.

Pritchett, W. K. (1993) *The Liar School of Herodotus*. Amsterdam.

Pucci, P. (1987) *Odysseus Polytropos*. Ithaca and London.

(1998) *The Song of the Sirens*. Lanham.

(2002) "Theology and poetics in the *Iliad*," *Arethusa* 35: 17–34.

Purcell, N. (1995) "Eating fish: The paradoxes of seafood," in *Food in Antiquity*, eds. J. Wilkins, D. Harvey, and M. Dobson. Exeter: 132–49.

Quincey, J. H. (1981) "Another purpose for Plato, *Republic* I," *Hermes* 109: 300–15.

Raaflaub, K. A. (1980) "Des freien Bürgers Recht der freien Rede," in *Studien zur antiken Sozialgeschichte: Festschrift für F. Vittinghoff*, eds. W. Eck, H. Galsterer, and H. Wolff. Köln-Wien: 7–57.

(1996) "Equalities and Inequalities in Athenian Democracy," in Ober and Hedrick (1996) 139–74.

(1998) "The transformation of Athens in the fifth century," in Boedeker and Raaflaub (1998) 15–41.

(2001) "Political thought, civic responsibility, and the Greek polis," in Arnason and Murphy (2001a) 72–117.

(2004) *The Discovery of Freedom in Ancient Greece*. R. Franciscono, tr. Chicago/London.

Rabel, R. J. (1982) "Apollo in the vulture simile of the *Oresteia*," *Mnemosyne* 35: 324–6.

(1984) "The lost children of the *Oresteia*," *Eranos* 82: 211–13.

(1997) *Plot and Point of View in the Iliad*. Ann Arbor.

Rabinowitz, N. S. (1981) "From force to persuasion: Aeschylus' *Oresteia* as cosmogonic myth," *Ramus* 10: 159–91.

(1993) *Anxiety Veiled: Euripides and the Traffic in Women*. Ithaca/London.

Race, W. H. (1993) "First appearances in the *Odyssey*," *TAPA* 123: 79–107.

Rachels, J. (1990) *Created from Animals: The Moral Implications of Darwinism*. Oxford/New York.

Rahn, H. (1953) "Tier und Mensch in der Homerischen Auffassung der Wirklichkeit," *Paideuma* 5: 274–97, 431–80.

(1967) "Das Tier in der homerischen Dichtung," *Studium Generale* 20: 90–105.

Rankin, H. D. (1983) *Sophists, Socratics and Cynics*. Totowa, NJ.

Rappe, S. L. (1995) "Socrates and self-knowledge," *Apeiron* 28: 1–24.

Rawson, C. (1984) "Narrative and the proscribed act: Homer, Euripides and the literature of cannibalism," in *Literary Theory and Criticism. Festschrift Presented to René Wellek in Honor of his Eightieth birthday. Part II. Criticism*, ed. J. P. Strelka. Bern/Frankfurt: 1159–87.

Rawson, E. (1969) *The Spartan Tradition in European Thought*. Oxford.

Redfield, J. M. (1975) *Nature and Culture in the Iliad*. Chicago and London.

(1979) "The proem of the *Iliad*: Homer's art," *CP* 74: 95–110.

Reece, S. (1993) *The Stranger's Welcome: Oral Theory and the Aesthetics of the Homeric Hospitalilty Scene*. Ann Arbor.

Reeder, E. D. (ed.) (1995) *Pandora: Women in Classical Greece*. Baltimore.

Reeve, C. D. C. (1985) "Socrates meets Thrasymachus," *Archiv für Geschichte der philosophie* 67: 246–65.

(1988) *Philosopher-Kings: The Argument of Plato's Republic*. Princeton.

(1989) *Socrates in the Apology*. Indianapolis/Cambridge.

(2000) "Socrates the Apollonian?" in Smith and Woodruff (2000) 24–39.

Regan, T. (1983) *The Case for Animal Rights*. Berkeley.

(1991) *The Thee Generation*. Philadelphia.

(2001) *Defending Animal Rights*. Urbana and Chicago.

Rehm, R. (1994) *Marriage to Death: The Conflation of Wedding and Funeral Rituals in Greek Tragedy.* Princeton.

Reichman, J. B., S. J. (2000) *Evolution, Animal 'Rights', The Environment.* Washington, D.C.

Reinhold, M. (1976) "The generation gap in antiquity," in *The Conflict of Generations in Ancient Greece and Rome*, ed. S. Bertman. Amsterdam: 15–54.

Renehan, R. (1981) "The Greek anthropocentric view of man," *HSCPh* 85: 239–59.

  (1987) "The *Heldentod* in Homer: One heroic idea," *CP* 82: 99–116.

  (1993) "A note on Plato *Apology* 27B4–5," *CP* 88: 318–19.

Rhodes, P. J. (2000) "Oligarchs in Athens," in Brock and Hodkinson (2000a) 119–36.

Richardson, B. E. (1969) *Old Age Among the Greeks.* New York.

Richardson, N. J. (1974) *The Homeric Hymn to Demeter.* Oxford.

  (1980) "Literary criticism in the exegetical scholia to the *Iliad*: A sketch," *CQ* 30: 265–87.

Richardson, S. (1990) *The Homeric Narrator.* Nashville.

Rifkin, J. (1992) *Beyond Beef.* New York.

Rist, J. M. (1982) *Human Value: A Study in Ancient Philosophical Ethics.* Leiden.

Ritvo, H. (1987) *The Animal Estate: The English and Other Creatures in the Victorian Age.* Cambridge, MA.

Robb, K. (ed.) (1983) *Language and Thought in Early Greek Philosophy.* La Salle, Il.

  (1993) "*Asebeia* and *sunousia*: the issues behind the indictment of Socrates," in Press (1993a) 77–106.

Roberts, D. H. (1985) "Orestes as fulfillment, *teraskopos*, and *teras* in the *Oresteia*," *AJP* 106: 283–97.

Roberts, J. T. (1994) *Athens on Trial. The Antidemocratic Tradition in Western Thought.* Princeton.

Robinson, R. (1953) *Plato's Earlier Dialectic.* 2nd edition. Oxford.

Robinson, T. M. (1987) *Heraclitus: Fragments.* Toronto/Buffalo/London.

Rocco, C. (1997) *Tragedy and Enlightenment.* Berkeley.

Rochette, B. (1997) "Grecs, Romains et barbares: à la recherche de l'identité ethnique et linguistique des Grecs et des Romains," *RBPh* 75: 37–57.

Rogers, L. J. (1997) *Minds of Their Own: Thinking and Awareness in Animals.* Sydney/Boulder.

Rogers, L. J. and Kaplan, G. (2000) *Communication in Birds, Mammals, and Other Animals.* Cambridge, MA.

Rohde, E. (1925). *Psyche. The Cult of Souls and Belief in Immortality among the Greeks.* 8th edition. W. B. Hillis, tr. London.

Roisman, H. M. (1994) "Like father like son. Telemachus' KERDEA," *RhM* 134: 1–22.

Rollin, B. E. (1981) *Animal Rights and Human Morality.* Buffalo, NY.

  (1998) *The Unheeded Cry: Animal Consciousness, Animal Pain and Science.* Expanded edition. Ames, Iowa.

Romaine, S. (1999) *Communicating Gender.* Mahwah, NJ/London.

Romilly, J. de. (1975) *Magic and Rhetoric in Ancient Greece.* Cambridge.

(1993) "Les barbares dans la pensée de la Grèce classique," *Phoenix* 47: 283–92.

Romm, J. S. (1992) *The Edges of the Earth in Ancient Thought*. Princeton.

Roochnik, D. L. (1990) *The Tragedy of Reason: Toward a Platonic Conception of Logos*. New York/London.

Rose, G. P. (1979) "Odysseus' barking heart," *TAPA* 109: 215–30.

Rose, H. J. (1956) "Divine misgivings," *HThR* 49: 63–72.

Rose, P. W. (1997) "Ideology in the *Iliad*: polis, basileus, theoi," *Arethusa* 30: 151–99.

(2003) "'The conquest continues': towards denaturalizing Greek and Roman imperialisms," *CW* 96: 409–15.

Rosellini, M. and Saïd, S. (1978) "Usages de femmes et autres nomoi chez les 'sauvages' d'Hérodote: essai de lecture structurale," *Annali della Scuola Normale Superiore di Pisa*. 8: 949–1005.

Rosen, R. M. and Farrell, J. (eds.) (1993) *Nomodeiktes: Greek Studies in Honor of Martin Ostwald*. Ann Arbor.

Rosenbloom, D. (1995) "Myth, history, and hegemony," in Goff (1995). 91–130.

Rosenmeyer, T. G. (1982) *The Art of Aeschylus*. Berkeley.

Rosivach, V. J. (1994) *The System of Public Sacrifice in Fourth-Century Athens*. American Classical Studies 4. Atlanta.

(1999) "Enslaving *barbaroi* and the Athenian ideology of slavery," *Historia* 48: 129–57.

Rosner, J. A. (1976) "The speech of Phoenix: *Iliad* 9.434–605," *Phoenix* 30: 314–27.

Ross, S. D. (1989) *Metaphysical Aporia and Philosophical Heresy*. Albany.

Rossetti, L. (1993) "'If we link the essence of rhetoric with deception': Vincenzo on Socrates and rhetoric," *Ph&Rh* 26: 311–21.

Roth, P. (1993) "The theme of corrupted *xenia* in Aeschylus' *Oresteia*," *Mnemosyne* 46: 1–17.

Rothwell, K. S. (1995) "Aristophanes' *Wasps* and the sociopolitics of Aesop's fables," *CJ* 93: 233–54.

Rowe, C. (1998) "Democracy and Sokratic-Platonic philosophy," in Boedeker and Raaflaub (1998) 241–53.

Rozokoki, A. (2001) "Penelope's dream in book 19 of the *Odyssey*," *CQ* 51: 1–6.

Rudd, R. (1992) *Biology, Ethics and Animals*. Oxford.

Ruffell, I. (2000) "The world turned upside down: Utopia and utopianism in the fragments of old comedy," in Harvey and Wilkins (2000) 473–506.

Ruijgh, C. J. (1991) *Scripta Minora I*. Amsterdam.

Rundin, J. (1996) "A politics of eating: Feasting in early Greek society," *AJP* 117: 179–215.

(1998) "The vegetarianism of Empedocles in its historical context," *Ancient World* 29: 19–36.

Ruprecht, L. A., Jr. (2001) "Why the Greeks?" in Arnason and Murphy (2001a) 29–55.

Russo, J. and Simon, B. (1968) "Homeric psychology and the oral epic tradition," *JHI* 29: 483–98.

Rutherford, R. B. (1986) "The philosophy of the *Odyssey*," *JHS* 106: 145–62.

(1995) *The Art of Plato: Ten Essays in Platonic Interpretation*. Cambridge, MA.

Ryder, R. D. (1989) *Animal Revolution: Changing Attitudes towards Speciesism.* Oxford.

Ryle, G. (1966) *Plato's Progress.* Cambridge.

Saayman, F. (1993) "Dogs and lions in the *Oresteia*," *Akroterion* 38: 11–18.

Sachs, A. (1933) "Die Meleager erzählung in der *Ilias*," *Philologus* 88: 16–29.

Sacks, K. S. (1990) *Diodorus Siculus and the First Century.* Princeton.

Saïd, E. W. (1994) *Orientalism.* New York.

Saïd, S. (1979) "Les crimes des prétendants, la maison d'Ulysse et les festins de l'*Odyssée*," in *Études de Littérature Ancienne*, ed. S. Saïd. Paris: 9–49.

(1983a) "Concorde et civilisations dans les Euménides. (Euménides, vv. 858–866 et 976–987)," in *Théâtre et Spectacles dans l'Antiquité.* Leiden: 97–121.

(1983b) "Féminin, femme et femelle dans les grands traités biologiques d'Aristote," in *La Femme dans les sociétés antiques*, ed. E. Lévy. Leiden: 93–123.

(1985) "Usages de femmes et sauvagerie dans l'éthnographie grecque d'Hérodote à Diodore et Strabon," in *La Femme dans le Monde Méditerranéen I: Antiquité.* Lyon: 137–50.

(1991) (ed.) *ΕΛΛΗΝΙΣΜΟΣ: Quelques jalons pour une histoire de l'identité grecque.*

(1998) "Tragedy and politics," in Boedeker and Raaflaub (1998) 275–95.

(2001) "The discourse of identity in Greek rhetoric from Isocrates to Aristides," in Malkin (2001a) 275–99.

Sajavaara, K. and Lehtonen, J. (1997) "The silent Finn revisited," in Jaworksi (1997) 263–83.

Sale, (W.) M. (1989) "The Trojans, statistics, and Milman Parry," *GRBS* 30: 341–410.

(1994) "The government of Troy: Politics in the *Iliad*," *GRBS* 35: 5–102.

(2001) "The oral formulaic theory today," in Watson (2001) 53–80.

Sallares, R. (1991) *The Ecology of the Ancient Greek World.* London and Ithaca.

Sancassano, M. L. (1997) *Il serpente e le sue immagini.* Como.

Sansone, D. (1975) *Aeschylean Metaphors for Intellectual Activity. Hermes* Einzelschriften 35. Wiesbaden.

Sapontzis, S. F. (1987) *Morals, Reason, and Animals.* Philadelphia.

Sarpaki, A. (1992) "The palaeoethnobotanical approach: The Mediterranean triad or is it a quartet?" in Wells (1992) 61–76.

Sassi, M. M. (2001) *The Science of Man in Ancient Greece.* P. Tucker, tr. Chicago/London.

Sattel, J. W. (1983) "Men, inexpressiveness, and power," in *Language, Gender and Society*, eds. B. Thorne et al. London/Tokyo: 118–24.

Savage-Rumbaugh, S. (1997) "Why are we afraid of apes with language?" in Scheibel and Schopf (1997) 43–69.

Saxonhouse, A. W. (1978) "Comedy in Callipolis: Animal imagery in the *Republic*," *APSR* 72: 888–901.

(1992) *Fear of Diversity: The Birth of Political Science in Ancient Greek Thought.* Chicago/London.

(1996) *Athenian Democracy: Modern Mythmakers and Ancient Theorists*. Notre Dame/London.

Sayre, K. M. (1995) *Plato's Literary Garden: How To Read a Platonic Dialogue*. Notre Dame/London.

Schaps, D. (1977) "The woman least mentioned: Etiquette and women's names," *CQ* 22: 323–30.

(1993) "Aeschylus' politics and the theme of the *Oresteia*," in Rosen and Farrell (1993) 505–15.

(1998) "What was free about a free Athenian woman?" *TAPA* 128: 161–88.

Scheibel, A. B. and Schopf, J. W. (eds.) (1997) *The Origin and Evolution of Intelligence*. Boston.

Scheid-Tissinier, E. (1993) "Télémaque et les prétendants. Les νέοι d'Ithaque," *AC* 62: 1–22.

Schein, S. (1970) "Odysseus and Polyphemus in the *Odyssey*," *GRBS* 11: 73–83.

(1982) "The Cassandra scene in Aeschylus' *Agamemnon*," *G&R* 29: 11–16.

(1984) *The Mortal Hero*. Berkeley.

Schlosser, E. (2001) *Fast Food Nation*. Boston/New York.

Schlunk, R. R. (1976) "The theme of the suppliant-exile in the *Iliad*," *AJP* 97: 199–209.

Schmid, W. T. (1998) *Plato's Charmides and the Socratic Idea of Rationality*. Albany.

Schmidt, J.-U. (2002) "Thersites und das Politische Anliegen des Iliasdichters," *RhM* 145: 129–49.

Schmiel, R. (1972) "Telemachus in Sparta," *TAPA* 103: 463–72.

Schmitt, A. (1990) *Selbständigkeit und Abhängigkeit menschlichen Handelns bei Homer*. Mainz.

Schmitt Pantel, P. (ed.) (1992a) *A History of Women in the West. Vol. 1. From Ancient Goddesses to Christian Saints*. Cambridge, MA.

(1992b) "The woman's voice," in Schmitt Pantel (1992a) 473.

Schmitz, C. (2001) "'Denn Auch Niobe...' – Die Bedeutung der Niobe-Erzählung in Achills Rede (V 599–620)," *Hermes* 129: 145–57.

Schnapp, A. (1997) "Images of young people in the Greek city-state," in *A History of Young People in the West. Vol. I: Ancient and Medieval Rites of Passage*, eds. G. Levi and J.-C. Schmitt. C. Naish, trs. Cambridge, MA/London: 12–50.

Schnapp-Gourbeillon, A. (1981) *Lions, héros, masques: les représentations de l'animal chez Homère*. Paris.

Schofield, M. (1986) "Euboulia in the *Iliad*," *CQ* 36: 6–31.

(1991) "Heraclitus' theory of soul and its antecedents," in Everson (1991) 13–34.

(1992) "Socrates versus Protagoras," in Gower and Stokes (1992) 122–36.

Schrade, H. (1952) *Götter und Menschen Homers*. Stuttgart.

Schulkin, J. (2000) *Roots of Social Sensibility and Neural Function*. Cambridge, MA/London.

Schusterman, R. J. and Gisiner, R. C. (1997) "Pinnipeds, porpoises, and parsimony: Animal language research viewed from a bottom-up perspective," in Mitchell et al. (1997) 370–82.

Scobie, A. (1983) *Apuleius and Folklore*. London.

Scodel, R. (1982) "The autobiography of Phoenix: *Iliad* 9.444–95," *AJP* 103: 128–36.

   (1989) "The word of Achilles," *CP* 84: 91–9.

   (1994) "Odysseus and the stag," *CQ* 44: 530–4.

   (1998) "The removal of arms, the recognition with Laertes, and narrative tension in the *Odyssey*," *CP* 93: 1–17.

   (2001) "The suitor's games," *AJP* 122: 307–27.

   (2002) *Listening to Homer: Tradition, Narrative, and Audience.* Ann Arbor.

Scott, D. (1999) "Platonic pessimism and moral education," *OSAPh* 17: 15–36.

Scott, G. A. (2000) *Plato's Socrates as Educator.* Albany.

   (2002) (ed.) *Does Socrates Have a Method?* University Park.

Scott, J. A. (1917) "The journey made by Telemachus and its influence on the action of the *Odyssey*," *CJ* 13: 420–8.

Scott, W. C. (1974) *The Oral Nature of the Homeric Simile. Mnemosyne* Suppl. 28. Leiden.

   (1984) *Musical Design in Aeschylean Theater.* Hanover/London.

Scully, S. (1990) *Homer and the Sacred City.* Ithaca/London.

Scurlock, J. (2002) "Animals in ancient Mesopotamian religion" and "Animals in ancient Mesopotamian sacrifice," in Collins (2002) 361–403.

Seaford, R. (1994) *Reciprocity and Ritual. Homer and Tragedy in the Developing City-State.* Oxford.

   (1995) "Historicizing tragic ambivalence: the vote of Athena," in Goff (1995) 202–21.

   (2000) "The social function of Attic tragedy: A response to Jasper Griffin," *CQ* 50: 30–44.

Sealey, R. (1990) *Women and Law in Classical Athens.* Chapel Hill/London.

   (1987) *Dialogue and Discovery: A Study in Socratic Method.* Albany.

Segal, C. P. (1962) "Gorgias and the psychology of the *logos*," *HSCPh* 66: 99–155.

   (1963) "Nature and the world of man in Greek literature," *Arion* 2: 19–53.

   (1971) *The Theme of the Mutilation of the Corpse in the Iliad. Mnemosyne* Suppl. 17. Leiden.

   (1978) "The menace of Dionysus: Sex roles and reversals in Euripides' *Bacchae*," *Arethusa* 11: 185–202.

   (1981) *Tragedy and Civilization: An Interpretation of Sophocles.* Cambridge, MA.

   (1986) "Greek tragedy and society: A structuralist perspective," in *Greek Tragedy and Political Theory*, ed. J. P. Euben. Berkeley: 43–75.

   (1994) *Singers, Heroes, and Gods in the Odyssey.* Ithaca.

Seibel, A. (1995) "Widerstreit und Ergänzung: Thersites und Odysseus als Rivalisierende Demagogen in der Ilias (B 190–264)," *Hermes* 123: 385–97.

Seiler, H. (1953) "Ἄνθρωποι," *Glotta* 32: 225–36.

Severyns, A. (1948) *Homère III. L'artiste.* Bruxelles.

   (1966) *Les dieux d' Homère.* Paris.

Seyfarth, R. M. and Cheney, D. L. (1997) "Communication and the minds of monkeys," in Scheibel and Schopf (1997) 27–42.

Shaw, B. D. (1982–3) "'Eaters of flesh, drinkers of milk': The ancient Mediterranean ideology of the pastoral nomad," *Ancient Society* 13–14: 5–31.

Shaw, M. (1975) "Female intruder: Women in fifth-century drama," *CP* 70: 255–66.

Sheppard, J. T. (1922) "The prelude of the *Agamemnon*," *CR* 36: 5–11.

Shettleworth, S. J. (1998) *Cognition, Evolution, and Behavior*. New York/Oxford.

Shipp, G. P. (1972) *Studies in the Language of Homer*. Cambridge.

Sideras, A. (1971) *Aeschylus Homericus. Untersuchungen zu den Homerismen der Aischyleische Sprache*. Hypomnemata 31. Göttingen.

Sidwell, K. (1996) "Purification and pollution in Aeschylus' *Eumenides*," *CQ* 46: 44–57.

(2000) "From old to middle to new? Aristotle's *Poetics* and the history of Athenian comedy," in Harvey and Wilkins (2000) 247–58.

Sier, K. (1992) "Die Rolle des Skythen in den Thesmophoriazusen des Aristophanes," in Müller, Sier, and Werner (1992) 63–83.

Sifakis, G. M. (1971) *Parabasis and Animal Choruses*. London.

Sifianou, M. (1997) "Silence and politeness," in Jaworksi (1997) 63–84.

Sikes, E. E. (1914) *The Anthropology of the Greeks*. London.

Silk, M. S. (1974) *Interaction in Poetic Imagery*. Cambridge.

(1995) "Nestor, Amphitryon, Philocleon, Cephalus: The language of old men in Greek literature from Homer to Menander," in Martino and Sommerstein (1995) 165–214.

(2000) *Aristophanes and the Definition of Comedy*. Oxford.

Simoons, F. J. (1994) *Eat Not This Flesh: Food Avoidances from Prehistory to the Present*. 2nd edition. Madison.

Sinclair, R. K. (1988) *Democracy and Participation in Athens*. Cambridge.

Singer, P. (1986) "Animals and the value of life," in *Matters of Life and Death*, ed. T. Regan. 2nd edition. New York: 339–80.

(1990) *Animal Liberation*. 2nd edition. New York.

Sinos, D. (1980) *Achilles, Patroklos and the Meaning of Philos*. Innsbrucker Beiträge zur Sprachwissenschaft 29. Innsbruck.

Sissa, G. (1990) *Greek Virginity*. A. Goldhammer, tr. Cambridge, MA.

Skinner, M. B. (1993) "Woman and language in archaic Greece, or why is Sappho a woman?" in *Feminist Theory and the Classics*, eds. N. S. Rabinowitz and A. Richlin. New York/London: 124–44.

Skousgaard, S. (1979) "Genuine speech vs. chatter: A Socratic problematic," in *Plato: True and Sophistic Rhetoric*, ed. K. V. Erickson. Amsterdam: 375–83.

Skydsgaard, J. E. (1980) "Non-slave labour in rural Italy during the late republic," in *Non-Slave Labour in the Greco-Roman World*. Proceedings of the Cambridge Philological Society Suppl. vol. 6, ed. P. Garnsey. Cambridge: 65–72.

(1988) "Transhumance in ancient Greece," in Whittaker (1988) 75–86.

Smith, A. (1984) "Did Porphyry reject the transmigration of human souls into animals?" *RhM* 127: 276–84.

Smith, L. R. (1995) "The interrogation of Meletus," *CQ* 45: 372–88.

Smith, N. D. (1991) "Aristotle's theory of natural slavery," in *A Companion to Aristotle's Politics*, eds. D. Keyt and F. D. Miller, Jr.: Oxford/Cambridge, MA. 142–55.

Smith, N. D. and Woodruff, P. B. (eds.) (2000) *Reason and Religion in Socratic Philosophy*. Oxford/New York.

Smith, O. (1965) "Some observations on the structure of imagery in *Aeschylus*," *C&M* 26: 10–72.

Smith, W. (1988) "The disguises of the gods in the *Iliad*," *Numen* 35: 161–78.

Snell, B. (1960) *The Discovery of the Mind*. T. G. Rosenmeyer, tr. New York.

Sobkowiak, W. (1997) "Silence and markedness theory," in Jaworksi (1997) 39–61.

Solmsen, F. (1954) "The 'gift' of speech in Homer and Hesiod," *TAPA* 85: 1–15.

(1955) "Antecedents of Aristotle's psychology and scale of beings," *AJP* 76: 148–64.

Sommerstein, A. H. (1980) "The naming of women in Greek and Roman comedy," *Quaderni di Storia* 11: 393–418.

(1995) "The language of Athenian women," in Martino and Sommerstein (1995) 61–85.

(1996) *Aeschylean Tragedy*. Bari.

Sorabji, R. (1993) *Animal Minds & Human Morals*. Ithaca.

Sourvinou, C. (1971) "Aristophanes, *Lysistrata*, 641–647," *CQ* 21: 339–42.

Sourvinou-Inwood, C. (1986) "Myth as history: The previous owners of the Delphic oracle," in *Interpretations of Greek Mythology*, ed. J. Bremmer. Totowa, NJ: 215–41.

(1995) *'Reading' Greek Death To the End of the Classical Period*. Oxford.

(2003) *Tragedy and Athenian Religion*. Lanham.

Sowa, C. A. (1984) *Traditional Themes and the Homeric Hymns*. Chicago.

Spelman, E. V. (1983) "Aristotle and the politicalization of the soul," in *Discovering Reality*, eds. S. Harding and M. B. Hintikka. Holland/Boston/London: 17–30.

Spence, I. G. (1993) *The Cavalry of Classical Greece*. Oxford.

Spiegel, M. (1988) *The Dreaded Comparison*. Philadelphia.

Stager, L. E. (1998) "Forging an identity: The emergence of ancient Israel," in *The Oxford History of the Biblical World*, ed. M. D. Coogan. Oxford/New York: 90–131.

Stanford, C. (2001) *Significant Others: The Ape-Human Continuum and the Quest for Human Nature*. New York.

Stanford, W. B. (1939) *Ambiguity in Greek Literature*. Oxford.

(1972) *Greek Metaphor*. New York.

Steinberger, P. J. (1997) "Was Socrates guilty as charged?" *AncPhil* 17: 13–29.

Steiner, D. (2001) "Slander's bite: *Nemean* 7.102–5 and the language of invective," *JHS* 121: 154–8.

Steiner, D. T. (1994) *The Tyrant's Writ: Myths and Images of Writing in Ancient Greece*. Princeton.

Steiner, G. (1967) *Language and Silence: Essays on Language, Literature and the Inhuman*. New York.

Stemmer, P. (1992) *Platons Dialektik: Die früheren und mittleren Dialoge*. Quellen und Studien zur Philosophie 31. Berlin/New York.

Stern, P. (1993) *Socratic Rationalism and Political Philosophy*. New York.

Stokes, M. C. (1992) "Socrates' mission," in Gower and Stokes (1992) 26–81.

Stone, I. F. (1988) *The Trial of Socrates*. Boston/Toronto.

Stramaglia, A. (1995) "Le voci dei fantasmi," in Martino and Sommerstein (1995) 193–228.

Strauss, B. (1986) *Athens After the Peloponnesian War*. Ithaca.

Sullivan, L.-L. (1997) "Athenian impiety trials in the late fourth century B.C.," *CQ* 47: 136–52.

Sullivan, S. D. (1988) *Psychological Activity in Homer: A Study of Phrên*. Ottawa.

　(1989) "The psychic term *noos* in Homer and the *Homeric Hymns*," SIFC 7: 152–95.

　(1995a) *Psychological and Ethical Ideas: What Early Greeks Say. Mnemosyne* Suppl. 144. Leiden.

　(1995b) "The relationship of speech and psychic entities in early Greek poetry," *Prometheus* 21: 228–40.

　(1996) "The psychic term ἦτορ: its nature and relation to person in Homer and the *Homeric Hymns*," *Emerita* 64: 11–29.

　(1997) *Aeschylus' Use of Psychological Terminology: Traditional and New*. Montreal.

Sultan, N. (1999) *Exile and the Poetics of Loss in Greek Tradition*. Lanham.

Susanetti, D. (1991) "Silenzio, Socrate sta pensando," *Lexis* 7–8: 113–33.

Suter, A. (1991) "Language of gods and language of men: The case of Paris/Alexandros," *Lexis* 7–8: 13–25.

Swain, S. (1996) *Hellenism and Empire: Language, Classicism, and Power in the Greek World AD 50–250*. Oxford.

Tacon, J. (2001) "Ecclesiastic *thorubos*: Interventions, interruptions, and popular involvement in the Athenian assembly," *G&R* 48: 173–92.

Tannen, D. (1993) "The relativity of linguistic strategies: Rethinking power and solidarity in gender and dominance," in *Gender and Conversational Interaction*, ed. D. Tannen. New York/Oxford: 165–88.

Tannen, D. and Saville-Troike (eds.) (1985) *Perspectives on Silence*. Norwood, New Jersey.

Taplin, O. (1977) *The Stagecraft of Aeschylus*. Oxford.

　(1978) *Greek Tragedy In Action*. Berkeley/Los Angeles.

　(1986) "Homer's use of Achilles' earlier campaigns in the *Iliad*," in *Chios: A Conference at the Homereion in Chios*, eds. J. Boardman and C. E. Vaphopoulou-Richardson. Oxford: 15–19.

　(1990) "Agamemnon's role in the *Iliad*," in Pelling (1990) 60–82.

　(1992) *Homeric Soundings*. Oxford.

Tarkow, T. A. (1981) "Thematic implications of costuming in the *Oresteia*," *Maia* 32: 153–65.

Tarrant, D. (1946) "Imagery in Plato's *Republic*," *CQ* 40: 27–34.

Teeter, E. (2002) "Animals in Egyptian religion," in Collins (2002) 335–60.

Teloh, H. (1986) "The importance of interlocutors' characters in Plato's early dialogues," *BACAP* 2: 25–38.

Tester, K. (1991) *Animals and Society: The Humanity of Animal Rights*. London/New York.

Thalmann, W. G. (1984) *Conventions of Form and Thought in early Greek Epic.* Baltimore and London.

(1985) "Speech and silence in the *Oresteia*, I: *Agamemnon* 1025–1029," *Phoenix* 39: 99–118; 221–37.

(1988) "Thersites: Comedy, scapegoats, and heroic ideology in the *Iliad*," *TAPA* 118: 1–28.

(1998a) "Female slaves in the *Odyssey*," in Joshel and Murnaghan (1998) 22–34.

(1998b) *The Swineherd and the Bow. Representations of Class in the Odyssey.* Ithaca/London.

Thesleff, H. (1984) "Plato and inequality," in Kajanto (1984) 17–29.

Thomas, K. (1983) *Man and the Natural World.* New York.

Thomas, R. (1989) *Oral Tradition and Written Record in Classical Athens.* Cambridge.

(1992) *Literacy and Orality in Ancient Greece.* Cambridge.

(2000) *Herodotus in Context: Ethnography, Science and the Art of Persuasion.* Cambridge.

(2001) "Ethnicity, genealogy, and Hellenism in Herodotus," in Malkin (2001a) 213–33.

Thommen, L. (1999) "Spartanische Frauen," *MH* 56: 129–49.

Thompson, D. W. (1936) *A Glossary of Greek Birds.* London.

Thornton, A. (1984) *Homer's Iliad: Its Composition and the Motif of Supplication.* Hypomnemata 81. Göttingen.

Thornton, B. (1999) *Plagues of the Mind.* Wilmington, Delaware.

(2000) *Greek Ways: How the Greeks Created Western Civilization.* San Francisco.

Thür, G. (1977) *Beweisführung von den Schwurgerichtshöfen Athens: Die Proklesis zur Basanos.* Wien.

Todd, S. and Millett, P. (1990) "Law, society and Athens," in *Nomos: Essays in Athenian Law, Politics, and Society*, eds. P. Cartledge, P. Millett, and S. Todd. Cambridge: 1–18.

Tomasello, M. (1999) *The Cultural Origins of Human Cognition.* Cambridge, MA/London.

Tompkins, D. P. (1993) "Archidamus and the question of characterization in Thucydides," in Rosen and Farrell (1993) 99–111.

Torey, Z. (1999) *The Crucible of Consciousness.* Oxford.

Trédé, M. (1991) "Quelques définitions de l'hellénisme au IVe siècle avant J.-C. et leurs implications politiques," in Saïd (1991) 71–80.

Tsagarakis, O. (1982) *Form and Content in Homer. Hermes* Einzelschriften 46. Wiesbaden.

(2000) *Studies in Odyssey 11. Hermes* Einzelschriften 82. Stuttgart.

Turner, C. (2001) "Perverted supplication and other inversions in Aeschylus' Danaid trilogy," *CJ* 97: 27–50.

Tyrrell, W. B. (1984) *Amazons: A Study in Athenian Mythmaking.* Baltimore.

Tyrrell, W. B. and Bennett, L. J. (1999) "Pericles' muting of women's voices in Thuc. 2.45.2," *CJ* 95: 37–51.

Umphrey, S. (1982) "Eros and Thumos," *Interpretation* 10: 382–422.

Valk, M. H. A. L. H. van der. (1953) "Homer's nationalistic attitude," *AC* 22: 5–26.

(1985) "Homer's nationalism, again," *Mnemosyne* 38: 373–6.

Vander Waerdt, P. A. (ed.) (1994a) *The Socratic Movement*. Ithaca/London.

(1994b) "Socrates in the *Clouds*," in Vander Waerdt (1994a) 48–86.

Vasiliou, I. (2002) "Socrates' reverse irony," *CQ* 52: 220–30.

Vasunia, P. (2001) *The Gift of the Nile: Hellenizing Egypt from Aeschylus to Alexander*. Berkeley et al.

Vauclair, J. (1996) *Animal Cognition*. Cambridge, MA/London.

Vegetti, M. (1979) *Il coltello e lo stilo: animali, schiavi, barbari e donne alle origini della razionalità scientifica*. Milan.

Vérilhac, A.-M. (1985) "L'image de la femme dans les épigrammes funéraires grecques," in *La Femme dans le Monde Méditerranéen I: Antiquité*. Lyon: 85–112.

Vermeule, E. (1979) *Aspects of Death in Early Greek Art and Poetry*. Berkeley.

Vernant, J.-P. (1981a) "The myth of Prometheus in Hesiod," in Gordon (1981) 43–56.

(1981b) "Sacrifice and alimentary codes in Hesiod's myth of Prometheus," in Gordon (1981) 57–79.

(1988) *L'individu, la mort, l'amour*. Paris.

(1989) "At man's table: Hesiod's foundation myth of sacrifice," in Detienne and Vernant (1989) 21–86.

Vidal-Naquet, P. (1981) "Hunting and sacrifice in Aeschylus' *Oresteia*," in *Tragedy and Myth in Ancient Greece*, J.-P. Vernant and P. Vidal-Naquet. J. Lloyd, tr. Atlantic Highlands, New Jersey: 150–74.

(1986) *The Black Hunter*. A. Szegedy-Maszak, tr. Baltimore/London.

(1997) "The place and status of foreigners in Athenian tragedy," in Pelling (1997a) 109–19.

(2001) "Beasts, humans and gods: The Greek view," in Arnason and Murphy (2001a) 127–37.

Vivante, P. (1971) *The Homeric Imagination*. Bloomington.

(1982) *The Epithets in Homer*. New Haven/London.

Vlastos, G. (1946) "On the pre-History in Diodorus," *AJP* 67: 51–9.

(1971a) (ed.) *The Philosophy of Socrates*. Garden City, NY.

(1971b) "Introduction: The paradox of Socrates," in Vlastos (1971a) 1–21.

(1981) *Platonic Studies*. Princeton.

(1991) *Socrates: Ironist and Moral Philosopher*. Ithaca.

(1994) *Socratic Studies*, ed. M. Burnyeat. Cambridge.

Vogt, J. (1975) *Ancient Slavery and the Ideal of Man*. T. Wiedemann, tr. Cambridge, MA.

Voltaire. (1972) *Philosophical Dictionary*. T. Besterman, tr. London.

Waal, F. de. (2001) *The Ape and the Sushi Master. Cultural Reflections by a Primatologist*. New York.

Wackers, P. (1988) "Mutorum animalium conloquium or, why do animals speak?" *Reinardus* 1: 163–74.

Walbank, F. W. (1951) "The problems of Greek nationality," *Phoenix* 5: 41–60, reprinted in his *Selected Papers: Studies in Greek and Roman History and Historiography.* (1985) Cambridge: 1–19.

Walcot, P. (1978a) *Envy and the Greeks: A Study of Human Behavior.* Warminster.

(1978b) "Herodotus on rape," *Arethusa* 11: 137–47.

Waldron, T. P. (1985) *Principles of language and mind.* London.

Walkerdine, V. (1985) "On the regulation of speaking and silence: Subjectivity, class and gender in contemporary schooling," in *Language, Gender and Childhood,* eds. C. Steedman, C. Urwin, and V. Walkerdine. London/Boston/Henley: 203–41.

Wallace, R. W. (1996) "Law, freedom, and the concept of citizens' rights in democratic Athens," in Ober and Hedrick (1996) 105–19.

(1998) "The sophists in Athens," in Boedeker and Raaflaub (1998) 203–22.

Wallach, J. R. (1996) "Socratic citizenship," in Prior (1996) vol II: 69–91.

(2001) *The Platonic Political Art.* University Park, PA.

Wallman, J. (1992) *Aping Language.* Cambridge.

Warden, J. (1971) "ΨΥΧΗ in Homeric death-descriptions," *Phoenix* 25: 95–103.

Wathelet, P. (1998) "Les Troyens vus par Homère," in Isebaert and Lebrun (1998) 292–305.

Watkins, C. (1970) "Language of gods and language of men: Remarks on some Indo-European metalinguistic traditions," in *Myth and Law Among the Indo-Europeans,* ed. J. Puhvel. Berkeley: 1–17.

(1986) "The language of the Trojans," in *Troy and the Trojan War,* ed. M. J. Mellink. Bryn Mawr, PA: 45–62.

Watson, J. (ed.) (2001) *Speaking Volumes: Orality and Literacy in the Greek and Roman World. Mnemosyne* Suppl. 218. Leiden.

Watson, W. (1995) "Dogma, skepticism, and dialogue," in Gonzalez (1995a) 189–210.

Watts, R. J. (1997) "Silence and the acquisition of status in verbal interaction," in Jaworksi (1997) 97–115.

Webb, S. H. (1998) *On God and Dogs: A Christian Theology of Compassion for Animals.* New York/Oxford.

Wees, H. van. (1992) *Status Warriors: War, Violence and Society in Homer and History.* Amsterdam.

(1995) "Princes at dinner," in Crielaard (1995) 147–82.

Wells, B. (ed.) (1992) *Agriculture in Ancient Greece.* Stockholm.

Wender, D. (1973) "Plato: misogynist, paedophile, and feminist," *Arethusa* 6: 75–90.

(1978) *The Last Scenes of the Odyssey. Mnemosyne* Suppl. 52. Leiden.

Werner, J. (1992) "Zur Fremdsprachenproblematik in der griechisch-römischen Antike," in Müller, Sier, and Werner (1992) 1–20.

West, E. J. M. (1995) "Plato's audiences, or how Plato replies to the fifth-century intellectual mistrust of letters," in Gonzalez (1995a) 41–60.

West, M. L. (1961) "Hesiodea," *CQ* 11: 130–45.

(1979) "The parodos of the *Agamemnon,*" *CQ* 29: 1–6.

(1997) *The East Face of Helicon.* Oxford.

West, S. (1989) "Laertes revisited," *PCPS* 35: 113–43.

West, T. G. (1979) *Plato's Apology of Socrates.* Ithaca.

Whallon, W. (1958) "The serpent at the breast," *TAPA* 89: 271–5.

(1961a) *The Homeric Epithets. YCS* 17: 97–142.

(1961b) "Why is Artemis angry?" *AJP* 82: 78–88.

(1969) *Formula, Character, and Context.* Washington, D.C.

(1980) *Problem and Spectacle: Studies in the Oresteia.* Heidelberg.

(1993) "The herm at *Agamemnon* 55–56: stocks and stones of the *Oresteia*," *Hermes* 121: 496–9.

White, S. A. (1995) "Thrasymachus the diplomat," *CP* 90: 307–27.

Whitehead, D. (1977) *The Ideology of the Athenian Metic.* Proceedings of the Cambridge Philological Society. Suppl. vol. 4. Cambridge.

Whitman, C. H. (1958) *Homer and the Heroic Tradition.* New York.

Whittaker, C. R. (ed.) (1988) *Pastoral Economies in Classical Antiquity.* Proceedings of the Cambridge Philological Society. Suppl. Vol. 14. Cambridge.

Whittaker, H. (1999) "The status of Arete in the Phaeacian episode of the *Odyssey*," *Sym. Osl.* 74: 140–50.

Wickert-Micknat, G. (1982) *Die Frau.* Archaeologia Homerica III.R. Göttingen.

Wiedemann, T. E. J. (1983) "ἐλάχιστον . . . ἐν τοῖς ἄρρεσι κλέος: Thucydides, women, and the limits of rational analysis," *G&R* 30: 163–70.

(1986) "Between men and beasts: Barbarians in Ammianus Marcellinus," in *Past Perspectives*, eds. I. S. Moxon, J. D. Smart, and A. J. Woodman. Cambridge/New York: 189–201.

Wilkins, J. (1990) "The state and the individual: Euripides' plays of voluntary self-sacrifice," in *Euripides, Women, and Sexuality*, ed. A. Powell. London: 177–94.

(1993) "Social status and fish in Greece and Rome," in Mars and Mars (1993) 191–203.

(1997) "Comic cuisine: Food and eating in the comic polis," in Dobrov (1997) 249–68.

(2000a) *The Boastful Chef: The Discourse of Food in Ancient Greek Comedy.* Oxford.

(2000b) "Edible choruses," in Harvey and Wilkins (2000) 341–54.

Willcock, M. M. (1964) "Mythological paradeigma in the *Iliad*," *CQ* 14: 141–54.

(1977) "Ad hoc invention in the *Iliad*," *HSCP* 81: 41–53.

(1983) "Antilochos in the *Iliad*," in *Mélanges Edouard Delebecque.* Intr. C. Froidefond. Aix-en-Provence: 479–85.

Williams, B. (1993) *Shame and Necessity.* Berkeley.

Willis, R. (ed.) (1990) *Signifying Animals: Human Meaning in the Natural World.* London/New York.

Wilson, D. F. (1999) "Symbolic violence in *Iliad* Book 9," *CW* 93: 131–47.

(2002) *Ransom, Revenge, and Heroic Identity in the Iliad.* Cambridge.

Wilson, J. R. S. (1995) "Thrasymachus and the *thumos*: A further case of prolepsis in *Republic* I," *CQ* 45: 58–67.

Winkler, J. J. and Zeitlin, F. I. (eds.) (1990) *Nothing to Do With Dionysos? Athenian Drama in Its Social Context*. Princeton.

Winnington-Ingram, R. P. (1983) *Studies in Aeschylus*. Cambridge.

Winterbottom, M. (1989) "Speaking of the gods," *G&R* 36: 33–41.

Wirshbo, E. (1993) "On critically looking into Snell's Homer," in Rosen and Farrell (1993) 467–77.

Wise, S. M. (2001) *Rattling the Cage: Toward Legal Rights for Animals*. Cambridge, MA.

  (2002) *Drawing the Line: Science and the Case for Animal Rights*. Cambridge, MA.

Wittgenstein, L. (1958) *Philosophical Investigations*. G. E. M. Anscombe, tr. New York.

Wohl, V. (1998) *Intimate Commerce: Exchange, Gender, and Subjectivity in Greek Tragedy*. Austin.

Wolfe, C. (2003) *Animal Rites: American Culture, the Discourse of Species, and Posthumanist Theory*. Chicago/London.

Wood, D. (1999) "*Comment ne pas manger* – deconstruction and humanism," in *Animal Others: On Ethics, Ontology, and Animal Life*, ed. H. P. Steeves. Albany: 15–35.

Wood, E. M. and Wood, N. (1996) "Socrates and democracy: A reply to Gregory Vlastos," in Prior (1996) vol. II: 45–68.

Woodhead, A. G. (1967) "ΙΣΕΓΟΡΙΑ and the council of 500," *Historia* 16: 129–40.

Woodruff, P. (1987) "Expert knowledge in the *Apology and Laches*; what a general needs to know," *BACAP* 3: 79–115.

  (2000) "Socrates and the irrational," in Smith and Woodruff (2000) 130–50.

Worman, N. (1999) "Odysseus *panourgos*: The liar's style in tragedy and oratory," *Helios* 26: 35–68.

  (2001) "This voice which is not one: Helen's verbal guises in Homeric epic," in Lardinois and McClure (2001) 19–37.

  (2002) *The Cast of Character: Style in Greek Literature*. Austin.

Wyatt, W. F., Jr. (1988) "Homer in performance: *Iliad* 1.348–427," *CJ* 83: 289–97.

  (1989) "The intermezzo of *Odyssey* 11 and the poets Homer and Odysseus," *SMEA* 27: 235–50.

Yamagata, N. (1991) "Phoenix's speech – is Achilles punished?" *CQ* 41: 1–15.

  (1994) *Homeric Morality. Mnemosyne* Suppl. 131. Leiden/New York/Köln.

  (1998) "Odyssean parenthood," in Paisi-Apostolopoulou (1998) 277–81.

Yamamoto, D. (1998) "Aquinas and the animals: Patrolling the boundary?" in Linzey and Yamamoto (1998) 80–9.

Yonezawa, S. (1995–6) "The purpose of Socratic logoi: Egocentrism and altruism in Socrates," *Platon* 47–8: 62–7.

Yunis, H. (1998) "The constraints of democracy and the rise of the art of rhetoric," in Boedeker and Raaflaub (1998) 223–40.

Zafiropoulos, C. A. (2001) *Ethics in Aesop's Fables*. Leiden.

Zak, W. F. (1995) *The Polis and the Divine Order*. Lewisburg.

Zanker, G. (1994) *The Heart of Achilles*. Ann Arbor.

(1998) "Beyond reciprocity: The Akhilleus-Priam scene in *Iliad* 24," in Gill, Postlethwaite, and Seaford (1998) 73–92.

Zeitlin, F. I. (1965) "The motif of the corrupted sacrifice in Aeschylus' *Oresteia*," *TAPA* 96: 463–508.

(1978) "The dynamics of misogyny: Myth and mythmaking in the *Oresteia*," *Arethusa* 11: 149–84, reprinted in Zeitlin (1996) 87–119.

(1990) "Thebes: Theater of self and society in Athenian drama," in Winkler and Zeitlin (1990) 130–67.

(1996) *Playing the Other: Gender and Society in Classical Greek Literature.* Chicago/London.

Ziolkowski, J. M. (1993) *Talking Animals: Medieval Latin Beast Poetry, 750–1150.* Philadelphia.

Zwerdling, D. 2002. "Fast food and animal rights: McDonald's new farm," American Radio Works. June.

Zyskind, H. (1992) "Plato's *Republic* Book 1," *Ph&Rh* 25: 205–21.

Index

Achilles 39–40, 44, 106
  and Agamemnon 121–3, 127, 128–9
  and language 115, 119–67
  and Odysseus 127, 162
  and Patroclus 3, 44, 124, 145, 155, 160, 164
  and Priam 143–66
  as "beast" 134–43
  quality of his voice 123, 125, 221
  similar to Telemachus 119–20
  Socrates' interpretation of 269, 290
aegis 126, 129
Aegisthus 224–6, 252–3
Aeneas 128
Aeschines 180
Aeschylus 18, 74, 178–9, 212
  Agamemnon 217–33
  Eumenides 236–58
  Libation Bearers 233–6
  on free speech 178, 182
  on the Other 182, 200, 201
  Oresteia 215
Aesop 15, 26
Agamemnon 74, 149, 162, 232, 235
  see also Achilles; Aeschylus
age *see* speech
agênôr 45
agriophônous 64
Ajax 268
alalêtos 66
Alcibiades 2, 172, 310–11
  see also Plutarch
Alcinous 75–6
  his gold and silver dogs 41
Allen, D. S. 271
Allen, Woody 13
Amazons 173, 250
amphasiê 97
Anacreon 186
Anaxagoras 322
Andromache 69–71, 159

animals
  and justice, *see dikê*
  and non-human animal duality 23–9
  and rationality 10
  and the unjust, *see* Plato
  as markers of status 1–2
  in comedy 3, 13, 14, 15–16
  in diet 2–3, 12–13, 14, 52
  in fables 14–15, 44
  in the golden age 12–14
  in omens 40, 229–31
  in prophecy 40, 210
    see also Xanthus
  in sacrifice 2–3, 210–12, 230, 247–8
  lack of language 5–6
  modern debate over rights of 316–33
  souls of *see psuchê, thumos, phrenes, noos*
  talking 13–16, 210
    see also Xanthus
  women associated with 190
  see also Aeschylus; Homer; *logos*; Plato; silence; speech
anthropology, Greek versions of 26–8
Anticleia 59
  her description of death 47
Antilochus 39, 97–9
Antinous, *see* suitors
Antiphon 10, 195, 206
Anytus 299–300
Apollo 129, 240
Apuleius 59
Aquinas 321
Archilochus 223
Archippus 15
Arete 74–6
argument from marginal cases 326–8
Argus (Odysseus' dog) 49–50
Aristarchus 69, 70
Aristophanes 15, 178, 181
  and the Other 188, 200, 204, 207, 208

387